D. Lischinski
G. W. Larson (eds.)

Rendering Techniques '99

Proceedings of the Eurographics Workshop
in Granada, Spain,
June 21 – 23, 1999

Eurographics

SpringerWienNewYork

Dr. Dani Lischinski
Institute of Computer Science,
The Hebrew University of Jerusalem,
Jerusalem, Israel

Dr. Greg Ward Larson
Silicon Graphics Inc.,
Mountain View, CA, USA

Typesetting: Camera-ready by authors
Printing: Novographic, A-1238 Wien
Binding: Papyrus, A-1100 Wien

Printed on acid-free and chlorine-free bleached paper

SPIN: 10734669

With 212 partly coloured Figures

ISSN 0946-2767
ISBN-13: 978-3-211-83382-7   e-ISBN-13: 978-3-7091-6809-7
DOI: 10.1007/ 978-3-7091-6809-7

Preface

This book contains the proceedings of the 10th Eurographics Workshop on Rendering, which took place from the 21st to the 23rd of June, 1999, in Granada, Spain. Originally an outgrowth of the annual Eurographics meeting, the workshop was organized by a dedicated group of researchers who felt there was insufficient opportunity at Eurographics and Siggraph to exchange ideas specifically on rendering. Over the past 9 years, the workshop has become renown as an international watershed for top quality work in this field, attracting between 50 and 100 attendees each year to share their latest research.

This year we received a total of 63 submissions. Each paper was carefully reviewed by two of the 25 international programme committee members, as well as two external reviewers, selected by the co-chairs from a pool of 71 individuals. (The programme committee and external reviewers are listed following the contents pages.) In this new review process, all submissions and reviews were handled electronically, with the exception of videos submitted with a few of the papers. This streamlined the review process considerably, while reducing the costs and confusion associated with courier delivery of hundreds of papers.

The overall quality of the submissions was very high, but due to space and time constraints, only 28 papers were accepted, and they are contained in this book. Additionally, this book contains two invited papers, one by Donald P. Greenberg (Cornell University) and one by Stuart Green (LightWork Design Ltd). Almost all papers are accompanied by color images, which appear at the end of the book.

The subfields of rendering represented in this volume are indeed varied. There are papers concerning the "classical" rendering workshop topics: radiosity and Monte Carlo global illumination algorithms and illumination models, alongside papers on near-interactive ray tracing, hardware-assisted rendering algorithms, techniques for acquisition and modeling from images, image-based rendering, novel shadow algorithms, and inverse lighting and design. As in previous years, we expect these proceedings to become an invaluable resource for both rendering researchers and practitioners.

We wish to thank the organizing chairman Carlos Ureña Almagro and his colleagues at the University of Granada for their help in the production of the proceedings, and for taking care of all the local organization aspects of the workshop. Thanks go also to the Spanish Ministry of Education and Culture (Ministerio de Educación y Cultura — Gobierno Español), the Andalusian Education and Science Council (Consejería de Educación y Ciencia — Junta de Andalucía), and the Spanish Chapter of Eurographics for providing funding for the workshop.

Finally, we wish to thank all of the authors who submitted their work to the workshop, and the programme committee members and external reviewers for all the time and energy they invested in the review process. The quality of research between these covers reflects the efforts of many individuals, and their work is their gift to the community. It has been our honor to receive this gift.

Greg Ward Larson
Dani Lischinski

June, 1999

Contents

International Programme Committee

External Reviewers

Author Index

Disruptive Technologies in Computer Graphics:
Past, Present, and Future

Donald P. Greenberg
Program of Computer Graphics
Cornell University

The history and famous landmarks of computer graphics hardware are well known. Starting with Ivan Sutherland's Sketchpad system in the early 1960's, the first generation of computer graphics hardware consisted of calligraphic (vector) displays capable of drawing complex three-dimensional wireframe models at interactive rates. In the early 1970's expensive color frame buffers with the capability for displaying static color images were introduced. Although more and more intelligence was added to these frame buffers, Jim Clark's geometry engine and the first graphics workstations were not introduced until the 1980's. During the 1970's, only the very costly and specialized hardware used for military and aerospace simulations was capable of real-time surface color display.

By the 1990's, very high-end graphics servers evolved, but the computer graphics hardware industry previously occupied by numerous workstation vendors rapidly became dominated by the use of personal computers with high-performance graphics accelerator boards. Today we can purchase even lower cost systems from game manufacturers with startling real-time graphics capabilities. The differentiation between the high-end and low-end systems is now getting more difficult to perceive.

From an algorithmic point of view, at least with respect to rendering, much research of the first decade was devoted towards solving the visible surface or hidden surface problem. The Gouraud and Phong lighting algorithms were introduced in the early 1970's. The first scan-line algorithms and the z-buffer approach as well as texturing algorithms quickly followed. The computational requirements for global illumination were too excessive to attempt. It was not until 1979 that Whitted's ray tracing algorithm was published, and Cornell's first radiosity images appeared in 1984. Much of the research during the following decade concentrated on light reflection models, physically-based rendering, and stochastic methods to accurately simulate light interaction. Today we can produce accurate photorealistic images of startling quality, complex scenes with textures, shadows, shading and all of the subtle effects of global inter-reflections. Because the modeling tasks are so difficult and because image acquisition techniques have become so commonplace, these object-based algorithms are now being supplemented or replaced by image-based rendering algorithms, even further improving the image quality.

During this same forty-year time period, computing environments have also changed dramatically. From the early 1960's to the mid-1970's the information technology industry was dominated by batch computing and time-sharing systems. Starting at research laboratories and universities, the next decade was marked by distributed computing based on the introduction and rapid acceptance of the mini-computer. With the advent of microprocessors and Ethernet during the past fifteen years, the environments have gradually transformed to environments of networked personal computers. Today, we are dependent on open systems consisting of clients and servers and the use of parallel computing, and as devices become smaller, we are rapidly moving into the decade of information appliances.

At each stage of this evolutionary process, more powerful, more efficient, more compact, and cheaper devices have replaced the functionality and performance of the previous era. Perhaps just as significantly, the leading manufacturers in one era did not recognize the potential impact of the new technologies of the following era. Note the change in the dominant suppliers as the mainframes were replaced by mini-computers, or the minis were replaced by microprocessor-based personal computers. The same phenomena can be observed in the mass storage sectors. As noted by Clayton Christiansen in his book, 'The Innovators Dilemma", these are examples of a typical 'disruptive technology".

It is interesting to examine the progress, the change, and the disruptions in computer graphics, not just by identifying the historical landmarks by themselves, but within the context of the available computer technologies, as well as the cost structures associated with those technologies. This evaluation can not only explain the changes of the past, but perhaps help in recognizing the changes which will occur in the future.

Although actual comparisons are much more complicated, I have chosen four major criteria for context and comparisons: memory capacity, processing power, bandwidth, and display resolution.

For each of these independent variables, it is important to consider not only the absolute performance or capabilities, but also the economic efficiencies in terms of unit costs (e.g. Megabytes per dollar for memory, MIPS or FLOPS per dollar for processing). When examined in this context, the evolutionary changes in computer graphics are easily explained.

Since the improvements in each of these four parameters occur at different rates, at any point in time, the lack of performance in one category creates the current impediment. The bottlenecks then become cyclical, explaining, in the words of Ivan Sutherland, 'the wheel of reincarnation".

To clarify my concepts, it is helpful to understand the original optimization procedures applied to manufacturing processes, building construction, etc. Critical path methods (CPM) consist of first finding the longest path in terms of time through a system. Without violating any of the precedent relationships, optimal solutions next find the most cost-effective means to shorten this path. For example, in a construction process, where does one assign additional labor to most cost-effectively truncate the total time to completion?

The analogy is similar to the primary goal in the design of computer graphics systems. How do we compute the image in the shortest time, or in the graphics pipeline, create the most complex images in real time? Although graphics hardware designers have been balancing their pipelines for each changing technology, it should be noted that the models are also changing. The first pipelines were balanced for 1000 pixel polygons, but we are now approaching 10 pixels per polygon. Should the system stay the same?

With an increase in memory density of five orders of magnitude, an increase in processing capacity of four orders of magnitude and a bandwidth increase of three orders of magnitude, all occurring at different rates and times, the systems and architectures change. Perhaps, more importantly, the costs efficiencies of the memory, processing, and bandwidth components further exaggerate the rates of change. Only display resolution has remained relatively constant with less than an order of magnitude increase.

But the graphics industry is technology driven, and we can with some degree of confidence predict the change in technology. How will this effect the future graphics hardware and algorithms?

With free memory, and ample processing power, the implications include different architectures and buffering schemes, an increase in image based rendering, and greater emphasis on perceptual approaches to reduce computational complexity. Display resolution will vastly increase, displays will be omnipresent and ultimately real-time, pixel-based, and global illumination algorithms will replace the standard graphics pipeline.

Perceptually-informed accelerated rendering of high quality walkthrough sequences

Karol Myszkowski, Przemyslaw Rokita and Takehiro Tawara

University of Aizu, Aizu Wakamatsu 965-8580, Japan

Abstract. In this paper, we consider accelerated rendering of walkthrough animation sequences using combination of ray tracing and Image-Based Rendering (IBR) techniques. Our goal is to derive as many pixels as possible using inexpensive IBR techniques without affecting the animation quality. A perception-based spatio-temporal Animation Quality Metric (AQM) is used to automatically guide such a hybrid rendering. The Pixel Flow (PF) obtained as a by-product of the IBR computation is an integral part of the AQM. The final animation quality is enhanced by an efficient spatio-temporal antialiasing, which utilize the PF to perform a motion-compensated filtering.

1 Introduction

Rendering of animated sequences proves to be a very computation intensive task, which in professional production involves specialized rendering farms designed specifically for this purpose. While the progress in efficiency of rendering algorithms and increasing processor power are very impressive, with a similar pace the requirements imposed by the complexity of rendered scenes also increase. Effectively, rendering timings reported for the final antialiased frames are still counted in tens of minutes or hours.

It is well-known in the video community that the human eye is less sensitive to higher spatial frequencies than to lower frequencies, and this knowledge was used in designing video equipment [9]. It is also the conventional wisdom that the requirements imposed on the quality of still images must be higher than for images used in an animated sequence. Another intuition is that the quality of rendering can be usually relaxed as the velocity of a moving object (image pattern) increases. These observations are confirmed by systematic psychophysical experiments investigating the sensitivity of the human eye for various spatio-temporal patterns [16, 28]. For example, the perceived sharpness of moving low resolution (or blurred) patterns increases with velocity, which is attributed to the higher level processing in the visual system [30]. This means that all techniques that attempt to speed up rendering of every single frame separately cannot account for the eye sensitivity variations resulting from the temporal considerations. Effectively, computational efforts can be easily wasted on processing image details which cannot be perceived in the animated sequence. In this context, a global approach involving both spatial and temporal dimensions appears promising [23] and relatively unexplored research direction.

This research is an attempt to develop a framework for the perceptually-informed accelerated rendering of antialiased animated sequences. In our approach, computation is focused on those selected frames (keyframes) and frame fragments (inbetween frames), which strongly affect the whole animation appearance by depicting image details readily perceptible by the human observer. All pixels related to these frames and frame fragments are computed using a costly rendering method (we use ray tracing as the final pass of our global illumination solution), which provides images of high quality. The remaining pixels are derived using an inexpensive method (we use IBR techniques [21, 20, 25]). Ideally, the differences between pixels computed using the slower and faster methods should not be perceived in animated sequences, notwithstanding that such differences can be readily seen when the corresponding frames are observed as still images. The spatio-temporal perception-based quality metric for animated sequences is used to guide frames computation in the fully automatic and recursive manner. The special care is taken for efficient reduction of spatial and especially annoying temporal artifacts, which occasionally can be observed even in the professionally produced animated sequences.

In our approach, the Pixel Flow (PF) computed as the motion vector field is the key point of the overall animated sequence processing. It is computed using the IBR techniques, which guarantee its very good accuracy and high speed of processing for the synthetic images[1]. The PF is used in our technique in three ways:

- To reproject pixels from the ray traced keyframes to the image-based inbetweens.
- To improve temporal considerations of our perception-based animation quality metric.
- To enhance animation quality by performing antialiasing based on motion-compensated filtering.

Obviously, the best cost-performance is achieved when the PF is used in all three processing steps. However, since all these steps are only loosely coupled, and the costs of computing PF are very low, other scenarios are also possible e.g., fully ray traced animation can be filtered with motion compensation.

In this paper, we narrow our discussion to the production of high-quality walkthrough animations (only camera animation is considered), although some of solutions proposed by us can be used in a more general animation framework (refer to [23] for discussion of problems with global illumination in this more general case). We assume that walkthrough animation is of really high quality involving complex geometry and global illumination solutions, and thus it incurs significant costs for a single frame rendering (e.g., about 170 minutes in the example chosen as a case study in this research [1]). We make also other reasonable assumptions such as: animation path and all camera positions are known in advance, ray tracing (or other high quality rendering method) for selected pixels is available, depth (range) data for every pixel are inexpensive to derive for every frame (e.g., using z-buffer), and object identifiers for every pixel can be easily accessed for every frame (e.g., using item buffer).

In the following section, we discuss previous work on improving performance of animation rendering and perception-based video quality metrics. Then we describe efficient methods of inbetween frames computation we have used in our research. Section 4 describes our 3D antialiasing technique based on the motion-compensated filtering. In Section 5 we present our animation quality metric. Section 6 and the accompanying Web page [1] show results obtained using our approach. Finally, we conclude this work.

2 Previous work

In this research our objective is the reduction of time required for rendering frames, in particular, inbetween frames, which can be derived from the high-quality keyframes.

---

[1]For the natural image sequences the optical flow can be derived [27], which is more costly and usually far less accurate.

In this context, we discuss previous work on exploiting various forms of frame-to-frame coherence to speedup rendering and enhance image quality. To our knowledge, a method that automatically selects keyframes minimizing distortions visible by the human observers has not been presented yet. We review the perceptually-informed video quality metrics which could be used to guide rendering of inbetween frames.

2.1 In-between frame generation

Frame-to-frame coherence has been widely used in computer animation to speedup computations. Here we limit our discussion to techniques dealing with camera animation. Early research focused mostly on speeding up ray tracing by interpolating images for views similar to a given keyframe [2, 3]. These algorithms involved costly procedures for cleaning up image artifacts such as gaps between pixels (resulting from stretching samples reprojected from keyframes to inbetween frames), and occlusion (visibility) errors. For example, Adelson and Hodges [2] traced rays between the viewing position and the reprojected intersection point for every pixel to check for visibility errors. In this respect, recently developed IBR techniques are more efficient: the 3-D warping and warp ordering algorithms proposed by McMillan [21] efficiently solve the problem of visibility, and the "splatting" technique developed by Shade *et al.* [25] is fast and fills well gaps between resampled pixels.

Special treatment is required for objects occluded in the reference image (keyframe) and visible in the derived images (inbetween frames). Shade *et al.* [25] and Lischinski [18] warped a number of reference frames into the selected view (usually it is one of the reference views) and built the Layered Depth Image (LDI) structure in which the subsequent layers of occluded pixels were stored. The LDI structure is very compact because redundancies resulting from multiple reference images are removed, but rendering of these reference images can be costly. Mark *el al.* [20] and Darsa *et al.* [7] proposed techniques which fit well to the walkthrough applications. Compositing between just two warped frames computed along the animation path is performed. All algorithms discussed reduce significantly the problem of occlusions, however, some perceptible errors are still likely to appear when an object occluded in all reference frames becomes visible in desired views.

Processing of specular surfaces for inbetween frames using interpolation techniques is a hard problem. For a majority of ray tracing-based interpolation techniques all pixels depicting objects with specular properties are recomputed [2]. On the other hand, a vast majority of IBR techniques was developed for diffuse environments [21, 20, 25] and only few solutions handling more general reflectance functions were proposed. The light field [17] and Lumigraph [13] techniques are suitable for rendering of glossy objects. A dense grid of images is used to store lighting outgoing in all directions from a bounded region of space. It is not clear how to handle occlusions between objects if navigation is freely allowed within this bounded region [18]. This problem can be solved and more crisp images can be obtained using the surface light field approach [22] in which geometry is explicitly represented. View-dependent lighting is stored in a huge volume of textures attached to every glossy surface. In general, all light field-like techniques require a huge number of images that must be precomputed and stored to achieve a reasonable quality of derived images. This can be very costly, in particular, in applications dealing with synthetic images of high quality. Even with a huge number of precomputed images, sharp mirror reflections are hard to obtain in this framework. The most promising in this context is technique proposed by Lischinski and Rappoport [18] who capture directional distribution of reflected lighting in multiple specialized

LDI-like structures which make possible recomputation of glossy and specular effects for changing views fully within the IBR framework. This solution seems to be especially suitable for interactive applications dealing with compact (localized in space) objects and requiring full freedom in selecting views.

In our application, scenes might be of substantial geometrical extent and visual complexity (textures and geometrical details) which would require LDIs of high resolution (this means high rendering cost to prepare such LDIs) to secure the high quality of rendering and to cover the full scene extent. On the other hand, since only the predefined set of views is processed during walkthroughs, these requirements can be relaxed for some LDIs storing the view-dependent light component, which are referenced less frequently or are not referenced at all. Automatic generation of an adaptive LDI representation accommodating for these requirements still remains an open research problem [18].

The Multiple Viewpoint Rendering technique [15] seems to be an interesting alternative to the traditional rendering, but to make it practical in our walkthrough application further research is required to enable less constrained camera motion within large environments.

2.2 Pixel flow applications in animation rendering

The Pixel Flow found many successful applications in video signals processing [27] and animated sequences compression [14]. Also, some applications in computer animation have been shown. Zeghers *el al.* [31] used the linear interpolation between densely placed keyframes, which was performed along the PF direction. To avoid visible image distortions only a limited number of inbetween frames could be derived (the authors showed examples for one or three consecutive inbetweens only). Shinya [26] proposed the motion-compensated filtering as the antialiasing tool for animation sequences. Zeghers *el al.* and Shinya used animation information to compute the PF between images, and visibility computations were performed explicitly for every pixel. Using IBR techniques the PF computation is greatly simplified for walkthrough sequences, and the visibility is handled automatically.

2.3 Video quality metrics

In recent years, a number of video quality metrics based on the spatio-temporal vision models have been proposed. One of the main motivations driving development of such metrics was the need to evaluate the performance of digital video coding and compression techniques in terms of artifacts visible to the human observer [8, 29]. In this study, we are interested in general purpose metrics which are applicable for synthetic image sequences. Such an ideal metric should account for important characteristics of the Human Visual System (HVS) such as the multi-resolution structure of the early stages of human vision, spatio-temporal sensitivity to contrast, and visual masking [9]. One commonly used approach is to extend a still image quality metric into the time domain [19, 29]. A practical problem here is the lack of separability of spatio-temporal Contrast Sensitivity Function (CSF) [16] (it is separable only at high spatial and temporal frequencies [28]). In practice, spatial and temporal channels are modeled separately by a filterbank, and the spatio-temporal interaction is then modeled at the level of respective gains of the filters [8, 29].

Another practical problem is computational cost and memory requirements involved in processing in the time domain. Usually two temporal channels are considered [8, 19] to account for transient (low-pass) and sustained (band-pass with a peak frequency around 8 Hz) mechanisms [28].

Lack of comparative studies makes difficult evaluation of the actual performance of discussed metrics. It seems that the Sarnoff Just-Noticeable Difference (JND) Model [19] is the most developed (the Tektronix, Inc. product PQA-200 Picture Quality Analyzer test instrument includes so called JNDmetrix which is based on this technology), while a DCT-based model proposed by Watson [29] is computationally efficient and retains many basic characteristics of the Sarnoff model [6]. In this research, we decided to use our own metric of animated sequence quality, which takes advantage of the PF that is readily available in our application.

3 Rendering of the animation

Rendering of animation sequence is one of the key factors affecting time required for the overall animation production. For rendering techniques relying on keyframing, the overall animation rendering time depends heavily upon the efficiency of inbetween frames computation, which usually significantly outnumber the keyframes. In this section, we outline briefly our approach to the generation of inbetween frames. Then, we describe our algorithm for managing computation of the complete animation.

3.1 Inbetween frames generation

When selecting appropriate walkthrough rendering methods, their overall costs should be taken into account. On this ground, we reject some fast rendering techniques which require very costly preprocessing, e.g., the light field and other similar techniques [17, 13, 22]. Also, since in walkthroughs the spatial range of camera motions may be quite substantial and the viewing directions may change significantly, we think that in this case the cost-performance of the LDI technique [25] is not so attractive. The LDI data structures provide information for a rather limited space of possible observer locations and viewing directions. Effectively, the ratio between the number of derived images and the number of images used to building LDI might be low.

This reasoning focused our attention on simpler solutions, which use very simple data structures and do not require intensive preparatory computations. To account for proper PF computation and occlusion relations we use the 3D warping and warp ordering algorithms developed by McMillan [21], which require just the reference image and the corresponding range data. The formulation of McMillan's warping equation fits very well to camera model used in ray tracing, which simplifies the compositing of IBR-based and ray traced pixels. To reduce gaps between stretched samples during image reprojection we use the adaptive "splatting" technique proposed by Shade *el al.* [25]. To remove holes resulting from occluded objects we blend two keyframes as proposed by Mark *et al.* [20]. Pixels depicting objects occluded in the two keyframes are computed using ray tracing.

Since specular effects are usually of high contrast and they attract the viewer attention when observing a video sequence [24], the special care is taken to process them properly. We use our perception-based animation quality metric to decide for which objects with strong glossy or transparent properties pixels must be recomputed using ray tracing.

3.2 Managing inbetween frames generation

In our approach, rendering of walkthrough sequences is designed as a recursive procedure. In the initialization step, the whole walkthrough is decomposed into segments S of uniform length (a reasonable length is selected, e.g., 25 subsequent frames). Then every segment S is processed separately.

The recursive procedure for processing segment S is as follows. The first frame k_0 and the last frame k_{2N} are generated using ray tracing (keyframes are shared by two neighboring segments and are computed only once). Then 3D warping [21] is performed, and we generate two frames corresponding to k_N as follows: $k'_N = Warp(k_0)$ and $k''_N = Warp(k_{2N})$. Using the perception-based animation quality metric (AQM) we compute the map of perceptible differences between k'_N and k''_N. This quality metric incorporates the PF between frames k_{N-1} and k_N, and k_N and k_{N+1} to account for temporal sensitivity of the human observer.

In an analysis process, at first we search for perceptible differences in images of objects with strong specular, transparent and glossy properties, which we identify using the item buffer of frame k_N (in Section 6 we provide details on setting the thresholds of AQM response, which are used by us to discriminate between the perceptible and imperceptible differences). All pixels depicting objects for which the significant differences are reported in the perceptible differences map will be recalculated using ray tracing. We mask out those pixels from the map. In the same manner, we mask out holes composed of pixels which could not be derived from the reference images using 3D warping. If the masked-out difference map still shows significant discrepancies between k'_N and k''_N then we split the segment S in the middle and we process recursively two resulting sub-segments using the procedure described in the previous paragraph. Otherwise, we blend k'_N and k''_N (with correct processing of depth [25]), and ray trace pixels for remaining holes and masked out specular objects to derive the final frame k_N. In the same way, we generate all remaining frames in S. To avoid the image quality degradation resulting from multiple resamplings, we always warp the fully ray-traced reference frames k_0 and k_{2N} to derive all inbetween frames in S.

We evaluate the animation quality metric only for frame k_N. We assume that derivation of k_N applying the IBR techniques is the most error-prone in the whole segment S because its minimal distance along the animation path to either the k_0 or k_{2N} frames is the longest one. This assumption is a trade off between the time spent for rendering and for the control of its quality (we discuss the costs of AQM in Section 6), but in practice, it holds well for typical animation paths.

Figure 1 (see Appendix/Color Section) summarizes computation and compositing of an inbetween frame. We used the dotted line to mark those processing stages that are performed only once for segment S. The remaining processing stages are repeated for all inbetween frames.

As the final step, we perform our spatio-temporal antialiasing. To speedup rendering phase all pixels (including those that have been ray traced) are not antialiased until this last stage of processing.

4 Image enhancement

Composing still images of high quality into an animated sequence might not result in equally high quality of animation because of possible temporal artifacts. On the other hand, proper temporal processing of the sequence makes possible relaxing the quality of frames without perceptible degradation of the animation quality, which effectively means that simpler and faster rendering methods can be applied.

It is well-known that aliasing affects the quality of images generated using rendering techniques. This concerns as well images obtained using IBR methods which additionally may exhibit various kind of discontinuities (such as holes resulting from the visibility problems). These discontinuities can be significantly reduced using techniques like splatting and image compositing introduced above, but anyway in the resulting images in many places instead of smooth transitions - jagged unwanted edges and contours will be easily perceptible (refer to the enclosed animation samples [1]).

Aliasing is also inherent to all raster images with significant content. Images obtained in computer graphics, or in general - all digital images, are the sampled versions of their synthetic or real world continuous counterparts. Sampling theory states that a signal can be properly reconstructed from its samples if the original signal is sampled at the Nyquist rate. Due to limited resolution of output devices such as printers and especially CRTs the Nyquist rate criterion in computer graphics is rarely met - and the image signal cannot be represented properly with a restricted number of samples.

From the point of view of signal processing theory - discontinuities and aliasing artifacts described above are high frequency distortions. This suggests the possibility of replacing the traditional, computationally-expensive antialiasing techniques - like unweighted and weighted area sampling and super-sampling, by an appropriate image processing method. Such an approach was tried by Shinya [26], who derived the sub-pixel information improving efficiency of antialiasing from the image sequences by tracking a given sample point location along the PF trajectories. In his approach, Shinya emphasized temporal filtering (his filter has ideal antialiasing properties when its size is infinite), which lead to filters of very wide support (Shinya acquired temporal samples from 32 subsequent frames of animation). In our research, we have found that by treating both aspects - spatial and temporal in a balanced way, we were able to improve both quality and efficiency of antialiasing. We have obtained a very efficient and simple antialiasing and image quality enhancement method based on low pass filtering using spatial convolution. Spatial convolution is a neighborhood operation - i.e. a result at each output pixel is calculated using the corresponding input pixel and its neighboring pixels. For the convolution, this result is the sum of products of pixel intensities and corresponding weights from the convolution mask. The values in the convolution mask determine the effect of convolution by defining the filter to be applied. Those values are derived from the point spread function of the particular filter - in the case of low pass filtering, typically it will be the Gaussian function (for more details on convolution see, e.g., [12]). In our case - i.e., in the case of a sequence of images composing an animation, we have to consider not only the spatial but also temporal aspect of aliasing and discontinuities. The proper way of solving the problem is to filter the three dimensional intensity function (composed of a sequence of frames) not along the time axis - but along the pixel flow - i.e. the PF introduced earlier it this paper (results and differences between those approaches can be seen on the enclosed animation samples [1]). Such filtering technique, known also as the motion compensated filtering, was earlier used in video signals processing [27], image interpolation [31], and image compression [14].

In practice, we used a separable Gaussian filter with the maximum support size of 5×5 in spatial and 9 temporal domains. The main idea that enabled us to use it in a context of antialiasing in a sequence of computer generated images (coming both from ray tracer and IBR) was to use the IBR technique to obtain the PF in a computationally inexpensive way.

The drawback of such a motion-compensated filtering (as well as the other solutions [26, 31, 27]) is incorrect processing of directional lighting effects, which are especially objectionable for crisp mirror reflections. Indeed, motion of the reflected/refracted patterns over specular surfaces as a function of camera motion does not correspond to motion of these surfaces in the image plane which is described by the PF. Since estimation of the optical flow for reflections and refractions is quite involved, we used the following trade-off which worked well in walkthroughs that we tested. We reduced the size of temporal filter support for objects with strong directional reflectance/refraction properties.

The PF obtained from IBR gives us the sub-pixel accuracy (coordinates are calculated using floating point arithmetic). We have modified the standard spatial convolution algorithm to accommodate this feature. For each input pixel of the temporal filter the value is calculated as a weighted average of 4 pixels in the proximity of the input point (weights are proportional to the distance between neighboring pixel center and this point position).

It is well-known that low pass filtering as a side effect is causing blurring and in fact - a loss of information in the processed signal or image. In our case we have to consider that the content and the final quality of the resulting animation is to be judged by a human observer. We were quite fortunate to find that with pixels velocity increase there is an increase of perceived sharpness (see also [30]) - for example, an animation perceived as sharp and of a good quality can be composed of relatively highly blurred frames. I.e., each still frame considered separately would be judged as blurred and unacceptable by the human observer. As a result, the case of animation excessive blurring introduced by our antialiasing technique is compensated by the perceptual phenomena. This fact was also confirmed by our AQM predictor.

The antialiasing technique we developed in the scope of this research proved to be efficient and computationally inexpensive. Achieved quality can be evaluated on the enclosed animation samples [1], and the comparison of timings between traditional methods and our antialiasing approach can be found in Section 6.

5 Animated sequence quality metric

Before we move to the description of our metric of the animated sequence quality, we recall some well-known relationships between sensitivity to temporal fluctuations and moving patterns [28], which lie at the foundation of our approach.

5.1 Spatio-velocity vs. spatio-temporal considerations

Let $f(x, y, t)$ denote the space-time distribution of an intensity function (image) f, and r_x and r_y denote the horizontal and vertical components of the velocity vector $\vec{r}$, which is defined in the xy plane of f. For simplicity we assume that the whole image f moves with constant velocity $\vec{r}$, and the same reasoning can be applied separately to any finite region of f that moves with a homogeneous, constant velocity [31]. The intensity distribution function $f_{\vec{r}}$ of the image moving with speed $\vec{r}$ can be expressed as:

$$f_{\vec{r}}(x, y, t) = f(x - r_x t, y - r_y t, 0) \tag{1}$$

Let $F(u, v, \omega)$ denote the 3D Fourier transform of $f(x, y, t)$, where u and v are spatial frequencies and ω is temporal frequency. Then the Fourier transform $F_{\vec{r}}$ of the image moving with speed $\vec{r}$ can be expressed as:

$$F_{\vec{r}}(u, v, \omega) = F(u, v)\delta(r_x u + r_y v - \omega) \tag{2}$$

This equation shows the relation between the spatial frequencies and the temporal frequencies, resulting from the movement of the image along the image plane. For example, we can see that a given flickering pattern characterized by the spatial frequencies u and v, and the temporal fluctuation ω is equivalent to the steady pattern of the same spatial frequencies, but moving along the image plane with speed $\vec{r}$ such that

$$r_x u + r_y v = \omega \tag{3}$$

This relationship between the velocity of an image pattern and its temporal frequency was used by Kelly [16] in his experimental derivation of spatio-velocity CSF. Kelly measured contrast sensitivity at several fixed velocities of traveling waves of various spatial frequencies. Kelly found that the constant velocity CSF curves have very regular shape at any velocity greater than about 0.1 degree/second. This made easy fitting an analytical approximation to the contrast sensitivity data derived by Kelly in the psychophysical experiment. Obviously, equation (3) can be used to convert the analytical representation of the spatio-velocity CSF into the spatio-temporal CSF, which is commonly used in many applications including video quality metrics.

Kelly performed his psychophysical experiments with stabilization of the retinal image to eliminate the eye movements. Effectively in this case, the retinal image velocity depended exclusively on the velocity of the image pattern motion. However, in the natural observation conditions the spatial acuity of visual system is affected also by the eye movements of three types: smooth pursuit, saccadic, and natural drift. Tracking of moving image patterns with smooth-pursuit eye movements makes possible compensating for the motion of an object of interest, which leads to reducing of the retinal velocity and improving acuity. The smooth pursuit movements make also possible to keep the retinal image of an object of interest in the foveal region, in which the ability of resolving spatial details is the best. The smooth-pursuit eye movement is affected by saccades, which shift the eye's focus of attention and may occur every 100-500 milliseconds [24]. The saccadic eye movements are of very high velocity (160-300 deg/sec), and effectively the eye sensitivity is near zero during this motion [5]. During intentional gaze fixation the drift eye movements are present, and their velocity can be estimated as 0.15 deg/sec [16, 5].

Daly [5] pointed out that a direct use of spatio-temporal CSF as developed by Kelly leads to underestimating of the human vision sensitivity because of ignoring the target tracking by the eye movements. Daly extended the Kelly's spatio-velocity CSF to account for the eye movements, and showed the way to transform it into the spatio-temporal CSF.

We found that in our application it is more convenient to include directly the spatio-velocity CSF to our animation quality metric. The following reasons may justify our approach:

- The widely used spatio-temporal CSF was in fact derived from the Kelly's spatio-velocity CSF, which was measured for moving stimuli (the traveling wave).
- As Daly have shown [5] accounting for the eye movements is more straightforward for a spatio-velocity CSF than for a spatio-temporal CSF.
- It is not clear whether the vision channels are better described as spatiotemporal or spatiovelocity [16, 6].
- The PF provides us directly with velocity information for local image regions.

The following section describes the animation quality metric developed in this research.

5.2 Animation Quality Metric

As the framework of our Animation Quality Metric (AQM) we decided to expand the perception-based visible differences predictor for static images proposed by Eriksson *el al.* [11]. The architecture of this predictor was validated by Eriksson *el al.* through psychophysical experiments, and its integrity was shown for various contrast and visual masking models [11]. Also, we found that responses of this predictor are very robust, and its architecture was suitable for incorporation of the spatio-velocity CSF.

Figure 2 illustrates the processing flow of AQM. A pair of compared animation frames undergoes an identical initial processing. At first, the original pixel intensities are compressed by the amplitude non-linearity and normalized to the luminance levels of the CRT display (the maximum luminance of 100 cd/m^2 was assumed). Then decomposition into spatial and orientation channels is performed using the Cortex transform proposed by Daly [4], and contrast in every channel is computed (the global contrast definition [11] in respect to the mean luminance value of the whole image was assumed). In the next stage, the spatio-velocity CSF was computed according to the Kelly model. Then the visual masking is modeled using the threshold elevation approach [11]. The final stage is error pooling across all channels.

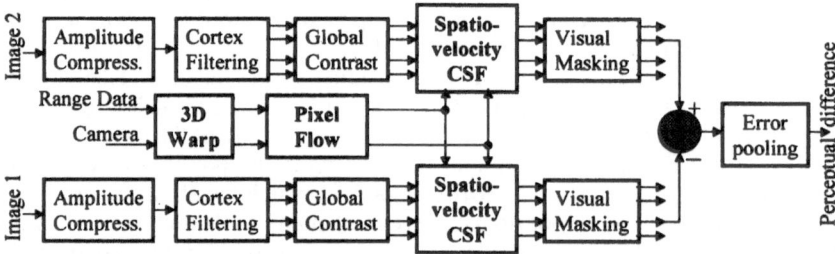

Fig. 2. Animation Quality Metric. The spatio-velocity CSF is based on velocity information for every pixel. For this purpose the Pixel Flow is computed for the next and previous frames along the animation path in respect to the input Image1 (or Image2 which should closely correspond to Image1). This requires the camera parameters for all three involved frames and the range data of Image1.

Since all stages of AQM are standard and well described in the provided references, we narrow further discussion to our extensions in respect to the predictor, which was originally proposed by Eriksson *el al.* We start by recalling the formula describing the Kelly spatio-velocity CSF model with its later extensions introduced by Daly [5]:

$$CSF(\rho, r) \doteq c_0(6.1 + 7.3|\log(c_2 r/3)|^3)c_2 r(2\pi c_1 \rho)^2 \exp(-4\pi c_1 \rho(c_2 r + 2)/45.9) \tag{4}$$

where ρ is spatial frequency in cycles per degree, r is retinal velocity in degrees per second, and $c_0 = 1.14$, $c_1 = 0.67$, $c_2 = 1.7$ are coefficients introduced by Daly [5] to adapt the Kelly model to the typical levels of CRT display luminance (around 100 cd/m^2). The CSF values are calculated for the center frequency ρ of each Cortex frequency band. The resulting values are used to normalize contrasts in every frequency-orientation channel into the Just Noticeable Differences (JND) units [19, 4]. The retinal velocity is estimated as the difference of the image velocity r_I and the eye movement velocity r_E [5]:

$$r = r_I - r_E = r_I - \min(0.82 r_I + r_{Min}, r_{Max}) \tag{5}$$

where $r_{Min} = 0.15$ is the estimated eye drift velocity, $r_{Max} = 80$ the maximum velocity of the smooth eye pursuit, and the coefficient 0.82 is experimentally derived efficiency of the eye tracking for a simple stimuli on the CRT display [5]. In general, the estimate of retinal velocity given by equation (5) is very conservative because it assumes that the eye is tracking all moving image elements at the same time. However, it cannot be considered as the upper bound of the eye sensitivity, because for the lower spatial frequencies the sensitivity may increase with the increasing retinal velocity [1], i.e., when the eye tracking efficiency is reduced. To account for this phenomena the eye movements can be ignored, in which case $r = r_I$. This assumption is actually made by many video quality metrics [8, 19, 29]. To get more conservative measure of the eye sensitivity these two estimates of the retinal velocity can be used and the maximum value of the sensitivity which depends on the image spatial contents can be selected.

The practical question arises how to estimate r_I. In our framework it becomes very easy because the PF derived using IBR techniques is available. For a given frame we use two estimates of the PF in respect to the previous and subsequent frames. We derive the retinal velocity vector for every pixel as the average of these estimates.

It is well-known that the image is maximally blurred in the direction of retinal motion, and the spatial acuity is retained in the direction orthogonal to the retinal motion direction [10]. To account for this characteristic of the visual system we project the retinal velocity vector to the direction of the filter band orientation.

6 Results

As the case study in this research we selected the walkthrough animation in an atrium of the University of Aizu [1]. The main motivation for this choice were interesting occlusion relationships between objects that are challenging for the IBR rendering. Also, a vast majority of surfaces in the atrium exhibits some view-dependent reflection properties including mirror-like and transparent surfaces, which made inbetween frames calculation more difficult. In such conditions, the AQM guided selection of keyframes and glossy objects within inbetween frames to be recomputed was more critical, and wrong decisions concerning these issues could be easy perceptible.

For our experiments we selected a walkthrough sequence of 200 frames. The resolution of each frame was 640 × 480 (to accommodate for the NTSC standard). At the initialization step, we split this walkthrough into eight segments S of 25 frames each.

As described in Section 3.2 for every segment S we run the AQM once to decide upon the specular objects which require recomputation. The AQM is calibrated in such way that 1 JND unit corresponds to a 75% probability that an observer can perceive the difference between the corresponding image regions (such a probability value is the standard threshold value for discrimination tasks [4]). If a group of connected pixels representing an object (or a part of an object) exhibits the differences bigger than 2 JND (93.75% probability of discrimination) we select such an object for recalculation. If for an object the differences below 2 JND are reported by the AQM then we estimate the ratio of pixels exhibiting such differences to all pixels depicting this object. We assume that if the ratio is bigger than 25% then we select such an object for recomputation - 25% is an experimentally selected trade-off value, which makes possible the reduction of the number of specular object requiring recomputation, at expense of some potentially perceptible image artifacts. These artifacts are usually hard to notice unless the observer attention is specifically directed to a given image region. The graph in Figure 3a depicts the percentage of pixels that are selected for recomputation in our walkthrough sequence. The percentage includes also pixels which cannot be properly derived using the IBR techniques, which usually are a small fraction of all recomputed pixels (in average 0.3% for our animation).

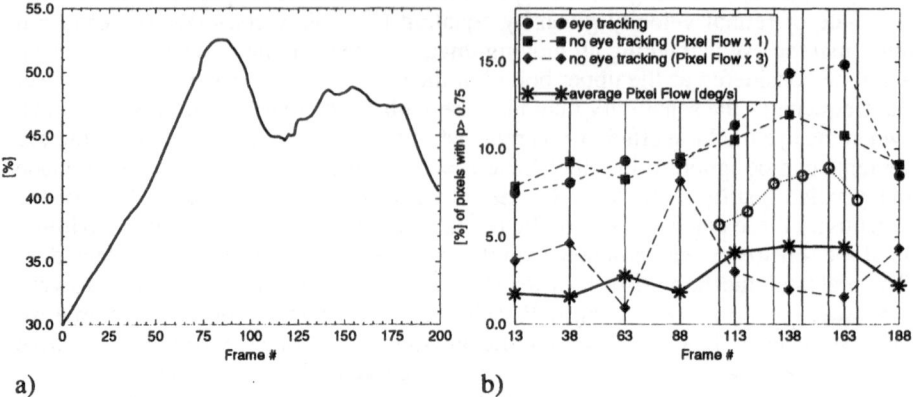

a)   b)

Fig. 3. a) The percentage of pixels to be recalculated by ray tracing. b) The AQM prediction of the perceived differences between warped images of two neighboring reference frames taking into account various retinal image velocity. Also, the average Pixel Flow velocity expressed in [degree/second] units is shown. Lines connecting the symbols were added for the figure readability and they do not have any meaning for unmarked frames.

After masking out the pixels to be recomputed, the decision upon further splitting of S is taken using the AQM predictions for the remaining pixels. The predictions are expressed as the percentage of unmasked pixels for which the probability p of detecting the differences is greater than 0.75. Based on experiments that we conducted, we decided to split every segment S when the percentage of such pixels is bigger than 10%. When computing the AQM predictions that we used to decide upon segment splitting, we assumed good tracking of moving image patterns with the smooth-pursuit eye movements (the retinal velocity is computed using equation (5)). The filled circles in Figure 3b show such predictions for the inbetween frames located in the middle of every initial segment S. Three segments with the AQM predictions over 10% were split and the empty circles show the corresponding reduction of predicted perceptible differences. We performed also experiments assuming higher levels of the retinal velocity when observing our walkthrough animation. The filled squares in Figure 3b show the AQM predictions when the retinal velocity is equal to the PF (the eye movements are ignored). For all segments that we selected for splitting based on the smooth-pursuit eye movements assumption, the AQM predictions exceeded the threshold of 10% as well when the eye movements were ignored. As we discussed in Section 5.2, although in general the eye sensitivity is improving when the eye tracking is enabled, however, for some image patterns the eye sensitivity can be better when the eye tracking is disabled (refer to the AQM predictions for the inbetween frame #38). The filled diamonds marks show the AQM prediction assuming that the original velocity of PF was multiplied by the factor three (the eye movements are ignored). Effectively, this corresponds to three times faster display of our animation. As expected, in general the perceivability of image artifacts decreases with the velocity. The graph shown with the thick line shows the average PF values in [degrees/second] units, which were measured for the selected inbetween frames.

To evaluate efficiency of our animation rendering system we compared the average time required for a single frame of the atrium walkthrough. All timings were measured on the MIPS 195 MHz processor. For an antialiased frame (with adaptive supersampling) the required rendering time was about 170 minutes, and for the corresponding non-antialiased frame which was used as a keyframe for our image-based rendering took about 40 minutes. The average rendering time using our compositing of IBR and ray traced images was about 27 minutes (in average 43.9% of pixels were ray traced per frame). This included rendering keyframes, the AQM processing (which required 9 minutes to process a pair of frames, mostly because the Fast Fourier Transform of 1024×512 images was involved as the result of processing our 640×480 frames), IBR rendering (which requires about 12 seconds to warp and blend two reference frames). The motion-compensated 3D filtering added an overhead of 10 seconds per frame.

The most significant speedup was achieved by using our spatio-temporal antialiasing technique and avoiding the traditional adaptive supersampling. Our inbetween frames rendering technique added further 30% of speedup for the scene built mostly from surfaces exhibiting view-dependent reflectance properties. Even better performance can be expected for environments in which specular objects are depicted by a moderate percentage of pixels.

7 Conclusions

In this work, we proposed an efficient approach to rendering animated walkthrough sequences of high quality. Our contribution is in developing a fully automatic, perception-based guidance of the inbetween frames computation, which minimizes the number of pixels computed using costly ray tracing, and seamlessly (in terms of perception of animated sequences) replace them by pixels derived using inexpensive IBR techniques. Also, we have shown two useful applications of the Pixel Flow obtained as a by-product of IBR processing: (1) to estimate the spatio-velocity Contrast Sensitivity Function which made possible incorporation of temporal factors into our perceptually-informed image quality metric, (2) to perform the spatio-temporal antialiasing with motion-compensated filtering based on image processing principles (in contrast to traditional antialiasing techniques used in computer graphics). We integrated all these techniques into a balanced animation rendering system.

As the future work we plan to conduct validation of our AQM in psychophysical experiments. Also, we believe that our approach has some potential in automatic selection of reference frames used in IBR systems. As the future work we plan to investigate this issue.

Acknowledgments

Special thanks to Scott Daly for his stimulating comments on video quality metrics.

References

1. www.u-aizu.ac.jp/labs/csel/aqm. *The Web page accompanying to this paper.*
2. S.J. Adelson and L.F. Hodges. Generating exact ray-traced animation frames by reprojection. *IEEE Computer Graphics & Applications*, 15(3):43–52, 1995.
3. C. Chevrier. A view interpolation technique taking into account diffuse and specular inter-reflections. *The Visual Computer*, 13(7):330–341, 1997.
4. S. Daly. The Visible Differences Predictor: An algorithm for the assessment of image fidelity. In A.B. Watson, editor, *Digital Image and Human Vision*, pages 179–206. MIT Press, 1993.

5. S. Daly. Engineering observations from spatiovelocity and spatiotemporal visual models. In *Human Vision and Electronic Imaging III*, pages 180–191. SPIE Vol. 3299, 1998.

6. S. Daly. personal communication. 1999.

7. L. Darsa, B.C. Silva, and A. Varshney. Navigating static environments using image-space simplification and morphing. In *1997 Symposium on Interactive 3D Graphics*, pages 25–34. ACM SIGGRAPH, 1997.

8. C.J.van den Branden Lambrecht. *Perceptual models and architectures for video coding applications*. Ph.D. thesis, 1996.

9. C.J.van den Branden Lambrecht and O. Verscheure. Perceptual quality measure using a spatio-temporal model of the human visual system. pages 450–461. SPIE Vol. 2668, 1996.

10. M.P. Eckert and Buchsbaum G. The significance of eye movements and image acceleration for coding television image sequences. In A.B. Watson, editor, *Digital Image and Human Vision*, pages 89–98. Cambridge, MA: MIT Press, 1993.

11. R. Eriksson, B. Andren, and K. Brunnstrom. Modelling of perception of digital images: a performance study. pages 88–97. Proceedings of SPIE Vol. 3299.

12. R.C. Gonzalez and R.E. Woods. *Digital image processing*. Addison-Wesley, 1993.

13. S.J. Gortler, R. Grzeszczuk, R. Szeliski, and M.F. Cohen. The lumigraph. In *SIGGRAPH 96 Conference Proceedings*, Annual Conference Series, pages 43–54, 1996.

14. B.K. Guenter, H.C. Yun, and R.M. Mersereau. Motion compensated compression of computer animation frames. In *SIGGRAPH '93 Proceedings*, volume 27, pages 297–304, 1993.

15. Michael Halle. Multiple viewpoint rendering. In *SIGGRAPH 98 Conference Proceedings*, Annual Conference Series, pages 243–254, 1998.

16. D.H. Kelly. Motion and Vision 2. Stabilized spatio-temporal threshold surface. *Journal of the Optical Society of America*, 69(10):1340–1349, 1979.

17. M. Levoy and P. Hanrahan. Light field rendering. In *SIGGRAPH 96 Conference Proceedings*, Annual Conference Series, pages 31–42, 1996.

18. D. Lischinski and A. Rappoport. Image-based rendering for non-diffuse synthetic scenes. In *Proceedings of Eurographics Rendering Workshop '98*, pages 301–314, 1998.

19. J. Lubin. A human vision model for objective picture quality measurements. In *Conference Publication No. 447*, pages 498–503. IEE International Broadcasting Convention, 1997.

20. W.R. Mark, L. McMillan, and G. Bishop. Post-rendering 3D warping. In *1997 Symposium on Interactive 3D Graphics*, pages 7–16. ACM SIGGRAPH, 1997.

21. L. McMillan. *An Image-Based Approach to 3D Computer Graphics*. Ph.D. thesis, 1997.

22. G. Miller, S. Rubin, and D. Poncelen. Lazy decompression of surface light fields for pre-computed global illumination. In *Rendering Techniques '98 (Proceedings of Eurographics Rendering Workshop '98)*, pages 281–292, 1998.

23. J. Nimeroff, J. Dorsey, and H. Rushmeier. Implementation and analysis of an image-based global illumination framework for animated environments. *IEEE Transactions on Visualization and Computer Graphics*, 2(4):283–298, 1996.

24. W. Osberger, A.J. Maeder, and N. Bergmann. A perceptually based quantization technique for MPEG encoding. pages 148–159. Proceedings of SPIE Vol. 3299, 1998.

25. J.W. Shade, S.J. Gortler, L. He, and R Szeliski. Layered depth images. In *SIGGRAPH 98 Conference Proceedings*, pages 231–242, 1998.

26. M. Shinya. Spatial anti-aliasing for animation sequences with spatio-temporal filtering. In *Computer Graphics (SIGGRAPH '93 Proceedings)*, volume 27, pages 289–296, 1993.

27. A. Murat Tekalp. *Digital video Processing*. Prentice Hall, 1995.

28. A.B. Watson. Temporal sensitivity. In *Handbook of Perception and Human Performance, Chapter 6*. John Wiley, New York, 1986.

29. A.B. Watson. Toward a perceptual video quality metric. In *Human Vision and Electronic Imaging III*, pages 139–147. Proceedings of SPIE Vol. 3299, 1998.

30. J.H.D.M. Westerink and C. Teunissen. Perceived sharpness in moving images. pages 78–87. Proceedings of SPIE Vol. 1249, 1990.

31. E. Zeghers, S. Carre, and K. Bouatouch. Faster image rendering in animation through motion compensated interpolation. In *Graphics, Design and Visualization*, pages 49–62, 1993.

Editors' Note: see Appendix, p. 355 for colored figures of this paper

Interactive Rendering using the Render Cache

Bruce Walter†, George Drettakis†, Steven Parker‡

†iMAGIS[1]-GRAVIR/IMAG-INRIA
B.P. 53, F-38041 Grenoble, Cedex 9, France
‡University of Utah

Abstract.
Interactive rendering requires rapid visual feedback. The *render cache* is a new method for achieving this when using high-quality pixel-oriented renderers such as ray tracing that are usually considered too slow for interactive use. The render cache provides visual feedback at a rate faster than the renderer can generate complete frames, at the cost of producing approximate images during camera and object motion. The method works both by caching previous results and reprojecting them to estimate the current image and by directing the renderer's sampling to more rapidly improve subsequent images.
Our implementation demonstrates an interactive application working with both ray tracing and path tracing renderers in situations where they would normally be considered too expensive. Moreover we accomplish this using a software only implementation without the use of 3D graphics hardware.

1   Introduction

In rendering, interactivity and high quality are often seen as competing and even mutually exclusive goals. Algorithms such as ray tracing [29] and path tracing [14] are widely used to produce high-quality, visually compelling images that include complex effects such as reflections, refraction, and global illumination. However, they have generally been considered too computationally expensive for interactive use.

Interactive use has typically been limited to lower-quality, often hardware accelerated rendering algorithms such as wireframe or scan-conversion. While these are perfectly adequate for many applications, often it would be preferable to achieve interactivity while preserving, as much as possible, the quality of a more expensive renderer. For example, it is desirable to use the same renderer when editing a scene as will be used for the final images or animation.

The goal of this work is to show how high quality ray-based rendering algorithms can be combined with the the high framerates needed for interactivity, using only a level of computational power that is widely and cheaply available today. Once achieved, this creates a compelling visual interface that users quickly find addictive and are reluctant to relinquish. In the typical visual feedback loop, as illustrated in Figure 1(a), the expense of the renderer often strictly limits the achievable framerate[2].

The *render cache* is a new technique to overcome this limitation and allow interactive rendering in many cases where this was previously infeasible. The renderer is shifted out of the synchronous part of the visual feedback loop and a new display process introduced to handle image generation as illustrated in Figure 1(b). This greatly

---

[1] iMAGIS is joint project of CNRS, INPG, INRIA and Université Joseph Fourier.

[2] In this paper we will use framerate to mean the rate at which the renderer or display process can produce updated images. This is usually slower than the framerate of the display device (e.g., a monitor or CRT).

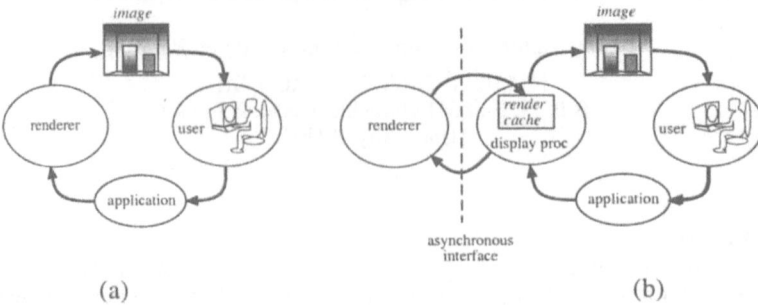

Fig. 1. (a) The traditional interactive visual feedback loop where the framerate is limited by the speed of the renderer. (b) The modified loop using the *render-cache* which decouples display framerate from the speed of the renderer.

reduces the framerate's dependence on the speed of the renderer. The display process, however, does not replace the renderer and depends on it for all shading computations.

The display process caches recent results from the renderer as shaded 3D points, reprojects these to quickly estimate the current image, and directs the renderer's future sampling. Reprojection alone would result in numerous visual artifacts, however, many of these can be handled by some simple filters. For the rest we introduce several strategies to detect and prioritize regions with remaining artifacts. New rendering samples are concentrated accordingly to rapidly improve subsequent images. Sampling patterns are generated using an error diffusion dither to ensure good spatial distributions and to mediate between our different sampling strategies.

The render cache is designed to make few assumptions about the underlying rendering algorithm so that it can be used with different renderers. We have demonstrated it with both ray tracing [29] and path tracing [14] rendering algorithms and shown that it allows them to be used interactively using far less computational power than was previously required. Even when the renderer is only able to produce a low number of new samples or pixels per frame (e.g., 1/64th of image resolution), we are able to achieve satisfactory image quality and good interactivity. Several frames taken from an interactive session are shown in Figure 2.

1.1 Previous Work

The render cache utilizes many different techniques and ideas to achieve its goal of interactivity including progressive refinement for faster feedback, exploiting spatio-temporal image coherence, using reprojection to reuse previously results, image space sparse sampling heuristics, decoupling rendering and display framerates, and parallel processing. The contribution of the render cache is to show how these ideas can be adapted and used simultaneously in a context where *interactivity* is considered of paramount importance, in a way that is both novel and effective.

One way to provide faster visual feedback and enhanced interactivity is to provide the user with approximate intermediate results rather than waiting for exact results to be available. This is often known as progressive refinement and has been used by many researchers (e.g., the "golden thread" of [3] or progressive radiosity [9]).

Many researchers have explored ways to exploit spatio-temporal image plane coherence to reduce the computational costs in ray tracing sequences of images. With a fixed

Fig. 2. Some frames from an interactive editing session using the render cache. The user is given immediate feedback when changing the viewpoint or moving objects such as the mug and desk lamp in this ray traced scene. While there are some visual artifacts, object positions are rapidly updated while other features such as shadows update a little slower. The user can continue to edit and work without waiting for complete updates. On a single processor, this session ran at ∼5fps and lasted about one minute. No graphics hardware acceleration was used. See Appendix for larger color images.

camera, changing materials or moving objects can be accelerated by storing partial or complete ray trees (e.g., [25, 13, 6]).

Sequences with camera motions can be handled by storing the rendered points and reprojecting onto the new camera plane. There are several inherent problems with reprojection including that the mapping is not a bijection (some pixels have many points map to them and some have none), occlusion errors (if the reprojected point is actually behind an occluding surface in the new view), and non-diffuse shading (a point's color may change when viewed from a different angle). Many different strategies for mitigating these problems have been proposed in the image-based literature (e.g., [8, 18, 17, 16, 26]), which relies heavily on reprojection.

Reprojection has also been used in ray tracing to accelerate the generation of animation sequences (e.g., [2, 1]). These methods save considerable computation by reprojecting data from the previous frame and only recomputing pixels which are potentially still incorrect. At a high level their operations are similar to those of the render cache but their goal (i.e. computing exact frames) is different. Our goal of interactivity requires the use of fast reconstruction heuristics that work reasonably well even in the presence of inexact previous frames and a prioritized sparse sampling scheme to best choose the limited number of pixels that can be recomputed per frame.

Sparse or adaptive image space sampling strategies (e.g., [21, 19, 11, 5]) can greatly reduce ray tracing costs. While most work has concentrated on generating single images, some researchers have also considered animations (e.g., using a uniform random sampling to detect changed regions [2] or uniform deterministic sampling in an interactive context [4]). The render cache introduces a new sampling strategy that combines several different pixel update priority schemes and uses an error diffusion dither [10] to mediate between our conflicting goals of a uniform distribution for smooth image refinement and concentrating samples in important regions for faster image convergence.

Parallel processing is another way to accelerate ray tracing and global illumination rendering (e.g., see [24] for one survey). Massive parallel processing can be used to achieve interactive ray tracing (e.g., [20, 22]), but this is an expensive approach. A better alternative is to combine parallel processing with intelligent display algorithms. For example, Parker et. al. [22] who used frameless rendering [4] to increase their framerate, could benefit from the render cache which produces better images and requires significantly fewer rays per frame.

The Post-Rendering 3D Warp [16] is an alternative intelligent display process. It displays images at a higher framerate than that of the underlying renderer by using

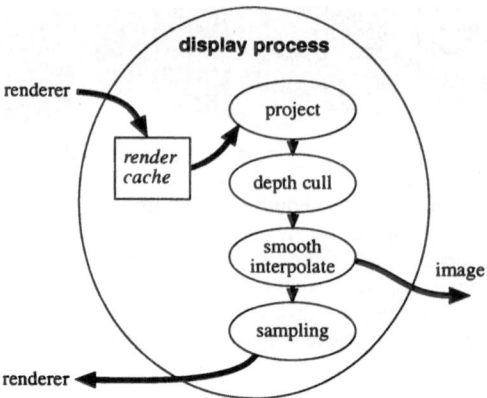

Fig. 3. The display process: The render cache receives and caches sample points from the renderer, which are then projected onto the current image plane. The results are filtered by the depth culling and interpolation steps to produce the displayed image. A priority image is also generated which is used to choose which new samples will be requested from the renderer.

image warping to interpolate from neighboring (past and future) rendered frames. One drawback is that the system must predict far enough into the future to render frames before they are needed for interpolation. This is trivial for a pre-scripted animation, but extremely difficult in an interactive context.

Another example is the "holodeck" [15] which was designed as a more interactive front end for Radiance [28]. It combines precomputation, reprojection, and online uniform sampling to greatly increase interactivity as compared to the Radiance system alone. Unlike the render cache though, it is not designed to handle dynamic scenes or long continuous camera motions and uses a less sophisticated sampling strategy.

2 Algorithm Overview

Our display process is designed to be compatible with many different renderers. The main requirement is that the renderer must be able to efficiently compute individual rays or pixels. Thus, for example, ray tracing like renderers are excellent candidates while scan conversion renderers are not. The display process provides interactive feedback to the user even when the renderer itself is too slow or expensive to produce complete images at an interactive rate (though the number of visual artifacts will increase if the renderer would take more than a few seconds to produce a full image).

There are several essential requirements for our display process. It must rapidly generate approximations to the current correct image based on the current viewpoint and the data in the render cache. It must control which rays or samples are rendered next to rapidly improve future images. It also must manage the render cache by integrating newly rendered results, and discarding old data when appropriate or necessary.

Image generation consists of projection, depth culling, and interpolation/smoothing steps. Rendered points from the cache are first projected onto the current view plane. We try to enforce correct occlusion both within a pixel by using a z-buffered projection, and among neighboring pixels using the depth culling step. The interpolation step fills in small gaps in the often sparse point data and produces the displayed image.

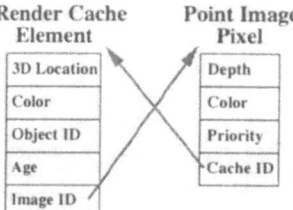

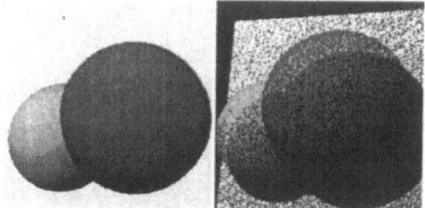

Fig. 4. The fields in the render cache and point image. Each point or element in the render cache contains a 3D location, a color, and an object id all provided by the renderer. They also have an age which is incremented each frame and an image id field which tells which pixel (if any) this point currently maps to. Each pixel in the point image contains a depth, a color, a priority, and the cache id of the point (if any) that is currently mapped to this pixel.

Fig. 5. Results of z-buffered point projection for a simple scene containing a white plane behind two diffuse spheres. The points generated for one viewpoint (left) are projected on the image plane for a new viewpoint (right). Notice that there are many gaps where no point projected onto a particular image (shown as black) and some points of the lighter plane are showing through gaps in the darker sphere points which should be occluding them.

Simultaneously, the display process also builds a *priority image* to guide future sampling. Because we expect that only a small subset of pixels can be rendered per frame, it important to direct the rendered sampling to maximize their benefit. Each pixel is given a priority value based on the relative value of rendering a new sample at that pixel. We then use an error diffusion dither [10] to choose the new samples to request. Using a dither both concentrates more samples in important regions and ensures that the samples are well spaced and distributed over the entire image. A diagram of the display process steps is shown in Figure 3.

3 Image Generation

Images are generated in our display process by projecting rendered points from the render cache onto an augmented image plane called *point image* (see Figure 4 for corresponding data fields). The projection step consists of a transform based on the current camera parameters as specified by the application program and z-buffering to handle the cases when more than one point maps to the same pixel. Whenever a point is mapped to a pixel, their corresponding data fields (see Figure 4) are updated appropriately including writing the point's color, depth, and a priority based on its age to the pixel.

The raw results of such a projection will contain numerous artifacts as illustrated in Figure 5. We handle some of the simpler kinds of artifacts using some filters while relying our sampling algorithm and newly rendered samples to resolve the more difficult artifacts in future frames. We have deliberately chosen to use only fast, simple techniques and heuristics in our system to keep its computational requirements both as light and consistent as possible.

3.1 Depth Culling and Smoothing/Interpolation

Some of the points, though formerly visible, may currently lie behind an occluding surface (e.g., due to object or camera motion). Visual artifacts, such as surfaces incorrectly "showing through" other surfaces, occur if such points are not removed (see Figure 6).

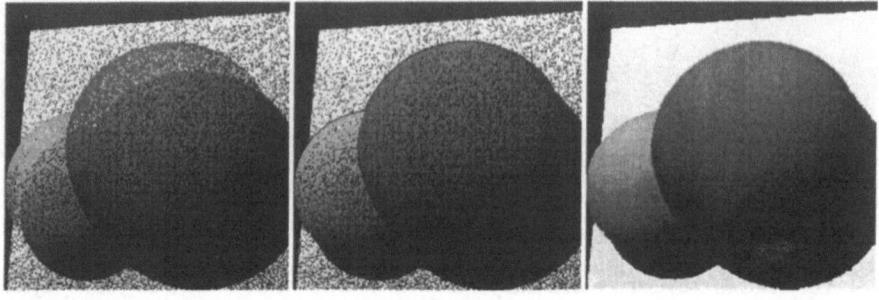

Fig. 6. Image reconstruction example: The raw projected points image (left) from Figure 5 is filtered by our depth-cull (middle) and interpolation (right) to produce an image that gives the correct impression that the surfaces are opaque and continuous.

Projection only removes occluded points if a point from the occluding surface maps to the same pixel. We remove more occluded points using a depth culling heuristic that searches for points whose depth is inconsistent with their neighbors.

Each pixel's 3x3 neighborhood is examined and an average depth computed, ignoring neighboring pixels without points. If the point's depth is significantly different from this average, then it is likely that we have points from different surfaces and that the nearer surface should now be occluding the farther one. Based on this assumption, we remove the point (i.e. we treat it as if no point had mapped to this pixel) if its depth is more than some threshold beyond the average depth (currently we use 10%). This heuristic both correctly removes many points which should have been occluded and falsely removes some genuinely visible points near depth discontinuity edges. Fortunately the incorrect removal artifacts are largely hidden by the interpolation step.

Next we use an interpolation and smoothing filter to fill in small gaps in the point image (see Figure 6). For each pixel, we again examine its 3x3 neighborhood and perform a weighted average[3] of the corresponding colors. The weights are 4, 2, and 1 for center, immediate neighbor, and diagonal neighbors respectively, and pixels without points receive zero weight. This average becomes the pixel's displayed color except when there are no points in the neighborhood making the average invalid. Such pixels either retain the color they had in the previous frame or are displayed as black depending on the user's preference.

The quality of the resulting image depends on how relevant the cached points are to the current view. Actions such as rapid turning or moving through a wall can temporarily degrade image quality significantly. Fortunately the sparse sampling and interpolation tend to quickly restore image quality. Typically the image quality becomes usable again by the time that just one tenth of the cache has been filled with relevant points.

4 Sampling

Choosing which samples the renderer should compute next is another essential function of the display process. Since we expect that the number of new samples computed per frame to be much smaller than the number of pixels in the displayed image (typically by a factor between 8 and 128), it is important to optimize the placement of these sparse

---

[3] As described the system performs some slight smoothing even in fully populated regions. If this is considered objectionable, smoothing could easily be disabled at those pixels that had a point map to them.

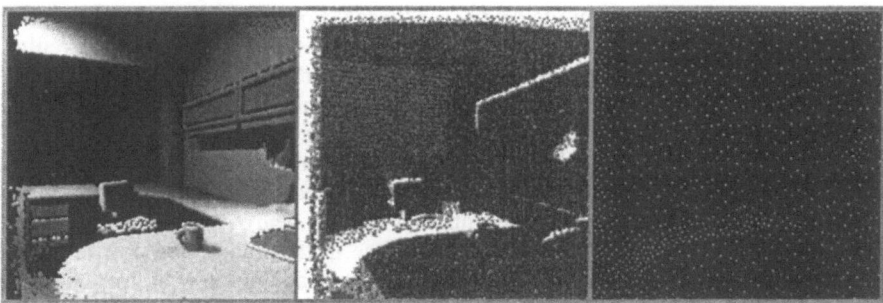

Fig. 7. A image produced by the display process (left) along with its corresponding priority image (middle) and the dithered binary image specifying which sample locations will be requested next from the renderer. In this case the user is moving toward the upper left and the high priority regions are due to previously occluded regions becoming visible. Note that the dithering algorithm causes new samples to be concentrated in these high priority regions while staying well spaced and distributed over the entire image region.

samples. Samples are chosen by first constructing a grayscale sampling *priority image* and then applying an error diffusion dither algorithm. We use several heuristics to give high priority to pixels that we suspect are likely to contain visual artifacts.

The priority image is generated simultaneously with image reconstruction. Each point in the render cache has an age which starts at zero and is incremented each frame. When a point in the render cache maps to a pixel, that pixel's priority is set based on the point's age. This reflects the intuition that it is more valuable to recompute older samples since they are more likely to have changed. The priority for other pixels is set during the interpolation step based on how many of their neighbors had points map to them. Pixels with no valid neighbors receive the maximum possible priority while pixels with many valid neighbors receive only a medium priority. The intuition here is that it is more important to sample regions with lower local point densities first.

Choosing sampling locations from the priority image is equivalent to turning a grayscale image into a binary image. We want our samples to have a good spatial distribution so that the image visually refines in a smooth manner by avoiding the clumping of samples and ensuring that they are distributed over the whole image. We also want to concentrate more samples in high priority regions so that the image converges more quickly. A uniform distribution would not properly prioritize pixels, and a priority queue would not ensure a good spatial distribution. Instead we utilize a simple error diffusion dithering algorithm [10] to create the binary sample image (see Figure 7). The dithering approach nicely mediates between our competing sampling goals at the cost of occasionally requesting a low priority pixel.

In our implementation, scanlines are scanned in alternating directions and the priority at each pixel compared to a threshold value (total priority / # samples to request). If above threshold, this pixel is requested as a sample and the threshold subtracted from its priority. Any remaining priority is then propagated, half to the next pixel and half to the corresponding pixel on the next scanline.

4.1 Premature Aging

By default, points age at a constant rate, but it is often useful to prematurely age points that are especially likely to be outdated or obsolete. Premature aging encourages the system to more quickly recompute or discard these points for better performance.

A good example is our color change heuristic. Often a new sample is requested for a pixel which already contains a point. We consider this a *resample*, record the old point's index in the sample request, and ensure that the requested ray passes exactly through the 3D location[4] of the old point. We can then compare the old and new colors of resampled pixels to detect changes (e.g., due to changes in occlusion or lighting). If there is a significant change, then it is likely that nearby pixels have also changed. Therefore, we prematurely age any points that map to nearby pixels. In this way we are able to automatically detect regions of change in the image and concentrate new samples there. Another example is that we prematurely age points which are not visible in the current frame since it is likely that they are no longer useful.

4.2 Renderer and Application Supplied Hints

While we want our display process to work automatically, we also want to provide ways for the renderer and application to optionally provide hints to increase the display process' effectiveness. For example, the renderer can flag some points as being more likely to change than others and thus should be resampled sooner. The display process then ages these points at a faster rate. Some possible candidates are points on a moving objects, points in their shadows, or points which are part of a specular highlight. Together with the resample color change optimization, this can greatly improve the display process's ability to track the changes in such features.

The noise inherent in Monte Carlo renderers can cause the display process to falsely think that a sample's color has changed significantly during resampling. Falsely triggering the color change heuristic can prematurely age still valid points and wastefully concentrate samples in this region. To avoid this, the renderer can provide a hint that specifies the expected amount of noise in a result. This helps the display process to distinguish between significant color changes and variation simply due to noise.

We have also added a further optimization to help with moving objects. The application can provide rigid body transforms (e.g., rotation or translation) for objects. The display process then updates the 3D positions of points in the render cache with the specified object identifiers. This significantly improves the tracking of moving objects as compared to resampling alone though resampling is still necessary.

4.3 Cache Management Strategy

We use a fixed size render cache that is slightly larger than the number of pixels to be displayed. Thus each new point or sample must overwrite a previous one in the cache. The fixed size cache helps keep the computational cost low and constant. In dynamic environments, this also ensures that any stale data will eventually be discarded.

New points or samples that are resamples of an old point (see above) simply overwrite that point in the cache. Since the old point is highly likely to be either redundant or outdated, this simple strategy works well.

For other new points, we would like to find some no longer useful point to overwrite. One strategy is to replace the oldest point in the cache as it is more likely to be obsolete. However, we decided that doing this exactly would be unnecessarily expensive. Instead we examine a subset of the cache (e.g., groups of 8 points in a round robin order) and replace the oldest point found.

---

[4]Otherwise requested rays are generated randomly within the pixel to reduce aliasing and Moiré patterns.

5   Implementation and Results

We have implemented our display process and a simple test application that allows us to change viewpoints and move objects. The display process communicates with renderers using a simple abstract broker interface. This abstract interface allows us to both easily work with different renderers (two ray tracers and two path tracers so far) and to utilize parallel processing by running multiple instances of the renderers simultaneously. The broker collects the sample requests from the display process, distributes them to the renderers when they need more work and gathers rendered results to be returned to the display process. It is currently written for shared memory parallel processing using threads, though a message passing version for distributed parallel processing is also feasible.

The render mismatch ratio is a useful measure of the effectiveness of the render cache and our display process. We define this ratio as the number of pixels in a frame divided by the number of new samples or pixels produced by the renderer per frame. It is render cache's ability to handle higher mismatch ratios that allows us to achieve interactivity while using more expensive renderers and/or less computational power.

Working with a mismatch ratio of one is trivial; render and display each frame. Mismatch ratios of two to four can easily be handled using existing techniques such as frameless rendering [4]. The real advantage and contribution of the render cache is its ability to effectively handle higher mismatch ratios. In our experience, the render cache works well for mismatch ratios up to 64 and can be usable at even higher ratios. In many cases this allows us to achieve much greater interactivity with virtually no modification to the renderer. Performance in particular cases will of course depend on many factors including the absolute framerate, scene, renderer, and user task.

5.1   Results

Our current implementation runs on Silicon Graphics workstations using software only (i.e. we do not use any 3D graphics hardware). Our experience shows that the render cache can achieve interactive ray tracing even on single processor systems whose processing power to equivalent to that of today's PC computers. Specialized or expensive hardware is not required, though we can also exploit the additional rendering power of parallel processing when available.

Timings for the display process running on a 195Mhz R10000 processor in an SGI Origin 2000 are shown in Table 1. The display process can generate a 256x256 frame in 0.07 seconds for a potential framerate of around 14 frames per second. In a uniprocessor system, the actual framerate will be lower because part of the processors time must also be devoted to the renderer. In this case, we typically split the processors time evenly between the display process and the renderer for a framerate of around 7 fps. Even on a multiple processor machine it may be desirable to devote less than a full processor to the display process in order to increase the number of rendered samples produced.

Using larger images is trivial though it reduces the framerate. The time to produce each frame scales roughly linearly with the number of pixels to be displayed since all the data structures sizes and major operations are linear in the number of pixels.

We have tested the render cache in various interactive sessions using both ray tracing [29] and path tracing [14] renderers and on machines ranging from one to sixty processors. Some images from example sessions are shown in Figures 2 and 8 (see color plates in Appendix) and videos are available on our web page[5].

---

[5] http://www-imagis.imag.fr/Publications/walter

Initialize buffers	0.0046 secs
Point projection	0.0328 secs
Depth cull	0.0085 secs
Interpolation	0.0139 secs
Display image	0.0027 secs
Request new samples	0.0053 secs
Update render cache	0.0027 secs
Total time	0.0705 secs

Table 1. Timings for the display process' generation of a 256x256 image produced on a single 195Mhz R10000 processor. The display process is capable of producing about 14 frames per second in this case, though the actual framerate may be slower if part of the processors time is also devoted to renderering.

In all cases tested, the render cache provides a much more interactive experience than any other method using the same renderers that we are aware of (e.g., [22, 4]). The reprojection correctly tracks motion and efficiently reuses relevant previously rendered samples. While there are visual artifacts in individual frames, the prioritized sparse sampling smoothly refines the images and allows us to quickly recover from actions that make the previous samples irrelevant (e.g., walking through a wall). We still rely on the renderer for all shading calculations and need it to produce an adequate number of new samples per frame. Compared to previous methods though, we require far fewer new samples per frame to maintain good image quality.

All the sessions shown in Figure 8 used 320x320 resolution and ran at around 8 fps. The first three sessions used ray tracing and between two and four R10000 processors. An image from a sequence where the user walks through a door in Greg Larson's cabin model is shown in the upper left. In the upper right, an ice cream glass has just been moved in his soda shoppe model, and its shadows are in the process of being updated. In the lower left, the camera is turning to the right in a scene with many ray traced effects including extensive reflection and refraction.

The lower right of Figure 8 shows a path tracing of Kajiya's original scene. Path tracing simulates full global illumination and is much more expensive. The four processor version (shown) is no longer really adequate as too few new samples are rendered per frame resulting in more visual artifacts. Nevertheless, interactivity is still much better than it would be without the render cache. We have demonstrated good interactivity even in this case when using a sixty processor machine.

6 Conclusions

The render cache's modular nature and generic interfaces allows it to be used with a variety of different renderers. It uses simple and fast algorithms to guarantee a fast consistent framerate and is designed for interactivity even when rendered samples are expensive and scarce. Reprojection and filtering intelligently reuse previous results to generate new images and a new directed sampling scheme tries to maximize the benefits of future rendered results.

Our prototype implementation has shown that we can achieve interactive framerates using software only for low but reasonable resolutions. We have also shown that it can enable satisfactory image quality and interactivity even when the renderer is only able to produce a small fraction of new pixels per frame (e.g., between 1/8 and 1/64 of the pixels in a frame). We have also demonstrated it working with both ray tracing and path tracing and efficiently using parallel processors ranging from two to sixty processors. Moreover, we have shown the render cache can handle dynamic scenes including moving objects and lights.

We believe that the render cache has the potential to significantly expand the use of ray tracing and related renderers in interactive applications and provide interactive users with a much wider selection of renderers and lighting models to choose from.

6.1 Future Work

There are many ways in which the render cache can be further improved. Higher framerates and bigger images are clearly desirable and will require more processing power. With its fixed-size regular data structures and operations, the render cache could benefit from the small-scale SIMD instructions that are becoming common (e.g., AltiVec for PowerPC and SSE for Pentium III). It is also a good target for graphics hardware acceleration as its basic operations are very similar to those already performed by current graphics hardware (e.g., 3D point projection, z-buffering, and image filtering).

The lack of good anti-aliasing is one clear drawback of the render cache as presented here. Unfortunately since anti-aliasing is highly view dependent, we probably do not want to include anti-aliasing or area sampling within individual elements in the render cache [8]. This leaves supersampling as the most obvious solution though this will considerably increase the computational expense of the display process.

Although the render cache works well for renderer mismatch ratios up to 64, more work is needed to improve its performance at higher ratios. Some of the things that will be needed are interpolation over larger spatial scales, better very sparse sampling, and methods to prematurely evict obsolete points from the render cache.

Because the render cache works largely in the image plane, it is an excellent place to introduce perceptually based optimizations and improvements. Some examples include introducing dynamic tone mapping models (e.g., [27, 23]) or using perceptual based sampling strategy (e.g., [5]).

We also like to see our display process used with a wider variety of renderers such as Radiance [28], bidirectional path tracing, photon maps[12], and the ray-based gather passes of multipass radiosity methods [7].

Acknowledgements
We would like to thank people at the Cornell Program of Computer Graphics and especially Eric Lafortune for helpful early discussions on reprojection. We are indebted to Peter Shirley for many helpful comments and contributions. Also thanks to Greg Larson for making his mgf library and models available and special thanks to Al Barr for resurrecting from dusty tapes his original "green glass balls" model as used in Jim Kajiya's original paper.

References

1. S. J. Adelson and L. F. Hodges. Generating exact ray-traced animation frames by reprojection. *IEEE Computer Graphics and Applications*, 15(3):43–52, May 1995.
2. S. Badt. Two algorithms taking advantage of temporal coherence in ray tracing. *The Visual Computer*, 4(3):123–132, Sept. 1988.
3. L. D. Bergman, H. Fuchs, E. Grant, and S. Spach. Image rendering by adaptive refinement. In *Computer Graphics (SIGGRAPH '86 Proceedings)*, volume 20, pages 29–37, Aug. 1986.
4. G. Bishop, H. Fuchs, L. McMillan, and E. J. Scher Zagier. Frameless rendering: Double buffering considered harmful. In *Computer Graphics (SIGGRAPH '94 Proceedings)*, pages 175–176, July 1994.

30

5. M. R. Bolin and G. W. Meyer. A perceptually based adaptive sampling algorithm. In M. Cohen, editor, *SIGGRAPH 98 Conference Proceedings*, pages 299–310, July 1998.

6. N. Brière and P. Poulin. Hierarchical view-dependent structures for interactive scene manipulation. In *SIGGRAPH 96 Conference Proceedings*, pages 83–90, Aug. 1996.

7. S. E. Chen, H. Rushmeier, G. Miller, and D. Turner. A progressive multi-pass method for global illumination. In *SIGGRAPH 91 Conference Proceedings*, pages 165–174, July 1991.

8. S. E. Chen and L. Williams. View interpolation for image synthesis. In J. T. Kajiya, editor, *Computer Graphics (SIGGRAPH '93 Proceedings)*, volume 27, pages 279–288, Aug. 1993.

9. M. F. Cohen, S. E. Chen, J. R. Wallace, and D. P. Greenberg. A progressive refinement approach to fast radiosity image generation. *Computer Graphics*, 22(4):75–84, August 1988. ACM Siggraph '88 Conference Proceedings.

10. R. W. Floyd and L. Steinberg. An adaptive algorithm for spatial greyscale. In *Proceedings of the Society for Information Display*, volume 17(2), pages 75–77, 1976.

11. B. Guo. Progressive radiance evaluation using directional coherence maps. In M. Cohen, editor, *SIGGRAPH 98 Conference Proceedings*, pages 255–266, July 1998.

12. H. W. Jensen. Global illumination using photon maps. In *Rendering Techniques '96*, pages 21–30. Springer-Verlag/Wien, 1996.

13. D. A. Jevans. Object space temporal coherence for ray tracing. In *Proceedings of Graphics Interface '92*, pages 176–183, May 1992.

14. J. T. Kajiya. The rendering equation. In D. C. Evans and R. J. Athay, editors, *Computer Graphics (SIGGRAPH '86 Proceedings)*, volume 20, pages 143–150, Aug. 1986.

15. G. W. Larson. The holodeck: A parallel ray-caching rendering system. In *Second Eurographics Workshop on Parallel Graphics and Visualisation*, Rennes, France, Sept. 1998.

16. W. R. Mark, L. McMillan, and G. Bishop. Post-rendering 3D warping. In *1997 Symposium on Interactive 3D Graphics*, pages 7–16. ACM SIGGRAPH, Apr. 1997.

17. N. Max and K. Ohsaki. Rendering trees from precomputed Z-buffer views. In *Eurographics Rendering Workshop 1995*. Eurographics, June 1995.

18. L. McMillan and G. Bishop. Plenoptic modeling: An image-based rendering system. In R. Cook, editor, *SIGGRAPH 95 Conference Proceedings*, pages 39–46, Aug. 1995.

19. D. P. Mitchell. Generating antialiased images at low sampling densities. In M. C. Stone, editor, *Computer Graphics (SIGGRAPH '87 Proceedings)*, pages 65–72, July 1987.

20. M. J. Muuss. Towards real-time ray-tracing of combinatorial solid geometric models. In *Proceedings of BRL-CAD Symposium*, 1995. http://ftp.arl.mil/ mike/papers/.

21. J. Painter and K. Sloan. Antialiased ray tracing by adaptive progressive refinement. In *Computer Graphics (SIGGRAPH '89 Proceedings)*, pages 281–288, July 1989.

22. S. Parker, W. Martin, P. Sloan, P. Shirley, B. Smits, and C. Hansen. Interactive ray tracing. In *Symposium on Interactive 3D Computer Graphics*, April 1999.

23. S. N. Pattanaik, J. A. Ferwerda, M. D. Fairchild, and D. P. Greenberg. A multiscale model of adaptation and spatial vision for realistic image display. In *Computer Graphics*, July 1998. ACM Siggraph '98 Conference Proceedings.

24. E. Reinhard, A. Chalmers, and F. W. Jansen. Overview of parallel photo-realistic graphics. In *Eurographics '98 State of the Art Reports*. Eurographics Association, Aug. 1998.

25. C. H. Séquin and E. K. Smyrl. Parameterized ray tracing. In J. Lane, editor, *Computer Graphics (SIGGRAPH '89 Proceedings)*, volume 23, pages 307–314, July 1989.

26. J. W. Shade, S. J. Gortler, L. He, and R. Szeliski. Layered depth images. In M. Cohen, editor, *SIGGRAPH 98 Conference Proceedings*, pages 231–242, July 1998.

27. G. Ward. A contrast-based scalefactor for luminance display. In P. Heckbert, editor, *Graphics Gems IV*, pages 415–421. Academic Press, Boston, 1994.

28. G. J. Ward. The RADIANCE lighting simulation and rendering system. *Computer Graphics*, 28(2):459–472, July 1994. ACM Siggraph '94 Conference Proceedings.

29. T. Whitted. An improved illumination model for shaded display. *Communications of the ACM*, 23(6):343–349, June 1980.

Editors' Note: see Appendix, p. 356 for colored figures of this paper

Interactive Ray-Traced Scene Editing Using Ray Segment Trees

Kavita Bala   Julie Dorsey   Seth Teller

Laboratory for Computer Science
Massachusetts Institute of Technology
{kaybee,dorsey,seth}@graphics.lcs.mit.edu

Abstract. This paper presents a ray tracer that facilitates near-interactive scene editing with incremental rendering; the user can edit the scene both by manipulating objects and by changing the viewpoint. Our system uses object-space radiance interpolants to accelerate ray tracing by approximating radiance, while bounding error. We introduce a new hierarchical data structure, the *ray segment tree* (RST), which tracks the dependencies of radiance interpolants on regions of world space. When the scene is edited, affected interpolants are rapidly identified— typically in 0.1 seconds—by traversing these ray segment trees. The affected interpolants are updated and used to re-render the scene with a 3 to 4× speedup over the base ray tracer, even when the viewpoint is changed. Although the system does no pre-processing, performance is better than for the base ray tracer even on the first rendered frame.

Keywords: Ray tracing, radiance interpolation, scene manipulation, incremental rendering

1 Introduction

Ray tracing is a popular technique for producing high-quality imagery. Ray tracers typically support specular and diffuse reflectance functions, and general geometric primitives, producing high quality view-dependent images. However, this quality is achieved by compromising interactivity; ray tracing is not commonly used in interactive applications such as editing and viewing because of the high cost of computing each frame.

In recent years, strides have been made in facilitating interactive scene manipulation with ray tracing. Several researchers have developed ray tracers supporting scene editing that incrementally render parts of the scene that might be affected by a change. Cook's shade trees [4] maintain a symbolic evaluation of the local illumination at each pixel of a frame. When an object's material properties are changed, if the shade trees remain the same, they are re-evaluated with the new material properties. Séquin and Smyrl [9] extend these shade trees to include reflections and refractions. Their trees represent the entire radiance contribution by the scene at each pixel. In their system, changes to an object's material properties (e.g., color, specular coefficient) are the only user-specified edits permitted. Murakami and Hirota [8] and Jevans [7] extend these techniques to support geometry changes (e.g., object is moved) by associating rays with the voxels they traverse. A scene change affects voxels and their associated rays.

More recently, Brière and Poulin [3] introduced a system that maintains *color trees* and *ray trees* to separately accelerate updates to object attributes and geometry. Attribute changes involve adjustments to an object's color, reflection coefficient etc., while geometry changes include changes such as moving an object. Their system reflects attribute changes in about 1-2 seconds, and geometry changes in 10-110 seconds.

All of the above techniques are *pixel-based*; that is, additional information is maintained for each pixel and used to recompute radiance as the user edits the scene. The chief drawback of these systems is that they are completely view-dependent; while a user can edit the scene, he cannot adjust the viewpoint. Also, for high resolution images, the memory requirements can be large.

Another related area of research is the use of line or ray space to accelerate editing and rendering in global illumination algorithms. Arvo and Kirk [1] represent bundles of rays as 5D bounding volumes that are used to accelerate ray-object intersections, but do not accelerate shading or editing. In the context of editing for radiosity applications, Dretakkis and Sillion [5] augment the link structure of hierarchical radiosity with additional line-space information to track links affected by the addition or deletion of objects. The hierarchical link structure, and hence the implicit line space, makes it possible to identify affected regions rapidly when an object is edited. Their system is not pixel-based; therefore, a user can change the viewpoint after an update. However, their algorithms apply only to radiosity systems for scenes with diffuse materials.

In previous work [2, 11] we presented a system to accelerate ray tracing using per-object 4D *radiance interpolants* used to approximate radiance, while guaranteeing bounds on error. A radiance interpolant records view-dependent radiance for a set of rays that intersect an object. The system uses an error predicate to guarantee that the interpolant approximates radiance for every ray covered by that set of rays to within a user-specified error bound. For each pixel, the system finds the interpolant that covers that eye ray, and if it exists, uses it to interpolate radiance. Interpolants are built lazily and adaptively as needed and stored in 4D trees called *linetrees*. When the viewpoint changes, some interpolants from the previous frame are reused. Thus, our system accelerates ray tracing while allowing the viewpoint to move; however, objects in the scene cannot be modified.

In this paper, we present a system that supports interactive scene editing *while permitting changes in the viewpoint*. Our work draws on the work of Brière and Poulin, Dretakkis and Sillion, and our previous work on radiance interpolants, while providing additional functionality. Our system builds radiance interpolants to accelerate rendering by approximating radiance. When an object is updated, only a subset of global line space is affected. We introduce space-efficient hierarchical *5D ray segment trees* to track the regions of ray space that affect an interpolant. When the scene is edited, trees are traversed to rapidly identify and invalidate the interpolants that are affected by the edit. When a new frame is rendered from the same or a different viewpoint, interpolants that are still valid are reused to accelerate rendering.

First, we review 4D per-object interpolants in Section 2. In Section 3, we show how to augment interpolants to support interactive scene editing, and describe how these augmented interpolants can be used with global linetrees to track the regions of line space affected by an interpolant. In Sections 4 and 5, we address the limitations of the 4D global linetrees by using 5D ray segment trees, and explain how these trees can be used to find all interpolants that might be affected by a scene edit. Finally, we present results in Section 6, and conclude with a discussion of future work in Section 7.

2 Radiance Interpolants

In this section, we review how 4D radiance interpolants are used to accelerate ray tracing by exploiting spatial coherence, both object and screen-space, and also temporal coherence. The key idea of this system is to accelerate ray tracing by approximating radiance while guaranteeing error bounds. Every ray intersecting an object has an associated radiance. Assuming that a ray intersects an object, and the object is surrounded by a transparent medium, the ray can be parameterized using four coordinates. The space of all such rays is the four-dimensional space of directed lines, called *line space*. A radiance interpolant represents the radiance of an object over a region of line space; the interpolant is said to *cover* that region of line space. The region of line space covered by an interpolant is a four-dimensional hypercube, and every ray covered by the interpolant lies inside the hypercube. The interpolant records a radiance sample for each of the sixteen vertices of the hypercube. The radiance associated with any ray covered by the interpolant is then approximated by quadrilinearly interpolating these radiance samples. When radiance is coherent, radiance interpolants are an efficient way to compute and represent the radiance of a scene.

Radiance interpolants have two important properties for interactive scene editing:

- Interpolants do not depend on the viewpoint; therefore, the viewpoint can be changed freely without invalidating them. As long as rays from the current viewpoint are covered by an interpolant, the interpolant can be reused.
- An update to the radiance samples stored in an interpolant effectively updates radiance for *all* rays covered by that interpolant. Thus, interpolants are an efficient way to structure the update of radiance information when a scene is edited.

2.1 Ray parameterization

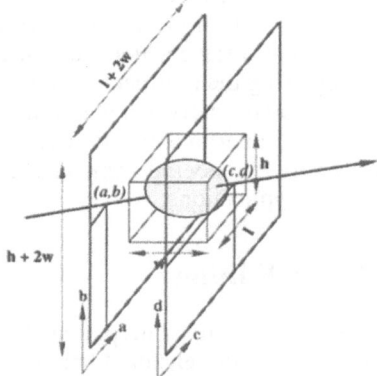

Fig. 1. Ray parameterization in 3D. The ray is parameterized by (a, b, c, d), its intercepts with the front and back faces of the expanded face pair.

Every ray intersecting an object is parameterized by four coordinates (a, b, c, d), which are the intercepts that it makes with two parallel faces surrounding that object (see Figure 1). To completely cover the space of rays that intersect the object, six pairs of parallel faces are considered. Each face pair is defined by two parallel faces and a principal direction that is perpendicular to the faces. The principal directions of the six face pairs are $\pm\hat{x}$, $\pm\hat{y}$ and $\pm\hat{z}$. Every ray intersecting o is uniquely associated with the face pair whose principal direction is closest to the ray's direction; that is, the principal direction onto which the ray has the maximum positive projection. To ensure that every ray associated with a face pair intersects both parallel faces, the faces are sized as shown in Figure 1. Once the face pair associated with a ray is identified, the ray is intersected with its front and back faces to compute its (a, b) and (c, d) coordinates respectively.

2.2 4D Radiance Interpolants

When rendering a pixel, the system must be able to find an interpolant (if any) that covers the eye ray corresponding to that pixel. To accelerate interpolant lookup, interpolants are stored in *linetrees* that are the 4D analogues of octrees. There is a linetree associated with each face pair of an object. For every eye ray, once the object it intersects is known, an interpolant is found by walking recursively down from the root of the linetree of the appropriate face pair. The radiance for the eye ray is then quadrilinearly interpolated using the radiance samples in the interpolant.

Interpolation error arises from discontinuities and non-linearities in the radiance function. An *error predicate* is tested to automatically detect both these conditions. An interpolant is not constructed if the error predicate indicates conservatively that its interpolation error would exceed a user-specified bound. The error predicate uses information about ray trees [3] to identify the regions of line space that have smoothly varying radiance that is approximated well by quadrilinear interpolation. The error predicate ensures that linetrees are subdivided adaptively; interpolants cover large regions of line space where radiance varies smoothly, and conversely, where radiance changes rapidly, interpolants cover small regions of line space. Thus, adaptive subdivision of linetrees prevents erroneous interpolation while allowing reuse when possible. Currently, the error predicate only supports convex objects, as discussed in Section 7.

Visibility determination at pixels is another important function of the ray tracer and is needed in order to find the correct interpolant for an eye ray. We use a conservative algorithm for *reprojection* of linetree cells to accelerate visibility determination. This algorithm exploits the temporal frame-to-frame coherence in the user's viewpoint, while guaranteeing that the correct visible surface is detected for each pixel. A fast scan-line algorithm accelerates rendering using the reprojected linetrees. See [2] for details.

This algorithm has the important property that it is entirely on-line; no pre-processing is necessary to construct radiance interpolants. Radiance interpolants are generated lazily and adaptively as the scene is rendered from various viewpoints. This on-line property is useful for interactive applications.

3 Interpolants and Scene Editing

In this section, we describe how to identify interpolants that are affected by an object edit. First, we present a *global* four-dimensional parameterization of rays and show that the region of line space affected by an object edit is a subset of global line space. We then describe how a hierarchical global linetree can be used to rapidly identify and invalidate the interpolants affected by an object edit.

3.1 Global Line Space Parameterization

Global line space is the space of all directed lines that intersect the scene. In the previous section, we presented a four dimensional parameterization of rays intersecting an object. We use a similar parameterization for rays intersecting the scene, except that the face pairs (as shown in Figure 1) surround the scene, and $w \times l \times h$ is the size of the bounding box of the entire scene. As explained in Section 2, every ray intersecting the scene is associated with a face pair, and the ray is parameterized by the four intercepts it makes with the two parallel faces of the face pair. Note that per-object line space coordinates can be easily transformed into global line space coordinates.

For simplicity, we explain ideas in 2D in this paper; the extension of these ideas to

3D is straightforward. Each 2D ray is represented by two intercepts (a, c) that it makes with a pair of parallel 2D line segments; this representation is a 2D analogue of the ray parameterization in Section 2.1. For example, in Figure 2-(a), the horizontal lines surrounding the circle represent a 2D face pair for *global line space*. Four such face pairs are needed to represent all the rays that intersect the scene.

3.2 Line Space affected by an Object Edit

A basic intuition is that interpolants can be updated efficiently to reflect an object edit because an object edit affects a contiguous subset of line space, as shown in Figures 2-(a) and (b). On the left in Figure 2-(a), a circle C in world space, a ray that intersects C, and its associated face pair are shown. On the right is a Cartesian representation of 2D line space. Every directed line in world space is a point in line space. The set of rays that intersects the circle in world space corresponds to the interior of a hyperbola in line space as shown on the right in Figure 2-(a) (See Appendix A for details). When the circle is edited, the radiance of every ray in the shaded region of line space could be affected. Therefore, every interpolant that includes a ray in the shaded region should be updated. If all the rays covered by an interpolant lie outside this hyperbola the interpolant is not affected and can be reused. In the next section, we explain how to find the rays covered by an interpolant.

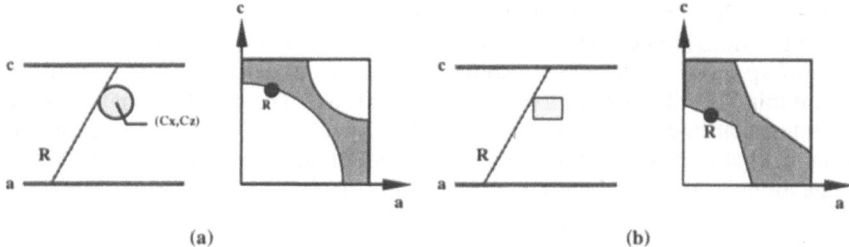

Fig. 2. When the circle or rectangle are edited, the shaded region of line space (on the right of the corresponding figures) is affected.

If instead of a circle, a rectangle is edited (shown in Figure 2-(b)), an hourglass-shaped region (similar to a hyperbola) of line space is affected by the edit. The important point is that the region of line space affected by an edit is a well-defined subset of line space that can be identified efficiently using a hierarchical tree to represent line space. This is true for object edits in 3D world space (4D line space) as well.

3.3 Interpolant Dependencies

Interpolants are an efficient way to structure the update of radiance when a scene is changed, since an update to the radiance samples of the interpolant effectively updates the radiance for all rays covered by the interpolant. In this section, we explain how interpolants are affected by scene editing.

First we review the concept of ray trees, which are important for understanding interpolant dependencies. In a Whitted ray tracer [13], when the radiance for a ray is computed, an associated ray tree can be built that records all the sources of radiance that contributed to the total radiance of the ray [2, 3, 9]. Each internal node in the

36

ray tree corresponds to an intersection of a ray with a surface, and the leaf nodes are lights. An arc of a ray tree represents a *ray segment* from a surface to either another surface or a light. A ray tree node has position-independent and position-dependent information [3]. The position-independent information includes the object intersected by the ray, a list of every light that contributes to the radiance at that point, and a list of every occluder that blocks some light. The position-dependent component includes the point of intersection of the ray, the normal at that point, texture coordinates (if the object is textured), and pointers to the reflected and refracted ray trees (if they exist). These reflected and refracted ray trees are computed recursively. To conserve memory, the position-independent information in ray trees is shared when possible [2, 3].

In our earlier work [2], the error predicate used the sixteen radiance samples and their associated ray trees to determine if the interpolant approximates radiance to within a user-specified error bound over the region of line space that is *covered* by the interpolant. To detect radiance discontinuities, the error predicate requires that the position-independent components of the sixteen extremal ray trees be the same. Since the object associated with the interpolant is convex, every ray covered by the interpolant is bounded by the extremal rays, even after one or more reflections. An additional shaft-cull [6] then guarantees that *every* ray covered by the interpolant also shares the same position-independent ray tree component.

The sixteen extremal ray trees differ only in their position-dependent information. Consider one set of sixteen corresponding arcs from the extremal ray trees; each arc is a ray segment. The corresponding ray segment of every interior ray lies in the 3D volume bounded by these sixteen ray segments. Therefore, when a scene edit affects that 3D volume of space, the interpolant should be invalidated to guarantee correctness. We represent this 3D volume conservatively as a shaft [6]. The set of all shafts represented by an interpolant's ray trees is similar to the *tunnels* used by Brière and Poulin [3], although in that work ray dependencies are captured only for a fixed viewpoint. In Plate A, some tunnels associated with interpolants for the three-sphere scene are shown.

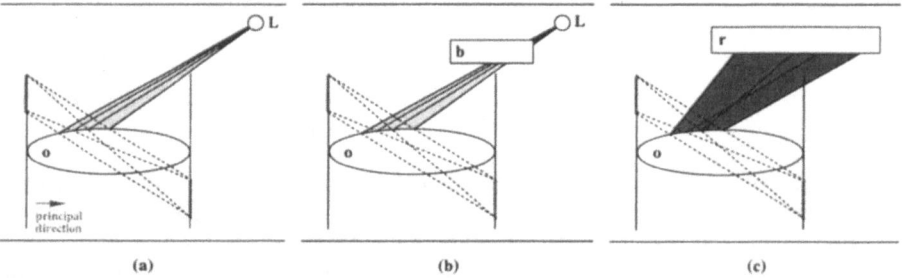

Fig. 3. Rays that affect an interpolant: (a) Light rays, (b) Occluder rays, (c) Reflected rays.

Now we consider the different types of ray-tree arcs and the 3D volumes they cover. Figure 3 depicts three such arcs, corresponding to unoccluded light rays, occluded light rays, and reflected rays. In the figure, the ellipse *o* is the object for which an interpolant *I* is built. The interpolant is associated with the face pair shown as two vertical line segments surrounding *o*. The dotted lines show the four extremal rays (in 2D) that are used to build *I*. The two horizontal lines at the top and bottom of the scene show one of the face pairs of global line space. The volume that affects each arc (and therefore affects the interpolant) is shaded in each figure.

In Figure 3-(a), the four extremal rays intersect *o*, and their radiance is evaluated by shooting rays to the light L which is visible to every ray covered by I. Therefore, I depends on the shaded region shown in the figure. In Figure 3-(b), the light rays for the interpolant are all occluded by the same occluder b. If b is opaque, I depends only on the occluder b. If b is transparent, I depends on the shaded region shown in the figure. In Figure 3-(c), the volume of space that affects the arcs corresponding to reflections in the interpolant is shaded. Thus, the regions of world space that affect an interpolant can be determined using the ray trees associated with the extremal rays of the interpolant. An interpolant can become invalid only if the scene edit affects one of these regions.

3.4 Finding Affected Interpolants using Global Linetrees

Given a scene edit, we want to efficiently identify the interpolants that could be affected by the edit. We now discuss how global line space can be used to track the regions of 3D space that affect an interpolant. This is similar to the approach taken by Drettakis and Sillion [5] for radiosity systems.

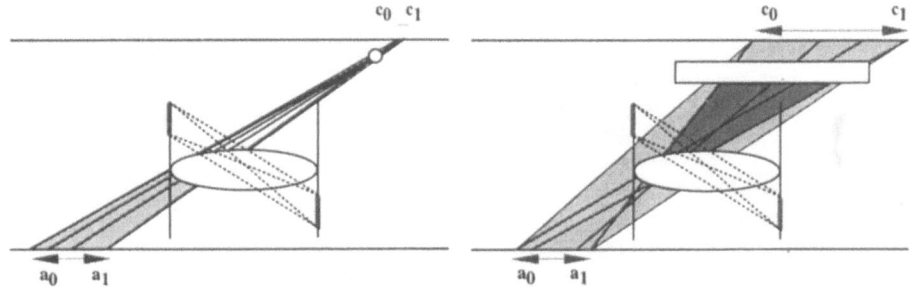

Fig. 4. Global line space for: (a) Light rays, (b) Reflected rays.

When the scene is edited, the edit affects a 3D volume. An interpolant depends on that 3D volume if any tunnel associated with the interpolant intersects that volume. We would like to rapidly identify all such tunnels. Each of the tunnel sections is contained in some region of global line space. This region can be characterized conservatively by extending the sixteen extremal rays that define the tunnel section until they intersect the appropriate global face pair. For example, Figures 4-(a) and (b) show this computation in 2D. In Figure 4-(a), the four extremal rays from the object o to the light L are extended to intersect a global face pair (shown as horizontal lines surrounding the scene). The a and c ranges of these intersections are computed. The corresponding rectangular region in line space, $[a_0, a_1] \times [c_0, c_1]$, is a conservative characterization of the volume that affects the interpolant. In the figure, this region of line space is shown in medium gray. Similarly, in Figure 4-(b), the extremal reflected rays are intersected with the global face pair and the medium gray region shows the corresponding region of line space. This characterization is conservative because it covers a larger 3D volume than its tunnel section. In the next section this characterization is made more precise.

In 4D, each tunnel section of an interpolant is conservatively represented by 8 coordinates (a_0, b_0, c_0, d_0) — (a_1, b_1, c_1, d_1) that define a 4D bounding box in line space. The tunnel sections affected by an object edit can be rapidly identified in the following manner: a linetree is constructed for each face pair of global line space. Each node of the linetree corresponds to a 4D bounding box in line space. A leaf node in the linetree contains pointers to every interpolant that *depends* on the region of line space represented by the node. In other words, for every interpolant included in the linetree node, the 4D bounding box of the linetree node intersects the 4D bounding box that conservatively represents at least one of the interpolant's tunnel sections. This hierarchical linetree can be used to rapidly identify the interpolants affected by an object edit.

4 Interpolants and Ray Segments

The previous section described a data structure that conservatively tracks the regions of line space that affect an interpolant. However, this representation is too conservative. In this section, we introduce a 5D parameterization of rays to address this limitation, and describe *ray segment trees* that improve on the linetrees of the previous section.

4.1 Limitations of Line Space

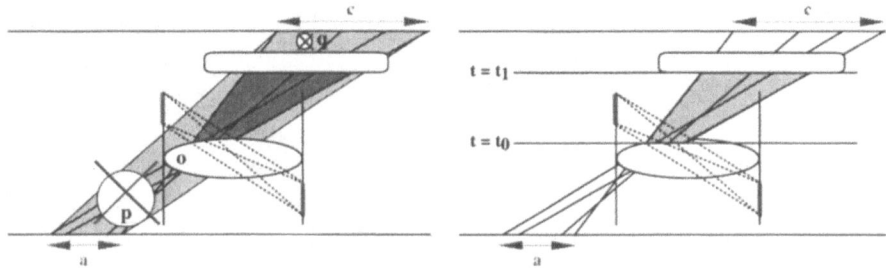

Fig. 5. (a) Line space vs. Ray space, (b) using the extra distance dimension t.

The main disadvantage of the 4D representation of lines is that it is too conservative. This problem is illustrated in Figure 5-(a), which shows an interpolant for o. The tunnel section corresponding to reflected rays from o is shown in dark gray, while the corresponding conservative line space representation is shown in light gray. When the circles p and q are edited, they intersect the 4D bounding box represented by the tunnel section. Therefore, o's interpolant, stored in some leaf of the global linetree, is flagged as a potential candidate for invalidation. However, o's interpolant is only affected by changes in the dark gray region and this invalidation is unnecessary. We address this problem by introducing an extra parameter t for rays. Intuitively, this parameter represents the distance along the 4D lines. In Figure 5-(b), the light gray line space region is bounded by $t = t_0$ and $t = t_1$. Using this extra parameter, o's interpolant is not flagged for invalidation when the circles are updated.

4.2 Global ray segment trees

To efficiently identify the interpolants that are affected by an edit, the system maintains six *global ray segment trees* (RSTs). Each RST node stores ten coordinates $(a_0, b_0, c_0, d_0, t_0)$ to $(a_1, b_1, c_1, d_1, t_1)$ that define a 5D bounding box in ray segment space. The t dimension represents the distance along the principal direction of the face pair. The front face of the face pair is at $t = 0$ and the back face is at $t = 1$. The root node of the tree spans the region from $(0, 0, 0, 0, 0)$ to $(1, 1, 1, 1, 1)$. When an RST node is subdivided, each of its five axes is subdivided simultaneously. Each of the 32 children of the RST node covers the region of 5D ray space that includes all rays from its front face to its back face. While this branching factor may seem high, the tree is sparse, keeping memory requirements modest.

Figure 6 shows RST nodes for 2D rays. The parent node from (a_0, c_0, t_0) to (a_1, c_1, t_1) is shown on the top left, and a-c-t ray segment space (a three dimensional unit cube) is shown on the top right. The parent represents all rays entering its front face and leaving its back face. When the parent is subdivided, the rays represented by its eight children are as shown. Children 0 through 3 correspond to the ray segments that start at the front face at $t = t_0$ and end at the middle face at $t = \frac{t_0 + t_1}{2}$. Similarly, children 4 through 7 start at the middle face and end at $t = t_1$. When the parent is subdivided, truncated segments of the parent's rays (shown in black in the figure) lie in different children.

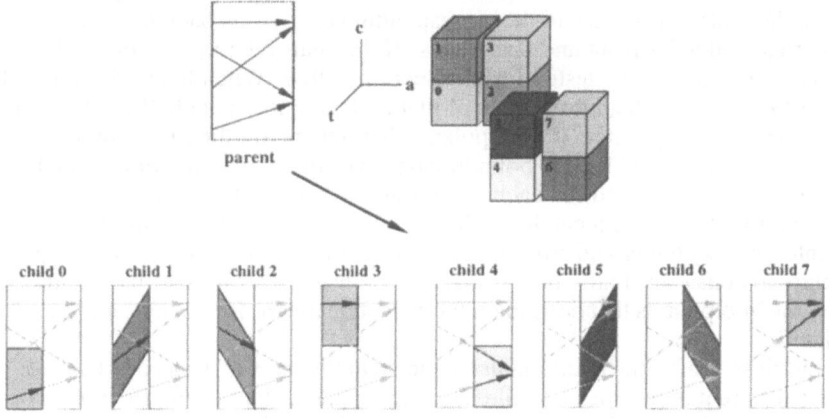

Fig. 6. Subdivision of Ray Segment Trees.

4.3 Inserting interpolants in the RSTs

RSTs are populated with interpolants by a recursive insertion algorithm that starts from the root RST node. For each tunnel section of the interpolant, its sixteen extremal rays are intersected with the current RST node to compute a 5D bounding box that includes the tunnel section. If this bounding box intersects a leaf RST node, a pointer to the interpolant is inserted in the node. For a non-leaf node, the algorithm recursively inserts the interpolant into the children of the RST node that intersect its 5D bounding box. As described in Section 3, the leaf node in an RST stores a list of pointers to every interpolant that *depends* on the region of ray segment space covered by that node and a list of the 5D bounding boxes of the interpolant's corresponding tunnel section.

5 Using Ray Segment Trees

In this section, we describe how interpolants affected by an object edit are rapidly identified and invalidated using RSTs. Brière and Poulin [3] describe two main categories of object edits: attribute changes (including changes to an object's color, specular or diffuse coefficient), and geometry changes (including insertion or deletion of an object). In their work, attribute and geometry changes are handled using different mechanisms, since attribute changes can be dealt with rapidly, while geometry changes require more time. In our work, RSTs permit rapid identification of affected interpolants; therefore, we use the same mechanism to identify affected interpolants for both types of changes.

5.1 Identifying Affected Interpolants

When an object is edited, we use 3D shafts [6] to identify every region of ray segment space, and therefore every associated interpolant, that is affected by the edit. The identification algorithm is recursive and starts at each of the six root RST nodes with a world-space region v (the object's bounding box) that is affected by an object edit. For each RST node visited recursively, a shaft is built enclosing the 3D volume between the front and back face of the node. The shaft consists of six planes: four planes from each edge of the node's front face to the corresponding edge of its back face, and two planes that correspond to its front and back faces. If the shaft intersects v, the children of the RST node are recursively tested for intersection with v. When the shaft of a RST node does not intersect v, the descendants of that node are not visited. If the RST node is a leaf, it has a list of pointers to interpolants that depend on the 3D volume represented by the node's shaft, and the 5D bounding boxes of their corresponding tunnel sections. A 3D shaft is constructed for each such tunnel section. If that shaft intersects v, the interpolant is flagged as a candidate for update. Our approach is similar to the shafts presented by Drettakis and Sillion [5], though they implicitly use the radiosity link structure to construct shafts. In [3], shafts are constructed for pixel-based rays. Plate A shows the interpolants that depend on the reflective mirror for the museum scene shown in Plate B.

One class of affected interpolants (depicted in Figure 3-(c)), can be identified rapidly using a different mechanism. While building an interpolant for o, if a light is occluded by an opaque object b, that tunnel section of the interpolant can only be affected when b moves. Therefore, we maintain a separate list of interpolants for occluders; when b is edited, its list of interpolants is marked for invalidation.

5.2 Interpolant Invalidation

The algorithm to identify affected interpolants is conservative: it might flag interpolants for update even if they are not affected by an object edit, because shaft culling against the edited object's bounding box is conservative. Therefore, we perform an additional check on the position-independent component of the interpolant's ray tree to determine if the interpolant is affected by the edit. For example, when o's color is edited, the edit affects an interpolant I if either I is o's interpolant, or I depends on o indirectly, for example through reflections. For a geometry change, such as the deletion of an object o, an interpolant I should be invalidated if I is o's interpolant, or o appears in the ray tree of I, for example, as an occluder or a reflection. Note that, as in [3], we treat an object movement as a deletion from its old position and an insertion to its new position.

When an interpolant is invalidated, the memory allocated to the corresponding object's linetree node is automatically garbage collected and the node itself is marked for deletion. If recursively, all that linetree node's siblings are also invalid, their space is reclaimed, and therefore, the parent is reclaimed. For example, consider an object o_1 that blocks the light to another object o_2, causing o_2's linetrees to be subdivided around o_1's shadow. When o_1 is deleted, o_2's interpolants are compacted, so that no unnecessary subdivision of o_2's linetrees takes place around the shadow that no longer exists.

To support rapid editing for attribute changes, interpolants could be augmented to include extra information such as the surface normal and point of intersection, for each of the sixteen extremal rays. Using this extra information, the interpolants could be updated by computing the difference in radiance due to the change in o's material properties. However, this extra position-dependent information increases the memory requirements of interpolants. Therefore, we invalidate interpolants for both attribute and geometry changes and lazily recompute them as needed.

6   Performance Results

We have extended our accelerated interpolant ray tracer to maintain and use RSTs for scene editing. The interpolant ray tracer, and the base ray tracer it is compared with, both implement classical Whitted ray tracing [13] with textures and use the Ward isotropic local shading model [12]. The system can handle convex primitives such as cubes, spheres, cylinders, cones, disks and polygons, and CSG union and intersection operations on these primitives. The base ray tracer contains several standard performance optimizations (see [2] for details).

Our timing results were obtained for the museum scene shown in Plate B. The scene has more than 1100 primitives (a tesselation of these primitives requires about 500k polygons). All timing results are reported for frames rendered at 1200×900 resolution on a single 250MHz processor of an SGI Infinite Reality. We report results for three edits (shown in Plate B): the top of the sculpture is deleted (Edit-(a)), the bottom of the sculpture is deleted (Edit-(b)), a green cube is moved in on the right (Edit-(c)). Camera translations and rotations correspond to small adjustments of the viewpoint; a forward translation is by 0.2 feet (the room size is 45×30 sq. ft.), while a rotation is by 2.5°. When the user changes the viewpoint, new interpolants are built as required.

Plate B shows the impact of edits on interpolants. On the left, rendered images are shown, and on the right are error-coded images showing the regions of interpolation failure and success. Green and yellow pixels are not interpolated due to radiance discontinuities such as shadow edges and object silhouettes. Magenta pixels are not interpolated because of adaptive error-driven subdivision. Pixels that are successfully interpolated are shown in dark blue. The red pixels show the interpolants that are invalidated and rebuilt when the scene is edited. For example, after Edit-(a), the top of the sculpture and the shadow behind it are updated; the new interpolants lazily built to cover those pixels are shown in red. After Edit-(b), the interpolants associated with the bottom of the sculpture and its reflection in the mirror are found and invalidated.

In Table 1, we present results for time and memory usage for scene edits. A change to the viewpoint is considered a scene edit, except that no interpolants are invalidated by the viewpoint change. This is because interpolants do not explicitly depend on the current viewpoint. For each of the edits, traversing the RSTs and invalidating the corresponding linetrees is extremely fast, on the order of *a tenth of a second*. Depending on the type of edit, and its impact on interpolants, updating interpolants lazily while re-rendering a frame takes 26 to 28 seconds. Of this time, building new interpolants lazily, shown in red in the plate, takes 1 to 3 seconds. Similar results are obtained when the object's attributes (e.g., color) are changed. As the camera position is changed, frames are rendered in 26 to 31 seconds, depending on the camera movement; the greater the reuse of interpolants from the previous frame, the shorter the rendering time.

The memory requirements of this system are modest: each edit requires an additional 0.6 to 1 MB of memory. Camera movements typically require 0.7 to 2.1 MB of memory, depending on the type and extent of the movement. Additionally, in [2], we

Edit	Base ray tracer	Interpolant ray tracer with RSTs		
		Time (in secs)		Memory (in MB)
		Traverse RSTs and Invalidate linetrees	Update and Re-render	
Edit-(a)	109.0	0.11	25.6	0.7 M
Edit-(b)	108.6	0.10	28.2	1.0 M
Edit-(c)	109.2	0.09	27.4	0.6 M
Pan camera	108.2	—	26.9	0.7 M
Step forward	108.5	—	31.2	2.1 M

Table 1. Time and memory usage for edits and camera movements.

Ray Tracer System	Time (in secs)	Memory (in MB)
Base	109.0	—
Interpolant	79.5	18.0 M
Interpolant with RSTs	80.4	23.5 M

Table 2. Time and memory usage for ray tracers supporting interpolants and RSTs.

have implemented a least-recently used (LRU) memory-management technique to limit memory used for interpolants to a user-specified maximum. This technique imposes a performance penalty of only 1% when memory usage is restricted to 40MBs. This LRU system can be easily extended to limit the memory used for RSTs.

Table 2 shows system performance when rendering the first frame. Unlike in [3], the ray tracer using interpolants is 25% faster than the base ray tracer *even on the first frame*: interpolants exploit the spatial coherence within a frame. Note that our algorithm is an on-line algorithm; no pre-processing is needed to build either linetrees or RSTs. The overhead of creating RSTs is small: less than 1 second. For the first frame, interpolants require 18 MBs of memory, while RSTs require an additional 5.5 MBs. Subsequent frames require much less memory, as shown in Table 1.

7   Conclusions and Future Work

We have presented an incremental ray tracer for scene manipulation that permits the user to edit the scene and the current viewpoint. The system maintains ray segment trees to track the dependencies of interpolants on regions of world space. When the scene is edited, the RSTs are rapidly traversed, in roughly a tenth of a second, to identify and invalidate the interpolants affected by the edit. The interpolants are rebuilt as needed. For full-screen images, the scene is re-rendered with 3 to 4× speedup over the base ray tracer. For small adjustments to the viewpoint, incremental rendering is effective. For large changes in the camera position and even for the first frame, the system is still faster than the base ray tracer.

We believe this is a promising approach to support scene editing in ray tracers. There are several extensions that will improve the system. To support faster re-rendering when the scene is edited without changing the viewpoint, we could add screen-space acceleration structures similar to those described by Brière and Poulin [3]. Since interpolants succeed for a large number of pixels (e.g., 90% for the museum scene), these acceleration structures will only be maintained for the small fraction of the pixels that fail interpolation. Therefore, we expect that they will significantly accelerate rendering when the camera is not moved, while having modest memory requirements. These screen-space structures can be invalidated when the camera moves, and re-built as necessary. With this optimization, we expect that both attribute and geometry changes will require less than 3-5 seconds for fixed viewpoints.

One constraint of the interpolant ray tracer is that it can only guarantee error bounds for convex primitives. Interpolants are not built for non-convex or transparent primitives; therefore, rendering of these primitives is not accelerated. For scene editing, the screen-space structures discussed above could still be used to rapidly update these objects. However, we would like to accelerate the rendering of non-convex and transparent objects when the viewpoint changes as well. In [2], we discuss how to extend the error predicate to support non-convex objects by using linear interval arithmetic. We are currently extending our system to support parametric patches and transparent objects.

8 Acknowledgements

We would like to thank Andrew Myers for many useful discussions. This work was supported by an Alfred P. Sloan Research Fellowship (BR-3659), an NSF CAREER award (CCR-9624172), an NSF CISE Research Infrastructure award (EIA-9802220), a ONR MURI Award (SA-15242582386) and a grant from the Intel Corporation.

References

1. ARVO, J., AND KIRK, D. Fast Ray Tracing by Ray Classification. In *Computer Graphics (SIGGRAPH '87 Proceedings)*, pp. 196–205.
2. BALA, K., DORSEY, J., AND TELLER, S. Radiance Interpolants for Accelerated Bounded-Error Ray Tracing. In *ACM Transactions on Graphics (1999, to appear)* (See graphics.lcs.mit.edu/~kaybee/publications.html).
3. BRIÈRE, N., AND POULIN, P. Hierarchical View-dependent Structures for Interactive Scene Manipulation. In *Computer Graphics (SIGGRAPH '96 Proceedings)*, pp. 83–90.
4. COOK, R. L., PORTER, T., AND CARPENTER, L. Distributed Ray Tracing. In *Computer Graphics (SIGGRAPH '84 Proceedings)* (July 1984), vol. 18, pp. 139–147.
5. DRETTAKIS, G., AND SILLION, F. X. Interactive Update of Global Illumination Using a Line-Space Hierarchy. In *Computer Graphics (SIGGRAPH '97 Proceedings)*, pp. 57–64.
6. HAINES, E., AND WALLACE, J. Shaft Culling for Efficient Ray-Traced Radiosity. In *Proc. 2nd Eurographics Workshop on Rendering* (May 1991).
7. JEVANS, D. Object Space Temporal Coherence for Ray Tracing. In *Proceedings of Graphics Interface '92* (Toronto, Ontario, May 1992), pp. 176–183.
8. MURAKAMI, K., AND HIROTA, K. Incremental Ray Tracing. In *Photorealism in Computer Graphics*, K. Bouatouch and C. Bouville, Eds. Springer-Verlag, 1992.
9. SÉQUIN, C. H., AND SMYRL, E. K. Parameterized Ray Tracing. In *Computer Graphics (SIGGRAPH '89 Proceedings)*.
10. SOMMERVILLE, D. M. Y. *An Analytical Geometry of Three Dimensions*. University Press, Cambridge, 1959.
11. TELLER, S., BALA, K., AND DORSEY, J. Conservative Radiance Interpolants for Ray Tracing. In *Seventh Eurographics Workshop on Rendering* (June 15-17 1996), pp. 258–269.
12. WARD, G. J., RUBINSTEIN, F. M., AND CLEAR, R. D. A Ray Tracing Solution for Diffuse Interreflection. In *Computer Graphics (SIGGRAPH '88 Proceedings)*, pp. 85–92.
13. WHITTED, T. An Improved Illumination Model for Shaded Display. *CACM 23*, 6 (1980), 343–349.

A Appendix

In this appendix, we characterize the region of line space affected by an object edit. In 2D, the region of line space affected by an object edit is a hyperbola. We then extend this result to an object edit in 3D — the region of 4D line space affected by the edit can be characterized by a fourth-order equation.

A.1 In 2D

Consider a scene and its four global segment pairs. In Figure 2-(a), one of the four segment pairs (the pair of thick horizontal lines), with $+\hat{z}$ as principal direction, is shown on the left. When an object o is edited, every ray that passes through o is affected by the edit. We prove that the region of line space (shown as a square on the right of the figure) affected by updates to o is a hyperbola in 2D.

A ray $\mathbf{R}$ is specified by its intercepts $[a, c]$ on its associated segment pair. Without loss of generality, $\mathbf{R} = [c-a, 1]$. If $\mathbf{R}$ is a ray on the boundary of the region of line space affected by the edit, it satisfies two additional constraints: $\mathbf{R}$ intersects the circle o at some point $\mathbf{P} = [X, Z]$, and $\mathbf{R}$ is tangential to the circle at $\mathbf{P}$. We have three constraints: $\mathbf{P}$ lies on $\mathbf{R}$, $\mathbf{R}$ is perpendicular to the normal at $\mathbf{P}$, $\mathbf{P}$ lies on the circle.

$$[X, Z] = [a, -\frac{1}{2}] + t[c - a, 1], \mathbf{R} \cdot \mathbf{N} = 0, (X - C_x)^2 + (Z - C_z)^2 = R^2$$

Eliminating t, X and Z:

$$[(c - a)C_z + (\frac{a + c}{2} - C_x)]^2 - R^2[1 + (c - a)^2] = 0 \tag{1}$$

Equation 1 is a second order equation in a and c; the discriminant of the equation satisfies the condition of a hyperbola [10]. Thus, when a circle o is edited, the region of 2D line space affected by the edit is a hyperbola — i.e., the rays in the shaded region on the right in Figure 2-(a) are affected by the edit. The parameters of the hyperbola can be derived from o's location and radius.

A.2 In 4D

A similar derivation identifies the region of 4D line space affected by an edit to a 3D sphere o. Each ray $\mathbf{R}$ associated with the face pair with principal direction $+\hat{z}$ is specified as $[c - a, d - b, 1]$. The region of 4D space affected by an edit to a 3D sphere is characterized by the following equation:

$$[(c - a)C_z + (\frac{a + c}{2} - C_x)]^2 + [(d - b)C_z + (\frac{b + d}{2} - C_y)]^2$$
$$-R^2[1 + (c - a)^2 + (d - b)^2]$$
$$+[(c - a)(\frac{b + d}{2} - C_y) - (d - b)(\frac{a + c}{2} - C_x)]^2 = 0$$

While the first two lines of the equation are exactly the 4D generalization of a 2D hyperbola, the third line introduces fourth-order cross terms. Thus, when a 3D sphere o is edited, the region of 4D line space affected by the edit is not a hyperboloid, but it is specified by a fourth-order equation. Every ray *inside* the surface represented by this equation could potentially be affected by the object edit.

Editors' Note: see Appendix, p. 357–358 for colored figures of this paper

Decoupling Polygon Rendering from Geometry using Rasterization Hardware

Rüdiger Westermann, Ove Sommer, Thomas Ertl

University of Utah, University of Stuttgart

Abstract. The dramatically increasing size of polygonal models resulting from 3D scanning devices and advanced modeling techniques requires new approaches to reduce the load of geometry transfer and processing. In order to supplement methods like polygon reduction or geometry compression we suggest to exploit the processing power and functionality of the rasterization and texture subsystem of advanced graphics hardware. We demonstrate that 3D-texture maps can be used to render voxelized polygon models of arbitrary complexity at interactive rates by extracting isosurfaces from distance volumes. Therefore, we propose two fundamental algorithms to limit the rasterization load: First, the model is partitioned into a hierarchy of axis-aligned bounding boxes that are voxelized in an error controlled multi-resolution representation. Second, rasterization is restricted to the thin boundary regions around the isosurface representing the voxelized geometry. Furthermore, we suggest and simulate an OpenGL extension enabling advanced per-pixel lighting and shading. Although the presented approach exhibits certain limitations we consider it as a starting point for hybrid solutions balancing load between the geometry and the rasterization stage and we expect some influence on future hardware design.

1 Introduction

Despite the tremendous attention that is currently paid to volume graphics we still find polygonal models dominating the field of interactive computer graphics. Recent hardware advances brought performance rates of about 5 million textured triangles per second to low priced PC graphics adapters and the development does not seem to have reached its peak. Nevertheless are 3D scanners and advanced animation systems the source of models composed of millions of polygons which prohibit real-time rendering on even the most expensive high-end systems. Coping with that level of complexity is still an important field of computer graphics research and the investigated approaches fall into three broad classes. *Polygonal simplification* reduces the number of triangles to be used in level-of-detail representations of small or distant objects. *Visibility processing* eliminates polygons which are not in the viewing frustum or which are occluded by other objects before they are sent down the graphics pipeline. *Texturing* conveys visual detail within a polygon allowing larger and fewer triangles to be used in a scene. While the first two approaches offload vertex processing from the geometry engine to a preprocessing step in the CPU, does the third approach substitute geometry processing by rasterization.

Modern graphics architectures try to support the latter by increasing the performance of the rasterization and texturing subsystem. Silicon Graphics' InfiniteReality system [11] introduced virtual textures and efficient loading and paging of 64 MByte texture memory as well as fill rates of about 800 million pixels per second. 3D PC graphics adapters like Nvidia's Riva TNT claim 180 million pixels per second and provide fast texture loading through a AGP2X bus and single pass multi-texturing. Our approach for rendering large polygonal models, which we present in this paper, tries to exploit this tremendous processing power in the rasterization hardware. However, instead of working with 2D textures, we follow the ideas of volume graphics. That means, rather than reducing the geometric representation in such a way that the number of available primitives still approximates the original data sufficiently, we aim in developing a volumetric model that provides an alternative approach for the rendering of complex polygonal models.

2 Overview and related work

The basic idea of volume graphics as introduced in [2, 6, 7, 14] is to represent graphics objects on a 3D raster of volume primitives called voxels, thus repeating the 2D transition from vector graphics to raster graphics now in 3D. One of the advantages of this technique is the decoupling of the rendering complexity from the complexity of the geometry. It comes at the additional cost of the 3D scan conversion of the objects and the related aliasing errors as well as the high memory and processing demands of rendering the voxelized representation, which up to now limited the broad success of volume graphics. Interactive rendering of high resolution volumes became practical only recently based on sophisticated algorithms [9], dedicated hardware architectures [8, 12] or 3D-texture slicing available in medium to high-end graphics workstations [1].

The basic idea of texture-based volume rendering is the compositing of planes perpendicular to the viewing direction with the plane pixels trilinearly interpolated from a 3D scalar texture and transformed to RGBα by a lookup-up table. It proved to be a valuable tool for the visualization of medical and scientific data, but the lack of lighting capabilities made it hard to render objects with opaque surfaces. However, using the alpha test, the stencil buffer and a few more OpenGL extensions, it turned out that isosurfaces can be extracted from a volume and rendered with diffuse lighting as fast as traditional texture slicing [15]. It is a slightly modified and extended version of this method that we use in our paper to render shaded polygonal surfaces.

In order to transform the rendering problem into a isosurface extraction task we have to voxelize the polygonal scene in a special way. Gibson [3] has shown that the inaccuracies of surface renderings from intensity-based volumes can be overcome by means of distance maps. The distance-to-closest-surface function varies smoothly across surfaces and can be used to determine the surface as the zero-value isosurface of the distance volume and the normals from its derivatives. While there are many other sophisticated approaches for voxelizing meshes [2, 6] we follow a rather straightforward implementation of distance maps since efficient voxelization is not a main concern of our method.

One of the advantages of volume rendering as opposed to isosurface extraction in visualization applications is, that potentially every voxel will contribute to the final image and no volumetric information in between surfaces is lost. Therefore it is usually no waste of rasteriziation resources that the 3D texture slicing algorithm renders polygons which cover the entire volume. This is no longer true for volume rendering of voxelized polygonal models because in general there are many empty voxels in the bounding volume of the entire object. We overcome this problem by partitioning the scene into a hierarchy of axis-aligned bounding boxes. The efficient determination of bounding box hierarchies is a widely investigated problem in computer graphics, but since it is not in the main focus of our approach, we follow the ideas suggested in [4]. Having bounding boxes available that provide a tight enclosing of a group of polygons we can dramatically decrease the rasterization load by slicing many small 3D textures with fewer empty voxels instead of a large one.

The set of bounding boxes serves for a further improvement in our approach since we do not have to voxelize with the same resolution in each box. Instead we start out with a very coarse voxelization and determine the approximation error by estimating the one-sided Hausdorff distance [5] of the isosurface to the original polygonal representation. Only if the error exceeds a certain threshold do we continue with the next finer resolution. Thus, we get coarse 3D textures for very smooth surfaces and a fine resolution for highly curved parts. However, we have to invest some effort to guarantee continuity across neighboring boxes.

Although the use of bounding boxes as described dramatically decreases the number of operations that have to be performed in the rasterization unit we still recognize a considerable waste of resources. Since the voxelized models are opaque the distance values inside do not contribute to the final image but have to be rasterized as well. In order to avoid the processing of structures inside the model we developed a technique particularly designed to render thin boundary regions. We construct two coarse meshes: an outer one which entirely covers the original model and an inner one which is enclosed by it. Then we tessellate the area between the two meshes within each slicing plane and we render only the generated triangles. In this way the rasterization is restricting to the thin region around the isosurface that represents the voxelized geometry.

Subsequent shading is then performed in image space implementing the lighting evaluations in software on a per-pixel basis. Some evaluations are already supported by the OpenGL imaging subset, others could be efficiently accomplished using an proposed OpenGL extension. The outlined extension works independently of our volumetric approach, but it enables high quality lighting and shading evaluations on a per-pixel basis only using gradient textures.

We now describe the organization of the rest of the paper. Section 3 explains the core algorithm we developed to adaptively convert polygonal meshes into multi-resolution distance volumes. Section 4 focuses on the details of rendering the models by extracting isosurfaces from the 3D textures. Finally, we present some results and draw some conclusions.

3 A volumetric model for polygonal rendering

Just recently, 3D textures have been established as fundamental rendering primitives in volume visualization [1], but even more importantly they have proved to be an effective tool for the rendering of isosurfaces on a per-pixel basis thereby avoiding any polygonal representation [15]. As a consequence, previous work on the voxelization of polygonal models [2, 7, 14] gains a completely new relevance. No longer is the rendering of large scale volume data too slow to allow for interactive frame rates, which up to now prohibited its break through in practical applications.

However, the use of voxelized models still exhibits certain limitations due to the fact that in general these models contain large parts covered with redundant information, i.e. empty voxels as shown in Figure 1, which demand the rasterization hardware to no purpose. In order to avoid the encoding and thus the processing of empty regions we propose an adaptive voxelization based on axis aligned bounding boxes.

3.1 Axis aligned bounding boxes

In [4] oriented bounding boxes have been introduced for fast and robust collision detection between arbitrary parts of complex scenes. The construction of a bounding box

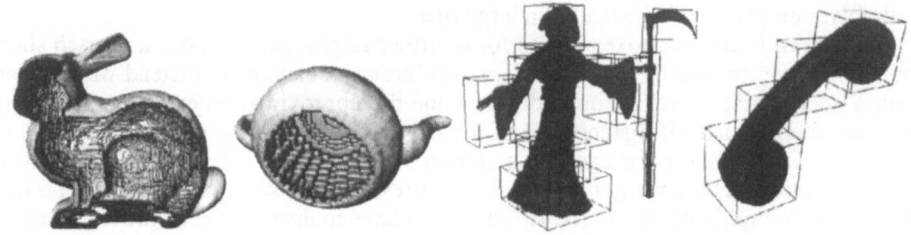

Fig. 1. The left two images demonstrate sparse volumetric representations as they usually result from voxelizing polygonal models. The right two images show axis aligned bounding boxes for different models.

hierarchy allows for efficient determination of interferences by recursively traversing the underlying tree structure. Although oriented bounding boxes provide much tighter bounds for the enclosed objects compared to axis aligned bounding boxes (AABB) we are not sure whether this kind of representation can be effectively integrated into our approach due to reasons described later on.

As a consequence our partitioning strategy is actually restricted to axis aligned bounding boxes, but it slightly differs from the one proposed in [4]. During the top-down construction of the hierarchical data structure we split each box that contains more than a given number of primitives into two smaller boxes each of them enfolding a disjunct subset of the primitives. In order to keep the space covered by adjacent boxes as small as possible we choose a dividing plane that is orthogonal to the main axis along the largest dimension of the AABB (cf. Figure 1) instead of selecting the axis that is orthogonal to the largest eigenvector of the covariance matrix.

In the actual implementation, however, we do not consider the hierarchical tree structure. Although the entire hierarchy is generated only a particular level is used further on.

3.2 Distance volumes

Once the underlying domain has been partitioned into a number of axis aligned bounding boxes we start building our volumetric model. Each partition is converted into a scalar volume consisting of the distance-to-closest-surface function at every grid point. A detailed description of the fundamental algorithms to voxelize surfaces and to encode polygonal descriptions in volume data by means of distance maps can be found in [2, 3, 6, 14] and will not be discussed in this work.

Some of the nice features distance maps offer are the smooth variation of the internal representation across surfaces, the encoding of the original surface model by the zero-values and the low variation of surface gradients calculated from the distance map. 3D distance volumes thus offer an attractive alternative to encode polygonal meshes in a volumetric representation at the same time allowing for the quite optimal reconstruction of the converted models. Putting together distance volumes and axis aligned bounding boxes we are now able to adaptively convert arbitrary polygonal scenes into volumetric models thus considerably reducing the memory requirements and the rasterization operations to be performed.

Fig. 2. The terrain model was converted into a signed distance volume considering different error tolerances. For the right model the Hausdorff distance between the reconstructed isosurface and the original one was below 5% of the maximal height of the terrain.

3.3 Error controlled voxelization

In this paragraph we will address the problem of accurately encoding the original polygonal representation in a distance volume. Obviously, the accuracy by which the scene can be reconstructed depends on the geometry, e.g. the curvature of the underlying mesh, and the resolution of the generated distance map.

Although one could think about a theoretical investigation of the relation between the curvature and the voxel size necessary to adequately reconstruct the surface from its voxelized counterpart, this approach seems to be rather cumbersome due to the less intuitive meaning of the curvature and the fact that it is quite difficult to obtain adequate curvature bounds in advance for arbitrary meshes.

A more intuitive and stable algorithm to compute a measure for the maximum deviation of the approximating mesh from the original one is based on the estimation of the one-sided Hausdorff distance between the two meshes. By calculating the maximal distance between vertices on one mesh and triangles of the other one we obtain an intuitive upper bound for the introduced approximation error. Although the calculation of the one-sided Hausdorff distance is numerically intensive it can be easily integrated in our volumetric approach.

At the beginning of the voxelization process we start out with a coarse volume resolution and we compute the signed distance values for each grid point. In order to efficiently perform the calculation of the maximal distance between the original mesh and the newly generated one we exploit the fact that the isosurface passing through the volume can be extracted separately for each cell by a Marching Cubes algorithm [10]. For each vertex on the original mesh all volume cells within the desired maximal deviation are traversed. If the minimal distance between the vertex and the triangles generated by the Marching Cubes algorithm is above the tolerance or if no surface was found the procedure stops and the voxelization is performed on the next finer grid (see Figure 2).

3.4 Multi-resolution representation

In general it might occur that the volume resolution in adjacent boxes will differ because parts of the geometry have been voxelized according to different error tolerances or because regions with high oscillations have been separated from rather smooth ones. In order to guarantee continuous transitions some extra effort has to be made.

For example, in Figure 3 two cells from different resolution levels are supposed to share one boundary face. Although both cells consist of the same values at the corner vertices the continuity of the scalar field does not in general guarantee the continuity of the isosurface if extraction is performed on different levels. This can clearly be seen from the fact that the isocurve on the common face is approximated by a straight line from the coarser side while it is a broken line with several segments on the finer side. To

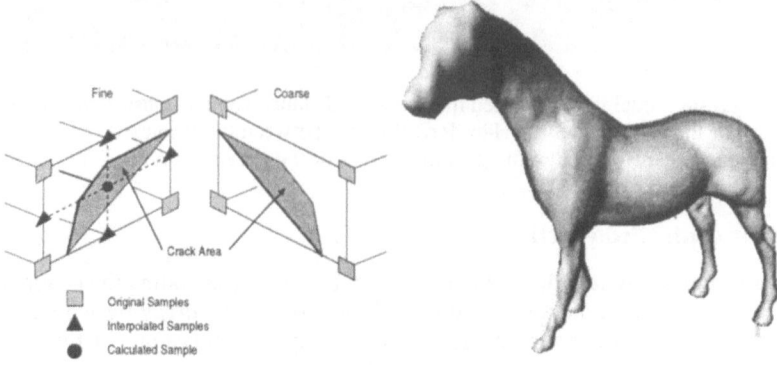

Fig. 3. Left: cracks in the piecewise linear approximation to the isosurface occur at common cell faces where cells from different octree levels meet — even if edge-compatibility is guaranteed. Right: the voxelization process is performed with varying resolution. From the tail to the head the horse has been converted into distance volumes with decreasing resolution. Three different resolution levels were used.

maintain a *continuous* scalar field even if the extraction level changes, the scalar values at those cell faces where a level transition occurs are properly adjusted: Whenever a cell is adjacent to a coarser level cell, the data values on the cell edges are linearly interpolated between the voxel values at the coarser level. The distance function for the midpoint, however, has to be recalculated in order to obtain the same surface on either of both sides. This can easily be achieved by considering the line equation obtained from the intersection with the coarser cell edges and the already interpolated data values.

If we allow for the resolution between adjacent distance volumes to only differ about a factor of two we can always guarantee a continuous transition. A huge amount of memory can be saved by adjusting the volume resolution with respect to the geometry of the data to be voxelized or if a LOD representation is desired (i.e. Figure 3).

4 Rendering surfaces from distance volumes

Once the volumetric model consisting of the distance-to-closest-surface function has been created its use in practical applications still depends on how fast it can be rendered. Since in the voxel data the original mesh is represented by the isosurface at zero-value, for a particular view it is sufficient to re-sample the volume along the lines of sight and to determine the first sample where the isovalue is hit.

4.1 Volume re-sampling via 3D textures

Most efficiently the re-sampling of large scale volume data can be accomplished by exploiting 3D texture mapping hardware that allows for the interpolation of texture samples with about some hundred MOps per second on high-end graphics workstations. Although at this time hardware accelerated 3D texture mapping is only supported on a few particular architectures we expect the same functionality to be available on low-end architectures like PCs in the near future.

The key idea in volume rendering via 3D texture maps is to re-sample the data on clipping planes that are oriented orthogonal to the viewing plane and to blend the results appropriately [1]. By only slightly modifying this approach it can be employed to render lighted isosurfaces [15]. Each distance volume has to be converted into a RGBα texture, which stores the gradient components and the distance values as the scalar material values in the color channels and the alpha channel, respectively. Note that all components have to be properly scaled and translated to the range (0,1) in order to fit into the internal texture format.

By slicing the texture in front-to-back order and by exploiting the OpenGL alpha-test and the depth-test it is guaranteed that only the first hit with the isosurface is rendered into the frame buffer. Finally, the gradient components and the distance value of the surface points are resident in the pixel values. The diffusely lighted surface points (cf. Figure 4) are obtained by multiplying each pixel value with a $4x4$ matrix. The matrix is initialized in order to transform the gradients back to the range (-1,1), to rotate them with respect to the rotational part of the model view matrix and to perform the calculation of the inner product with the light direction. The matrix multiplication is accomplished by a single per-pixel copy operation with a properly initialized color matrix.

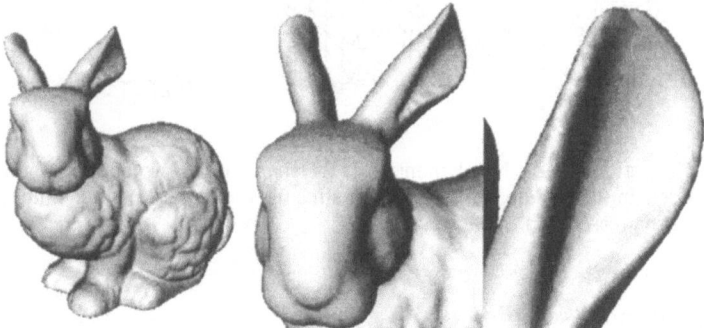

Fig. 4. All images show the isosurface at zero distance rendered with an inter-slice distance of one voxel. Note that the isosurface won't be hit exactly, but that we can arbitrarily decrease the inter-slice distance in order to get more accurate results.

The major benefit of this approach is that any polygonal representation is completely avoided at run-time. Thus the complexity of the rendering process is raster bound and does not depend on the complexity of the surface to be reconstructed. However, there are still a few problems that have to be addressed.

4.2 Rendering thin boundary regions

Although in the proposed framework we are only interested in re-sampling the texture around the isosurface at zero distance a huge number of operations is performed in regions that do not represent the surface. Bounding boxes as introduced already help to make these regions smaller by defining tight bounds around the object, but the texture is also rendered inside the object although the reconstructed samples consist of redundant information.

Consequently, the re-sampling should be restricted to the thin region around the isosurface at zero-distance. Therefore we need to find two approximating meshes for which the minimal deviation from the original one is above a certain tolerance, but one of them completely covers and the other one is completely enclosed by the original model. Then the region between the two meshes exactly covers the relevant texture samples.

Again, from the volumetric representation by means of distance values these two meshes can be reconstructed in a quite efficient way. Let us consider the original mesh to be scan-converted into a signed distance representation at a very coarse resolution. In general, the original surface *cannot* be reconstructed properly due to the insufficient resolution of the underlying grid. Nevertheless, the approximating meshes can be reconstructing from the distance volume according to different isovalues. If the voxel size is supposed to be one, then the two surfaces encoded by distance values 1 and -1 comply with the requirements. We reconstruct these surfaces by means of the Marching Cubes algorithm but we place vertices on the edge midpoints. Thus the surface will most likely to be consisting of many planar triangles that can be collapsed in order to effectively decimate the meshes (see Figure 5).

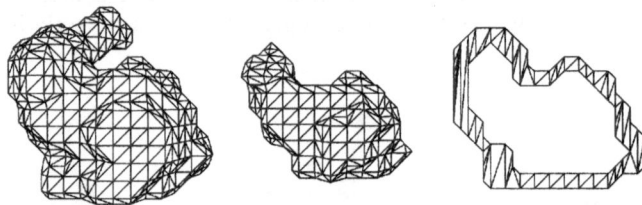

Fig. 5. The illustrations on the left demonstrates the shape of the two approximating meshes for the bunny model. In the middle, for a particular slice the region between the outer mesh and the inner one has been tessellated.

4.3 Clipping and tessellation

Once the two approximating meshes have been constructed the boundary region between them needs to be tessellated. In general, this can be accomplished in two ways: in a preprocessing step by approximating the region by 3D primitives, e.g. cubes or tetrahedra, as in the SGI-Volumizer [13], or in turn during rendering by tessellating the contours that result from clipping both meshes with the slicing planes (see right image in Figure 5).

In our implementation we chose the latter one since we found it attractive to inherit the various techniques already developed for the efficient handling of triangle meshes. We proceed by calculating the sectional polygons with the outer and the inner mesh for each slicing plane. This yield pairs of contours, one inside the other. For the tessellation of the boundary region we utilized the OpenGL tessellation utilities for computing trapezoidal decompositions of concave polygons with multiple holes.

We further exploit an active edge data structure including topological information that allows us to efficiently find those triangles of the approximating meshes that intersect with a certain clipping plane. Initially, once the two meshes have been constructed, to each vertex the appropriate texture coordinate is assigned, which has to be used to texture the newly generated triangles. The intersection procedure thus interpolates vertex positions and texture coordinates.

In case that multiple inner and outer contours are generated or the outer contour is enclosed by the inner one a simple in-out test yields the appropriate pairs to be tessellated. Note that self-intersecting contours cannot occur due to the way they are reconstructed from the distance volume.

With these modifications on hand we are now prepared to considerably decrease the load in the rasterization unit. Only those regions that are close to the isosurface at zero-distance are re-sampled by rendering the appropriate triangles. Concerning the overhead that is spent to generate sectional contours and to tessellate the boundary region we will show in the results section that this doesn't effect the overall performance noticeable. At this point let us just summarize that the use of distance volumes allows us to generate the approximating meshes in a coarse resolution with as few triangles as desired.

4.4 Rendering multiple distance volumes

Although multiple axis aligned distance volumes can be rendered in random order due to the depth comparison of fragments some additional issues have to be considered:

Alignment: When adjacent bounding boxes are not coherently aligned to each other the reconstruction process no longer guarantees continuous transitions. However, if the resolution of each distance volume is constrained to be a multiple of an initial size Δ_{Vox} we can quite easily achieve that cells from adjacent volumes always coincide by just translating and scaling the bounding box appropriately. Now the interpolation method will always yield the same results where bounding boxes overlap or share a common edge. Note that boxes must have an overlap of at least one voxel due to the treatment of texture boundaries by OpenGL. Therefore bounding boxes are appropriately scaled in advance.

Slicing: In order to continuously re-sample the surface at bounding box transitions it is necessary to choose a unique inter-slice distance Δs for the texture based rendering. However, since slices used to re-sample different volumes usually do not coincide we constrain their position in such a way that they are always in a distance $k \cdot \Delta s$, $k \in Z$, from the viewing plane. This strategy allows for the reconstruction of continuous surfaces even if a multi-resolution representation has to be rendered.

We should also mention that for each bounding box the two approximating meshes for the included geometry have to be constructed. In order to apply the proposed tessellation strategy we have to guarantee that a closed surface is maintained at the boundary faces. This is accomplished by clipping the entire mesh with the bounding boxes and by re-tessellating by means of the outlined technique.

4.5 Per-pixel lighting and shading

Hardware accelerated per-pixel shading as proposed in [15] only allows for up to three diffuse light sources. In general, however, in order to simulate realistic lighting and shading effects a more sophisticated lighting model should be provided.

Remember that when the rendering process via 3D textures has been finished the normalized and properly transformed gradients are contained in the pixel components. Instead of performing lighting calculations on a per-vertex or per-fragment basis before fragments are drawn to the frame buffer we propose an OpenGL extension $glShadePixelEXT(x_{min}, y_{min}, x_{max}, y_{max}, mat)$, which enables per-pixel shading thus decoupling the complexity from the scene complexity. A chunk of pixel values is read from the color buffer, then it is multiplied with the matrix *mat* and the resulting values are interpreted as per-pixel normals for which standard OpenGL lighting is performed. Color values generated in this way are drawn back into the color buffer.

Although this extension is actually not available we simulate it in software. The appropriate pixels are read into main memory. Thereby the color matrix is initialized with *mat* in such a way that the components in main memory represent the correctly rotated gradients in the range $(0,1)$. We now retrieve the current OpenGL state, perform the lighting calculations and write the results back into the color buffer.

Obviously, the software simulation is rather inefficient, but on the other hand we should note that lighting calculations are entirely performed on a per-pixel basis. Thus the complexity does not depend on the complexity of the scene and scales only with the image resolution. The images in Figure 8 outline the results of simulating the Phong lighting model using the proposed algorithm.

5   Results and Analysis

In this section we show results for different models and we analyze some of the main features of our approach. All tests were run on a SGI Onyx2 BaseReality with one R10000, 195 MHz processor, 64 MB texture memory and 256 MB main memory.

Table 1 shows detailed results of the proposed adaptive voxelization technique with respect to memory requirements, rendering complexity and frame rates. The models we compare to each other are illustrated in the top row of Figure 6. The approximation error is given with respect to the longest axis of the models bounding box. The adaptive tessellation technique was not used in these examples.

Table 1: Model characteristics, memory use and timings for different polygonal models

	dino	car	horse
#Triangles	110K	150K	210K
#BBoxes	16	128	16
Preprocessing (min)	1.1	1.6	2.1
Memory use	3MB	6MB	9MB
Hausdorff Distance	$\leq 1\%$	$\leq 2\%$	$\leq 1\%$
Frames per sec	8.8	6.8	5.7
#Rendered triangles	1.0K	1.6K	2.3K

We observe that for all examples the memory use is moderate compared to the amount that is originally occupied by the polygonal representation. For example, storing the horse data set as a triangle mesh without any topological information would require approximately 5 MB. Although in the presented examples our adaptive voxelization strategy roughly needs twice this amount we expect to achieve considerably better results if we further increase the number of bounding boxes. Additionally we have to consider that tighter bounding volumes will obviously result in less operations to be performed in the rasterization unit, but that the CPU will be loaded more heavily in order to clip the slicing planes. In the demonstrated examples, however, this time was negligible compared to the overall rendering times.

Also from Table 1 it can be observed that our approach is still slower than pure polygon rendering. This loss in the rendering performance can be explained by the fact that although we already did considerably reduce the number of operations to be performed in the rasterization unit the capacity of the rasterization hardware still prohibits more optimal frame rates.

The last row of Table 1 should demonstrate the gains of our method in terms of the load in the geometry unit in more detail. Note that only the polygons that result from clipping the slicing planes against the bounding boxes have to rendered. As a consequence only about 1% of the original number of primitives had to be converted into fragments and finally displayed. In this way we effectively decouple the geometry unit from the complexity of the underlying mesh, which we see as one of the most challenging features to be considered in the design of future graphics hardware.

In order to demonstrate the improvements that can be achieved by integrating the proposed adaptive tessellation technique, for the horse data set we constructed the approximating meshes as illustrated in Figure 7. The outer mesh consists of 420 triangles and the inner one of 266 triangles. Rendering was performed using 200 slices. The calculation of intersection points and the tessellation of the sectional contours took approximately 0.1 seconds.

Since re-sampling is effectively restricted to the thin boundary region around the surface we saved about 85% of the rasterization operations. The frame rates were increased accordingly, from 5.7 fps up to 8.8 fps. The additional number of triangles introduced by tessellating the boundary region was 9.3K. Still, this amount is considerably smaller than the original number of triangles to be rendered, but at the same time the rasterization load is dramatically reduced.

Finally, the images in Figure 8 illustrate the results of per-pixel shading simulated in software. For a 500x500 viewport it took roughly 0.3 seconds to read the pixel values, to perform the lighting calculations and to write the shaded pixels back into the color buffer. We should note that even without constructing a bounding box representation the rasterization load for the rendering of the dragon data sets was reduced of about 76% using the tessellation technique.

6 Conclusion

We have presented a general approach that demonstrates how large polygonal models can be rendered from a volumetric representation with significantly reduced geometry transfer and processing. Although there are some deficits of our approach:

- Colored models can only be rendered by a two-pass algorithm, the rendering of surface texture is not yet worked out but may benefit from multi-texture functionality that will be available soon.
- Realistic lighting effect have to be simulated in software including expensive frame buffer access.
- The approach is restricted to static scenes since it requires a great deal of preprocessing.
- Sharp edges can only be modeled by dramatically increasing the resolution of the volumetric representation.

we are convinced that the ideas we presented could be influential for future graphics algorithm and hardware developments:

- We have demonstrated that there are new challenges and applications in which 3D textures can be used effectively. So far, the use of volume textures was more or less exclusively limited to volume rendering applications.
- The proposed adaptive tessellation technique has great influence on volume visualization algorithms since it allows one to reduce rasterization load by focusing on the relevant parts.

- We believe that some of the described limitations can be overcome by even faster access to textures and advanced features like single-pass multi-texturing.
- With dedicated volume graphics boards being announced we expect new relevance for all voxel algorithms and we are investigating ways of performing hardware accelerated voxelization.
- With dedicated graphics boards enabling hardware supported per-pixel shading we believe that our approach might streamline an important future direction leading to graphics architectures that render normals as color values issued on a per-vertex basis and perform the lighting and shading calculations in image space.
- We will consider hybrid approaches where the load is balanced in between the geometry stage and the rasterization stage by rendering LOD representations either as polygonal or as volumetric models. For example, in mesh decimation high resolutional parts with low curvature could be rendered from the volumetric representation while high curvature parts are still rendered as triangles.

References

1. B. Cabral, N. Cam, and J. Foran. Accelerated Volume Rendering and Tomographic Reconstruction Using Texture Mapping Hardware. In *ACM Symposium on Volume Visualization '94*, pages 91–98, 1994.
2. S. Cohen and A. Kaufman. Scan-Conversion Algorithms for Linear and Quadratic Objects. In *1990 Symposium on Volume Visualization*, pages 280–301. IEEE, 1990.
3. S. Gibson. Using Distance Maps for Accurate Surface Reconstruction in Sampled Volumes. In *1998 Symposium on Volume Visualization*, pages 23–30. ACM, 1998.
4. S. Gottschalk, M.C. Lin, and D. Manocha. OBBTree: A Hierarchical Structure for Rapid Interference Detection. *ACM Computer Graphics, Proc. SIGGRAPH '96*, 1996.
5. H. Hoppe. View-Dependant Refinement of Progressive Meshes. *ACM Computer Graphics, Proc. SIGGRAPH '97*, 1997.
6. J. Huang, R. Yagel, V. Filippov, and Y. Kurzion. An Accurate Method for Voxelizing Polygon Meshes. In *1998 Symposium on Volume Visualization*, pages 119–126. ACM, 1998.
7. A. Kaufman. Efficient algorithms for 3D scan-conversion of parametric curves, surfaces and volumes. *ACM Computer Graphics, Proc. SIGGRAPH '87*, 1987.
8. Knittel, G and Straßer, W. A Compact Volume Rendering Accelerator. In Kaufman, A. and Krüger, W., editor, *1994 Symposium on Volume Visualization*, pages 67–74. ACM SIGGRAPH, 1994.
9. P. Lacroute and M Levoy. Fast Volume Rendering Using a Shear-Warp Factorization of the Viewing Transform. *Computer Graphics, Proc. SIGGRAPH '94*, 28(4):451–458, 1994.
10. W.E. Lorensen and H.E. Cline. Marching Cubes: A High Resolution 3D Surface Construction Algorithm. *ACM Computer Graphics, Proc. SIGGRAPH '87*, 21(4):163–169, 1987.
11. J. Montrym,.D. Baum, D. Dignam, and C. Migdal. Infinite Reality: A Real-Time Graphics System. *Computer Graphics, Proc. SIGGRAPH '97*, pages 293–303, July 1997.
12. H. Pfister and A. Kaufman. Cube-4 - A Scalable Architecture for Real-Time Volume Rendering. In R. Crawfis and Ch. Hansen, editors, *1996 Symposium on Volume Visualization*, pages 47–54. ACM SIGGRAPH, 1996.
13. IRIS InSight Silicon Graphics Publication. *OpenGL Volumizer Programmer's Guide*. 1997.
14. S. Wang and A. Kaufman. Volume sampled voxelization of geometric primitives. In *Visualization 1993*, pages 78–84. IEEE, 1993.
15. R. Westermann and T. Ertl. Efficiently using graphics hardware in volume rendering applications. *ACM Computer Graphics, Proc. SIGGRAPH '98*, 1998.

Editors' Note: see Appendix, p. 359 for colored figures of this paper

Hierarchical Image-Based Rendering using Texture Mapping Hardware

Nelson Max, University of California, Davis, max2@llnl.gov
Oliver Deussen, University of Magdeburg, deussen@isg.cs.uni-magdeburg.de
Brett Keating, University of California, Davis, brettk1@home.com

Abstract. Multi-layered depth images containing color and normal information for subobjects in a hierarchical scene model are precomputed with standard z-buffer hardware for six orthogonal views. These are adaptively selected according to the proximity of the viewpoint, and combined using hardware texture mapping to create "reprojected" output images for new viewpoints. (If a subobject is too close to the viewpoint, the polygons in the original model are rendered.) Specific z-ranges are selected from the textures with the hardware alpha test to give accurate 3D reprojection. The OpenGL color matrix is used to transform the precomputed normals into their orientations in the final view, for hardware shading.

1. Introduction

Image-based rendering using depth images has become a promising technique for rendering real-world scenes acquired as images, or models with very high polygon counts. Our strategy is to reproject for a new viewpoint one or more precomputed images. This involves using the depth at each pixel, together with the pixel address, to reconstruct a 3D surface point. This point is multiplied by a matrix Q, which is the product of the inverse of the viewing matrix for the precomputed view and the viewing matrix for the desired new view, and then projected into the new view.

Chen and Williams [1] achieve the reprojection using texture flow, which is coherent on large areas where the same smooth surface is visible. For scenes containing vegetation, where the depth varies discontinuously with high spatial frequency, it is more effective to transform each pixel independently, usually in software. McMillan and Bishop [2] showed that a single image can be processed in a "painter's" order that does not require a z-buffer for the output image, and Shade *et al.* [3] extended this to multiple z-layers at each pixel. Max [4] and Shade *et al.* [3] used the multiple layers to include more of the depth complexity in the pre-computed images, which might become "disoccluded" in the new view.

Recently, Schaufler[5, 6] has shown how to reproject single layer z-buffer images using texture mapping hardware, by storing the depth in the alpha channel, and testing it for equality during multiple passes through the texture. The alpha channel of the texture is loaded by reading back the depth buffer of the precomputed view. During rendering, it is scaled by a factor that compresses the 8 or 12 bit alpha range into a smaller number of integer values. For each of these integers n, a polygon covering the corresponding depth layer in the precomputed view is transformed into the new view by the matrix Q, and rendered with the alpha test set to transmit only those pixels with alpha equal to n. The color channels of the texture were used by Schaufler to store preshaded colors. Here we use them to store unshaded color (diffuse reflectivity) in one pass, and to store normal components in a second pass.

Max [7] reprojected precomputed images of various subparts of a tree, organized in a hierarchical model. These were adaptively selected according to the detail needed for the current viewpoint. This scheme requires shading during or after reprojection, because the subparts are used in the hierarchical model at various orientations. Westermann and Ertl [8] show how the color matrix can be used with a surface-normal texture to reorient the normal and shade the surface in hardware.

In the current work, we have combined the techniques of [5], [7], and [8] into a completely hardware-based method to reproject and shade hierarchies of images. The standard z-buffer hardware is used for final visibility determination, so the input can be processed in any order. The next section explains the basic reprojection scheme, and the following one deals with the shading.

2. The hierarchical reprojection algorithm

The hierarchical model uses the standard philosophy of constructing complex objects from repeated instances of subparts, each scaled, translated, and/or rotated into position by a 4 x 4 matrix. Several systems for modeling vegetation use this hierarchical philosophy, together with a substantial amount of randomness, so that many geometrically inequivalent subobjects are used at each level of the hierarchy. Here, since each subobject must have images precomputed in several views and used as textures, this randomness must be very limited, as in Brownbill [9], so that only one or two inequivalent objects are used at each level. Our system can parse and render from input files that contain both the hierarchical objects of Max [7] and those in the Rayshade format [10], such as produced by Brownbill[9] and Lintermann and Deussen [11].

In order to decide whether to reproject an object as a whole, the reprojected size of the precomputed pixel closest to the viewpoint is compared to a threshold, which is approximately the size of an output pixel. If the reprojected size is less than the threshold, reprojection will provide sufficient detail, so the whole object is reprojected. Otherwise, the algorithm goes deeper into its detailed description, in terms of subobjects. If a part of the model is so close to the viewer that no precomputed image has enough detail, the polygons in the original model are rendered.

In Max [7], the threshold was fairly small, in order to avoid gaps between reprojected pixels. Shade *et al.* [3] filled in these gaps by reprojecting each input pixel as an appropriately sized "splat" of several output pixels. Texture mapping hardware can automatically find the nearest precomputed texture pixel for a reprojected output pixel, so gaps solely from texture resampling are less of a problem. (Nearest neighbors must be used, rather than the smoother linear or mip-map texture interpolation, because interpolating or averaging the depth in the alpha channel could lead to meaningless results when the correct depth is discontinuous.)

The key step is to reproject a precomputed image, using the alpha test. As shown in [5], even though this alpha test is for equality to a single value, it can be made to give some overlap in the z-ranges for adjacent layers, in order to reduce visible gaps between them when viewing slanted smooth surfaces. However this does not completely eliminate gaps from surfaces which are at too steep a slant in the precomputed view, and cannot show surfaces that are occluded in the precomputed image. Both Schaufler [5, 6] and Max[4, 7] reproject several views to help solve these problems. In this paper we use all six views along the positive and negative directions on the x, y, and z axes. This guarantees that every surface will be positioned (although possibly not visible) in at least one pair of images at an angle which is not too slanted, and also that thin round objects like twigs can have all sides represented. The same six views were also used for image based rendering by Lischinski and Rappaport[12].

Shade *et al.* [3] and Max[4, 7] used multiple depth layers in the precomputed images, whose depths were stored individually in a sorted list at each pixel, and thus could not be easily generated in standard z-buffer hardware. To take advantage of hardware rendering, we slice the object by hardware z clipping into multiple slabs, and reproject each of them by the method of Schaufler[5]. Since each slab is viewed from both the front and the back (in two of the six fixed viewing directions) this completely handles slabs with a depth complexity of two (*i. e.* a viewing ray intersects at most two surfaces per slab). The RGBA images for the multiple slabs are placed together in a single texture for each precomputed view. These are each loaded as a separate texture object, using OpenGL texture binding.

A related technique was described by Meyer and Neyret[13]. They made many more z-clipped slabs and put each in a separate texture. In general, a smooth closed surface intersects a slab in a collection of strips, each bounding an interior region of pixels. Meyer and Neyret filled in these interior regions with opaque textured pixels, and thus eliminated the cracks visible in our method when the surface is viewed at a steep angle. However, since our bottleneck is in the loading of many different textures, this method is impractical for us.

We preprocess each frame by going once through the hierarchical model doing no rendering, but instead accumulating a list of reprojection matrices Q for the multiple instances of each precomputed view of each object. In a second pass, we go through all the precomputed views in order, and for each non-empty list, we bind the appropriate texture and reproject all the instances using it. This reduces texture swapping. We also render in the hardware pipeline the polygonal descriptions for parts of objects that are so close that resampling is inadequate. In a third pass, we similarly reproject or render all the surface-normal images and use them for shading, as described below. The scene parser must repeatedly read the same object description files, so these are first loaded once into memory, and then processed from there.

3. Normals and shading

To precompute a separate RGBA texture, with the x, y, and z components of the surface normal in the R, G, and B components of the texture, standard color interpolation is used while rendering the polygons in the model. The polygonal tessellations for curved surfaces must be fine enough so that when the vertex normals are interpolated in hardware, they remain approximately unit vectors. The polygon vertex colors are set by scaling and biasing the normal components (N_x, N_y, N_z), from the range [-1, 1] into the range [0, 1], as in Westermann and Ertl [8], so that

$$(red, green, blue) = (.5 + .5*N_x, \; .5 + .5*N_y, \; .5 + .5*N_z) . \tag{1}$$

When the precomputed texture is reprojected into a new view, these normals must be rotated into their new positions, using M_{rot}, the rotation part of the reprojection matrix Q, after scaling and translation are removed. This is done using the 4 x 4 color matrix, an SGI OpenGL extension in the "imaging pipeline", which multiplies the RGBA values from an array in memory as they are being stored into the texture table.

If $L = (L_x, L_y, L_z)$ is the vector to a light source at infinity, we used the color matrix

$$
CM = \begin{bmatrix} L_x & L_y & L_z & 0 \\ L_x & L_y & L_z & 0 \\ L_x & L_y & L_z & 0 \\ 0 & 0 & 0 & 1 \end{bmatrix} M_{rot} .
\tag{2}
$$

To remove the scale and bias of equation (1), we used a post-color-matrix scale of 2, and a post-color-matrix bias equal to minus the sum of the entries in one of the identical first three row of CM. (Westermann and Ertl [8] did this instead by multiplying the product in equation (2) on the right by an appropriate constant matrix, but this assumed that alpha is always 1, while we are using alpha to store the depth.) The color data are automatically clamped to [0, 1] before being stored in the texture map. This sets the shading value to zero for surfaces facing away from the light source, and gives the shaded image that would result if all the model surfaces were perfectly diffuse white.

This black and white shaded image is multiplied by the unshaded color image by copying it over the color image, using a blending weight of zero for the source image, and a blending weight of the source color for the destination image. During this image copy (we used an image read and write) we used a bias of *ambient*, and a scale of (1. - *ambient*), in order to add ambient illumination to the final image.

The same lists of reprojection matrices Q for each needed object view are used for reprojecting the normal textures. Each texture is loaded into system memory only once per non-empty list, but since the color matrix is only in the imaging pipeline, not the fragment pipeline, the texture map has to be reloaded from memory with a different color matrix for each different matrix Q on the list.

4. Results and future work

Figure 1 (see color section at the rear of this volume) shows a view of a maple forest, produced in 5 minutes by this method, using one 195 Mhz R10000 processor on an SGI Onyx, InfiniteReality. Figure 2 shows the hardware rendering of the complete model of 955,871 subobjects with 17,205,476 polygons, which took 11 minutes. Much of this time was spent in the software traversal of the deepest levels of the hierarchy. It took about 3 hours to prerender the colors, normals, and depths in the 6 orthogonal views, each with 6 depth slabs, for the five levels in the hierarchical model. The complete polygonal models were used. Much of this time could be saved, at some cost in accuracy, if reprojections of prerendered lower levels of the hierarchy were used in prerendering the higher levels. The precomputed textures were stored on disc as run length encoded SGI image files, requiring 15.4 megabytes.

Our goal was to produce complex images like those in Deussen *et al.* [14], so we extended the parser of Max[7] to read Rayshade files. Figure 3 shows a forest containing a mixture of the maple trees in figure 1, with oak trees modeled by the system of Lintermann and Deussen[11]. It took 46 seconds to render, using only the precomputed images of the whole trees. A polygon rendering took 20 minutes. Figure 4 shows a closer view, which took 109 seconds because it also needed precomputed views of branches. Figures 5 is a close-up showing textured leaves, and figure 6 is a long view.

Because normals are represented in the precomputed images, it should be possible to use bump-mapped texture for the bark on the tree trunks and branches, which would make them look more realistic.

Currently, our leaf polygons have only one normal, which can become reversed when the wrong side of the leaf is visible. If the normals were transformed by M_{rot} alone, to form a normal image, instead of using equation (2) to take their dot product with L, then a software post-process could reverse the normals that point away from the viewer. Also, given a corrected normal image, table look-ups, perhaps using "pixel textures", could be used to produce the radiance-based shading of Max et al. [15]. Since the "shadow buffer" of Williams [16] can also be generated by image-based rendering, it should be possible to add post-process shadows to this algorithm, as in Max et al. [15], but the quantization of the depth onto the parallel planes used in the reprojection technique might cause artifacts in the shadows.

The accuracy in reprojecting using the alpha test depends on the spacing of the polygonal layers into which the depth is quantized. This depends on the total number of layers from all the slabs, but not on the number of slabs sliced from the object. So the cost in textured pixels ("fragments") is not increased with multiple slabs; only the texture storage and transfer costs increase. The speed/quality trade-offs involved in setting these two quantities should be further explored.

In the "standard" layered depth images of Shade[3] and Max[4, 7], the first layer at a pixel contains the surface, if any, closest to the viewpoint. The next layer contains the surface, if any, just behind the first one, and so forth. Each layer could potentially involve the entire depth range of the object, so the fragment cost could grow in proportion to the number of layers. However, no surfaces would be lost from occlusion, even if only one view were taken along each of the three positive x, y, and z axis directions, instead of the six positive and negative ones. It is difficult to precompute such images with current hardware, but possible in software. If the bottleneck is in texture loading rather than in fragment processing, as it is in our current implementation, the "standard" layered depth images should be considered. Future hardware which permits rendering from compressed textures, or at least loading texture maps from compressed data in memory, should alleviate this current bottleneck, since most of each slab or layer is empty and transparent. Concurrent prefetches of texture from disc should also help.

Acknowledgments

This work was performed under the auspices of the U. S. Department of Energy by Lawrence Livermore National Laboratory under contract W-7405-ENG-48. Mark Duchaineau provided the X-window management software, and Dan Schikore, Rüddiger Westermann, Gernot Schaufler, Brian Cabral, and Mark Duchaineau gave helpful information and suggestions. Jan Nunes and Ross Gaunt helped record the videotape.

References

1. Chen, Shenchang Eric, and Lance Williams, "View Interpolation for Image Synthesis", ACM Computer Graphics Proceedings, Annual Conference Series 1993, pp. 279 - 288.

2. McMillan, Leonard, and Gary Bishop, "Plenoptic Modeling: An Image-Based rendering System", ACM Computer Graphics Proceedings, Annual Conference Series 1995, pp. 39 - 46.

3. Shade, Jonathan, Steven Gortler, Li-wei He, and Richard Szeleski, "Layered Depth Images", ACM Computer Graphics Proceedings, Annual Conference Series 1998, pp. 231 - 242.

4. Max, Nelson and Keiichi Ohsaki, "Rendering Trees from Precomputed Z-Buffer Views", in "Rendering Techniques '95 (Hanrahan and Purgathofer, eds.) Springer, Vienna (1995) pp. 74 - 81.

5. Schaufler, Gernot, "Per-Object Image Warping with Layered Imposters", in "Rendering Techniques '98" (Drettakis and Max, eds.) Springer, Vienna (1998) pp. 145 - 156.

6. Schaufler, Gernot, "Image-based Object Representation by Layered Impostors", Proceedings of ACM Symposium on Virtual Reality Software and Technology '98, Nov. 1998, Taipei, Taiwan, pp 99-104.

7. Max, Nelson, "Hierarchical Rendering of Trees from Precomputed Multi-Layer Z-Buffers", in "Rendering Techniques '96 (Pueyo and Schröder, eds.) Springer, Vienna (1996) pp. 165 - 174.

8. Westermann, Rüdiger and Thomas Ertl, "Efficiently Using Graphics Hardware in Volume Rendering Applications", ACM Computer Graphics Proceedings, Annual Conference Series 1998, pp. 169 - 177.

9. Brownbill, Andrew, "Reducing the storage required to render L-system based models", Master's Thesis, The University of Calgary, 1996.

10. Kolb, Craig, "Rayshade", http://graphics.stanford.edu/~cek/rayshade.

11. Lintermann, Bernd, and Oliver Deussen, "Interactive Modelling of Plants", IEEE CG&A Vol. 19 No. 1 (1999).

12. Lischinski, Dani, and Ari Rappoport. "Image-Based Rendering for Non-Diffuse Synthetic Scenes, in "Rendering Techniques '98" (Drettakis and Max, eds.) Springer, Vienna (1998) pp. 301 - 314.

13. Meyer, Alexander, and Fabrice Neyret, "Interactive Volume Textures" in "Rendering Techniques '98" (Drettakis and Max, eds.) Springer, Vienna (1998) pp. 157 - 168.

14. Deussen, Oliver, Pat Hanrahan, Bernd Lintermann, Radomír Mech, Matt Pharr, and Przemyslaw Pruisinkiewicz, "Realistic modeling and rendering of plant ecosystems", ACM Computer Graphics Proceedings, Annual Conference Series 1998, pp. 275 - 286.

15. Max, Nelson, Curtis Mobley, Brett Keating, and En-Hua Wu, "Plane-Parallel Radiance Transport for Global Illumination in Vegetation", in "Rendering Techniques '97" (Dorsey and Slusallek eds.) Springer, Vienna (1997) pp. 239 - 250.

16. Williams, Lance "Casting Curved Shadows on Curved Surfaces", Computer Graphics, Vol. 12, No. 3 (1978 Siggraph Conference Proceedings) pp. 270 - 274.\

Editors' Note: see Appendix, p. 360 for colored figures of this paper

Towards Interactive Photorealistic Rendering of Indoor Scenes: A Hybrid Approach

Tushar Udeshi and Charles D. Hansen

Dept. of Computer Science
University of Utah
{tudeshi, hansen}@cs.utah.edu

Abstract. Photorealistic rendering methods produce accurate solutions to the rendering equation but are computationally expensive and typically non-interactive. Some researchers have used graphics hardware to obtain photorealistic effects but not at interactive frame rates. We describe a technique to achieve near photorealism of simple indoor scenes at interactive rates using both CPUs and graphics hardware in parallel. This allows the user the ability to interactively move objects and lights in the scene. Our goal is to introduce as many global illumination effects as possible while maintaining a high frame rate. We describe methods to generate soft shadows, approximate one-bounce indirect lighting, and specular reflection and refraction effects.

1 Introduction and previous work

Research in photorealistic rendering has concentrated on numerically solving the rendering equation[9]. Ray tracers[22] use Monte Carlo methods while radiosity systems[6] use finite element methods. These give accurate solutions but are computationally expensive. Classic radiosity methods typically converge faster to a solution to the rendering equation than ray tracers but cannot account for specular reflection and refraction. Moreover, they are mainly used with planar geometry. Ray tracers obviate both these limitations but require path tracing[9] to get indirect illumination effects which introduces noise and is computationally expensive.

Many interactive environments such as Virtual Building Systems[1] rely on precomputation of static environments to form progressive radiosity solutions. These suffer from large computational overhead and unchangeable geometry. Even in incremental radiosity solutions[3], geometry changes require significant recomputation time. Moreover these solutions do not account for specular reflection and refraction.

Systems based on ray tracing are mostly non-interactive. Recently Parker et al.[14] developed an interactive ray tracer. However it does not account for indirect illumination. Moreover, moving objects must be spatially bounded which implies that all motion is known *a priori*.

Hardware-based solutions, which are interactive, are inherently of lower quality due to the limited feature set of the graphics accelerator. Diefenbach[5] demonstrated techniques of using graphics hardware to get specular reflection, refraction, caustics and transparency but not at interactive frame rates.

In this paper, we describe techniques of using both graphics hardware and multiple CPUs in parallel to achieve near photorealistic rendering of simple indoor scenes[1] at

---

[1]Up to 10,000 polygons and eight area light sources

interactive rates of one to ten frames a second. The user has the flexibility to interactively move both lights and scene geometry. We have developed our application on a SGI Reality Monster with eight Infinite Reality^{TM} graphics pipes and 64 MIPS R10000 processors. Our goal is to make use of all these resources to introduce global illumination effects while keeping the image generation as interactive as possible. The near photorealistic effects we have introduced are soft shadows, approximate one bounce indirect lighting and specular reflection and refraction effects.

1.1 Shadow generation algorithms

Shadows play a key role in the overall realism of computer-generated images because they provide important visual cues about the 3D arrangement of objects. Today's graphics hardware supports directional and point lights, Lambertian surfaces, and Gouraud or Phong shading. However it does not take visibility into account while shading; thus shadows are not an inherent rendering feature. There are three algorithms which make use of graphics hardware to calculate visibility: projective texture, shadow buffer and shadow volume. We give a brief description of these algorithms in the following paragraphs.

Projective textures. This algorithm has been used to generate soft shadows during walk-throughs[8]. To find the shadows cast on a particular polygon P, with respect to a light source L, all other polygons in the scene are projected on to P, with L as the center of projection. This can be done in hardware by fixing the view point at L and setting the view frustum so that P is tightly bounded at its base. Then P is rendered with lighting enabled and all other polygons in the scene are rendered only with ambient light. The image thus obtained is then texture mapped onto P. Hence for p polygons and l point light sources, $O(lp^2)$ polygons need to be rendered to determine visibility. This algorithm works well for walk-throughs in static scenes but is unsuitable for scenes with moving objects.

Shadow map / Shadow buffer algorithm. Shadow maps use the depth buffer and projective texture mapping to create a screen space method for shadowing objects[15, 16, 23]. The scene is rendered from a light source L and also from the eye. The depth values of pixels from the eye are transformed to the light-view coordinate system and then compared to depth values recorded from the light corresponding to the same region in object space. If the depth value from the light is less, that pixel is inferred to to be in shadow with respect to L. Hence for l point light sources and p polygons, $O(lp)$ polygons need to be rendered to determine visibility.

This technique has the advantage that occluders can have arbitrary geometry. However it suffers from aliasing problems. The number of pixels a particular object occupies when seen from the light is different from that when seen from the eye. Hence we do not have a one to one correspondence of pixels in the two images and so aliasing effects can be seen. This effect is illustrated in Figure 1. Another drawback of this algorithm is that omni-directional lights require multiple renderings of the scene in order to cover the entire scene. Also, even if one object in the scene moves, the entire shadow map needs to be recalculated. Therefore, this algorithm is not suitable for dynamic scenes.

Shadow volume algorithm. The shadow volume algorithm [4] is an object-space technique for generating shadows. A shadow volume, defined with respect to an occluder O and a point light source L, is that region in space where L is blocked by O.

Fig. 1. "Shadow Acne"(aliasing artifacts) caused by shadow map algorithm.

Consider a ray shot from the view point into the scene. If the ray enters a shadow volume but does not leave it before intersecting with an object in the scene, the corresponding pixel can be concluded to be in shadow.

For l light sources and p polygons, the number of shadow volumes generated is $O(lp)$ in the worst case. Shadows are generated with object space precision. There are a few subtleties associated with this algorithm. A solution to these is given in Section 2.

We use multiple pipes and CPUs to implement both the shadow map and the shadow volume algorithm. The details are in Section 4.1.

1.2 Indirect lighting

As Appel[2] recognized, greater realism requires global illumination models, which account for inter-reflection of light between surfaces. Studies[19] have shown that indirect illumination also gives an important visual cue signaling contact between two surfaces.

Radiosity systems give accurate solutions for indirect lighting in diffuse scenes but not at interactive rates. Several systems use a static, precomputed radiosity solution for indirect lighting. While this is acceptable for walk-throughs and minor scene geometry changes, it is unsuitable for scenes in which light sources can move.

Keller[10] suggested a method to get fast solutions for indirect illumination by using hardware-assisted particle tracing. Particles are shot from the light in software. When a particle hits a diffuse object in the scene at a point P, the scene is rendered by the hardware with a virtual light source placed at P. With this technique, a very good approximation for indirect illumination is obtained in much shorter time compared to the physically-based ray tracing and radiosity methods. However, this technique did not run at interactive rates.

We use a similar technique for approximate one-bounce indirect illumination. We use a hardware-accelerated energy shoot approach as used in progressive radiosity. The algorithm is described in detail in Section 3.

1.3 Specular effects

In real scenes, we often encounter objects made of specular materials such as glass and metal. The specular reflection and refraction associated with these materials is view-dependent.

Diefenbach implemented reflection and refraction using graphics hardware[5]. The scene is rendered from a virtual view point to get the reflected/refracted image which is then projected onto the original image. This gives a good approximation for reflective surfaces. However for refraction, this approach is an acceptable approximation only if the rays incident on to the refractive surface are *para-axial* [7], which requires all refractive surfaces to be perpendicular to the line of sight vector. This approach cannot be used for non-planar surfaces. Moreover each reflective/refractive surface visible from the eye generates a virtual eye point, thus requiring an extra rendering of the scene. This technique is too computationally expensive for interactive applications.

Ofek et al.[13] demonstrated a technique to render curved, reflective surfaces using both the CPU and the graphics hardware. A *reflection image* is generated by creating and rendering virtual objects corresponding to reflections of scene objects. This *reflection image* is then merged into the primary image.

Ray tracing inherently accounts for reflection and refraction. We use multiple CPUs to ray trace the specular regions in the scene. Graphics hardware is used to speed it up further. This is described in detail in Section 4.3.

2 Soft shadow generation using shadow volumes

The shadow volume algorithm[4] is well suited for today's graphics hardware if the scene is composed of planar geometry. In this case, a shadow volume is a truncated semi-infinite pyramid and is bounded by what we call *shadow quads*. This is shown in Figure 2. A shadow quad is constructed from rays cast from the light source, intersecting the vertices of an edge, then continuing outside the scene.

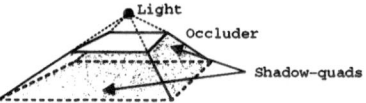

Fig. 2. The shaded area shows the shadow volume generated by an occluder due to a light source. The shadow volume is a semi-infinite pyramid bounded by quadrilaterals (shadow quads).

Consider a ray shot from the eye into the scene. An intersection with a front-facing shadow quad implies that the ray has entered a shadow volume . Similarly an intersection with a back-facing shadow quad indicates an exit from a shadow volume. Hence, for each pixel we need to determine the number of front-facing shadow quads minus the number of back-facing shadow quads which are closer to the eye than any object in the scene. We refer to this as *s-count*. If the *s-count* of a particular pixel is positive, we infer that the pixel is in shadow. Heidmann[18] used the stencil buffer to determine *s-count* for each pixel. In our implementation we use the red channel in the back buffer to maintain this count. The scene is rendered in the front buffer and the depth values copied into the back buffer. The color buffer of the back buffer is cleared. Shadow quads are assigned a color of $(1, 0, 0)$. All front-facing shadow quads are first rendered with additive blending enabled and then all back-facing shadow quads are rendered with subtractive blending enabled. Note that these are rendered with depth-testing enabled and the depth mask set to FALSE. Consequently, the red channel of a particular pixel is modified by a shadow quad only if the shadow quad is closer to the view point than any object in the scene. The stencil buffer is used to resolve the shadow volume straddling the view plane issue as described in Section 2.1.

This is an object space algorithm and hence independent of the view point. Thus, shadow quads need not be recalculated when the view point changes. If shadow quads are constructed from each edge, the number of shadow quads generated will be very large. This number can be reduced by constructing shadow quads only from silhouette edges. However this can be done only with convex geometry as shown in Figure 3. Also face-edge data needs to be maintained which increases storage requirements.

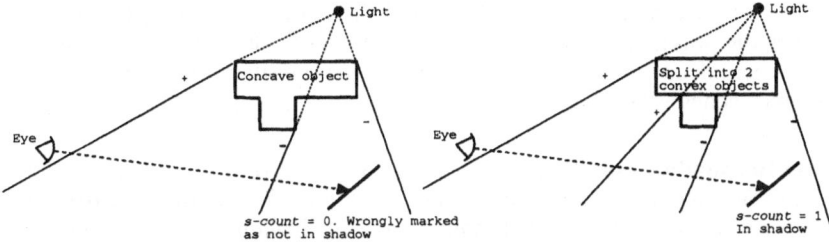

Fig. 3. Convex geometry needed for shadow volume algorithm. *s-count* is incremented when ray intersects with front-facing shadow quads (marked +) and decremented when intersected with back-facing shadow quads (marked -).

2.1 Shadow volume straddling the view plane

If the entire view plane is inside a shadow volume, then the *s-count* can be incremented by one for each pixel. We can determine the number of such shadow volumes with respect to a light source l by shooting a ray from the view point to l and keeping track of the number of light-facing objects which the ray intersects. *s-count* can then be initialized to this count for all pixels before drawing the shadow quads. However, as demonstrated in Figure 4, a shadow volume can straddle the view plane and the shadow quads are clipped at the boundaries of the view frustum. Consequently, not all pixels on the view plane are inside this shadow volume. The *s-count* of only those pixels which lie inside this clipped shadow volume should be corrected. Correcting *s-count* for all pixels will not work.

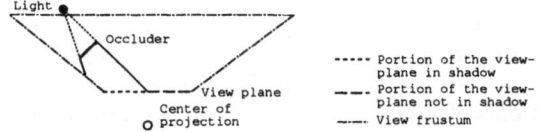

Fig. 4. A clipped shadow volume may straddle the view plane.

Consider a ray shot from the view point into the scene. The number of intersections with back-facing shadow quads minus those with front facing shadow quads is the number of shadow volumes which enclose the corresponding pixel in the view plane. Note that the ray intersection with scene geometry is ignored. We refer to this as the pixel's *g-count*. Note that both *g-count* and *s-count* are non-negatively clamped. Incrementing *s-count* by *g-count* for each pixel increments the *s-count* by the number of shadow volumes which enclose that pixel. This has the effect of registering an entry into these shadow volumes. In our implementation, we maintain *g-count* in the stencil buffer. When drawing front-facing shadow quads, the stencil test is set to decrement regardless of the outcome of the depth test. The stencil test is similarly set to increment while drawing back-facing shadow quads. Front-facing shadow quads are drawn first and then back-facing ones. This is achieved in hardware by rendering the polygons once with back-face culling enabled and once with front-face culling enabled, i.e. we need to make two passes over the polygon data, but each shadow quad is rendered only once. At the end of this process, the red channel has the *s-count* value and the stencil buffer has the *g-count* value for each pixel. The only other method we know of which addresses this issue requires the shadow quads to be drawn twice[5] (with four passes made over the polygon data). As shown in Section 5, drawing the shadow quads is the bottleneck of our implementation. Hence, drawing them twice would deteriorate performance considerably.

Capping the shadow volumes. The shadow volumes drawn are open at both ends. This may cause incorrect values of *g-count*. In Figure 5a, the ray shot from the view point towards the object O does not intersect any shadow quad and hence O is wrongly marked as not in shadow. This is because the ray passes through the open end of the shadow volume near the light. Note that this can occur only if the light is in front of the view plane. Similarly, the ray passes through the open end of the shadow volume away from the light in Figure 5b and this can occur only if the light is behind the view plane. One technique[5] suggested to resolve this issue was to extend the shadow quads to the light while determining *g-count*. However this gives incorrect results if the eye is between the light and the occluder. In this case, all visible objects are marked in shadow. In fact, even the occluder will be marked as being in its own shadow! This is illustrated in Figure 6. It also fails to cap the end of the shadow volume away form the light as shown in Figure 5b.

We cap the shadow volumes by drawing light-facing scene polygons for the case in which the light is in front of the eye, as shown in Figure 5a, and drawing a perspective projection with the light as the center, of every light-facing polygon when the light is behind the eye, as shown in Figure 5b. The rendering of these is done with stencil test enabled so that *g-count* is corrected and the color mask set to FALSE so that *s-count* is not modified.

Figure 7 shows the shadows generated under a table with and without the shadow volume correction.

Approximating the shadow volume capping. While the above solution always works, there is a performance degradation because every light-facing polygon, or its projection, needs to be drawn once for each light sample. However, note that a shadow volume needs to be capped only if it encloses at least one pixel of the view plane, i.e. only shadow volumes constructed by polygons which occlude the light sample from some region of the view plane need to be capped. We determine these occluding polygons by sampling the view plane and shooting rays from these samples towards the light source; all objects intersected are tagged. Only shadow volumes generated from silhouette edges of tagged polygons are capped. However, a few occluding objects can sometimes be missed by the ray tracing which cause incorrect shadows. We decided to include this feature because it resulted in a large performance gain. The user can toggle this approximation off if correctness is required at all times.

3 Approximate indirect lighting

On the SGI Infinite Reality^{TM} graphics system, with p graphics pipes, we can have as many as $8p$ light sources. These can be used to simulate one-bounce reflected light. In

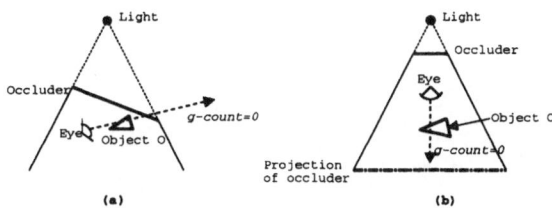

Fig. 5. If shadow volume is not capped Object O is wrongly considered to be in shadow(a) Light is in front of the eye: Occluder can cap the shadow volume (b) Light is behind the eye: projected occluder will cap shadow volume.

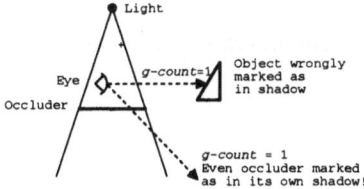

Fig. 6. Problem of extending the shadow volumes to the light for capping the shadow volumes.

our implementation, we tessellate polygons in the scene into elements of equal area for the indirect lighting pass. We approximate the one-bounce reflected light from those polygon elements which reflect maximum energy. The polygon elements are sorted, by multiple CPUs in parallel, in descending order of the energy they reflect. The energy an element P receives directly from a differential area light source dl is directly proportional to the form-factor from dl to P. Therefore, this form-factor multiplied by the reflectivity of P and the emissivity of dl is a measure of the energy which is received from dl and reflected by P.

We use a *single-plane* algorithm[17] to calculate the form-factors. Each polygon is assigned a weight initialized to zero. A wide-perspective *item buffer*[21] is rendered with dl as the center of projection. The form-factor from dl to each pixel in the *item buffer* is precomputed in a map with the help of Nusselt Analog. The weight of a polygon P is the the sum of form-factors of pixels that display P in the item buffer multiplied by the reflectivity of P and the emissivity of dl. Multiple CPUs are used to sort the polygon elements based on their assigned weight. We note that a full sort is not required. We only require the $8p$ polygon elements having the highest weight. Each pipe approximates the one bounce reflected light of 8 polygon elements by rendering the scene with light sources placed at the centroids of these elements. The light source direction is set to that of the normal of the polygon and the intensity is set proportional to the assigned weight. The scene rendered with these virtual light sources is blended into the final display image to add in the indirect illumination effect.

We note that OpenGL lighting does not take visibility into account, so the virtual light sources may light regions in the scene which should not be lit. For example in Figure 8, object O should not be lit by the virtual light source. However the intensities of these virtual light sources are low. Thus, the incorrect illumination is not noticeable for most scenes.

(a) (b)

Fig. 7. Shadow under a table (a) No shadow volume correction (b) With shadow volume correction

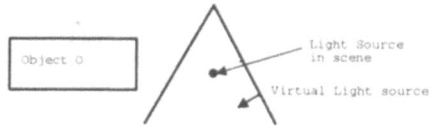

Fig. 8. Object O wrongly lit by virtual light source

4 Implementation details

We have developed our application on an SGI Reality Monster^{TM} which has 64 CPUs and 8 Infinite Reality graphics pipes. The user can select the number of pipes and CPUs to use with the restriction that the number of pipes should be greater than or equal to the number of area light sources in the scene. The user can also choose between the shadow buffer and shadow volume algorithm. The latter is generally faster and gives more accurate shadows but the former should be used if the model is not convex. If the user chooses the shadow volume algorithm, the faster approximate shadow volume capping as described in Section 2.1, can also be selected. The accuracy of soft shadows depends on how finely the light is sampled. More samples give more accurate shadows but result in a performance degradation. This can also be specified by the user. The user also has the option of selecting which global illumination effects are desired among soft shadows, indirect lighting and reflection/refraction.

Each pipe generates shadows from a few light samples and also contributes to the indirect lighting with 8 virtual light sources. Figure 10 (see color plate) shows the different stages in the rendering pipeline and Figure 11 (see color plate) shows the images generated by the different pipes before compositing. The following sections give implementation details.

4.1 Shadow generation

The scene is rendered into the front buffer, with one point light source which is a jittered random sample of the area light source. OpenGL supports only per-vertex lighting calculation. The polygons in the scene are uniformly tessellated with a threshold on their area only while doing the direct lighting shading.

Soft shadows are generated by sampling the light source into point light samples.

The light samples are uniformly distributed between all pipes. A binary image is generated for each light sample, i.e. the image is divided into regions lit by the point light sample and those that are not. These binary images are accumulated in the accumulation buffer to generate a gray-level image which is blended onto the front buffer to give shadows. Typically we sample the light source using 9 point light sources which produces only ten levels of gray. When the eye zooms into a shadow, discontinuities and Mach bands can be observed . To alleviate this effect, we convolve the grey level image with a 7×7 square average filter before blending into the front buffer. Convolution is supported by the graphics hardware and therefore does not introduce noticeable overhead.

Shadow map. The shadow map algorithm has been implemented as an OpenGL extension on SGI machines and is called the SGIX_SHADOW extension. The coordinate transformation of depth values from eye-view to light-view coordinates, comparison of the two corresponding depths and filtering are all implemented in hardware.

Theoretically, one rendering of the scene from the eye and one from each light sample should be enough to generate the shadow map for multiple light samples. However, the shadow map algorithm implemented by the SGIX_SHADOW extension, uses 3D texture mapping. A texture can be mapped only if geometry is drawn and so the scene needs to be rendered once from the eye and once from the light for each point light source sample.

We tried to avoid this cost by implementing the algorithm ourselves. A pure software-based implementation proved to be too slow. So we attempted to perform the coordinate transformation in hardware. We first render the scene so that the color at each pixel represented the object space coordinates at that point. This is done using 3D texture mapping. Using automatic texture coordinate generation, the texture coordinates are set proportional to the corresponding object space coordinate and scaled from 0 to 1. The texture map is then set so that the red channel is proportional to the x coordinate in object space, the green to y and the blue to the z coordinate. We call the image rendered using this texture mapping a *coordinate buffer*.

The scene is then rendered from the point light sample and the depth buffer read into a memory buffer MD. The color matrix is loaded with the product of the light-view perspective matrix and the model-view matrix as well as the scaling and biasing required to convert back to object coordinates and then the *coordinate buffer* is read into another memory buffer MB. In this pixel transfer process, we thus perform the coordinate transformation required. Now the red, green and blue color channels in MB represent the x, y and z normalized device coordinates respectively. The red and green channels of each pixel are converted to window coordinates (a scale followed by a bias) and the green channel is compared with the corresponding value in MD. However, this technique gave incorrect shadows especially at points of contact. This is because we only had 10 bits per color channel, which was not enough precision to represent the object space coordinates accurately in the *coordinate buffer* and so transformed depth values had significant errors.

Shadow volume. The CPUs extract the silhouette edges of the scene with respect to the light samples. This needs to be done only if a light has moved or the object to which the edge belongs has moved since the last frame. Let $\overline{n_1}$ and $\overline{n_2}$ be the normals to the two faces bounded by an edge. Let $\overline{v}$ be a vector from the light source to any point on the edge. Then the edge is a silhouette if $(\overline{n_1}.\overline{v}) * (\overline{n_2}.\overline{v})$ is negative. The shadow quads are calculated for the silhouette edges and stored with the edge data.

Each pipe is assigned a few samples of one area light source. If approximate shadow volume capping is enabled, jittered samples from the view plane are determined and rays are shot from these to the light source. These rays determine which objects need to be drawn to cap the shadow volumes. Else, all shadow volumes are capped.

The depth buffer is copied from the front to the back buffer and all shadow volumes generated from the assigned light samples are drawn and capped as described in Section 2. The stencil buffer, which stores *g-count*, is read into memory and then additively blended into the red channel of the back buffer, which stores *s-count*. A positive red channel value for a pixel implies that the pixel is in shadow. This binary image is accumulated in the accumulation buffer. The above process is repeated for all light samples. The red channel of the accumulation buffer then varies from 0 to the number of samples assigned to that pipe, say s, with 0 representing totally unoccluded and s representing totally occluded. We extract a gray-scale image from the accumulation buffer using the color matrix and then blend onto the front buffer.

The advantage of this algorithm over the shadow map algorithm is that there is load sharing between CPUs and graphics pipes: CPUs are used for silhouette edge detection and shadow quad construction while the graphics pipes are used for drawing shadow quads and determining which areas in the scene are in shadow. Also, shadows are generated with object space precision.

4.2 Indirect lighting

If there are l lights in the scene, the first l pipes render an item buffer from the point of view of the centroid of the lth light. These are read into shared memory and the polygon elements sorted by multiple CPUs as described in Section 3. Then, the graphics hardware is used to render the scene with virtual light sources to approximate one-bounce indirect illumination.

4.3 Ray tracing for specular surfaces

The techniques suggested in Section 1.3 are mainly implemented in graphics hardware. In our implementation the graphics hardware is heavily used for shadow generation and indirect lighting effects. Therefore, these methods are not suitable. We use hardware-assisted ray tracing performed by multiple CPUs to get these effects.

An item buffer[21] from the point of view of the eye is rendered by the last pipe with the specular objects tagged and read into shared memory. The master thread is then signaled to begin ray tracing. We use a standard master-slave implementation. The master assigns rows of the item buffer to idle CPUs. Each CPU scans through the row it is assigned to and spawns rays only for those pixels which are tagged. The first object that a ray intersects need not be determined since that information is determined from the item buffer.

If there are not enough CPUs available this ray tracing could become a bottleneck. In this case, when the hardware has finished the task of drawing shadows and indirect illumination, the image is read back into a memory buffer MB. Now whenever a ray hits a point P on a diffuse surface which is visible to the eye, the radiance at P can be retrieved from MB. Therefore, shadow rays need not be spawned which results in a performance gain.

The efficiency structure used is a uniform grid. This allows fast update in the event of geometry changes. After all rows in the image have been processed, the ray traced image is blended onto the display pipe.

4.4 Compositing

Each pipe generates a partial image, contributing to both indirect illumination and soft shadows. When all pipes finish their tasks, their partial images are composited onto the display pipe. If the ray tracing has not finished before the compositing of these images is completed, the composited image, which has the direct and indirect illumination components, is loaded into shared memory to assist the ray tracing, as discussed in Section 4.3. When ray tracing of specular surfaces is completed, the ray traced image is blended onto the display pipe.

The partial images rendered in the pipes are read into shared memory. The composition of these involves just an additive blending. We implemented this in two ways: hierarchical binary swap[11, 20] which used graphics hardware and software compositing. When enough CPUs are available, the latter results in a higher frame rate. This is because a few CPUs can be assigned to the task of compositing. If the time taken by these CPUs for compositing is less than the time taken to render a frame, the compositing time is almost completely hidden. However there is one frame of latency[2].

4.5 Usage of resources

We summarize the utilization of resources for each rendering stage in Table 1. Observe that a combination of CPUs and graphics pipes are used for each rendering stage. Traditional rendering is done only on graphics hardware or is solely software-based. Hence, our approach is a better utilization of available resources.

Task	CPUs utilized for	Graphics pipes utilized for
Direct lighting without visibility	None	Scene rendered from the eye with a single light.
Shadow volumes	Determining silhouette edges. Calculating shadow volume boundaries	Drawing the shadow quads to generate gray-level shadow-image
Shadow maps	None	Rendering the scene twice for each light sample.
Indirect lighting effect	Scanning item buffer. Assigning brightness to each polygon and sorting them.	Rendering item buffer from light. Rendering scene with 8 virtual light sources to simulate indirect bounce.
Specular surface rendering	Ray trace specular portions of the image.	Render item buffer from eye

Table 1. Distribution of tasks between CPUs and graphics pipes

5 Results

We present results of our implementation on three example scenes. The first is an office scene consisting of 4,083 polygons. The scene has 2 area light sources which were each sampled into 9 point lights. There were 52,335 shadow quads generated. This scene was

---

[2]In our implementation we found that 5 CPUs perform the compositing of a 680 × 480 image in less than .01 seconds.

SCI office, 512x512 image size, 18 light samples						
Pipes	Shadow (%)	Indirect Light(%)	Direct Light(%)	Specular (%)	Compos-ite(%)	HC (secs)	SC (secs)
2	65.38	20.01	6.306	2.692	4.173	0.4061	0.4041
4	46.65	26.63	9.883	3.136	11.34	0.2961	0.2625
8	28.22	28.00	11.39	4.141	25.79	0.2565	0.2093
Classroom, 512x384 image size, 36 light samples						
4	80.16	6.336	2.604	2.440	7.447	0.4816	0.4372
8	61.16	10.63	4.490	3.967	18.10	0.2937	0.2490
Cornell Box with glass sphere, 512x512 image size, 25 light samples						
1	73.10	17.49	2.945	6.299	0.02277	0.293	0.3175
2	50.98	24.11	4.173	5.731	14.73	0.2093	0.1981
4	29.22	31.17	4.780	6.830	27.73	0.1751	0.1444
8	14.98	31.56	5.158	6.683	41.27	0.1650	0.1322

Table 2. Rendering times for 3 scenes. HC: Total time using hardware-based binary swap. SC:Total time using software compositing.

rendered at over 4 frames a second using 8 graphics pipes and software composition. Timings are given in Table 2 and a snapshot shown in Figure 12 (see color plate).

The second is a classroom scene composed of 3,135 rectangles. There are 4 area light sources each of which were sampled into 9 light samples. The top of the table is reflective. This scene is the worst case scenario for the shadow volume algorithm as almost all edges are silhouette edges. There were totally 112,326 shadow quads generated. Even when using 8 pipes 61% of the time is used for shadow quad rendering! Results are summarized in Table 2 and the image is shown in Figure 9.

The third scene the Cornell Box. A glass sphere is added into the scene and the top of the small box is made reflective. The sphere is tessellated into 200 polygons for the purpose of generating shadow volumes. Note that the sphere is used directly for the ray tracing pass. The scene has 217 polygons and one area light source sampled into 25 point lights, generating 1,134 shadow quads. Timings are given in Table 2. The image can be seen in Figure 10 (see color plate).

For all three scenes, the graphics hardware proved to be the bottleneck i.e. the CPUs would finish their task before the hardware was ready to use it. However, if the scene is composed of a large number of specular objects, ray tracing could become the bottleneck. We observe that shadow generation time dominates. Fortunately, this time scales almost linearly with the number of pipes used. Rendering times for all other effects are independent of the number of pipes used.

6 Conclusion and future work

We have demonstrated techniques for performing near photorealistic rendering of simple dynamic indoor scenes at interactive rates. To our knowledge, no other system achieves these rendering rates for comparable dynamic scenes and with comparable image quality. We have also identified and given efficient solutions for various subtleties associated with the shadow volume algorithm. We observe that soft shadow generation has the maximum computational cost among all the photo-realistic effects

Fig. 9. Classroom scene rendered at 4 frames a second using 8 pipes and software compositing.

we have introduced. This is because area light sources need to be sampled into several point lights, which generates a large number of shadow volumes. Future work includes addressing this by using shadow volumes to divide the scene into three regions: totally occluded, partially occluded and totally unoccluded. This can be accomplished by rendering those shadow volumes which form umbral or penumbral boundaries, as described in [12]. The number of shadow volumes would be significantly reduced. However a fast way to render the partially occluded regions of the scene is still an open question.

Acknowledgments

This work was supported by the SGI Visual Super computing Center at the University of Utah, NSF grant 97-20192 and the Center for Simulation of Accidental Fires and Explosions, a DOE ASCI Level 1 Alliance Center. We would like to thank Peter Shirley, Brian Smits, Peter-Pike Sloan and Steven Parker for their helpful ideas.

References

1. John M. Airey, John H. Rohlf, and Frederick P. Brooks, Jr. Towards image realism with interactive update rates in complex virtual building environments. volume 24, pages 41–50, March 1990.
2. Arthur Appel. Some techniques for shading machine renderings of solids. In *AFIPS 1968 Spring Joint Computer Conf.*, volume 32, pages 37–45, 1968.
3. Shenchang Eric Chen. Incremental radiosity: An extension of progressive radiosity to an interactive image synthesis system. In Forest Baskett, editor, *Computer Graphics (SIGGRAPH '90 Proceedings)*, volume 24, pages 135–144, August 1990.

4. Franklin C. Crow. Shadow algorithms for computer graphics. volume 11, pages 242–248, July 1977.

5. Paul J Diefenbach. *Pipeline rendering: Interaction and realism through hardware-based multi-pass rendering.* PhD thesis, University of Pennnsylvania, 1996.

6. Cindy M. Goral, Kenneth E. Torrance, Donald P. Greenberg, and Bennett Battaile. Modelling the interaction of light between diffuse surfaces. In *Computer Graphics (SIGGRAPH '84 Proceedings)*, volume 18, pages 212–22, July 1984.

7. Paul S. Heckbert and Pat Hanrahan. Beam tracing polygonal objects. In Hank Christiansen, editor, *Computer Graphics (SIGGRAPH '84 Proceedings)*, volume 18, pages 119–127, July 1984.

8. Michael Herf and Paul S. Heckbert. Fast soft shadows. In *Visual Proceedings, SIGGRAPH 96*, page 145, Aug. 1996.

9. James T. Kajiya. The rendering equation. In David C. Evans and Russell J. Athay, editors, *Computer Graphics (SIGGRAPH '86 Proceedings)*, volume 20, pages 143–150, August 1986.

10. Alexander Keller. Instant radiosity. In Turner Whitted, editor, *SIGGRAPH 97 Conference Proceedings*, Annual Conference Series, pages 49–56. ACM SIGGRAPH, Addison Wesley, August 1997. ISBN 0-89791-896-7.

11. Kwan-Lui Ma, James S. Painter, Charles D. Hansen, and Michael F. Krogh. Parallel volume rendering using binary-swap image composition. *IEEE Computer Graphics and Applications*, 14(4), July 1994.

12. T. Nishita and E. Nakamae. Half-tone representation of 3-D objects illuminated by area sources or polyhedron sources. *Proc. COMPSAC 83: The IEEE Computer Society's Seventh Internat. Computer Software and Applications Conf.*, pages 237–242, November 1983.

13. Eyal Ofek and Ari Rappoport. Interactive reflections on curved objects. In Michael Cohen, editor, *SIGGRAPH 98 Conference Proceedings*, Annual Conference Series, pages 333–342. ACM SIGGRAPH, Addison Wesley, July 1998. ISBN 0-89791-999-8.

14. Steven Parker, William Martin, Peter-Pike Sloan, Peter Shirley, Brian Smits, and Chuck Hansen. Interactive ray tracing. In *Symposium on interactive 3D graphics*, April 1999. Accepted for publication.

15. William T. Reeves, David H. Salesin, and Robert L. Cook. Rendering antialiased shadows with depth maps. In Maureen C. Stone, editor, *Computer Graphics (SIGGRAPH '87 Proceedings)*, volume 21, pages 283–291, July 1987.

16. Mark Segal, Carl Korobkin, Rolf van Widenfelt, Jim Foran, and Paul E. Haeberli. Fast shadows and lighting effects using texture mapping. In Edwin E. Catmull, editor, *Computer Graphics (SIGGRAPH '92 Proceedings)*, volume 26, pages 249–252, July 1992.

17. Francois X. Sillion and Claude Puech. A general two-pass method integrating specular and diffuse reflection. In Jeffrey Lane, editor, *Computer Graphics (SIGGRAPH '89 Proceedings)*, volume 23, pages 335–344, July 1989.

18. Heidmann T. Real shadows - real time. In *IRIS Universe*, December 1991.

19. William B. Thompson, Peter Shirley, Brian Smits, Daniel J. Kersten, and Cindee Madison. Visual glue. Technical Report UUCS-98-007, Computer Science Department, University of Utah, March 1998. http://www2.cs.utah.edu/vissim/papers/glue/glue.html.

20. Tushar Udeshi and Charles D. Hansen. Parallel multipipe rendering for very large isosurface visualization. In *Joint EUROGRAPHICS - IEEE TCCG Symposium on Visualization*, May 1999.

21. Hank Weghorst, Gary Hooper, and Donald P. Greenberg. Improved computational methods for ray tracing. *ACM Transactions on Graphics*, 3(1):52–69, January 1984.

22. Turner Whitted. An improved illumination model for shaded display. *Communications of the ACM*, 23(6):343–349, June 1980.

23. Lance Williams. Casting curved shadows on curved surfaces. In *Computer Graphics (SIGGRAPH '78 Proceedings)*, volume 12, pages 270–274, August 1978.

Editors' Note: see Appendix, p. 361–362 for colored figures of this paper

Group Accelerated Shooting Methods for Radiosity

François Rousselle and Christophe Renaud

Laboratoire d'Informatique du Littoral
Université du Littoral Côte d'Opale
BP 719 62228 Calais Cedex France
roussell,renaud@lil.univ-littoral.fr

Abstract. The introduction of the Progressive Refinement method was the starting point of interactivity in the radiosity illumination process. Overshooting methods brought an important acceleration to the convergence particularly for scenes with a high mean reflectivity.

In this paper we present a new acceleration technique to PR and overshooting methods based on group shooting methods. The acceleration is obtained by occasionally selecting groups of interacting patches and by solving the subsystem built from this group.

This technique allows us to reduce the number of iterations that are required to solve the radiosity system and only involves a small computation overhead.

Comparing different algorithms for scenes with particular properties, we highlight interesting results of the Group Accelerated Shooting Methods especially when considering complex scenes with many occlusions.

1 Introduction

Many efforts to improve the radiosity method have been made since its introduction in 1984 by C. M. Goral & al. [1]. Progressive Radiosity [2] was the first step toward interactivity and overshooting methods [3] [4] [5] improved its convergence rate, especially for scenes with high mean reflectivity. However these methods still need more iterations than the total number of patches in the scene when a nearly exact solution of the system is needed.

In this paper we introduce a new approach based on group iterative methods [6]. Unlike Greiner & al. [7] who select sets of important patches to reduce the size of the radiosity system, we accelerate existing progressive methods by shooting from group of patches in order to improve the diffusion of light. Moreover, interactions between all the patches of the group are resolved.

In the next section we describe group iterative methods and notations used to simplify the expression of the system. Definitions of group Jacobi and group Gauss-Seidel methods are given with their cost in term of operation per iteration. Direct application of these methods to the radiosity system is discussed in the case of large scenes where the form factor matrix is unknown. Greiner's blockwise refinement method is described and discussed in the same case. Then we compare the group methods approach with bi-level [10] and hierarchical [11] radiosity methods and show that it does not relate to any of these two methods.

In the third section, after rewriting the equation of group Gauss-Seidel iteration by using the residual, we give algorithms for group Southwell, group Progressive Radiosity and group overshooting methods and briefly discuss their advantages and drawbacks.

We expose in section four the implementation of group shooting iterations into Progressive Radiosity and Xu's overshooting method followed by a discussion on the optimization of group construction and efficiency.

Finally, comparative results of some group accelerated progressive methods applied on three different scenes are presented.

2 Group iterative methods

Group iterative methods are an extension of point iterative methods using several equations of the system at a time. The resolution of a group of n equations instead of the successive resolution of these n equations leads to a better convergence of the unknowns to the solution but implies a much higher cost.

Let us consider a system of n linear equations :

$$\Phi B = E \Leftrightarrow \sum_{j=1}^{n} \varphi_{i,j} b_j = e_i \qquad i = 1, \ldots, n \tag{1}$$

Point Jacobi and point Gauss-Seidel iterations are resolution schemes considering one equation of the system at a time. For example the point Jacobi's $(k+1)^{th}$ iteration is the resolution of the ith equation below :

$$\varphi_{i,i} b_i^{(k+1)} = e_i - \sum_{j=1, j \neq i}^{n} \varphi_{i,j} b_j^{(k)}$$

$b_i^{(k+1)}$ is the only unknown while the b_j's are taken from the previous iteration.

Group Jacobi and group Gauss-Seidel iterations are successive resolution of groups of the system equations. For example group Jacobi's $(k+1)^{th}$ iteration restricted to a group built from equations i and j leads to the resolution of the following subsystem :

$$\begin{cases} \varphi_{i,i} b_i^{(k+1)} & + & \varphi_{i,j} b_j^{(k+1)} & = & e_i & - & \sum_{t=1, t \neq i, t \neq j}^{n} \varphi_{i,t} b_t^{(k)} \\ \varphi_{j,i} b_i^{(k+1)} & + & \varphi_{j,j} b_j^{(k+1)} & = & e_j & - & \sum_{t=1, t \neq i, t \neq j}^{n} \varphi_{j,t} b_t^{(k)} \end{cases}$$

$b_i^{(k+1)}$ and $b_j^{(k+1)}$ are the unknowns while the b_t's are taken from the previous iteration. Thus, a group iteration using n equations leads to the resolution of a subsystem of system (1) with n unknowns.

2.1 Notations and definitions

Using an ordered grouping $\pi : G_k, k = 1, \ldots, q$ of $I = \{1, \ldots, n\}$ we define $\Phi_{r,s}$ as the sub matrix of Φ consisting of rows $R_i, i \in G_r$ and columns $C_j, j \in G_s$. B_r is the sub vector of B consisting of elements $b_i, i \in G_r$, and E_r is the sub vector of E consisting of elements $e_i, i \in G_r$. Using these notations equation (1) is rewritten as :

$$\sum_{s=1}^{q} \Phi_{r,s} B_s = E_r, \qquad r = 1, \ldots, q \tag{2}$$

Thus, an iteration of the group Jacobi solver is written as :

$$\Phi_{r,r} B_r^{(k+1)} = E_r - \sum_{s=1, s \neq r}^{q} \Phi_{r,s} B_s^{(k)}, \qquad r = 1, \ldots, q \tag{3}$$

In the same way, a group Gauss-Seidel iteration is written as :

$$\Phi_{r,r} B_r^{(k+1)} = E_r - \sum_{s=1}^{r-1} \Phi_{r,s} B_s^{(k+1)} - \sum_{s=r+1}^{q} \Phi_{r,s} B_s^{(k)}, \qquad r = 1, \ldots, q \tag{4}$$

2.2 Point versus group methods for radiosity

In the case of radiosity, point iterative methods previously described are known as gathering methods. Each iteration corresponds to the energy gathering from the scene to the patch associated with the unknown of the equation being solved. Group iterative methods correspond to group gathering. The resolution of the subsystem of Φ associated to the group G_r composed of m equations corresponds to the 'simultaneous' gathering from the scene to the m patches associated with the unknowns of the equations. By 'simultaneous' we mean that this group gathering also resolves the interactions between the m patches involved in this group, this leads to a better estimation of their radiosities than m successive gathering steps.

But group iterative methods have a higher cost in term of number of operations per iteration. Considering the group G_r associated to m equations of the system, we need approximatively m^3 operations to compute $\Phi_{r,r}^{-1}$ using a Gauss elimination method and approximatively $2nm^2$ operations to compute the unknowns of group Jacobi or group Gauss-Seidel iteration. Compared to the $3n$ operations that are required for a point Jacobi or point Gauss-Seidel iteration (even $2n$ in the radiosity case where $\varphi_{i,i} = 1$), the benefit of group methods over point methods vanishes in the general case. In fact, group iterative methods are used when Φ can be partitionned in groups with special properties permitting the resolution of each iteration in $O(n)$ operations. For example [8] gives a procedure to solve directly the subsystem when $\Phi_{r,r}$ is a symmetric and positive definite tridiagonal matrix.

Another problem of gathering methods is the lack of interactivity during the process. Most nowadays radiosity scenes consist of tens or even hundreds of thousands of patches and need a lot of time for form factors computation. Each iteration step of a gathering method requires all the form factors matrix to be available, each row of the matrix allowing the radiosity of a unique patch to be updated. Thus, one have to wait almost an entire iteration step to have a first idea of what the result of illumination will be.

In 1988 Cohen & al. [2] introduced the progressive refinement method also called progressive radiosity (PR) which shoots energy from a patch, and updates the radiosities of all the visible patches at each iteration by using a column of the form factors matrix. This method was proved to be an equivalent of the Southwell iterative method in [9]. Several overshooting methods [3] [4] [5] increased the convergence speed of PR by anticipating the amount of energy which will come back to the shooting patch in future iteration steps, and shooting it along with the current unshot radiosity. Xu's method gives the best acceleration by considering direct illumination plus an estimation of the energy due to multiple reflections in the scene before shooting.

These methods introduce interactivity during the process as a few shooting steps give a first idea of the illumination of the scene. But they also need more than n iteration steps to give a result close to the exact solution. They involve multiple selections of the same shooting patches requiring several computation of the same form factors since the whole matrix cannot be stored in memory. Moreover these methods do not converge in the same manner, it is difficult to compare for example scenes from PR and Xu's methods before the convergence is achieved. When stopping PR and Xu's methods at the same RMS error, the scene computed by Xu's method has a much higher contrast than PR solution. The patches well exposed to light sources have radiosities much closer to the exact solution than the less exposed ones. On the contrary, the more uniform illumination of the PR algorithm leads to a better solution in term of visualisation since the error with the exact solution is well distributed among all patches of the scene. Xu's method has a good convergence rate in term of mean error measure but not in term of maximum error measure. The overshooting term added to the unshot radiosity permit the acceleration of convergence only for patches that are visible from the shooting patch.

2.3   Blockwise refinement

Greiner & al. proposed in [7] a method also based on the selection of groups of important patches. The Blockwise Refinement approach solves the radiosity system by selecting in turn a small set of patches. An approximate solution of the whole system is computed for this set of patches taking into account the exact interactions between the selected patches and all other patches, and an approximation for the interactions between the others patches. This solution is refined by selecting other sets of patches that successively correct the error introduced by the approximation.

This method implies a matrix of unshot radiosities to be stored in order to keep the energy exchanges between the different patches. Thus, this method does not fit the resolution of large systems where a $n \times n$ matrix for each wavelength cannot be stored.

The comparison of Blockwise Refinement with other methods is done considering the number of floating points operations needed by the resolution of the system. This implies that all form factors are already known and that their computation is not taken into account. This does also not apply to the resolution of large systems.

Taking the form factors computation into account, our goal is to obtain a method that takes advantage both of the interactivity of shooting methods and of the accelerated convergence provided by group resolution without any $n \times n$ matrix storage. Group shooting methods described in the next section are a step towards this goal.

2.4   Comparison with substructuring and hierarchical methods

The notion of group exposed in this paper is very different from the grouping of surface elements into patches proposed in the bi-level radiosity method or even from the hierarchical organization of surfaces and energy exchanges of the hierarchical radiosity method.

In the bi-level radiosity method, a coarse meshing of the scene in N patches is subdivided in M surface elements $(M \gg N)$ for patches presenting a high radiosity gradient. A patch can be considered an element itself or consisting of a group of elements. The elements are the energy receivers thus capturing details of the illumination, while the patches are the emitters. The elements that are derived from a patch do not have any interaction between themselves unlike our groups. In our approach, groups are built from elements which exchange energy in order to accelerate the diffusion of this energy. In bi-level radiosity, groups are built in order to reduce the size of the system.

The solution obtained by the bi-level radiosity method is comparable to the solution obtained by a complete resolution of a system implying a $M \times M$ matrix constructed with all the elements, but requires only the use of a $M \times N$ matrix. This method can be viewed as a simplification of the system by compressing the matrix Φ by merging columns.

The hierarchical organization of surfaces and energy exchanges of the hierarchical radiosity method results in reducing the number of form factors needed to $O(n)$ [12]. Thus, this hierarchical organization can be viewed as a compression technique of the form factors matrix reducing the complexity of the system.

The aim of group methods is to accelerate the convergence of the iterate not by reducing the size or complexity of the system but by relaxing several unknowns at a time.

3 Group shooting methods

3.1 Group Southwell

Southwell and Gauss-Seidel relaxation methods are very similar. The only difference is that in Gauss-Seidel, the equations of the system are considered successively while in Southwell, the order in which the equations are selected is performed according to a residual criterion. Unlike group Gauss-Seidel where an iteration step consists in the resolution of all the groups of equations using equation (4), a group Southwell iteration step solves only one group of equations. The $(k+1)^{th}$ Southwell iteration step using a group r computes $B^{(k+1)}$ where $B_r^{(k+1)}$ is updated using the equation (6) described below and $B_s^{(k+1)} = B_s^{(k)}$ for all $s \neq r$.

The residual vector $R^{(k)}$ defined by

$$R^{(k)} = E - \Phi B^{(k)} \tag{5}$$

is computed at each iteration and the element of $R^{(k)}$ with the greatest absolute value defines the next group of equations to consider.

From equation (4) and using the iteration numbering described above, group Southwell iteration can be written using the residual R :

$$
\begin{aligned}
B_r^{(k+1)} &= \Phi_{r,r}^{-1}(E_r - \sum_{s=1, s\neq r}^{q} \Phi_{r,s} B_s^{(k)}) \\
B_r^{(k+1)} &= \Phi_{r,r}^{-1}(E_r - \sum_{s=1}^{q} \Phi_{r,s} B_s^{(k)} + \Phi_{r,r} B_r^{(k)}) \\
B_r^{(k+1)} &= \Phi_{r,r}^{-1} R_r^{(k)} + B_r^{(k)}
\end{aligned}
\tag{6}
$$

Thus, each unknown is updated using its value from the previous iteration. The residual can also be updated instead of directly computed from its definition :

$$R_s^{(k+1)} = E_s - \sum_{l=1}^{q} \Phi_{s,l} B_l^{(k+1)}$$

$$R_s^{(k+1)} = E_s - \sum_{l=1, l \neq r}^{q} \Phi_{s,l} B_l^{(k)} - \Phi_{s,r} B_r^{(k+1)}$$

$$R_s^{(k+1)} = E_s - \sum_{l=1, l \neq r}^{q} \Phi_{s,l} B_l^{(k)} - \Phi_{s,r} (B_r^{(k)} + \Phi_{r,r}^{-1} R_r^{(k)})$$

$$R_s^{(k+1)} = E_s - \sum_{k=1}^{q} \Phi_{s,k} B_k^{(k)} - \Phi_{s,r} \Phi_{r,r}^{-1} R_r^{(k)}$$

$$R_s^{(k+1)} = R_s^{(k)} - \Phi_{s,r} \Phi_{r,r}^{-1} R_r^{(k)} \qquad (7)$$

From equations (6) and (7), group Southwell algorithm is presented below :

    for all i
     $b_i = 0$
     $r_i = e_i$
    while not converged
      choose group r with largest $\| R_r \|$
      $B_r = B_r + \Phi_{r,r}^{-1} R_r$
      for all groups $s \neq r$
       $R_s = R_s - \Phi_{s,r} \Phi_{r,r}^{-1} R_r$
     $R_r = 0$
    display image using b_i as intensity of patch i

3.2 Group PR and group overshooting

We can express group PR in the group Southwell form using ∇B_r and ΔB_r as the shot and unshot radiosities of group r and A_r as the surfaces vector of patches belonging to group r :

    for all i
     $\nabla b_i = 0$
     $\Delta b_i = e_i$
    while not converged
      choose group r with largest $\| \Delta B_r . A_r^T \|$
      compute form factors columns corresponding to group r
      $\nabla B_r = \nabla B_r + \Phi_{r,r}^{-1} \Delta B_r$
      for all groups $s \neq r$
       $\Delta B_s = \Delta B_s - \Phi_{s,r} \Phi_{r,r}^{-1} \Delta B_r$
     $\Delta B_r = 0$
    display image using $\nabla b_i + \Delta b_i$ as intensity of patch i

Finally, replacing the shot radiosity vector ∇B by $B = \nabla B + \Delta B$ we get the following group PR algorithm :

    for all i
     $b_i = e_i$
     $\Delta b_i = e_i$
    while not converged

choose group r with largest $\| (\Delta B_r[+\Delta B_r^+].A_r^T \|$
compute form factors columns corresponding to group r
compute $\Phi_{r,r}^{-1}$
for all groups s
 $\Delta rad = -\Phi_{s,r}\Phi_{r,r}^{-1}(\Delta B_r[+\Delta B_r^+])$
 $\Delta B_s = \Delta B_s + \Delta rad$
 $B_s = B_s + \Delta rad$
$\Delta B_r = 0[-\Delta B_r^+]$
display image using b_i as intensity of patch i

Group overshooting is achieved by considering ΔB_r^+ (term inside the [ ] in the previous algorithm) computed by the different overshooting methods.

Each resolution of the subsystem consisting of a group of size m allows a faster convergence than the m shooting steps of the patches composing the group. As explained in section 2.2, interactions between all the patches composing a group are resolved. Thus, unshot radiosities of patches within the group are all set to 0 after an iteration of group PR, which is not the case after the shooting steps of point PR. In the same manner, unshot radiosities of patches within the group are all set to $-\Delta B_r^+$ after an iteration of a group overshooting method.

Group shooting methods are suitable for large scenes illumination because they only require the storage of m columns of Φ, m corresponding to the size of the largest group.

3.3 Group building

All group methods described in sections 2.2 and 3 use an ordered grouping as described in section 2.1. The system is therefore partitioned before starting the resolution. But in order to define well suited groups for the radiosity system we have to consider the unshot radiosity values which vary all along the resolution. It is thus preferable to construct groups dynamically during the resolution of the system. Instead of having several groups chosen at the beginning of the algorithm we construct one group at the beginning of each iteration. This leads to the algorithm below :

choose m the size of the group
for all i
 $b_i = e_i$
 $\Delta b_i = e_i$
while not converged
 construct group r with the m patches having largest $\| (\Delta b_i[+\Delta b_i^+]).a_i \|$
 compute form factors columns corresponding to the patches of the group
 compute $\Phi_{r,r}^{-1}$
 for all patches j
  $\Delta rad = -\Phi_{j,r}\Phi_{r,r}^{-1}(\Delta B_r[+\Delta B_r^+])$
  $\Delta b_j = \Delta b_j + \Delta rad$
  $b_j = b_j + \Delta rad$
 $\Delta B_r = 0[-\Delta B_r^+]$
display image using b_i as intensity of patch i

The cost of solving of a group is not a problem when restricting to small size as compared to the number of patches in the scene. In fact, the time spent in computing form factors is much more important than the time spent in solving the subsystems (see section 5).

But those group shooting methods result in a lack of interactivity since the time elapsed between each update of the radiosities is much more important than in the case of point shooting methods. Using a group of size m, we have to wait for the computation of m columns of the form factors between each update.

4 Group accelerated shooting methods

Our goal is to find an interactive method suited to large scenes illumination and that converges to an accurate solution in a time smaller than the time required to compute the form factors matrix. The interactivity is conserved from the existing shooting methods and the acceleration of convergence is obtained from the periodic use of group shooting steps.

4.1 First approach

Giving a scene, we choose the size of the group, typically from 20 to 50 in our experimentations. It determines the number of form factors columns stored into memory. The chosen shooting method is then started and each column of the form factors matrix computed to shoot energy from a patch is stored. We keep the same order of selection of shooting patches as the shooting method.

When the number of stored patches and form factors columns reaches the size of the group, the subsystem generated by these patches is solved. The time spent solving this subsystem is measured and compared to the computation time of form factors in order to compute a frequency of group resolution applications which ensure a small overhead for the shooting method. The determination of the frequency is based on computation time because we cannot estimate precisely the cost of form factors computation in term of operations. It is not only dependent on the method used nor the number of patches in the scene but also of its geometry.

Then, at the beginning of each new iteration, the older patch stored in the group is deleted along with its corresponding form factors and replaced by the new shooting patch and its form factors. The resulting algorithm is outlined below. The m first shooting steps, the resolution of the resulting subsystem and the computation of the frequency of group resolution are not detailed in order to clarify the algorithm reading.

> choose m the size of the group
> for all i
> $b_i = e_i$
> $\Delta b_i = e_i$
> do m shooting steps and store each shooting patch along with its form factors
> solve the subsystem generated by these m patches
> compute the frequency of group resolution
> while not converged
>   choose patch i with max $| \Delta b_i . a_i [+\Delta b_i^+] |$
>   if patch i is not already stored in memory
>   compute the form factors column $F_{*,i}$
>   replace oldest patch and ff's in the group with patch i and $F_{*,i}$
>   if the number of shooting steps matches the frequency of group resolution
>   compute $\Phi_{r,r}^{-1}$
>   for all patches j

$$\Delta rad = -\Phi_{j,r}\Phi_{r,r}^{-1}(\Delta B_r[+\Delta B_r^+])$$
$$\Delta b_j = \Delta b_j + \Delta rad$$
$$b_j = b_j + \Delta rad$$
$$\Delta B_r = 0[-\Delta B_r^+]$$

else
 for all patches j
$$\Delta rad = -\varphi_{j,i}(\Delta b_i[+\Delta b_i^+])$$
$$\Delta b_j = \Delta b_j + \Delta rad$$
$$b_j = b_j + \Delta rad$$
$$\Delta b_i = 0[-\Delta b_i^+]$$

display image using b_i as intensity of patch i

Generally, source patches have low reflectivities in radiosity scenes. Considering these patches in a group is useless and has no gain as compared to successive shooting steps because there is almost no energy transfer between them. Thus, it is preferable to shoot from all source patches before starting the construction of the group.

4.2 Optimisation of groups

By storing columns of the matrix Φ instead of columns of the form factors matrix we would save some operations needed to compute $\Phi_{j,r}$ during the group r resolution. But storing columns of Φ requires much more memory since it is proportionnal to the number of wavelenghts used to illuminate the scene. We did not choose this solution because the quality of groups constructed during the resolution can be improved using the memory available in the host machine.

Indeed, we store as much patches and form factors as possible that will be used to build the groups. The size of the group is not changed but the choice of patches included in the group is no longer set by the shooting method. For the optimized algorithm presented in section 5, the group were constructed by choosing among all the patches available in memory those having the maximum $\Delta b_i.a_i$ ($|(\Delta b_i + \Delta b_i^+).a_i|$ for overshooting methods).

But the amount of unshot energy is not always a sufficient criterium to ensure a significant speedup. The advantage of using groups is to simultaneously illuminate a great number of patches and to resolve all the interactions due to multiple reflections between the patches within the groups. It is thus essential for our acceleration method to construct the groups by maximizing the number of visible patches from the group and the amount of energy exchange between patches of the group. We are currently working on new techniques for group building based on the knowledge of the form factors stored in memory in order to suit best to these criteria.

5 Comparison of the algorithms

We use the normalized Root Mean Square error metric to compare the convergence of each method. The computational cost of each step of the different methods is dominated by the form factor computation. For the different scenes we used, the mean cpu time spent for shooting the energy is 1% in the case of PR and Xu and 4% to solve the subsystems in the case of group accelerated shooting methods, the rest of the time being spent for form factors computation. Thus, we simply use iteration steps to present each method.

We have selected three different scenes for comparing the performances of the algorithms. The first one called multi-cubes contains 480 patches and has a mean reflectivity of 0.44 (see figure 4). It is built from a large external cube including 64 smaller cubes that generate a lot of occlusions. The comparison of PR, Xu, group accelerated PR and group accelerated Xu with or without the storage of more patches than required by the group is shown in figure 1. All group accelerated methods perform very well all along the iterations giving an important acceleration at the beginning of the convergence and leading to a very good solution in less than n iteration steps. This kind of scene where light propagation is difficult seems to be well handled by our method. In this case group shooting is interesting since it allows an update of a larger number of patches than the sole shooting patch of PR or Xu's method.

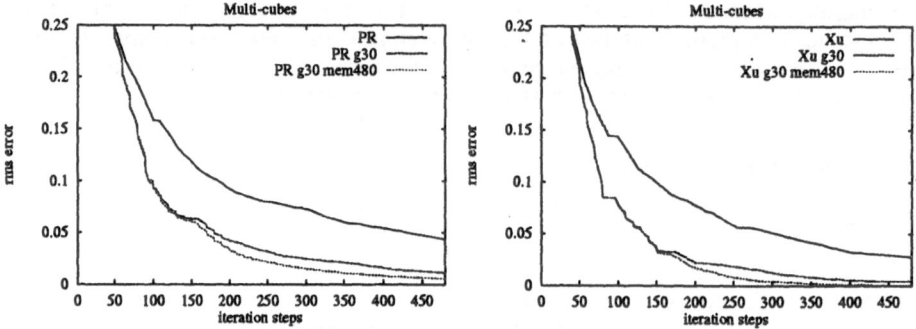

Fig. 1. Convergence for multi-cubes scene. On the left side : PR, PR g30 : group accelerated PR using groups of size 30 and PR g30 m480 : use the main memory to store all the patches and form factors. On the right side : Xu, Xu g30 : group accelerated Xu using groups of size 30 and Xu g30 m480 : store 480 patches and form factors columns

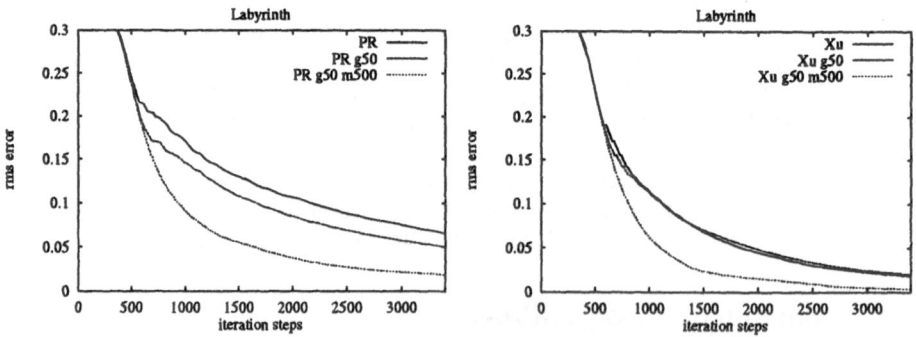

Fig. 2. Convergence for labyrinth. PR, PR g50 and PR g50 m500 on the left side. Xu, Xu g50 and Xu g50 m500 on the right side

The second scene is called labyrinth (see figure 5). It contains 3362 patches and has a mean reflectivity of 0.59. This scene is a good example of the benefit of storing several patches in order to improve groups efficiency without having to change their size when the scene has more patches (see figure 2). Again, group accelerated Xu with storage of 500 patches leads to a nearly converged solution in n iteration steps.

The last scene, shown in figure 6 is an office. It contains 10991 patches and has a mean reflectivity of 0.43. Group accelerated PR converges faster than PR, but the difference appears to be very small (see figure 3). Group accelerated Xu does not provide any acceleration even by storing some additionnal rows into memory. These poor results can be explained by several reasons. The main one is that the patches that appear in a group have a very small size as compared to the scene dimensions. Consequently when the group's patches are homogeneously distributed through the scene (which does not include a large number of occlusions) the resolution of this group does not provide any large updates both for group and group-outside patches. Furthermore we used a low number of patches per group (50) as compared to the total number of patches for this scene. Using a much more larger number of pacthes per group should provide better results. But it implies a larger computationnal cost for solving the group subsystem. We studed some new resolution techniques in [13] which could allow us to use larger group for our approach.

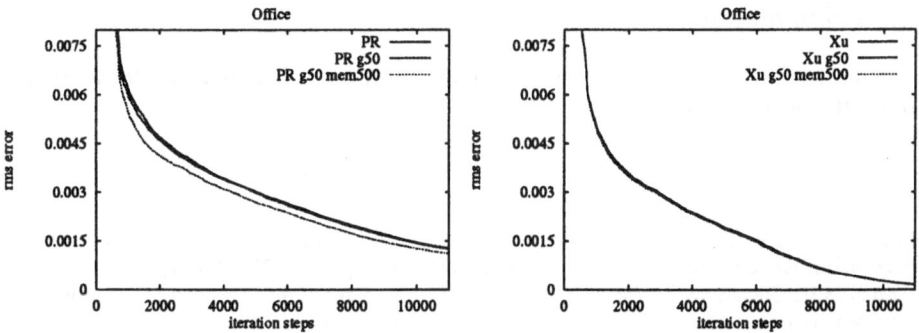

Fig. 3. Convergence for office. PR, PR g50 and PR g50 m500 on the left side. Xu, Xu g50 and Xu g50 m500 on the right side

6 Conclusion

In this paper we presented a new approach for accelerating existing shooting methods. Periodically, during the iteration of the shooting algorithm, we choose a group of important patches that have been stored into memory and solve the subsystem composed of the equations corresponding to these patches.

Shooting from groups of patches increases the diffusion of light through the scene by updating more radiosities and resolving all interactions inside the group. This method shows very good results especially in scenes with high occlusions where classical progressive algorithms have a very low convergence rate. Our results show that near-convergence can be obtained in less shooting iterations than the total number of patches in the scenes.

Studying accurately the group building choices is one of the next stage of our work. We used simple criteria for choosing both a shooting patch and patches of a group. Those criteria are too closed from the shooting algorithms ones and seems to be inefficient in some cases like the office scene. Some group properties are today under investigation in order to built the "best" group, providing the best speedup with a low computation cost.

88

Fig. 4. Multi-cubes scene, 480 patches, mean reflectivity 0.44

Fig. 5. Labyrinth scene, 3362 patches, mean reflectivity 0.59

Fig. 6. Office scene, 10991 patches, mean reflectivity 0.43

Acknowledgements

We would like to thank the referees for their helpful comments which allowed us to improve the quality of our paper.

References

1. Goral C.M., Torrance K.E., Greenberg D.P., Battaile B. : Modeling the interaction of light between diffuse surfaces. ACM Computer Graphics, 18(3):pp. 213-222, July 1984.
2. Cohen M.F., Chen S.E., Wallace J.R., Greenberg D.P. : A progressive refinement approach to fast radiosity image generation. ACM Computer Graphics, 22(4):75-84, August 1988.
3. Feda M., Purgathofer W. : Accelerating radiosity by overshooting. Proceedings of Third Eurographics Workshop on Rendering, 21-32, May 1992.
4. Shao M.Z., Badler N.I. : Analysis and Acceleration of Progressive Refinement Radiosity Method. Proceedings of Fourth Eurographics Workshop on Rendering, 247-258, June 1993.
5. Xu W., Fussell D. : A Fast Solver of Radiosity Equation Systems. Proceedings of Pacific Graphics, 1994.
6. Young D.M. : Iterative Solution of Large Linear Systems. Academic Press, New York, 1971.
7. Greiner G., Heidrich W., Slusallek P. : Blockwise Refinement - A New Method for Solving the Radiosity Problem. Proceedings of Fourth Eurographics Workshop on Rendering, 233-245, June 1993.
8. Hageman L.A., Young D.M. : Applied Iterative Methods. Academic Press, 1981.
9. Gortler S.J., Cohen M.F., Slusallek P. : Radiosity and Relaxation Methods: Progressive Refinement is Southwell Relaxation. Technical Report CS-TR-408-93, Department of Computer Science, Princeton University, Princeton, NJ, February 1993.
10. Cohen M.F., Greenberg D.P., Immel D.S., Brock P.J. : An Efficient Radiosity Approach for Realistic Image Synthesis. IEEE Computer Graphics and Applications, 6(3):pp. 25-35, March 1986.
11. Hanrahan P., Saltzman D., Aupperle L. : A Rapid Hierarchical Radiosity Algorithm. ACM Computer Graphics, 25(4):pp. 197-206, August 1991.
12. Sillion F.X., Puech C. : Radiosity and Global Illumination. Morgan Kaufmann Publishers, 1994.
13. Leblond M., Rousselle F., Renaud C. : Accelerating Convergence of Radiosity Solvers through Hybridation. Submitted to Pacific Graphics'99.

Gathering for Free in Random Walk Radiosity

Mateu Sbert*, Alex Brusi* and Philippe Bekaert°

* Institut d'Informàtica i Aplicacions, Universitat de Girona
Lluis Santaló s/n, E 17071 Girona
e-mail: mateu@ima.udg.es

° Department of Computer Science, Katholieke Universiteit Leuven
Celestijnenlaan 200 A, B-3001 Leuven, Belgium
e-mail: Philippe.Bekaert@cs.kuleuven.ac.be

Abstract. We present a simple technique that improves the efficiency of random walk algorithms for radiosity. Each generated random walk is used to simultaneously sample two distinct radiosity estimators. The first estimator is the commonly used shooting estimator, in which the radiosity due to self-emitted light at the origin of the random walk is recorded at each subsequently visited patch. With the second estimator, the radiosity due to self-emitted light at subsequent destinations is recorded at each visited patch. Closed formulae for the variance of the involved estimators allow to derive a cheap heuristic for combining the resulting radiosity estimates. Empirical results agree well with the heuristic prediction. A fair error reduction is obtained at a negligible additional cost.

Keywords: radiosity, Monte Carlo, random walk

1 Random walk estimators for radiosity

We first review the two random walk estimators for radiosity that will be combined in §2. A discussion of the technique and its results are presented in §3.

1.1 The shooting estimator

The distribution of light power P_i in a scene, discretised in patches i, can be obtained by solving the following system of linear equations[1]:

$$P_i = \Phi_i + \sum_j P_j F_{ji} R_i \tag{1}$$

$$= \sum_{j_0} \Phi_{j_0} \delta_{j_0 i} + \sum_{j_0, j_1} \Phi_{j_0} F_{j_0 j_1} R_{j_1} \delta_{j_1 i} + \sum_{j_0, j_1, j_2} \Phi_{j_0} F_{j_0 j_1} R_{j_1} F_{j_1 j_2} R_{j_2} \delta_{j_2 i} + \cdots$$

Now consider a random variable $\hat{b}_{is}^S$ taking values $\hat{b}_{is}^S(\mathbf{J})$ with probability $p^S(\mathbf{J})$ where

$$A_i \hat{b}_{is}^S(\mathbf{J}) = \delta_{s j_0} \frac{\Phi_s}{p_s} \cdot \sum_{k=1}^n R_{j_k} \delta_{j_k i} \tag{2}$$

$$p^S(\mathbf{J}) = p_{j_0} \cdot F_{j_0 j_1} R_{j_1} \cdots F_{j_{n-2} j_{n-1}} R_{j_{n-1}} F_{j_{n-1} j_n} (1 - R_{j_n}). \tag{3}$$

$\mathbf{J}$ denotes any sequence $j_0, \ldots, j_n, n \geq 1$ of patches. Such a random variable can be sampled by generating random walks $\mathbf{J}$ with origin selection probability p_{j_0}, transition

---

[1]The meaning of all symbols used in this paper is tabulated in table 1.

P_i	Total power emitted by patch i
Φ_i	Self-emitted power; $\Phi_T = \sum_s \Phi_s$
A_i	Area; $A_T = \sum_i A_i$ is the total surface area
R_i	Reflectivity; $R_{ave} = (1/A_T)\sum_i A_i R_i$ is the area-average reflectivity
B_i	Total radiosity emitted by i;
E_i	Self-emitted radiosity; $E_{ave} = \Phi_T/A_T$: average self-emitted radiosity
b_i	Non-self-emitted radiosity $b_i = B_i - E_i$
b_{is}	Radiosity on i due to self-emitted radiosity on source s; $b_i = \sum_s b_{is}$
$\hat{b}_{is}$	An estimator for b_{is}; $\hat{b}_i = \sum_s \hat{b}_{is}$; $\hat{b}_i^S$: shooting estimator, $\hat{b}_i^G$: gathering estimator.
$E[\hat{b}_{is}]$	Expectation of the estimator $\hat{b}_{is}$
$V[\hat{b}_{is}]$	Variance of the estimator $\hat{b}_{is}$
$\mathbf{J}$	A sequence of patches $j_0, \ldots, j_n$ (used to denote a random walk)
$\hat{b}_{is}(\mathbf{J})$	Contribution of the random walk $\mathbf{J}$ to the estimator $\hat{b}_{is}$
p_i	Probability of starting a random walk on i
$p(\mathbf{J})$	Probability of generating the random walk $\mathbf{J}$
δ_{ij}	Kronecker's delta: 1 if $i = j$ and 0 if $i \neq j$
ξ_i	Incident power received back at i due to emission of one unit of power by i

Table 1. Symbols used in this paper. Symbols like $i, s, j_0, \ldots, j_n$ denote a patch.

probabilities equal to the form factor F_{kl} from patch k to patch l and survival probabilities equal to the reflectivity R_k on each patch k. The transitions can be simulated using local lines, as in [8], or global lines [7]. If such a random walk originates at s, a contribution of $R_i\Phi_s/A_i p_s$ is recorded each time the patch i is visited. No contribution is recorded at the origin j_0 itself of a random walk however.

It can be shown that the expectation $E[\hat{b}_{is}^S] = \sum_{\mathbf{J}} \hat{b}_{is}^S(\mathbf{J}) p^S(\mathbf{J})$ of this random variable equals the radiosity b_{is} on i due to self-emitted radiosity on the source s. The sums $\hat{b}_i^S(\mathbf{J}) = \sum_s \hat{b}_{is}^S(\mathbf{J})$ over all sources s in the scene yield an estimator $\hat{b}_i^S$ for the total non-self-emitted radiosity b_i. It can be shown that the variance is given by [4, 5]:

$$V[\hat{b}_i^S] = \frac{R_i(1 + 2R_i\xi_i)}{A_i} \sum_s \frac{\Phi_s}{p_s} b_{is} - b_i^2. \tag{4}$$

This random walk estimator leads to a "discretised" version of the particle tracing algorithm [2]. In an implementation, incident particles are "warped" to a uniformly chosen other position on each hit patch. It is closely related to various other Monte Carlo radiosity algorithms.

1.2 The gathering estimator

A similar random walk estimator can be derived from the radiosity equations:

$$B_i = E_i + \sum_j R_i F_{ij} B_j \tag{5}$$

$$= \sum_{j_0} \delta_{ij_0} E_{j_0} + \sum_{j_0, j_1} \delta_{ij_0} R_{j_0} F_{j_0 j_1} E_{j_1} + \sum_{j_0, j_1, j_2} \delta_{ij_0} R_{j_0} F_{j_0 j_1} R_{j_1} F_{j_1 j_2} E_{j_2} + \cdots$$

Consider the random variable $\hat{b}_{is}^G$ taking values $\hat{b}_{is}^G(\mathbf{J})$ with probability $p^G(\mathbf{J})$ where

$$\hat{b}_{is}^G(\mathbf{J}) = \delta_{ij_0} \frac{R_i}{p_i} \cdot \sum_{k=1}^{n} E_{j_k} \delta_{j_k s} \tag{6}$$

$$p^G(\mathbf{J}) = p_{j_0} \cdot F_{j_0 j_1} R_{j_1} \cdots F_{j_{n-2} j_{n-1}} R_{j_{n-1}} F_{j_{n-1} j_n} (1 - R_{j_n}). \tag{7}$$

Again, $\mathbf{J}$ denotes a sequence of patches $j_0, \ldots, j_n, n \geq 1$. The random variable $\hat{b}_{is}^G$ can be sampled by generating random walks as for sampling $\hat{b}_{is}^S$. This time however, only walks originating from i instead of s will contribute. If originating at i, a contribution $R_i E_s$ is recorded every time the light source s is visited during the random walk. Also in this case, only visits $j_k = s$ for $k \geq 1$ count.

It can be shown that the expectation $E[\hat{b}_{is}^G]$ equals b_{is} as well. The sums $\hat{b}_i^G(\mathbf{J}) = \sum_s \hat{b}_{is}^G(\mathbf{J})$ over all sources s yield an estimator $\hat{b}_i^G$ for b_i with variance [4]:

$$V[\hat{b}_i^G] = \frac{R_i}{p_i} \sum_s (E_s + 2b_s) b_{is} - b_i^2. \tag{8}$$

This random walk estimator leads to an algorithm that is similar to ray-tracing. No next event estimators (shadow rays) are traced however and incident particles are "warped" to a uniformly chosen new point on each hit patch. Instead of using next-event estimators, direct illumination can be used as a source light distribution rather than self-emitted illumination. Direct illumination can be computed first using a depth-one shooting pass [6]. A more advanced such "smoothing" pass is proposed in [1].

2 The new algorithm: gathering for free

2.1 Simultaneous shooting and gathering

Consider first a fixed pair of patches s and i. Consider any random walk $\mathbf{J} = j_0, \ldots, j_n$, $n \geq 1, j_0 = s, j_n = i$ originating at s and being absorbed on i, but furthermore generated as described above. The probabilities $p^S(\mathbf{J})$ (3) and $p^G(\mathbf{J})$ (7) are identical for each such a random walk. They can therefore be used to sample both estimators $\hat{b}_{is}^S$ and $\hat{b}_{si}^G$ simultaneously: to "gather" an amount of radiosity $\hat{b}_{si}^G(\mathbf{J})$ (6) at s from i[2] while "shooting" an amount of radiosity $\hat{b}_{is}^S(\mathbf{J})$ (2) from s to i.

Each random walk can however be used to obtain gathering or shooting contributions to the total non-self-emitted radiosity b_{j_k} at *every* visited patch j_k (see figure 1):

- Shooting: the radiosity due to all sources s is estimated by generating random walks from each source s with probability $p_s = \Phi_s/\Phi_T$. A contribution $R_{j_k}\Phi_T/A_{j_k}$ is recorded at every visited patch $j_k, k \geq 1$ (no contribution at the origin);
- Gathering: the radiosity at s is estimated more efficiently by recording a gathering contribution at s for every visited patch $j_k, k \geq 1$. Moreover, since each sub-path $j_k, \ldots, j_n, k \geq 1$ is an independent path for every visited patch j_k [3], it is allowed to accumulate a gathering contribution at each $j_k, k < n$ for each subsequently visited patch $j_l, l > k$[3]. In short, a gathering contribution of $R_{j_k}(E_{j_{k+1}} + \cdots + E_{j_n})$ shall be recorded at each $j_k, k = 0, \ldots, n-1$.

In an implementation, shooting and gathering contributions shall be accumulated separately on each patch i. Eventually, the shooting contributions at i shall be divided by the total number N of random walks. The gathering contributions at i shall be divided by the number of gathering contributions N_i^G at i. After adding self-emitted radiosity E_i, two independent estimates B_i^S and B_i^G for the radiosity on each path i are obtained.

---

[2]Note the switch of indices compared to (6).

[3]It is possible to use the sub-paths for shooting as well, but this results in increased variance.

92

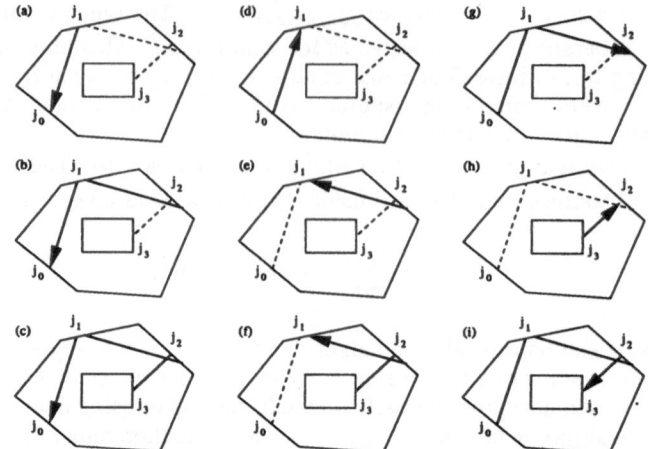

Figure 1. Contributions of a random walk j_0, j_1, j_2, j_3: (a,b,c) gathering at j_0; (d) shooting at j_1; (e,f) gathering at j_1; (g) shooting at j_2; (h) gathering at j_2; (i) shooting at j_3.

The gathering estimates B_i^G are obtained at negligible extra computation cost. Storage requirements are however slightly higher due to the need to store the count of gathering contributions N_i^G per patch as well as two radiosity estimates instead of one.

2.2 Combination of the radiosity estimates

The optimal combination $\alpha_i B_i^S + \beta_i B_i^G$ is obtained by chosing $\alpha_i + \beta_i = 1$ with each coefficient inverse proportional to the variance of the corresponding estimators:

$$\frac{\beta_i}{\alpha_i} = \frac{V[\hat{b}_i^S]/N}{V[\hat{b}_i^G]/N_i^G}. \tag{9}$$

Closed formulae for the variances $V[\hat{b}_i^S]$ and $V[\hat{b}_i^G]$ were given above. Unfortunately, these formulae require very detailed knowledge of the radiosity solution, which is not available in practice. Near-optimal weights can be obtained however by using approximations for the variances in (9).

A very simple but reasonably good heuristic for determining the weights is obtained by introducing the following assumptions:

- The origin selection probability for the random walks is $p_s = \Phi_s/\Phi_T$ in (4), and only those random walks that yield a gathering contribution at patch i are counted in N_i^G ($p_i = 1$ in (8));
- $R_i \xi_i$, the fraction of power received back at i due to own emission, is small in (4);
- $\sum_s (E_s + 2b_s)b_{is} \approx (\sum_s A_s(E_s + 2b_s)/A_T) \cdot \sum_s b_{is}$ in (8);
- After a smoothing pass, almost every patch i can be considered a source [6, 1], so that $\sum_s A_s b_s \approx \sum_i A_i b_i \approx \frac{R_{ave}\Phi_T}{1-R_{ave}}$;

With these assumptions, the following approximation for (9) is obtained:

$$\frac{\beta_i}{\alpha_i} \approx \frac{N_i^G A_T}{NA_i} \cdot k \approx \frac{B_i}{E_{ave}} \cdot k \quad \text{with optimal } k = \frac{1-R_{ave}}{1+R_{ave}}. \tag{10}$$

The second alternative follows from $E[N_i^G] = NP_i/\Phi_T$, which is easy to prove, and suggests the use of a (a-posteriori) radiosity estimate, e.g. $B_i^S \approx B_i$, instead of N_i^G.

3 Results and discussion

The combination is asymptotically unbiased. Since $E[\alpha_i B_i^S + \beta_i B_i^G] = E[B_i^S + \beta_i(B_i^G - B_i^S)]$ and $E[B_i^S] = B_i$, the bias is given by $E[\beta_i(B_i^G - B_i^S)]$. Since $\beta_i \leq 1$, the bias is bounded by $E[|B_i^G - B_i^S|] = \sqrt{\frac{2}{\pi}(V[\hat{b}_i^S]/N + V[\hat{b}_i^G]/N_i^G)}$ for sufficiently large N and N_i^G so that the central limit theorem applies.

The heuristic weights are reasonable. Figure 2 show that in three tested scenes with average reflectivity $0.2, 0.45$, and 0.8 the choice of k in (10) is near to the optimal choice indeed. The assumptions in §2.2 are satisfied well in these scenes.

Fair error reduction at nearly no additional cost. In the tested scenes, a mean square error (MSE) reduction of 9.8%, 19%, and 49% respectively was observed. Resulting images for the scene with average reflectivity 0.8 are shown in figure 3. A reduction of the MSE by 49% does not translate in dramatic improvements in visual appearance. The reduction of the error is however obtained at nearly no additional computation cost. With shooting only, 49% more random walks would be needed in order to achieve a given error level.

Related work. In [9], heuristics are presented for combining an a-priori known number of samples of a single integrand drawn from several probability distributions. In our case, we deal with samples of two distinct sums drawn from a single probability distribution. It is possible to reformulate the problem so that the heuristics in [9] can be applied when gathering to/shooting from only the origin of the paths. The heuristics in [9] cannot be used for combining shooting and gathering over all sub-paths: this would require that the probability that a random walk visits any patch is known in advance. These probabilities are proportional to the flux P_i of the patches, which is the result to be computed. For our combination heuristic, a a-posteriori radiosity estimate is sufficient.

4 Conclusion

The combination of a shooting random walk estimator with a corresponding gathering estimator which can be sampled at negligible additional cost can yield fair a error reduction. The technique was presented for the most commonly used shooting estimator, but can be used equally well with other random walk radiosity estimators as well as with similar estimators for general environments. The main area for improvement is in the development of more elaborate heuristics to combine the estimates by better approximation of the variance formulae.

References

1. F. Castro, R. Martínez, and M. Sbert. Quasi monte carlo and extended first shot improvement to the multi-path method for radiosity. In *Proceedings of SCCG'98, Budmerice, Slovakia*, April 1998.
2. S. Pattanaik and S. Mudur. Computation of global illumination by Monte Carlo simulation of the particle model of light. *Third Eurographics Workshop on Rendering*, pages 71–83, May 1992.
3. R. Y. Rubinstein. *Simulation and the Monte Carlo method*. J. Wiley and sons, 1981.

94

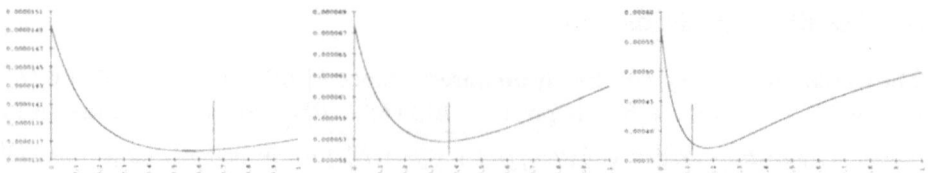

Figure 2. Mean square error (vertical axis) against combining factor k in (10) for a scene with average reflectance 0.2 (left), 0.45 (middle) and 0.8 (right). The vertical line indicates the proposed value for k. The scene with reflectance 0.8 is shown in figure 3.

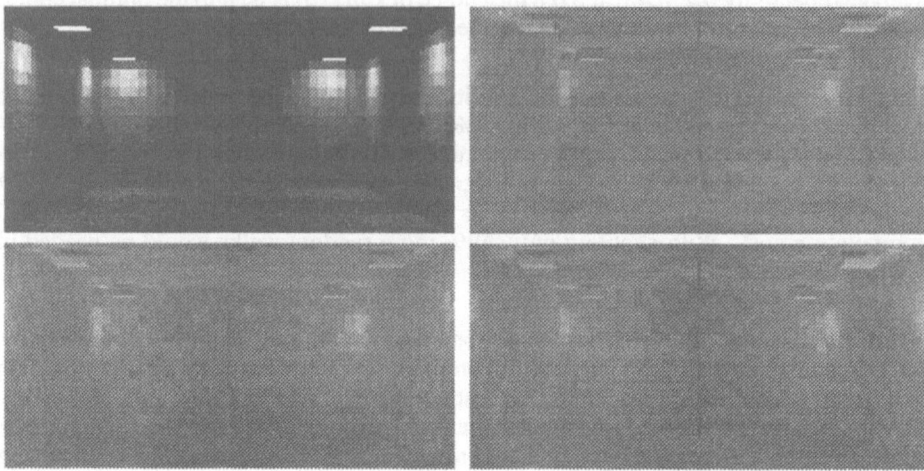

Figure 3. Top left: direct illumination used as the source distribution; Top right: Indirect illumination by combining shooting (bottom left) and gathering (bottom right).

4. M. Sbert. Error and complexity of random walk Monte Carlo radiosity. *IEEE Transactions on Visualization and Computer Graphics*, 3(1):23–38, March 1997.
5. M. Sbert. Optimal source selection in shooting random walk monte carlo radiosity. *Computer Graphics Forum*, 16(3):301–308, August 1997. Proc. Eurographics '97.
6. M. Sbert. *The use of global random directions to compute radiosity. Global Monte Carlo methods.* PhD thesis, Universitat Politècnica de Catalunya, Barcelona, March 1997. Available from http://ima.udg.es/~mateu.
7. M. Sbert, X. Pueyo, L. Neumann, and W. Purgathofer. Global multipath monte carlo algorithms for radiosity. *The Visual Computer*, 12(2):47–61, 1996.
8. P. Shirley. Radiosity via ray tracing. In James Arvo, editor, *Graphics Gems II*, pages 306–310. Academic Press, San Diego, 1991.
9. E. Veach and L. Guibas. Optimally combining sampling techniques for Monte Carlo rendering. In *Computer Graphics (ACM SIGGRAPH'95 conference proceedings)*, 1995.

Acknowledgements

This project has been funded in part with grant number TIC 98-0856-C03-02 of the Spanish Government, and Flemish-Catalan Joint-Action of CUR-Generalitat de Catalunya. The last author acknowledges financial support by a grant from the "Flemish Institute for the Promotion of Scientific-Technological Research in Industry" (IWT #941120) and the Flemish fund for scientific research (NWO-Vl #G.0105.96). Thanks to Frank Suykens for animated discussions.

Information Theory Tools
for Scene Discretization

Miquel Feixas*, Esteve del Acebo*, Philippe Bekaert† and Mateu Sbert*

*Institut d'Informàtica i Aplicacions, Universitat de Girona
feixas|acebo|mateu@ima.udg.es
†Department of Computer Science, Katholieke Universiteit Leuven
Philippe.Bekaert@cs.kuleuven.ac.be

Abstract. Finding an optimal discretization of a scene is an important but difficult problem in radiosity. The efficiency of hierarchical radiosity for instance, depends entirely on the subdivision criterion and strategy that is used. We study the problem of adaptive scene discretization from the point of view of information theory. In previous work, we have introduced the concept of mutual information, which represents the information transfer or correlation in a scene, as a complexity measure and presented some intuitive arguments and preliminary results concerning the relation between mutual information and scene discretization. In this paper, we present a more general treatment supporting and extending our previous findings to the level that the development of practical information theory-based tools for optimal scene discretization becomes feasible.

Keywords: information theory, radiosity, adaptive scene discretization

1 Introduction

From the point of view of Information Theory (IT) [4, 7], the discretization of a scene into patches in the radiosity method can be understood as the encoding or compression of a continuous signal over a discrete channel with the consequent distortion or information loss. The continuous signal corresponds to the (continuous) radiosity function $B(x)$ on the surfaces of the scene. The discrete channel is represented by a Markov Chain, with states corresponding to the patches into which the scene is discretized. The transition probabilities essentially correspond to the form factors.

To each discretization can be associated a quantity, *mutual information*, which quantifies the information transfer or information gain in a system. From the IT point of view, the optimal discretization corresponds with the one with minimal loss of information, or vice versa, the one with the highest mutual information. The most common distortion measure is the mean square error (MSE) or equivalently the L_2 norm. We can expect that the optimal discretization should give a minimum MSE.

Mutual information was proposed as a scene complexity measure in [9]. In [9] we also presented some intuitive arguments and preliminary results concerning the relation between mutual information and scene discretization. In this paper, we present a theorem that solidifies this previous work and allows to extend it to the level that the development of practical IT-based tools for scene discretization becomes feasible. We derive the optimal discretization for some simple scenes and common patch configurations. A heuristic for the patch-to-patch case is given, which can be used as an oracle for subdivision. We give also some evidence that the optimal mutual information discretization corresponds well to an optimal mean square error discretization.

The organisation of the paper is as follows: In section 2 we present a brief overview of our previous work [1, 8, 9] on the subject. In section 3 we present a general setting with its application to visibility, radiosity and importance. In section 4 we develop heuristics for good discretizations. In section 5 a proposal for a new subdivision oracle is presented and finally in section 6 we present our conclusions and future work.

2   An IT framework for the analysis of scene complexity

In this section we briefly review some basic concepts introduced in [1, 8, 9].

Complexity. Complexity reflects "the difficulty of describing a system, the difficulty of reaching a goal, the difficulty of performing a task, and so on" [14]. Over the last twenty years several complexity measures have been proposed from different fields to quantify the degree of structure or correlation of a system [10]. We study this concept of complexity from the point of view of IT [4, 7].

Markov Chains. In general, a Markov Chain is a sequence of random variables (sets of values or events with associated probabilities) $X^k, k = 0 \ldots \infty$ in which each $X^k, k \geq 1$ depends only on the previous X^{k-1} and not on the ones before. A Markov Chain is often characterized by a set of *states* labelled $i = 1, \ldots, n$. The random variables X^k indicate the probability of finding an imaginary particle in each state i after k steps from an initial distribution given by X^0. In each step, the imaginary particle makes a transition from its current state i to a new state j with *transition probability* P_{ij}. Under certain conditions (which are fulfilled in the context of this paper), the probabilities of finding the particle in each state i converge to a *stationary distribution* $w = (w_1, \ldots, w_n)$ after a number of steps. The stationary, or equilibrium probabilities w_i fulfil the relation $w_i = \sum_{j=1}^{n} w_j P_{ji}$. For the Markov Chains we deal with in this paper, the stationary distribution also satisfies another (balance or reciprocity) relation $w_i P_{ij} = w_j P_{ji}$.

Markov Chains for studying scene visibility complexity. In [9], we studied *discrete scene visibility* complexity by letting the states $i = 1, \ldots, n_p$ correspond to the patches of a scene and the transition probabilities P_{ij} with the form factors F_{ij}. n_p denotes the number of patches. It can be shown [9] that the stationary probabilities of the resulting Markov Chain are given by $w_i = A_i/A_T$, the relative area of the patches i of the scene (A_i is the area of patch i, A_T is the total scene surface area).

When the states form a countable set, as above, the Markov Chain is called a *discrete* chain. When the states are not countable, the chain is called *continuous*. For instance, when taking infinitesimal areas dx at each point x on the surfaces S of the scene as the states and differential form factors $F(x, y)$ with $x, y \in S$ as transition probabilities, a continuous Markov Chain with stationary distribution $w(x) = 1/A_T$ results. We have used this Markov Chain to study *continuous scene visibility* complexity.

Shannon entropy. The Shannon entropy of the stationary distribution (w_i) of a discrete Markov Chain is defined as $H_p = -\sum_{i=1}^{n} w_i \log w_i$. In the case of discrete scene visibility:

$$H_p = -\sum_{i=1}^{n_p} \frac{A_i}{A_T} \log \frac{A_i}{A_T}. \tag{1}$$

The Shannon entropy, which we will call the (discrete) *positional entropy* in this case, reflects the uncertainty on the position (patch) of a particle travelling an infinite random walk with transition probabilities equal to the form factors. The logarithms are taken in base 2 and we take $0 \log 0 = 0$.

For a continuous Markov Chain, e.g. for studying continuous visibility complexity, the sum $\sum_{i=1}^{n}$ shall be replaced by an integral over the uncountable set of states.

Entropy rate. The entropy rate of a Markov Chain with transition probability matrix (P_{ij}) and stationary probability distribution (w_i) is defined as $H_s = -\sum_{i=1}^{n} \sum_{j=1}^{n} w_i P_{ij} \log P_{ij}$. Applied to scene visibility:

$$H_s = -\sum_{i=1}^{n_p} \sum_{j=1}^{n_p} \frac{A_i}{A_T} F_{ij} \log F_{ij}. \tag{2}$$

The scene visibility entropy rate measures the average uncertainty that remains about the patch j visited next (*destination* patch) when an imaginary particle undergoing an infinite random walk, with the form factors as transition probabilities, is known to be on a given patch i (*source* patch).

Mutual information. Mutual information is defined as the difference of Shannon entropy and entropy rate: $I_s = H_p - H_s$. The *discrete scene visibility mutual information*

$$I_s = \sum_{i=1}^{n_p} \sum_{j=1}^{n_p} \frac{A_i F_{ij}}{A_T} \log \frac{F_{ij} A_T}{A_j} \tag{3}$$

can be interpreted as the amount of information that the destination patch conveys about the source patch, and vice versa. I_s *is a measure of the average information transfer in a scene* [9].

Continuous versus discrete mutual information. By discretizing a scene into patches, a distortion or error is introduced. In a way, to discretize means to equalize. Obviously, the maximum accuracy of the discretization is obtained when the number of patches tends to infinity and the size of the patches tends to zero.

Mutual information between two continuous random variables X and Y is the limit of the mutual information between their discretized versions [7, 11]. In our case, discrete scene visibility mutual information I_s (3), converges to *continuous scene visibility mutual information* I_s^c when the maximum patch size tends to zero [9]:

$$I_s^c = \int_{x \in S} \int_{y \in S} \frac{1}{A_T} F(x, y) \log(A_T F(x, y)) dx dy \tag{4}$$

I_s^c expresses with maximum accuracy the information transfer or correlation in a scene. This is an *absolute* measure of the complexity of scene visibility. On the other hand, discrete mutual information I_s expresses the complexity of a discretized scene, which is always lower than the corresponding I_s^c.

Scene radiosity complexity. Measures for the complexity of a scene, taking also diffuse illumination into account besides visibility, can be obtained by using a different pair of discrete and continuous Markov Chains [9] (see also §3.4 below).

3 Mutual information and patch subdivision

In [9] we presented intuitive arguments and preliminary results suggesting that between different discretizations of the same scene the most precise one will be the one that has the highest mutual information I_s, i.e., the one that best captures information transfer or has minimum information loss. We presented experiments for scene visibility and radiosity complexity.

In this section, we present a theorem (§3.1) that supports our preliminary findings and allows to derive more exact predictions of the gain in mutual information resulting from subdivision of scene patches. We first study the problem for a general scene complexity Markov Chain (§3.2) and next consider the application to scene visibility (§3.3), radiosity (§3.4) and importance (§3.5).

3.1 State refinement and continuous versus discrete mutual information

Theorem 1 *Consider a discrete Markov chain over a set of states labelled $i, j = 1, \ldots, n$, with transition probability matrix $P = (P_{ij})$ and stationary distribution $w = (w_1, w_2, \ldots, w_n)$ which satisfies the reciprocity relation $w_i P_{ij} = w_j P_{ji}$ $\forall i, j$. When a state i is refined into m sub-states i_k, $k = 1, \ldots, m$ such that*

    (a) $w_{i_k} P_{i_k j} = w_j P_{j i_k}$ $\forall i_k, j$ (reciprocity relation with the sub-states);
    (b) $P_{ji} = \sum_{k=1}^{m} P_{j i_k}$ $\forall j$ (the sub-states i_k "cover" i),

mutual information increases (or remains the same). (Proof in appendix A.)

Corollary 1 *Continuous mutual information I^c of a scene which fulfils the conditions of the above theorem is the least upper bound to discrete mutual information I.*

Proof: Continuous mutual information between two continuous random variables X and Y is the limit of the discrete mutual information between their discretized versions [7]. The statement that I^c is the least upper bound to I then immediately follows from the above theorem. $\qquad\square$

3.2 Patch-to-patch increase in mutual information

If we consider a scene with planar patches, the increase in mutual information between two planar patches i and j when subdividing i into m sub-patches is

$$(\Delta I)_{ij} = 2 \left(\left(\sum_{k=1}^{m} w_{i_k} P_{i_k j} \log \frac{P_{i_k j}}{w_j} \right) - w_i P_{ij} \log \frac{P_{ij}}{w_j} \right)$$

$$= 2 \left(\left(\sum_{k=1}^{m} w_{i_k} P_{i_k j} \log P_{i_k j} \right) - w_i P_{ij} \log P_{ij} \right) \tag{5}$$

This can be obtained from (10) and (11) in appendix A , where the second half of these formulae is null, and from the conditions of the theorem. For a regular subdivision, $w_{i_k} = \frac{w_i}{m}$, we have

$$(\Delta I)_{ij} = 2 \left(\left(\frac{w_i}{m} \sum_{k=1}^{m} P_{i_k j} \log P_{i_k j} \right) - w_i P_{ij} \log P_{ij} \right)$$

and it can be shown that the *theoretical* maximum possible increase in I happens when for all k except one $P_{i_k j} = 0$. The one not null can be shown to be equal to $m P_{ij}$. Thus the maximum possible increase in I is given by

$$max((\Delta I)_{ij}) = 2(w_i P_{ij} \log m P_{ij} - w_i P_{ij} \log P_{ij}) = 2 w_i P_{ij} \log m \qquad (6)$$

If we sum over j, we will obtain the maximum possible increase when dividing a given patch i

$$\sum_j max((\Delta I)_{ij}) = \sum_j 2 w_i P_{ij} \log m = 2 w_i \log m$$

Thus a heuristic to pick a patch to subdivide regularly, lacking any other knowledge, would be to take the one with maximum w.

3.3 Application to visibility

Taking $w_i = \frac{A_i}{A_T}$ and $P_{ij} = F_{ij}$, it is easy to see that the hypotheses of theorem 1 are fulfilled. Thus, from (5), the increment of mutual information is in this case

$$
\begin{aligned}
(\Delta I)_{ij} &= 2 \left(\left(\sum_{k=1}^m \frac{A_{i_k}}{A_T} F_{i_k j} \log \frac{F_{i_k j} A_T}{A_j} \right) - \frac{A_i}{A_T} F_{ij} \log \frac{F_{ij} A_T}{A_j} \right) \\
&= 2 \left(\left(\sum_{k=1}^m \frac{A_{i_k}}{A_T} F_{i_k j} \log F_{i_k j} \right) - \frac{A_i}{A_T} F_{ij} \log F_{ij} \right) \qquad (7)
\end{aligned}
$$

Thus, the maximum increase upon a regular subdivision is

$$max((\Delta I)_{ij}) = 2 \frac{A_i}{A_T} F_{ij} \log m$$

and the maximum possible increase when dividing a given patch i is $2 \frac{A_i}{A_T} \log m$.

3.4 Application to radiosity

In the radiosity setting, we consider the following transition probabilities

$$P_{ij} = \frac{\int_{S_i} \int_{S_j} F(x_i, x_j) B(x_i) B(x_j) dx_i dx_j}{\int_{S_i} B(x_i) \frac{B(x_i) - E(x_i)}{R(x_i)} dx_i}$$

These are the extension to the continuous case of the discrete null variance probabilities (see below) and fulfil $\sum_j P_{ij} = 1$ due to the additivity of the integral over its domain S, where $S = \cup_j S_j$, and the fact that the radiosities fulfil the diffuse rendering equation

$$B(x_i) = E(x_i) + R(x_i) \int_S F(x_i, x) B(x) dx$$

It can be easily checked that the equilibrium probabilities are

$$w_i = \int_{S_i} B(x_i) \frac{B(x_i) - E(x_i)}{R(x_i)} dx_i$$

and the reciprocity relation is trivially fulfilled. The normalising factor of w_i is

$$\sum_j \int_{S_j} B(x_j) \frac{B(x_j) - E(x_j)}{R(x_j)} dx_j = \int_S B(x) \frac{B(x) - E(x)}{R(x)} dx$$

If we divide patch i into i_1 and i_2 it is easy to prove, due to the additivity of the integrand, that the hypotheses of the theorem 1 are fulfilled. The radiosity case reverts to the visibility case when $B(x) = k$, where k is a constant, and this happens whenever $\forall x$ $E(x) = k(1 - R(x))$.

Now let us suppose radiosities and reflectivities are constant along each patch. In this case $w_i = A_i B_i \frac{(B_i - E_i)}{R_i}$ and $P_{ij} = \frac{R_i F_{ij} B_j}{B_i - E_i}$. These quantities can be considered a kind of generalized area and form factor respectively, by analogy with the visibility case in section 3.3. The P_{ij} probabilities were found to be the null variance transition probabilities for a gathering random walk in [17].

3.5 Application to importance

The continuous importance $I(x)$, given initial importance $V(x)$, is the solution to the integral equation for importance on a point x [16]:

$$I(x) = V(x) + \int_S R(y) F(x, y) I(y) dy$$

Consider now the transition probability

$$P_{ij} = \frac{\int_{S_i} \int_{S_j} F(x_i, x_j) R(x_i) R(x_j) I(x_i) I(x_j) dx_i dx_j}{\int_{S_i} R(x_i) I(x_i) (I(x_i) - V(x_i)) dx_i}$$

Similarly to the radiosity case, we have $\sum_j P_{ij} = 1$ due to the additivity of the integral over its domain S, where $S = \cup_j S_j$, and the fact that importances fulfil the importance integral equation. The equilibrium probabilities w_i are (without normalising)

$$w_i = \int_{S_i} R(x_i) I(x_i) (I(x_i) - V(x_i)) dx_i$$

and the reciprocity relation is fulfilled. If we divide patch i into i_1 and i_2, similarly to radiosity, the hypotheses of the theorem are fulfilled. It can be seen that for $R(x) I(x) = k$ for all x, that happens when we take $V(x) = k(\frac{1}{R(x)} - 1)$, the importance case reverts to the visibility case.

Now let us suppose importances and reflectivities are constant along each patch. In this case $w_i = A_i R_i I_i (I_i - V_i)$ and $P_{ij} = \frac{R_j F_{ji} I_j}{I_i - V_i}$. When $V_i = \delta_{ik}$ we have the null variance transition probabilities for a shooting random walk [17].

4 Results and discussion

In this section we discuss how mutual information varies for some common patch configurations and some simple scenes (§4.1). We also provide some evidence that an optimal subdivision obtained by mutual information maximization corresponds well to an optimal subdivision in terms of mean square error (§4.2).

4.1 Maximal mutual information subdivision for some common configurations

The following results can be obtained from (7), form factor properties and closed form formulae for the unoccluded form factors [6, 18, 12]:

Partially occluded pair of patches (figure 1a). Consider the subdivision of patch i into two sub-patches:

1) Of all subdivisions of i with one sub-patch totally occluded to j, the maximum mutual information increase corresponds to the discontinuity mesh (see appendix B.1).

2) When the point-to-point form factor $F(x, y)$ is approximately constant for x in the unoccluded part of i and y in j, the maximum increase in mutual information corresponds to the discontinuity mesh (see appendix B.2).

Two square patches with common edge (figure 2). Consistent with observations in [5], orthogonal splitting (figure 2(b)) leads to only a small gain in mutual information. Nothing is gained by orthogonal splitting in the middle. When splitting along a line parallel with the common edge (figure 2(a)) the maximum gain in mutual information results when splitting at a 40% relative distance from the edge (figure 2(c)).

Three square patches with common edges (figure 3). The maximum gain is obtained at a distance 39% from the edge. The small displacement (from 40% to 39%) towards the edge with respect to the previous case is due to the small positive gradient of mutual information for the orthogonal subdivision (see figure 2(b), squares).

Empty cube (figures 4 and 5). The resulting maximum mutual information subdivision is a bit displaced towards the edges with respect to the regular one. Figure 5 shows an example with more subdivisions.

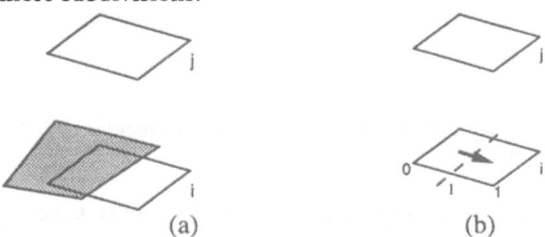

(a) (b)

Figure 1. (a) Partially occluded patch pair. (b) (§4.2) Subdivision of a patch perpendicular to the radiosity gradient. The position of the cutting line is parametrized by the relative distance $0 \leq l \leq 1$ to one edge.

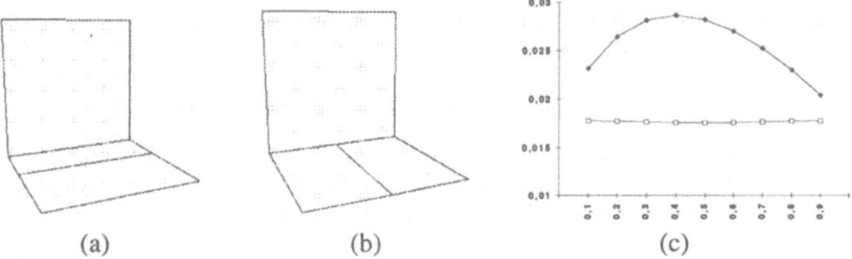

(a) (b) (c)

Figure 2. Mutual information on vertical axis (c) when dividing orthogonal (b,squares) and parallel (a,diamonds) to the common edge. Horizontal axis represents the displacement from the common edge (a) or one side edge (b).

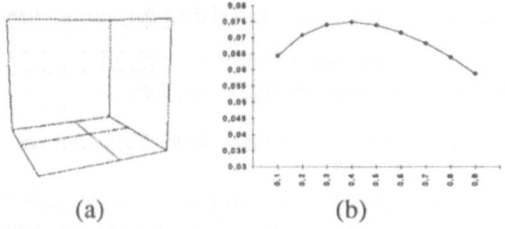

(a)   (b)

Figure 3. Mutual information on vertical axis (b) when subdividing a patch in a corner (a). Horizontal axis represents the distance from the parallel division to one common edge.

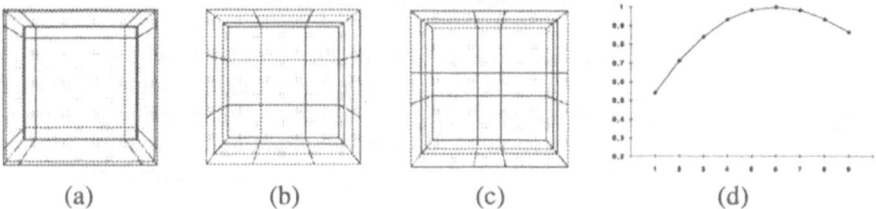

(a)   (b)   (c)   (d)

Figure 4. (d) Mutual information on vertical axis for an empty cube. Horizontal axis represents the relative displacement of a nearest subdivision to a common edge, ranging from 0 to 10. (b) corresponds to the optimal case, with value near to 6, (a) with value 2 and (c) with value 8.

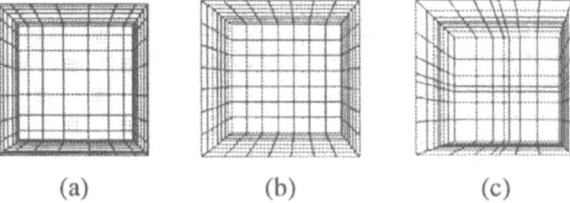

(a)   (b)   (c)

Figure 5. An empty cube with (a) optimal ($I = 1.3569$), (b) regular ($I = 1.3331$) and (c) "bad" ($I = 1.2554$) subdivision.

4.2 Mutual information maximization and mean square error

Consider two square patches, i and j, with the following characteristics: B_j is constant over j, $F(x, y)$ is approximately constant for $x \in S_i$, $y \in S_j$ and the reflectivity is constant along each patch. Consider now that the radiosity on patch i varies along one axis parallel to one edge of i, $B(l) = l^n B$, for B constant and l between 0 and 1 parametrizes the patch (figure 1(b)). The increase in mutual information when dividing patch i into sub-patches i_1 and i_2 is given by (5)

$$2(w_{i_1} P_{i_1 j} \log P_{i_1 j} + w_{i_2} P_{i_2 j} \log P_{i_2 j} - w_i P_{ij} \log P_{ij})$$

where in the radiosity case quantities w and P have to be substituted by the values given in section 3.4. The maximum increase in mutual information results when splitting patch i perpendicular to the gradient (this is, across a line $l = k$). The optimal value for l is found by optimising the expression:

$$l^{n+1} \log \frac{1}{l} + (1 - l^{n+1}) \log \frac{1 - l^{n+1}}{1 - l^{n+2}}.$$

For $n = 1, 2, 3, 4$ the optimal values correspond to $l = 0.48, 0.61, 0.68, 0.74$.

Consider now the subdivision problem from the point of view of minimising the L_2 error (or MSE error) on patch i, when assuming constant values for the radiosities on the sub-patches (equal to the average of the continuous radiosity function $B(x)$). After some algebra again, it can be shown that the optimal solution satisfies:

$$2nl^n - l^{n-1} - \ldots - l^2 - l - 1 = 0.$$

For $n = 1, 2, 3, 4$ the optimal values are $l = 0.5, 0.64, 0.72, 0.77$.

We have seen with this example that, in the absence of a form factor gradient, the subdivision cuts along the radiosity gradient and the optimal value that corresponds to maximum increase in mutual information is very near to the minimum L_2 error.

5 Towards a mutual information based oracle for subdivision

It can be seen that for the constant radiosity case the increase in mutual information is given by

$$(\Delta I)_{ij} = 2B_i B_j ((\sum_{k=1}^{m} (A_{i_k} F_{i_k j} \log F_{i_k j}) - A_i F_{ij} \log F_{ij}))$$

Thus, for a regular subdivision and from (6), the maximum possible increase is

$$\begin{aligned} max((\Delta I)_{ij}) &= 2B_i B_j ((\frac{A_i}{m} m F_{ij} \log(m F_{ij})) - A_i F_{ij} \log F_{ij})) \\ &= 2B_i B_j A_i F_{ij} \log m \propto B_i B_j A_i F_{ij} \end{aligned}$$

Thus the quantity $B_i B_j A_i F_{ij}$ expresses the maximum potential gain of mutual information between two patches when subdividing one of them. However, this can be really far from the real gain obtained, when for instance the form factors are fairly equal in the subdivisions, as could be with two parallel patches at some distance and without occlusions. Thus, the use of this quantity as an oracle for subdividing is not recommended. Better, the full expression for ΔI should be used, or at least some information on form factor gradients along subdivisions should be taken into account, the larger the gradient the larger the increase in mutual information.

One could also consider which is the patch with more potential gain in mutual information with respect to all other patches. In this case we sum over j

$$\sum_j B_i B_j A_i F_{ij} = A_i B_i \frac{B_i - E_i}{R_i}$$

this is, the one with the larger generalized area. Thus, in lack of any other information, a heuristic would be to look for the largest generalized area patch to subdivide.

Summarising, an oracle proposal for hierarchical radiosity subdivision is the following:

- A patch of the pair (i, j) will be candidate to subdivide only when the quantity $B_i B_j A_i F_{ij} > \epsilon_1$. This discards subdivisions with small potential increment of mutual information.

- If a pair (i, j) is considered, we pick from both the one corresponding to

$$max(A_i B_i \frac{B_i - E_i}{R_i}, A_j B_j \frac{B_j - E_j}{R_j})$$

this is, the one with the highest potential mutual information increase.
- A patch of the pair (i, j), say i, is finally subdivided only if the estimated gradient in form factors between the subdivisions and j is larger than a given threshold ϵ_2. This intends to guarantee a real increase in mutual information.

As a cheap gradient estimator we could use the differences between point-to-point form factors from the center of the subdivisions to the center of the j patch.

We remark here that the first step in the oracle is analogous to the power oracle $B_j R_i A_j F_{ji}$ [13, 3], the second step can be seen as an extension to the heuristics of dividing the patch with larger area, and the third step is analogous to the various gradient oracles used in hierarchical radiosity literature [5]. Obviously, the last step in the oracle can be refined to incorporate the exact form of the mutual information function, but at a much higher cost due to the numerical instabilities of the log function.

6 Conclusions and future research

In this paper we have taken one step further in our application of information theory to study the scene complexity. A general theorem on the increase of mutual information upon subdivision of the scene is presented, with application to visibility, radiosity and importances. The kind of subdivision driven by mutual information maximization is analysed, and shown that it has good properties, such as dividing across visibility and radiosity gradients. Also, evidence has been given on the minimization of MSE error by mutual information driven subdivision. Finally, a subdivision oracle based on the maximum mutual information increase has been presented and its potential utility in hierarchical radiosity justified.

Future research will be directed to analyse more precisely the interplay between MSE and mutual information. Also, the application to hierarchical radiosity of the proposed oracle will be undertaken, and the balance between cost and accuracy in subdivision for oracles reproducing the mutual information function more faithfully will be studied.

Acknowledgements

Many thanks to Roel Martínez and Joaquim Gelabertó. This project has been funded in part with grant numbers TIC 98-586-C03 and TIC-98-973-C03 of the Spanish Government and catalan-flemish joint action number ABM/acs/ACI98-19. The third author acknowledges financial support by a grant from the "Flemish Institute for the Promotion of Scientific-Technological Research in Industry" (IWT #941120) and the Flemish fund for scientific research (NWO-Vl #G.0105.96).

References

1. E. del Acebo, M. Feixas and M. Sbert. "Form Factors and Information Theory". *Proceedings of 3IA'98*, Limoges, April 1998.
2. R. Badii and A. Politi. *Complexity. Hierarchical structures and scaling in physics*. Cambridge University Press, 1997.

3. Ph. Bekaert, L. Neumann, A. Neumann, M. Sbert and Y. D. Willems. "Hierarchical Monte Carlo Radiosity". 9th *Eurographics Workshop on Rendering*, pp. 259–268, Vienna, Austria, June 1998.

4. R. E. Blahut. *Principles and practice of Information Theory*. Addison-Wesley, 1987.

5. A. Campbell. "Modelling Global Diffuse Illumination for Image Synthesis". PhD thesis, Dept. of Computer Science, University of Texas at Austin, 1991.

6. M. F. Cohen and J. R. Wallace *Radiosity and Realistic Image Synthesis*. Academic Press, 1993.

7. T. M. Cover and J. A. Thomas. *Elements of Information Theory*. Wiley, 1991.

8. M. Feixas, E. del Acebo and M. Sbert. "Entropy of scene visibility". *WSCG'99*, Plzen, 1999.

9. M. Feixas, E. del Acebo, Ph. Bekaert and M. Sbert. "An information theory framework for the analysis of scene complexity". To appear in Eurographics'99 Proceedings. Available in *http://ima.udg.es/~mateu*.

10. D. P. Feldman and J. P. Crutchfield. "Statistical Measures of Complexity: Why?". *Physics Letters A*, 238:244–252, 1998.

11. D. P. Feldman. "A brief introduction to: Information Theory, Excess Entropy and Computational Mechanics". Department of Physics, University of California, July 1997. Available in *http://leopard.ucdavis.edu/dave/index.html*.

12. A. S. Glassner. *Principles of digital image synthesis*. Morgan Kaufmann Publishers, San Francisco, 1995.

13. P. Hanrahan, D. Salzman and L. Aupperle. "Rapid hierarchical radiosity algorithm". *Computer Graphics (Proc.Siggraph'91)*, 25(4):197-206, 1991.

14. W. Li. "On the relationship between complexity and entropy for Markov chains and regular languages". *Complex Systems*, 5(4):381-399, 1991.

15. D. Lischinski, F. Tampieri and D. Greenberg. "Combining Hierarchical Radiosity and Discontinuity Meshing". SIGGRAPH'93 Proceedings, 1993.

16. S. Pattanaik and S. Mudur. "Adjoint Equations and Random Walks in Illumination Computation". ACM Transactions on Graphics, Vol. 14, No. 1, January 1995.

17. M. Sbert, A. Brusi, R. Tobler and W. Purgathofer. "Random Walk radiosity with generalized transition probabilities", Research Report IIiA-98-07-RR, Institut d'Informàtica i Aplicacions, Universitat de Girona, 1998. Available in *http://ima.udg.es/~mateu*.

18. F. X. Sillion and C. Puech. *Radiosity and Global Illumination*. Morgan Kaufmann Publishers, San Francisco, 1994.

A Proof of theorem 1

Let us imagine a discrete random walk with discrete mutual information

$$I = \sum_{i=1}^{n} \sum_{j=1}^{n} w_i P_{ij} \log \frac{P_{ij}}{w_j} \qquad (8)$$

We must show that, if any state is discretized into m sub-states, the discrete mutual information I' of the new random walk fulfils $\Delta I = I' - I \geq 0$. Without loss of generality we divide the nth state into m sub-states $n_1, n_2, \ldots, n_m$. Thus, we have

$$I' = \sum_{i=1}^{n-1} \sum_{j=1}^{n-1} w_i' P_{ij}' \log \frac{P_{ij}'}{w_j'} + \sum_{i=1}^{n-1} \sum_{k=1}^{m} w_i' P_{in_k}' \log \frac{P_{in_k}'}{w_{n_k'}}$$

$$+ \sum_{k=1}^{m} \sum_{j=1}^{n-1} w_{n_k}' P_{n_k j}' \log \frac{P_{n_k j}'}{w_j'} + \sum_{k=1}^{m} \sum_{l=1}^{m} w_{n_k}' P_{n_k n_l}' \log \frac{P_{n_k n_l}'}{w_{n_l}'} \qquad (9)$$

where $w_i = w_i'$ for $1 \leq i < n$, $w_n = \sum_{k=1}^{m} w_{n_k}'$, $P_{ij} = P_{ij}'$ for $1 \leq i, j < n$ and $P_{in} = \sum_{k=1}^{m} P_{in_k}'$ for $1 \leq i < n$. Because of $w_i P_{ij} \log \frac{P_{ij}}{w_j} = w_j P_{ji} \log \frac{P_{ji}}{w_i}, \forall i, j$, we have

$$I = 2 \sum_{i=1}^{n-1} \sum_{j=i+1}^{n} w_i P_{ij} \log \frac{P_{ij}}{w_j} + \sum_{i=1}^{n} w_i P_{ii} \log \frac{P_{ii}}{w_i} \tag{10}$$

Then

$$I' - I = 2 \sum_{i=1}^{n-1} \left(\sum_{k=1}^{m} w_i P_{in_k} \log \frac{P_{in_k}}{w_{n_k}} - w_i P_{in} \log \frac{P_{in}}{w_n} \right)$$

$$+ \sum_{k=1}^{m} \sum_{l=1}^{m} w_{n_k} P_{n_k n_l} \log \frac{P_{n_k n_l}}{w_{n_l}} - w_n P_{nn} \log \frac{P_{nn}}{w_n} \tag{11}$$

where the coincident terms in I and I' have been deleted. Applying the above hypotheses and the concavity of the logarithm function for non-negative numbers

$$\sum_{i=1}^{n} a_i \log \frac{a_i}{b_i} \geq \left(\sum_{i=1}^{n} a_i \right) \log \frac{\sum_{i=1}^{n} a_i}{\sum_{i=1}^{n} b_i} \tag{12}$$

we can conclude that

$$\Delta I = I' - I \geq 0$$

B Discontinuity meshing

B.1 Subdivision in occluded part

Patch i is divided into sub-patches i_a and i_b, where i_b is totally occluded and i_a has one part i_c unoccluded and one part i_d occluded. Then, from (7) and taking $A_T = 1$ without loss of generality,

$$
\begin{aligned}
(\Delta I)_{ij} &= 2 \left(A_{i_a} F_{i_a j} \log \frac{F_{i_a j}}{A_j} + A_{i_b} F_{i_b j} \log \frac{F_{i_b j}}{A_j} - A_i F_{ij} \log \frac{F_{ij}}{A_j} \right) \\
&= 2 \left((A_{i_c} F_{i_c j} + A_{i_d} F_{i_d j}) \log \frac{(F_{j i_c} + F_{j i_d})}{(A_{i_c} + A_{i_d})} - A_i F_{ij} \log \frac{F_{ij}}{A_j} \right) \\
&= 2 \left(A_{i_c} F_{i_c j} \log \frac{F_{j i_c}}{(A_{i_c} + A_{i_d})} - A_i F_{ij} \log \frac{F_{ij}}{A_j} \right)
\end{aligned}
\tag{13}
$$

The maximum is obtained when $A_{i_d} = 0$, i.e. when subdivision is made according to discontinuity meshing.

B.2 Subdivision in unoccluded part

Patch i is divided into sub-patches i_a and i_b, where i_a is totally unoccluded and i_b has one part i_c occluded and one part i_d unoccluded. Then, from (7) and taking $A_T = 1$,

$$
\begin{aligned}
(\Delta I)_{ij} &= 2 \left(A_{i_a} F_{i_a j} \log \frac{F_{i_a j}}{A_j} + A_{i_b} F_{i_b j} \log \frac{F_{i_b j}}{A_j} - A_i F_{ij} \log \frac{F_{ij}}{A_j} \right) \\
&= 2 \left(A_{i_a} F_{i_a j} \log \frac{F_{i_a j}}{A_j} + A_{i_d} F_{i_d j} \log \frac{F_{j i_d}}{(A_{i_d} + A_{i_c})} - A_i F_{ij} \log \frac{F_{ij}}{A_j} \right) \\
&\leq 2 \left(A_{i_a} F_{i_a j} \log \frac{F_{i_a j}}{A_j} + A_{i_d} F_{i_d j} \log \frac{F_{j i_d}}{A_{i_d}} - A_i F_{ij} \log \frac{F_{ij}}{A_j} \right)
\end{aligned}
\tag{14}
$$

where the right hand of the inequality corresponds to the mutual information increase in the discontinuity meshing case, where we have taken by hypothesis $F_{i_a j} = F_{i_d j}$.

Geospecific rendering of alpine terrain

Simon Premože   William B. Thompson   Peter Shirley

Department of Computer Science
University of Utah
Email: {premoze,thompson,shirley}@cs.utah.edu

Abstract. Realistic rendering of outdoor terrain requires both that the geometry of the environment be modeled accurately and that appropriate texturing be laid down on top of that geometry. While elevation data is widely available for much of the world and many methods exist for converting this data to forms suitable for graphics systems, we have much less experience with patterning the resulting surface. This paper describes an approach for using panchromatic (grayscale) aerial imagery to produce color views of alpine scenes. The method is able to remove shading and shadowing effects in the original image so that shading and shadowing appropriate to variable times of day can be added. Seasonal snow cover can be added in a physically plausible manner. Finally, 3–D instancing of trees and brush can be added in locations consistent with the imagery, significantly improving the visual quality.

1 Introduction

Sophisticated techniques exist for converting real-world elevation data into a *terrain skin* appropriate for graphical rendering [7, 10, 11, 17]. In most such systems, however, visual realism suffers because of the stylized texture maps or simplistic coloring used to pattern the terrain skin. To improve image quality, some high-end real-time visual simulators now support *geospecific texturing* in which texture maps are derived from aerial images registered to the terrain skin. Software techniques are also available for draping large aerial images over terrain data [5].

While draping aerial imagery onto a terrain skin adds a great deal of visual richness (Figure 1), visual realism still suffers in a number of important ways. Available high-resolution imagery is almost always panchromatic. Shadowing in the source imagery makes rendering views for times of day other than when the imagery was acquired problematic. Similar problems occur when simulating views at different times of year, particularly in alpine terrain when snow cover is an issue. Finally, texture mapping with aerial imagery in and of itself does not provide the fine scale three-dimensionality that is critical to perceiving a sense of scale over long distances. In the case of alpine environments, in particular, the three-dimensionality of trees is apparent even over distances of several kilometers.

The rendering shown in Figure 2 (see Color Plate) was produced by starting with the same source data as used to generate Figure 1. Using no additional data, terrain types and vegetation cover were mapped and this information was used to color the image. Existing shadows were removed and new shadows, appropriate to a different time of day, were added. Three-dimensional trees and brush were added at locations consistent with their appearance in the original aerial image. Finally, snow cover was added in locations appropriate for a particular time of year.

Fig. 1. *A traditional drape of panchromatic aerial imagery onto an elevation grid*

1.1 The nature of the data

Geospecific rendering of terrain requires information about both the geometry and the photometry of the scene. Raw information about the geometric shape of the terrain itself is most often available as a *Digital Elevation Model* (DEM), in which elevation values are represented in a rectangular grid. The highest resolution widely available elevation data[1] for the continental U.S. are United States Geological Survey (USGS) 7.5-Minute DEMs [24]. Elevation values with a nominal precision of 1m are provided at 30m intervals (*post spacing*) on the ground. The 7.5-Minute DEMs are created by optically scanning contour maps and then fitting an approximation surface. They are subject to a number of systematic distortions that, depending on the technology used when a particular DEM was produced, can result in the actual resolvability of ground features being far worse than the 30m post spacing might suggest.

The most direct way to render geospecific photometry is to start with an image of the area to be rendered. Perspective effects make it difficult to register conventional aerial imagery with elevation data. As a result, an *orthorectification* process is often performed, in which the perspective image is warped to remove the effects of lens projection, camera orientation, and terrain. The result is an image that is effectively a scaled orthographic projection. The USGS provides 1m resolution panchromatic *Digital Orthoimagery* (DOQ) for much of the continental U.S. [23]. No comparable source for color orthoimagery exists, although aerial survey companies can produce such imagery on a custom basis with significant cost. Satellite images are often used to render terrain. While not true color imagery as that term is commonly used, multi-spectral satellite data can be converted to an RGB format that closely approximates perceptual color. In addition, much work has gone into the classification of multi-spectral satellite data to determine properties such as vegetation cover. See [3] for an example of using this for terrain rendering. Unfortunately, the resolution of available multi-spectral satellite data is at best on the order of 20m on the ground [1, 20].

If actual imagery of the terrain being rendered is to be used, the available choices are usually limited to false-colored multi-spectral satellite data of limited resolution or USGS high-resolution panchromatic orthoimagery. Since visual realism in terrain rendering depends in part on high resolution texturing, it is important to explore whether or

---

[1]http://edcwww.cr.usgs.gov/doc/edchome/ndcdb/ndcdb.html

not panchromatic orthoimagery can be effectively utilized. Can realistic color be generated? Can we get enough information about ground cover to add detail not resolved in the imagery? Can we remove shadows and shading effects so as to simulate views at times other than when the original imagery was acquired? Can we simulate seasonal effects not present in the original imagery?

1.2 System overview

We developed a modeling and rendering environment that meets the goals and considerations described above (Figure 3). Input consists of terrain elevation data and orthophoto data. These two sources of information are used as input by a pattern classification system to categorize each pixel in the image into one of a set of possible classes (e.g., rock, snow, tree, etc.). The classifier is also capable of identifying shadowed regions in the original image, together with unshadowed areas of the same class. This is sufficient to enable a deshadowing process in which shadowed areas of a given type are made to be visually similar to the corresponding unshadowed regions. The classification is also used to develop explicit geometric models for larger objects such as trees. Finally, a physically-based snow simulation is used to compute snow cover for a given date. All of these are combined to form a terrain skin covered by a colored texture map and a set of geospecific vegetation models.

The major obstacles that must be crossed to create such a system include:

- removing shadows and shading effects from orthoimagery (Sections 2.1 and 2.3),
- classifying the pixels in orthoimages into categories (Section 2.2),
- adding seasonal effects (Section 3),
- adding geometry for the major vegetation in the appropriate locations.

2 Normalizing and classifying orthoimages

Orthoimages are produced from conventional aerial photographs and are subject to all of the common problems of the photographic process. Though care is taken to use images taken when the sun angle is high, shadows still occur. This is particularly true in images of alpine terrain due to the steep slopes that are often present. To determine surface type at each location in an orthoimage, it is desirable to first reduce those brightness effects in the image that are due to shading rather than surface reflectivity. In order to render a view with a simulated sun angle different from the actual sun angle when the image was acquired, this same shading normalization must be accompanied by a process that removes the existing shadows.

2.1 Removing shading effects

To use aerial imagery in the rendering of terrain as it would appear at different times of day, we need to minimize the luminance variability in the source imagery that is due to illumination effects at the time the imagery was acquired. If we had a way to recover surface albedo from luminance, this would also aid in determining what sort of surface cover was present at a given location in the image. Given Lambertian surfaces, a known distribution of illumination, and surface orientation at every point, it is straightforward to determine surface reflectances. In practice, we know none of these properties. Surface reflectance is far from Lambertian, illumination depends not only

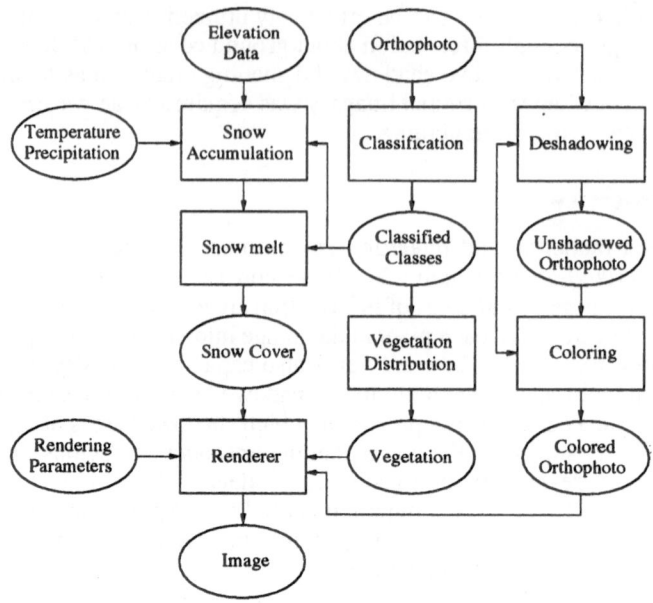

Fig. 3. Scene synthesis flow graph

on sun angle but also on complex, weather dependent variations in sky brightness, and DEMs provide only low resolution information about surface orientation.

Nevertheless, shading effects can be reduced by applying a normalization based on the cosine of the angle between the approximate surface orientation, as specified in a DEM, and an estimate of the direct illumination direction. Sun angle is often provided with satellite data. For USGS orthoimages, it must be estimated from the imagery. Computer vision shape-from-shading methods can be used to solve this problem [4]. If shadows are present and one or more matches can be established between points on shadow generating contours and the corresponding point on the trailing edge of the shadow, then the direction of direct illumination can be inferred from the DEM-specified elevations of the corresponding points.

2.2 Classifying orthoimages

Figure 4 shows a 480m by 340m section of an orthoimage of an area of the Wasatch Mountains near Salt Lake City, Utah. Included within the image are regions of pine trees, brush, talus, rock cliffs, and snow. The pine trees are surrounded by an understory consisting of dirt, grass, and shrub. Portions of talus, cliff, and snow are in shadow. Each of these classes of surface cover has a distinct coloration. Given the panchromatic brightness at each pixel and the corresponding surface type, it is straightforward to produce a relatively accurate color version of the image.

Image brightness can yield a rough categorization of these regions: pine is dark, talus a mid-gray, and snow is bright. A quantitative examination of image values, however, quickly demonstrates that thresholding cannot adequately separate the classes of interest, no matter how carefully the thresholds are chosen. Computer vision techniques based on 2–D shape analysis are not likely to succeed either, given the complexity of

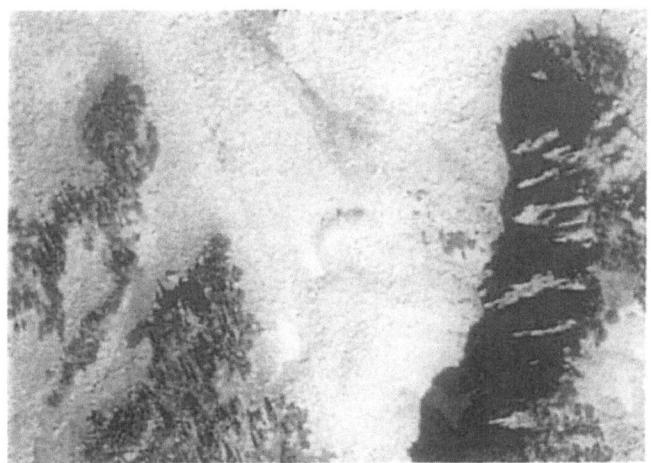

Fig. 4. *480m by 340m section of an orthoimage of the Wasatch Mountains*

the images. Instead, we have successfully used a pattern classification approach similar to that used to classify multi-spectral satellite data.

For each pixel in the deshaded orthoimage, we computed eight features:

1. pixel brightness
2. average neighborhood brightness
3. minimum neighborhood brightness
4. maximum neighborhood brightness
5. elevation
6. slope
7. aspect
8. angle to southern occluder

Features 2–4 allow consideration of brightness within a local context. Features 5–8 are computed by interpolating 30m DEM values. Feature 7 measures the direction a given point on a slope is facing, an important determinant of vegetation cover. Feature 8 measures the angle from a given point to the southern skyline. Larger values increase the likelihood that the point will be in shadow when the image was acquired.

A simple normal distribution, maximum likelihood Bayes classifier [22] proved sufficient, avoiding the need for complex training procedures, hand tuning of parameters, or other manual adjustments. This classifier assumes that the values of each feature for each class are generated by a normally distributed random process, possibly involving correlation between different features. Population statistics, $p(\mathbf{x}|C_k)$, are computed for feature values, represented as a vector $\mathbf{x}$, given that the features came from a particular class, C_k. Since the feature values arising from a given class are assumed to be normally distributed, their statistics are completely characterized by a mean vector, μ_k, and a covariance matrix, Φ_k. Given the *a priori* likelihood of each class, $P(C_k)$, the minimum error classifier is achieved by assigning the class C_k such that:

$$P(C_k|\mathbf{x}) \geq P(C_j|\mathbf{x}) \ \forall \ j \neq k.$$

Fig. 5. *Classification results of orthoimage in Figure 4*

Bayes law is used to convert this to a discriminant function formulation, in which C_k is chosen maximizing:

$$g_k = -\frac{1}{2}\mathbf{x}^t[\Phi_k]^{-1}\mathbf{x} + \mathbf{x}^t[\Phi_k]^{-1}\mu_k - \frac{1}{2}\mu_k^t[\Phi_k]^{-1}\mu_k + \ln P(C_k) - \frac{1}{2}\ln|\Phi_k|.$$

For each class, several hundred image locations were selected manually to form a training set, in a process requiring only a few minutes of time. Statistics on the distributions of feature values for the training set were determined and used to form the discriminant functions for the maximum likelihood Bayes classifier, assuming all *a priori* probabilities to be equal. This classifier was then used to categorize each pixel location in the full orthoimage. A final decluttering step reclassified very small regions based on the dominant surrounding class.

Classification results are shown in Figure 5. While ground-truth validation has not been done, spot checking of the results corresponds closely with what would be expected from a careful examination of the orthoimage. The actual statistical distribution characterizing the features is almost certainly not multi-variate normal. The fact that the classifier still performed well is an indication that the features for each class are well separated in a statistical sense. As is often the experience in pattern recognition, appropriately chosen features allowed the use of a simple classifier.

2.3 Removing shadows

While the aerial imagery used to generate orthoimages is chosen to minimize shadows, shadowing is still present. As would be expected, the severity of this problem increases

Fig. 6. *Figure 4 deshaded, colored, and with shadows removed*

with the ruggedness of the terrain. These shadows need to be removed and replaced by simulated shadows resulting from a different illumination direction if we want to use the imagery to texture a terrain scene for a date/time different from when the source image was taken. Given accurate information about the direction of incident direct illumination and high resolution elevation data, expected shadow locations could be easily computed. In practice, we seldom have either and so another approach is needed.

The maximum likelihood classifier does a good job of identifying shadow areas and can even categorize different surface covers within the shadowed regions. This can be used to remove the photometric effects of shadowing, even when the direction of illumination is not known. For purposes of visual rendering, it is enough to renormalize shadowed portions of the orthoimage to have a brightness distribution statistically similar to unshadowed regions of the same surface type. In practice, it appears to be enough to standardize the mean and standard deviations of the shadowed regions.

To improve the visual qualities of our talus texture, we apply image processing. The real talus exhibits shadowing and highlights from individual stones. Most of this is lost in the blurring of the photographics process. To add some shading variation, we apply two steps. First, we apply mean-variance normalization. Because the dynamic range in the shadows is so low, the variance normalization effectively translates quantization noise into uncorrelated additive noise. We then apply a gaussian blur, thus adding correlation to the noise for an appearance that more resembles the mid-size rocks of talus.

Often, shadow boundaries in orthoimages exhibit a penumbra-like effect, though at a scale much larger than the shadow penumbra that would be generated by a light source the angular extent of the sun. The causes of this phenomenon are not clear, but are likely due to a combination of interreflection, variations in sky brightness, and photographic dodging done as a pre-processing step in orthophoto preparation. Whatever the cause, these shadow fringes are visually distracting and can generate ground type misclassifications. Fortunately, it is an easy matter to replace dark pixels near classified shadow regions with lighter pixels slightly farther away, largely eliminating the problem.

Figure 6 shows the results of deshading and shadow removal applied to Figure 4 and followed by coloring based on the classification shown in Figure 5.

3 Modeling snow cover

In alpine environments, snow cover is the predominant seasonal effect. Snow cover normally develops from a series of winter storms and is modified by the action of rain, wind and melting. Thus, to show seasonal effects not present in the original orthoimagery, we need to simulate effects such as snow accumulation, snow ablation and melt. In mountainous areas, the amount of snow present at any given location is highly variable. This is particularly noticeable in late spring and early summer, as southern and western aspects melt out exposing the underlying ground, while north facing slopes are still covered in deep snow.

3.1 Snow accumulation

Snow accumulation and loss is controlled primarily by atmospheric conditions and the elevation and slope of the terrain [9]. Atmospheric processes of interest are precipitation, deposition, condensation, turbulent transfer of heat and moisture, radiative exchange and air movement. Land features influence snow accumulation by slope, orientation, and by shadowing properties. These factors act together and are related to each other [2]. For example, mountain ranges interrupt the winds that can redistribute the snow into drifts, slope and aspect influence incoming solar radiation and humidity, and latitude and elevation control air and ground temperature.

The variability of snow cover is commonly considered on three geometric scales [9]:

- *Regional scale*: large areas with linear distances up to 1000km in which dynamic meteorological effects such as wind flow around barriers and lake effects are important
- *Local scale*: areas with linear distances of 100m to 1000m in which accumulation may be related to the elevation, aspect and slope of the terrain and to the canopy and crop density, tree species, height and extent of the vegetative cover
- *Microscale*: distances of 10m to 100m over which accumulation patterns result primarily due to surface roughness

For our simulations, we consider only local scale and microscale.

3.2 Snow ablation and melt

The rate of snow melt is dependent on energy availability, which is mostly in the form of radiation [13]. Cold snowpacks have a negative energy balance, but warming causes the snowpack to become isothermal (0°C) and additional energy results in positive energy balance and melt. Daily snow melt in forested areas is considerably less than melt in open areas, as forests protect the snow cover from solar radiation and wind. Canopy warming can increase longwave radiation, but the net effect of forest is reduction in melt. Rain falling on snowpack may accelerate its melt rate, but intense sunshine of late spring and summer is the principal melting energy source.

Most operational procedures for snow melt prediction rely on ambient air temperature as the index of the energy available for melt. The *temperature index* is usually used to characterize the level of the energy balance because it is superior to other simple methods for the full energy balance at the snow surface [6]. The most common expression relating snow melt to the temperature index is:

$$M = C_m(T_{air} - T_{melt}),$$

where M is the daily snow melt (mm/day), C_m is the melt rate factor (mm/$^\circ$C per day), T_{air} is the daily ambient temperature ($^\circ$C) and T_{melt} is the threshold melt temperature ($^\circ$C). The critical melt temperature is often set to 0°C but can be optimized for a particular location. In our simulations the melt temperature was set to 0°C.

3.3 Snow cover simulation

Our model divides the height field into a grid storing the amount of snow as *snow water equivalent*. This is the depth of water that would be obtained by melting the snow cover. Snow is first deposited by elevation and then is melted in a simulation that varies temperature with height and available radiation. The available radiation is based on surface orientation and the times of day it is shadowed. The shadowing is computed at the center of each grid cell.

Ambient air temperature is a fundamental component of the calculations for snow accumulation, melt and evapotranspiration. Temperature data at specified base elevation is provided as user input and contains: (i) minimum, (ii) maximum, and (iii) average temperature. An average environmental lapse rate can also be user specified, but we adopted a rate of -0.6°C per 100m [15]. Warm air advection can make a standard lapse rate inadequate for temperature predictions in alpine environment [19]. However, over time fluctuations about the mean lapse rate will tend to even out.

Elevation is believed to be the single most important factor in snow cover distribution. Precipitation data at specified base elevation is provided as user input and contains: (i) amount of precipitation, and (ii) precipitation density (1 g/cm^3 for rain). Elevation rise from the base elevation is treated very simply using an optional user specified lapse rate. We adopted a 10% increase in precipitation per 100m. As with air temperature, the simplified precipitation distribution assumptions are less likely to pose problems over long time periods.

The amount of snow accumulated depends on the balance between rain and snowfall [19]. The usual method to classify precipitation is to set a threshold ambient air temperature (T_{snow}) above which all precipitation is assumed to be rain. For every simulation time step, we determine precipitation type from ambient air temperature. If precipitation is snow, the snow water equivalent is computed from snowfall and density, and accumulated. If precipitation is rain no accumulation occurs and the simulation continues to melting phase.

The major variables controlling the snow melt factor are determined using the relationship suggested by Eggleston et al. [14]:

$$C_m = k_m k_v R_I (1 - A),$$

where k_m (≈ 0.4) is a proportionally constant, k_v is a vegetation transmission coefficient for radiation, R_I is a solar radiation index, and A is the snow albedo. The change in snow albedo with time t (days) is described by

$$A = 0.4[1 + e^{-k_e t}],$$

where k_e ($\approx 0.2/day$) is a time constant. A fall of new snow increases the albedo to 0.8 while rain reduces it to 0.4. The vegetation transmission coefficient k_v is computed as

$$k_v = e^{-4C_v},$$

where C_v is the vegetation canopy density.

R_I is the ratio of the radiation received by a surface with a given slope and aspect, normalized to that received by a horizontal surface at the same latitude and time of year. Note that only the ratio of energies needs to be computed. A slightly modified method of Swift [21] is used for this computation. For periods of rain the melt factor C_m is adjusted as follows:

$$C_m(rain) = C_m + 0.00126 P_{rain},$$

where P_{rain} is amount of rainfall (mm).

Every simulation time step, if the ambient air temperature (T_{air}) is greater than the threshold melt temperature (T_{melt}), the melt rate factor C_m is computed and the snowpack water equivalent is adjusted accordingly. When the simulation is done, grid cells with non-zero snow water equivalent are assumed to have snow cover. We do not model snow depth so we use the snow cover information only to decide where to render snow in the final image. Adding snow to regions that are uncovered in the original orthoimage is straightforward, since at a distance snow appears as a relatively diffuse reflector except for glancing illumination and viewing angles. Subtracting snow that was on the ground when the aerial image was shot is a bit more complicated. However, since almost all of the raw imagery is acquired in summer to minimize sun angle effects, we can be pretty much assured that the underlying surface cover is rock or talus.

4 Results

Figure 7 (see Color Plate) shows renderings produced for a 2km by 2km region in the Wasatch Mountains. This particular region was selected because it includes both rugged and fairly gentle terrain, significant shadowing, a fairly wide range of surface types, and slopes of varying aspect, all within a relatively compact area. The sole source data utilized was standard issue USGS DEM elevation and DOQ image data. A classification map was created as described in Section 2.2. This was used for deshadowing, coloring, and for seeding a plant growth simulation in the manner of Deussen et al. [16], with the individual plants represented using ellipsoids in the spirit of Gardner [8]. For a given time of year, a snow simulation is run and the appropriate parts of the colored orthotexture are replaced with snow color. The texture and plant data was input to a Monte Carlo path tracer [12] with a sky model similar to that used by Preetham et al. [18] that appropriately controls illumination based on time/date/place.

Figure 7(a) and 7(b) show renderings with and without explicit plant geometry. Figure 7(c) and 7(d) show variation of appearance at different times of day. Figure 7(e) and 7(f) show variation of appearance at different times of year. Figure 7(e) and 7(f) show variation due to seasonal effects. Higher resolution images are available on our web page at http://www2.cs.utah.edu/vissim/alpineTerrain.

5 Acknowledgments

Thanks to Steve Parker for his last minute hardware support and to A. J. Preetham for the use of his sky model code. This work was supported by NSF grants 97-20192, 97-31859 and CDA-96-23614.

Fig 2. A rendering of the same data as used to generate Figure 1,
after processing using the techniques from this paper.

a. Image without explicit plant geometry.

b. Image with explicit plant geometry.

c. Rendering for winter morning.

d. Rendering for winter afternoon.

e. Late spring.

f. Early summer.

Fig 7. Renderings of a 2km by 2km region in the Wasatch Mountains
at different time of day/year.

References

1. AERIAL-IMAGES, INC. http://www.aerial-images.com. 615 Hillsborough Street, Raleigh, NC 27603, USA.
2. BARRY, R. G. *Mountain Weather and Climate*. Methuen, London, UK, 1981.
3. BRIVIO, P. A., FURINI, P., RIGHETTI, M., AND MARINI, D. Synthesis of multispectral images of natural landscape. In *Eurographics Workshop on Rendering* (1991).
4. BROOKS, M. J., AND HORN, B. K. P. Shape and source from shading. In *Shape from Shading*, B. K. P. Horn and M. J. Brooks, Eds. MIT Press, Cambridge, MA, 1989.
5. CLINE, D., AND EGBERT, P. Interactive display of very large textures. In *Proceedings of IEEE Visualization '98* (Oct. 1998), pp. 343–350.
6. FERGUSON, R., AND MORRIS, E. Snowmelt modelling in the Cairngorms. *Earth Sci.*, 78 (1987), 261–267.
7. FOWLER, R. J., AND LITTLE, J. J. Automatic extraction of irregular network digital terrain models. In *SIGGRAPH 79 Conference Proceedings* (1979), Annual Conference Series, ACM SIGGRAPH, pp. 207–218.
8. GARDNER, G. Y. Simulation of natural scenes using textured quadric surfaces. In *Computer Graphics (SIGGRAPH '84 Proceedings)* (July 1984), H. Christiansen, Ed., vol. 18, pp. 11–20.
9. GRAY, D. M., AND MALE, D. H., Eds. *Handbook of Snow*. Pergamon Press, 1981.
10. HOPPE, H., DeROSE, T., DUCHAMP, T., McDONALD, J., AND STUETZLE, W. Mesh optimization. In *Computer Graphics (SIGGRAPH '93 Proceedings)* (Aug. 1993), J. T. Kajiya, Ed., vol. 27, pp. 19–26.
11. HOPPE, H. H. Smooth view-dependent level-of-detail control and its application to terrain rendering. In *Proceedings of IEEE Visualization '98* (Oct. 1998), pp. 343–350.
12. KAJIYA, J. T. The rendering equation. In *Computer Graphics (SIGGRAPH '86 Proceedings)* (Aug. 1986), D. C. Evans and R. J. Athay, Eds., vol. 20, pp. 143–150.
13. KELLY ELDER, J. D., AND MICHAELSEN, J. Snow accumulation and distribution in an alpine watershed. *Water Resources Research 27*, 7 (1991), 1541–1552.
14. K.O. EGGLESTON, E. I., AND RILEY, J. Hybrid computer simulation of the accumulation and melt processes in a snowpack. Technical Report PRWG65-1, Utah State University, Logan, UT, USA, 1971.
15. LEEMANS, R., AND CRAMER, W. The HASA climate database for mean monthly values of temperature, precipitation and cloudiness on a terrestrial grid, 1991. RR-91-18, HASA, Laxenburg.
16. OLIVER DEUSSEN, PAT HANRAHAN, BERND LINTERMAN, RADOMIR MĚCH, MATT PHARR AND PRZEMYSLAV PRUSINKIEWICZ. Realistic modeling and rendering of plant ecosystems. In *SIGGRAPH 98 Conference Proceedings* (July 1998), pp. 275–286.
17. POPE, C. N., VUONG, M., MOORE, R. G., AND COWSER, S. S. A whole new CCTT world. *Military Simulation and Training*, 5 (1995).
18. PREETHAM, A. J., SHIRLEY, P., AND SMITS, B. A practical analytic model for daylight. In *SIGGRAPH* (1999). To Appear.
19. ROHRER, M. Determination of transition air temperature from snow to rain and intensity of precipitation. In *WMO IASH ETH International Workshop on Precipitation Measurement* (Oct. 1989), pp. 475–582.
20. SPOT IMAGE CORPORATION. http://www.spot.com. 1897 Preston White Drive, Reston, VA 20191, USA.
21. SWIFT, L. W. Algorithm for solar radiation on mountain slopes. *Water Resources Research 12*, 1 (1976), 108–112.
22. TOU, J. T., AND GONZALEZ, R. C. *Pattern Recognition Principles*. Addison-Wesley, Reading, MA, 1974.
23. U.S. GEOLOGICAL SURVEY. Standards for digital orthophotos, December 1996.
24. U.S. GEOLOGICAL SURVEY. Standards for digital elevation models, January 1998.

Editors' Note: see Appendix, p. 363 for colored figures of this paper

Multiple Textures Stitching and Blending on 3D Objects

C. Rocchini, P. Cignoni, C. Montani

Istituto di Elaborazione dell'Informazione – C.N.R.
Email: `cignoni|montani|rocchini@iei.pi.cnr.it`

R. Scopigno

CNUCE – C.N.R.
Email: `r.scopigno@cnuce.cnr.it`

Abstract. In this paper we propose a new approach for mapping and blending textures on 3D geometries. The system starts from a 3D mesh which represents a real object and improves this model with pictorial detail. Texture detail is acquired via a common photographic process directly from the real object. These images are then registered and stitched on the 3D mesh, by integrating them into a single standard texture map. An optimal correspondence between regions of the 3D mesh and sections of the acquired images is built. Then, a new approach is proposed to produce a smooth join between different images that map on adjacent sections of the surface, based on texture blending. For each mesh face which is on the adjacency border between different observed images, a corresponding triangular texture patch is resampled as a weighted blend of the corresponding adjacent images sections. The accuracy of the resampling and blending process is improved by computing an accurate piecewise local registration of the original images with respect to the current face vertices. Examples of the results obtained with sample Cultural Heritage objects are presented and discussed.

1 Introduction

An accurate digital representation of both the shape and the pictorial detail of 3D objects is mandatory in many applications. An example is certainly the acquisition of 3D objects in the Cultural Heritage field. The accuracy required is so high that standard CAD systems do not produce accurate enough models, and in any case accurate modeling is very time consuming. Automatic acquisition is therefore becoming the solution to the problem, and many different technologies have been proposed [15]. Accuracy and resolution of the available devices are in general very good, and allow the acquisition of highly detailed models.

One critical point is how do we acquire *pictorial detail* and how do we link it to the shape description [1, 11, 12, 9, 19, 20, 18, 16, 17, 26, 13] (hereafter, we assume that shape is represented by a standard triangle mesh encoding). The term *pictorial detail* can be used to represent different concepts: from texture color observed on the object surface, which strongly depends on the lighting conditions, to object surface reflectance properties, computed by removing highlights and diffuse shading or even by computing a bidirectional reflectance distribution function (BRDF).

Texture mapping has been used in graphics as an early approximation of *image-based modeling*. In our case, we want to acquire automatically the pictorial detail of a complex surface, by extracting texture-maps from real world [23] and by pasting them on standard textured three-dimensional models. The same problem was investigated previously[1] by Soucy et al. [22].

Some problems we may find in current 3D scanning technology, with respect to detail acquisition, are: the existence of devices with no pictorial detail acquisition capability; possible insufficient accuracy or resolution of the pictorial detail acquired; complexity of the integration of multiple scans process, especially if we want the final mesh to integrate smoothly and accurately the acquired pictorial detail [9, 20, 17, 13].

In our approach, shape and pictorial detail acquisition are de-coupled. This to allow the use, out of the many available, of the 3D scanning technology which is more adequate to process the target object. In this paper we focus mainly on the acquisition and management of pictorial detail, and in particular on how we can map and integrate on a standard textured mesh the detail contained in a set of images taken from different view points. Our approach can be classified as a *hybrid image-based modeling* one. The construction of a panoramic image to be used in *image-based rendering* shows some similarities with the process proposed in this paper, where the seamless join of images taken from the real world is one of the goals [24, 14, 5, 16, 21].

We propose the integration of different techniques (range scanning, image processing, inverse texture-mapping and surface-based 3D graphics) to extract pictorial detail from images and to past it on a standard triangle-based mesh. An optimal correspondence between regions of the 3D mesh and sections of the acquired images is built. In particular, a new approach is proposed to produce a smooth join between different images that maps on adjacent sections of the surface (where it is crucial to preserve discontinuity of pictorial detail, e.g. edges or lines, and continuity of chromatic content). This is done by applying an accurate piecewise local registration of the observed images: an overlapping region is defined on the mesh, and a local registration is computed for each vertex in this region. For each mesh face which is in the overlapping region, texture blending is operated by resampling a new texture patch, obtained as a weighted blend of the corresponding adjacent images.

The paper is organized as follows. In the next section we introduce the four constituent phases of our approach, presented in detail in the following sections. The *vertex-to-image* binding phase is presented in Section 3. The determination of a potentially optimal decomposition of the mesh in contiguous areas that map to the same texture image is described in Section 4. The management of texture blending on the frontier faces is introduced in Section 5. Finally, all active texture patches are packed in a single rectangular texture, see Section 6. Issue related to the quality of the final texture mapping obtained are briefly discussed in Section 7. An evaluation of the proposed approach is presented in Section 8 and concluding remarks are in the last section.

2 Texture Stitching and Blending

Our approach de-couples shape and detail acquisition. We assume that the shape of the considered object has been acquired using whichever type of scanning device. A triangle mesh M becomes one of the inputs of our detail acquisition process; it can be either the original range-scan mesh or a partially simplified one.

The pipeline of the processing phases is as follows.

---

[1]A comparison between our approach and the one by Soucy et al. [22] is not easy, because not sufficient detail is given in their paper regarding the technique they use to integrate different texture images on a single mesh.

Pictorial detail acquisition and registration
Our detail acquisition methodology requires only inexpensive hardware: a digital still camera or a high-resolution video camera. To acquire pictorial detail we shot images from a set of different view points. The set of viewpoints is defined such that each area of the sample object is visible at least from one viewpoint.

Then, all the different views are registered with respect to the object shape M. This is a well known problem, and we adopt a classical approach [25] based on the interactive selection of corresponding point pairs. The output of this phase is the definition, for each set of images taken from the same view, of the associated camera calibration and pose parameters.

Texture Stitching
In this phase all the detail images are stitched on the shape mesh and partially fused, to generate a single textured triangle mesh. Intuitively, we built an optimal patchwork of images subsections such that all of the object surface is covered and adjacent image subsections join smoothly on the object surface (both in terms of color and pictorial detail continuity). The texture patching process works on the mesh vertices, and it is composed of four sub-phases (described in detail in the next sections):

1. *vertex–to–image* **binding:**
   for each mesh vertex v, we detect the subset of *valid* images that contain a *valid* projection of vertex v. Among all valid images, we select initially as *target* image the one which is most orthogonal to surface M in v;

2. **patch growing:**
   the *vertex-to-image* relation is iteratively refined, by visiting the vertex adjacency graph, to obtain an optimal texture patching. We iteratively change the *vertex-to-image* links, among the possible valid ones, to obtain larger contiguous sections of mesh M that map to the same target image (i.e. such that all the three vertices of each triangular face in the mesh section are linked [if possible] to the same image, and adjacent faces are linked [if possible] to the same image);

3. **patch boundary smoothing:**
   The previous step produces some faces that have vertices associated with different images. We call these faces *frontier* faces, i.e. faces which are on the border of adjacency between different target image sub-sections. Particular attention is paid to prevent the production of discontinuity in the representation of pictorial detail. Therefore, we first apply a *local registration* to all of the vertices of the frontier faces; second, we resample a new triangular texture patch for each of these faces. This new texture patch is computed as a weighted composition of the corresponding triangular sections in the associated target images;

4. **texture-patches packing:**
   All the target image sub-sections and the set of resampled triangular texture patches are packed into a single rectangular texture map, and texture coordinates in the triangle mesh are updated accordingly.

3 *Vertex–to–image* binding

The goal of this phase is to assign to each mesh vertex v both a *valid image set* and a *target image*, given the set of input images. The *valid image set* for a vertex v is defined as the subset of images $I_v = \{i_k\}$ such that v is *visible* in i_k and it is a *non-silhouette* vertex.

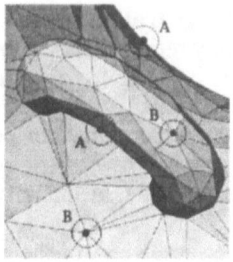

Fig. 1. Classification of the mesh vertices with respect to a given image i_k: (A) silhouette vertices, (B) non-silhouette vertices.

To verify if a vertex v is **visible** in a given image i_k we must check that: the projection of v on the image plane is contained in the image i_k, AND the normal vector in v is directed towards the viewpoint (i.e. the angle between the normal and the view direction has be lower than $\pi/2$), AND there are no other intersections of mesh M with the line that connect v and the viewpoint.

Possible mesh intersections on the line of sight are tested in the current implementation by adopting a ray casting approach, accelerated by means of a uniform grid data structure [10]. The use of an hardware-accelerated z-buffer solution is also feasible (but will produce results dependent on the rasterization resolution).

Moreover, vertices are classified with respect to a given image as: **silhouette** and **non-silhouette** vertices. In the first case, at least one face oriented opposite to the view point should exist in the fan of triangles in M that are incident in v (see Figure 1). We avoid including in the *valid set* images in which v is classified as a silhouette vertex because possible small registration errors on v are easy to notice on these images.

If for a given a vertex v the valid image set is empty, then the *vertex–to–image binding* module will request that the user takes some more images, showing the area that has not been sampled.

If, conversely, we have multiple images in the valid set, we initially select as *target image* the one such that the angle between the surface normal in v and the view direction is the smallest one, that is the image showing the lowest projective distortion with respect to a small mesh area centered in v. See in Figure 2 an example of how much distortion can be introduced while mapping an image to a nearly orthogonal mesh section.

4   Patch growing

In the previous *vertex-to-image* binding phase we worked on each mesh vertex independently, without considering vertex and face adjacency. Mesh faces are mapped to a given texture and classified as follows:

if the three vertices of a triangular face f are all linked to the same target image i_k, then face f is mapped on image i_k with texture coordinates equal to the projection of its vertices on i_k; this face is called **internal** face;

if, conversely, the vertices of f are linked to two (or even three) different target images, then face f is classified as a **frontier** face.

Because some aliasing might be introduced while resampling texture patch for *frontier* faces (multiple images composition might introduce some degradation and smooth-

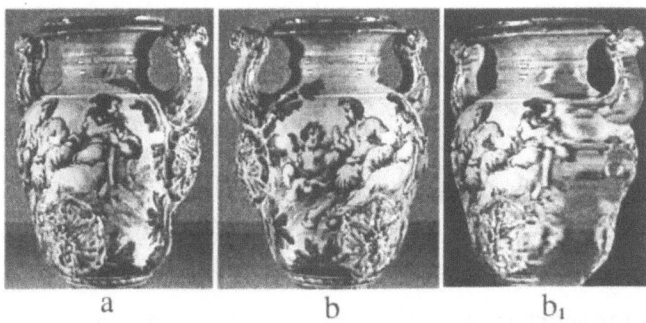

a   b b_1

Fig. 2. An example of two *target images*, (*a*) and (*b*); if we map image (*b*) on the mesh and render a synthetic image (*b₁*) using the same viewpoint of image (*a*), then we may note how poor and distorted is the detail retrieved in the right-most side of the mesh; obviously, mapping image (*a*) on this mesh section can give a much better local representation of the detail.

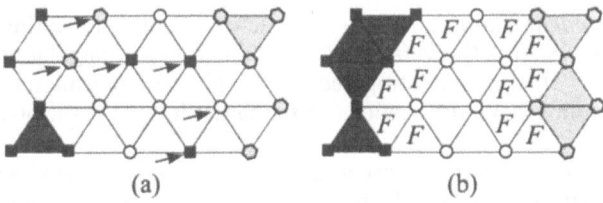

(a)   (b)

Fig. 3. Iterative local optimization of texture coverage on a sample mesh subsection: vertices are initially assigned to three target images (represented by an hexagon, a square and a circle). Then, we select a set of frontier vertices (indicated with arrows) and change their target images, obtaining configuration (b), which now correspond to a local minimum. Frontier faces are indicated with an *"F"* in (b).

ing, due to possible miss-alignment and color variation, see Subsection 5), we need to minimize the percentage of frontier faces and produce a mapping where contiguous areas of the mesh will be mapped, as much as possible, on contiguous areas of the same image.

A greedy iterative algorithm is therefore applied that analyzes each single vertex and changes the target image association (i.e. the *vertex-to-image* link) if this updates reduces the global number of frontier faces. During the iterative process a vertex can change multiple times its target image, until we get a minimum (see Figure 3). The results produced in our experiments were very good (see an example in Figure 10 in color plate and the results in Section 8). The few small isolated red regions in the figure remain after patch growing because, in this particular case, they are visible only from the red-coded image. A similar approach has been adopted in [20] to optimize the face–to–image mapping, but it is based on a more simple single step evaluation phase.

A different approach proposed by Marschner builds texture patches by taking into account only the mesh topology [13]. A disadvantage of Marschner's approach is that a complete resampling is needed to build each circular texture maps; conversely, because in our approach resampling is limited to the frontier faces only (see Section 5), our output textures are noticeably less blurred.

124

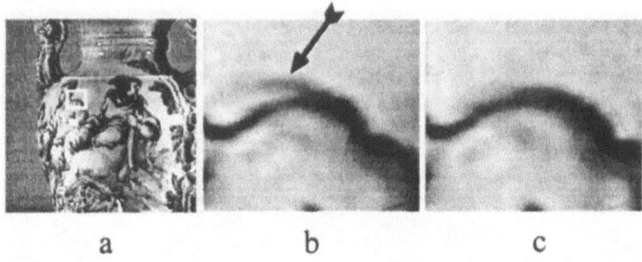

a   b   c

Fig. 4. Local registration phase: the section of the vase surface marked in image (a) is represented (magnified) in images (b) and (c); an example of the ghost effect generated by a slight miss-alignment is shown in the composite texture section shown in (b), while the more precise texture section generated after *local registration* is shown in (c).

5   Patch boundary smoothing

Other *view-dependent texture mapping* approaches blend at rendering time multiple weighted textures [8, 16]. Conversely, we resample a new triangular texture patch for each *frontier* face. This patch is computed as a weighted composition (or cross-fading) of the corresponding triangular sections of the target images associated with the face vertices.

Let us suppose that a set of three target images i_a, i_b, i_c is associated with the vertices v_1, v_2, v_3 of a given frontier face f. For each vertex of f we have the corresponding texture coordinates to the three target images. To build the corresponding triangular texture patch we have firstly to decide its resolution (in texel units); this depends on the corresponding resolution of the target images sections, to avoid to loose information while blending the images.

Then, the frontier face f is scan-convert (using the above sampling step). For each sampling point produced by the scan conversion, represented by its baricentric coordinates:
$$p = \alpha \, v_1 + \beta \, v_2 + \gamma \, v_3 \,, \quad \text{with} \quad \alpha + \beta + \gamma = 1 \,,$$
we determine the corresponding three color values $i_a[\bar{p}_a], i_b[\bar{p}_b], i_c[\bar{p}_c]$ in the three target images. The color c_p to be assigned to p (and stored in the texture patch) is therefore computed as a composition of these three values, weighted using the barycentric coordinate factors:
$$c_p = \alpha \, i_a[\bar{p}_a] + \beta \, i_b[\bar{p}_b] + \gamma \, i_c[\bar{p}_c] \,.$$

The sampling point p might be not visible on one of the target images, due to a possible intersection of the mesh M with the line of sight; in this case, the color contained in this image is relative to another section of the mesh and therefore the contribution of this image is not added (i.e. the corresponding barycentric coordinate is set to zero). Visibility is therefore checked for each sampling point and each target image, by tracing rays from p to the viewpoints.

The detection of the triangular section in each target images which correspond to a frontier face is critical, because we do not want to introduce discontinuity in the representation of detail. A potential problem can be an insufficient accuracy of the *Image Registration* phase, due to: (a) an imprecise selection of the corresponding point pairs; (b) the use of a simplified camera model that does not take into account all the possible non-radial distortions of the real camera lenses; (c) the use of limited numeric precision in the computations of the camera parameters. These misalignments may produce

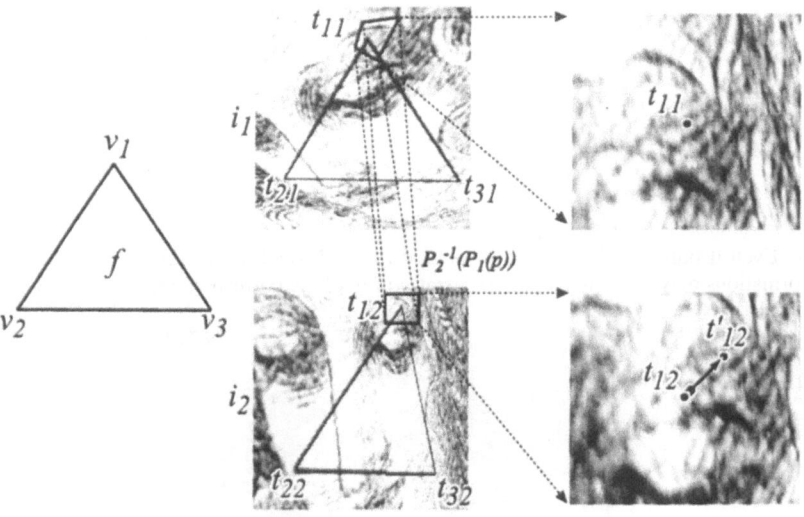

Fig. 5. Local registration of the texture coordinates of a frontier face vertices that maps on different target images.

ghost effects in the resampled triangular texture patches. Ghost effects are more easily perceivable if the pictorial detail contains very thin lines or abrupt changes of the color information (see an example in Figure 4). The vase used in our experimentation is a very challenging object, because the pictorial detail is composed by many thin painted lines.

To reduce drastically this possible aliasing we apply a *local registration* step which works on each single vertex of the frontier faces (in contrast to the *Image Registration* phase, which works on the entire image). The goal of the *local registration* is to remove small miss-alignments that can be introduced during the different phases of our overall acquisition pipeline. Our solution is completely automatic and adopts an image-processing approach (see Figure 5).

Shum and Szelinski noticed a similar problem in the registration of multiple images for the construction of panoramic mosaics [21]. They propose a local alignment solution which removes ghosting effects by dividing the images in patches, aligning the center points of corresponding patches on different images, and then warping the images.

Our solution, conversely, is *mesh-centered*, in the sense that we start from the geometric model and limit the texture warping and blending to the area associated to frontier faces. For each frontier face we simply compute a local registration of the texture coordinates of its vertices with respect to [at most] the three target images onto which the frontier face maps. Let us see how our approach works.

For each frontier face f of the mesh we have: the three target images i_1, i_2, i_3 associated with the three vertices v_1, v_2, v_3 of f; nine texture coordinates $t_{hk} \in \mathbf{R}^2$, where t_{hk} is the texture coordinate relative to the h-th vertex on the k-th image. For each image i_k is defined also a projection function $\mathcal{P}_k : \mathbf{R}^3 \rightarrow \mathbf{R}^2$ which computes the texture coordinate corresponding to each mesh point p (and obviously $t_{hk} = \mathcal{P}_k(v_h)$).

During the *local registration* phase we maintain fixed the texture coordinates t_{kk} (that is, for each vertex the corresponding coordinates on its target image remain fixed; e.g.

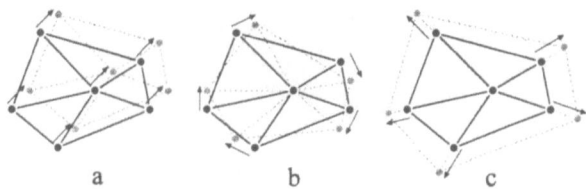

a   b   c

Fig. 6. Even if only translations are computed for each vertex, the combination of all of these transformations may result in a *affine transformation* of the corresponding target image section.

Fig. 7. As an example, a stripe of frontier faces is marked by the thick white polyline (on the left); the same *vase* section is rendered on the right.

vertex t_{11} in Figure 5). We process the vertices of face f one at the time. Starting from vertex v_1 of f, we compute an optimal translation of the texture coordinates t_{12} and t_{13} of the same vertex on the other two images. Each translation is computed by comparing independently a section of i_1 with the corresponding sections on i_2 and i_3. For example, to compute the optimal translation of t_{12}, we select on the target image i_2 a rectangular area centered on point t_{12} (see Figure 5); for each texel in this area, we compute the corresponding texel in i_1 (by projecting it firstly on mesh M using the inverse projection transformation $\mathcal{P}_2^{-1}$ associated with i_2, and then projecting the obtained 3D point again to the plane of i_1 using the associated projective mapping $\mathcal{P}_1$). Now we have two corresponding texture subsections, immersed in the same space of i_2, that can be aligned by maximizing the cross-correlation between these two image sections [3].

This process is iterated for each vertex, and returns six new texture mapping coordinates. An example of the improved texture obtained after local registration is shown in Figures 4 and 7.

Please note that even though for each vertex we compute a simple translation of its texture coordinates, the result of the application of different translations on a set of nearby vertices can also correct empirically a slight rotation or scaling error introduced in the *Image Registration* phase. An example is in Figure 6.

Obviously, if there are no features in the image sections considered then the *local registration* returns an identity transformation (but this is not a problem, because if the images have no discontinuity or features of interest, then the local registration is not

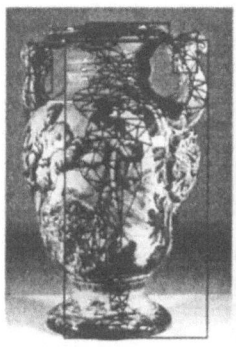

Fig. 8. On the left are shown (rendered wire-frame) the faces of M which are linked to a particular input image; in this case the corresponding texture section has an elongated shape, which can cause some space overhead in the final texture T_M (shown on the right).

needed at all).

6 Texture-patches packing

For each triangle in M we therefore have texture coordinates to either one of the initial images or one of the triangular texture patches corresponding to frontier faces. In this last sub-phase, all the target image sub-sections (e.g. the areas of the initial images that have faces mapped into) and the set of triangular texture patches are packed into a single rectangular texture map T_M, and texture coordinates in the triangle mesh are updated consequently. We store all the detail in a single texture map to allow space/time efficient rendering on standard graphics systems (e.g. OpenGL, VRML).

The first step is to extract from each target image the polygonal sections which have been linked to some faces of M. To simplify texture packing, we extract from each target image the minimal *rectangular* texture area that contains each needed section (see an example in Figure 8 in color plate, on the left). In case two rectangular areas on the same target image have a non-empty intersection, then we decide to store in T_M the bounding rectangle of their union *iff* the area of the union is smaller than the sum of the two areas (see an example in Figure 9).

As for the triangular texture patches, we join pairs of these patches to form rectangular areas (obviously, by joining pair of faces which have identical or similar size).

Then, all the rectangular texture sections are packed in a single texture T_M (see Figure 8 in color plate) by using a *cutting-stock* algorithm [2]. Even if more sophisticated solutions exist in literature for the polygonal area packing problem, this packing solution has been chosen because it is simple to implement and sufficiently efficient (at least, when the number of rectangular texture sections is not huge, as in the case of the meshes used in our experiments).

It is obvious that, once packed, a triangular texture has adjacent patches in the packed texture that are probably different from the ones assigned to the geo-topologically adjacent faces. A packed texture therefore might not produce a proper filtering across edges which are shared between all those triangle pairs that are now disjoint in the packed texture. But this problem can be simply overcome by a keen sampling of each

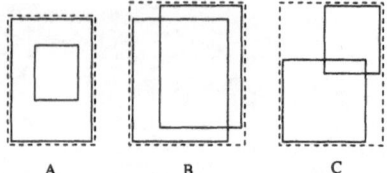

A   B   C

Fig. 9. The figure shows the possible combinatorial cases: in the case of configuration (A) and (B) we pack in T_M the bounding rectangle of the two sections (dashed area), because its size is smaller than the sum of the two areas; conversely, in case (C) it is more efficient to pack the two sections independently.

frontier face f. The associated triangular texture patch t_f is resampled few pixels larger than the required minimal size [7]. In this manner we ensure that at rendering time for each scan-converted pixel $p_i \in f$ we have that its texture coordinates are always internal to the associated discrete texture area t_f.

7 Perspective Distortion in Texture Mapping

One potential problem that can arise when mapping images taken from reality on a 3D geometry is the geometrical texture distortion that can be introduced. This because we have a non-linear perspective transformation and a corresponding bilinear texture interpolation (according to most hardware and software texture mapping systems). This means that without *image rectification* of the texture (taking into account the respective Z coordinates), textures mapped on a rendered face can appear distorted. This distortion decreases as the image viewpoint is closer to being orthogonal to the triangle face. The need to rectify textures to remove distortion also makes it difficult to merge rectangular textures, as pointed out in other papers.

In our case, the job is much simpler because we can assume to have a mesh described by small-area triangles (where triangle area is measured as the texel area of the corresponding texture subsection); in this case the distortion may be really small, and rectification may not be necessary.

Moreover, note that some recent hardware and API's now allow the use of perspective texture coordinates (u, v, w). These could be used to remove all the inherent distortion in an image-based texture map, using the distance from camera to vertex as the third w coordinate.

8 Evaluation of results

We report here the results obtained on two target objects. The first one is a ceramic *vase* of Albissola, with a height of around 40 cm. and a very complex pictorial detail (mostly thin painted lines). The *vase* geometry was acquired with a Cyberware 3030 range scanner. The mesh obtained was originally composed of 2M faces, and it was simplified down to 20,000 faces using the Jade 2.0 simplification code [6] with an accuracy of 0.17 mm. The second object is a small Capodimonte *statue* (around 25 cm. tall), whose geometry was acquired using a CT scanner. The geometry, reconstructed via iso-surface fitting on the volume model, is around 1.5M faces, and was simplified down to 10,000 faces. In both cases, detail mapping has been done starting from the simplified models.

Texture images have been acquired by using a KODAK DC210, a commercial digital still camera which can be driven by software and supports a sufficiently high acquisition resolution (1152x864) in true color. The detail of the *statue* model, that has a rather complex shape, was acquired by taking 14 different views. Conversely, only 8 views were sufficient for the *vase*.

Data processing times needed to perform the initial *Image Registration* are obviously user-dependent; in our case, the registration of each view is performed in less than 5 minutes. The automatic texture integration and patching process running time depends on the number of total images and the complexity of the object mesh (i.e. the number of faces and, only secondarily, the topologic complexity of the mesh). The running times needed to process the two test objects were 191 seconds for the *vase* and 132 seconds for the *statue* (on a SGI O2 R5000 180MHz).

The detail texture produced for the *vase* is shown in Figure 8 in color plate. A visual comparison of synthetic images and photographic images the real objects is in Figure 11 in color plate.

9 Conclusions

In this paper we have proposed a system for the semi-automatic acquisition of the pictorial detail of 3D free-form objects, and its integration with the 3D shape through standard texture-mapping. In particular, detail observed in a small set of photographic images is registered and patched on the input mesh (acquired with any automatic acquisition methodology). Advantages of the process are the very limited user-intervention required (i.e. selection of the view set, initial rough registration) and the high quality results obtained, due to the original texture patching process proposed. In particular, the global texture is produced as a patchwork of textures sections and gives a very precise representation of the observed detail because of the image-based local registration of the target images and the computation of resampled triangular texture patches for the frontier faces.

Some possible extensions on which we are now working are oriented to the reduction of the possible chromatic variations between overlapping images (possible either by increasing the width of the frontier region, or by adopting a multiresolution approach which blends only low frequency texture information [4]).

Acknowledgements
This work was partially financed by the *Progetto Finalizzato Beni Culturali* of the Italian National Research Council (CNR). Special thanks to Giovanni Braccini and Simona del Corona for the tomographic acquisition of the Capodimonte statue.

References

1. R. Baribeau, M. Rioux, and G. Godin. Color reflectance modeling using a polychromatic laser sensor. *IEEE Trans. on P.A.M.I.*, 14(2):263–269, 1992.
2. J.E. Beasley. An exact two-dimensional non-guillotine cutting tree search procedure. *Operation Research*, 33(1):49–64, 1985.
3. L. Gottesfeld Brown. A survey of image registration techniques. *ACM Computing Surveys*, 24(4):325–376, Dec. 1992.
4. P. J. Burt and E. H. Adelson. A multiresolution spline with application to image mosaics. *ACM Transactions on Graphics*, 2(4):217–236, October 1983.

130

5. S.E. Chen. Quicktime VR - an image-based approach to virtual environment navigation. *Comp. Graph. Proc., Annual Conf. Series (Siggraph '95)*, pp.29–38, 1995.
6. A. Ciampalini, P. Cignoni, C. Montani, and R. Scopigno. Multiresolution decimation based on global error. *The Visual Computer*, 13(5):228–246, June 1997.
7. P. Cignoni, C. Montani, C. Rocchini, R. Scopigno, and M. Tarini. Preserving attribute values on simplified meshes by re-sampling detail textures. Technical Report IEI-B4-37-12-98, IEI – C.N.R., Pisa, Italy, Dic. 1998.
8. P. Debevec, Y. Yu, and G. Borsukov. Efficient view-dependent image-based rendering with projective texture-mapping. *Rendering Techniques '98*, page 14. Springer Wien, 1998.
9. P.E. Debevec, C.J. Taylor, and J. Malik. Modeling and rendering architecture from photographs: A hybrid geometry- and image-based approach. *Comp. Graph. Proc., Annual Conf. Series (Siggraph '96)*, pp.11–20, Addison Wesley, 1996.
10. W.R. Franklin, N. Chandrasekhar, M. Kankanhalli, M. Seshan, and V. Akman. Efficiency of uniform grids for intersection detection on serial and parallel machines. In *New Trends in Computer Graphics – CGI '88*, pp.288–297, Geneva, Switzerland, 1988. Springer-Verlag.
11. G. Kay and T. Caelli. Inverting an illumination model from range and intensity maps. *CVGIP - Image Understanding*, 59(2):183–201, March 1994.
12. J. Lu and J. Little. Reflectance function estimation and shape recovery from image sequence of a rotating object. In *Proc. of Int. Conference on Computer Vision*, pp.80–86, 1995.
13. S.R. Marshner. *Inverse rendering for computer graphics*. PhD thesis, Cornelle Univ., 1998.
14. L. McMillan and G. Bishop. Plenoptic modeling:an image-based rendering system. In *Comp. Graph. Proc., Annual Conf. Series (Siggraph '95)*, pp.39–46. ACM Siggraph, 1995.
15. M. Petrov, A. Talapov, T. Robertson, A. Lebedev, A. Zhilyaev, and L. Polonsky. Optical 3D digitizers: Bringing life to the virtual world. *IEEE CG&A*, 18(3):28–37, May – June 1998.
16. K. Pulli, M. Cohen, T. Duchamp, H.Hoppe, L. Shapiro, and W. Stuetzle. View-based rendering: Visualizing real objects from scanned range and color data. In *Proceedings of 8th Eurographics Workshop on Rendering (St. Etienne, France)*, pp.23–34, June 1997.
17. H. Rushmeier, F. Bernardini, J. Mittleman, and G. Taubin. Acquiring input for rendering at appropriate levels of detail: digitizing a pietá. *Rendering Techniques '98*, Springer Wien, 1998.
18. H. Rushmeier, G. Taubin, and A. Gueziec. Applying shape from lighting variation to bump map capture. In P. Slusallek J. Dorsey, editor, *Eurographics Rendering Workshop 1997*, pp.35–44. Springer Wien, June 1997.
19. Y. Sato and K. Ikeuchi. Reflectance analysis for 3D computer graphics model generation. *Graphical models and image processing: GMIP*, 58(5):437–451, September 1996.
20. Y. Sato, M.D. Wheeler, and K. Ikeuchi. Object shape and reflectance modeling from observation. *Comp. Graph. Proc., Annual Conf. Series (Siggraph '97)*, pp.379–388, 1997.
21. H.-Y. Shum and R. Szeliski. Construction and refinement of panoramic mosaics with global and local alignment. In *In Sixth International Conference on Computer Vision (ICCV'98), Bombay*, pp.953–958, 1998.
22. M. Soucy, G. Godin, R. Baribeau, F. Blais, and M. Rioux. Sensors and algorithms for the construction of digital 3d colour models of real objects. In *Proceedings Intl. Conf. on Image Processing*, pp.409–412, 1996.
23. R. Szeliski. From images to model (and beyond): a personal retrospective. In *Vision Interface '97*, pp.126–137. Canadian Image Processing and Pattern Recognition Society, 1997.
24. R. Szeliski and H.Y. Shum. Creating full view panoramic image mosaic and environment maps. *Comp. Graph. Proc., Annual Conf. Series (Siggraph '97)*, pp.251–257, 1997.
25. R. Tsai. A versatile camera calibration technique for high accuracy 3D machine vision metrology using off-the-shelf TV cameras and lenses. *IEEE Journal of Robotics and Automation*, RA-3(4), August 1987.
26. Y. Yu and J. Malik. Recovering photometric properties of architectural scenes from photographs. In Michael Cohen, editor, *SIGGRAPH 98 Conference Proceedings*, Annual Conference Series, pp.207–218. ACM SIGGRAPH, Addison Wesley, July 1998.

Editors' Note: see Appendix, p. 364 for colored figures of this paper

132

direction to the incident irradiance I at a particular wavelength λ from an incident solid angle $d\omega_i$ about a given illumination direction. Representing the incident and exitant directions in spherical coordinates according to Figure 1,

$$f_r(\theta_i, \phi_i, \theta_e, \phi_e, \lambda) = \frac{dL(\theta_e, \phi_e)}{dI(\theta_i, \phi_i)}. \tag{1}$$

The BRDF is thus a function of five variables, but its domain is reduced somewhat by a symmetry called *reciprocity*, which states that reversing the light's path does not change the reflectance:

$$f_r(\theta_1, \phi_1, \theta_2, \phi_2, \lambda) = f_r(\theta_2, \phi_2, \theta_1, \phi_1, \lambda).$$

In this paper we will concentrate on the important class of *isotropic* materials, for which the reflectance is independent of rotating the incident and exitant directions about the surface normal. For these surfaces, the BRDF depends only on $\Delta\phi = \phi_e - \phi_i$, rather than on ϕ_i and ϕ_e separately, which reduces the domain from five to four variables:

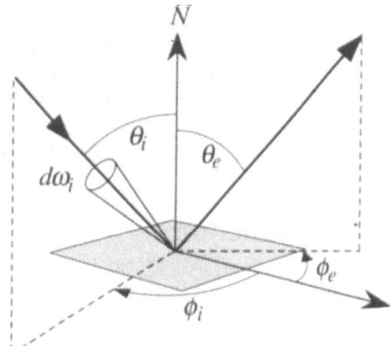

Fig. 1. Geometry of surface reflection.

$$f_r(\theta_i, \phi_i, \theta_e, \phi_e, \lambda) = f_r(\theta_i, \theta_e, \Delta\phi, \lambda). \tag{2}$$

In computer graphics, the wavelength dependence of BRDF is of interest only for the purposes of determining colors seen by human observers, so the continuous wavelength dimension can often be replaced with an appropriate discrete set of three measurements (R, G, B), further reducing the isotropic BRDF to a vector-valued function of three variables.

3 Overview of Method

A straightforward device for measuring isotropic BRDFs is shown in Figure 2a, illustrating the three mechanical degrees of freedom required. A flat sample is illuminated by a light source, and a detector measures the complete distribution of reflected light by moving around the entire hemisphere. To measure a full BRDF, this process must be repeated many times, moving the light source each time to measure a different incidence angle.

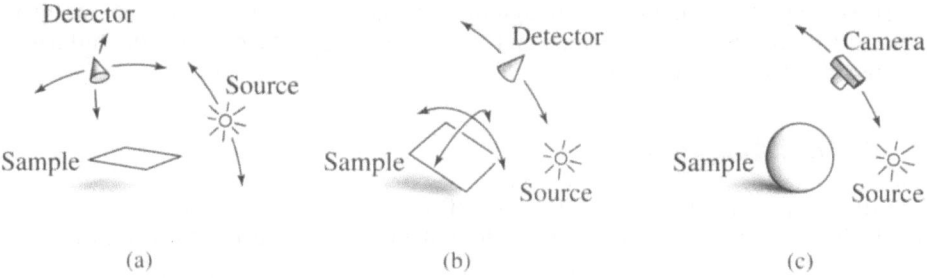

(a) (b) (c)

Fig. 2. Three BRDF measurement devices, including our image-based approach (c).

Image-Based BRDF Measurement
Including Human Skin

Stephen R. Marschner* Stephen H. Westin Eric P. F. Lafortune
Kenneth E. Torrance Donald P. Greenberg
Program of Computer Graphics
Cornell University

Abstract: We present a new image-based process for measuring the bidirectional reflectance of homogeneous surfaces rapidly, completely, and accurately. For simple sample shapes (spheres and cylinders) the method requires only a digital camera and a stable light source. Adding a 3D scanner allows a wide class of curved near-convex objects to be measured. With measurements for a variety of materials from paints to human skin, we demonstrate the new method's ability to achieve high resolution and accuracy over a large domain of illumination and reflection directions. We verify our measurements by tests of internal consistency and by comparison against measurements made using a gonioreflectometer.

1 Introduction

To render accurate images reliably and easily, the reflectance of surfaces must be simulated accurately. The most direct way to ensure correct simulation is to use physical reflectance measurements. Such measurements can guide the choice of parameters for existing reflectance models, and if they are sufficiently complete they can be used as input for renderers or provide the basis for entirely new models. To completely capture the reflectance of an opaque surface, one must measure the *bidirectional reflectance distribution function* (BRDF). BRDF measurements have traditionally been made with purpose-built devices known as *gonioreflectometers*, which are rare and expensive.

This paper presents a system that measures reflectance quickly and completely without special equipment. The method works by taking a series of photographs of a curved object; each image captures light reflected from many differently oriented parts of the surface. By using a curved test sample and an imaging detector, and by using automated photogrammetry to measure the camera position, we eliminate the precise mechanisms needed to position the source and detector in a conventional gonioreflectometer. By knowing the sample shape and the light source position, we can analyze the photographs to determine the sample's BRDF. With only a light source and a digital camera, objects of known, regular shape can be measured; adding a 3D geometry scanner extends the technique to cover a whole class of surfaces, including human skin, that are impractical to measure by other methods. Although the apparatus is simple and the measurement rapid, the resulting data are accurate and can be very complete, covering the full hemisphere almost to grazing angles.

2 BRDF Background

The BRDF, f_r, completely describes the reflectance of an opaque surface at a single point. Its value measures the ratio of the radiance L exiting the surface in a given

---

*Current address: Microsoft Research, One Microsoft Way, Redmond, WA 98052-6399

Because only the relative positions of the sample, source, and detector are relevant, all the same measurements could be made using the device of Figure 2b, in which the sample rotates with two degrees of freedom but the detector has only one and the source is fixed. The number of degrees of freedom remains the same, and all the same configurations of source, sample, and detector can be achieved.

If we replace the flat sample with a curved one, we can acquire data from many sample orientations simultaneously. Since every part of the sample's surface has a different orientation, we can use a camera to measure different parts of the surface instead of rotating the sample, as shown in Figure 2c. In this device, the two dimensions of the image sensor substitute for the two degrees of freedom of sample rotation. If there is sufficient curvature, we can make all the same measurements as the other devices, and by measuring two degrees of freedom in parallel we can greatly reduce the measurement time while increasing the sampling density.

This is the essence of image-based BRDF measurement: in an image of a curved object taken using a small light source, every pixel is in effect a BRDF measurement. Given a 3D model of the sample, camera, and light source, we can determine the incident and exitant directions for each pixel relative to the surface normal, as well as the irradiance due to the light source. Together with the radiance measured by the camera, these are all the data required to compute the BRDF.

Because a single image will only cover a two-dimensional subset of the possible BRDF configurations, many images are required to measure the whole domain. In the case of an isotropic BRDF, we are filling up the three-dimensional domain of the BRDF by measuring two-dimensional sheets, so we will need a one-dimensional sequence of images, with the camera or light source positioned differently in each.

4 Related Work

Traditionally [19,21], the three or four angular dimensions of the BRDF are handled by specialized mechanisms that position a light source and a detector at various directions from a flat sample of the material to be measured. Because three or four dimensions must be sampled sequentially, reflectance measurements are time-consuming, even with modern computer controls. Even a sparse sampling of the incident and exitant hemispheres can take several hours.

More recently, image-based methods have been used to speed measurements by gathering many angular samples at once. These methods, including the method presented in this paper, use a two-dimensional detector—the image sensor of a digital camera—to measure a two-dimensional range of angles simultaneously, leaving one or two dimensions of angle to be sampled by sequential measurements.

These can be categorized in two groups: those that attempt to measure the BRDF over its entire bihemispherical domain and those that measure some useful subset. The BRDF over an appropriate subset of the domain can be used to deduce characteristics of the surface microgeometry or to find parameters for a low-dimensional BRDF model.

One example of measuring a subset of the domain is the work of Karner et al. [15], who use images of a planar sample to measure the BRDF over a limited range of interesting angles. They use these data to fit coefficients for a simple reflectance model.

Ikeuchi and Sato [14] estimate reflectance model parameters using a surface model from a range scanner and a single image from a video camera. They use a curved sample to capture a larger range of incidence and exitance angles, but their data are still constrained to the angles provided by the illumination and view directions of a single image. Sato et al. [20] extend this method to deal with spatial variations in BRDF by

acquiring a sequence of images while the sample rotates. The image sequence provides samples along a one-dimensional path for each surface point; a simple reflectance model is fit to these data.

The surface optics literature also includes a number of approaches to measure a subdomain of the BRDF rapidly; these are generally used to deduce physical parameters of the surface itself, such as feature size on integrated circuits [12] or surface roughness [3], and often measure only at a single wavelength.

Ward describes a device [23] that is able to measure the complete BRDF of anisotropic materials. His camera captures the entire exitant hemisphere at once with a hemispherical mirror and a fisheye lens. The source and sample are moved mechanically to cover all incident angles.

More recently, Lu, Koenderink, and Kappers [17] use a cylindrical sample to give broad angular coverage in the incident plane, using multiple images with different source positions to cover all angles.

Like these other image-based systems, the system presented in this paper uses a camera to sample a two-dimensional set of angles in a single measurement, so it shares their advantages in speed and sampling density over traditional approaches. It can be thought of as a combination and extension of the techniques of Ward and Lu et al. By adopting a curved sample, it avoids the fisheye lens and hemispherical mirror of Ward's method and permits measurements much closer to grazing.[1] By using samples with compound curvature, we extend coverage from the incidence plane to the entire BRDF domain. We go beyond both of these techniques in allowing hand-held positioning, which obviates any precision source positioning mechanism, and in extending the technique to arbitrary convex objects. The method of this paper was derived from that in the dissertation of the first author [18], but it works with more general shapes, requires less equipment, and is simpler to use.

The following sections describe the specifics of our system, give the results of measuring several materials, and demonstrate the accuracy of those results by comparing them to measurements from a gonioreflectometer of verified accuracy.

5 Method

Our image-based technique can measure the BRDF of two different classes of objects: simple geometric shapes, for which the 3D shape can be defined analytically, and irregular shapes, for which the 3D model is provided by a range scanner.

Geometric shapes, such as spheres and cylinders, can be modeled and aligned precisely, giving r .easurements with low error. This approach also requires less equipment, since a range scanner is not required. However, only certain materials can be measured using these shapes—typically only paints or other man-made finishes that can be applied to such an object.

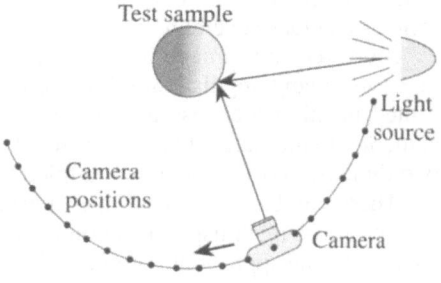

Fig. 3. Schematic of measurement setup.

If a 3D description of the sample shape is available, we can measure any convex object that has a uniform BRDF. Since we no longer have to control the geometry, it becomes possible to measure many more interesting materials. This generality has a cost, however: the limitations of the scanner introduce geometric errors that lead to noise in our results.

---

[1] Ward's device covers angles of up to 45° to 75°, depending on azimuth angle [10].

We use a hand-held camera to photograph the sample from a sequence of positions, with a single stationary light source providing the only illumination. The camera moves from a position next to the light source, which allows measurement of near-retroreflection, to opposite the light source, where we measure grazing-angle reflection (Figure 3). A few additional photographs, described below, are also taken to measure the location and intensity of the light source. In all, a typical measurement session, including the range scan and all the photographs, takes about half an hour.

The equipment we use to make our measurements includes:

- A digital still camera using a 1.5 megapixel CCD sensor with an RGB color filter array (Kodak DCS 420).
- A simple industrial electronic flash, rated at 400 W-sec output (Photogenic Machine Co. EP377).
- A structured-light range scanner, for measurements of irregularly-shaped samples (Cyberware 3030/PS).

From each pixel in each measurement image we derive one sample somewhere in the domain of the BRDF; the locations of the samples are determined by the geometry of the sample's surface and the arrangement of camera, source, and sample. As explained in Section 3, each image measures a two-dimensional set of BRDF configurations, but we take multiple images (typically about 30) from different positions to cover the full three-dimensional BRDF.

5.1 Calibration

Turning the camera images into accurate BRDF measurements requires both geometric and radiometric calibration. Geometric calibration establishes the relative positions of the light source, sample, and camera for each measurement image, and radiometric calibration determines the irradiance due to the source and the relationship between pixel values and radiance reflected from the sample.

Geometric calibration. Geometric calibration is done with photogrammetric techniques, using machine-readable targets that are placed on a structure positioned near the sample [18 (Appendix C)]. These targets are located and identified automatically in each image using ID codes embedded in the targets. The information that must be derived from the target locations includes:

- The position of the light source.
- The camera pose for each measurement image.
- The pose of the sample.

The poses of the camera are found from the image-plane target locations using bundle adjustment[2] [4, 7, 18 (Appendix B)]. Since our targets are recognized automatically and coded with unique ID numbers, no manual intervention is needed to establish correspondence between points in the various images.

There are three sets of targets: the *sample targets*, fixed with respect to the sample, the *source targets*, fixed with respect to the source, and the *stationary targets*, fixed in the room. The positions of the camera in the room are obtained using the stationary

---

[2]Bundle adjustment takes the image-plane projections of m points in n images and computes the m 3D locations of the points and the n camera poses by solving a nonlinear system of equations.

targets. Three extra images that include both the stationary targets and the source targets allow us to extract the position of the source in the room. The sample targets are used to determine the position of the sample relative to the camera positions. With the knowledge of these three relationships, the incident and exitant directions relative to the surface normal can be computed for any point on the sample. When measuring the skin of a human subject, which may change position from one image to the next (see Section 6.4), the sample position is determined separately for each frame, but when measuring inanimate samples the stationary targets are redundant, and are used only to improve position estimates. Gortler et al. [9] also used encoded targets to determine camera pose, but we have extended the technique to find sample and source positions; we also use more targets to cover a wide angular range robustly.

Radiometric calibration. In order to make BRDF measurements for each pixel, we must know the radiance reflected to the camera and the irradiance due to the source. To use a digital camera to measure radiance we must characterize both the optoelectronic conversion function (OECF), which relates the digital count reported for a pixel with the image-plane exposure, and the flat-field response, which relates the image-plane exposure to radiance in the scene. We used a calibrated reference source (Labsphere CSTM-USS-1200) to measure each of these camera characteristics.

To measure the OECF, we removed the camera lens to expose the CCD sensor directly to the source. We used a variable iris aperture and individual control of the four lamps in the source to vary irradiance through a range of more than 1600:1. A previously calibrated digital camera was used as a reference.

To measure the flat-field response, we remounted the lens (which is the principle source of flat-field variation) and took a series of exposures with the source appearing at various positions on the image plane. By fitting a biquadratic function to these images, we approximated the spatial variation across the image plane and were able to compensate for it. This procedure differs from that used previously [18 (Appendix A)] in order to reduce flare associated with the lens used here.

To determine the irradiance at each location on the surface, we approximated the source as a single point.[3] In order for this model to be valid, the source must be small compared to the distance to the sample, and its angular intensity distribution must be uniform. We measured the angular distribution of the source by capturing calibrated images of a flat, uniform surface illuminated by the flash and verified that, with an additional diffuser, it is sufficiently uniform over the range of angles we use. To get the absolute magnitude of the BRDF correct, we measured the intensity of the light source relative to the camera's three color sensitivities by photographing a diffuse white reference sample (a calibrated Spectralon target from Labsphere, Inc.) in a known position.

5.2 Data processing

Processing the measurement images to extract BRDF samples involves two steps. First, the photogrammetric targets are used to determine the geometric arrangement of the sample, camera, source, and reference white target. Second, all this information is given to a *derenderer*, which computes the BRDF values.

---

[3]While the real source only approximates a point, compensating for its solid angle requires a deconvolution process that is not trivial. We follow accepted practice of reporting our raw measurements and the solid angle of the source, which is a circle subtending 1.3×10^{-3} steradians. The solid angle of the camera's aperture, $\approx 6 \times 10^{-5}$ steradians, is negligible by comparison.

We begin by extracting the target positions in each image. This gives us the 2D image positions of the targets visible in each image and their correspondence in different images. This information is used to solve a bundle adjustment system, which computes the poses of all the cameras and the 3D locations of all the targets. It then remains to locate the model of the sample in the same coordinate system. For a cylindrical sample, a cylinder is automatically fit to the 3D locations of the sample targets, which are attached to the sample's surface. If the sample is a sphere, the user manually specifies points on the boundary of the sample in 3 or 4 images, and a tangent sphere is fit to the corresponding rays to define the sample model. For a sample of arbitrary shape, we scan the sample and the sample targets together. The targets can then be automatically recognized in the luminance image produced from the scan and transformed to their 3D positions within the scan. A rigid-body transformation aligns these scanned 3D positions with the 3D positions of the corresponding targets in the bundle adjustment results, putting the scanned 3D geometry in the same coordinate system as the camera and source positions.

The derenderer is derived from a ray-tracing renderer, and its input is a scene description including the cameras, the light source, and a model of the sample. It uses standard rendering techniques [8] to find the intersection point of each pixel's viewing ray with the sample surface and to compute the irradiance due to the source. Rather than using a BRDF value to compute the radiance reflected to the pixel, as a renderer would, the derenderer instead divides the pixel's measured radiance by the irradiance to obtain the BRDF value. The derenderer's output is a list of BRDF samples, each including the incident direction, the exitant direction, and the BRDF value for that configuration. Separate sample sets are generated from the camera's red, green, and blue pixels.

If a range scan is providing the model of the sample, the points from the scanner are tessellated to define the surface for ray intersection. To reduce the effects of scanner noise, we derive a normal to compute the BRDF at each point by fitting a plane to a weighted set of nearby points.

6 Results

We have used our image-based system to measure the BRDFs of several materials. Here, we present three materials: matte gray paint, a squash, and human skin. The matte gray paint, applied to a cylinder, allows us to verify that our BRDF measurements are accurate by comparing them with gonioreflectometer measurements. The squash and human skin demonstrate the measurement of two surfaces impractical to measure in a traditional gonioreflectometer. We have measured other materials ranging from paints to felt, a few of which are shown in rendered images.

For each of the samples, we show measurements in the incidence plane for several values of θ. Plotted with the measurements is a slice of a smooth BRDF reconstructed using local quadratic regression in the BRDF's 3D domain [5]. This technique defines a smooth, continuous function over the entire BRDF domain that follows the samples and interpolates across unsampled areas. Each curve is a slice of a 3D function fit to all the data points, not just a fit to the points visible with it. Since the curve accounts for more points than are shown, it may sometimes diverge slightly from the points. In these plots, backward scattering is on the left and forward on the right; the specular direction is marked by a vertical gray line.

6.1 Gray cylinder

To verify the correctness of our measurements, we painted a section of aluminum tubing (outside diameter 6 inches) with a sprayed gray primer. The resulting sample has a very uniform surface and is well modeled by an ideal cylinder. We measured its geometry and position using a strip of photogrammetric targets along each edge; a typical measurement image is shown in Figure 4. Because a cylinder curves only along one direction, the resulting data lie very near a two-dimensional slice of the three-dimensional (isotropic) BRDF domain; this allows us to concentrate our measurement points on the incidence plane.

Figure 6 summarizes the results of the gray cylinder measurement. Note the low noise and broad coverage—the results seem reliable out to at least 80°. The raw points shown include measurements both in the forward direction (all θ_e for the θ_i indicated on each plot) and in the reciprocal direction (all θ_i for the indicated θ_e): the scatter shown includes any deviations from reciprocity. The low scatter serves as a first validation of our measurements, since the reciprocal measurements are independent.

We measured a matching flat sample using a gonioreflectometer [6] designed according to ASTM recommendations [1] and verified to an accuracy of 5%. The gonioreflectometer results are plotted with a dashed line. Note the good correspondence to our image-based measurements; this independent measurement further validates the correctness of our method.

6.2 Squash

Having verified the accuracy of our technique, we applied it to more interesting objects. One of these, a squash, illustrates some of the strengths of our method. There is no practical way to obtain a flat sample of this surface to use in a traditional gonioreflectometer.

A typical measurement image is shown in Figure 5. Below the squash, one can see the support structure containing the sample targets (see Section 5.1); the stationary targets can be seen above it. Figure 5 also indicates the approximate subset of the geometry used in the derendering process. The top was truncated by the limits of our 3D scanner; we deleted the lower part to reduce computation time and storage demands. Even this small subset of the available data results in over 300,000 BRDF samples per channel.

The first column of Figure 7 shows the coverage obtained with this sample. The dots are plotted in a polar coordinate system, with radius indicating θ_e or θ_i and angle indicating $\Delta\phi$ ($\Delta\phi = 0$ is at the bottom; the incidence plane, where $\Delta\phi = 0$ or 180° is marked by the vertical line). We include both the forward measurements (fixed θ_i) and reciprocal measurements (fixed θ_e); reciprocity allows us to use these points to help fill the hemisphere. The points in each plot fall on rings, each consisting of samples from one measurement image. The rings appear because the angle between the illumination and viewing direction is nearly constant within each image. There are never any data within a small circle around the incident direction because we cannot physically place the camera at the source position to measure exact retroreflection.

Because of the squash's compound curvature, much of the BRDF domain is sampled. There are some gaps in the coverage; had we scanned the entire rounded end of the squash, we would have covered the entire hemisphere well. The reconstructed curves in the incidence-plane plots (Figure 7, second column) show that the dataset as a whole defines a smooth function that describes an interesting and plausible BRDF, with an off-specular forward scattering lobe but also a non-Lambertian base color. The data

Fig. 4. A typical measurement image from the gray cylinder dataset.

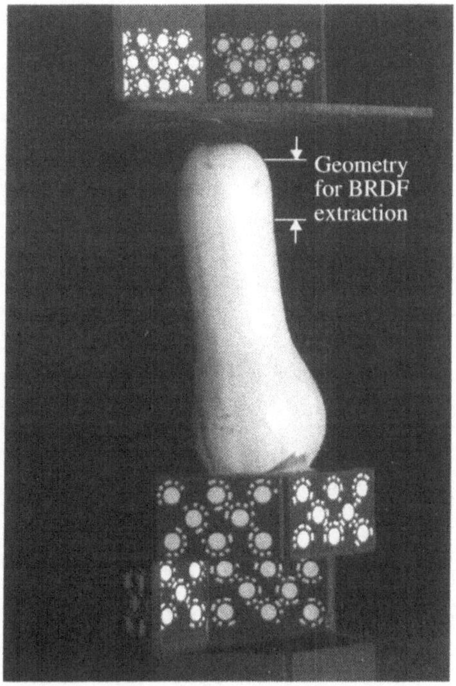

Fig. 5. A typical measurement image from the squash dataset.

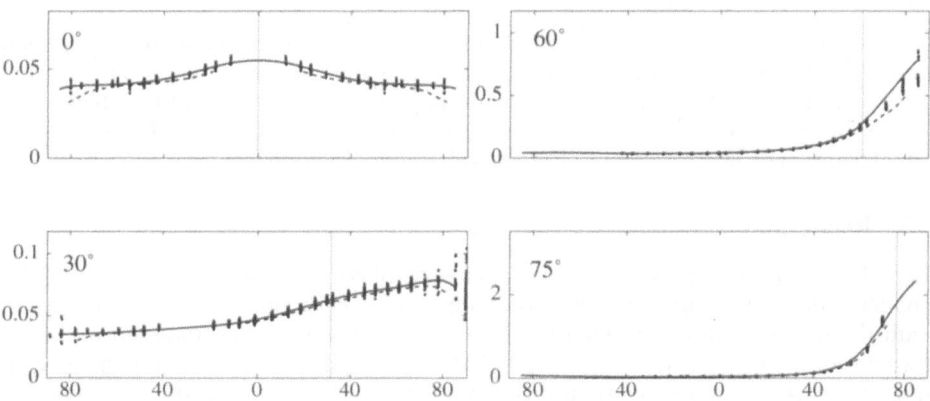

Fig. 6. Summary of results from 29 images of the gray cylinder. Points: raw measurements including reciprocal data. Solid line: local polynomial fit. Dashed line: gonioreflectometer results.

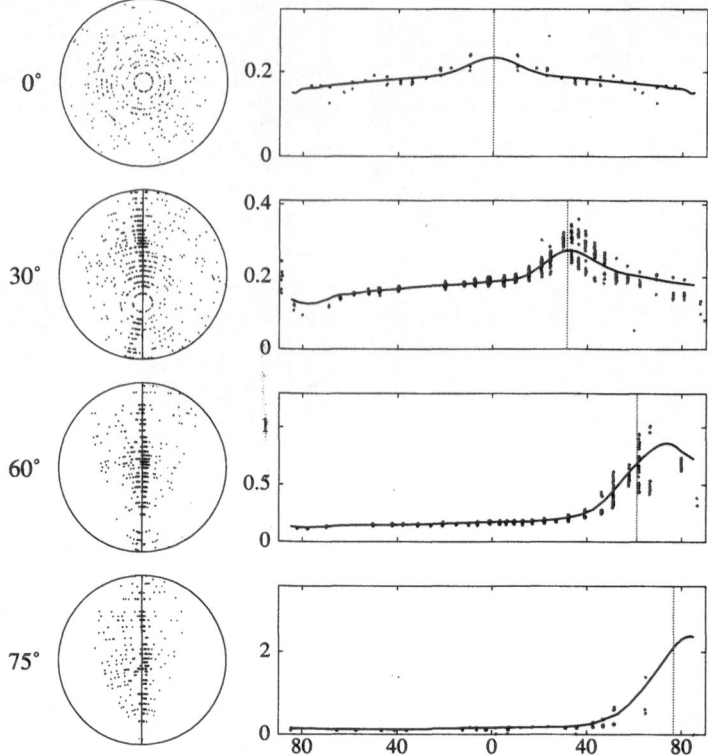

Fig. 7. Summary of results for the squash dataset. Left column: sample coverage; right column: raw data and local polynomial fit.

contain considerably more noise than do the gray cylinder data, as might be expected given the irregular nature of the surface, the noise in the 3D scanner data, and the finite precision of aligning the scanner data with the images. The slight surface blemishes visible in Figure 5 will affect the scatter plots, but have much less influence on the smoothed BRDF, as they cover only a small fraction of the surface.

6.3 Renderings

Plate 1 (see Appendix) shows some visual results of our reflectance measurements. To condense the data for tractable rendering times, the measurements were approximated with the representation presented by Lafortune et al. [16], using three cosine lobes (besides the diffuse term) for each BRDF.[4] Of course, the same data could be used in more sophisticated representations or for studies of surface optics and development of new parametric models.

The scene is rendered with Monte Carlo path tracing. It is illuminated by one over-head light source and two smaller light sources in the background, one on each side of the scene. All object surfaces show reflectances measured by our method: gray primer

---

[4]Because local polynomial reconstruction is slow and difficult to use for stochastic sampling, we did not use it for the renderings.

Fig. 8. Measurement setup.

on the floor, an unglazed ceramic on the flowerpot, blue and metallic red paints on the puzzle, and black felt on the hat. Even those surfaces that seem Lambertian in this image display distinctive directional behavior; the floor, for example, shows no visible shadows from the back lights in a Lambertian approximation.

6.4 Human skin

We adapted our method to measure the skin of human subjects. To our knowledge, our measurements are only the second angle-resolved reflectance measurements of living human skin; Cader and Jankowski have used a gonioreflectometer-like device to measure UV reflectance [2]. Our method, however, obtains many more BRDF samples in a short time (typically 20 minutes).

To accommodate a human subject, we attached our sample targets to a baseball cap worn backward by the subject. This fixes a field of targets to the subject's head; the geometry of the targets and the head together is obtained, as before, with the 3D range scanner. We selected a section of the forehead for derendering because it presents a relatively smooth, convex, uniform area of skin that is unlikely to deform during the measurement session. The hat positions the targets so as to make it easy to capture the forehead and all targets in each image.

Since the sample targets are no longer stationary, the stationary targets shown in Figure 8 provide a frame of reference for the positions of the camera, the subject, and the light source. Transforming everything into this frame for derendering allows us to accommodate minor movement of the subject's head without loss of measurement accuracy.

We measured skin BRDFs from several different subjects. Figure 9 shows coverage and incidence-plane slices of one of our data sets. Scatter is remarkably low, given the difficulties of precise geometric alignment and extracting reliable normals from noisy geometric data.

The BRDF itself is quite unusual; at small incidence angles it is almost Lambertian, but at higher angles strong forward scattering emerges. Note that the scale changes by a factor of 25 from the top row to the bottom. This scattering does not seem to correlate with the specular direction, so it cannot be simulated with a Phong function, nor would it be predicted by traditional rough-surface models such as those of Torrance and Sparrow [22] or He [13]. The only predictive model that might match these data is

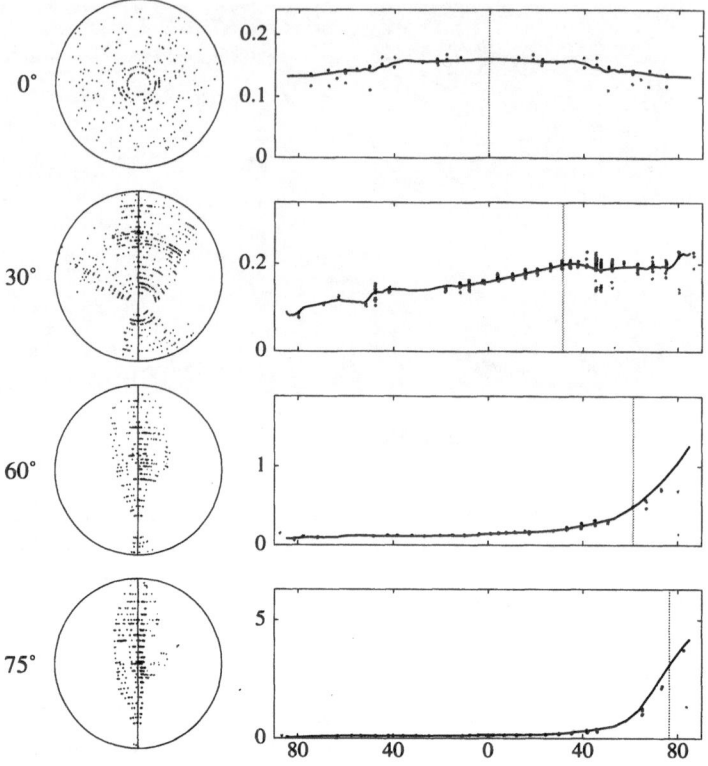

Fig. 9. BRDF of typical skin, showing coverage and scatter in raw data

the Monte Carlo simulation of Hanrahan and Krueger [11]; our data could be used to confirm or refine that method.

The renderings of Plate 2 (see Appendix) show the two extremes of our measurements to date: the BRDFs of a 43-year-old Caucasian male and a 23-year-old male from India, who exhibits not only a different skin color but also noticeably glossier skin.

7 Conclusion

This paper has described a simple technique that can measure the BRDFs of many materials using only a digital camera and a light source. We achieve accuracy rivaling that of a specialized gonioreflectometer but with much greater speed and resolution, and with one twentieth the equipment cost. In addition, the technique is versatile enough to measure living human skin. The technique is rapid because the two dimensions of a camera image sample two angular degrees of freedom instantaneously, leaving only one to be handled by sequential measurement. In a measurement session lasting under half an hour, our system can acquire hundreds of thousands of samples scattered over the full domain of an isotropic BRDF. The resulting data are internally consistent and agree closely with independent measurements.

Our technique demands samples with homogeneous BRDF, as do most traditional gonioreflectometers and almost all image-based techniques. We also require convex curved samples; this complements the capabilities of more conventional methods, which only work with flat samples. Just as some materials are most readily available as flat samples (e.g. various building materials), others, including most organic objects, are only available in curved samples.

Acknowledgments

The authors were supported by the National Science Foundation Science and Technology Center for Computer Graphics and Scientific Visualization (ASC-8920219) and by NSF Grant ASC-9523483. Dr. Marschner was also partly supported by the Hewlett-Packard Corporation, who also donated several of the workstations used in this work. In addition, we thank HP Laboratories for accommodating Dr. Marschner's work on this paper during his employment there. Measurement equipment was provided by NSF grant CTS-9213183 and by the Imaging Science Division of the Eastman Kodak Company. Special thanks to Grace Westin, Sebastian Fernandez, and Mahesh Ramasubramanian, who served as additional test subjects for skin BRDF measurements.

References

1. Standard practice for angle resolved optical scatter measurements on specular or diffuse surfaces. ASTM Standard E 1392-96.
2. A. Cader and J. Jankowski. Reflection of ultraviolet radiation from different skin types. *Health Physics*, 74(2):169–172, February 1998.
3. Raymond J. Castonguay. New generation high-speed high-resolution hemispherical scatterometer. In John C. Stover, editor, *SPIE Proceedings*, volume 1995, pages 152–165, July 1993.
4. J. H. Chandler and C. J. Padfield. Automated digital photogrammetry on a shoestring. *Photogrammetric Record*, 15(88):545–559, 1996.
5. J. Fan and I. Gijbels. *Local Polynomial Modeling and Its Applications*. Chapman and Hall, London, 1996.
6. Sing-Choong Foo. A gonioreflectometer for measuring the bidirectional reflectance of material for use in illumination computation. Master's thesis, Cornell University, 1997.
7. C. S. Fraser, M. R. Shortis, and G. Ganci. Multi-sensor system self-calibration. In *Videometrics IV*, pages 2–18. SPIE, October 1995.
8. A. Glassner, editor. *An Introduction to Ray Tracing*. Academic Press, London, 1989.
9. Steven J. Gortler, Radek Grzeszczuk, Richard Szeliski, and Michael F. Cohen. The lumigraph. In *Computer Graphics (SIGGRAPH '96 Proceedings)*, pages 43–54, August 1996.
10. Anat Grynberg and Greg Ward. A new tool for reflectometry. Monograph 161, Lawrence Berkeley Laboratory, July 1990.
11. Pat Hanrahan and Wolfgang Krueger. Reflection from layered surfaces due to subsurface scattering. In *Computer Graphics (SIGGRAPH '93 Proceedings)*, pages 165–174, August 1993.
12. Ziad R. Hatab, John R. McNeil, and S. Sohail H. Naqvi. Sixteen-megabit dynamic random access memory trench depth characterization using two-dimensional diffraction analysis. *Journal of Vacuum Science and Technology B*, 13(2):174–181, March/April 1995.
13. Xiao D. He, Kenneth E. Torrance, Francois X. Sillion, and Donald P. Greenberg. A comprehensive physical model for light reflection. *Computer Graphics (SIGGRAPH '91 Proceedings)*, 25(4):175–186, July 1991.
14. Katsushi Ikeuchi and Kosuke Sato. Determining reflectance properties of an object using range and brightness image. *IEEE Transactions on Pattern Analysis and Machine Intelligence*, 13(11):1139–1153, 1991.

15. Konrad F. Karner, Heinz Mayer, and Michael Gervautz. An image based measurement system for anisotropic reflection. *Computer Graphics Forum (Eurographics '96 Proceedings)*, 15(3):119–128, August 1996.

16. Eric P. F. Lafortune, Sing-Choong Foo, Kenneth E. Torrance, and Donald P. Greenberg. Non-linear approximation of reflectance functions. In *Computer Graphics (SIGGRAPH '97 Proceedings)*, pages 117–126, August 1997.

17. Rong Lu, Jan J. Koenderink, and Astrid M. L. Kappers. Optical properties (bidirectional reflectance distribution functions) of velvet. *Applied Optics*, 37(25):5974–5984, September 1998.

18. Stephen R. Marschner. *Inverse Rendering for Computer Graphics*. PhD thesis, Cornell University, 1998.

19. F. E. Nicodemus, J. C. Richmond, J. J. Hsia, I. W. Ginsberg, and T. Limperis. Geometric considerations and nomenclature for reflectance. Monograph 160, National Bureau of Standards (US), October 1977.

20. Yoichi Sato, Mark D. Wheeler, and Katsushi Ikeuchi. Object shape and reflectance modeling from observation. In *Computer Graphics (SIGGRAPH '97 Proceedings)*, pages 379–387, August 1997.

21. K. E. Torrance and E. M. Sparrow. Off-specular peaks in the directional distribution of reflected thermal radiation. *Transactions of the ASME*, 88:223–230, May 1966.

22. K. E. Torrance and E. M. Sparrow. Theory for off-specular reflection from roughened surfaces. *Journal of Optical Society of America*, 57(9):1105–1114, 1967.

23. Gregory J. Ward. Measuring and modeling anisotropic reflection. *Computer Graphics (SIGGRAPH '92 Proceedings)*, 26(2):265–272, July 1992.

Editors' Note: see Appendix, p. 365 for colored figures of this paper

Real-Time Rendering of Real World Environments

David K. McAllister, Lars Nyland, Voicu Popescu, Anselmo Lastra, Chris McCue

University of North Carolina at Chapel Hill, Department of Computer Science[1]

Abstract: One of the most important goals of interactive computer graphics is to allow a user to freely walk around a virtual recreation of a real environment that looks as real as the world around us. But hand-modeling such a virtual environment is inherently limited and acquiring the scene model using devices also presents challenges. Interactively rendering such a detailed model is beyond the limits of current graphics hardware, but image-based approaches can significantly improve the status quo.

We present an end-to-end system for acquiring highly detailed scans of large real world spaces, consisting of forty to eighty million range and color samples, using a digital camera and laser rangefinder. We explain successful techniques to represent these large data sets as image-based models and present contributions to image-based rendering that allow these models to be rendered in real time on existing graphics hardware without sacrificing the high resolution at which the data sets were acquired.

Keywords: image-based rendering, range data, 3D free-form objects, automatic object modeling

1   Introduction

Our goal is to walk freely in an interactively rendered, high-resolution, convincing environment acquired from the real world. We intend the prototype system presented here to be a point of reference from which others and we may advance the same goal. We have implemented an end-to-end image-based system to:

- rapidly and robustly acquire a high resolution image-based scene model,
- process the data as necessary to create a reasonably frugal representation, and
- render the scene with full detail, in real-time, onto a high-resolution display.

Our system acquires scenes consisting of a single large room containing free-form solid objects, intricate surfaces, and complex lighting. We first capture a color and shape representation of the whole scene using a laser rangefinder combined with a high-quality color CCD camera. We place the scanning rig in the scene and acquire a range scan with about ten million samples over 180° horizontally by 76° vertically. We then take a panorama of about ten color images from the same location as the rangefinder. We repeat this process for up to ten manually chosen positions. Each laser range scan takes about 20 to 30 minutes, followed by a few extra minutes to swap the camera and the rangefinder and take the color images.

The raw data must be processed in several steps to prepare a scene description suitable for real-time rendering. We first register each range scan against the others. using a straightforward method in which a user interactively selects three planes that two range scans have in common, and the rigid-body transformation is computed in closed form. This is done for each range scan in turn.

---

[1] E-mail: {davemc,nyland,popescu,lastra,mccue}@cs.unc.edu

We next register each color image with its range scan. Once this rigid-body transformation is known, the range data is projected onto the color image, converting it from scattered data in spherical coordinates to a regular parameterization on the plane, yielding color images with per-pixel depth.

One key aspect of our method is that we represent and process the scene in 2D instead of 3D. Three-dimensional scenes may be represented as a set of projections of the scene onto two-manifolds, such as image planes. This has the important storage and processing advantage that each sample only requires a single coordinate (typically depth) to be stored and computed since the other two coordinates are induced by the parameterization. Were it not for this image-based approach, we would never have been able to process and render scene models consisting of eighty million vertices.

Our depth images require several more phases of processing. We interpolate over small dropouts in the range data and flag larger missing regions (usually caused by absorption or specular reflection of the laser light) as low confidence. We approach the familiar problem of detecting surface discontinuities in a depth image using both a heuristic filter and a novel image reprojection approach.

We now merge the several depth and color images into a single image-based scene model. Again, we use a 2D projection-based approach because of its speed and its easily induced connectivity constraints. We project each depth image onto every other image, using depth comparisons to measure where the images contain the same surface and where they are distinct. For redundant regions we choose the better surface sampling and cull the others. The resulting scene representation is a set of partial depth images whose union is the set of all surfaces scanned from any position.

We render this image-based scene model using several methods – point primitives that approximate splats, triangle meshes with compositing by confidence, and a Voronoi region primitive with novel properties. The renderer runs well on commercial OpenGL-compliant hardware, but can take advantage of special-purpose primitives on PixelFlow [Eyles 1997] to obtain higher quality rendering and better performance.

The data sets shown in this paper are taken from rooms in our building – a reading room, a laboratory and a cluttered office (see Appendix). Each is a single room in which we controlled the lighting. The scenes contain plants as examples of our technique's ability to acquire free-form surfaces if sampled adequately. A major goal of our research is to acquire outdoor scenes as well as indoor. We believe our current system could be used outdoors under strict conditions described in the conclusions.

Following a section on related work, we describe the system in the order in which it is used: data acquisition, processing, and then rendering. We then present performance results and conclude with some observations and future directions.

2 Related Work

Several previous systems have shared our goal of acquiring a model of a real environment for purposes that include rendering novel views. The systems acquire geometry using either computer vision methods or laser range scanning. Of the vision methods, [Sara 1998], [Teller 1998], and [Debevec 1996] use photogrammetry or sparse correspondence to derive shape from camera images. [Laveau 1994] and [Rander 1997] both use dense correspondence to compute depth or disparity. [Laveau 1994], [Teller 1998], and [Debevec 1996] all use significant manual effort to create the model. All these systems yield both color and geometry, usually represented as a coarse polygonal model with texture maps of the surfaces, which are assumed to be diffuse. [Laveau 1994] and [Teller 1998] instead create an image-based model.

The other common method of acquiring an environment's geometry is a scanning laser rangefinder. The system of [El-Hakim 1997] is probably the most similar to our own, with a major difference being that we use far fewer measurement devices – only the laser and one color camera, and depend on these two devices to provide all registration parameters. Range data acquisition systems for environments are commercially available from K^2T, Cyra, and Acuity Research, each of which sells time-of-flight laser rangefinders. All of these have range accuracy in millimeters, however their maximum measurable range varies from 15m to 100m. The Acuity rangefinder is a kit, but Cyra's Cyrax scanner and K^2T's SceneModeler both come as complete products with software to produce 2D and 3D standard format environment models. These two systems do not currently provide color, but only point clouds or simplified polygonal models.

Another class of scanning systems scans objects, rather than whole environments. This distinction will become important in our approaches to several aspects of this work. The most advanced object scanning systems are probably those of [Rushmeier 1998] and [Sato 1997]. Both are able to provide more surface detail than just diffuse color, and both use controlled lighting. [Sato 1997] returns coarse specular surface properties, which is an important step, but since the system acquires shape from silhouette, currently the object must be small enough to fit on a turntable. The [Rushmeier 1998] system cleverly acquires bump maps by controlling the lighting, then simplifies the geometry heavily, leaving the detail in the texture and bump maps. Unlike these two systems, we will make no attempt to derive surface material properties of the many objects in the scenes that we scan since our current goal of acquiring a scene and rendering it exactly as it originally appeared does not require relighting. These two systems as well as commercial object scanning systems from Cyberware, Real3D, and Minolta typically use range image registration systems like [Besl 1992], and important variants such as [Turk 1994], followed by meshing systems like [Curless 1996]. Promising recent work by [Whitaker 1998] robustly generalizes this method, but typically imposes surface smoothness constraints.

We represent and render our scene using an image-based model, rather than the typical simplified polygonal mesh with textures. The Light Field [Levoy 1996] and Lumigraph [Gortler 1996] image-based models consist of a dense set of rays regularly parameterized over four dimensions, typically a 2D grid of 2D images. These models have been acquired for real objects, but not for real environments. When they are, we expect the results to be very pleasing, since they will automatically reproduce view-dependent lighting effects for the original lighting.

Other image-based models represent a scene using sparse images, augmented with camera parameters or range images. These systems store far less data by assuming that surface radiance is view-independent. [Chen 1993] and [Chen 1995] constrain the viewer to positions for which the model can accurately reconstruct a view. [McMillan 1995], [Rademacher 1998] and [Shade 1998] allow any viewpoint to be reconstructed, but exhibit artifacts due to an incomplete model. The latter two systems and ours each use different means of representing a more complete model than the original system.

3 Data Acquisition

To acquire color and range scans of real environments, we have assembled a system consisting of a rangefinder, a high-resolution digital camera and a pan-tilt unit. All of these components are controlled by a PC and were put together on a cart, with the rangefinder placed approximately at eye-level, (see Appendix). We manually place the scanning rig in locations that attempt to maximize the amount of visible detail. The range and color data have a relatively high resolution of 20 to 25 samples per degree, requiring about 250MB for the raw data from a single 180° x 90° panorama. The total cost of the hardware was less than $35,000. To share our experience in building this acquisition system we will describe each component.

3.1 Scanning, Panning Laser Rangefinder System

The scanning laser rangefinder is an infrared 8mw Acuity Research LIR-4000. It is a time-of-flight (as opposed to triangulation) rangefinder that modulates the laser light to set up an interference pattern, determining the distance from the frequency of the best interference. The rangefinder can measure distances from 0 to 15m at up to 50,000 range readings per second, with precision better than 1cm. A mirror, 45° off-axis, rotates about a shaft with a 2000-position encoder to sweep out a plane.

The pan-tilt unit, a Directed Perception PTU-70-15, has a very clean interface, making programming very simple. The stepping resolution is 14,000 steps in 180°, or about 78 positions per degree, but we typically take data at every third or fourth position. The spinning mirror and panning motor combine to allow the laser to sweep out a longitude-latitude sphere.

The data produced for each rangefinder sample includes range, intensity of the returned laser light, the ambient light subtracted out, and the shaft-encoder position. Using a slower sampling rate and shorter maximum measurable range improves the range data quality, since it can find the proper interference frequency more quickly. We typically acquire 16k to 25k samples per second, with a maximum measurable range of 6m, and the mirror spinning approximately 4 RPS.

During acquisition, raw data is streamed to disk. This consists of the range, the angles of the mirror and panning unit, and the strength of the reflected laser light. The samples are not regular in longitude and latitude, since the rangefinder and scanning mirror are not synchronized.

As with any rangefinder, system calibration has taken considerable effort. For instance, we have determined that the pan-tilt unit includes about 14,039 steps in 180°, not 14,000. The 45° mirror actually has an angle of 44.8°. While these discrepancies may seem small, an error of several centimeters occurs for objects only 3m away. Other values that require calibration are the shaft encoder position of the horizon and the rotation of the pan-tilt unit caused by the weight of the rangefinder. We have experiments to calibrate these factors and we apply corrections in software.

3.2 Digital Camera

In order to capture color imagery, we remove the laser from the pan-tilt unit and replace it with a Canon EOS2000 digital camera (also sold as the Kodak DCS520). The camera is built on a 35mm single-lens reflex body, has a resolution of 1728 by 1152 pixels with up to 12 bits of color data per channel, and an IEEE 1394 (Firewire) interface. We use a Canon 14mm flat-field lens for several reasons. First, the camera's CCD sensor is not as large as a 35mm-film image, so any lens on this camera will have a narrower field of view than on a film camera. Second, since we fix the focus and aperture for all images in the panorama, we require a large depth-of-field. Our typical setting is f/11, allowing us to focus the lens such that everything between 0.5m and infinity is in focus.

We built a mount that makes the camera's nodal point coincide with that of the laser and both devices rotate about this point. This was key to achieving high quality registration of color and range data (see Section 4.2). We mount the camera vertically and pan the camera to acquire color images covering the field scanned by the laser.

3.3   Camera Calibration

Knowing the camera parameters is crucial for registration of color and range and for rendering with the resulting images. Although the camera parameters could be determined during the registration of the color and range images, the registration is more robust and efficient when the intrinsic camera parameters are determined beforehand. We used the [Tsai 1986] camera calibration algorithm to find the intrinsic parameters of our camera and lens, which is modeled as a simple planar pinhole with one coefficient of radial distortion.

The calibration routine takes in three-space points and their projections on the image plane. The fiducials are the corners of black and white checkerboard squares on a 1 x 2-meter planar grid. We mounted the camera on an optical rail perpendicular to the grid and took images at several positions along the 1-meter rail in order to change the depth of the fiducials, yielding a total of 1460 fiducials.

The fiducial image locations are detected automatically at sub-pixel precision by correlating a single checkerboard square template with the image. The template is divided into four parts by two lines that pass through its center. The slopes of the two lines and the center coordinates are all varied to optimize the correlation.

Since the camera has a wide-angle lens and a high resolution CCD, the radial distortion is significant. The corners of the image are thirty pixels closer to the image center than they would be for a pinhole camera. Before the images are used, they must be undistorted using the radial distortion coefficient determined by calibration.

The measured calibration error was quite small. The 3D locations of the fiducials were projected using the calibrated camera parameters and their distance to the actual image plane locations was computed. The mean distance was 0.66 pixels, with a max of 5.09 pixels. Then the 2D fiducials were projected to three-space using their original three-space depth and the calibration results, and their distance to the actual 3D locations was computed. The mean was 0.62 mm and the max was 2.94 mm. The entire calibration experiment was done twice with almost identical results. This and the small measured error lead us to believe that the camera calibration is quite accurate enough for our application, which is confirmed by the rendering results.

4   Processing

Once the color images and range scans have been acquired they must be converted into a form suitable for efficient storage and image-based rendering. This includes registering all scan positions into a common reference frame, finding each color image's rotation relative to the rangefinder, creating a depth image for each color image based on the range scan, marking surface discontinuities in each depth image and finally culling redundant image portions, yielding a final image-based model.

4.1   Registration of Multiple Positions

Since several scans of the room will be combined into a single model we must register them into a common coordinate system. The registration process will yield a transformation matrix that rigidly translates and rotates a scan to match the others.

We register a pair of scans by manually identifying corresponding planar surfaces in the range data, then use their plane equations to align them. First we map the points from spherical to Cartesian coordinates and then select in each scan three non-parallel planar surfaces that exist in both. The best-fit plane (in the least squares sense) is calculated for each of the selected surfaces using code from [Eberly 1998]. Once these planes are known, a rotation makes the first plane from each scan parallel to each other, a second rotation makes the other two planes as nearly parallel as is possible, and finally a translation aligns the scans. Since each selected plane includes about 50,000 samples, the best-fit plane is robustly computed and, assuming the three are fairly linearly independent, the resulting transformation makes corresponding planes parallel to within 0.5°. Scene features that are far from the selected planes are sometimes misregistered by several centimeters because of imperfect calibration of the scanning rig. We wanted to evaluate this new approach on indoor scenes, but will probably replace it with a deformation-based registration method.

4.2 Registration of Color and Range Data

The laser rangefinder data is used to provide a depth value for each pixel of the color images, and the resulting color-depth images will be used in rendering. Since the color images were taken with a different device than the range scans, the two must be registered, matching each range sample with the right color pixel. We take care to place the camera's nodal point at the same physical location as the laser's center of rotation, and to rotate both devices about this point. This homographic relationship simplifies the registration to the camera's three rotations relative to the laser. Having no translation greatly increases the quality of our registration and of our final images because it bypasses a projective warp and the associated image resampling.

We use fairly standard image-processing techniques to register each color image with the spherical range image. Simply, we want to find the orientation of the camera image that best correlates with the rangefinder image. Since we have the infrared intensity image, it would seem that we could correlate this directly with the color image (or perhaps with a grayscale representation or just the red channel of the color image). But the illumination of the two images is so different that simple image correlation gives poor results. Specifically, the laser image is illuminated directly by the laser itself; it has no shadows, the entire scene is equally illuminated, and specularities occur in different places than in the normally lit scene.

Instead of correlating the images directly, we correlate edges of the color and range images. The color photograph has high edge strength nearly everywhere in the image because of the high spatial frequency of the natural scene and because of noise in the camera's sensor. In order to find just the salient edges we preprocess the color image using a variable conductance diffusion filter. See [Yoo 1993] for details, but briefly a VCD filter is similar to convolving the image with a gaussian (a standard low-pass filter), but VCD also attenuates each pixel's weight on the pixel at the center of the filter kernel by a gaussian evaluated at their distance in color space[2]. This causes pixels to blend with their neighbors (reducing high frequencies or edge strength), but pixels blend less across sharp boundaries (salient edges) because the boundary in color space is too great. Salient edges act as insulators to the blurring operation, hence the name variable conductance diffusion. Since this operation does not have a closed form solution it is performed iteratively[3]. The total process takes about one minute for a 2Mpixel image.

---

[2] We use RGB, but another color space such as LUV may give better results.
[3] We performed six iterations, with an image space gaussian of st. dev. 2.5 pixels and a color space gaussian of st. dev. 3.5 intensity values (on 0 to 255).

We then apply an edge detector to the VCD-blurred color image and list the edge pixels that had a partial derivative in either axis for any color channel greater than a threshold. We match these edges against the spherical laser image after correcting them for the barrel distortion in the color image (see Section 3.3).

We prepare the spherical range image for correlation by running an edge detector on the laser intensity image and on the range image and storing the combined result as an edge image[4]. To provide a smoother gradient for the image correlation optimization process we convolve the edge image with a kernel that has very broad support (we chose 21 pixels) and a steeply increasing gradient near the center of the kernel. This makes potential solutions have a better error value when they are near the solution (so the optimizer knows it is close), but the best solution has a significantly smaller error than any approximate solution.

The registration proceeds by optimizing the correlation of the edge images. We optimize for the three angles orienting the planar camera image relative to the spherical laser image. Imagine rotating the planar image, looking through each of its edge pixels to sample the corresponding location on the spherical edge image. The objective function is the sum of the squares of the sampled edge strengths. We use a downhill simplex optimization algorithm, but an abundance of local minima force us to restart often, which is done with a variant of simulated annealing in which the algorithm evaluates many solutions and then refines on several of the better solutions. The entire registration process takes about ten minutes for one color image. This optimization algorithm converges given a nearby approximation that can be obtained from the pan-tilt unit's position, or a manual guess. See Appendix for a result.

4.3 Planar Projection

We now create a planar, pinhole image with per-pixel range. This involves two stages. We first undistort the color image to correct for barrel distortion (see Section 3.3), resampling using a bilinear basis function.

Then, given the rotation resulting from each color image's registration process, we are prepared to create the range map for this color image. Note that the data returned from the rangefinder must be filtered before being used because some surfaces do not return accurate values, and noise causes outliers. Also, the rangefinder integrates its sample over a finite aperture, rather than point sampling, due to the continuous mirror rotation during the sampling period. Thus, when sampling a silhouette edge, the returned range value will generally be a point floating in space between the two surfaces. Also, the range samples are not regularly located in longitude and latitude – each has an arbitrary theta and phi. In order to filter the range samples to address all these issues, we first regularize the data on a planar grid. We project the raw, scattered rangefinder samples onto the image plane using a bilinear basis for the support of each splat, and store for each pixel a list of all range samples that touch the pixel and their associated weights. Changing the size of the splat controls the size of dropouts that are filled. We must then properly filter this layered range image, which is a difficult problem. Convolving range images with standard filters creates additional unwanted outlying range values [Shade 1998]. Our approach is to cluster each pixel's list of samples, using a threshold to direct the clustering. The weighted mean of the largest-weight cluster becomes the pixel's range value. This method allows proper

---

[4] Since the IR image is perfectly registered with the range image, the two can be summed without confusing the resulting edge image.

filtering of range samples in the interior of a surface, but avoids creation of floating samples at silhouette edges because the two sides will fall into different clusters. This method works well on standard, solid surfaces of the type that our scenes include, but is no improvement over current methods for areas of very high range frequency.

We now have the finished range image. We chose to represent the range values as generalized disparity [McMillan 1995], which is the distance from the center-of-projection (COP) to the pixel on the image plane divided by the distance from the COP to the surface sampled. This is a simple conversion from the range value. Range values are inappropriate for rendering because range cannot be projected onto a view plane using a projective transformation, but generalized disparity can.

We also store a flag byte for each pixel with information needed when processing or rendering this pixel. One flag bit marks bad pixels (invalid color value, invalid range value, etc.). We store the color, range, and flag components and the image's camera matrix (described below) in a TIFF file variant. A full-resolution image is approximately 13 MB and takes about three minutes to create.

4.4 Finding Silhouette Edges

One method we use to reconstruct an image from the projected pixels of a source image is to treat the source image as a regular mesh and rasterize the mesh, similar to [Mark 1997]. As they note, when this mesh is projected to other viewpoints it can tear at silhouette edges. It is inappropriate to interpolate across silhouette edges because the interpolated surface does not really exist in the environment. We must detect silhouette edges and mark them using flag bits to avoid rasterizing these false surfaces or "skins". We present two methods for detecting silhouette edges in range images.

Our first approach is similar to a common solution from the range scan literature – reject all polygons that are at grazing angles (cf. [Pulli 1997]). This heuristic works well for solid surfaces. We use a similar, more efficient heuristic, based on range images being locally planar except at silhouettes. To quickly detect planarity we note that generalized disparities of equidistant, collinear pixels increase linearly only when they sample points on a line (or a plane) in 3D. A formal proof is straightforward, but the key is that generalized disparity is inversely proportional to eye-space Z. Simply convolving directional second derivative operators with the generalized disparity map yields a surface planarity map. We mark all pixels with planarity below a threshold as silhouette edges. Since depth and range do not vary linearly in perspective images they are less appropriate for planarity detection than generalized disparity.

Our second method detects only those silhouette edges that are truly skins (false surfaces assumed to exist because we have no data indicating otherwise), versus those surfaces that happen to be viewed very obliquely. A false surface may occlude some real surface seen in another view. Thus, we can detect a mesh triangle as a skin by viewing it from the viewpoint of some other source image and comparing Z buffers to detect occlusions. For example, in Figure 1, to detect the skins in source image **A** we warp it to the viewpoint of source image **B**, computing the projected Z as part of the warp. We reconstruct the projected samples using a regular triangle mesh. We refer to the image resulting from warping A to B as A'. Now, any pixel whose Z value in **B** is greater than in A' indicates a skin in image A since the Z value of the pixel in **B** is in effect making the statement that space is empty up to this given Z value. But the pixel from A' claims to exist in that empty space, so we mark as a skin the mesh triangle in A that projected to this pixel. This useful notion of range images making a statement about empty space is used for other purposes in [Curless 1996] and elsewhere.

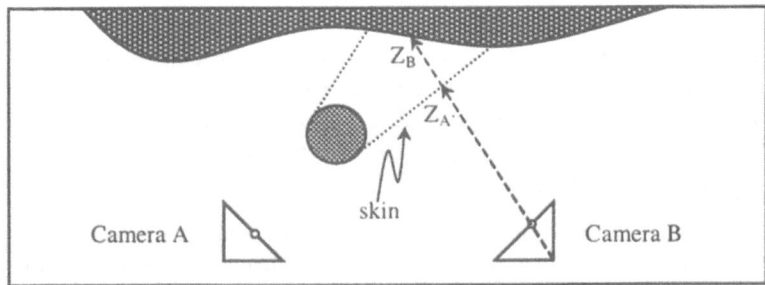

Fig. 1. Finding silhouette edges in image A by projecting it to the viewpoint of image B. Pixels with $Z_B > Z_{A'}$ indicate skins in image A.

The algorithm warps each source image **A** in the model to the point of view of all other images **B**, comparing Z-buffer **B** with the warped Z-buffer **A'**. For the pixels failing the Z test[5], we flag a skin in the source image. This is easily done by rasterizing an item buffer for **A'** indicating which mesh triangle of **A** is visible (see Appendix). Since one skin may occlude another skin, we must repeatedly warp **A** to **B** until a warp can be done with no skins found. We then warp **A** to the next image **B**. The running time is quadratic in the number of images. For our data sets of 40 to 100 images, the whole process takes less than an hour with high-end graphics hardware. This algorithm is well-suited to graphics hardware because the core of the algorithm involves rasterizing triangle meshes and comparing Z buffers.

This method worked well and gave results similar to the planarity heuristic. No skins were marked incorrectly. Some skins were not found because no source image could "see through" that skin. In practice, this works well. If the source images are assumed to represent the region from which a user will see the environment, keeping these skins will prevent the user from ever seeing disocclusion errors that could have been filled using a skin. Another practical value of this reprojection-based silhouette edge finder is that it gives rise to a whole class of range image processing algorithms based on projecting one range image to the point of view of another. This lets model processing and other typically-3D operations be performed in image space where pixel connectivity and occlusion properties are known. [Seitz 1998] includes similar goals, but computes correspondence between pixels in different source images using a cleverly-created explicit voxel representation instead of a reprojection warp.

4.5 Image Tile Primitives

In order to process and render from portions of source images instead of from entire images, we use an image tile primitive. A tile is a higher-order primitive than a pixel sample, but smaller than a whole image. We use tiles for culling redundant imagery from the data set, view-frustum culling, and distributing the work over parallel rendering hardware. Tiles can be any size, and do not all need to be the same size, though our standard size is 32x32 pixels. Tiles need to be large enough that overhead is negligible, but small enough that culling on a per-tile basis is efficient. [Grossman 1998] used image tiles with goals similar to ours, but stored different per-pixel data such as a surface normal.

A tile primitive contains the color, disparity, and flag bits of each pixel, plus the minimum and maximum disparity values and the 4x4 matrix **M** that projects the tile's pixels to their 3D locations. This matrix is the concatenation of three matrices:

---

[5] We perform a soft Z comparison using glPolygonOffset, to allow for error and discreteness in the images. We then draw the image again using wide lines to account for error in X and Y.

$$\mathbf{M} = \mathbf{R}\,\mathbf{E}\,\mathbf{T} \tag{1}$$

T is the offset of this tile within the full image, allowing pixels to be indexed relative to the tile. **E** is the camera matrix determined in Section 3.3, describing the projection of a pixel to a point in space. **R** is the transformation of this camera pose in world space from the registration process of Section 4.2.

4.6 Culling Redundant Scene Data

Since each surface may appear in multiple source images we select one image to represent each piece of surface, and cull the others from our representation. Our tile culling preprocess loads all source images and evaluates each tile, deciding whether to include it in the final scene description, or cull it. First, the tiles are ranked by their intrinsic quality: We count how many pixels are flagged as skins or as having low-confidence range values. We compute the tile's average range value as a metric of sampling density. And we compute the range variance, as a metric of viewing angle – the lower the variance the less oblique the viewing angle.

We step through the tiles from worst to best, attempting to reject each tile by projecting it to the point of view of each other source image and comparing the two in that image space. As in finding silhouette edges (see Section 4.4), we compare Z values in the space of the second image. For pixels whose projected Z is similar to that stored in the image (which we sample bilinearly), the two pixels sample the same surface. For these pixels we compare their quality (their range and viewing angle), and keep the higher quality pixel. By adding a threshold when comparing, we vary how aggressively the tiles are culled. After projecting a tile to all source views, if all its pixels have been rejected, we can cull the entire tile. We believe that this approach to combining multiple source images into a scene description has great potential that we have not fully explored. One of its advantages is that it is non-redundant, similar to a Layered Depth Image [Shade 1998], and yet is constructed without resampling the pinhole camera source images, unlike an LDI. The rendering efficiency is basically equivalent to that of an LDI.

5 Rendering

A simple interactive application allows the user to explore the image-based environment. The application is implemented using OpenGL and runs on a Silicon Graphics Onyx2 with InfiniteReality2 graphics, or on PixelFlow [Eyles 1997]. With smaller data sets, the application also runs on a PC.

The application's rendering primitive is an image tile. To render a tile we first concatenate the tile's projection matrix **M** (see Section 4.5) with the OpenGL model-view matrix **V** and projection matrix **P**.

$$\mathbf{C} = \mathbf{P}\,\mathbf{V}\,\mathbf{M} \tag{2}$$

The matrix **C** maps points in the image tile of the form $<x, y, 1, d(x,y)>$ to points in homogeneous space. $d(x,y)$ is the generalized disparity at point x,y.

Using this transformation matrix, the program attempts to trivially reject tiles that project entirely off-screen. The extrema of the x, y, and disparity dimensions of the tile form a bounding volume, which is projected and clipped against the screen. View frustum culling simply rejects the entirely off-screen tiles. From typical viewpoints, approximately 65% of all tiles are rejected at this stage. Using a standard-sized tile, the cost of the culling test is less than 1% of the cost of projecting all the tile's pixels.

On PixelFlow, we wrote a custom primitive [Olano 1998] to incrementally transform the x, y, and z columns of the matrix, so each pixel requires only the multiplication with the disparity coordinate, which varies arbitrarily from pixel to pixel [McMillan 1995]. This incremental transformation reduces the cost to one fourth of the multiplication operations of a standard vertex. Converting from NDC space to screen space using the OpenGL viewport and depth range transformations [Neider 1993] finishes the transformation. Note that this transformation yields a screen-space Z value, which will be used in compositing.

One problem in McMillan-style image-based rendering is correctly resolving visibility when projecting multiple source images into a single output image. The occlusion-compatible image traversal order allows any individual image to resolve self-occlusions but provides no means of compositing multiple source images. An inverse warping renderer [McMillan 1997] addresses this problem by searching all source images to find the front-most surface at each pixel, as in ray tracing, but incurs a cost penalty. The Layered Depth Image [Shade 1998] resolves visibility *a priori* by resampling onto an intermediate layered image [Max 1996] and then using the occlusion-compatible order. Our approach is to use standard Z-buffer composition to resolve visibility. This allows compositing of standard geometric primitives with image-based primitives. Z-buffering hardware is ubiquitous and the additional cost of computing Z at each sample is minimal.

Once the source image samples have been projected to the screen, the last remaining issue is reconstructing an image from this scattered data. For this interactive system, we have explored several reconstruction strategies.

5.1 Point-Based Reconstruction

Our simplest reconstruction method is to render each sample using GL_POINTS. On the SGI IR2 this is fairly fast if the primitives are placed in display lists. However, the reconstruction quality is worse than rendering as triangles because we have poor control over each sample's footprint. Also, most graphics hardware does not properly accelerate point primitives although it is becoming increasingly important to do so.

5.2 Triangle Mesh Reconstruction

An image tile can be treated as a regular mesh, with the tile pixel positions and range values dictating the mesh vertex positions, and the pixel colors being used as the vertex colors [Mark 1997]. Each square of the mesh can be interpolated using a bilinear patch or simply using two triangles. Many people have used this approach to render height fields on graphics hardware [Taylor 1993].

Our mesh never exists explicitly as 3D geometric primitives, but is projected from the source-image tile directly to the screen. The pixel colors are linearly interpolated across the mesh. When the tile pixels being interpolated are samples of a single continuous surface, this method works quite well and provides excellent reconstruction quality. Reconstruction algorithms for image-based rendering often exhibit gaps when the source image pixels project sparsely onto the screen because the algorithms use a splat size with too small a support for the given projection. Reconstructing by linearly interpolating adjacent samples as we do here avoids these gaps. But in order to avoid interpolating across disocclusions, we check the skin bits of each sample (see Section 4.4) and cull mesh triangles that cross silhouette edges.

5.3 Compositing by Confidence

Since many different source images may view a given surface in the scene, we cull the redundant image area as a preprocess, but some overlaps remain to prevent seams. These overlap regions cannot be satisfactorily resolved by the Z composite because, being images of the same surface, they have nearly identical Z values. We want to composite in the way that gives the best results in regions of overlap. An alpha composite is a common choice here (cf. [Pulli 1997]), but the results are often blurry.

We implemented on PixelFlow a quality-based compositing operation similar to the confidence compositing in [Mark 1997]. Our method primarily composites by Z, but when two instances of a surface exist, the better-sampled surface remains visible. Our sampling quality metric is the screen-space density of the projected samples – the denser the sampling, the higher the resolution of the rendered frame. We measure sampling density for each triangle to be rasterized as the triangle's area, which is already computed as part of triangle rasterization. To implement this compositing efficiently we scale the triangle's area and add it to the Z value of each vertex, yielding Z'. When rasterizing the triangle we interpolate Z' instead of Z and perform the depth composite on Z' values. This takes no more work per pixel than depth compositing and required no change to our graphics hardware. This method is also order-independent, unlike alpha compositing. The result of this composite is that larger triangles (worse-sampled surfaces for this projection) will be pushed back more in Z than smaller triangles and so will lose to denser samplings of the same surface.

5.4 Quadratic Splat Primitive

When samples project sparsely onto the screen (less than one source sample per screen pixel) the continuous interpolation provided by triangle mesh reconstruction is a significant quality advantage over other reconstruction methods. However, in many systems like ours the samples often project more densely than one source sample per screen pixel. Reconstructing as triangles is inefficient since their area is often smaller than half a pixel. Both the transformation and rasterization work are overkill. A geometrically simpler primitive such as a point would alleviate this inefficiency [Levoy 1985; Grossman 1998], and would be applicable whenever the screen density of primitives approximates or exceeds the screen's pixel density (as in high-resolution image-based or volume rendering).

We have developed and implemented on PixelFlow a primitive that reconstructs the image from the projected samples by rasterizing each sample as a solid-colored circle that has a quadratic falloff in depth. One of these quadratic splats can be rasterized in less than one third the clock cycles needed to rasterize two triangles per sample. The falloff in depth normally causes each pixel to receive the color of the closest sample. This is similar to the technique of rendering Voronoi regions by rasterizing a cone for each sample [Haeberli 1990], which [Larson 1998] used for reconstruction in image-based rendering. Unlike cones for Voronoi regions, our splat centers do not all have the same Z value. Rather, they have the sample's Z value at the center and increase quadratically toward the circle's edge. This allows compositing for visibility and reconstruction to both be done with a single Z composite.

Figure 2 shows an example of reconstructing samples from two images using the quadratic splat primitive. Note that both source images contribute to the final image, with source image 1 having a greater contribution because it is better sampled.

The primitive's quadratic shape approximates the central lobe of a gaussian splat's alpha component, as used in volume rendering [Westover 1990] but the

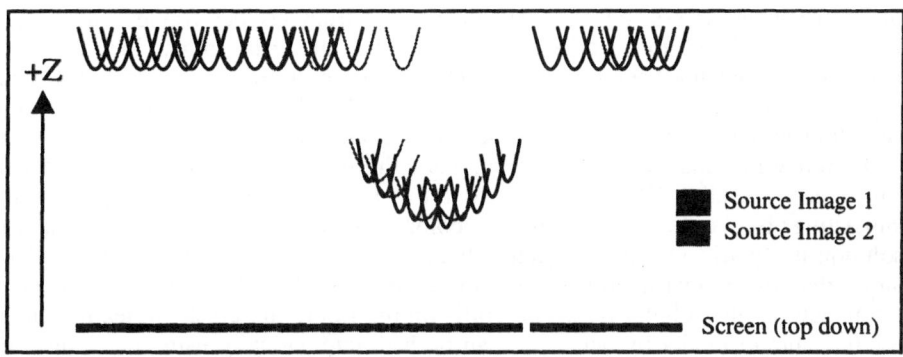

Fig. 2. The results of compositing two images reconstructed using quadratic splat primitives, shown as a top-down view of screen space.

primitives can be rendered in any order, instead of sorting them back to front or vice-versa. The reconstruction of the scattered samples is piecewise-constant, but since the samples will usually project more densely than the screen pixels and since we supersample the screen [Molnar 1991], the flat-color regions are properly filtered to prevent artifacts of piecewise-constant reconstruction like aliasing and Mach banding.

Our quadratic splat primitive, implemented on an edge equation-based rasterizing system, is actually a much simpler primitive than even a single triangle. Other edge equation-based systems like InfiniteReality [Montrym 1997] could probably implement circle or quadratic splat primitives with very little added hardware.

Samples in the interior of a surface tend to have Voronoi region-shaped footprints, but to avoid artifacts at silhouette edges we must bound the radius of the circle. If the radius is too large, silhouette edges will look scalloped. If the radius is too small, gaps will appear in the surfaces. The correct radius is a function of the projected area of a source image pixel. Since the projection of a source image pixel will be an ellipse, but our splats are only circles, the radius must be approximate.

Our approximation is based on the average scaling of the composite projection matrix C from Equation 2. We compute this as the cube root of the determinant of the 3x3 principal submatrix of C, times the average scaling of the viewport transformation (computed similarly), divided by the w coordinate of the projected sample. Since only the w coordinate varies per sample, we can compute each sample's projected area with just one multiply. [McMillan 1997] suggests a similar method that is less efficient but yields elliptical splats. [Shade 1998] uses one multiply and a lookup table that is recomputed each frame. Their method has the advantage of taking the sample's normal into account, but it is unsuitable for rendering from tiles because it would take much longer to compute the lookup table than to render the entire tile.

6 Results

Rendering performance is acceptable, but not quite what we are hoping for. We timed an 800-frame sequence with each of the four rendering methods. It averaged 549 visible tiles (1024 pixels per tile) per frame. We always render at 1920x1080 resolution, with four samples per pixel on PixelFlow and one on InfiniteReality2. On the IR2 the average frame rate was 12.14 frames per second for points and 6.21 for triangle meshes. On a sixteen-node PixelFlow, the average frame rate was 8.47 frames per second for confidence-composited triangles and 12.43 for quadratic splats. For the triangle mesh rasterizers, this is more than 1.1M triangles per frame – after view frustum culling. PixelFlow works best as a retained-mode machine, since the high-speed interface has not been completed. This limits the size of the data sets we can view on that machine. We plan to double the size of PixelFlow, but would prefer to be able to transfer data on demand as the viewpoint changes.

The rendering quality is quite good, with the quadratic splat yielding the best results (see Appendix). We plan to improve this reconstruction method by including compositing by confidence. Acquired color and geometry represented at full resolution is significantly more detailed than an equivalent synthetic model, and we believe that the rendering results are more realistic. Details such as crooked or sagging ceiling tiles, clutter on desks, spills on the floor, and cracks in leather chairs are intractable to model by hand, but can be had automatically using an acquisition system.

The data from the laser are excellent, except for problems with specular or very dark surfaces. The spatial resolution of the range data is as high as we need at this time, but some small calibration errors remain. Registration of multiple range scans using planes works well on indoor scenes, but barring perfect rangefinder calibration, we will have to deform the scans to make them align. We intend to implement a deformation based on the calibration parameters of the rangefinder, rather than a generic three-space deformation like [Curless 1996].

Registration of color and range usually works but occasionally the optimization does not converge without manually adjusting the starting parameters. Our plans for the future include building a device that captures color and range from the same location, at the same time, thus eliminating the need for color/range registration.

7   Conclusions

Through the creation of this system we learned and observed several things that are worth sharing. Assembling the laser rangefinder and writing the software was much more difficult than we expected. It has taken a man-year to get good results, and we are still fighting subtle calibration errors. We compensate in software for some of the hardware's weaknesses such as missing range data, but more work is required.

The area of image-based model representations for large environments requires additional research. Most systems represent an environment as a simplified polygonal mesh with textures. This is adequate for scenes without much detail in the geometry, but is less appropriate for scenes with geometric detail like plants, clutter, and people. Our approach preserves the sampled geometric detail by using an image-based model, but the model is represented in terms of the images that acquired the model. The only benefits of this are that it is easy to implement, does not require resampling of the images, and is more compact and efficient to render than an equivalent polygon model. We would prefer a representation that unifies the model and fully implies the connectivity while still being compact to store and efficient to render by using an incremental transformation. Our results also indicate that capturing directional exitant radiance and representing it in the model will yield more satisfying images, although this is not the system's primary weakness right now.

One of our major goals is to acquire outdoor scenes. Some obstacles can be overcome, but some are difficult to solve, regardless of technology. It is difficult to keep outdoor scenes static when wind blows and people walk through the scene. The motion of the sun, even over just 15 minutes, leads to difficulties in acquiring consistent color. Color acquisition must become quicker, or perhaps scenes could be acquired on overcast days or at night. But the acquisition of multiple panoramas of a single scene will always require that they be taken one at a time to avoid seeing the acquisition devices, unless the devices become so small as to be unobtrusive.

The most significant performance bottleneck we encountered in this research was the rendering. We would like to see faster and more flexible point primitives in graphics hardware, such as points whose size is defined in model space instead of screen space and points with an application-defined alpha or depth falloff. Much experimentation remains to be done in this area. We are investigating special-purpose hardware for image-based rendering, but hopefully this work shows the advantage of certain small changes to existing graphics hardware.

We would like to thank Kurtis Keller and John Thomas for their help building the scanning rig, Chun Fa Chang and Chris Wynn for early software work on the PixelFlow application, and the UNC IBR group for assistance and ideas. We are grateful for funding from Integrated Device Technologies Corp., DARPA under order #E278 and NSF under grant #MIP-961. We are grateful for equipment donations from Intel Corp. and Hewlett-Packard Corp.

8 References

Besl, P. J. and N. D. McKay. A Method for Registration of 3-D Shapes. *IEEE Transactions on Pattern Analysis and Machine Intelligence* **14**(2): 239-256, 1992.

Chen, E. QuickTime VR - An Image-Based Approach to Virtual Environment Navigation. *Proc. of SIGGRAPH '95*, Los Angeles, CA, August, 1995.

Chen, E. and L. Williams. View Interpolation for Image Synthesis. *Proc. of SIGGRAPH '93*, Anaheim, CA, August, 1993.

Curless, B. and M. Levoy. A volumetric method for building complex models from range images. *Proc. of SIGGRAPH '96*, New Orleans, LA, August, 1996.

Debevec, P. E., C. J. Taylor, et al. Modeling and Rendering Architecture from Photographs. *Proc. of SIGGRAPH '96*, New Orleans, LA, August, 1996.

Eberly, D. MAGIC: My Alternate Graphics and Image Code. *http://www.magic-software.com*, 1998.

El-Hakim, S. F., P. Boulanger, et al. Sensor Based Creation of Indoor Virtual Environment Models. *Intl. Conf. on Virtual Systems and MultiMedia - VSMM'97*, Geneva, Switzerland, September, 1997.

Eyles, J., S. Molnar, et al. PixelFlow: The Realization. *SIGGRAPH/Eurographics Workshop on Graphics Hardware*, Los Angeles, CA, August, 1997.

Gortler, S. J., R. Grzeszczuk, et al. The Lumigraph. *Proc. of SIGGRAPH '96*, New Orleans, LA, August, 1996.

Grossman, J. P. and W. Dally. Point Sample Rendering. *Proc. of Eurographics Workshop on Rendering*, Vienna, Austria, June, 1998.

Haeberli, P. Paint By Numbers: Abstract Image Representations. *Proc. of SIGGRAPH '90*, Dallas, TX, August, 1990.

Larson, G. W. The Holodeck: A Parallel Ray-caching Rendering System. *Proc. of Eurographics Workshop on Parallel Graphics and Visualisation*, September, 1998.

Laveau, S. and O. Faugeras. 3-D Scene Representation as a Collection of Images and Fundamental Matrices. *Proc. of Intl. Conf. on Pattern Recognition*, Jerusalem, Israel, 1994.

Levoy, M. and P. Hanrahan. Light field rendering. *Proc. of SIGGRAPH '96*, New Orleans, LA, August, 1996.

Levoy, M. and T. Whitted. The Use of Points as a Display Primitive. Univ. of North Carolina, Computer Science, Technical Report 85-022, 1985.

Mark, B., L. McMillan, et al. Post-Rendering 3D Warping. *Proc. of Symposium on Interactive 3D Graphics*, Providence, RI, April, 1997.

Max, N. Hierarchical Rendering of Trees from Precomputed Multi-Layer Z-Buffers. *Proc. of Eurographics Workshop on Rendering*, Porto, Portugal, June, 1996.

McMillan, L. An Image-based Approach to Three-Dimensional Computer Graphics. Univ. of North Carolina, Computer Science, Ph.D. Dissertation, 1997.

McMillan, L. and G. Bishop. Plenoptic Modeling: An Image-Based Rendering System. *Proc. of SIGGRAPH '95*, Los Angeles, CA, August, 1995.

Molnar, S. Efficient Supersampling Antialisasing for High-Performance Architectures. Univ. of North Carolina, Computer Science, Technical Report 91-023, 1991.

Montrym, J. S., D. R. Baum, et al. InifiniteReality: A Real-Time Graphics System. *Proc. of SIGGRAPH '97*, Los Angeles, CA, August, 1997.

Neider, J., T. Davis, et al. OpenGL Programming Guide, Addison Wesley, 1993.

Olano, M. and A. Lastra. A Shading Language on Graphics Hardware: The PixelFlow Shading System. *Proc. of SIGGRAPH '98*, Orlando, FL, July, 1998.

Pulli, K., M. Cohen, et al. View-based Rendering: Visualizing Real Objects from Scanned Range and Color Data. *Proc. of Eurographics Workshop on Rendering*, St. Etienne, France, June, 1997.

Pulli, K., T. Duchamp, et al. Robust Meshes From Multiple Range Maps. *Intl. Conf. on Recent Advances in 3-D Digital Imaging and Modeling*, Ottowa, ON, 1997.

Rademacher, P. and G. Bishop. Multiple-Center-of-Projection Images. *Proc. of SIGGRAPH '98*, Orlando, FL, July, 1998.

Rander, P., P. J. Narayanan, et al. Virtualized Reality: Constructing Time-Varying Virtual Worlds from Real World Events. *Proc. of IEEE Visualization '97*, Phoenix, AZ, October, 1997.

Rushmeier, H., F. Bernardini, et al. Acquiring Input for Rendering at Appropriate Levels of Detail: Dgitizing a Pieta. *Proc. of Eurographics Workshop on Rendering*, June, 1998.

Sara, R., R. Bajcsy, et al. 3-D Data Acquisition and Interpretation for Virtual Reality and Telepresence. *Proc. of IEEE Workshop on Computer Vision for Virtual Reality Based Human Communications*, Bombay, India, January, 1998.

Sato, Y., M. D. Wheeler, et al. Object Shape and Reflectance Modeling From Observation. *Proc. of SIGGRAPH '97*, Los Angeles, FL, July, 1997.

Seitz, S. M. and K. N. Kutulakos. Plenoptic Image Editing. *Proc. of ICCV'98*, 1998.

Shade, J., S. Gortler, et al. Layered Depth Images. *Proc. of SIGGRAPH'98*, Orlando, FL, August, 1998.

Taylor, R. M., W. Robinett, et al. The Nanomanipulator: A Virtual-Reality Interface for a Scanning Tunneling Microscope. *Proc. of SIGGRAPH '93*, Anaheim, CA, August, 1993.

Teller, S. MIT City Scanning Project. *http://graphics.lcs.mit.edu/city/city.html*, 1998.

Tsai, R. Y. An Efficient and Accurate Camera Calibration Technique for 3D Machine Vision. *Proc. of IEEE Conf. on Computer Vision and Pattern Recognition*, Miami Beach, FL, 1986.

Turk, G. and M. Levoy. Zippered Polygon Meshes from Range Images. *Proc. of SIGGRAPH '94*, Orlando, FL, August, 1994.

Westover, L. Footprint Evaluation for Volume Rendering. *Proc. of SIGGRAPH '90*, Dallas, TX, August, 1990.

Whitaker, R. T. A Level-Set Approach to 3D Reconstruction from Range Data. *Intl. Journal of Computer Vision* 29(3): 203-231, 1998.

Yoo, T. S. and J. M. Coggins. Using Statistical Pattern Recognition Techniques to Control Variable Conductance Diffusion. Information Processing in Medical Imaging (Lecture Notes in Computer Science 687). H. H. Barrett and A. F. Gmitro. Berlin, Springer-Verlag: 459-471, 1993.

Editors' Note: see Appendix, p. 366 for colored figures of this paper

Computing Visibility for Triangulated Panoramas

Chi-Wing Fu[†]
cwfu@cse.cuhk.edu.hk

Tien-Tsin Wong[‡]
ttwong@acm.org

Pheng-Ann Heng[†]
pheng@cse.cuhk.edu.hk

[†]The Chinese University of Hong Kong
[‡]Hong Kong University of Science and Technology

Abstract. A visibility algorithm for triangulated panoramas is proposed. The algorithm can correctly resolve the visibility without making use of any depth information. It is especially useful when depth information is not available, such as in the case of real-world photographs. Based on the optical flow information and the image intensity, the panorama is subdivided into variable-sized triangles, image warping is then efficiently applied on these triangles using existing graphics hardware. The visibility problem is resolved by drawing the warped triangles in a specific order. This drawing order is derived from epipolar geometry. Using this partial drawing order, a graph can be built and topological sorting is applied on the graph to obtain the complete drawing order of all triangles. We will show that the time complexity of graph construction and topological sorting are both linear to the total number of triangles.

1 Introduction

In this paper, we focus on solving the visibility problem in warping a given reference panorama to generate the desired panorama from a new viewpoint. Given an image together with its depth information, image as viewed from another viewpoint can be synthesized by reprojecting each pixel [2, 10]. Since multiple pixels may be mapped to the same location in the new image, visibility has to be resolved. The most straightforward method is depth-buffering. However, in some cases, the depth information may not be available or not accurate. This is especially common for real-world photographs. In that case, only the correspondences or optical flow information can be determined.

McMillan [13, 12] proposed a clever solution to the visibility problem. Once the mapping of pixels from the reference image to the desired image is known (either by pixel reprojection [2, 10] or by finding the point correspondences [6] or optical flow [14, 5]), the image can be warped correctly. *No* depth-buffering is needed. The visibility is solved by mapping pixels in a specific order. Due to the nature of the drawing order, only small image entities, such as pixels, can be applied. However, warping images in a pixel-by-pixel manner (*pixel-based warping*) is time-consuming and cannot utilize existing graphics hardware. Moreover, gaps occur between adjacent pixels after they are warped. If the image is subdivided into larger image entities (triangles) and the mapping is then applied on them instead of pixels, we can make use of graphics hardware to accelerate the image warping. The gap problem can also be solved at the same time. We call this triangle-by-triangle image warping the *triangle-based warping*. Unfortunately, McMillan's drawing order cannot be applied to larger entities. We introduce a visibility sorting algorithm to find out the ordering of triangles for image warping. We will also show that the time complexity of the algorithm is linear to the number of triangles.

In this paper, we propose a triangle-based visibility algorithm for image types which satisfy the *mapping criterion* described in Section 5. Planar perspective images satisfy this mapping criterion. Hence cube-based panoramas formed by six planar perspective images can be warped correctly using the proposed algorithm. Although cylindrical panoramas do not satisfy this criterion, approximated results can be obtained by applying the algorithm. The approximated results do not exhibit any noticeable artifact.

In Section 2, some related work are discussed and compared. We then have a brief overview of epipolar geometry in Section 3. In Section 4, details of the image triangulation are described. Based on the epipolar geometry, the drawing order of all triangles is derived in Section 5. Section 6 shows the results of our implementation. Finally, some conclusions and future directions are drawn in Section 7.

2 Related Work

Chen and Williams [2] warped images by reprojecting each pixel onto the new image. Depth-buffering is used to solve the visibility. Darsa *et al.* [3] subdivided the depth image into variable-sized triangles and performed reprojection on each of them. Again in their work, the visibility is solved by depth-buffering. Seitz and Dyer [16] introduced the view morphing which can correctly interpolate two different views based on image morphing [1]. Additional information such as the position of the camera and the correspondences of some feature points are required.

McMillan [11, 13, 12] first proposed a drawing order to solve the visibility without using depth-buffering. The problem is solved by drawing pixels in a specific order. The drawing order is derived from epipolar geometry. Mark and Bishop [7] studied the memory access pattern of McMillan's pixel drawing ordering. The difference between McMillan's and ours is that his drawing ordering is *only* valid for pixel-sized image entities. In our work, there is no restriction on the size of image entities. In this sense, our work can be regarded as an extension of McMillan's pixel drawing order.

If pixels are forwardly mapped to the new image, gaps will appear in between those pixels. Laveau and Faugeras [6] used a backward mapping, which maps pixels from the desired image back to the reference image, in order to prevent the appearance of gap. It is similar to the backward texture mapping. Mark *et al.* [9] solved the gap problem by two methods, namely splatting and modeling the image as a triangular mesh. To prevent gap using splatting, the footprint of pixel must be large enough. However large footprint may excessively blur the image. They also suggested to model the image as a triangular mesh to prevent the gap. Since McMillan's drawing order can only be applied to pixel-sized entities, they have to subdivide the image into pixel-sized triangles by connecting neighboring three pixel samples as in Figure 1(a). Hence a 512×512 image may be subdivided into more than five hundred thousand triangles. Even with the assistance of graphics hardware, the warping is still slow. Note that their triangular mesh approach is different from the one proposed in this paper. Their triangles are still in pixel size while our triangles can be in arbitrary size and shape. Figure 1 shows the differences. Shade *et al.* [17] further extended the usage of McMillan's drawing order to image with multiple layers of depth values.

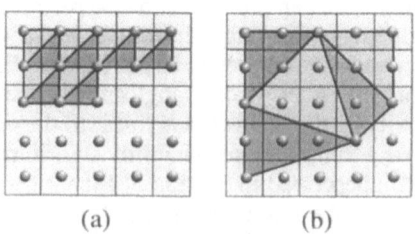

(a)   (b)

Fig. 1. Comparison of the (a) pixel-sized and (b) arbitrary-sized triangulation.

3   Epipolar Geometry

Given a viewpoint (or center of projection), image synthesis is accomplished by firing bundle of rays from the viewpoint to the surrounding and sampling radiances received along the rays. If a rectangular plane is placed in front of the viewpoint, a planar perspective image can be formed by projecting the radiance values onto this plane. The rectangular plane is one kind of *projection manifold*, more specifically, a planar projection manifold. Similarly, other geometry can be used as the projection manifold, such as cylinder or sphere. Since the viewpoint is a point in space and the rays are fired from the viewpoint, a sphere is the most natural and general form of projection manifold which can record the radiance received along any ray. Radiances recorded by any other projection manifold can always be reprojected onto the spherical projection manifold.

From now on, we focus on the discussion of spherical projection manifold due to its generality. Consider a spherical image I_c captured with the center of projection at $\dot{c}$. We use the dot notation $\dot{a}$ to denote a 3D position and the arrow notation $\vec{a}$ to denote a 3D directional vector. A desired spherical image I_e is generated with a new center of projection at $\dot{e}$. Figure 2 shows the geometry in both 3D and 2D.

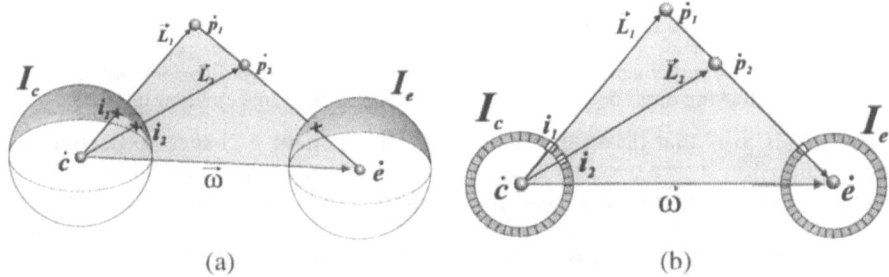

Fig. 2. The geometry of two cameras (a) in 3D and (b) in 2D.

Each pixel i in the image I_c stores the radiance along the ray $\vec{L}$ which is fired from $\dot{c}$ passing through the pixel window associated with i. Now, let's choose an arbitrary pixel i_1 from image I_c. A ray $\vec{L_1}$ is associated with it. The intersection point $\dot{p}_1$ associated with i_1 must lie somewhere on the ray $\vec{L_1}$. To generate a new view from $\dot{e}$, $\dot{p}_1$ has to be reprojected onto I_e. The plane constructed by $\dot{c}$, $\dot{e}$ and $\dot{p}_1$ is known as *epipolar plane* in computer vision literature. The vector, $\vec{\omega}$, originated from $\dot{c}$ pointing towards $\dot{e}$ is called *positive epipolar ray* while the vector, $-\vec{\omega}$, originated from $\dot{c}$ pointing to the opposite direction is called *negative epipolar ray*.

Now let's choose another pixel i_2 from image I_c. Occlusion happens only when $\dot{p}_1$ and $\dot{p}_2$ are reprojected onto the same location in I_e (see Figure 2). If $\dot{p}_2$ does not lie on the epipolar plane associated with $\dot{p}_1$, $\dot{p}_1$ and $\dot{p}_2$ will never occlude each other. Hence occlusion happens only when $\dot{c}$, $\dot{e}$, $\dot{p}_1$ and $\dot{p}_2$ all lie on the same plane. Moreover the necessary condition of $\dot{p}_2$ occluding $\dot{p}_1$ is $\dot{e}$, $\dot{p}_1$ and $\dot{p}_2$ are collinear and $\dot{p}_2$ is in between $\dot{p}_1$ and $\dot{e}$, as illustrated in Figure 2.

From Figure 2, we know that $\dot{p}_2$ will never be occluded by $\dot{p}_1$ as viewed from $\dot{e}$ no matter where the exact positions of $\dot{p}_1$ and $\dot{p}_2$ are. Therefore, if we always draw $\dot{p}_1$ before $\dot{p}_2$ during reprojection, the visibility problem is solved without comparing their depth values. And hence, if we can identify those pixels whose intersection points may occlude each other and derive the drawing order, the visibility problem can be solved without depth-buffering.

To identify the pixels which may occlude each other, we first intersect the epipolar plane with the spherical projection manifold (image I_c). The intersection curve on the sphere is called the *epipolar line*. Figure 3(a) illustrates the terminologies graphically. When the positive epipolar ray $\vec{\omega}$ intersects with the projection manifold I_c, the intersection point on the projection manifold is known as *positive epipole*. Figure 3 denotes it by a positive sign. On the other hand, the intersection point of the negative epipolar ray and the sphere is known as *negative epipole* and denoted by a negative sign. Note all epipolar lines terminated at two epipoles. Moreover, each epipolar line must be a half of the great circle (Figure 3(c)) as the epipolar plane passes through the center of the sphere, $\dot{c}$.

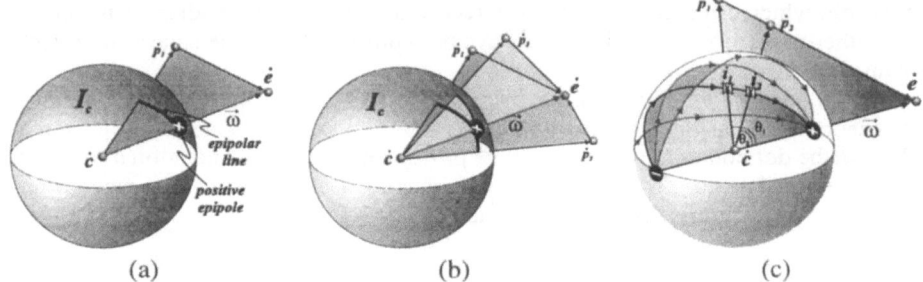

$$(a) \qquad\qquad (b) \qquad\qquad (c)$$

Fig. 3. (a) & (b): The epipolar line is the intersection of the projection manifold and the epipolar plane. (c): The drawing order between two pixels that lie on the same epipolar line.

All pixels in I_c that lie on the same epipolar line have a chance to occlude each other. Figure 3(c) shows two pixels, i_1 and i_2, lying on the same epipolar line. As their associated intersection points $\dot{p}_1$ and $\dot{p}_2$ are on the same plane with $\dot{c}$ and $\dot{e}$, they may occlude each other. Moreover, $\dot{p}_1$ will never occlude $\dot{p}_2$ as $\dot{p}_1$'s angle of derivation θ_1 is greater than, θ_2 of $\dot{p}_2$ (see Figure 3(c)). In other words, if i_2 is closer to the positive epipole on the epipolar line than i_1, i_1 will never occlude i_2. Hence we should always draw i_1 first. Arrows on the epipolar line in Figure 3(c) indicate the drawing order of pixels.

Based on the pattern of epipolar lines on the sphere, McMillan [11] derived a drawing order for pixel-sized image entities. Since the epipolar line can only tell the ordering of small image entities that lie on it, the drawing order only works for pixel-sized image entities. The drawing order cannot be easily extended to larger entities such as triangles which occupy a bundle of epipolar lines.

4   Image Triangulation

4.1   Optical Flow

Before the image is warped, the 2D image has to be first triangulated. To do so, we make use of the optical flow. Consider two images $I_c(x,y)$ and $I_e(x,y)$ of the same scene but with different viewpoints $\dot{c}$ and $\dot{e}$, one can determine the image correspondences between two images using existing computer vision techniques. These correspondences allow us to calculate the two dimensional *optical flow vector* [14, 5] for each pixel, *i.e.* the 2D pixel movement from I_c to I_e. The optical flow of a pixel i is defined as

$$\vec{f} = \begin{pmatrix} x_e - x_c \\ y_e - y_c \end{pmatrix}, \tag{1}$$

where (x_c, y_c) is the image coordinate of i in I_c,
$\quad (x_e, y_e)$ is the image coordinate of i in I_e.

If the optical flow vectors of two neighboring pixels are close, it is very likely that the intersection points associated with these pixels are on the same object. On the other hand, if the optical flow vectors are not close, the intersection points are more likely to be on different objects with different distances from the viewpoint. During image warping, they are very likely to be moved away from each other. Hence, one criterion of triangulating the image is to separate those pixels with large difference in optical flows. Otherwise, serious distortion will result during image warping. Hence we want to locate the regions with large variation in optical flow between neighboring pixels. To do so, we calculate a function F for each pixel,

$$F(x,y) = \max(|\frac{\partial^2 \vec{f}}{\partial x^2}|, |\frac{\partial^2 \vec{f}}{\partial y^2}|). \tag{2}$$

Function F is defined as the maximum of the magnitudes of two second order partial derivatives of the optical flow vectors along dimensions x and y.

4.2 Image Gradient

Besides the optical flow, image intensity is also used during triangulation. Regions with edges (sharp intensity change) are perceptually more noticeable to humans. A distortion in the edge region is more noticeable than the same distortion in the non-edge region. In other words, the tolerance of distortion in the region with different image content should be different. To quantify this factor, we first convert the color image to grayscale by transforming RGB to $Y_t IQ$ color space. The Y_t is then used as the grayscale version of the image. The standard grayscale conversion [4] is

$$I'_c = 0.299I_c^R + 0.587I_c^G + 0.114I_c^B, \tag{3}$$

where I_c^R, I_c^G, and I_c^B are the R, G and B values from image I_c.

To locate edge region, we simply apply the standard Laplacian operator, ∇^2, to the grayscale image I'_c and obtain function G,

$$G(x,y) = \nabla^2 I'_c(x,y) = \frac{\partial^2 I'_c}{\partial x^2} + \frac{\partial^2 I'_c}{\partial y^2}. \tag{4}$$

Both optical flow and image gradient are important criteria for triangulating the image. They are combined in the following potential function $P(x,y)$, which tells us where should we place the vertices of triangles.

$$P(x,y) = \alpha F^*(x,y) + (1-\alpha)G^*(x,y), \tag{5}$$

where $\alpha \in [0,1]$ is a weight, $\alpha = 0.7$ is a good choice,
$\quad F^*$ and G^* are the normalized F and G, they are normalized to range $[0,1]$.

The larger the potential value of the pixel, the larger the potential that the pixel is on the silhouette of an object. Figures 10(a) and (b) show the reference panorama and the corresponding potential map calculated by Equation 5.

4.3 Triangulation

To triangulate the image, we stochastically distribute the vertices of triangles onto the potential map. The pixel with larger potential value has a larger chance of receiving a vertex. Then Delaunay triangulation [15] is applied to obtain the initial triangular mesh.

The initial triangular mesh is further refined to reduce the visual artifact during the actual image warping. A triangle is split into two smaller triangles if its *sum of potential* exceeds a pre-defined threshold τ_p. The sum of potential, ρ, of a triangle t is defined as the total sum of potential value of pixels within this triangle t.

$$\rho(t) = \sum_i P(x_{p_i}, y_{p_i}) \qquad \forall p_i \in t, \tag{6}$$

where p_i is a pixel inside the triangle t. The subdivision continues until all triangles satisfy the sum of potential requirement. Figure 10(c) shows the final triangular mesh.

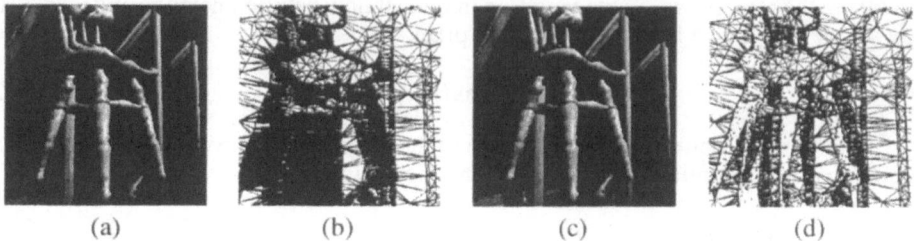

     (a)   (b)   (c)   (d)

Fig. 4. Excessive stretching near the object silhouette during the image warping due to the triangle connectivity.

Note that all triangles are now connected. Therefore no gap can be found during image warping. However, another artifact appears if all triangles are connected together. Figures 4(a) and (b) show that triangles near the silhouette of the object are excessively stretched. During image warping, some of the occluded regions become visible. Since no information is available, these areas should be left blank instead of filling them with the excessively stretched triangles. This kind of artifact usually appears near the silhouette of an object. Hence it can be reduced by disconnecting the triangles at object silhouette. Again, the disconnection can be done with the guidance of function F as the map indicates object silhouette. If the common edge shared by two neighboring triangles is located at a region with average potential value above a user-defined threshold τ_c, these neighboring triangles shall be disconnected. Figure 4(c) and (d) show the result. Mark and Bishop [8] proposed an efficient reconstruction technique for filling this kind of holes. The process of triangulation can be done off-line. Once it has been done, the triangular mesh will not be changed during the actual image warping.

5 Image-based Visibility Sorting

5.1 Ordering of Two Triangles

Epipolar geometry provides sufficient information for us to resolve the visibility problem when warping triangles. Our algorithm resolves the visibility problem of triangles on the surface of the sphere. Hence, we need to project a triangle in the image to a spherical triangle on the surface of the sphere which encloses viewpoint $\dot{c}$.

Each 2D image must be related to an implicit projection manifold. For examples, a planar perspective image is related to a planar projection manifold. A cylindrical panoramic image is related to a cylindrical projection manifold. As the image triangulation algorithm discussed in the previous section triangulates the image in 2D, the validity of the proposed algorithm relies on one criterion of mapping (from 2D to sphere): *any straight line on the 2D surface must be mapped to one geodesic curve on the sphere and vice versa* (Figure 5). A geodesic curve connecting two points on the sphere is the shortest path on sphere from one point to another. It must also be a segment of the great circle of sphere. Two dimensional images resulted from planar projection manifold satisfy the above mapping criterion. Hence the proposed algorithm is applicable to cube-based panorama. On the other hand, a straight line on the 2D unfolded cylindrical or spherical panoramic image may not be mapped to a geodesic curve on the sphere.

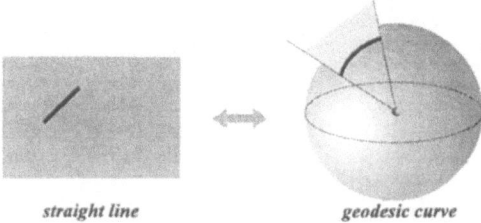

straight line   geodesic curve

Fig. 5. Mapping criterion: a straight line in 2D can be mapped to a geodesic curve on the sphere.

If an image can be projected onto the sphere and the mapping satisfies the above criterion, a triangle in the image can always be mapped to a spherical triangle on the sphere. Each edge of the spherical triangle must be a geodesic curve. Consider two arbitrary spherical triangles, t_1 and t_2, obtained by triangulating the 2D image and being mapped onto the sphere. We can determine whether they may occlude each other, by checking the bundles of epipolar lines they occupy. Let's call the bundle of epipolar lines occupied by a triangle the *epipolar band*. Figure 6(a) shows the epipolar bands occupied by two spherical triangles in light gray. If their epipolar bands do not overlap (Figure 6(a)), no occlusion will occur between them. There is no element (pixel) in these two spherical triangles sharing any common epipolar line. Hence the order of drawing these two spherical triangles is irrelevant. On the other hand, if the two epipolar bands overlap (Figure 6(b)), some elements from these spherical triangles lie on the same epipolar line. Hence occlusion may happen after image warping. Therefore, the ordering of these triangle does matter. In the specific example of Figure 6(b), t_1 may occlude t_2 as t_1 is closer to the positive epipole than t_2 in the overlapping region. We now define two ordering relations of spherical triangles:

Definition 1 *If all elements in a spherical triangle t_1 must be drawn before any element in another spherical triangle t_2 in order to preserve the correct visibility, we say t_1 must be drawn before t_2 and denote this ordering relation as $t_1 \rightarrow t_2$.*

Definition 2 *If the drawing order between the elements in spherical triangle t_1 and the elements in another spherical triangle t_2 is irrelevant, the drawing order between these two spherical triangles are also irrelevant. We denote this ordering relation as $t_1 \leftrightarrow t_2$.*

Since all the spherical triangles are the result of triangulating an image as viewed from the viewpoint $\dot{c}$, they all must be visible, non-overlapping and connected as viewed from $\dot{c}$. Instead of considering the ordering of any two arbitrary spherical triangles, we first consider the ordering between each pair of neighboring spherical triangles which share a common edge as in Figure 7. Now we will show that the ordering of any two neighboring spherical triangles can be determined by the position and orientation of spherical triangles.

Theorem 1 *Given two neighboring spherical triangles which share a common edge, a plane that passes through the center of projection $\dot{c}$ and the shared edge (which is a geodesic curve) can be constructed (see Figure 8). It divides the sphere into two*

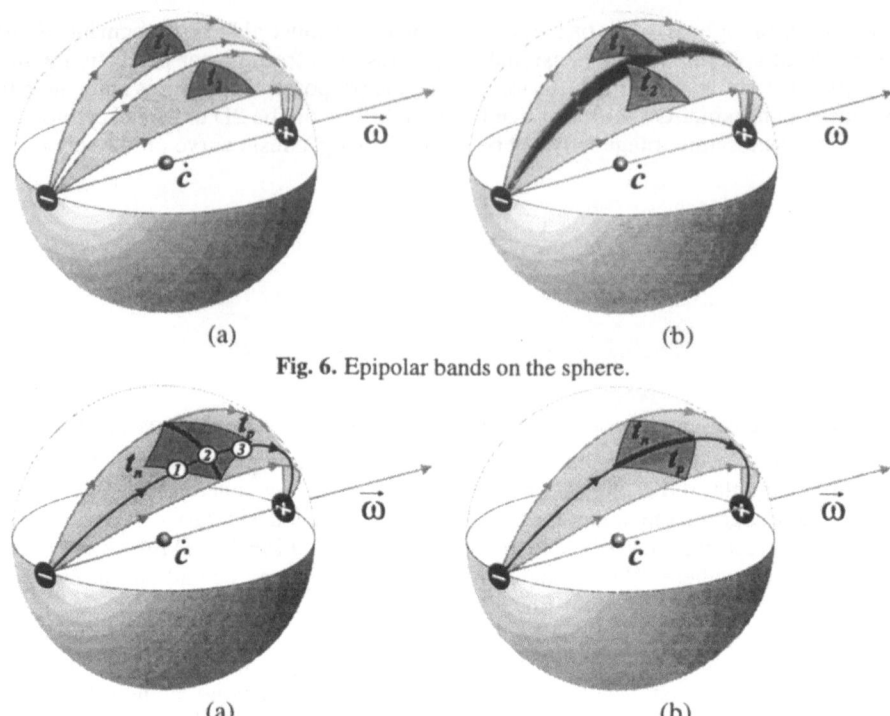

Fig. 6. Epipolar bands on the sphere.

(a) (b)

Fig. 7. a) The epipolar line starting from the negative epipole must always enter t_n before t_p if it cuts both t_n and t_p. b) If the epipoles and the shared edge lie on the same plane, the ordering of t_n and t_p is irrelevant.

equal halves and separates two spherical triangles. The spherical triangle with the positive epipole on its side should be drawn later during warping. On the other hand, the triangle with the negative epipole on its side should be drawn first during warping. If the epipoles (positive and negative) lie exactly on the constructed plane, the ordering of these two triangles is irrelevant.

Proof: Due to the mapping criterion, all edges of spherical triangle must be geodesic curves. These geodesic curves lie in the planes that pass through the center of the sphere. Therefore one can always separate two neighboring spherical triangles by constructing a plane that contains the shared common edge and the sphere center. This is also why we need the mapping criterion. Let's denote the spherical triangle with the positive epipole on its side as t_p and the other as t_n as shown in Figure 7(a). Now let's draw a geodesic curve from the negative epipole to the positive epipole. Since the negative epipole is on the same side as t_n, whenever this geodesic curve passes through both t_n and t_p, it should first pass through t_n, then the shared edge and finally t_p (Figure 7(a)). Therefore whenever there are elements in t_n which are sharing a common epipolar line (geodesic curve) with some elements in t_p, elements in t_n should be closer to the negative epipole than those elements in t_p. Hence, no element in triangle t_n will occlude any element in t_p and we must draw t_n before t_p during warping, *i.e.* $t_n \rightarrow t_p$.

When both epipoles and the shared edge lie on the same plane, epipolar bands of t_n and t_p have no intersection (Figure 7(b)). One can always separate the epipolar bands of these two spherical triangles by a plane that contains the shared edge, the center of sphere, and the two epipoles. In other words, no element in t_n and t_p shares any common epipolar line. Therefore, their ordering is irrelevant and we say $t_n \leftrightarrow t_p$.

Hence, the drawing order of two spherical triangles t_1 and t_2 can be determined by checking on which side of the constructed plane the negative epipole resides. This can be done with some simple vector mathematics. Figure 8 illustrates the mathematical symbols used in the following equations. Vectors $\vec{e}_a$ and $\vec{e}_b$ are the vectors from the center of projection, $\dot{c}$, to the two endpoints of the shared common edge. Vectors $\vec{v}_1$ and $\vec{v}_2$ are the vectors from $\dot{c}$ to the unshared vertices of spherical triangles t_1 and t_2 respectively.

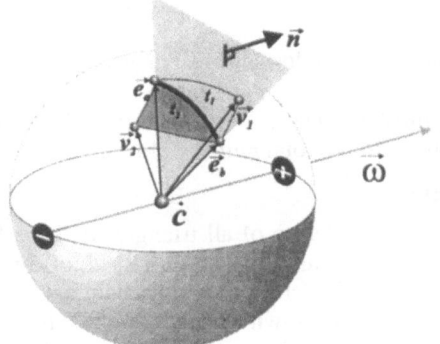

Fig. 8. Mathematical symbols used for the calculation of drawing order.

$$\vec{n} = \vec{e}_a \times \vec{e}_b \qquad \beta = \vec{n} \cdot \vec{\omega} \qquad \gamma = \vec{n} \cdot \vec{v}_1$$

Based on the values of β and γ, the drawing order is determined as follows:

1. If $\beta = 0$, $\vec{\omega}$ is orthogonal to $\vec{n}$. In other words, the epipoles and the shared edge must be on the same plane. Hence, the drawing order of t_1 and t_2 is irrelevant, *i.e.* $t_1 \leftrightarrow t_2$.
2. If β and γ have the same sign (either both are positive or negative), t_2 is on the same side as the negative epipole. Hence $t_2 \rightarrow t_1$.
3. If β and γ have the different signs, t_1 is on the same side as the negative epipole. Hence $t_1 \rightarrow t_2$.

5.2 Graph Construction

Using the method described, one can always derive the drawing order of two neighboring triangles. This ordering can be further extended to cover any two arbitrary triangles from mesh by constructing a drawing order graph. By representing each triangle as a node and the relation $\rightarrow$ as a directed edge in the graph, we can construct a graph of drawing order. No edge is needed to represent the relation $\leftrightarrow$ as the ordering is irrelevant. Note the constructed graph may contain disjointed subgraphs. Figure 9(a) shows seven connected triangles. The drawing order of each pair of neighboring triangles are shown as arrows crossing the shared edges between neighboring triangles. The constructed graph is shown in Figure 9(b). Figure 9(c) shows two valid drawing orders derived from the example graph. Note there is no unique ordering for the same graph.

In the actual implementation, there is no need to construct the graph explicitly. The graph can be implicitly represented as a set of ordering relation between each pair of neighboring triangles. Hence, for each shared edge, we determine the drawing order between neighboring triangles using Theorem 1. The time complexity of graph construction is obviously $O(E)$ where E is the number of shared edges. As each triangle

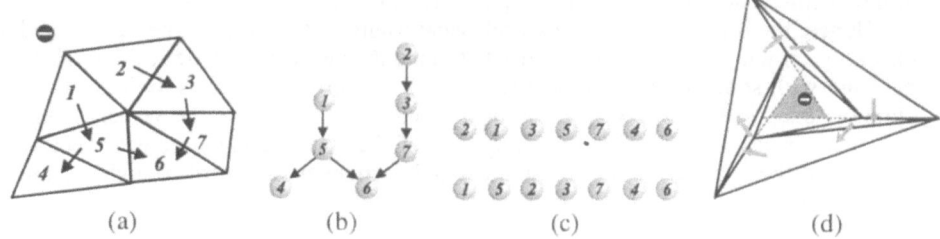

Fig. 9. (a), (b) & (c):Construction of drawing order graph. (d): Cycle may exist in the graph.

has three edges, E is at most $3N$ where N is total number of triangles. Hence, the time complexity should be linear to the total number of triangles.

5.3 Topological Sorting

The final step to find out the ordering of all triangles is to perform a topological sort on the drawing order graph. Basically it is a two-pass algorithm. Before describing the algorithm in detail, let's define the terminology. A triangle (node) is called degree zero if there is no triangle needed to be drawn before it, *i.e.* it is not on the right hand side of any $\rightarrow$ relation. It is called degree 1 if one of its three neighbors has to be drawn before it. A triangle is at most of degree three.

In the first pass of algorithm, it looks for all zero-degree triangles and put them into a pool. In the second pass, one triangle t_1 in the pool is picked, output and removed from the pool. Then for each neighboring triangle t_2 of t_1, such that $t_1 \rightarrow t_2$, decrease the degree of t_2 by one. If the degree of t_2 drops to zero after deduction, put it into the pool. The process of picking and drawing continues until no more triangle is left. The algorithm is shown on the right. The example graph in Figure 9(b) is sorted using this algorithm.

```
// First pass
Pool_0 = 0
For each triangle t of degree zero
    Pool_0 = Pool_0 U {t}
For each triangle t of degree one
    Pool_1 = Pool_1 U {t}

// Second pass
While there exists triangle not output
    If Pool_0 ≠ 0
        Pick a triangle t_1 from Pool_0 and output
    else there is cycle
        Randomly pick a triangle t_1 from Pool_1
        and output it
    For each neighbor triangle of t_2 s.t.  t_1 → t_2
        Decrease the degree of t_2 by one.
        If the degree of t_2 is zero
            Pool_0 = Pool_0 U {t_2}
        If the degree of t_2 is one
            Pool_1 = Pool_1 U {t_2}
```

It seems that the graph will be a directed acyclic graph. However cycles do exist in extremely rare cases. Figure 9(d) shows one special example of triangulation such that cycle exists. If the projected epipole (projected onto reference image) locates inside the gray region, cycle will occur. In practice, cycles seldom occur and no cycle was found in all our experiments. However, the above algorithm does handle the case when cycle is found. It randomly picks a triangle of degree one, draws it on the screen and hence breaks the cycle. A pool of degree-one triangle is setup for this purpose. This approach may result in visual artifact.

The time complexity of the first pass of algorithm is $O(N)$. Since each triangle will be put into the pool and picked out from the pool at most once, the time complexity of the second pass is also linear. Hence the topological sorting is linear. The time complexity of the whole visibility sorting algorithm is also linear to the number of triangles.

6 Results

In our implementation, we use a cylindrical panorama to record the environment. Although we have mentioned before that cylindrical panorama does not satisfy the mapping criterion, approximated results without noticeable artifacts can be obtained. To apply the proposed algorithm to cylindrical panorama, the edges of triangles should not be too long, especially horizontal edges near the top and the bottom of the unfolded panorama.

Determining accurate optical flow is a well-known hard problem. Since our work mainly concentrates on solving visibility, we obtain the accurate optical flow map by reprojecting pixels using depth values. But no depth value is used in the following visibility determination.

As the image is being warped, originally occluded regions become visible and these areas are left blank as there is no information. To minimize the unfilled region, multiple reference panoramas are warped to the same position and then blended together. Figures 13(a) and (c) show the warped results of two reference panoramas. They are warped to the same position. The green regions highlight the blank areas. Figure 13(e) shows the result of blending Figures 13(a) and (c). Figures 13(b) and (d) show the corresponding warped triangulation together with the drawing order. To distinguish one triangle from another, three distinct colors are used to color the neighboring triangles. The intensity of the triangle indicates the drawing order. The darker the color, the earlier is the triangle in the drawing order.

Table 1 shows the timing for visibility sorting and rendering. The desired image is a planar perspective image while the reference image is a cylindrical panorama. All the timings are recorded on an SGI Octane with CPU MIPS R10000/250MHz and MXE graphics accelerator. As expected, major computation is spent on visibility sorting (graph construction + topological sorting). Rendering only occupies a minor portion of the time as it is assisted with graphics accelerator. Nevertheless, the overall image warping can still be done at interactive speed. Note that the visibility sorting is not necessary if the user does not change the walking direction $\tilde{\omega}$.

Figure 11 shows the result of warping and blending panoramas of an attic scene. Note how the pillars and the chair correctly occlude the background objects. The correctness of resultant visibility demonstrates the validity of the proposed algorithm. The times below the images indicate how far the image has been warped. When the time equals to zero, no warping is done. The image is simply the first reference panorama. When the time equals to 0.5, both the first and the second reference panoramas are warped to the middle position. When the time equals to 1.0, the image is simply the second reference panorama. Another set of warping panoramas of a city scene is shown in Figure 12. Note how forwardly moving buildings occlude neighboring buildings.

Data set	Reference pano. image resolution	Desired pers. image resolution	Number of triangles	Build graph (sec.)	Topology sort (sec.)	Average Rendering time (sec.)
attic	1024×256	512×512	54611	0.1190	0.0879	0.0577
city	1024×256	512×512	53550	0.1160	0.0853	0.0557

Table 1. Timing of triangle-based image warping.

7 Conclusions and Future Directions

In this paper, we propose a triangle-based visibility algorithm without using depth information. Grouping pixels to form triangles allows image warping to be done in an efficient manner. Hardware graphics board can further accelerate the rendering of warped image. Moreover, the gap problem due to pixel-based image warping is also removed simultaneously. Both graph construction and topological sorting in the visibility algorithm have a linear time complexity and only need to be performed whenever the user changes $\tilde{\omega}$.

We have only described how image warping can be done correctly for triangles. The merging of two warped images usually exhibits visual discontinuity due to the surface properties of the objects and illumination configuration during image capturing. Therefore, how to merge two warped images seamlessly is another important issue. In some cases (especially complex scene), holes (unfilled pixels) will still exist even multiple images are warped and merged. The sampling scheme (placement of the panorama nodes) requires further investigation.

Acknowledgements

This work is supported by Hong Kong Government RGC CRCs Scheme Grant No. CRC4/98. We would like to thank all anonymous paper reviewers for their valuable comments and pointing out the error.

Web Availability

The warped images and movies of tested scenes can be found at the following web pages: http://www.cs.ust.hk/~ttwong/papers/panowalk/panowalk.html and http://www.cse.cuhk.edu.hk/~cwfu/papers/panowalk/panowalk.html

References

1. T. Beier and S. Neely. Feature-based image metamorphosis. In *Computer Graphics (SIGGRAPH '92 Proceedings)*, volume 26, pages 35–42, July 1992.
2. S. E. Chen and L. Williams. View interpolation for image synthesis. In *Computer Graphics (SIGGRAPH '93 Proceedings)*, pages 279–288, 1993.
3. L. Darsa, B. C. Silva, and A. Varshney. Navigating static environments using image-space simplification and morphing. In *Proceedings of the 1997 Symposium on Interactive 3D Graphics*, pages 25–34, April 1997.
4. R. Hall. *Illumination and Color in Computer Generated Imagery*. Springer-Verlag, 1988.
5. B. Horn. *Robot Vision*. MIT Press, 1986.
6. S. Laveau and O. Faugeras. 3-D scene representation as a collection of images. In *Proceedings of the Twelfth International Conference on Pattern Recognition (ICPR '94)*, pages 689–691, October 1994.
7. W. R. Mark and G. Bishop. Memory access patterns of occlusion-compatible 3d image warping. In *Proceedings of the 1997 Siggraph/Eurographics Workshop on Graphics Hardware*, pages 35–44, August 1997.
8. W. R. Mark and G. Bishop. Efficient reconstruction techniques for post-rendering 3d image warping. Technical report, University of Northern Carolina at Chapel Hill, March 1998. UNC CS #TR98-011.
9. W. R. Mark, L. McMillan, and G. Bishop. Post-rendering 3d warping. In *Proceedings of the 1997 Symposium on Interactive 3D Graphics*, pages 7–16, April 1997.
10. N. Max and K. Ohsaki. Rendering trees from precomputed Z-buffer views. In *Eurographics Rendering Workshop 1995*. Eurographics, June 1995.
11. L. McMillan. Computing visibility without depth. Technical report, University of North Carolina, October 1995. UNC Computer Science TR95-047.
12. L. McMillan. *An Image-Based Approach to Three-Dimensional Computer Graphics*. PhD thesis, Department of Computer Science, University of North Carolina at Chapel Hill, 1997.

13. L. McMillan and G. Bishop. Plenoptic modeling: An image-based rendering system. In *Computer Graphics (SIGGRAPH '95 Proceedings)*, pages 39–46, August 1995.

14. K. Prazdny. On the information in optical flows. *Computer Vision, Graphics and Image Processing*, 22(9):239–259, 1983.

15. F. P. Preparata and M. I. Shamos. *Computational Geometry, An Introduction*. Springer-Verlag, 1985.

16. S. M. Seitz and C. R. Dyer. View morphing. In *Computer Graphics (SIGGRAPH '96 Proceedings)*, pages 21–30, 1996.

17. J. Shade, S. Gortler, L. He, and R. Szeliski. Layered depth images. In *Computer Graphics (SIGGRAPH '98 Proceedings)*, pages 231–242, July 1998.

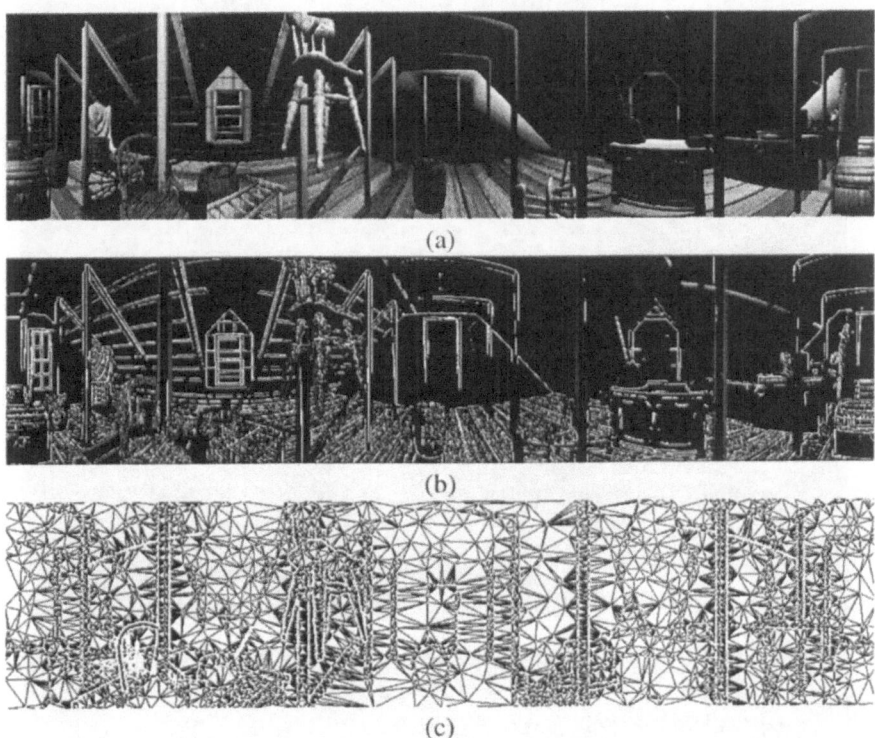

(a)

(b)

(c)

Fig. 10. Triangulation of the panorama. a) The reference panorama, b) the potential map, and c) the triangulated mesh.

174

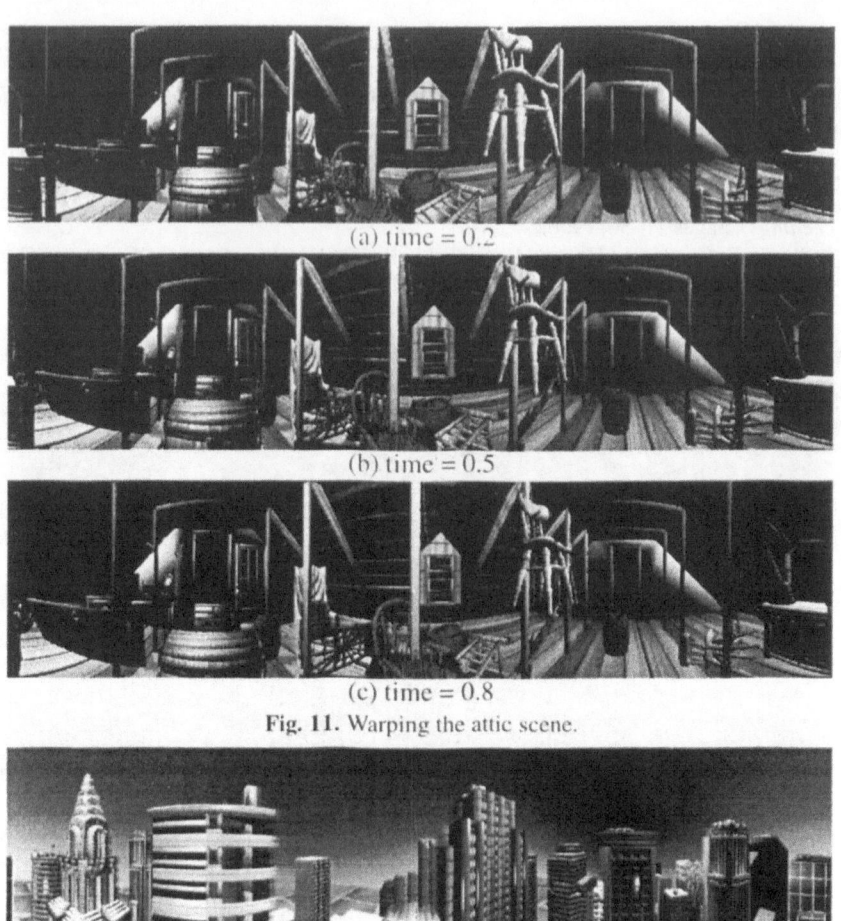

(a) time = 0.2

(b) time = 0.5

(c) time = 0.8

Fig. 11. Warping the attic scene.

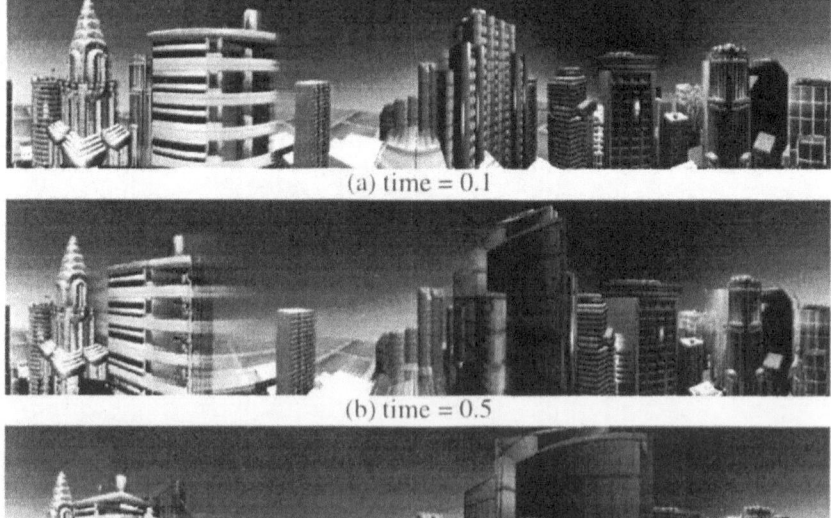

(a) time = 0.1

(b) time = 0.5

(c) time = 0.8

Fig. 12. Warping the city scene.

Editors' Note: see Appendix, p. 367 for colored figures of this paper

Efficient Displacement Mapping
by Image Warping

Gernot Schaufler
Computer Graphics Group, MIT
Cambridge, MA 02139
gs@graphics.lcs.mit.edu

Markus Priglinger
GUP, JK University
A – 4040 Linz, Austria
mprigl@gup.uni-linz.ac.at

Abstract. While displacement maps can provide a rich set of visual detail on otherwise simple surfaces, they have always been very expensive to render. Rendering has been done using ray-tracing and by introducing a great number of micro-polygons. We present a new image-based approach by showing that rendering displacement maps is sufficiently similar to image warping for parallel displacements and displacements originating form a single point. Our new warping algorithm is particularly well suited for this class of displacement maps. It allows efficient modeling of complicated shapes with few displacement mapped polygons and renders them at interactive rates.

1 Introduction and Motivation

Displacement mapping as introduced by Cook provides rich geometric and visual detail without requiring the user to model them explicitly [6]. In contrast to other texture mapping techniques, not only the appearance of a surface is altered, but the surface itself is displaced by an amount specified in a texture map.

While displacement mapping reduces the burden on the modeling side, it increases the effort necessary to obtain images from the model. Little published work exists on the rendering of displacement mapped surfaces [13] and two approaches are commonly taken: micro-polygons and ray-tracing. Both of these methods are very time consuming and, therefore, more efficient alternatives are desirable.

This paper introduces such an alternative by making the observation that displacement mapping is sufficiently similar to warping an image with depth. The pixel colors describe the optical surface properties and the depth specifies how much the surface deviates from the image plane. These displacements can either be applied perpendicular to the normal of a flat surface using an orthographic projection, or they can be made to emanate from a single point — namely the center of projection in a perspective image. Image warping takes the displaced surface points to the same location in the image as first displacing them in 3D and then projecting them onto the image plane.

Current warping algorithms have difficulties in reconstructing the final image, both in regions of depth discontinuities and where the object's surface was not sufficiently sampled. We introduce a novel warping algorithm that overcomes these problems for the case of images representing displacement maps. In this restricted family of images, depth differences in adjacent pixels are always meant to represent a surface slope, and therefore, must be treated as being connected.

We begin with a discussion of previous work on rendering displacement maps and warping depth images. Next, we describe how the epipolar geometry relating two images can be exploited to implement an efficient warping algorithm well suited for displacement maps. Our interactive system allows the user to cover arbitrary geometry with displacement maps. For rendering, these displacement maps are warped into the final image and composited using a depth buffer, which handles displacement mapped geometry efficiently in traditional scan-line renderers. We then present images and performance measurements in the results section. Finally, we discuss limitations and possible extensions for more general shading.

2 Previous Work

Since the introduction of displacement maps in 1984 by Cook [6], they have been rendered using micro-polygons [7] and using ray-tracing [13, 19, 24]. By subdividing displacement-mapped geometry into micro-polygons and displacing their vertices, a great deal of additional geometry is introduced that makes the model time-consuming to render. A fine subdivision is usually necessary to capture the details of the displacement map. The only system capable of doing this described in the literature is the REYES image rendering architecture [7], but it suffers from additional problems if the displacements excessively increase the size of the triangles. Ray-tracing is a costly rendering technique in itself and ray-tracing inverse displacement maps has been described as only being practical for objects of the complexity of tori or sweeps [13]. The authors of [13] expect the rendering time for more complex surfaces "to become prohibitive." Pharr et al. have presented an approach to handle micro-polygons in ray-tracing [20, 21].

Image-based rendering (IBR), on the other hand, is very efficient for detailed scenes because its algorithmic complexity is independent of the complexity of the rendered scene. The complexity is determined by the number of samples in the reference images and the desired images. IBR evolved from re-projections of environment maps for perspective viewing [3], via image interpolation [4], to image warping [16].

There are two strategies in image warping: forward mapping and backward mapping. Forward mapping loops over the pixels in the reference image and projects each one into the desired image. Splatting can compensate for mismatches in the images' sampling densities. Grossman provides an alternative solution [11]. Forward mapping is usually preferred, because it can be implemented more efficiently. Backward mapping loops over the pixels in the desired image and finds the corresponding samples in the reference image. Since the mapping is not invertible, a search must be performed. The epipolar geometry limits the extent of this search adversely affecting its time complexity [17]. Popescu has accelerated warping by parallelization [22].

Two approaches leading in the direction of our method have been published, namely view-dependent texture mapping [8] and ray-tracing height-fields [1, 5, 10, 15]. Debevec uses stereo algorithms to obtain displacement maps for building facades, and renders them with view-dependent texture mapping by blending between the images taken from different view angles. Height-fields can be rendered efficiently by sweeping a ray upwards in each pixel column of the image keeping track of how the intersection with the terrain recedes into the distance.

3 Forward Image Warping

Assume points in the image space of a pinhole camera (as in [17] and shown in Figure 1) are converted to 3D Euclidean space through multiplication by 3 by 3 matrix P as given in Equation (1):

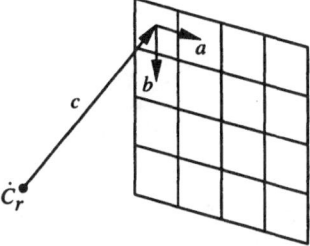

Fig. 1. A pinhole camera with center of projection $\dot{C}_r$.

$$Px = [a\ b\ c]\begin{bmatrix} u \\ v \\ 1 \end{bmatrix} = \begin{pmatrix} a_x & b_x & c_x \\ a_y & b_y & c_y \\ a_z & b_z & c_z \end{pmatrix}\begin{pmatrix} u \\ v \\ 1 \end{pmatrix} \tag{1}$$

$$x_d = \delta(x_r)P_d^{-1}(\dot{C}_r - \dot{C}_d) + P_d^{-1}P_r x_r \tag{2}$$

$$\delta(x) = \frac{|Px|}{depth} = \frac{1}{w} \tag{3}$$

The forward warping Equation (2) takes samples $x_r = (u, v)$ described by a color and a disparity $\delta(x_r)$ as its input (see Equation (3)). Equation (2) maps them from a reference image (denoted by subscript r) into a desired image (denoted by subscript d, see Figure 2). The workings of the forward warping equation are shown in Figure 3 (reproduced from [14]). The figure shows a cross-section of Figure 2 known as the epipolar plane — the plane containing the two cameras' centers of projection and the 3D point $\dot{X}$.

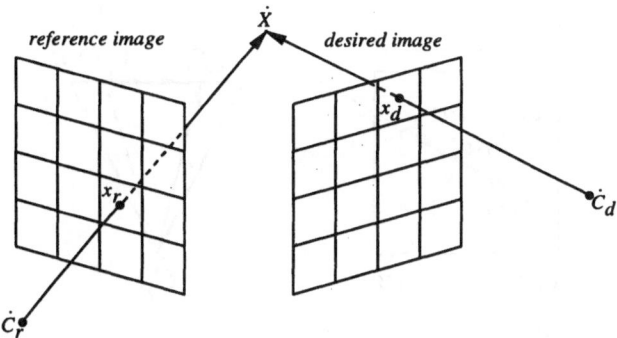

Fig. 2. Point $\dot{X}$ as seen in the reference image and in the desired image.

Subjecting every sample x_r to the warping equation will usually result in holes in the desired image because of different sampling densities in the reference and desired images. This is the main reason why inverse warping is desirable, as it makes sure that every pixel in the desired image is computed.

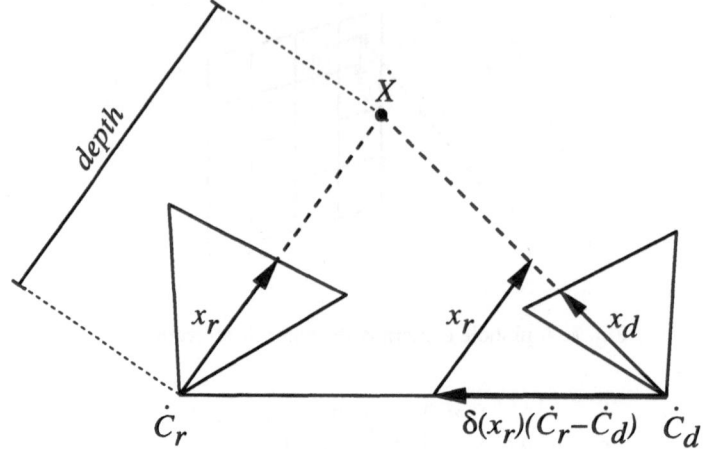

Fig. 3. Illustration of the forward warping equation in the epipolar plane.

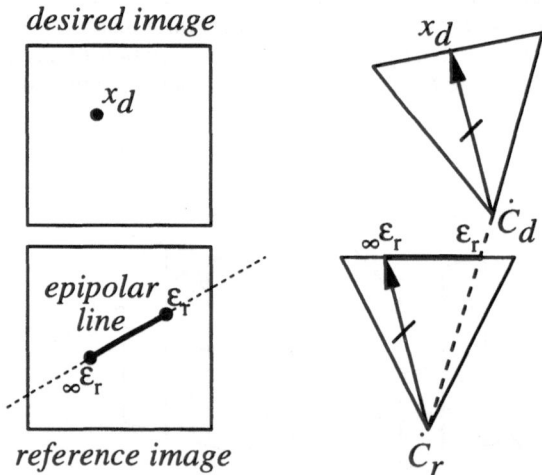

Fig. 4. Inverse warping: the epipolar line's extent in the reference image.

4 Inverse Image Warping

Two points in the reference image play an important role in which samples correspond to a pixel in the desired image — the epipole ϵ_r and the projection of the pixel's point at infinity $_\infty\epsilon_r$. They are determined by the viewing ray through a particular pixel in the desired image. Their geometric interpretation is illustrated in Figure 4 and Equation (4).

$$\epsilon_r = P_r^{-1}(\dot{C}_d - \dot{C}_r) \quad _\infty\epsilon_r = P_r^{-1}P_d x_d \tag{4}$$

The epipole ϵ_r is the intersection of the baseline connecting the two cameras $\dot{C}_r$ and $\dot{C}_d$ (also the ray's origin) with the reference image plane. The point $_\infty\epsilon_r$ is the projection of the ray's point at infinity into the reference image. These two points delimit the segment on the epipolar line, where the point x_r corresponding to the point x_d must lie (see Figure 4). The extent of this line segment must be searched to obtain x_r for every pixel in the desired image [17].

Our approach to inverse image warping (or backward mapping) differs from previous work [8, 14, 17] by making the observation that points x_d on epipolar lines in the desired image share the same corresponding epipolar line in the reference image. Therefore, there is great coherence between the searches for corresponding points when considering adjacent points along the epipolar line in the desired image [23].

This observation is inspired by the ray-casting of height-fields mentioned in the previous work section [1, 5, 10, 15]. In "image-warping terminology," height-fields are orthographic reference images. As long as the viewing direction in the desired image is horizontal, vertical pixel columns lie on epipolar lines in the desired image. The coherence along them can be exploited by sweeping a ray upwards in every pixel column, and the search for the intersection of the next ray's pixel with the terrain can start where the intersection for the last ray was found.

The same is true for warping the points along an epipolar line in an inverse warper. Figure 5 shows how the rays through the points along an epipolar line scan the samples in the reference image for correspondences. Instead of searching the complete segment between x_r and $_\infty\epsilon_r$ for every pixel, a match is typically found within a bounded number of steps starting from the match of the last pixel processed. Consequently, the expected runtime complexity of inverse warping is reduced from $O(n^3)$ to $O(n^2)$ for n by n reference and desired images. Instead of warping individual samples we warp epipolar lines as a whole.

5 Implementation

In order to warp a complete perspective image we need to cover the whole image with epipolar lines. For this we locate the epipoles in both images (see Figure 6). Then we trace epipolar lines from the border of the images towards the epipole in the case of a true epipole (the baseline connecting the two cameras pierces the image plane from the back) or from the epipole to the image border in the case of an antipode [9] (the baseline pierces the image plane from the front).

There are nine regions (A-I) in and around the image where the epipole can lie. This results in different numbers of image border-lines (a-d) that must be walked to cover the desired image. Table 1 summarizes these cases and Figure 7 shows the case of the epipole ϵ_d in region I. We use Bresenham's line rasterization algorithm to walk along

180

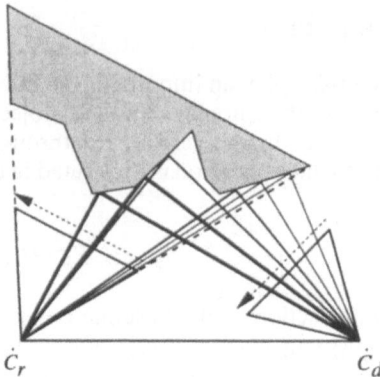

Fig. 5. Rays scanning the displacement map of the reference image along epipolar lines in both the reference and the desired image.

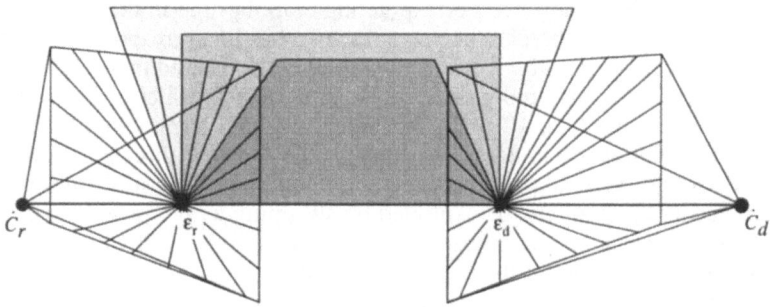

Fig. 6. The family of epipolar planes through the baseline covers both the reference and desired image with epipolar lines.

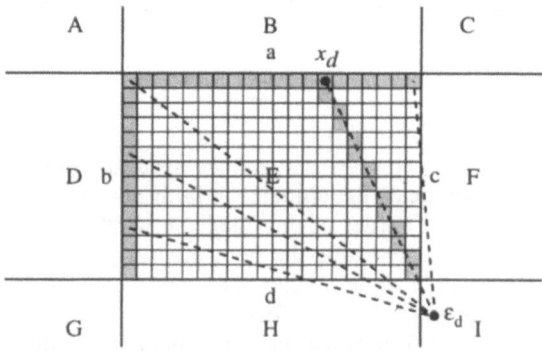

Fig. 7. Covering a raster image with epipolar lines.

the epipolar lines in the raster images [2]. In order to process every pixel in the desired image only once, we mark the processed pixels with a flag.

ϵ_d in region	A	B	C	D	E	F	G	H	I
border walks	2	3	2	3	4	3	2	3	2
borders	c, d	b, d, c	b, d	a, c, d	a, c, d, b	a, b, d	a, c	b, a, c	b, a

Table 1. Different cases depending on which region contains the epipole ϵ_d.

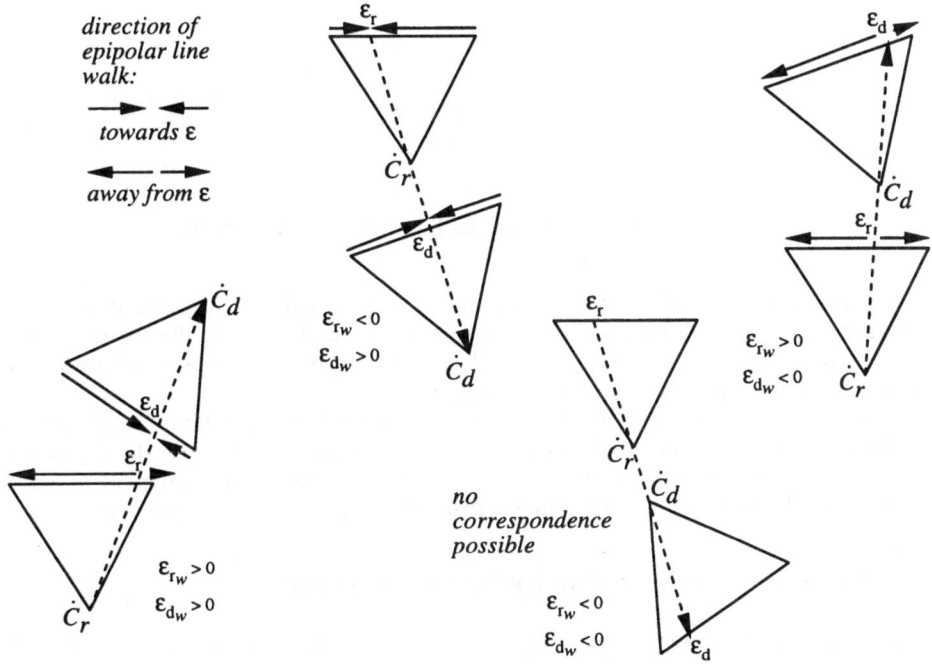

Fig. 8. The four different cases of walking order along epipolar lines.

Figure 8 summarizes the four cases of the walking direction along epipolar lines for both the reference image and the desired image. They are distinguished by the homogeneous coordinate of the images' epipoles (making the point an epipole or an antipode). Figure 9 depicts the five cases when clipping the epipolar line to the reference image results in a non-empty line segment. Notice how in some cases — a), b) and d) — points outside the segment connecting ϵ_r and $_\infty\epsilon_r$ are considered. When warping epipolar lines instead of individual points, the sign of the homogeneous coordinate of $_\infty\epsilon_r$ can change along the line. In warping algorithms, which consider a single point at a time different, the sign of $_\infty\epsilon_r$'s homogeneous coordinates correspond to different walking orders along the epipolar line in the reference image. This behavior is achieved when warping whole epipolar lines by continuing to search for correspondences beyond $_\infty\epsilon_r$. A different sign of the homogeneous coordinate takes $_\infty\epsilon_r$ to the other side of ϵ_r along the epipolar line and the search must proceed in the other direction. However, this is exactly the direction we have started with when the sign was still different.

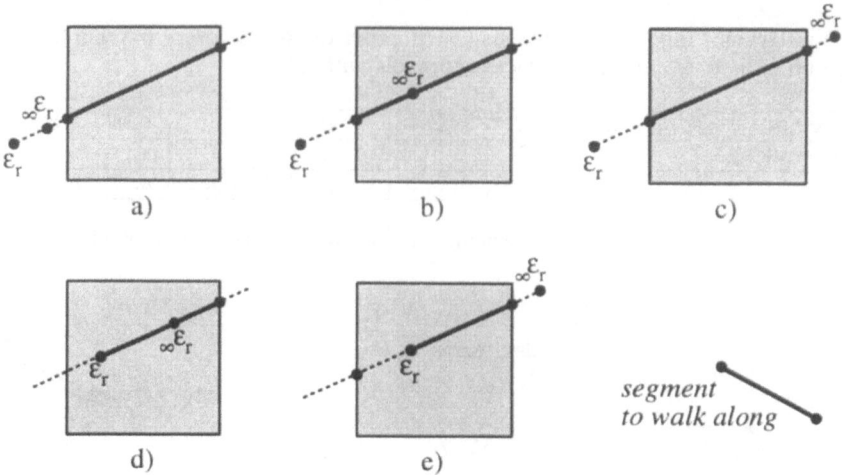

Fig. 9. Clipping the epipolar line to the reference image.

In order to know whether a correspondence of x_d with x_r was found, a minimal disparity $_{min}\delta(x_r)$ is determined from the warping equation. If the disparity $\delta(x_r)$ stored for x_r is larger than $_{min}\delta(x_r)$, then a correspondence exists. Otherwise the search along the epipolar line must continue.

Once a correspondence has been found, we calculate x_{d_w} (the homogeneous coordinate of the point in the desired image) and optionally convert it to depth using Equation (3) so that the depth test can be carried out in the desired image. For a scene entirely made up of displacement maps, disparity values can be compared instead.

6 Displacement Mapping by Image Warping

Displacement mapping by image warping is compatible with two classes of displacement maps: height-fields (orthographic projections) and displacements originating from a single point (perspective projections with the single point being the center of projection). Such displacement maps can be rendered using image warping. This is not as severe a restriction as it sounds because the directions of the displacements are usually irrelevant as long as the surface ends up at the desired 3D location. So even the displacements for a free-form surface could be done in this way — only the displacements may not always be in the direction of the surface normal. The restriction is that every ray in the reference image must not have more than one intersection with the desired surface. Otherwise, the surface will self-occlude and cause undesired rubber-sheets.

Figure 10 shows a simple example of how a displacement-mapped globe is built from a sphere by displacing a cube with six perspective depth images. The center of projection for all the six images is the center of the sphere and all the images have horizontal and vertical fields of view of ninety degrees. From left to right Figure 10 shows the frusta of the six images positioned in the cube, the rays of the reference images originating from the center of the sphere, the color image of the earth's texture, and the displacements.

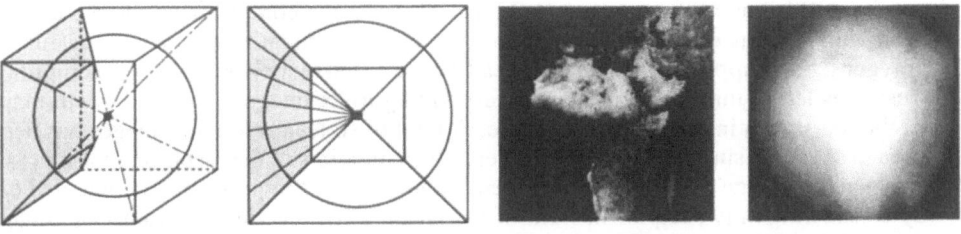

Fig. 10. An example of creating a displacement-mapped globe with six reference images. The frusta of these perspective images are arranged as a cube.

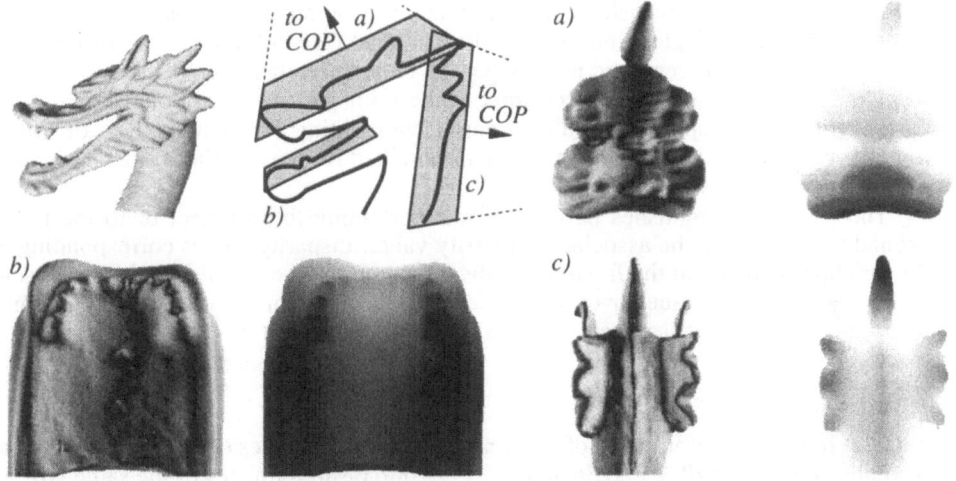

Fig. 11. Covering a dragon head with displacement maps — the arrows point to the centers of projection (COP). Both the texture (left) and the displacements (right) are shown for frusta a) – c).

Figure 11 illustrates how one would plan to cover the complex surface of a dragon head with reference images in order to obtain displacement maps for a hand-full of polygons. The upper left shows the head and a cross-section with three exemplified frusta labeled a) through c). Their corresponding RGB images (left) and depth maps (right) are shown in the rest of the figure. A total of sixteen reference images has been used to cover the surface of the dragon head. Not all points of the displacement-mapped polygon (the image plane) need to be used as samples. The required part is stenciled out by considering only samples in front of the far plane of the view-frustum. The image on the right of Figure 12 shows the polygons to be displaced into the dragon's head (see the color section).

7 Results

We implemented a program for the interactive placement of frusta on the surface of arbitrary geometry and the warper described in sections 4 and 5. The renderer uses the warper to map multiple displacement maps into the final image where they are composited using a depth buffer.

7.1 Interactive Frustum Placement

Figure 12 shows two screenshots of the interactive program used to place frusta on the displacement-mapped globe and on the dragon head (see color section). In this program, the geometry is rendered using OpenGL and the frusta are created and modified using the mouse. In the lower left corner of these images, the view obtained from the current frustum is displayed to guide the user with editing the frustum. Sets of frusta, together with the RGB and the depth images obtained from using them in a perspective projection, can be saved to a file.

The warper distinguishes between pixels pertaining to an object or to the background by examining the associated disparity value: disparity values corresponding to the far clipping plane of the frustum are the background pixels. This would allow us to "paint" far disparity values over unwanted image sections in order to avoid the aforementioned rubber-sheet artifacts. Currently, we do not exploit this possibility.

7.2 Warping Performance

Table 2 shows the performance of warping the reference images of our models taken at resolutions of 128x128, 256x256 and 512x512 into desired images of the same size on a 250 MHz R10000 processor. Note that in image warping for displacement mapping the individual displacement maps cover only a small fraction of the desired image. Therefore, restricting the epipolar line walk to those image sections will avoid a warping cost directly related to the number of displacement maps used.

The table lists the warping performance for the views given in Figure 13 (in the color section). Notice that $O(n^3)$ growth in the rendering time does not occur when increasing both the reference and desired image dimensions by a factor of two. In practice, variations in the warping performance can occur due to the position of the epipoles in the desired image as classified in Table 1. Also, the clipping of epipolar lines and the rejection of epipolar lines for which no correspondence is possible in the reference image account for some variation.

Model	Fig.13	ref. imgs.	resolution	time (sec)
Torus	top	6	128x128	0.0503
			256x256	0.2013
			512x512	0.7752
Globe	n/a	6	128x128	0.0523
			256x256	0.2911
			512x512	0.8362
Dragon	bottom	16	128x128	0.0842
			256x256	0.3218
			512x512	1.2276

Table 2. Warping performance in seconds on a R10000 processor running at 250 MHz.

8 Conclusions and Future Work

In this paper, we described a method to achieve interactive rendering of displacement mapped geometry by inverse image warping. The proposed warping algorithm is particularly suited for rendering displacement maps, because it always treats the samples in the reference images as being connected. Epipolar geometry is exploited to reduce the algorithmic complexity from $O(n^3)$, in previously described inverse warpers, to $O(n^2)$ making the performance comparable to forward warping.

Much work remains to be done in the field of obtaining the displacement maps of interesting objects. Stereo algorithms could be applied to acquire displacement maps for approximate geometry of real-world objects. 3D paint programs [12, 25] could be used by artists to paint displacements directly onto simple geometry to increase their visual richness, much in the way the terrain was created in the game *Myst* [18].

In terms of shading, simply warping color values from the reference images into the desired image restricts the lighting to be entirely static. We would like to apply techniques such as deferred shading and shadow maps in order to obtain a more dynamic lighting. Further, the image quality could be improved by applying interpolation schemes on the reference samples instead of picking the closest one.

We would also like to investigate whether avoiding a much denser sampling of the images around the epipole could significantly speed up the warping. Squares centered around the epipole could be used to define additional border lines from which epipolar lines are traced only up to the next inner square allowing to trade denser sampling for more frequent epipolar line setup.

Acknowledgments

We would like to thank the Stanford University Computer Graphics Group for making the dragon appearing in this paper available in their Stanford 3D Scanning Repository.

References

1. Barr, A., *"Ray-Tracing Deformed Surfaces"*, SIGGRAPH '86, pp 287-296.
2. Bresenham, J. E., *"Algorithm for Computer Control of a Digital Plotter"*, IBM Systems Journal 4(1), July 1965, pp 25-30.
3. Chen, S. E., L. Williams, *"View Interpolation for Image Synthesis"*, SIGGRAPH '93, pp 279-288.

186

4. Chen, S. E., *"Quicktime VR - An Image-Based Approach to Virtual Environment Navigation"*, SIGGRAPH '95, pp29-38.

5. Cohen-Or, D., E. Rich, U. Lerner, V. Shenkar, *"A Real-Time Photo-Realistic Visual Flythrough"*, IEEE Transactions on Visualization and Computer Graphics, Vol. 2, No. 3, September 1996, pp 255-265.

6. Cook, R. L., *"Shade Trees"*, SIGGRAPH '84, pp 223-231.

7. Cook, R. L., L. Carpenter, E. Catmull, *"The Reyes Image Rendering Architecture"*, SIGGRAPH '87, pp 95-102.

8. Debevec, P. E., C. J. Taylor, J. Malik, *"Modeling and Rendering Architecture from Photographs"*, SIGGRAPH '96, pp 11-20.

9. Faugeras, O., *"Three-Dimensional Computer Vision: A Geometric Viewpoint"*, MIT Press, Cambridge, Massachusetts, 1993.

10. Fishman, B., B. Schachter, *"Computer Display of Height Fields"*, Computers and Graphics, Vol 5 Number 2-4 1980, pp 53-60.

11. Grossman J.P., W. J. Dally, *"Point Sample Rendering"*, Proceedings of the 9th Eurographics Workshop on Rendering, June 29 - July 1, 1998, Vienna, Austria, pp 181-192.

12. Hanrahan, P., P. Haeberli, *"Direct WYSIWYG Painting and Texturing on 3D Shapes"*, SIGGRAPH '90, pp 215-223.

13. Logie J. R., J. W. Patterson, *"Inverse Displacement Mapping in the General Case"*, Computer Graphics Forum, 14 5, December 1995, pp 261-273.

14. Marcato, R.W., *"Optimizing an Inverse Warper"*, Master's Thesis, Massachusetts Institute of Technology, May 1998, pp 35-37.

15. Max, N., *"Vectorized Procedural Models for Natural Terrain: Waves and Islands in the Sunset"*, SIGGRAPH '81, pp 317-324.

16. McMillan, L., G. Bishop, *"Plenoptic Modeling: An Image-Based Rendering System"*, SIGGRAPH '95, pp 39-46.

17. McMillan, L., *"An Image-Based Approach to Three-Dimensional Computer Graphics"*, Ph.D. Dissertation, University of North Carolina, April 1997.

18. Miller, R., Miller, R., *"The Making of Myst"* , Video accompanying the adventure game *"Myst"* by Cyan, Inc.

19. Patterson J. W., S. G. Hoggar, J. R. Logie, *"Inverse Displacement Mapping"*, Computer Graphics Forum, 10 2, June 1991, pp 129-139.

20. Pharr, M., P. Hanrahan, *"Geometry Caching for Ray-Tracing Displacement Maps"*, Proceedings of the 7th Eurographics Workshop on Rendering 1996, pp 31-40.

21. Pharr, M., C. Kolb, R. Gershberg, P. Hanrahan, *"Rendering Complex Scenes with Memory-Coherent Ray-Tracing"*, SIGGRAPH '97, pp 101-108.

22. Popescu, V., A. Lastra, D. Aliaga, M. de Oliveira, *"Efficient Warping for Architectural Walkthroughs using Layered Depth Images"*, IEEE Visualization '98, pp 211-215.

23. Priglinger, M., *"Re-projecting Images with Depth"*, Master's Thesis, Johannes Kepler University Linz, September 1998 (in German).

24. Taillefer, F., *"Fast Inverse Displacement Mapping and Shading in Shadow"*, Graphics Interface '92 Workshop on Local Illumination, Vancouver, May 1992, pp 53-60.

25. Williams, L., *"3D Paint"*, Proceedings of the Symposium on Interactive 3D Graphics 1990, pp 225-234.

Editors' Note: see Appendix, p. 368 for colored figures of this paper

Light Field Techniques for Reflections and Refractions

Wolfgang Heidrich[†], Hendrik Lensch[†], Michael F. Cohen[*], Hans-Peter Seidel[†]

[†]Max-Planck-Institute for Computer Science
{heidrich,lensch,seidel}@mpi-sb.mpg.de

[*]Microsoft Research
mcohen@microsoft.com

Abstract. Reflections and refractions are important visual effects that have long been considered too costly for interactive applications. Although most contemporary graphics hardware supports reflections off curved surfaces in the form of environment maps, refractions in thick, solid objects cannot be handled with this approach, and the simplifying assumptions of environment maps also produce visible artifacts for reflections.
Only recently have researchers developed techniques for the interactive rendering of true reflections and refractions in curved objects. This paper introduces a new, light field based approach to achieving this goal. The method is based on a strict decoupling of geométry and illumination. Hardware support for all stages of the technique is possible through existing extensions of the OpenGL rendering pipeline. In addition, we also discuss storage issues and introduce methods for handling vector-quantized data with graphics hardware.

1 Introduction

Reflections and refractions are important visual effects that have not been handled appropriately in interactive applications. Highly reflective or transparent objects can be thought of as a lens that transforms incoming rays into outgoing rays in some new direction. Consider a glass pitcher half full of water. A ray of light entering the pitcher may be reflected and/or refracted many times, eventually leaving the pitcher in some new direction. (We will ignore the fact that some of the energy may be absorbed and the ray may split into a tree of subrays.) Unfortunately, it is not possible to compute this mapping from rays in to rays out in real time for complex objects. However, for static objects, this map can be computed offline and reused at each frame at render time if we can find a way to efficiently represent this mapping and provide fast lookup methods.

The light field [13] and Lumigraph [6] image based rendering approaches faced a similar problem. In this work it was recognized that one could precompute all the light leaving the convex hull of an object and then quickly lookup appropriate values to create any image of the object. This 4D mapping from rays out from an object to colors was the central structure of these methods.

A key idea in the current work is to replace the mapping from rays to colors as found in the Lumigraph with a mapping from rays to rays. In other words, replace the RGB color triplet with four numbers representing a new ray direction. Storing this mapping in the form of a Lumigraph allows us to use all the methodologies developed in [13] and [6].

This completely decouples the illumination from the geometry, and allows us to exchange the environment and the refracting/reflecting object independently of each other. Such a separation also has the advantage that some extra blurring for the indirect illumination will in most cases be tolerable since direct illumination is visually much more important than indirect illumination for almost all scenes. This means that one can get away with a lower resolution light field, which saves memory and reduces the acquisition cost.

After a discussion of previous work, we first introduce some notation for light fields, and then describe our technique for rendering reflections and refractions in Section 4. We then turn to the hardware rendering of vector-quantized light fields [13] in Section 5, and discuss our approaches in Section 6.

2   Previous Work

Producing approximate reflections and refractions at interactive rates has been done with environment maps [2]. The inherent assumption is that what is seen in a reflection is sufficiently far away from the reflector. This assumption breaks down in many scenes.

Environment maps can also be used for refractions at thin surfaces. A thin surface is one, for which the thin lens approximation holds (see [3]). This approximation assumes that the entry and exit points of each ray coincide. It does not hold for objects like glass balls, but it can be used for windows or spectacle lenses.

Only recently have researchers started to develop algorithms that do not have these restrictions. A commonly used technique for rendering mirror reflections in planar objects is given in [5]: with a simple affine model/view matrix, the scene is mirrored at the planar reflector. This mirrored scene is rendered at every pixel where the reflector is visible in the current view. It is possible to realize multiple reflections by repeating this process as explained in [5].

For curved objects the geometric transformations yielding the reflected geometry are more complex. Rather than transforming the complete object with a single affine transformation, a different transformation is required for each point on the reflected object. In [16] an algorithm is introduced, in which all vertices of the reflected geometry are individually transformed in software. This approach only works at interactive frame rates for relatively smooth objects that are either concave or convex.

As mentioned above, the light field [13] and Lumigraph [6] approaches are based on a dense sampling of the plenoptic function [1], which describes the flow of light in a scene. This way, the light field outside the convex hull of an object in empty space can be represented as a 4-dimensional function in the parameters u, v, s, and t. The parameterization of this function is a topic of ongoing research [4], but typically the 2-plane parameterization explained in Section 3 is used [6, 13]. The advantage of the light field approach is that images of the scene from new camera positions can simply be computed by interpolating radiance values in 4 dimensions. This is a very inexpensive operation that can be further accelerated through the use of OpenGL-compliant graphics hardware, as has been shown in [6] and [19].

The disadvantage of this method is that it involves large memory requirements to store the 4D data structures. A light field of moderate resolution can easily have a size of multiple Gigabytes. The authors of [13] have proposed to use vector quantization (VQ) to compress the data. VQ has some interesting advantages over other compression methods that make it attractive for compressing light fields. Firstly, decompression is a constant time operation, and secondly the different entries can be decompressed independently of each other and in arbitrary order (random access). In Section 5 we describe how the hardware accelerated rendering algorithm for light fields [6] can be extended to the direct rendering of vector-quantized light fields. This means that the light fields do not have to be decompressed before hardware rendering, which is particularly interesting since texture RAM is typically a scarce resource.

The Lumigraph [6] extends the concept of a light field by adding some geometric information which helps compensating for artifacts that arise from the use of quadrilinear interpolation for the reconstruction. A coarse polygon mesh is stored together with the images. The mesh is used to first find the approximate depth along the ray to be reconstructed, and then this depth is used to correct the weights for the interpolation. This depth corrected rendering can also be accelerated with graphics hardware [6].

Miller [15] attempts to overcome blurring artifacts by introducing a parameterization in which the u and v parameters of the light field are the surface parameters of the reflecting object, and s and t parameterize the hemisphere of directions over the surface point (u, v). The authors call this a *surface light field* because the (u, v) parameters are directly attached to the surface of the reflector. This is particularly well suited to mostly diffuse objects with well defined surface parameters.

In addition to this different parameterization, [15] also introduces a block-based compression scheme which achieves higher compression ratios than VQ, but is also more complicated and requires the decompression of a complete block of values. This decompression has to be performed in software during the resampling process used for generating the texture maps.

Both light field representations reach their limits when it comes to mirror reflections and narrow specular highlights from light sources. These will in both approaches still result in some amount of unwanted blurring, due to the limited (s, t) resolution of the light field.

This problem is fixed by another approach for using light fields to render reflections [14]. There, the authors introduce the concept of *image-based ray-tracing* to render mirror reflections. In this work, a light field not only stores radiance values, but also geometric information such as depth and normal. The method proceeds by tracing rays through a light field of layered depth images [18]. This method is computationally expensive and cannot be performed in real time on contemporary hardware.

3 Light Fields

Our work builds strongly on the light field [13], and the Lumigraph [6]. A light field is a dense sampling of the 5-dimensional plenoptic function [1], which describes the radiance at every point in space in every direction. Since radiance does not change along a ray in empty space (e.g., outside the convex hull of an object), the dimensionality can be reduced by one, if an appropriate parameterization is found, that reflects this property.

The so-called 2-plane parameterization used by [13] and [6] representation fulfills this requirement. It represents a ray via its intersection points with two parallel planes. Since each of these points is characterized by two parameters in the plane, this results in a 4-dimensional function that is sampled through a regular grid on each plane (see Fig. 1).

One useful property of the 2-plane parameterization is that all the rays passing through a single point on the (s, t)-plane form a perspective image of the scene, with the (s, t) point being the center of projection. Thus, a light field can be considered a 2-dimensional array of images with eye points regularly spaced on the (s, t)-plane.

Moreover, since we assume that the sampling is dense, the radiance along an arbitrary ray passing through the two planes can be interpolated from the known radiance values in nearby grid points. Each such ray passes through one of the grid cells on the (s, t)-plane and one on the (u, v)-plane. These are bounded by four grid points on the respective plane, and the radiance from any of the (u, v)-points to any of the (s, t)-points is stored in the data structure. This makes for a total of 16 radiance values, from which the radiance along the ray can be interpolated quadri-linearly. As shown in [6], this can also be done in hardware.

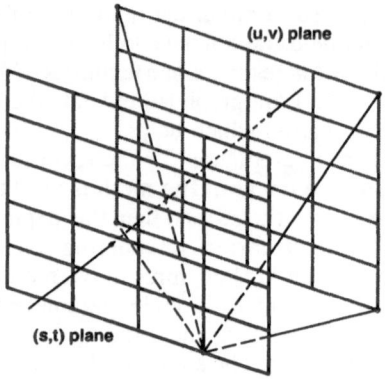

Fig. 1. A light field can be parameterized as a 2-dimensional array of images taken from a regular grid of eye points on the (s, t)-plane through a window on the (u, v)-plane.

For each eye point on the (s, t)-plane, the hardware rendering algorithm draws the grid cells surrounding the eye point using graphics hardware. The alpha values of the polygon vertices are set to 1 at the eye point and to 0 everywhere else. Furthermore, each rendered polygon is textured with the (u, v)-slice corresponding to the eye point, and these textures are weighted by the alpha values of the polygons. This combination of alpha blending and texture mapping with bi-linear interpolation yields the desired reconstruction.[1] This hardware algorithms is many times faster than a purely software-based approach. For example, on an SGI O2 the hardware renderer can achieve approximately 25 frames per second in full screen resolution. This number is almost independent of light field resolution.

The possibility to use graphics hardware for rendering is also what distinguishes the 2-plane parameterization from most other parameterizations that have been proposed for light fields (see, for example [4]). For us, this is the reason to use the 2-plane parameterization.

4 Decoupling Geometry and Illumination

As stated above, the core of the proposed method is to separate the geometry and the illumination of an object into two distinct image-based data structures. The first data structure is a 2-plane parameterized "light field" containing a mapping from incoming rays to outgoing rays based on the geometry and refractive properties of the object. The outgoing rays are stored in the form of a color coded direction. The illumination corresponding to this outgoing ray can either be provided in the form of an environment map or in the form of another light field.

Thus, to render a complete image, first the geometry light field is rendered, yielding an image of color coded ray directions. These can then be used to look up the illumination from an environment map, to trace new rays into a scene, or lookup a color from a second light field describing the surrounding scene.

When using environment maps, the geometry light field can directly contain the 2D texture coordinates for the entry in the environment map that corresponds to the

---

[1] As pointed out in [6] quadri-linear interpolation is not possible due to the use of Gouraud shading for the interpolation of the alpha values across polygons. However, the described algorithm yields a close approximation.

refracted ray direction. The format for these values depends on the specific parameterization used for the environment map. For example, for a spherical environment map [7], the texture coordinates are given as the x and y components of the normalized halfway vector $\vec{h} = (h_x, h_y, h_z)^T$ between the refracted viewing ray $\vec{v}$ and the z-axis (see Fig. 2).

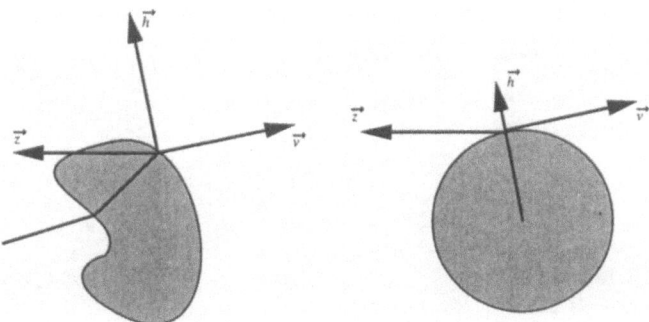

Fig. 2. The texture coordinates that correspond to a certain ray direction $\vec{v}$ in a spherical environment map are given by the normalized halfway vector $\vec{h}$ between $\vec{v}$ and the z-axis (left). This is because a spherical map is the image of a small, reflective sphere as seen by an orthographic camera looking into the negative z-axis. The vector $\vec{h}$ corresponds to both the point on the sphere where $\vec{v}$ is the reflection of $\vec{z}$, and to the sphere's surface normal in that point.

In our implementation we use the parabolic parameterization presented in [10]. It has the advantage of providing a more uniform sampling of the hemisphere of directions than the spherical parameterization, and the texture coordinates are less expensive to compute. The texture coordinates of the parabolic parameterization are given as h_x/h_z and h_y/h_z, which means that a simple division suffices to compute the texture coordinates instead of a vector normalization. While the advantage of a uniform sampling is essential, the performance benefits are not significant in our case.

Independent of how the illumination is represented, the first step in the algorithm is the hardware-based rendering of the geometry light field as described in [6] and [19]. Afterwards, the framebuffer contains an image with the color coded texture coordinates for the environment map holding the illumination information. Now the framebuffer contents are read back to main memory and for each pixel the texture coordinates need to be used to look up the illumination from the environment map, before the resulting image is written back to the framebuffer, yielding the final image.

The texture lookup can be achieved in one of the following two ways. Firstly, it can be performed in software. This is a relatively inexpensive operation, that is feasible even on low end platforms, as shown below. Alternatively, the graphics hardware can be employed for the texture lookup, using an extension that is available from SGI. The so-called *pixel texture extension* [17, 8] modifies the rendering pipeline in such a way that the color values of the pixels in an image can be interpreted as texture coordinates, which are then in turn used to texture each individual pixel. This feature can be applied during so-called *pixel transfer operations*, that is, during the transfer of images to and from the framebuffer, and is exactly the functionality required for our algorithm. Although pixel textures are currently a proprietary extension from SGI, their usefulness is demonstrated by several applications, and will hopefully result in a more widespread availability of this extension.

Fig. 3 shows images that were generated using this approach. The left image represents the color coded texture coordinates reconstructed from the geometry light field. The light field itself was generated using ray-tracing. Center and right represent the final result after the application of the environment map. This method is very fast, and achieves between 15 and 20 fps. on an Octane MXE using the pixel texture extension. The same images can be rendered with the software method at about 10 frames per second on an SGI O2 with a 175 MHz R10k (images are of size 400×400 pixels).

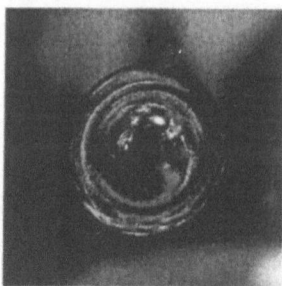

Fig. 3. Light fields rendering with decoupled geometry and illumination, the latter being provided through an environment map. Left: color coded texture coordinates for the environment map, as extracted from the geometry light field. Center/right: final renderings.

4.1 Illumination from Light Fields

Instead of using an environment map to store the illumination, it is also possible to use a second light field. The advantage of this approach is the additional dependency on the surface location, which allows for the proper handling of objects close to the refractor. As stated above, the use of environment maps for illumination is typically not of interest for implementing reflections. If the illumination is stored in light fields, however, the situation is different, because the near field effects that can be achieved with this method exceed the possibilities of traditional geometry-based rendering with environment maps.

To store the illumination in a light field, the geometry light field has to contain the correct 4-dimensional ray direction u, v, s, and t referencing into the illumination light field. The ray direction can be color coded into the R, G, B and A channels of the geometry light field. The exact coordinates, of course, again depend on the parameterization of the illumination light field.

The rendering algorithm proceeds similarly to the case where the illumination is stored in an environment map. First, the geometry light field is rendered using hardware acceleration. Then, the framebuffer contents are read back to main memory. The ray lookup for determining the illumination is either performed in software, or using pixel textures and 4-dimensional texture mapping. The latter method will be described in more detail in Section 5.

4.2 Realistic Materials

So far, we have only considered either reflections or refractions, which is mandated by the fact that the geometry light field can only store either the coordinates for the reflection or for the refraction part. However, it is possible to combine the two parts using multi-pass rendering, and also to develop models for more complicated materials, such as glossy reflections and the inclusion of a Fresnel term. These multi-pass techniques have been introduced for geometry-based rendering in [11] and [9], but they directly translate to the image-based rendering techniques presented in this paper. Please refer to the listed publications for the details. Fig. 4 gives an example of these techniques.

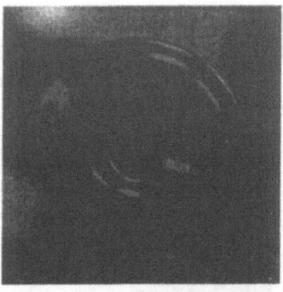 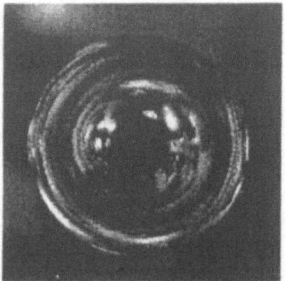 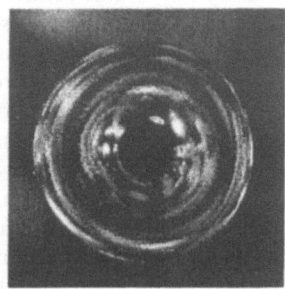

Fig. 4. The glossy torus on the left is the result of a geometry rendering with a prefiltered environment map. The torus in the center represents the refraction part. Both parts have been weighted by the appropriate Fresnel term. The right image shows the combination of the two parts.

5 Hardware Rendering of Vector-quantized Light Fields

One of the fundamental problems of light fields and Lumigraphs is the large memory consumption. For practical applications of these techniques it is therefore mandatory to compress the data sets. The problem with current implementations of compression schemes is that the hardware cannot directly deal with the compressed data. As a consequence, the required parts of the light field have to be decompressed before the hardware can be used. This is unfortunate since the texture RAM is a particularly scarce resource in many systems. If it is too small to hold the required parts of the light field, these need to be swapped in and out for every frame, which consumes large amounts of bandwidth, and results in serious performance penalties. The major reason why the hardware rendering of light fields performs so well on O2s (see Section 3), is that on this platform the texture RAM resides in main memory and is thus almost unlimited.

In the following we describe two slightly different methods for rendering vector-quantized light fields directly in hardware without the need to decompress them beforehand. VQ compresses a light field by replacing the color values of an adjacent block of pixels by a single index into a lookup table containing the color values. An often used configuration is to choose the block size as 2^4 and the table size as 2^{16}, meaning that 2 samples in each of the parametric directions u, v, s, and t are subsumed in a block, and all 16 RGB colors in the block are replaced by a single 2 Byte color index. This yields a compression ratio of $1 : 24$ (neglecting the size of the lookup table). The advantage of VQ over other compression techniques is that the basic structure of the data set is preserved: a light field is a 4-dimensional array of samples. A vector-quantized light field with the above parameters is a 4-dimensional array of color indices, but the resolution is reduced by a factor of 2 in each parametric direction. Instead of having a single lookup table that yields the complete 2^4 block of color values for each index, it is also possible to use 16 different tables, where each only returns a single color value. This is one table for all combinations of odd/even sample locations in the four parametric directions u, v, s, and t.

This property can be used for two related algorithms of rendering compressed light fields, using a hardware extension that is currently available. This extension is the so-called *texture color table*, which, in contrast to all the other color tables in the OpenGL pipeline, is *not* a pixel transfer operation, but takes place *after* the texture lookup and filtering. This extension is available on all SGI systems, and has in the past been used primarily for volume rendering (see, e.g. [20]).

This extension allows us to store the light field as a set of one-component textures. Then, multiple rendering passes with different color lookup tables are used to reconstruct the colors. Special care has to be taken for the interpolation of these color values. The difficulty is that the color in each pixel needs to be interpolated from the colors resulting from lookups in all the color tables. This can be achieved through alpha blending, as described below.

Let us assume for a moment that only the resolution on the (s, t)-plane, the plane of eye points, has been halved by the VQ algorithm. Then, the rendering is a trivial extension of the algorithm described in Section 3. The only difference to the algorithm there is that the correct texture color table needs to be loaded before polygons surrounding the (s, t)-sample point are rendered. Since in this situation there are only four different color tables, the (s, t)-samples can be ordered in such a way that only 4 changes of the color table are required for every frame (all samples with even s and even t have one table, all samples with even s and odd t another, and so forth).

Now, if the resolution on the (u, v)-plane is also halved, then it is necessary to interpolate the color values for a pixel in the (u, v)-plane between images generated by four different table lookups. This is achieved by rendering the basis functions for a bi-linear interpolation into the alpha channel, and then multiplying this basis function with the result of a nearest-neighbor sampled image resulting from a single table lookup. Repeating this process four times with four different lookup tables and the four corresponding basis functions, and summing up the results in the framebuffer, yields the correctly reconstructed image.

Fig. 5. Top: the 2×2 texture used to render the basis functions into the alpha buffer. Bottom: The set of basis functions for one color table. This image was generated by applying bilinear texture filtering to several replicated copies of the texture from the left.

To render the basis functions into the alpha channel, we specify a single 2×2 texture in which exactly one pixel is one, and the others are zero. By replicating this texture according to the resolution of the (u, v)-plane in the original light field, and by using bi-linear texture mapping, the basis functions for, say, all odd u and all even v samples can be rendered. If the same texture is shifted by one texel in subsequent rendering passes, the other basis functions can be rendered as well. Fig. 5 illustrates this method. The cost of this technique is about four times the cost of rendering an uncompressed light field, so that the method only pays off if the texture RAM is too small to hold the complete data set. The color plates show a comparison of the uncompressed light field rendering with vector-quantized data sets.

Another hardware-accelerated algorithm for rendering light fields that might become interesting in the future, is 4-dimensional texture mapping. Currently, this feature is supported on some high-end SGI machines. With 4D texture mapping the rendering of 2-plane parameterized light fields becomes extremely simple. The (s, t) grid is projected down on the (u, v)-plane to compute the texture coordinates for the corner vertices of the (u, v)-grid. Then (u, v)-plane is rendered as a single polygon with the precomputed 4D texture coordinates, and the light field as a texture.

4D texture mapping is also interesting in combination with the pixel texture extension, and can be applied in the reflection and refraction algorithm from Section 4.1. Here, the R, G, B, and A channels of each pixel in the image are interpreted as 4D texture coordinates u, v, s, and t.

The disadvantage of 4D texture mapping in the context of light field rendering is, that the whole light field needs to fit into the texture RAM. For practical applications this mandates the use of a compression technique, and VQ is again a good choice that allows us to exploit graphics hardware.

Since 4D texture mapping does not treat the (u, v)-plane differently from the (s, t)-plane like the algorithm from [6], the implementation is somewhat different than described above. What remains is the concept of using the alpha channel to render basis functions for the different lookup tables. This time, however, the basis functions are generated by 4D textures of resolution 2^4. In each of these textures, exactly two pixels are one and the others are zero. Fig. 6 illustrates this for a 2-dimensional "light field".

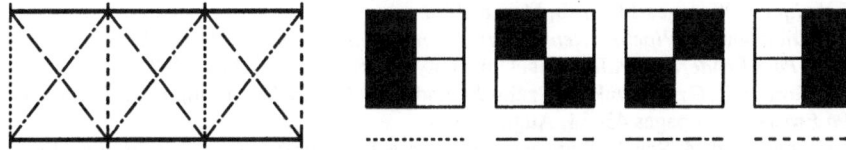

Fig. 6. The textures that comprise the basis functions for a 2D "light field", and the rays that each basis function corresponds to.

6 Discussion and Conclusion

In this paper we have explored practical techniques for applying light fields to the rendering of reflections and refractions on curved objects. Firstly, our method separates geometric and illumination information into two independent, image-based representations. The advantage of this approach is an increased flexibility for modeling. Image-based representations of objects can be positioned in a scene and lit by image-based representations of the illumination in that scene. Existing graphics hardware can be efficiently utilized for the implementation of the algorithm.

Secondly, we have described a technique for rendering vector-quantized light fields directly with graphics hardware. This approach is not limited to the rendering of reflections and refractions, but is a natural extension of the hardware algorithm presented in [6], and can therefore be used with all hardware light field renderers.

The techniques presented here rely on some OpenGL extensions that have not yet become mainstream features in low-end graphics hardware. However, all the extensions used have proven to be useful in several other applications as well [20, 12], so that it seems likely that some of these features will find their way into future graphics standards.

This idea of storing geometric information instead of simply color values in a light field can be extended even further. For example, if normal vectors are stored in the light field data structure, the local illumination for the object can be computed using the very same hardware techniques also applied to normal maps in [11] and [9]. With these techniques, it is possible to recompute the illumination for each point using complex materials models. This allows for image-based rendering with changing illumination, an area that has recently been of increased interest in the research community.

7 Acknowledgments

The environment map used in this paper is a resampled version of the cafe used in [7]. The Buddha light field is from the Stanford collection of light field data sets.

References

1. E. H. Adelson and J. R. Bergen. *Computational Models of Visual Processing*, chapter 1 (The Plenoptic Function and the Elements of Early Vision). MIT Press, Cambridge, MA, 1991.
2. J. F. Blinn and M. E. Newell. Texture and reflection in computer generated images. *Communications of the ACM*, 19:542–546, 1976.
3. M. Born and E. Wolf. *Principles of Optics*. Pergamon Press, Oxford, 6 edition, 1993.
4. E. Camahort, A. Lerios, and D. Fussell. Uniformly sampled light fields. In *Rendering Techniques '98*, pages 117–130, March 1998.
5. P. J. Diefenbach. *Pipeline Rendering: Interaction and Realism Through Hardware-based Multi-Pass Rendering*. PhD thesis, University of Pennsylvania, June 1996.
6. S. J. Gortler, R. Grzeszczuk, R. Szelinski, and M. F. Cohen. The Lumigraph. In *SIGGRAPH '96 Proceedings*, pages 43–54, August 1996.
7. P. Haeberli and M. Segal. Texture mapping as A fundamental drawing primitive. In *Fourth Eurographics Workshop on Rendering*, pages 259–266, June 1993.
8. P. Hansen. Introducing pixel texture. In *Developer News*, pages 23–26. SGI, May 1997.
9. W. Heidrich. *High-quality Shading and Lighting for Hardware-accelerated Rendering*. PhD thesis, University of Erlangen-Nürnberg, April 1999.
10. W. Heidrich and H.-P. Seidel. View-independent environment maps. In *Eurographics/SIGGRAPH Workshop on Graphics Hardware*, pages 39–45, 1998.
11. W. Heidrich and H.-P. Seidel. Realistic, hardware-accelerated shading and lighting. In *SIGGRAPH '99 Proceedings*, August 1999. See http://www.mpi-sb.mpg.de/~heidrich.
12. W. Heidrich, R. Westermann, H.-P. Seidel, and Th. Ertl. Applications of pixel textures in visualization and realistic image synthesis. In *Symposium on Interactive 3D Graphics*, 1999.
13. M. Levoy and P. Hanrahan. Light field rendering. In *SIGGRAPH '96 Proceedings*, pages 31–42, August 1996.
14. D. Lischinski and A. Rappoport. Image-based rendering for non-diffuse synthetic scenes. In *Rendering Techniques '98*, pages 301–314, June 1998.
15. G. Miller, S. Rubin, and D. Ponceleon. Lazy decompression of surface light fields for pre-computed global illumination. In *Rendering Techniques '98*, pages 281–292, March 1998.
16. E. Ofek and A. Rappoport. Interactive reflections on curved objects. In *SIGGRAPH '98 Proceedings*, pages 333–342, July 1998.
17. SGI. *Pixel Texture Extension*, December 1996. Specification document, available from http://www.opengl.org.
18. J. W. Shade, S. J. Gortler, L. He, and R. Szeliski. Layered depth images. In *SIGGRAPH '98 Proceedings*, pages 231–242, July 1998.
19. P.-P. Sloan, M. F. Cohen, and S. J. Gortler. Time critical Lumigraph rendering. In *Symposium on Interactive 3D Graphics*, 1997.
20. R. Westermann and Th. Ertl. Efficiently using graphics hardware in volume rendering applications. In *SIGGRAPH '98 Proceedings*, pages 169–178, July 1998.

Editors' Note: see Appendix, p. 369 for colored figures of this paper

Shadow Penumbras for Complex Objects by Depth-Dependent Filtering of Multi-Layer Depth Images

Brett Keating and Nelson Max

Lawrence Livermore National Laboratory and UC Davis

Abstract. This paper presents an efficient algorithm for filtering multi-layer depth images (MDIs) in order to produce approximate penumbras. The filtering is performed on a MDI that represents the view from the light source. The algorithm is based upon both ray tracing and the z-buffer shadow algorithm, and is closely related to convolution methods. The method's effectiveness is demonstrated on especially complex objects such as trees, whose soft shadows are expensive to compute by other methods. The method specifically addresses the problem of light-leaking that occurs when tracing rays through discrete representations, and the inability of convolution methods to produce accurate self-shadowing effects.

1   Introduction and Background

1.1   Introduction

Depth images are images that contain the depth of a visible object at each pixel, possibly along with other relevant scene information such as surface color. They are extremely common in computer graphics; the well-known and often-used z-buffer is a special case of a depth image. Depth images can be obtained synthetically by using a 3-D rendering engine, or they can be captured from real-life scenes by using special range-finding technologies or by finding correspondences between photographs.

An image-based rendering technique known as *view interpolation* uses depth images as input to synthesize new images [4]. This technique enjoys a rendering cost independent of geometric complexity. One major problem with view interpolation is the occurrence of holes in the synthesized images. To help solve this, Max extended the view interpolation technique to handle multiple depths at each pixel in a *multi-layer depth image* (MDI) [16]. MDIs contain additional important information about hidden surfaces at each viewpoint, which allows for reprojections that contain far less holes. Shade et al. proposed *layered depth images* (LDIs), which are multi-layer depth images optimized for rendering speed [24]. Each pixel in a layered depth image is called a *layered depth pixel*, each of which is a sorted collection of *depth pixels*.

The success of image-based rendering encouraged researchers to extend the technique so that it could produce general rendering effects, such as global illumination [14,17]. Also, image-based objects are beginning to be used in place of geometric objects [24]. This provides the motivation for the current work, which presents a technique for computing penumbras cast by image-based objects.

We propose a method for calculating penumbras that operates on a single multi-layer depth image, rendered from the point of view of the light source. Although image-based rendering motivates this work, the proposed method can be used in conjunction with virtually any rendering paradigm. We use an efficient incremental ray-tracing algorithm, similar to that used in [14]. The rays essentially perform an approximate integration operation on the visibility function, and this can be re-interpreted as a filtering scheme. Viewing the algorithm as a filtering scheme allows us to merge our algorithm with percentage-closer filtering [22], make direct comparisons with convolution methods [15,25], and weight the contribution of each ray to the final shadow.

1.2 Previous Work in Soft Shadow Calculation

The calculation of a penumbra can be viewed as the problem of computing the partial visibility of a light source from points on a surface. The darkness of the shadow cast by a light source at a point corresponds exactly to the occluded fraction of the source. Penumbra calculation is a difficult problem that has given rise to numerous different solutions, each with their own set of advantages and disadvantages [31].

Perhaps the most obvious approach to solving this problem would be to construct a frustum from a point on the surface back towards the light source. By doing so, one can clip objects to the frustum, effectively clipping objects against the extent of the light source. Tanaka et al. propose a fairly fast way to accomplish this calculation [27]. They use a ray-oriented buffer to cull much of the geometry in the scene. Then for the remaining objects, they use a fast silhouette generation algorithm in combination with a sophisticated clipping technique to quickly find the occluded area of the light source.

Discontinuity meshing is another exact method for calculating penumbra regions [7,11,13,26]. This technique partitions surfaces into regions within which all points view the light source as having the same topological configuration of vertices and edges. The visible area of the light source can be interpolated exactly within each of these regions. Collectively, these regions form a mesh known as a discontinuity mesh. Although this method is accurate, it can suffer from numerical instability and is also expensive to compute, especially for scenes containing a large number of objects. Discontinuity meshing methods are often used in a radiosity setting. There are several ways to compute soft shadows in radiosity, notably [5,21].

Since this problem tends to be expensive and difficult to solve exactly, much research has been done on finding approximate solutions [25,31]. Most of these solutions approximate an area light source by sampling its extent. One such approximation technique that can yield accurate soft shadows is distributed ray tracing [6]. This popular technique fires shadow rays from a point on a surface to sample points on a light source. The fraction of shadow at the surface point is equal to the proportion of rays that hit an intermediate object before reaching the light. This method is intuitive and completely general, however many rays are necessary to compute accurate penumbras. The current technique is closely related to this method, as is cone tracing [1].

The accumulation buffer is another method that samples the extent of the light source [9]. It does so by approximating it as a collection of point light sources. A visibility algorithm, such as a z-buffer, calculates a hard shadow (no penumbra) from the point of view of each point light source. These hard shadows are averaged in order to produce a soft shadow. This method requires many sample lights for adequate shadow quality, however view interpolation can be applied between samples to increase efficiency [4]. Other closely related approaches include [2,10].

Soft shadows have also been approximated using convolution techniques. These techniques use the fast Fourier transform to efficiently convolute an image of the light source with an image of the blockers, and the resulting blurred blocker image is projected onto receiver objects. Max applied the convolution technique to render penumbras caused by occluded sunlight and skylight underneath trees [15]. Soler et al. extended the convolution technique to more general situations, and utilized hardware to create soft shadows relatively quickly [25]. However, surfaces cannot accurately shadow themselves by this method.

Most of the above methods attempt to be completely general in their treatment of light sources. Other work has been done on specific types of light sources, such as sunlight or linear sources [20,28]. Our work addresses light sources that are moderately small in extent. A single MDI only gives completely accurate visibility from a single viewpoint, but the visibility is approximately correct for nearby viewpoints, as has been demonstrated by Max in [16] and Shade in [24]. Thus, a single MDI is adequate to approximate the visibility for all points on the light source if the light source occupies a reasonably small area. In this sense, our algorithm is not completely general and will not handle an arbitrarily large light source.

The remainder of the paper is organized as follows: Section 2 reviews the z-buffer shadow algorithm and percentage-closer filtering. Section 3 outlines the new method, and explains how filtering of depth buffer samples corresponds to the partial visibility of the light source. Section 4 provides implementation details and provides examples of penumbras rendered by this method. Section 5 concludes the paper with a discussion of the method's advantages and disadvantages, and directions for future work.

2   Z-Buffer Shadows and Percentage Closer Filtering

The z-buffer shadow algorithm is a two-pass technique originally conceived by Williams [29]. It is a hard shadow algorithm in that it only works for point light sources and does not produce penumbras. The scene is rendered into a z-buffer from the point of view of the light source, using coordinates we call *shadow space*. The depth is all that is entered into each z-buffer element during rendering, and a greater z-value indicates greater distance from the light. Assuming the scene has already been rendered into a z-buffer in camera space, we can compute shadows as a post-process by mapping each camera z-buffer point to a location in the shadow map. The z-value at that shadow map location is compared to the z-value of the mapped point. If the point's z-value is greater, the point is considered occluded and the illumination of the corresponding camera z-buffer entry is attenuated appropriately.

This shadowing technique enjoys great advantages while simultaneously suffering from major disadvantages. Its main advantage is that it can produce shadows for anything that can be represented in a depth buffer, which is almost everything. Even implicit surfaces, which are difficult to scan convert, can be placed in a depth buffer by ray casting or they can be tesselated. Another advantage is the algorithm's capability to be implemented in hardware, which was demonstrated by Segal et al. using texture-mapping hardware [23].

However, the shadows produced by the naïve approach are of poor quality. This is due to two different aliasing artifacts. The first artifact is a stair-stepping effect along the edge of the shadow, which is due to inadequate shadow buffer resolution. The second artifact is known as "surface acne," and it is due to inappropriate self-shadowing. In addition to these problems, the z-buffer shadow algorithm only works for point light sources, and cannot be used to generate accurate penumbras except as part of an accumulation-buffer type of scheme.

The above-mentioned aliasing problems can be reduced to a great extent by percentage-closer filtering [22]. This method samples the bounding box in shadow space of the transformed camera space pixel's area using jitter. Each sample's z-value is compared to the z-value of the transformed point, with a random bias added. If the sample's z-value is found to be lower, the sample is considered to be occluding the point. After the comparisons have been made, the proportion of occluding samples determines the fraction of shadowing.

The end result of the filtering is an antialiased shadow edge with the stair-stepping artifact removed. The random bias helps to remove the self-shadowing. The algorithm works well because of the properties of the stochastic sampling process. Jittering the samples effectively replaces the aliasing with random noise, which is a much less disturbing visual artifact.

One main criticism of the algorithm is the large amount of sampling parameters. Perhaps the most difficult parameters to adjust are the upper and lower bounds of the random bias. There is a fine line between too much surface acne and too much shadow displacement. Grant et al. developed an interesting solution to this problem involving the storage of normal vectors along with z-values in the depth buffer [8]. With the added normal information, the depth variation over a shadow map pixel can be modeled more accurately.

Woo proposed another solution to the bias problem, in which the average of the two closest depths is stored at each pixel instead of the closest depth [32]. By doing this, depth values are offset enough to prevent self-shadowing, but not so much as to prevent shadows on other possible receivers. Unfortunately this solution is not easily incorporated into the new method presented here due to the importance of knowing the actual surface depths.

Modifications to the percentage closer filtering algorithm can simulate penumbras by accounting for distances between objects in the scene. As a blocker's distance from a receiver increases, the shadow edge can be blurred more to account for the increased separation. Partial success in generating penumbras from a single z-buffer using this idea was presented in [12]. Another implementation of this idea was used to create the shadows in the movie ANTZ by Pacific Data Images [30].

3 Depth-Dependent Filtering

3.1 Overview

At this point, we will give a brief overview of the steps taken in the depth-dependent filtering algorithm. The next few subsections will explain in detail the reasons for each step of the process. Then, in section 4, the algorithm will be outlined in greater detail.

First, an MDI is obtained that represents the view from the center of the light source. This MDI is preprocessed by dividing the entire depth range uniformly into disjoint *depth buckets* along the direction of light propagation. Next, a pixel in camera space is transformed to the coordinate frame of the MDI. The pixel area is transformed as well. Points are chosen on the bounding box of the transformed pixel area using jittered sampling on a regular grid. After testing for self-shadowing by using a z-buffer shadow algorithm, a ray is traced to the light source from each of these sample points. The subdivision of the MDI helps make the ray tracing more efficient and more accurate.

3.2 Ray Tracing the MDI

The process of tracing shadow rays through a parallel-projected MDI is shown on the left in Fig. 1. In the figure, each column represents a layered depth pixel of the

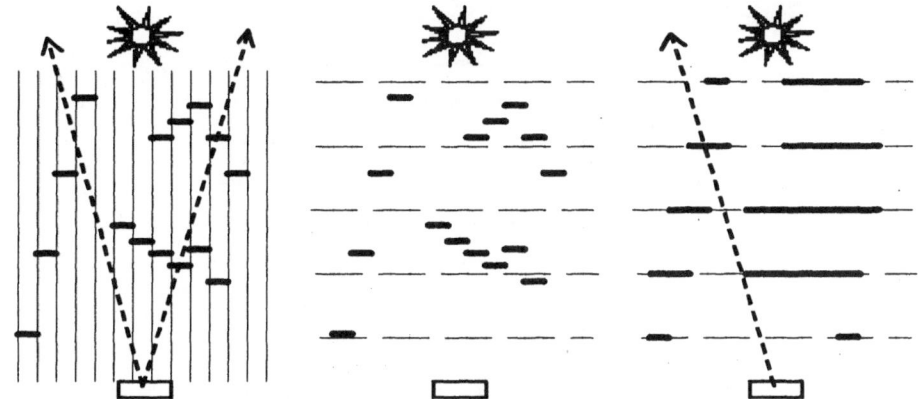

Fig. 1 The light leaking problem and reducing it by rounding to discrete depth levels

MDI. A thick black line across a layered depth pixel represents an individual depth pixel. This is a 2-D cross-section of the MDI, with depth varying vertically and the x-coordinate of the image varying horizontally. The shadow rays go to the light source from the shadow receiver, which is a pixel transformed from camera space to the MDI coordinate frame. Following the image-based ray tracing method used by Lischinski et al. [14], a ray intersects a depth pixel if the pixel's depth falls within the Z_{min} and Z_{max} of the ray as it crosses the layered depth pixel. The figure shows two rays, one that intersects a depth pixel and one that misses all depth pixels.

Notice that the depth pixels on the left seem to lie in a fairly straight line, indicating that they may all correspond to the same object. For example, a polygon that appears extremely slanted from the viewpoint of the light source may exhibit this behavior. With traditional ray tracing, the ray would intersect the object. However, note that with image-based ray tracing the object may be missed completely. This problem is known as *light-leaking*. To help reduce the light-leaking problem, we subdivide the MDI uniformly into separate regions of depth. We call these regions *depth buckets*. This is shown in the center of Fig. 1.

Instead of testing rays against depth pixels, we compute the intersection of a ray with the boundary between two buckets. Depth pixels from both buckets contribute to the boundary and form a blocker image. This essentially rounds each depth pixel to two discrete depths. The effect of doing this is shown at the right of Fig. 1, and notice that the light leak is removed. Although this changes the geometry of the scene, the net result is usually an imperceptible increase in the size of the shadow boundary. This problem is far less visually disturbing than having light appear to leak through a solid object.

In terms of implementation, we do not actually produce blocker images. Instead, we store a bitmask *at each layered depth pixel* that indicates which buckets contain depth pixels. For example, a 32-bit word can be used to describe 32 depth buckets at a pixel. The ray-object intersection method relies upon these bitmasks. When a ray intersects a depth bucket boundary, the intersection point occurs at a particular layered depth pixel. At this pixel, we check the two bits in the bitmask corresponding to the two buckets forming the boundary. Checking these two bits essentially checks for a ray-object intersection, and can be done with a single logic operation.

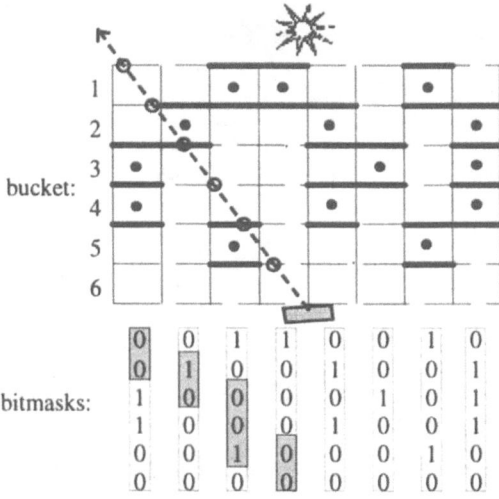

Fig. 2 Using bitmasks to perform ray-object intersections. Shaded bits are the ones checked at each layered depth pixel.

Fig. 2 graphically illustrates this process. Each black dot indicates that depth pixels are present in the relevant bucket at the relevant layered depth pixel. Thicker black lines indicate the depth pixel contributions to the boundary blocker images. Ray crossings at the boundaries are shown as small circles in the figure. The bits that are checked at each layered depth pixel are shaded. If the bit for either bucket is 1, we count that as a ray-object intersection.

Organizing the MDI into buckets in this fashion leads to several optimizations. First, it dramatically reduces the number of depth comparisons necessary for ray intersections at a layered depth pixel. Rather than iterate through the entire list of depths, we merely check the appropriate bits in a bitmask. Second, since all objects are assumed to be at uniformly spaced depths, we can step the rays through the MDI with uniform increments. These advantages, in concert with the reduction of light leaks, make this approach attractive despite the approximations made. A third important optimization uses the bitmasks to avoid unnecessary memory accesses. The range of layered depth pixels rays could hit is found, and the bitmasks of these pixels are *or*-ed together into a local variable. Since usually only a small proportion of buckets contain depth pixels, this variable can be used to cull a lot of processing and memory accesses.

The traced rays emanate from the transformed pixel area. We choose the emanation points by taking jittered samples of the transformed pixel area's bounding box. In our implementation, we trace one ray per jittered sample. We have found that for a given number of rays, the shadows visually look better if we do not also select the ray direction in a random fashion. In traditional

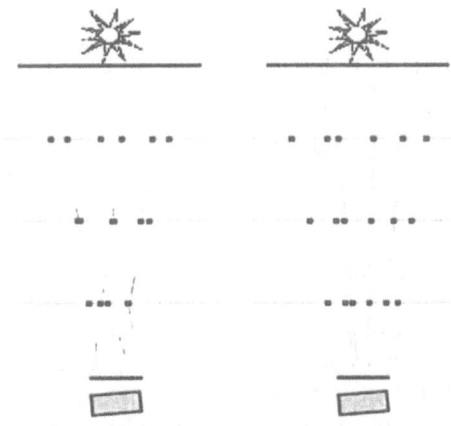

Fig. 3 Deterministic rays create similar patterns on blocker images.

distributed ray tracing, rays emanate from a surface with a random direction determined by the location of a random sample on the light source. In our implementation, we *deterministically* choose the ray direction based upon its starting location on the transformed pixel area. We choose the direction so that the rays intersect each blocker image with scaled versions of the same intersection pattern. By doing this, we are essentially correlating points on the pixel area with points on the light source, which is akin to a mapping operation. This is shown in Fig. 3. In the figure, the bottom line represents the receiver and the top line represents the light source.

Our method can be viewed as a solution to the problem of how to combine the effect of multiple blocker images. In [15,25], ad-hoc methods were used to combine occlusion from different overlapping blocker images. By using ray tracing, we are proposing a consistent and intuitive solution to the problem.

3.3 Filtering the MDI

Now that we have a method for tracing rays through the MDI, we can see how that method can be interpreted as a filtering method. This will be useful to us in several ways. First, we can easily incorporate pixel-area antialiasing by combining percentage closer filtering with our partial visibility algorithm. Second, we can adjust filter weights to approximate shaped light sources. Third, we can more directly compare our method with convolution methods for producing penumbras.

As mentioned in the previous section, the ray directions are chosen so that the intersection pattern is the same on each blocker image. However, as shown in Fig. 3, the pattern is scaled according to the relative distance from the transformed point. We can view this pattern as a *filter* that is performing area-averaging on each blocker image. Due to the way our ray directions have been chosen, the filters applied to the blocker images are all scaled versions of the same filter. Throughout the paper, the term *filter* will be used often to describe the area of a blocker image through which rays could possibly travel.

For the case of the parallel MDI, filter sizes for each blocker image are computed using the solid angle of the light source. The solid angle is used because the light source area is constant from all viewpoints, as with sunlight. In this case, visibility rays are confined to a cone of the same solid angle. For a particular transformed pixel, the volume of all possible rays will be the union of all such cones whose apex is a point on the transformed pixel area. The intersection of this volume with the blocker image plane yields the appropriate filter size for that blocker image.

This method can now be directly compared to convolution methods for calculating soft shadows. Convolution methods would convolute each blocker image with an image of the light source. We are convoluting each of these images with scaled versions of the same filter. Thus, by making the comparison between methods, our filter can be interpreted roughly as a representation of the image of the light source (it is really more like an approximate convolution of the pixel area and the light source image). If we change the weights on the filter, we can change the apparent shape of the light source. For example, if we set all corner weights on a filter to 1 and the remaining weights to 0, this would model four separate light sources at once. As another example, setting a row of filter weights equal to 1 and the rest 0 would model a linear source. An isotropic filter was used to model sunlight in the images provided in the color plates.

3.4 Self-Shadowing Surfaces

We do not discard the original depths contained in the MDI because we want to accurately produce self-shadowing effects. The z-buffer shadow algorithm is an excellent algorithm for computing self-shadows on complex surfaces, especially when percentage closer filtering is used. Since our algorithm is essentially based upon the z-buffer shadow algorithm (since we are using a multi-layer depth buffer), accurate self-shadows are possible if the actual depth pixels are accessed.

We mix the ray-tracing/filtering methods outlined above with a simple z-buffer shadow algorithm. The transformed pixel is mapped to a layered depth pixel location, as is done in the z-buffer shadow algorithm. Also, its depth occurs within the range of a particular depth bucket. Depth comparisons are made as in the z-buffer shadow algorithm, however only the depth pixels that are in that bucket and the next bucket are considered. The depth bias used in the z-buffer shadow algorithm may push the transformed point into the next bucket, in which case only depth pixels from the next two buckets are considered.

The depth pixels in these two buckets normally combine at their mutual boundary to form a blocker image. However, some of those depth pixels may actually be behind the transformed point. The depth comparisons serve to remove these pixels from the blocker image. To be consistent with our ray-tracing scheme, the appropriate filter size for the blocker image depth is used. Recall that the filter size on a blocker image determines the area through which visibility rays travel. In terms of implementation, this filter is applied using a method that closely mimics the percentage closer filtering algorithm.

3.5 Finite Light Sources

A perspective-projected MDI is used for the case of finite light sources. The actual 3-D Euclidean distance from the center of the light is stored in each depth pixel. This is done to ease the combination of the self-shadowing algorithm with the ray-tracing algorithm. If an orthographic projection was used, the z-buffer shadow

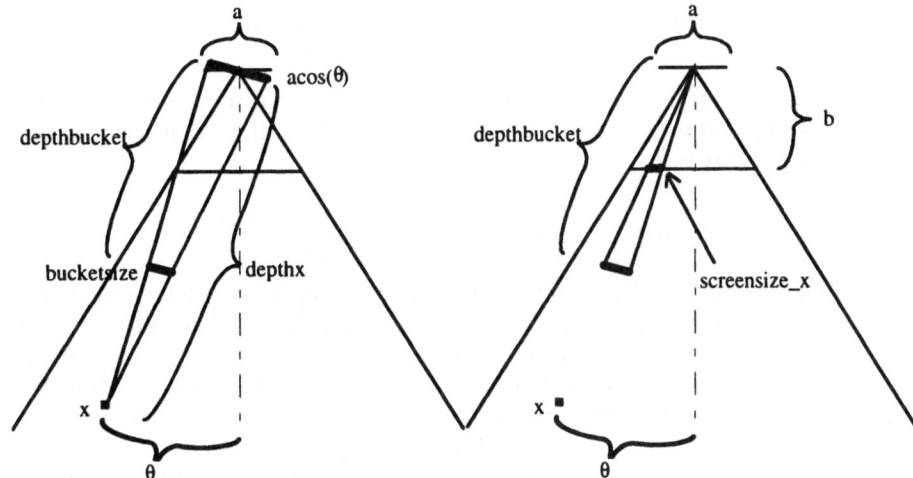

Fig. 4 Similar triangles argument for stepping rays through a perspective MDI.

algorithm would not accurately compute self-shadowing. Also, a perspective projection that stored a non-linear depth would complicate the ray-tracing algorithm.

By using a perspective projection and storing Euclidean depths, the algorithm is essentially the same as in the parallel case. The major difference is in the computation of the filter sizes. Intuitively, a square light on the ceiling will not appear to be square when viewed at an angle. Also, the filter will not grow linearly with depth as it did with a parallel light source.

We present a 2-D argument based on similar triangles to calculate the filter sizes for each depth bucket. We assume that the argument is independently valid for both dimensions of the filter. This is not entirely accurate, however it guarantees that the filter will remain rectangular.

At the left of Fig. 4 is a 2-D representation of the situation for finite light sources. The light is represented at the top of the figure by a line of length a. The transformed point occurs at $\mathbf{x}$, which is an angle θ from the center of the projection. The line across the upper part of the light source frustum is the screen onto which all depth pixels are projected. Each pixel address on the projection screen represents a layered depth pixel, each of which contains a list of depth pixels and a bucket bitmask. The volume containing all rays from $\mathbf{x}$ to points on the light source is drawn, and the line across it represents a bucket filter located at the minimum bucket depth.

Since depth is stored as Euclidean distance, uniform subdivisions in depth result in shell-like bucket regions. Thus, the filter size tangent to the shell is desired. Using the projected size of the light source, the filter size is found by similar triangles:

$$bucketsize = a\cos(\Theta) \cdot \left(\frac{depth_x - depth_{bucket}}{depth_x} \right)$$

However, this doesn't indicate how many layered depth pixels the filter covers. To find this, we use another similar triangles argument (see the right of Fig. 4). The projected size of the filter is given by:

$$bucketsize = depth_{bucket} \cdot \frac{screensize_x}{b}$$

Eliminating the intermediate variable *bucketsize*, we discover the relationship between $depth_x$, $depth_{bucket}$ and the parameters of the MDI. Using a geometric substitution for $cos(\theta)$:

$$screensize_x = \frac{ab}{\sqrt{x^2 + 1}} \cdot \left(\frac{depth_x - depth_{bucket}}{depth_x \cdot depth_{bucket}} \right)$$

To find the screen size in the y direction, we simply substitute y for x in the above equation. Obviously, there is a non-linear dependence of the projected filter size on the minimum bucket depth. Thus, constant additive increments cannot be used to step rays from boundary to boundary. However, the difference in depth between filters is kept constant. Let D denote this depth difference. Also, the minimum depth of a particular bucket will be some multiple of D, plus the distance from the light source to the minimum depth B of the closest bucket. If the minimum depth of a previous bucket is given by $KD+B$, then *screensize* of the next bucket can be calculated from the *screensize* of the previous bucket by using the following iteration:

$$screensize_{next} = screensize_{previous} + \frac{C}{(KD+B)((K-1)D+B)}$$

where $C=abDcos(\theta)$. The number K is simply the enumeration of the bucket, where $K=0$ indicates the closest bucket to the light source. This is a convenient representation, since C only needs to be calculated once per transformed pixel, and the enumeration of the buckets is readily available.

The above calculations compute the intersection of the volume of rays from a point with a blocker image. Recall that there are several sample points on the transformed pixel area from which rays can emanate. The actual filter size is found by considering all ray volumes emanating from the pixel. We calculate the ray intersection area from the center of the pixel and add half to each side of the pixel area. This is a good approximation to the actual area of intersection if the pixel area is small enough, which is usually the case.

4 Implementation Details and Results

4.1 Implementation Details

The entire visibility-testing algorithm is contained in a single routine. A skeletal pseudocode description is contained in Fig. 5. The input is the point to be shadowed in shadow space coordinates, and the bounding box of the transformed pixel area. The output is a percentage of shadowing, which is used to attenuate the illumination of the camera-space pixel or subpixel fragment. It is assumed that *pixel3D* occurs in the middle of the box defined by *pixelsize*. The variables *ray_x* and *ray_y* are coordinates of jittered samples in the box.

For clarity, one simple optimization was left out of the pseudocode. Before iterating through all depth pixels in the second *for* loop, it is a simple matter to check if any depth pixels exist in the current or next depth bucket by first checking the bitmask at *MDI[ray_x][ray_y]*. If the bitmask indicates there are no depth pixels in those buckets, there is no need to iterate through the depth pixels and the z-buffer self-shadowing test can be skipped.

The filter calculation details were also left out of the pseudocode for clarity. To compute the appropriate filter size at a boundary, the volume of possible rays must be considered. The distance of the transformed point to the boundary is used to increase the size of the filter according to the volume. For the example of an infinite light source with a specified solid angle, the filter would be increased on each side by this distance times the tangent of the angle. For finite light sources, the arguments outlined in Section 3.5 would be applied. Filters are recalculated for each transformed pixel, in order to guarantee smooth variation of penumbra width as the transformed pixel moves from one bucket to the next.

```
Shadow( MDI[len][wid], pixel3D, pixelsize )
  Find bucket that encloses pixel3D based upon pixel3D.z;
  Find filter size at closest boundary using pixelsize;
  For(i=all jittered samples on pixel=(ray_x,ray_y))
    Compute random bias;
    Adjust sample location and current bucket due to bias;
    For(d=all depth pixels in MDI[ray_x][ray_y])
      If(d.z<pixel3D.z-bias)&(d in current or next bucket)
        inshadow += filterweight[i]; next i;
      else shoot a ray
        while(bucket>=0)
          Increment ray_x, ray_y;
          If(MDI[ray_x][ray_y].bitmask shows intersection)
            inshadow += filterweight[i]; next i;
          Decrement bucket;
  return inshadow/total_filter_weight;
```

Fig. 5 Pseudocode description

A few words should be said about how the depth pixels are stored. As in [24], we compute the MDI by first inserting depths into a linked list at each layered depth pixel. This allows for quick insertion without copying or re-ordering. Then, we collapse the depth pixels into a compact data structure. We use an array of structs, and each struct contains 1) a memory offset into a linear depth array, which is given the value of −1 if the layered depth pixel is empty, 2) the number of depths attributed to this layered depth pixel, and 3) the bitmask describing the presence of depth pixels in each bucket. For a MDI with resolution P by Q with R bytes used in the bucket bitmask ($R=4$ for 32 buckets), the memory requirement is then $PQ(R+8)$ bytes, where it is assumed that 4-byte words are used for the memory offset and the depth count. Every MDI requires at least this much memory.

The depths are compactly stored in a linear depth array, and are only accessed as needed by using the memory offset. To iterate through all depths at a layered depth pixel, we first add the offset to the start of the array. To get the remaining depths, we increment this pointer a number of times equal to the number of depths stored at that layered depth pixel. The depth array has a memory requirement of $4S$, where a 4-byte word is used to store each depth and there are a total of S depth pixels in the entire MDI. Thus, the total memory requirement of the processed MDI is $PQ(R+8)+4S$. As an example, a 512x512 MDI with 32 buckets and an average of 4 depth pixels per layered depth pixel requires about 7 megabytes.

4.2 Discussion of Deterministic Ray Tracing

We have compared the results of our deterministic ray-tracing approach to that of tracing a random ray at each sample. We found that although intuitively it is more accurate to trace random rays, the shadows look worse due to additional noisiness in the shadow. This is a typical bias vs. variance problem. By preventing valid ray directions that may (or may not) reach the light source, we bias the size of the shadow in order to reduce the variance. This bias should not be confused with the depth bias used in the z-buffer shadow algorithm.

One way to understand the bias is to view it in terms of the direct correlation between points on the pixel and points on the light source. Essentially, we approximate the four-dimensional integral over the light source and the pixel as a two-dimensional integral, by constructing a one-to-one mapping between points in the two areas. The correlation introduced by the mapping makes the two-dimensional integral a biased approximation of the four-dimensional integral. Mathematically, the approximation can be described as follows:

$$\int\int V(\vec{x}, \vec{y})d\vec{x}d\vec{y} \approx \int V(\vec{x}, f(\vec{x}))d\vec{x}$$

In the above equation, $V(x,y)$ is the visibility function between points x on the pixel and points y on the light source. In the case of parallel light sources, y would represent a direction within the cone of the appropriate solid angle. The function $f(x)$ is a one-to-one function that maps each pixel point x to a unique point (or direction) y on the light source.

We chose $f(x)$ to be the rectangle-to-rectangle mapping $[Au, Bv] \rightarrow [Cu, Dv]$ where $[u, v]$ are in the range $[0,1]$, the pixel is a rectangle of dimensions AxB, and the light source is a rectangle (or a rectangular approximation to a cone of ray directions) of dimensions CxD. This mapping generates a fan-like distribution of rays emanating from the pixel area. It has several desirable properties. First, it is a one-to-one mapping. Second, the set of rays generated by this mapping fills the same volume as the original set of possible rays from the four-dimensional case. Third, it creates scaled versions of the same intersection pattern on each blocker image, as mentioned in Section 3.2.

By reducing the dimensionality of the integral, we are able to obtain a lower variance result with the same number of samples. We essentially perform Monte Carlo integration on the right hand side of the above equation by using stratified sampling over the pixel area. Stratification helps to reduce the variance compared to uniformly random sampling patterns [19]. Discussions of the relationship between the dimensionality of the sample space and the variance in computer graphics problems can be found in [18,19]. A variance measurement experiment involving four-dimensional double-area integration can be found in [18].

A comparison between tracing one random ray at each pixel sample versus tracing one correlated ray at each pixel sample is given in the color plate. By looking at the shadows of the poles, the variance difference is most noticeable. The variance presents itself as a noisy pattern in the penumbra. By comparing the shadows of the bush, the bias difference is most noticeable; certain areas that are illuminated in the random case are not present in the deterministic case, and the shape of illuminated areas are slightly different. Based upon comparisons like these, we decided that the bias error is more tolerable than the variance error for a given number of samples.

4.3   Results

All images were rendered using a program developed in-house in C++. The visibility algorithm used for rasterizing polygons in camera space was a modified version of the A-buffer [3], with 64 bits per pixel used for subpixel antialiasing. This algorithm was chosen for its close relationship to the MDI, and for its antialiasing. The program was executed on a 300Mhz Pentium II-based machine running Windows NT4, with 128 megabytes of RAM. All shadow computation times do not include the time spent rendering the MDI, since the MDI rendering process is independent of the shadow algorithm. We used a polygon-based renderer that typically produced an MDI in about a second. All times were found using the `clock` function. All rendering was done in software.

Each image was rendered at 256x256 resolution. Since our algorithm computes the shadow for each pixel individually, it is essentially an $O(pqNR)$ algorithm for each light source, where p and q are the dimensions of the final image, N is the number of buckets, and R is the number of rays per pixel. Thus, our algorithm fits in well with most of image-based rendering, since it is independent of geometric complexity.

We used 32 buckets in all situations, and 36 samples/rays per pixel. Increasing the number of buckets helps to increase accuracy to a point, but light-leaking becomes more of a problem and the efficiency begins to drop as the number of buckets gets higher. Using fewer buckets helps make the method faster, however the approximations made in geometry start to become more noticeable. We chose to use 32 buckets because it works well in most situations and fits neatly into a 32-bit word.

A standard resolution of 512x512 was used for all of the shadow MDIs. The speed of the algorithm is fairly insensitive to MDI resolution, however it can be sensitive to the number of depth pixels contained at a particular layered depth pixel. It is especially sensitive when there is a lot of self-shadowing, since it is for those cases that we must iterate through the entire list of depth values at a layered depth pixel.

To demonstrate the running time of the algorithm on a typical bad case, we used a dense tree, shown in the color plates. The filter size was selected to model sunlight. The MDI was allowed to contain any number of depth pixels at each layered depth pixel. For this model, the maximum number of depth pixels at a layered depth pixel was 112, and the average number over non-empty layered depth pixels was 19. The shadow was computed in 18.6 seconds. We feel that this is a fast time, since we are tracing rays through an enormous MDI. This shadow would be extremely difficult to compute using geometry-based methods, since the model contains 1,237,614 polygons.

The algorithm also tends to run slower if the size of the light source is larger. This is due to increased numbers of shadowed pixels and random memory accesses; thus it is not included in the algorithmic complexity argument given above. The color plates show a sunlight image, rendered in 2.5 seconds, and an image containing a parallel light with 10 times the sunlight solid angle, rendered in 9.5 seconds. For the finite light source examples, the light is modeled as a square source directly above the bush in the images. The poles are 30 units high, and the light source is positioned 25 units above them. The images show square light sources that are 4x4 and 8x8 in size, with shadows computed in 11.8 and 20.6 seconds, respectively. The field of view of the light sources was approximately 77 degrees.

A simulation of multiple light sources using a single filter is shown in the color plates as well, with a shadow computation time of about 4 seconds. The filter was an 8x8 filter, with each 3x3 corner isotropically weighted. Rays corresponding to zero filter weights were ignored.

5 Conclusions and Future Work

We have implemented a soft shadow algorithm that filters an MDI that represents the visibility from the light source. We have demonstrated how this algorithm efficiently traces rays through the MDI, and how the ray tracing corresponds to a filtering process. We have also shown how our algorithm relates to convolution methods, and how our algorithm intuitively blurs shadow edges according to the geometry of the scene.

Our algorithm has several advantages over other methods. It correctly produces self-shadowing for complex objects. In addition, the time complexity is independent of geometry. Also, it was designed to be applicable to image-based rendering situations, unlike most other soft shadow algorithms. The shadow computations are also reasonably fast given that the implementation is entirely in software.

Our algorithm also has several disadvantages. First of all, it is an approximation. However, approximate shadows are acceptable for many situations, as was argued in [25]. Another disadvantage is that our algorithm only works for light sources of moderate size. The fact that we are using MDIs makes this a high-memory-cost algorithm. The algorithm does not compute shadows at interactive rates, and the solution cannot be redisplayed interactively as in [10]. We feel that the shadow computation times could be improved if we could better exploit memory coherence.

Although we have reduced the light-leaking problem significantly, it has not been completely removed. The possibility still exists that light may leak through. A complete solution would treat the MDI used in the examples as a 512x512x32 collection of voxel-like slabs, and test against the sides of the slabs as well as the top and bottom. This would slow our implementation significantly, since it would be difficult to incorporate into our efficient bit-based scheme. We have yet to see light leaks happen for the types of light sources for which the algorithm was designed.

Like the z-buffer shadow algorithm, this algorithm suffers from resolution issues. If a particular area in the scene is sampled at high resolution in camera space (for example, objects very close to the camera in a perspective projection) but is sampled at a significantly lower rate in the MDI, the shadows will be of poor quality. Antialiasing over the pixel area is usually sufficient, but not in extreme situations. As a subject of future study, we are looking at ways to adaptively adjust the MDI resolution according to the relative positions and orientations of the camera, the light source and the surfaces in the scene.

The most noticeable artifact in the shadows is the random noise. We reduced the noise to a degree by putting a bias on the shadow size, which is less noticeable. Allowing multiple rays per pixel sample can reduce the noise without increasing bias, however this is significantly more expensive. We are currently working on image processing approaches based upon the wavelet transform to reduce noise as a post-process. This will hopefully allow us to use an unbiased integration scheme with fewer samples than is typically necessary, and still obtain penumbras with low noise levels.

6   Acknowledgements

This work was performed under the auspices of the U.S. Department of Energy by Lawrence Livermore National Laboratory under contract W-7405-ENG-48. Oliver Deussen provided the bush model and the tree model. Ross Gaunt and Jan Nunes recorded the video tape. We would like to also thank the reviewers, who added quite a bit to this paper through their constructive insights.

References

[1]   John Amanatides. Ray tracing with cones. *Computer Graphics*, 18(3):129-135, July 1984. Proc. SIGGRAPH '84.

[2]   Lynne Shapiro Brotman and Norman Badler. Generating soft shadows with a depth buffer algorithm. *IEEE CG&A*, 4(10):5-24, Oct. 1984.

[3]   Loren C. Carpenter. The A-Buffer, an anti-aliased hidden surface method. *Computer Graphics*, 18(3):103-8. Proc. SIGGRAPH '84.

[4]   Shenchang Eric Chen and Lance Williams. View interpolation for image synthesis. *Computer Graphics*, 27:279-88, August 1993. Proc. SIGGRAPH '93.

[5]   Michael F. Cohen and Donald P. Greenberg. The hemi-cube: A radiosity solution for complex environments. *Computer Graphics*, 19(3):31-40, July 1985. Proc. SIGGRAPH '85.

[6]   Robert Cook, Thomas Porter and Loren Carpenter. Distributed Ray Tracing. *Computer Graphics*, 18(3):137-145, July 1984. Proc. SIGGRAPH '84.

[7]   George Drettakis and Eugene Fiume. A fast algorithm for area light sources using backprojection. *Computer Graphics*, pp.223-30, 1994. Proc. SIGGRAPH '94.

[8]   Charles Grant and Michael Allison. Improvements on the depth buffer shadow algorithm. *Technical Report UCRL-102856*, Lawrence Livermore National Laboratory, January 1990.

[9]   Paul Haeberli and Kurt Akeley. The accumulation buffer: Hardware support for high-quality rendering. *Computer Graphics*, 24(4):309-18, August 1990. Proc. SIGGRAPH '90.

[10]   Paul S. Heckbert and Michael Herf. Simulating soft shadows with graphics hardware. Technical report TR CMU-CS-97-104, Carnegie Mellon University, January 1997.

[11]   Paul S. Heckbert. Discontinuity meshing for radiosity. *Rendering Techniques '92*, pp. 203-16, May 1992. Proc 3rd Eurographics Workshop on Rendering.

212

[12] Brett Keating. Extracting approximate sunlight penumbras from a single 3-D image (shadow z-buffer). Informal poster session, *Image-based rendering workshop*, Stanford University, March 23-25, 1998.

[13] Daniel Lischinski, Filippo Tampieri, and Donald P. Greenberg. Discontinuity meshing for accurate radiosity. *IEEE CG&A*, 12(6):25-39, November 1992.

[14] Dani Lischinski and Ari Rappoport. Image-based rendering for non-diffuse synthetic scenes. *Rendering Techniques '98*, pp. 301-14, June 1998. Proc. 9th Eurographics Workshop on Rendering.

[15] Nelson Max. Unified sun and sky illumination for shadows under trees. *CVGIP: Graphical Models and Image Processing*. 53(3):223-30, May, 1991.

[16] Nelson Max and Keiichi Ohsaki. Rendering trees from precomputed z-buffer views. *Rendering Techniques '95*, pp.74-81, June 1995. Proc. 6th Eurographics Workshop on Rendering.

[17] Nelson Max, Curtis Mobley, Brett Keating and En-Hua Wu. Plane-parallel radiance transport for global illumination in vegetation. *Rendering Techniques '97*, pp. 239-50, June 1997. Proc. 8th Eurographics Workshop on Rendering.

[18] Don P. Mitchell. Spectrally Optimal Sampling for Distribution Ray Tracing. *Computer Graphics*, 25(4):157-64, July 1991. Proc. SIGGRAPH '91.

[19] Don P. Mitchell. Consequences of Stratified Sampling in Graphics. *Computer Graphics*, pp. 277-80, August 1996. Proc. SIGGRAPH '96.

[20] Tomoyuki Nishita and Eihachiro Nakamae. Shading models for point and linear sources. *ACM Transactions on Graphics*, 14(2), 124-26, 1985.

[21] Tomoyuki Nishita and Eihachiro Nakamae. Continuous tone representation of three-dimensional objects taking account of shadows and interreflection. *Computer Graphics*, 19(3):23-30, July 1985. Proc. SIGGRAPH '85.

[22] William T. Reeves, David H. Salesin and Robert L. Cook. Rendering anti-aliased shadows with depth maps. *Computer Graphics*, 21(4):283-90, July 1987. Proc. SIGGRAPH '87.

[23] Mark Segal, Carl Korobkin, Rolf van Widenfelt, Jim Foran and Paul Haeberli. Fast Shadows and Lighting Effects Using Texture Mapping. *Computer Graphics*, 26(2):249-52, July 1992. Proc. SIGGRAPH '92.

[24] Jonathan Shade, Steven Gortler, Li-wei He and Richard Szeliski. Layered depth images. *Computer Graphics*, pp.231-42, July 1998. Proc. SIGGRAPH '98.

[25] Cyril Soler and François X. Sillion. Fast calculation of soft shadow textures using convolution. *Computer Graphics*, pp.321-32, July 1998. Proc. SIGGRAPH '98.

[26] A. James Stewart and Sherif Ghali. Fast computation of shadow boundaries using spatial coherence and backprojection. *Computer Graphics*, pp. 231-38, July 1994. Proc. SIGGRAPH '94.

[27] Toshimitsu Tanaka and Tokiichiro Takahashi. Fast analytic shading and shadowing for area light sources. Proc. EUROGRAPHICS '97, 16(3):C-231-40, 1997.

[28] Shinichi Takita, Kazufumi Kaneda, Toshio Akinobu, Haruhiko Iriyama, Eihachiro Nakame, and Tomoyuki Nishita. A simple rendering for penumbra caused by sunlight. *The Visual Computer*, 7(5) pp. 259-68, 1991.

[29] Lance Williams. Casting curved shadows on curved surfaces. *Computer Graphics*, 12(3):270-74, August 1978. Proc. SIGGRAPH '78.

[30] Daniel Wexler, Research & Development, Pacific Data Images. Personal communication, 1999.

[31] Andrew Woo, Pierre Poulin and Alain Fournier. A survey of shadow algorithms. *IEEE CG&A*, 10(6):13-32, Nov. 1990.

[32] Andrew Woo. The Shadow Depth Map Revisited. In David Kirk ed. <u>Graphics Gems III</u>. Academic Press, San Diego CA, pp. 338-42, 1992.

Approximating the Location of Integrand Discontinuities for Penumbral Illumination with Area Light Sources

Marc J. Ouellette   Eugene Fiume

Department of Computer Science
University of Toronto, Toronto, Canada
Toronto, ON   M5S 3G4   Canada
e-mail: {vv1|elf}@dgp.toronto.edu

Abstract. The problem of computing soft shadows with area light sources has received considerable attention in computer graphics. In part, this is a difficult problem because the integral that defines the radiance at a point must take into account the visibility function. Most of the solutions proposed have been limited to polygonal environments, and require a full visibility determination preprocessing step. The result is typically a partitioning of the environment into regions that have a similar view of the light source. We propose a new approach that can be successfully applied to arbitrary environments. The approach is based on the observation that, in the presence of occluders, the primary difficulty in computing the integral that defines the contribution of an area light source, is that of determining the visible domain of the integrand. We extend a recent shadow algorithm for linear light sources in order to calculate a polygonal approximation to this visible domain. We demonstrate for an important class of shadowing problems, and in particular, for convex occluders, that the shape of the visible domain only needs to be roughly approximated by a polygonal boundary. We then use this boundary to subdivide an area light source into a small number of triangles that can be integrated efficiently using either a deterministic solution, or a low degree numerical cubature.

Keywords: numerical cubatures, random seed bisection, area sources, soft shadows.

1   Introduction

The efficient computation of soft shadows due to area light sources remains one of the most challenging problems in computer graphics. The synthesis of realistic images depends on this computation; however, the discontinuities that arise, and the complexity of the visibility computation itself, can conspire to create renderings that are either too slow to compute or unsatisfactory in appearance. The problem of determining the direct illumination reaching a specific point from a given light source can be separated into two tasks: determining the visible portion of the source from that point, and calculating the reflected light due to this visible portion. In this paper, we propose a new solution to the first half of this problem, based on providing a polygonal approximation to the visible portion of the source. The resulting integrals can be solved efficiently using either an analytical solution for diffuse surfaces [10], or a numerical cubature of low degree. This algorithm naturally permits nonpolyhedral scene geometries.

In the general setting of area light sources, three main techniques have been used to determine the visibility of a source. The earliest techniques determined visibility of a source by either approximating it by point light sources [1], or by point sampling the source itself [4, 15]. This approach is subject to aliasing if too few samples are used. Images of a higher quality can be achieved using algorithms that use shadow volumes and/or discontinuity meshing to determine the exact visibility of a source [2, 3, 5, 7, 9, 14]. These techniques are very expensive and have only been designed to compute exact visibility for polygonal environments. Finally, shadow maps have also been used to texture map soft shadows, either by pre-calculating an approximation using multiple light source samples and combining them in an accumulation buffer [6], or, most recently, by convolving source and occluder images to produce a soft shadow texture[12, 13]. The latter algorithm can produce convincing shadows for environments with arbitrary types of objects; however, correct shadows are sometimes difficult to produce, for example, if a large occluder touches a receiver.

In this paper, we use *Random Seed Bisection* (RSB) and the *Two Discontinuity Finding* (TDF) algorithm developed in [11] to approximate the visible portion of a polygonal light source. RSB and TDF efficiently find the approximate location of (two or fewer) discontinuities in a one-dimensional integrand caused by (arbitrary) occluders. Given a triangular source, we use RSB and TDF to determine the number and approximate location of the discontinuities caused by occluders along each edge of the source. Given the number of discontinuities along each edge, we classify the triangle into one of six edge visibility configurations. Depending on the resulting configuration, we may compute one or two additional interior discontinuities. We then approximate the visible portion of the triangle using the polygonal boundary defined by the vertices and the discontinuities, and partition the visible domain into sub-triangles. Finally, we calculate the integral over each sub-triangle using either an analytical solution (in the case of a diffuse emitter and a diffuse surface), or a low degree numerical cubature.

This paper is organized as follows: in Section 2, we review the one dimensional discontinuity finding algorithms of [11]. In Section 3, we present the algorithm for calculating a polygonal approximation to the visible portion of a triangular light source. In Section 4, we present the extension of the algorithm to quadrilateral and general polygonal sources. In Section 5, we present results for triangular sources and a discussion of the algorithm developed. Finally, in Section 6, we present our conclusions.

2 One Dimensional Discontinuity Finding Algorithms

In this section, we briefly review the one dimensional discontinuity finding algorithms that were introduced in [11]. We want to find the approximate location of the discontinuities in a visibility function $V(x)$ defined over $[0, 1]$ such that $V(x) = 1$ if x is visible, and $V(x) = 0$ otherwise.

2.1 Random Seed Bisection

If V has at most one discontinuity in $[0, 1]$, then V has one discontinuity $\lambda \in [0, 1]$ iff $V(0) \neq V(1)$. In such a case, V is a step function, and given a tolerance ε, we calculate $\tilde{\lambda}$, the approximate location of λ, such that $\|\tilde{\lambda} - \lambda\| \leq \varepsilon$.

Suppose that V has exactly one discontinuity over an interval $[a, b]$ such that $V(a) \neq V(b)$. Let $m \in [a, b]$. If $V(a) \neq V(m)$, then V has a discontinuity over $[a, m]$, otherwise V has a discontinuity over $[m, b]$. The *Random Seed Bisection* (RSB) algorithm is based on this observation. In RSB, $[a, b]$ is initially set to $[0, 1]$, and m is set to a random seed taken from a uniform distribution over $[0, 1]$. At each iteration i, $V(m)$ is evaluated and compared to $V(a)$. The appropriate subinterval is chosen as the $(i + 1)^{st}$ interval, and

m is set to its midpoint. The iteration terminates when the $\|a - b\| < 2\varepsilon$, and we set $\tilde{\lambda} = m$. The expected error of RSB after n iterations is $(2/3)(1/2)^{n-1}$, which is almost optimal.

The function $E_n(\tilde{\lambda})$ is the expected value of $\tilde{\lambda}$ in terms of λ and of the number of iterations n. For RSB, $E_n(\tilde{\lambda})$ is a continuous function of λ over $[0, 1]$. Because $E_n(\tilde{\lambda})$ is continuous, we can use RSB to efficiently find the approximate location of a discontinuity for an integrand in a linear light source, while avoiding banding problems inherent to purely deterministic methods, as was shown in [11].

2.2 Two Discontinuity Finding Algorithm

Suppose that V has at most two discontinuities in $[0, 1]$. If $V(0) = V(1)$, then V has either zero or two discontinuities in $[0, 1]$. If we can find a point $m \in (0, 1)$ such that $V(0) \neq V(m)$, then we can use RSB to find a discontinuity on each side of m. The *Two Discontinuity Finding* (TDF) algorithm uses heuristics based on scene coherence to determine if such a point m exists. The heuristics either succeed in finding such a value m and we find two discontinuities, or they fail and we conclude that there are no discontinuities. Let P be the number of discontinuities detected in the integrand for the previous (and adjacent) pixel, and let these discontinuities be p_1 and p_2, if they exist. We have different heuristics based on the value of P.

State $P = 0$. Let v be a user-specified tolerance, and let $x_{-2} = 0$ and $x_{-1} = 1$. Choose a random value $x_0 \in [0, 1]$ and determine $V(x_0)$. If $V(x_0) \neq V(0)$, then let $m = x_0$ and return. Otherwise, at each step i, choose x_i as the midpoint of the largest subinterval $[x_a, x_b]$ such that $a, b \in [-2, i - 1]$ and there is no $c \in [-2, i - 1]$ such that $x_c \in (x_a, x_b)$, with ties being broken randomly. The iteration stops as soon as some $V(x_i) \neq V(0)$, in which case we let $m = x_i$ and return. If the largest subinterval becomes smaller than v, we stop and conclude that, probabilistically,[1] we have zero discontinuities, and return a failed status. We refer to this algorithm as the *Voronoi Search* (VS).

State $P = 1$. Since the previous pixel had one integrand discontinuity p_1, we had $V(0) \neq V(1)$. Since now $V(0) = V(1)$, one of the end points has changed visibility, say v_i. It is likely that if a change of visibility still occurs in the integrand, it does so between v_i and p_1. We let $m = (p_1 + v_i)/2$ and compute $V(m)$. If $V(m) \neq V(0)$, we return successfully. Otherwise, we use VS to look for a change of visibility between p_1 and v_i.

State $P = 2$. The integrand for the previous pixel had two discontinuities p_1 and p_2. It is likely that if we still have two discontinuities, the midpoint $m = (p_1 + p_2)/2$ will be such that $V(m) \neq V(0)$. If this is the case, return successfully. Otherwise, we use VS to look for a change of visibility in $[0, 1]$.

3 Triangular Shadow Algorithm

We now present an algorithm for finding the approximate shape of the visible portion of a triangular light source T for an important class of occluders. We define

---

[1] Specifically, there is no gap $G \subseteq [0, 1]$ of size $\|G\| > v$ such that $V(x) \neq V(0), \forall x \in G$.

the class of *Occluders Causing Two or fewer Discontinuities In Any Linear Subdomain* (OCTDIALS) to be the class of occluders that cause at most two discontinuities along any linear subdomain of T. Given T and a point to be shaded P, an occluder O is of class OCTDIALS(T, P) iff, given any line segment $L \subseteq T$, O causes at most two discontinuities in the visibility function of L, as seen from P. In a sense, this class includes any object, or collection of objects, that causes a locally convex occlusion of T as viewed from P. This class includes, but is not limited to, convex occluders and convex "visibility holes." In the remainder of this section, we will assume that any occluder O is of the class OCTDIALS(T, P).

We define the visibility function $V(\mathbf{x})$, $\forall \mathbf{x} \in T$, such that $V(\mathbf{x}) = 1$ if $\mathbf{x}$ is visible from P, and $V(\mathbf{x}) = 0$ otherwise. We can use RSB and TDF to determine efficiently the number and approximate location of discontinuities in $V(\mathbf{x})$ along any line segment $L \subseteq T$, and in particular, along the edges of T. Given the location of discontinuities along the edges of T, the location of T's vertices, and, if necessary, the location of one or two additional discontinuities inside T, we can approximate the visible domain of T with a polygonal boundary. We now formulate this approximation algorithm by examining the edge configurations and the configuration transitions.

3.1 Edge Configurations

The first step in approximating the visible domain of T is to find the number and approximate location of the discontinuities in $V(\mathbf{x})$ along the edges of T. Let the three vertices of T be $\mathbf{v_0}$, $\mathbf{v_1}$, and $\mathbf{v_1}$. Since the edges share these vertices, we first calculate $V(\mathbf{v})$ at each vertex $\mathbf{v}$. For each edge defined by a pair of vertices $\mathbf{v_i}$ and $\mathbf{v_j}$, we then compare $V(\mathbf{v_i})$ to $V(\mathbf{v_j})$. If the values are different, we use RSB to find the single discontinuity along this edge, otherwise we use TDF to find either zero or two discontinuities.

We classify T according to its *edge configuration*, that is, according to the number of discontinuities found along each edge. There are only two possible classes of vertex visibility: either all the vertices have the same visibility, or one vertex has a visibility that is distinct from the other two. This leads to a natural classification of the possible edge configurations.

If all vertices have the same visibility, then every edge has either zero or two discontinuities. We can then classify T into one of the following four configurations:

C_{000} : All three edges have zero discontinuities.
C_{002} : One edge has two discontinuities, two edges have zero discontinuities.
C_{022} : Two edges have two discontinuities, one edge has zero discontinuities.
C_{222} : All three edges have two discontinuities.

If a vertex $\mathbf{v}$ has a different visibility than the other two, then two edges have one discontinuity, and the other edge either has zero or two discontinuities. We can then classify T into one of the following configurations:

C_{011} : Two edges have one discontinuity, one edge has zero discontinuities.
C_{112} : Two edges have one discontinuity, one edge has two discontinuities.

If the visibility of the triangle is of type C_{000}, we will classify T as fully occluded if its vertices are occluded, and as fully visible otherwise. This assumption will fail only if the occluder O is entirely contained within the tetrahedron defined by P and T. Because of the unlikelihood of this happening, and because the resulting contribution to the penumbra may often be negligible, we have chosen to make this simplifying assumption.

Given a configuration of type C_{112} or C_{222}, we approximate the shape of the blocker by joining discontinuities with non-intersecting lines. These lines partition the triangle into visible and occluded polygons. Given a neighbourhood of pixels that have the same configuration, this type of approximation produces smooth varying shadows.

Unfortunately, given a configuration of type C_{002}, C_{011}, or C_{022}, simply joining the edge discontinuities can lead to dramatic discontinuities in the penumbral shadow. These discontinuities occur at the boundaries with other configurations, and correspond to the traditional discontinuities encountered in discontinuity meshing. To both understand and to alleviate these problems, we must examine the transitions that can happen between the various configurations.

3.2 Configuration Transitions

As we determine visibility from one pixel to the next, the occluder appears to move with respect to the source. We say that a transition pair exists between two configurations C_a and C_b iff it is possible for an occluder to be translated from position α to position β such that:

- At position α, the configuration due to the occluder is C_a.
- At position β, the configuration due to the occluder is C_b.
- For any position $\gamma = \alpha + s(\beta - \alpha)$ such that $s \in [0, 1]$, the configuration due to the occluder is either C_a or C_b.

There are only 8 possible transitions pairs,[2] and these are illustrated in Figure 1.

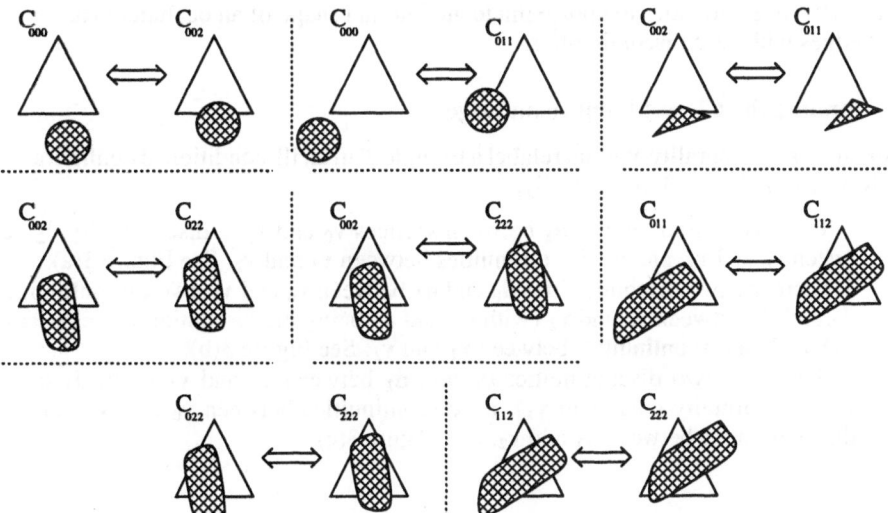

Fig. 1. Configuration Transition Pairs

If we simply use the discontinuities along the edges of T to approximate the shape of the occluder in each of the configurations, some transitions can become *ill-conditioned* (see [8]), in the sense that small changes in the location of the occluder can cause large changes in our approximation of the visible portion. The following transitions are

---

[2] If the fully-visible assumption about the C_{000} configuration is violated, other transitions are possible.

218

potentially ill-conditioned: $C_{002} \Leftrightarrow C_{011}$, $C_{002} \Leftrightarrow C_{022}$, $C_{002} \Leftrightarrow C_{222}$, $C_{011} \Leftrightarrow C_{112}$, and $C_{022} \Leftrightarrow C_{222}$. An ill-conditioned transition is illustrated in Figure 2. Notice that the approximation to the visible portion of the source suddenly increases in value in the last transition, as the occluder finally pierces the right edge.

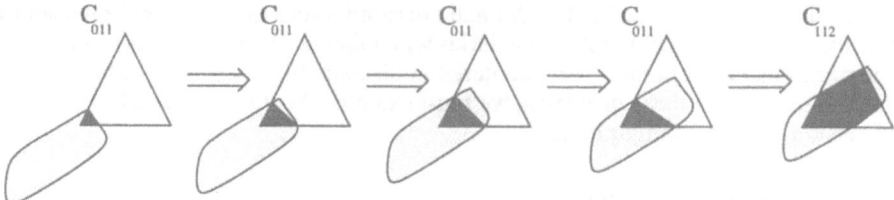

Fig. 2. Ill-Conditioned $C_{011} \Leftrightarrow C_{112}$ transition. Approximate visible domain shown in black.

The problem with the simple approximation is that it is impossible to maintain a consistent approximation across certain configuration transitions. To alleviate ill-conditioning, we must account for the shape of the occluder inside T. This is critical for the *ill-conditioned configurations* C_{002}, C_{011}, and C_{022}. These are the configurations that have one or two edges with zero discontinuities, and for which we have no information about the closeness of the occluder to these edges.

Our goal is to approximate the shape of the occluder such that the approximation varies smoothly across a region of pixels that have the same configuration, and varies continuously at the boundaries where the configuration changes. To achieve this goal, we use effective heuristics to approximate the internal shape of an occluder near one or more edges with zero discontinuities.

3.3 Finding the Closest Point to an Edge

Without loss of generality, we can relabel a triangle T in an ill-conditioned configuration as illustrated in Figure 3. Specifically,

C_{011} : There is a discontinuity $\mathbf{d}_1$ between vertices $\mathbf{v}_0$ and $\mathbf{v}_1$, a discontinuity $\mathbf{d}_2$ between $\mathbf{v}_0$ and $\mathbf{v}_2$, and no discontinuities between $\mathbf{v}_1$ and $\mathbf{v}_2$. See Figure 3(a).

C_{022} : There are two discontinuities $\mathbf{d}_0$ and $\mathbf{d}_1$ between $\mathbf{v}_0$ and $\mathbf{v}_1$, two discontinuities $\mathbf{d}_2$ and $\mathbf{d}_3$ between $\mathbf{v}_0$ and $\mathbf{v}_2$ (with $\mathbf{d}_1$ and $\mathbf{d}_2$ being the discontinuities closest to $\mathbf{v}_2$), and no discontinuities between $\mathbf{v}_1$ and $\mathbf{v}_2$. See Figure 3(b).

C_{002} : There are two discontinuities $\mathbf{d}_0$ and $\mathbf{d}_1$ between $\mathbf{v}_0$ and $\mathbf{v}_1$ (with $\mathbf{d}_1$ being the discontinuity closest to $\mathbf{v}_1$), no discontinuities between $\mathbf{v}_0$ and $\mathbf{v}_2$, and no discontinuities between $\mathbf{v}_1$ and $\mathbf{v}_2$. See Figure 3(c).

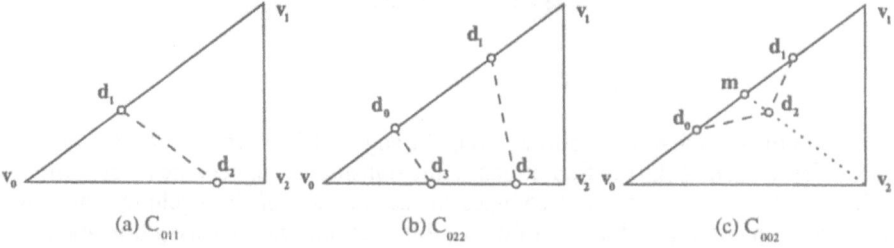

Fig. 3. Relabelling of ill-conditioned triangles, with dashed lines representing linear boundaries.

If a triangle is of type C_{002}, we let $\mathbf{m}$ be the midpoint between the discontinuities $\mathbf{d_0}$ and $\mathbf{d_1}$. Since the occluder is of class OCTDIALS(T, P), then $V(\mathbf{m}) \neq V(\mathbf{v_2})$, and we can use RSB to find a discontinuity $\mathbf{d_2}$ between $\mathbf{m}$ and $\mathbf{v_2}$. The triangle can then be split along the edge $\mathbf{m}$-$\mathbf{v_2}$, which results in two triangles of type C_{011}.

Given that any triangle of type C_{002} can be subdivided into two triangles of type C_{011}, we only need to be able to handle triangles of configuration type C_{011} and C_{022}, to effectively handle all ill-conditioned triangles. Examining Figure 3(a) and Figure 3(b), we see that approximating the internal shape of the visible domain of T can be expressed as follows: given the boundary of the occluder that extends from $\mathbf{d_1}$ to $\mathbf{d_2}$, find the point on this boundary that is closest to the edge $\mathbf{v_1}$-$\mathbf{v_2}$.

Let $\mathbf{v}(f) = \mathbf{v_1}(1 - f) + f\mathbf{v_2}$ be a parameterization of the edge $\mathbf{v_1}$-$\mathbf{v_2}$, where $f \in [0, 1]$. Let $\mathbf{d}(f)$ be the discontinuity between $\mathbf{v_0}$ and $\mathbf{v}(f)$ that is the furthest from $\mathbf{v_0}$. This is the intersection of the line $\mathbf{v_0}$-$\mathbf{v}(f)$ with the boundary of the occluder that extends from $\mathbf{d_1}$ to $\mathbf{d_2}$, and in fact, $\mathbf{d}(f)$ is the boundary curve. Let $D(f)$ be the perpendicular distance from $\mathbf{d}(f)$ to the edge $\mathbf{v_1}$-$\mathbf{v_2}$. Since the occluder is of class OCTDIALS(T, P), the function $D(f)$ can have only one of three possible shapes:

- Concave upward — if $D''(f) \geq 0$.
- Concave downward — if $D''(f) \leq 0$.
- Straight line — if $D''(f) = 0$.

Only if $D''(f) \geq 0$ can D have a minimum at m, with $\mathbf{d}(m)$ closer to the edge $\mathbf{v_1}$-$\mathbf{v_2}$ than both $\mathbf{d_1}$ and $\mathbf{d_2}$. How close $\mathbf{d}(m)$ is to the edge determines the ill-conditioning that would be inherent to an approximation of the visible domain were $\mathbf{d}(m)$ not to be taken into account. Since in practice this is the most common (and most difficult) type of ill-conditioning to detect, we now present an algorithm that determines if D is concave upward, and if so, finds the minimum m and the point $\mathbf{d}(m)$, within a tolerance μ.

In general, the boundary function $\mathbf{d}(f)$ is not explicitly available. However, we can use RSB to calculate $\mathbf{d}(f)$. First, we compute the intersection of the line $\mathbf{v_0}$-$\mathbf{v}(f)$ with the line $\mathbf{d_1}$-$\mathbf{d_2}$, giving the intersection point $\mathbf{i}$. Since the edge $\mathbf{v_1}$-$\mathbf{v_2}$ has no discontinuities, we know that $V(\mathbf{v}(f)) = V(\mathbf{v_1})$. We then compute $V(\mathbf{i})$, and compare it to $V(\mathbf{v}(f))$. If they are the same, the function $D(f)$ is not concave upward, and we cannot find a point on the boundary closer to edge $\mathbf{v_1}$-$\mathbf{v_2}$ than both $\mathbf{d_1}$ and $\mathbf{d_2}$. If they are different, we use RSB to find $\mathbf{d}(f)$, and then compute its perpendicular distance from the edge $\mathbf{v_1}$-$\mathbf{v_2}$.

Figure 4 contains the *Minimum Finding* (MF) algorithm. Given the tolerance μ, MF returns FALSE if the function is concave downward, otherwise returns TRUE and the approximate location of the minimum, within the specified tolerance. MF first determines if $D(f)$ is concave upward by examining a midpoint chosen randomly from a uniform distribution over $[0, 1]$, and comparing it to $D(0)$ and $D(1)$ to determine if the function can possibly be concave upward.

If the function is concave upward, MF iteratively refines the interval containing the minimum value of $D(f)$ by applying the *Mean Value Theorem* of calculus. The algorithm terminates when the interval is smaller than μ. The algorithm returns a TRUE value, and the midpoint m of the final interval is the location of the minimum of $D(f)$. The point on the boundary closest to the edge is then $\mathbf{d}(m)$.

If the point $\mathbf{d}(m)$ is closer to $\mathbf{v_1}$-$\mathbf{v_2}$ than both $\mathbf{d_1}$ and $\mathbf{d_2}$, it is used to refine the visible domain of the triangle. Since the occluder is of class OCTDIALS(T, P), the visible domain can be (uniquely) approximated by the polygonal boundary defined by the vertices of the triangle, the discontinuities, and the closest point $\mathbf{d}(m)$. The accuracy of $\mathbf{d}(m)$ is controlled by the tolerance μ, which in turn controls the continuity of the

```
        lo = 0; hi = 1; mid = choose randomly in [0,1]

        // If boundary is concave downward, return FALSE
        if( ( D(mid) > D(lo) ) and ( D(mid) > D(hi) ) ){
           return( FALSE );
        } else if( D(mid) > min(D(lo),D(hi)) ){
           // lineMid is the value of D(mid) if boundary is a line
           lineMid = ( D(lo)*(hi-mid) + D(hi)*(mid-lo) ) / (hi-lo);
           if ( D(mid) > maxMid ){
              // D(mid) above line, thus boundary is concave downward
              return( FALSE );
           }
        }
        while( (hi-lo) > tolerance ){
           if( D(mid) > min(D(lo),D(hi)) ){
              if( D(lo) < D(hi) ){
                 hi = mid;                    // Minimum is in [lo,mid]
              } else {
                 lo = mid;                    // Minimum is in [mid,hi]
              }
              mid = (lo+hi)/2;
           } else { // Test midpoints of lower and upper subintervals
              midlo = (lo+mid)/2; midhi = (hi+mid)/2;
              if( D(midlo) < D(mid) ){
                 hi = mid; mid = midlo;       // Minimum in [lo,mid]
              } else if( D(midhi) < D(mid) ){
                 lo = mid; mid = midhi;       // Minimum in [mid,hi]
              } else {
                 lo = midlo; hi = midhi;   // Minimum in [midlo,midhi]
              }
           }
        }
        // Desired point is mid, and distance from edge is D(mid)
        return( TRUE );
```

Fig. 4. Minimum Finding Algorithm

approximation of the visible domain of the triangle. As the occluder O gets closer to an edge with zero discontinuities, so does the point $\mathbf{d}(m)$, and thus the approximation to the visible domain gradually converges to the approximation that will result when the occluder finally pierces the edge. In Figure 5, the three types of boundaries and the resulting approximation to the visible domain are illustrated for a triangle of type C_{011}.

Similarly to RSB, MF uses a random initial subdivision to avoid banding artifacts. After the initial subdivision, the interval containing the minimum is reduced by half at each iteration. Each iteration requires at most two evaluations of $D(f)$, thus after n iterations, we have evaluated $D(f)$ at most $2n$ times, and the expected error is $O(1/2^{n-1})$.

Finally, a word of caution on the MF algorithm. Since MF relies on RSB, and since both are numerical algorithms, additional care must be exerted in controlling the error levels. As a rule of thumb [8], a nested numerical method should be roughly one order of magnitude more precise than the calling method. In our implementation, we have made the RSB routine (as used within MF) ten times as accurate as the MF routine.

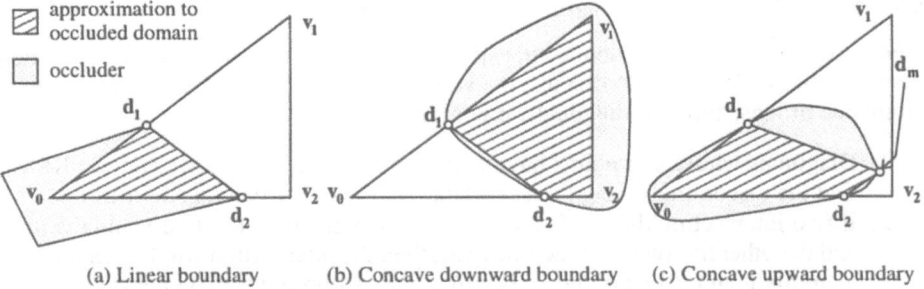

(a) Linear boundary   (b) Concave downward boundary   (c) Concave upward boundary

Fig. 5. Types of boundaries and resulting approximation of occluded domain.

4 Quadrilateral and General Polygon Algorithms

We now present an algorithm for finding the approximate shape of the visible domain of a (convex) quadrilateral light source Q. Since the four edges share the vertices of Q, we first compute visibility at all four vertices. We then use RSB and TDF to determine the number and approximate location of the discontinuities on the edges of Q.

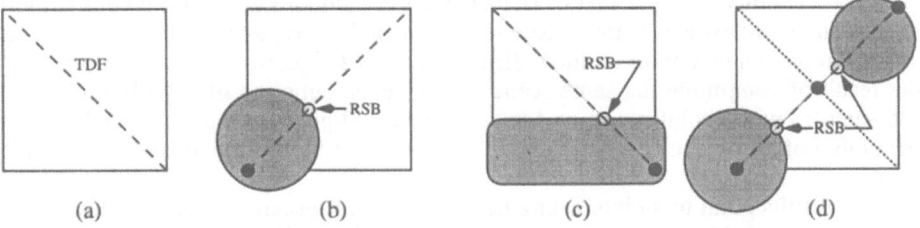

(a)   (b)   (c)   (d)

Fig. 6. Four possible vertex configurations for a quadrilateral light source.

Given the visibility at the vertices of Q, there are four different types of configurations possible. We enumerate the configurations and the criteria used to select the diagonal along which Q is subdivided and rendered as two triangles.

1. All four vertices have the same visibility. Choose a random diagonal and determine the number of discontinuities using TDF. See Figure 6(a).
2. One vertex has a different visibility than the other three. Choose the diagonal that has the vertex with a different visibility since we can use RSB to find the discontinuity, and avoid a call to the more expensive TDF routine. See Figure 6(b).
3. Two adjacent vertices have the same visibility and the other two vertices have the opposite visibility. Choose a random diagonal and find the discontinuity using RSB. See Figure 6(c).
4. Two diagonally opposite vertices have the same visibility and the other two vertices have the opposite visibility. Find the intersection point i of the two diagonals and determine its visibility. Choose the diagonal v_i-v_j whose end points have a different visibility than i, and use RSB to find the discontinuity between i and v_i, and to find the discontinuity between i and v_j. See Figure 6(d).

Once we have chosen the diagonal, we subdivide Q using this diagonal and render the light source as two triangles, using the algorithms of Section 3.

4.1 Extending to Polygons with More than 4 Sides

Our algorithm can also be extended in a straightforward manner to polygons with more than 4 vertices. The key is to first test the vertices for visibility and to split the polygon along one of these types of diagonals, if possible:

1. Diagonals whose end points have opposite visibilities, since we can use RSB to find the discontinuity (e.g., Cases 2 and 3 of the Quadrilateral Algorithm).
2. If two intersecting diagonals are such that one diagonal has two visible vertices and the other has two occluded vertices, then the intersection will have a different visibility than the end points of one diagonal. Choose this diagonal and use RSB to find the two discontinuities (e.g., Case 4 of Quadrilateral Algorithm).

5 Results and Discussion

In Figure 7, we show the result of illuminating three different types of objects with a triangular light source. The source is located parallel to the floor, above and slightly behind the objects. In Figure7(a), the image was computed using the heuristics designed in Section 3: RSB with a tolerance of $\varepsilon = 0.05$, TDF with a tolerance of $v = 0.25$, and MF with a tolerance of $\mu = 0.333$. The approximate visibility of the objects required about 26 visibility tests per pixel. The shadows are smooth within each configuration region, and seemless across the boundaries between these regions. Notice that the shadows are rendered nicely for all three different types of objects. In Figure7(b), we show the result of computing the same scene with a super sampling of slightly higher cost (28 samples with visibility testing for each pixel). Slight banding is noticeable in the penumbra of all objects, especially in the shadow cast by the sphere and by the tip of the cone.

Our results point to an interesting new direction of research involving the approximation of the visible domain of area light sources. We believe that one of the keys to the successful approximation of the visible domain of an integrand lies in the consistency of the approximation. The algorithms we have developed provide an approximate solution to the visible domain that is both smooth within a configuration region, and continuous as we move from one configuration to the other.

The *Minimum Finding* (MF) algorithm developed has several important properties. Ill-conditioned transitions are alleviated by allowing a more consistent approximation of the visible domain of the integrand. Banding is eliminated without sacrificing efficiency by the introduction of a random seed. The tolerance μ provides an effective mechanism for controlling the cost and quality of the approximation. For a given tolerance μ, the complexity of MF is nearly that of a pure bisection method, namely $O((\log 1/\mu)^2)$. This is a result of MF having the RSB method (which has a complexity of $O(\log 1/\varepsilon)$ for a tolerance of ε) embedded within a method of similar complexity. The squared complexity of MF (with respect to RSB) comes as no surprise, since doubling the dimensionality of an integration problem typically squares the cost of the solution. Finally, note that contrary to other sampling methods, the difference between a small occluder being detected or not is bounded by its actual contribution to the penumbral shadow, since the resulting occlusion will be approximated to within μ.

Many improvements are still possible to these approximation algorithms. In particular, approximating the internal shape of the occluder is a difficult (and expensive) problem to solve. Interesting areas of investigation to improve the algorithms presented in this paper include: taking advantage of scene coherence to speed up the outer loop

(a) RSB ($\varepsilon = 0.05$), TDF ($v = 0.25$), and MF ($\mu = 0.333$), with 26.2 visibility tests

(b) Super sampling with 28 samples

Fig. 7. Penumbral region comparison for locally convex occluders

of MF, and investigating more efficient methods for finding the minimum point on a concave upward boundary, such as perhaps the *Secant Method* [8].

Finally, an important area of future research is to determine how the algorithms presented in this paper can be extended to more complex computer graphics scenes. Assuming the convex occluder problem can be solved efficiently, how can this solution be extended to an arbitrary class of occluders and larger sets of discontinuity regions? In both cases, a possible approach would be to subdivide either the source or the occluder, so as to reduce the combinatorial complexity in the case analyses.

An interesting hybrid approach could combine the best properties of the algorithms we introduced, with those of shadow mapping techniques [12, 13]. An environment could be partitioned into classes of occluders best suited to each type, with the algorithm of this paper handling large occluders, particularly if an occluder and a receiver are abutting and causing few discontinuities in the integrand, and shadow mapping techniques used to approximate more complex occluders.

6 Conclusions

In this paper, we used the *Random Seed Bisection* (RSB) and the *Two Discontinuity Finding* (TDF) algorithms to approximate the location of discontinuities for polygonal light sources, and for the class of locally convex occluders. Given a triangular light source, we used RSB and TDF to determine the discontinuities along each edge, and to classify the triangle into one of six possible configurations. We introduced the *Minimum Finding* (MF) algorithm to approximate the shape of the visible domain within the triangle. Finally, we approximated the visible domain with a polygonal approximation using the discontinuities found. The resulting integrals can be solved efficiently using either a low degree numerical cubature, or in the case of diffuse surface and light sources, using an analytic solution. We then proposed an extension of these algorithms to general polygons. We believe that this an important first step in addressing the issue of the approximate knowledge of visible domains and its application toward efficient rendering of penumbral shadows.

7 Acknowledgments

The comments by the reviewers helped to improve the paper, and were much appreciated. We gratefully acknowledge the funding of NSERC and CITO in our research.

References

1. Brotman, L.S., Badler, N.I., "Generating Soft Shadows with a Depth Buffer Algorithm", *IEEE Computer Graphics and Applications*, 4(10), Oct. 1984.
2. Campbell, A.T., "Modeling Global Diffuse Illumination for Image Synthesis", Ph.D. Thesis, University of Texas at Austin, Dec. 1991.
3. Chin, N., Feiner, S., "Fast Object-Precision Shadow Generation for Area Light Sources Using BSP Trees", *ACM Computer Graphics (SIGGRAPH Symp. on Inter. 3D Graphics 1992)*.
4. Cook, R.L., Porter, T. and Carpenter, L., "Distributed Ray Tracing", *Computer Graphics*, 18(3), July 1984.
5. Drettakis, G., Fiume, E., "A Fast Shadow Algorithm for Area Light Sources Using Backprojection", *ACM SIGGRAPH Annual Conference Series*, July 1994.
6. Heckbert, P.S., Herf, M., "Simulating Soft Shadows with Graphics Hardware", *Technical Report CMU-CS-97-104*, Carnegie Mellon U., June 1997.
7. Hedley, D., Worrall, A., Paddon, D., "Selective Culling of Discontinuity Lines", *8th Eurographics Workshop on Rendering*, June 1997.
8. Kahaner, D., Moler, C., Nash, S., *Numerical Methods and Software*, Prentice Hall, Englewood Cliffs, New Jersey, 1989.
9. Lischinski, D., Tampieri, F., Greenberg, D., "Discontinuity Meshing for Accurate Radiosity", *IEEE C.G. & Appl.*, 12(6), Nov. 1992.
10. Moon, P., *The Scientific Basis of Illuminating Engineering*, McGraw-Hill, New York, 1936.
11. Ouellette, M.J., Fiume, E., "Approximating the Location of Integrand Discontinuities for Penumbral Illumination with Linear Light Sources", *Graphics Interface 99*, 1999.
12. Soler, C., Sillion, F.X., "Automatic Calculation of Soft Shadow Textures for Fast, High Quality Radiosity", *9th Eurographics Workshop on Rendering*, June 1998.
13. Soler, C., Sillion, F.X., "Fast Calculation of Soft Shadow Textures Using Convolution", *ACM SIGGRAPH Annual Conference Series*, July 1998.
14. Stewart, J.A., Ghali, S., "Fast Computation of Shadow Boundaries Using Spatial Coherence and Backprojections", *ACM SIGGRAPH Annual Conference Series*, July 1994.
15. Wallace, J.R., Elmquist, K.A., and Haines, E.A., "A Ray Tracing Algorithm for Progressive Radiosity", *Computer Graphics*, 23(3), July 1989.

Reducing Memory Requirements for Interactive Radiosity Using Movement Prediction

Frank Schöffel

Fraunhofer Institute for Computer Graphics
Darmstadt, Germany
schoeffe@igd.fhg.de

Andreas Pomi

vrcom GmbH
Darmstadt, Germany
apomi@vrcom.de

Abstract. The line-space hierarchy is a very powerful approach for the efficient update of radiosity solutions according to geometry changes. However, it suffers from its enormous memory consumption when storing shafts for the entire scene. We propose a method for reducing the memory requirements of the line-space hierarchy by the dynamic management of shaft storage. We store shaft information only locally for those parts of the scene that are currently affected by the geometry change. When the dynamic object enters new regions, new shaft data has to be computed, but on the other hand we can get rid of outdated data 'behind' the dynamic object. Simple movement prediction schemes are applied, so that we can provide shaft data to the radiosity update process in time when needed. We show how storage management and pre-calculation of shafts can be efficiently performed in parallel to the radiosity update process itself.

1 Introduction

Realistic global illumination simulations are applied more and more in three-dimensional computer-generated environments, e.g., in Virtual Reality applications. Due to its view-independent nature, the radiosity method is very well suited for illumination simulation in those applications. However, updating the illumination in interactive environments according to modifications in scene geometry is a demanding task, since radiosity updates are expensive to calculate. Interactive update rates are hard to achieve.

Several methods for updating radiosity solutions according to scene modifications have been presented in literature, both for progressive refinement radiosity and for hierarchical radiosity, amongst which the line-space hierarchy approach [5] is one of the most powerful ones. Although this method can provide very fast update rates in the context of hierarchical radiosity, it still has several drawbacks. Its high storage demand is the most important disadvantage, prohibiting a wide-spread use of the line-space approach for complex real-world scenes.

In this paper, we address this problem and propose a method for the dynamic management of storage, thus reducing storage requirements significantly and enabling the line-space hierarchy method to be applied even to complex scenes. In the original line-space hierarchy method, shafts are stored within the entire scene. Our method limits the spatial regions for which this data is stored to those regions in which interaction currently takes place. When an object is moved into new regions, missing shafts can be computed during radiosity update. To avoid this additional calculation, movement prediction schemes can be applied: The object movement is extrapolated for future frames, thus allowing to pre-compute shaft data so that it is available to the update process in time when needed. Furthermore, a garbage collector removes shafts that are no longer necessary behind the object. The method is scalable according to the storage available and can reduce storage requirements dramatically. It is especially useful when running on a multi-processor system, but can also be applied on single-processor machines when doing without movement prediction, taking into account slightly lower performance.

In the remainder of this paper, we briefly review previous work and then present our method for dynamic shaft management with movement prediction. We proceed with results of a first implementation and, finally, conclude and give an outlook on directions of future work.

2 Context and Previous Work

2.1 The radiosity method

The radiosity method simulates global illumination on a physical basis within diffuse environments. Improvements on the original algorithm [8] reduced the quadratic storage requirements: Progressive refinement radiosity [4] requires storage that is only linear in the number of patches, allowing radiosity simulations to be applied to complex environments. Hierarchical radiosity [10] simulates light transfer at different levels of accuracy and has also significantly less than quadratic storage costs. It subdivides the input polygons into *hierarchical elements* and creates *links*, across which energy is transferred between elements at appropriate levels. Links are initially established between all pairs of input polygons and refined according to the amount of energy transferred and other criteria. The quadratic cost of the initial linking phase is a major drawback of this method, which can be avoided by applying 'lazy linking' mechanisms [11] or clustering. The clustering approach [15][17] extends the hierarchy above the polygon level up to one single root element for the scene, and allows the efficient treatment of very complex environments.

2.2 Radiosity in dynamic environments

Since the radiosity process takes into account the whole scene geometry, the simulation has to be repeated whenever the geometry is modified, in order to maintain a consistent solution. However, the most important effects of geometry changes are often spatially limited, and coherence can be exploited in order to obtain an efficiently updated radiosity solution. Several approaches for fast radiosity updates have been proposed, some of which require the path of the dynamic object to be known in advance (e.g., [1]). These methods are obviously not suited for interactive applications, where the user may freely modify the scene, and therefore are not discussed in this paper.

Other approaches have been developed for both progressive refinement and hierarchical radiosity. Two very similar algorithms based on progressive refinement have been proposed by Chen [2] and George et al. [7]. These methods update an existing radiosity solution by shooting (possibly negative) 'correction values' to patches on which illumination has changed due to object movements, and they account for indirect effects by applying further iterations. In [13], an efficient data structure has been proposed by

Müller et al., enabling the efficient exploitation of coherence. However, these methods still cannot provide feedback at interactive rates for moderately complex environments.

For hierarchical radiosity, a first approach on dynamic updates was presented by Forsyth [6]. He proposed to move links up and down in the hierarchy, according to changes in occlusions and energy transfers. This idea was further developed by Shaw [14] to the idea of keeping track of link refinement and storing visibility information in 'ghost links' and 'shadow links'. Eventually, an efficient update algorithm for hierarchical radiosity and clustering, based on a line-space hierarchy, has been presented by Drettakis and Sillion [5].

2.3 The line-space hierarchy

This approach uses the line-space hierarchy for the rapid identification of links affected by a scene modification. The line-space between two hierarchical elements (which may be either patches or clusters) is represented by *shafts* [9] associated with the links.

While in traditional hierarchical radiosity a link that has been subdivided may be discarded, those links are kept in the line-space hierarchy but marked as *passive*. In contrast to *active* links, across which energy is transferred, passive links do not participate in energy transfer, but maintain a history of the link subdivision. The form-factor associated with these links is kept, in order to easily re-establish the links when needed.

Once an object is moved within the scene, one has to check the object's bounding boxes at its old and new position for intersection with the shafts in order to find which links are affected, descending in the shaft hierarchy. For the affected links, new form-factors have to be calculated and the links possibly have to be subdivided. On the other hand, some previous subdivisions may have become too fine and therefore passive links at higher levels have to be activated again. Finally, energy has to be gathered across the modified links, and a limited push-pull operation ensures a consistent global solution.

3 Reducing Memory Consumption by Movement Prediction

3.1 Memory requirements of the line-space hierarchy

Hierarchical radiosity approaches require a lot of memory when storing all links across which energy is transferred. For the line-space approach, memory requirements are even higher, since a complete hierarchy including passive links is kept, and usually shafts are stored for all links. While for hierarchical radiosity, link caching schemes can significantly reduce link storage [18], these methods cannot be applied to the line-space method for fast radiosity updates, where the complete link hierarchy is essential.

For fast identification of affected regions, shafts are needed to be available throughout the scene. Unfortunately, shafts are much more expensive in terms of storage than links: While a link just consists of a pointer to the element it transfers energy from and a form-factor, a shaft is made up of bounding boxes for the receiver and the sender, as well as a compound bounding box, a slab counter and up to eight slabs, altogether easily requiring more than 400 bytes per shaft, when assuming a float to be 8 bytes wide. Although this data of course can be compressed, the shafts still require a significant amount of memory. Thus, reducing the number of shafts will significantly reduce the overall memory consumption. Deleted shafts, of course, have to be re-calculated when needed for intersection tests during line-space traversal. A possible way to save this additional calculation time is to have a separate process providing shafts *just before* they are needed. Such a process could predict the regions in which shafts will be required in future frames and pre-calculate missing data.

3.2 Predicting object movement

For predicting future positions of a dynamic object that is moved interactively by a user just by looking at recent positions, literature offers many different methods. These approaches range from simple translation extrapolation and transformation matrix extrapolation to complicated prediction schemes taking into account kinematics and other constraints. For the purpose of roughly predicting regions into which the dynamic object will move, we do not need sophisticated methods like, e.g., Kalman filtering [12], but instead will use a fast and simple linear extrapolation of object movement.

Extrapolation. We define the translation vector $\vec{t}_0$ from the previous to the current object location by $\vec{t}_0 = \vec{c}_0 - \vec{c}_{-1}$, where $\vec{c}_0$ and $\vec{c}_{-1}$ are the bounding box centers of the dynamic object at the current and the previous position, respectively. $\vec{t}_0$ is added to the current position $\vec{p}_0$ of the dynamic object in order to obtain its position $\vec{p}_{+1}$ in the next frame. When adding $\vec{t}_0$ multiple times, we get the future positions for the next n frames:

$$\vec{p}_{+n} = \vec{p}_0 + n \cdot \vec{t}_0 \tag{1}$$

Jittered motion in interactive systems can be smoothened by considering not only *one* previous position, but the last m positions and translation vectors $\vec{t}_{-i}, i = 0, \ldots, m-1$:

$$\vec{p}_{+n} = \vec{p}_0 + \frac{1}{m} \sum_{i=0}^{m-1} \vec{t}_{-i} \tag{2}$$

In addition, the previous positions do not have to be weighted equally. For example, exponential weighting leads to the most recent positions being considered more important than older ones [3]. If not only previous bounding box positions are known, but also the object transformation matrices T_{-i}, then object rotation can be considered, too. For example, Eq. 1 then can be extended to:

$$\vec{p}_{+n} = T_0^n \cdot \vec{p}_0 \tag{3}$$

Compensating for prediction errors. The presented simple prediction scheme is fast to apply, but it may introduce errors since non-linear object movements cannot be covered very well. These errors, resulting in the predicted bounding box position being different from the actual one, are not crucial, since missing shafts can be generated *on-the-fly* during shaft testing (see Section 3.3). But, since missing shafts reduce update rates, we want to compensate for the prediction error: In order to keep things simple and fast, we scale the predicted object's bounding box by some factor $s > 1$.

Thus, the probability of missing affected shafts is reduced, but the appropriate values for s have to be chosen carefully: If s is too great, lots of unnecessary shafts will be generated, and if it is chosen too small, one might miss many affected shafts. An example for predicted bounding volumes is depicted in Fig. 4 (see Appendix). Note that for simplifying intersection tests we always use axis-aligned bounding boxes, even if the object is being rotated.

3.3 Dynamic shaft management

Since we do not store shafts for *all* links any longer, mechanisms are needed for calculating shafts when required. There are two reasons for a link not having shaft data available:

- The link has never been asked for its shaft before. This is true especially at initialisation time.
- The shaft once was available, but has been removed for saving memory.

Initially, there are virtually no shafts; a shaft is calculated only when required (or when predicted to be required). In a clustering environment, the only shaft available at startup time is the one associated with the self-link of the root cluster, which is identical with the scene's total bounding box (*root shaft*). For hierarchical radiosity without clustering, all top-level shafts (associated with the links resulting from the initial linking phase) are available and should be kept in storage. In the following, we describe the algorithm for a clustering environment, but it can also be applied directly to non-clustering hierarchical radiosity when considering all top-level shafts instead of just a single root shaft.

Shaft generation. One possible approach is to generate shafts at exactly the time when needed during line-space traversal. Moreover, it is not necessary to store a shaft at all—we can destroy it immediately after the intersection test has been finished and re-calculate it again when required. This approach minimises storage demands, but slows down line-space traversal significantly.

Therefore, it is preferable to minimise the number of shafts to be calculated on-the-fly by the update process, and to have missing shafts be provided automatically by the movement prediction process running in parallel. We use the bounding boxes predicted as described in Section 3.2 and check for intersection with existing shafts, starting with the root shaft and traversing the shaft hierarchy. For reducing the number of line-space traversals, we check for intersection with *all* predicted volumes for future frames in *one* traversal step. If more than one dynamic object exists, all predicted bounding boxes of all dynamic objects are used during the intersection test. If an intersection between any of the bounding boxes and a shaft is found, we store that shaft, and for passive links we descend in the hierarchy and test child links accordingly. Shafts that are not available for a child link are generated before testing. If such a newly created shaft intersects with a bounding box, we store it. Otherwise, we stop descending and may discard the shaft. This process is depicted in Fig. 1.

```
CreateShaftsOnPrediction (Helem p, IndexRange idx, BBoxList bbl)
{
    for each link L of p
    {
        Helem q = L→src
        if (TestAndCreateShaft (L→shaft, bbl))
            if ((L is passive) and (q→idx ⊆ idx))
                for each child node c of p
                    CreateShaftsOnPrediction (c, q→idx, bbl)
    }
}
```

Fig. 1. Checking for affected links and creating associated shafts.

Links of the dynamic object itself are always affected by the modification and therefore are calculated without checking. These shafts are trivial to detect since the dynamic object is known. However, care has to be taken to keep these shafts' geometry up-to-date during object movement.

Shaft deletion. Shafts which are not needed any longer should be deleted in order to save storage. However, it is not easy to decide which shafts are good candidates for deletion. Shafts can be outdated for several reasons:

- If a passive link is being re-established as *active*, all its child links, including the shafts, can be removed.
- Amongst the remaining links, many shafts can be deleted, too. For example, shafts located behind the dynamic object are very unlikely to be needed in the near future, when we assume the object not to turn around suddenly.
- Wrongly predicted shafts will never be used and therefore have to be deleted. This occurs, for example, when the object moves differently from the predicted path or when the user selects another object for interaction.

While the first category of outdated shafts is trivial to identify, shafts behind the dynamic object have to be searched for: These shafts intersect previous dynamic object bounding boxes, but not future ones. Identification of wrongly predicted shafts is quite hard. We suggest to establish a *garbage collector* that deletes shafts which have not been used for a certain time.

Garbage collection. In order to keep the total size of shaft storage approximately constant, about the same number of old shafts should be deleted when creating new shafts. We introduce a shaft counter N_{shafts} and a link counter N_{links}, and denote the rate of links with shaft data available by $P_{shafts} = \frac{N_{shafts}}{N_{links}}$. Defining a threshold $T_{shafts} \in [0, 1]$, we start the garbage collector whenever $P_{shafts} > T_{shafts}$.[1] This is checked after each line-space update.

The garbage collector removes those shafts which have not been used for the longest time. We add a new counter age to each shaft, and we reset this counter to its inital value 0 whenever the shaft is used for an intersection test. Once the garbage collector is triggered, it traverses the link hierarchy, incrementing ages of all existing shafts. Any shaft reaching a certain threshold age_{max} is deleted. The garbage collector may be stopped as soon as $T_{shafts} > P_{shafts}$, or when a lower threshold $T_{min,shafts}$ is reached by P_{shafts}, or it may resume, traversing the hierarchy completely. The process of garbage collection is outlined in Fig. 2.

```
GarbageCollect (Helem p, int age_max)
{
    for each child node c of p
        GarbageCollect (c, age_max)

    for each link L of p
    {
        if (L→shaft exists)
        {
            increment age_L→shaft
            if (age_L→shaft > age_max)
                DeleteShaft (L→shaft)
        }
    }
}
```

Fig. 2. The garbage collector.

---

[1] Alternatively, one could check for N_{shafts} exceeding some fixed maximum number of shafts. This allows for a fixed storage size being ensured and therefore should be preferred if memory is very limited.

Algorithm overview and parallelisation. After each radiosity update the dynamic shaft management is triggered. Firstly, the garbage collector is started if too many shafts are stored. In a second step, the movement prediction calculates future positions of the dynamic object. If more than one object is moving, we come up with a list of predicted bounding volumes for all dynamic objects for the next n frames. The line-space is traversed, and shafts are calculated as discussed above for the predicted object positions.

Although the proposed method can be applied on single processor machines for reducing memory consumption, it is especially useful if movement prediction and shaft management can be performed on a separate processor in parallel to the line-space update itself. Only in this case, shaft prediction can show to advantage, when compared to on-the-fly shaft generation. Since line-space update and shaft prediction/garbage collection can work independently, these tasks can be performed simultaneously by two processes, which we will refer to as *update process* and *shaft management process*. On the other hand, since both the shaft prediction and the update process traverse the same hierarchy, data access conflicts can occur. Therefore, data access has to be synchronised, e.g., by locking sub-trees of the hierarchy. But when both processes traverse the hierarchy in the same manner, there may occur many situations where the processes have to wait for each other, thus slowing down the whole update. To reduce the number of possible conflicts, we propose to organise hierarchy traversal in a way that both processes traverse the hierarchy in opposite directions, as shown in Fig. 3 (left). The simultaneous execution of the update process and the shaft management process is depicted in Fig. 3 (right).

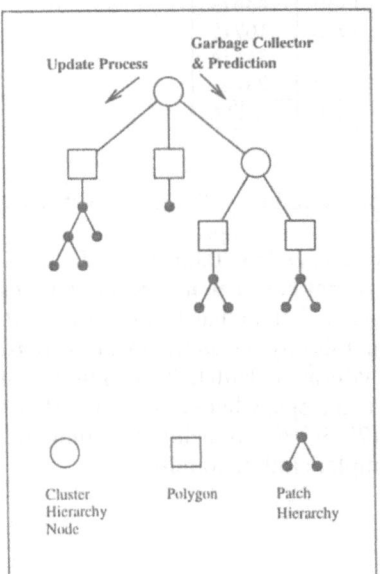
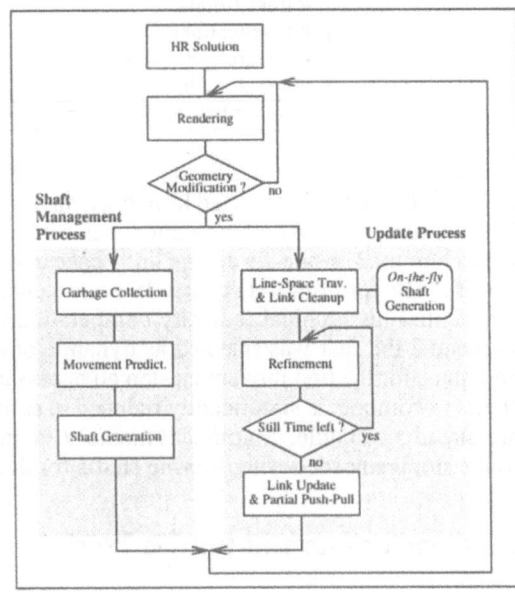

Fig. 3. Parallelisation of movement prediction and update process. Left: For avoiding conflicts, the link hierarchy is traversed by the update process and the shaft management process in opposite directions. Right: Performing shaft management in parallel to the line-space update. Missing shafts are generated *on-the-fly* during line-space traversal in the update process.

4 Results

We realised a first implementation in our hierarchical radiosity system without clustering. For movement prediction, we implemented a transformation matrix extrapolation scheme according to Eq. 3, accounting for both translation and rotation. We took into account only one previous object position and predict only one future position. Predicting future positions for $n > 1$ is difficult in practice in interactive environments, where users often change movement directions. For the scaling factor s of the predicted bounding boxes, values slightly greater than 1 usually proved to be useful ($s \in (1, 1.2]$); we applied a value of $s = 1.1$ to obtain the results presented in this paper.

Dynamic shaft generation and reduction is shown in Fig. 5 (see Appendix): Shafts do only exist in the region of the chair that forms the dynamic object. New shafts are added in the region into which the chair is moved, and outdated shafts are finally deleted by the garbage collector.

In the following, we report on shaft statistics for two test scenes. Scene 1 is the test environment shown in Fig. 5 (see Appendix), the more complex scene 2 is shown in Fig. 6 (see Appendix). We have simulated only one iteration of hierarchical radiosity in both example scenes. Statistics for the hierarchical solution are given in Table 1.

Table 1. Number of links for the two test scenes after initial hierarchical radiosity solution.

	scene 1	scene 2
# input polygons	227	1339
# links (total)	31130	43679
# passive links	7932	10715
# hierarchy elements	32108	31414
# hierarchy leaves	23679	23447
time for first HR iteration (sec)	81.4	129.6

Calculation times reported have been measured on an SGI Onyx IR with a 195 MHz R10000 processor. All computation was performed on the same processor, i.e., shafts were computed on-the-fly during line-space update when needed. Table 2 lists the number of shafts for both test scenes. In each scene, an object has been moved three times after initial hierarchical radiosity computation (in scene 1 the chair has been moved, in scene 2 the seat was selected as dynamic object). Initially, virtually no shafts exist and, thus, for the first movement step all necessary shafts are calculated. The number of shafts to compute is significantly reduced in subsequent steps, where most of the shafts are already available. Significant memory savings (79–95 %) are achieved, compared to the storage needed when storing shafts for the complete link hierarchy.

5 Conclusions and Future Work

We have presented a method for controlling the memory consumption for the line-space approach. We identified the shafts as the most memory-consuming part of the line-space data structure, which can be efficiently re-calculated instead of storing. In contrast to the straight-forward approach of not storing any shafts and re-calculating them when needed during line-space traversal, we have presented an approach for the dynamical management of shaft storage. A simple movement prediction is applied to

Table 2. Shaft statistics for test scenes 1 and 2, where objects have been moved in three steps.

move	scene 1			scene 2		
	1	2	3	1	2	3
# shafts at old pos.	1516	1392	1270	6208	6239	492
# shafts at new pos.	1392	1270	915	6239	492	485
# shaft tests	3128	2912	2728	18320	17586	6748
# shafts generated *on-the-fly*	1564	4	48	9160	152	355
# shafts already existing	0	1452	1316	0	8641	3019
# shafts deleted by garbage coll.	0	167	128	0	874	5538
# shafts (total)	1564	1401	1321	9160	8438	3255
shaft memory needed (MB)	0.88	0.79	0.74	5.15	4.75	1.83
shaft memory for *all* links (MB)	14.90	14.90	14.90	24.58	24.58	24.58
memory savings	94.1%	94.7%	95.0%	79.0%	80.7%	92.6%
time for line-space trav. (sec)	0.078	0.033	0.032	0.448	0.191	0.083
time for shaft generation (sec)	0.041	<0.001	0.002	0.239	0.004	0.011

let us know the necessary shafts for the next frames and prepare this data in time so that they are available to the line-space traversal when needed. Furthermore, a garbage collection is introduced to get rid of outdated shaft information. The presented approach is adjustable to the available memory size. Memory consumption can be reduced significantly, which allows to apply the line-space hierarchy method also to complex environments. We believe that even greater savings will be obtained when applying our method to more complex scenes than the test scenes described in the previous Section, and we therefore intend to do extensive tests on more complex real-world scenes.

While it is possible to apply this approach on a single processor machine for a better control of shaft storage, it comes to full advantage when the shaft pre-calculation and shaft deletion can be performed simultaneously with the line-space update itself on a separate processor. We have outlined how parallelisation can be organised. Even when performing shaft calculation on-the-fly, additional computation time turned out to be very small compared to line-space update time. Nevertheless, we intend to study in more detail the improvements achieved by parallel execution.

We feel that better prediction methods will not have great benefits in this context, since movements are not always smooth in interactive applications. Therefore, we chose a simple prediction method which is fast to perform. However, it should be investigated whether more exact movement prediction methods can improve the ratio of correctly predicted shafts, or if a rough but fast method performs better when combined with an efficient garbage collector.

An interesting direction for further research is to combine the presented approach with importance-driven approaches similar to [16]. Thus, update rates can be increased by focussing on the most 'important' regions of the scene first, and accordingly storage can be further reduced when only 'important' shafts are generated and held in memory.

Finally, of course, further parallelisation efforts can help to speed up the update process. For example, the line-space traversal itself could be split into parallel subtasks, and load balancing issues would then have to be investigated in order to gain maximum speed-up.

6   Acknowledgments

This work was funded in part by the European Union (Esprit LTR 24944: ARCADE). The authors wish to thank George Drettakis and François Sillion for fruitful dicussions and for providing helpful information about details on the line-space hierarchy.

References

1. Baum, D., Wallace, J., Cohen, M., Greenberg, D.: The back-buffer algorithm: an extension of the radiosity method to dynamic environments. *The Visual Computer*, 2(5):298–306, 1986.
2. Chen, S.: Incremental radiosity: An extension of progressive refinement radiosity to an interactive image synthesis system. *Computer Graphics (Proc. SIGGRAPH '90)*, 24(4):135–144, August 1990.
3. Chim, J., Lau R., Si, A., Leong, H., To, D., Green, M., Lam, M.: Multi-resolution model transmission in Distributed Virtual Environments. *Proceedings of the ACM Symposium on Virtual Reality Software and Technology (VRST '98)*, pages 25–33, November 1998.
4. Cohen, M., Chen, S., Wallace, J., Greenberg, D.: A progressive refinement approach to fast radiosity image generation. *Computer Graphics (Proc. SIGGRAPH '88)*, 22(4):75–84, August 1988.
5. Drettakis, G., Sillion, F.: Interactive update of global illumination using a line-space hierarchy. *Computer Graphics (Proc. SIGGRAPH '97)*, 31(3):57–64, August 1997.
6. Forsyth, D., Yang, C., Teo, K.: Efficient radiosity in dynamic environments. In Sakas, G. et al. (eds.): *Photorealistic Rendering Techniques*, pages 313–323, Springer-Verlag, 1995. Proc. 5th Eurographics Workshop on Rendering (Darmstadt, 1994).
7. George, D., Sillion, F., Greenberg, D.: Radiosity redistribution for dynamic environments. *IEEE Computer Graphics and Applications*, 10(4):26–34, July 1990.
8. Goral, C., Torrance, K., Greenberg, D., Battaile, B.: Modeling the interaction of light between diffuse surfaces. *Computer Graphics (Proc. SIGGRAPH '84)*, 18(3):213–222, July 1984.
9. Haines, E., Wallace, J.: Shaft culling for efficient ray-traced radiosity. Proc. 2nd Eurographics Workshop on Rendering (Barcelona, 1991). Proc. 2nd Eurographics Workshop on Rendering (Barcelona, 1991).
10. Hanrahan, P., Saltzman, D., Aupperle, L.: A rapid hierarchical radiosity algorithm. *Computer Graphics (Proc. SIGGRAPH '91)*, 25(4):197–206, August 1991.
11. Holzschuch, N., Sillion, F., Drettakis, G.: An efficient progressive refinement strategy for hierarchical radiosity. In Sakas, G. et al. (eds.): *Photorealistic Rendering Techniques*, pages 357–372, Springer-Verlag, 1995. Proc. 5th Eurographics Workshop on Rendering (Darmstadt, 1994).
12. Kalman, R.: A new approach to linear filtering and prediction problems. *J. Basic Eng., Series 82D*, pages 35–45, 1960.
13. Müller, S., Schöffel, F.: Fast radiosity repropagation for interactive virtual environments using a shadow-form-factor-list. In Sakas, G. et al. (eds.): *Photorealistic Rendering Techniques*, pages 339–356, Springer-Verlag, 1995. Proc. 5th Eurographics Workshop on Rendering (Darmstadt, 1994).
14. Shaw, E.: Hierarchical radiosity for dynamic environments. *Computer Graphics Forum*, 16(2)107–118, 1997.
15. Sillion, F.: A unified hierarchical algorithm for global illumination with scattering volumes and object clusters. *IEEE Trans. on Vis. and Comp. Graphics*, 1(3):240–254, Sep. 1995.
16. Smits, B., Arvo, J., Salesin, D.: An importance-driven radiosity algorithm. *Computer Graphics (Proc. SIGGRAPH '92)*, 26(4):273–282, July 1992.
17. Smits, B., Arvo, J., Greenberg, D.: A clustering algorithm for radiosity in complex environments. *Computer Graphics (Proc. SIGGRAPH '94)*, 28(2):435–442, July 1994.
18. Stamminger, M., Schirmacher, H., Slusallek, Ph., Seidel, H.-P.: Getting rid of links in hierarchical radiosity. In Ferreira, N., Göbel, M. (eds.): *Computer Graphics Forum (Proc. Eurographics '98)*, 17(3):C165–C174, 1998.

Editors' Note: see Appendix, p. 372 for colored figures of this paper

Space-Time Hierarchical Radiosity

Cyrille Damez and François Sillion

iMAGIS – GRAVIR/IMAG INRIA

Abstract. This paper presents a new hierarchical simulation algorithm allowing the calculation of radiosity solutions for time-dependent scenes where all motion is known *a priori*. Such solutions could, for instance, be computed to simulate subtle lighting effects (indirect lighting) in animation systems, or to obtain high-quality synthetic image sequences to blend with live action video and film. We base our approach on a Space-Time hierarchy, adding a life span to hierarchical surface elements, and present an integrated formulation of Hierarchical Radiosity with this extended hierarchy. We discuss the expected benefits of the technique, review the challenges posed by the approach, and propose first solutions for these issues, most notably for the space-time refinement strategy. We show that a short animation sequence can be computed rapidly at the price of a sizeable memory cost. These results confirm the potential of the approach while helping to identify areas of promising future work.

1 Introduction

Producing animated sequences has been a natural application of image synthesis since its inception, but remains an expensive endeavor, despite the impressive progress of computer performance over the years. A lot of effort has been devoted to the reduction of resource consumption for these calculations: Considering the large number of frames necessary even for a short movie sequence, shortening the production time carries an important economic value.

Interestingly, almost all animation systems to date still operate on a frame-by-frame basis, for understandable robustness and simplicity issues. Admittedly, and as we shall see below, more elaborate techniques trying to capitalize on temporal coherence are often more expensive in terms of memory usage. However even if this memory cost has appeared too expensive in the past, it is important to revisit such technological choices periodically in a period of fast change. Indeed, as computing power becomes cheaper by the day, memory prices are also decreasing in due proportion. Furthermore, while each and every frame of an animation must naturally be computed independently to reflect the appropriate position and parameters of the view at each time step, it seems promising to try and capitalize on the seemingly large temporal coherence in *illumination*, by computing lighting effects over a finite time range in a single calculation.

This paper therefore investigates the potential benefits of computing a radiosity solution over a time interval, taking into account all object movements and changes in the scene, and refining the calculation to precisely reflect the resulting illumination changes. We provide a formal framework for the derivation of space-time radiosity algorithms, and describe a hierarchical solution algorithm. The expected benefit of such a system is the ability to compute high-quality time-dependent radiosity solutions, in cases where all animation parameters are known *a priori*. In this case, and in contrast to dynamic update solutions for interactive uses, it will be possible to use the knowledge of the trajectories and changes to ensure the absence of visually distracting artifacts.

2   Previous work

Early attempts had been made to use space-time methods for ray tracing [9], by taking into account object motion when computing ray intersections. The gain then comes from the avoidance of multiple intersection tests, one for each frame. However the illumination is still computed frame-by-frame using a simple, local illumination model.

Similarly, limiting the amount of recomputation needed for computing radiosity solutions in dynamic scenes has been a subject of active research since the introduction of radiosity. Besuievsky *et al.* [2] performed Monte Carlo radiosity calculations in dynamic scenes by computing intersections with all frame-accurate positions of dynamic objects . Orti *et al.* [14]. predicted changes in visibility in a 2D world, but computed illumination at each frame.

For interactive applications, the main avenue has been the fast calculation of *updates* to an existing radiosity solution, in response to a change in the scene. Chen [3] and George *et al.* [8] performed incremental radiosity calculation by propagating energy corrections in the framework of progressive radiosity. Forsyth *et al.*[7], Shaw [15] and Drettakis *et al.* [5] attacked the issue of geometry modification, by reducing the set of links that require updating, in a hierarchical radiosity setting.

For non-interactive applications, where the movement of all objects is known in advance, Baum *et al.* [1] computed geometric shafts around the moving objects, and computed separately static and dynamic form factors. The latter were recomputed for every frame based on the actual position of the moving objects.

Incorporating time in the hierarchical radiosity framework will let us benefit from the separation between static and dynamic interactions, while maintaining the advantages of a hierarchical representation: namely, refinement will take into account the relative movement and speed of the objects, instead of re-evaluating the energy transfer at each and every frame. Furthermore, working on finite time intervals will let us apply global knowledge of motions and illumination changes to guide refinement.

3   Motivation for space-time calculations

In this section we review the potential benefits of a space-time hierarchical radiosity calculation. We start by recognizing the need for global illumination calculations for animated sequences: global illumination effects (indirect lighting) are key components in defining the "atmosphere" of a scene. Furthermore, realistic lighting is sometimes indispensable, when synthetic imagery must be combined with live action film: for instance a radiosity solution can be used to decide how to re-light actors, or as a background, influenced by the actors. This is particularly interesting for movie applications or in virtual sets.

3.1   A simple experiment demonstrating illumination coherence

We chose two test scenes with different lighting characteristics to investigate the amount of temporal coherence in the global illumination solution. We did not consider time varying light source properties (which can be treated by other means [8]), but focused on changing the geometry by moving objects.

The ACTOR scene (see Figure 1, left) shows a room with two objects moving. The size and movement of these objects were chosen to represent possible motion of human actors in a room, anticipating on the possible use of our technique for movie lighting or synthetic set applications. The LIGHT (see Figure 1, right) scene shows a similar room,

ACTOR scene.   LIGHT scene.

Fig. 1. Two test scenes chosen to illustrate situations that could be encountered in "real" applications. LIGHT has more obvious and large-scale illumination variations (both in space and time) due to the moving object near the right-hand light source.

but in which lighting conditions change dramatically in the entire scene over the course of the shot, because of a moving object in front of a light source. Both animations last 3 seconds or 75 frames.

In order to estimate the amount of CPU-time spent in redundant computations when computing a complete animated sequence frame by frame, we computed an independent radiosity solution for each frame, recording a complete view of the link hierarchy.

We then compared the link hierarchies and recorded the duration of validity of each link, by determining over how many frames it remained identical (we consider two links to be identical if they join the exact same elements, and they carry the same amount of energy within a threshold).

This allows us to compute, for any given duration, the amount of energy that was exchanged across links that were valid for that duration. The following table gives the proportion of energy (both for direct and indirect lighting) that was found to be constant during the *entire length* of the animation (*i.e.* traveling through links that were shared by every frame). The detail of the average amount of energy that remains valid seen as

Table 1. Proportion of energy constant during the entire animation

	Direct light	Indirect light
ACTOR	69.1%	49.5%
LIGHT	63.9%	42.7%

a function of the number of frame during which it is constant is given in Figure 2.

We can see that a large portion of light radiated in the scene needs only be computed once and for all. This is mostly due to links going from the light sources to the unoccluded parts of walls and static objects (the desk) for direct light, and between unoccluded part of the walls for indirect light. The fact that a significant number of links can be considered valid for more than one frame but not for the whole animation (especially for indirect lighting), makes a multi-resolution approach such as hierarchical radiosity particularly appealing. Note that in the LIGHT scene, significant energy is

238

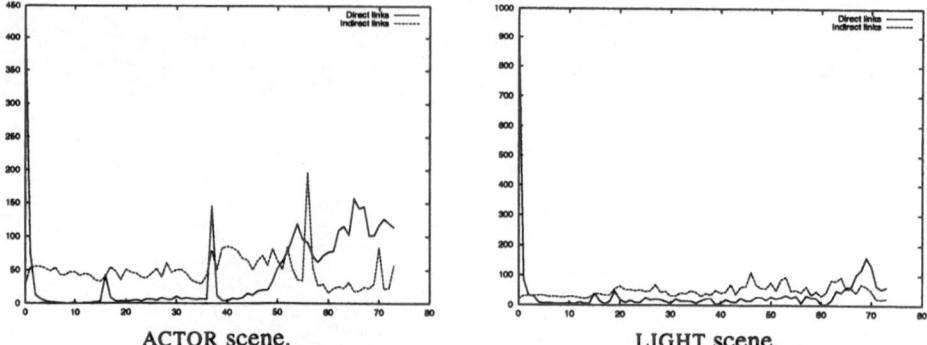

ACTOR scene.   LIGHT scene.

Fig. 2. Average amount of radiated energy with respect to the number of frames during which the associated link remains valid (arbitrary units). Because of scaling constraints, these figures does not include the links that remain valid for the whole animation.

carried by links that are valid for a single frame, reflecting the large amount of temporal change in direct lighting.

Another potential advantage of performing an integrated hierarchical radiosity solution over time is the ability to "play back" the animation in a virtual reality system or walkthrough application. In addition, having an integrated space-time hierarchy lets us combine coarse and fine object representations in both dimensions, without having to maintain separate structures as in the multi-resolution video application of [6].

4 A formal presentation of 4-dimensional radiosity

In this section we introduce notation and mathematical grounding for radiosity calculations over finite time intervals. Even though radiant energy exchanges are always considered instantaneous, which means that the radiosity balance equation at each time step is independent from all other time steps, space-time radiosity actually introduces temporal coupling between discrete radiating elements. This will allow us to build a hierarchical solution with elements of varying duration.

4.1 The 4D diffuse illumination equation

We want to compute the outgoing light for a set of ideally diffuse surfaces, for each moment in a given time interval. In other words, we want to find a function $B(x,t)$ giving us the radiosity of point x at time t, defined on $S \times T$, where S is the set of all points of all surfaces of the scene, and $T = [t1, t2]$ is the interval during which we want to render the scene.

We should be given two functions $M(x,t)$ and $N(x,t)$ with values over $\mathbb{R}^3$ giving us the position and outgoing normal of point x in space at time t. We should also be given the diffuse reflectance $\rho(x)$ of each point x, and the exitance $E(x,t)$ at point x at time t. Under those assumptions, the rendering equation [12] becomes :

$$\forall X = (x,t) \in (S \times T) \qquad B(X) = E(X) + \int_{Y=(y,t') \in (S \times T)} B(Y)\mathcal{K}(X,Y)dY \quad (1)$$

where

- $\mathcal{K}$ is a function defined over $(S \times T)^2$ by

$$\mathcal{K}((x,t),(y,t')) = \rho(x)k(x,y,t)V(x,y,t)\delta(t,t') \qquad (2)$$

- $\delta(t,t')$ is equal to 1 when $t = t'$ and 0 otherwise.
- k is the kernel function defined as :

$$k(x,y,t) = \frac{cos\theta(x,y,t)cos\theta(y,x,t)}{\pi r(x,y,t)^2} \qquad (3)$$

- $\theta(x,y,t)$ is the angle between the directions of $N(x,t)$ and $(M(y,t) - M(x,t))$
- $r(x,y,t)$ is the distance between $M(x,t)$ and $M(y,t)$
- $V(x,y,t)$ is equal to 0 whenever the ray joining $M(x,t)$ and $M(y,t)$ is intercepted by a surface of S at time t, and equal to 1 otherwise (*i.e.* visibility).

Note that equation (1) describes inter-temporal light exchanges since t can be different from t'. However the Dirac function $\delta(t,t')$ sets those exchanges to zero. Equation (1) in fact still governs the energy exchange equilibrium independently for each frame as is physically the case. However, the introduction of time will ease the development of our method.

4.2 Finite element formulation

We now derive the finite element formulation of 4D radiosity similarly to that of standard radiosity [17] [4]. Given a set of basis functions $(u_i)_{1 \leq i \leq N}$ and an inner product $\langle \ . \ \rangle$ we want to compute the approximation $\tilde{B}$ such that the residual

$$r(X) = \tilde{B}(X) - E(X) - \int_{Y \in (S \times T)} \tilde{B}(Y)\mathcal{K}(X,Y)dY \qquad (4)$$

is orthogonal to all the u_i.

Space-Time radiosity can then be expressed as a matrix equation comparable to the traditional radiosity equation :

$$MB = \epsilon \qquad (5)$$

with

$$\forall i \in [1,N] \qquad \epsilon_i = \langle E, u_i \rangle \qquad (6)$$

$$\forall (i,j) \in [1,N]^2 \ M_{i,j} = \langle u_i, u_j \rangle - \int_{X \in (S \times T)} u_i(X) \int_{Y \in (S \times T)} \mathcal{K}(X,Y)u_j(Y)dYdX \qquad (7)$$

4.3 4D radiosity with constant elements

We now derive the radiosity equation (5) in the case of constant basis function. We assume that our scene S is composed of polygons with rigid motion. We decompose these polygons into N disjoint spatio-temporal patches P_i over which radiosity is assumed constant.

The patches P_i are defined by their time domain $[t_i^1, t_i^2] \subset T$ and by their (possibly moving) geometry $Q_i^t \subset S$. Note that since the motion of Q_i^t is rigid, its area A_i is constant. Assume moreover that its reflectance ρ is constant in time and space. We use equation (7) to find the expression of M:

$$M_{i,j} = A_i(t_i^2 - t_i^1)\delta_{i,j} - \rho_i A_i(t_i^2 - t_i^1)\mathcal{F}_{i,j} \tag{8}$$

where $\mathcal{F}_{i,j}$, the spatio-temporal form-factor between P_i and P_j is:

$$\mathcal{F}_{i,j} = \frac{1}{A_i(t_i^2 - t_i^1)} \int_{[t_i^1,t_i^2]\cap[t_j^1,t_j^2]} \int_{P_i} \int_{P_j} \frac{cos\theta cos\theta'}{\pi r^2} V(x,y,t)dydxdt \tag{9}$$

Note that the time dependency of our radiosity coefficients B_i is now implicit through the time extension of u_i's support. Furthermore, inter-temporal interactions are now possible, since any two time intervals sharing a non-empty intersection can exchange radiosity. This is not a violation of physical laws but rather a byproduct of the underlying approximation performed in the discretization of the problem.

5   A space-time hierarchical radiosity algorithm

Let us now define an efficient approach to solve equation (5) in a time-dependent scene. As noted in section (3), a hierarchical algorithm allowing us to store multi-resolution information for both spatial and temporal variations would ensure that each interaction between objects can be represented with an appropriate level of precision. Thus we will be able to factor out redundant computation.

In order to build a hierarchical algorithm for space-time radiosity, we define :

- An adequate data structure to store the values of the radiosity function over space-time elements, allowing us to compute and obtain these values at various levels of precision both over space and time.
- A refinement method with a time specific approach.

We discuss below the issues raised by these two items, and present first solutions chosen in our current implementation. We also discuss possible improvements of these basic solutions.

5.1   Hierarchical data structure

As stated in Section 4.3, discrete elements are defined both by their geometrical description and their temporal description, the time interval of their validity, over which the radiosity is assumed constant, and referred to as their *time range*. They can therefore be split either in space (*e.g.* in four sub-patches for quads and triangles) or in time (by dividing the time range, leaving the geometry unchanged). Therefore an element in our hierarchy can have children either in space or in time. Currently, we do not allow our elements to be subdivided in time and in space simultaneously, since this would only reduce the depth of our hierarchy but not the number of hierarchical elements.

Figure 3 shows two scenarios for the possible subdivision of a space-time patch, in a simplified space with only one spatial dimension (therefore it shows two children elements created by a spatial splitting instead of four).

Considering memory consumption issues, note that we store separately the geometry mapping function M giving us the position of each vertex at a given time. Thus we do not have to store this position in our element description; the only data that needs

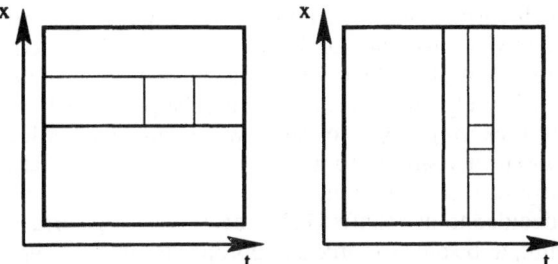

Fig. 3. Two examples of space/time hierarchy:

Left: An object is partially lit, therefore it is first subdivided spatially. At the end of our animation, a (small) shadow is briefly cast on its illuminated portion, inducing a temporal subdivision.

Right: An object is submitted to mainly uniform, though time-varying lighting conditions, therefore it is first subdivided in time. In the middle of the animation, a shadow is (briefly) cast on a small portion of its area.

to be created when time-splitting an element is its time extent and its radiosity value. Everything else can be shared between the two siblings and their parent.

We have implemented this space-time subdivision mechanism in a hierarchical radiosity simulator, using quadtree-like spatial subdivision and midpoint binary temporal subdivision. Note that more elaborate temporal subdivision schemes could easily be tried, in particular when information is available about a special event happening within the time range, to align the temporal boundaries to the event. For now, only surface patches are treated, but the notion of temporal refinement could be applied to other types of objects such as clusters.

With this hierarchical structure, the algorithm to solve equation 5 is the same as for classical hierarchical radiosity. From the original three parts composing an iteration (namely refine, push-pull, and gather), only the link refinement procedure needs specific changes in our case, which are described in section 5.2.

Once the solution computed, displaying the results for any given time t is straightforward. Leaf patches whose time interval contains t are found in the hierarchy and displayed with respect to their position (given by the function $M(t)$) and radiosity. This can be done rapidly.

5.2 Refinement

As in classical hierarchical radiosity, the refinement process is the most time-consuming part of each iteration, and inadequate refinement can produce an excessively heavy, yet inefficient hierarchy. The refinement pass requires a time specific approach be developed. We need to know whether a given link is a faithful enough representation of the light exchanged between two hierarchical elements, as in the purely spatial case. In addition, for the case where refinement is necessary, we need to know whether the elements' spatial or temporal extents are "responsible" for the inadequate representation, so as to be able to decide between time- and space-subdivision.

This decision is not easy in general, and can drastically impact the memory consumption as well as the time needed to compute the solution.

We chose a refinement criterion based on estimates of the variation of the form factor over the patch surface and time range. We proceed by sampling the radiosity kernel function k and visibility function V (cf. Section 4.1), as well as the radiosity of the sender if it is not a leaf of the hierarchy (this allows us to take into account indirect lighting variations). To rely only on sampling can be problematic: shadow edges can be missed, causing flickering edges, or shadow movements can leave stains. On the other hand we can expect visibility to not depend on time for a large number of links (*e.g.* between nearby surfaces that do not move or that have the same movement). As a consequence, we decided to use shafts [11] to detect moving surfaces between the two nodes of a given link, to be able to force an appropriate subdivision.

1. If both the source and the receiver of the considered link share the same movement, we build the shaft joining their bounding boxes. Then we hierarchically test objects that do not move in the same way to see if they intersect the shaft and cause "significant" occlusion, during a limited portion of the link's duration. When such transient blockers are found, we force time-refinement for this link.
2. In all other cases we sample the kernel function k and visibility function V. Then we compute the standard deviations of our sample set, considered with fixed time for various points and with varying time for fixed points. Finally we compare them first to a given threshold, to decide if we should refine, then one with each other, to decide which kind of refinement we apply.

Some optimizations are added to avoid unnecessary extensive sampling of both space and time:

- If both the source and receiver share the same motion, then the kernel function k does not depend on time (since we only consider rigid motions)
- If we detected that our shaft will never be crossed by a moving object then visibility does not depend on time

Unless there are very many large occluders moving around the scene, we can expect that a great number of links will benefit from these optimizations and therefore that the refinement test for these links will be as fast as if we were in a static scene.

5.3 Possible improvements

Improving the memory consumption of this algorithm could be achieved by taking advantage of the fact that computing the amount of light received by a patch only involves patches whose time extent overlap his own. Therefore it would be possible to find a hierarchy traversal method that could allow us to temporarily dump large parts of the hierarchy on disk, keeping only those needed in memory.

Another improvement that can be made addresses the fact that our hierarchy stores both time and space subdivisions, raising the following issue : it is possible that we might need to split an element in time (resp. in space) while it is already split in space (resp. in time) because of multiple or indirect light sources. For the moment we choose to push the interaction further down in the hierarchy until a leaf is found and the requested subdivision can be performed. This might lead to significant overcost as discussed in Section 6. A hierarchy maintenance pass could be added at the end of refinement that would be aimed at properly ordering our hierarchy to restrict this.

6 Results

We ran our algorithm on the two test scenes introduced in Section 3 (both animations are 3 seconds long, or 75 frames), and compared the results to the application of a static radiosity algorithm, for each frame, using the same spatial refinement parameters. Results (computed on a 250 MHz MIPS R10,000 processor) are summarized in the following table:

	Computation time		Memory usage	
	Space-Time	Static (per frame)	Space-Time	Static
ACTOR	335 s	11.5 s	112 Mb	11 Mb
LIGHT	671 s	18.1 s	237 Mb	14.3 Mb

In terms of quality, the solution obtained with space-time radiosity is almost identical to the frame-by-frame solution. Representative frames of both animations are shown in the color plates.

These results lead us to the following comments:

- The construction of a hierarchy representing the full length of the animation introduces a significant memory cost. Memory usage is greater than that of static calculation by a factor of about 10 (ACTOR) and 17 (LIGHT). Future efforts should therefore concentrate on making better use of available memory by scheduling calculations in order of increasing time, producing frames as time progresses and reclaiming memory on the fly.
- Our algorithm accelerates the calculation of a full-size animation clip, with the same illumination quality. Acceleration factors of about 2.5 (ACTOR) and 2 (LIGHT) are observed. This result is somewhat disappointing considering the increase in memory consumption and is clearly due to our intensive use of time-sampling during the evaluation of the oracle. In our first implementation attempts, we obtained acceleration factors of about 10 and 7, due to a different temporal sampling strategy which turned out to be unfair to the static version. The difference we observe shows that our current temporal sampling scheme (shooting significant numbers of rays distributed in time) heavily affects performance. Reducing the number of temporal visibility samples greatly decreases computation time, but damages the solution since occlusions can be missed, creating "holes" in moving shadows. Clearly, smarter techniques such as motion volumes should therefore allow large acceleration, similar to the use of shafts in the spatial dimensions.

Due to the hierarchical nature of the technique, the actual acceleration factor depends on the length of the sequence: in the example of the ACTOR scene, doubling the duration of the time interval (6 seconds, 150 frames) with equivalent movement resulted in a 55 % increase in computation time and 60 % increase in memory usage. This is an interesting result, similar to the well-known observation that spatial subdivision concentrates around shadow boundaries in static images, which means that additional subdivision is only performed in these limited areas when more detail is requested.

Note that this algorithm performs best for indirect lighting : an acceleration factor of 4 (ACTOR) and 3 (LIGHT) is observed when comparing only the time needed to obtain the indirect lighting in the dynamic and static calculations. This is due to the fact that indirect light exchanges vary more smoothly in time, as they do not induce sharp shadow edges movement.

We also observe that the LIGHT scene was specifically created to challenge our technique: direct illumination changes across the entire scene and during the entire duration of the cut; significant secondary illumination is due to the floor and wall areas near the lower light source, areas which are finely subdivided in time due to the shadow cast by the moving panel. Therefore this scene illustrates the difficulties encountered when these areas would warrant space-subdivision, but are already time-subdivided. Our current implementation forces the interactions to be pushed down the time hierarchy, with significant cost, but better solutions can certainly be found.

Beyond these numerical results, it is important to note that this framework opens the way for more elaborate refinement that will operate on the global knowledge of illumination variations across a time interval. Suppose the amount of energy flowing between a wall and an object is continuously increasing over a time interval, for instance because a light source is getting closer to the wall, and increases its radiosity. In the case of a frame-by-frame computation, there will be a discontinuous jump when the secondary illumination goes above the refinement threshold. If changes are computed incrementally [5], this will either be done from frame to frame, in which case the increment may be too small to be noticed, or with respect to a reference frame, which again introduces the risk of a discontinuous jump as we reach a threshold. Working over the full duration of a time interval, however, let us characterize illumination variations, and would allow us to apply knowledge of human perception to decide when additional detail or refinement is needed.

7 Conclusion and future work

In this paper, we have shown how the hierarchical radiosity algorithm can be extended to account for time-dependent scenes. The theoretical formulation of the time-dependent radiosity discretization provides a clear ground on which different approaches can be implemented. For instance, various time-space subdivision strategies can now be investigated, in particular to avoid explicit time-sampling of visibility and to address the problem of competing subdivisions in time and space.

The technique allows the calculation of animations equivalent to frame-by-frame computation, in a shorter time, at the cost of a much larger memory requirement. These results, obtained on a preliminary implementation, provide a proof that the concept is valid . From the restricted point of view of computing resources, our results are somewhat disappointing, considering the potential acceleration that should be drawn from the hierarchical formulation. However it should be stressed that a major advantage of space-time calculations is the potential ability to exploit the knowledge of temporal variations over finite time intervals to guide the subdivision. In this regard also, our refinement criterion is somewhat preliminary, and better, perceptually-based criteria are called for.

Our results also point us towards several very interesting areas for future research, which we are actively pursuing. In order of priority we can quote :

1. The derivation of good space-time refinement criteria that would avoid explicit time-sampling of visibility by taking into account object trajectories (*e.g.* using swept volumes, knowledge of the speed of the blocker, etc.). Extending our shaft-culling routine to estimate visibility between two objects with different motion. Using the shafts joining their motion volumes' bounding box, will certainly help us to do so.

2. Efficient treatment and maintenance of the hierarchy. Two directions of improve-

ment are : (a) introducing the ability to "space-subdivide" an element which is already "time-subdivided", with graceful management of different views of the hierarchy, and (b) optimizing the hierarchy according to perceptual and energy criteria, to remove unnecessary subdivision. Note that the latter optimization could perhaps be incorporated in the refinement criterion, but requires a global knowledge of all interactions in space. Therefore it is perhaps best left to a post-processing stage (after each refinement iteration). Both improvements would reduce the number of elements and links in the hierarchy and therefore the memory consumption and computation time as well.

3. Definition of a good ordering strategy for refinement, so as to allow efficient usage of memory, by processing energy exchanges roughly in the order in which they happen. This would facilitate garbage collection mechanisms, but is a non-trivial problem because of the global solution involving links of different "duration". A long-lived link can both influence a short-lived "early patch" and be influenced by a later patch. Such temporal influences are, of course, non-physical and should be kept minimal by appropriate refinement. A precise study of the allowable time approximations is therefore required.

4. Strategies for time dependent *clustering* [18, 16] have to be developed. As the complexity of scenes increases, this would be likely to change the pattern of hierarchical subdivision. While our subdivision trees are fairly balanced between time and space in the two tests scenes, for more complex scenes it would be more likely that time subdivision continues after space subdivision has stopped at an appropriate cluster level. Greater savings can then be expected. Amidst the problems that we are currently investigating is the fact that clusterisation is typically implemented as an *a priori* spatial subdivision of the scene. This means that we have to recursively duplicate all the objects in a cluster if we want to time-split the cluster.

5. Replacing mesh subdivision by textures [19, 10] is an effective means of avoiding the cost due to the subdivided hierarchy itself. In the case of time-dependent illumination, texture movies could be generated for this purpose, although a specific algorithm has yet to be proposed [13].

6. The use of a *shooting* approach [20, 10] would eliminate the need to store all the links in the solution, especially the links from primary light sources.

7. A precise comparison of this algorithm with Drettakis' and Sillion [5] dynamic update technique based on the line-space hierarchy would help to investigate the potential for time-dependent line space refinement.

8. The use of more elaborate finite elements for radiosity representation should be carefully studied. For instance, linear elements in the time direction could prove especially useful to avoid discontinuities. In general, reconstruction of a frame from a space-time radiosity solution should be carried out in a precise manner.

We believe that hierarchical computation of time-dependent global illumination can be put to efficient use if sufficient attention is devoted to all these issues, resulting in practical tools that will effectively accelerate lighting simulation for real applications such as movie lighting and virtual sets.

Acknowledgments

iMAGIS is a joint research project of INRIA, CNRS, INPG and UJF. This work was supported in part by the European union under the "ARCADE" ESPRIT LTR project, #24944.

References

1. Daniel R. Baum, John R. Wallace, Michael F. Cohen, and Donald P. Greenberg. The back-buffer algorithm : an extension of the radiosity method to dynamic environments. *The Visual Computer*, 2:298–306, 1986.

2. Gonzalo Besuievsky and Mateu Sbert. The Multi-Frame Lighting Method: A Monte Carlo Based Solution for Radiosity in Dynamic Environments. In *Rendering Techniques '96 (Proceedings of the Seventh Eurographics Workshop on Rendering)*, pages 185–194, New York, NY, 1996. Springer-Verlag/Wien.

3. Shenchang Eric Chen. Incremental radiosity: An extension of progressive radiosity to an interactive image synthesis system. *Computer Graphics*, 24(4):135–144, August 1990. Proceedings SIGGRAPH '90 in Dallas (USA).

4. Michael F. Cohen and John R. Wallace. *Radiosity and Realistic Image Synthesis*. Academic Press, Boston, 1993.

5. George Drettakis and François Sillion. Interactive update of global illumination using a line-space hierarchy. In *Computer Graphics Proceedings, Annual Conference Series:* SIGGRAPH '97 (Los Angeles, CA), pages 57–64. ACM SIGGRAPH, New York, August 1997.

6. Adam Finkelstein, Charles E. Jacobs, and David H. Salesin. Multiresolution video. In *Computer Graphics, Annual Conference Series: (ACM SIGGRAPH '96 Proceedings)*, pages 281–290, 1996.

7. David A. Forsyth, Chien Yang, and Kim Teo. Efficient Radiosity in Dynamic Environments. In *Fifth Eurographics Workshop on Rendering*, pages 313–323, Darmstadt, Germany, June 1994.

8. David W. George, François Sillion, and Donald P. Greenberg. Radiosity redistribution for dynamic environments. *IEEE Computer Graphics and Applications*, 10(4), July 1990.

9. Andrew S. Glassner. Spacetime ray tracing for animation. *IEEE Computer Graphics and Applications*, 8(2):60–70, March 1988.

10. Xavier Granier and George Drettakis. Controlling memory consumption of hierarchical radiosity with clustering. In *Graphics Interface*, June 1999.

11. Eric Haines and John Wallace. Shaft culling for efficient ray-traced radiosity. In *Eurographics Workshop on Rendering*, pages 122–138, 1991.

12. James T. Kajiya. The Rendering Equation. In *Computer Graphics (ACM SIGGRAPH '86 Proceedings)*, volume 20, pages 143–150, August 1986.

13. Ignacio Martin. Personal Communication.

14. Rachel Orti, Stephane Riviere, Fredo Durand, and Claude Puech. Radiosity for Dynamic Scenes in Flatland with the Visbility Complex. In *Computer Graphics Forum, Proc. EUROGRAPHICS '96*, volume 15, pages C237–C248. Blackwell, September 1996.

15. Erin Shaw. Hierarchical radiosity for dynamic environments. *Computer Graphics Forum*, 16(2):107–118, 1997. ISSN 0167-7055.

16. François Sillion. A unified hierarchical algorithm for global illumination with scattering volumes and object clusters. *IEEE Transactions on Visualization and Computer Graphics*, 1(3), September 1995. (a preliminary version appeared in the fifth Eurographics workshop on rendering, Darmstadt, Germany, June 1994).

17. François Sillion and Claude Puech. *Radiosity and Global Illumination*. Morgan Kaufmann publishers, San Francisco, 1994.

18. Brian Smits, James Arvo, and Donald P. Greenberg. A clustering algorithm for radiosity in complex environments. In *Computer Graphics Proceedings, Annual Conference Series:* SIGGRAPH '94 (Orlando, FL), pages 435–442. ACM SIGGRAPH, New York, July 1994.

19. Cyril Soler and François Sillion. Fast calculation of soft shadow textures using convolution. In *Computer Graphics Proceedings, Annual Conference Series:* SIGGRAPH '98 (Orlando, FL), pages 321–332. ACM SIGGRAPH, New York, July 1998.

20. Marc Stamminger, Hartmut Schirmacher, Philipp Slusallek, and Hans-Pieter Seidel. Getting rid of links in hierarchical radiosity. In *Computer Graphics Forum, Proc. EUROGRAPHICS '98*, pages 165–174. Blackwell, 1998.

Editors' Note: see Appendix, p. 373 for colored figures of this paper

Interactive Rendering with Arbitrary BRDFs using Separable Approximations

Jan Kautz and Michael D. McCool

Computer Graphics Laboratory; Department of Computer Science; University of Waterloo
Waterloo, Ontario, Canada N2L 3G1
{jnkautz,mmccool}@cgl.uwaterloo.ca
http://www.cgl.uwaterloo.ca

Abstract. *A separable decomposition of bidirectional reflectance distributions (BRDFs) is used to implement arbitrary reflectances from point sources on existing graphics hardware. Two-dimensional texture mapping and compositing operations are used to reconstruct samples of the BRDF at every pixel at interactive rates.*

A change of variables, the Gram-Schmidt halfangle/difference vector parameterization, improves separability. Two decomposition algorithms are also presented. The singular value decomposition (SVD) minimizes RMS error. The normalized decomposition is fast and simple, using no more space than what is required for the final representation.

1   Introduction

Traditionally hardware renderers only support the Phong lighting model [19] in combination with Gouraud shading. However, the Phong lighting model is strictly empirical and physically implausible. Gouraud shading also tends to undersample the highlight unless a highly tessellated surface is used.

In general, surface reflectance can be described using a bidirectional reflectance distribution, or BRDF. The reflectance equation describes the outgoing radiance $L_o(\hat{\omega}_o, \underline{x})$ in direction $\hat{\omega}_o$ at a surface point $\underline{x}$ as an integral over the irradiance $L_i(\hat{\omega}_i, \underline{x}) \cos_+ \theta_i$ at that surface point weighted by the BRDF $f(\hat{\omega}_o, \underline{x}, \hat{\omega}_i)$:

$$L_o(\hat{\omega}_o, \underline{x}) = \int_\Omega f(\hat{\omega}_o, \underline{x}, \hat{\omega}_i) L_i(\hat{\omega}_i, \underline{x}) \cos_+ \theta_i \, d\hat{\omega}_i,$$

with $\cos_+ \theta_i = \max(\hat{\omega}_i \cdot \hat{n}, 0)$ where $\hat{n}$ is the surface normal at $\underline{x}$ and Ω is the hemisphere of incoming directions. For M point sources, the reflectance integral reduces to

$$L_o(\hat{\omega}_o, \underline{x}) = \sum_{i=1}^{M} f(\hat{\omega}_o, \underline{x}, \hat{\omega}_i) \cos_+ \theta_i \frac{I_i}{r_i^2} \qquad (1)$$

where r_i is the distance to light source i and I_i is its intensity. While point sources are not ideal (glossy surfaces don't really look glossy unless they reflect the environment), we would still at *least* like to render surfaces at interactive rates using this model, with arbitrary BRDFs, evaluated at per-pixel resolution.

Neglecting $\underline{x}$ (and wavelength), BRDFs are parameterized by at least four degrees of freedom. Analytic evaluation of a BRDF is possible using programmable shaders

[18], but such capabilities are not yet widely available in hardware and measured data still cannot be used directly. Tabulated BRDFs could be implemented in hardware using four-dimensional texture maps, but this would be expensive: 50MB would be required for (the relatively low) resolution of 64^4 at three bytes per sample. To render multiple surfaces with different reflectance functions at interactive rates, a compressed representation that uses existing two-dimensional hardware texturing capabilities is desirable.

Recently separable decompositions have been proposed for compressing BRDFs [4, 5, 22]. Separable decompositions approximate (to arbitrary accuracy) a high-dimensional function f using a sum of products of lower-dimensional functions g_k and h_k:

$$f(x,y,z,w) \approx \sum_{k=1}^{N} g_k(x,y) h_k(z,w). \tag{2}$$

Separable decompositions are capable of high compression rates if good approximations can be found for small N. Separable representations are also much easier to evaluate pointwise than other representations, such as k-nearest neighbors [6], wavelets, or spherical harmonics [26].

As we will demonstrate, under certain changes of variables many BRDFs are highly separable, and so a small number N of low-dimensional functions can be used to represent them accurately. In fact, $N = 1$ has proven to be visually adequate for many interesting BRDFs; see colour Figure 12. Because of the simplicity of the reconstruction process, we can perform it at interactive rates using existing hardware support for texturing, compositing, and diffuse lighting. Of course, this method is also applicable to software rendering; fast evaluation of BRDFs can be performed using only a few texture lookups, multiplications and additions.

2 Overview

The technique described in this paper is composed of two distinct phases.

In the first phase a target BRDF is analyzed and a suitable separable representation found. Algorithms to accomplish this are discussed in Section 4.

Once a representation is found, it can be used in image synthesis. In this paper we focus on *interactive* rendering, on existing hardware, with respect to the point-source lighting model (eq. 1), although the separable representation of BRDFs is also very useful in software rendering.

The basic algorithm for hardware rendering replaces the evaluation of the BRDF by the sum of products of lower dimensional functions (substituting eq. 2 into eq. 1). The functions g_k and h_k are held in texture maps, the multiplications are done using either compositing or multitexturing, the cosine term is evaluated using diffuse lighting and texture modulation, and the summations (if $N > 1$ or more than one light source is required) are done with an accumulation buffer or compositing.

Hardware-accelerated interactive rendering imposes a number of constraints. The most serious is that the parameterization of the texture maps must be consistent with linear interpolation of texture coordinates so Phong shading (per-pixel tangent and normal interpolation) can be accurately approximated. These constraints interact with changes of variables that are useful for increasing the separability of BRDFs. Suitable parameterization choices and their effects on quality are discussed in Section 5. In Section 6 we describe briefly how the capabilities of existing graphics hardware can be exploited to achieve interactive rendering performance.

3   Prior Work

Representations of reflectance functions fall into two categories:

1. Parameterized models for specific kinds of BRDFs.
2. General approximation techniques.

The most familiar specialized parametric representation is probably the Phong model [19], which was one of the first reflectance models. Ward [25] has presented a more sophisticated model based on anisotropic Gaussian lobes fitted to various BRDFs. He *et al.* [7] have derived a physically based model based on Kirchhoff diffraction (called the HTSG model here), which also takes wavelength into account. Poulin and Fournier [20] have proposed a model based on self shadowing of microcylinders. There are other models, but we use these for examples in this paper.

There are also many BRDF approximation techniques. Schröder and Sweldens [23] have represented BRDFs using spherical wavelets. Koenderink *et al.* [12] have expressed BRDFs in terms of an orthonormal basis using Zernike polynomials. Lafortune *et al.* [13] have used an approximation based on the summation of generalized Phong cosine lobes. Cabral *et al.* [3] were the first to use spherical harmonics to represent BRDFs. Fournier [5] used a sum of separable functions for representing reflectance models.

None of the more general approximation models have been used in interactive rendering. The problem with many of the above representations is that interactive hardware implementations would require completely new hardware—they do not build on existing capabilities. The exception to this is Fournier's separable representation, which can be implemented using existing support for texture mapping and compositing.

To our knowledge there has only been one attempt to incorporate more sophisticated reflectance models into interactive rendering without general shader support. Heidrich and Seidel [8] analytically separated the Banks anisotropic model [2] and have proposed a single pass rendering algorithm using texture mapping. Our approach is similar but we consider the more general case of arbitrary BRDFs.

4   Decomposition

The first phase in the application of this technique is generation of a separable decomposition of each BRDF. Decomposition is done in advance of rendering, and need only be performed once per BRDF. The result is a compressed representation that can be stored until needed.

Neglecting position and wavelength dependence, a general anisotropic BDRF f is a function of four degrees of freedom corresponding to incident direction $\hat{\omega}_i$ and view direction $\hat{\omega}_o$. In Section 5 we will look at several reparameterizations that can increase the effective separability of a BRDF, so assume that the parameters of the BRDF are $\mathbf{x} = \mathbf{P}_x(\hat{\omega}_i, \hat{\omega}_o)$ and $\mathbf{y} = \mathbf{P}_y(\hat{\omega}_i, \hat{\omega}_o)$ for vector functions $\mathbf{P}_x$ and $\mathbf{P}_y$.

A separable decomposition approximates a multivariate function f as a sum of products of functions g_k and h_k of lower dimensionality:

$$f(\hat{\omega}_i, \hat{\omega}_o) = f_P(\mathbf{P}_x(\hat{\omega}_i, \hat{\omega}_o), \mathbf{P}_y(\hat{\omega}_i, \hat{\omega}_o));$$

$$f_P(\mathbf{x}, \mathbf{y}) \approx \sum_{k=1}^{N} g_k(\mathbf{x}) h_k(\mathbf{y}). \tag{3}$$

Our method does *not* assume that a BRDF is single-term separable. A BRDF can *always* be represented accurately using a separable expansion, if enough terms are used. However, we have found that a good approximation can be achieved with only a few terms and often a single term *is* sufficient if a good parameterization can be found.

We will consider two algorithms for finding appropriate functions g_k and h_k: singular value decomposition and normalized decomposition. The singular value decomposition (SVD) can produce optimal approximations, but is relatively expensive in time and space. We have developed an approach called normalized decomposition (ND), which is a much simpler technique that can produce good decompositions in time linear in the number of BRDF samples taken. It uses no more space than required to store the output factors.

4.1 Singular Value Decomposition

Given a matrix M, the singular value decomposition (SVD) [1, 21] of M is the factorization $M = USV^T$ where the columns of $U = [u_k]$ and $V = [v_k]$ are orthonormal and $S = \text{diag}(\sigma_k)$ is a diagonal matrix of singular values σ_k. The matrix product USV^T can be written as a sum:

$$M = \sum_{k=1}^{K} \sigma_k u_k v_k^T.$$

Note that each term $u_k v_k^T$ is an *outer product*, i.e. a matrix whose elements are products of an element of u_k and an element of v_k.

The singular values σ_k are positive and monotonically decreasing in magnitude. Truncating the above sum results in an optimal root mean square approximation of M.

Assume we have a tabulated, reparameterized BRDF $f_P(x, y)$ that has been sampled at some collection of $K \times K$ parameter values. Define a matrix $M = [m_{ij}]$ with $m_{ij} = f_P(x_i, y_j)$; in other words, let x be constant for each row of the matrix, and let y be constant for each column:

$$M = \begin{pmatrix} f_P(x_1, y_1) & \cdots & f_P(x_1, y_K) \\ \vdots & \ddots & \vdots \\ f_P(x_K, y_1) & \cdots & f_P(x_K, y_K) \end{pmatrix}$$

If we interpolate u_k and v_k of the SVD factorization of this matrix into the two-dimensional functions $u_k(x)$ and $v_k(y)$ and then truncate the series at $N < K$ terms, we have the approximation

$$f_P(x, y) \approx \sum_{k=1}^{N} \sigma_k u_k(x) v_k(y).$$

There are several major drawbacks to the SVD. First, it always results in a least root mean square approximation of M; it is not possible to specify a fundamentally different norm.

Secondly, the expansion contains negative factors that are not compatible with the strictly positive nature of reflectance, nor most graphics hardware. For the first term these negative values can usually be cancelled out, but not for later terms.

Finally, the memory consumption of the matrix M grows rapidly with the desired resolution. If we sample the BRDF 64 times along each parameter, the resulting matrix consumes about 67MB, assuming 4 bytes (a float) per sample. If we sample the BRDF 128 times in each dimension, the matrix would take up about 1GB. The resulting texture maps would be only 64×64 or 128×128 pixels in size. Smaller texture maps than this may result in visual artifacts.

4.2 Normalized Decomposition

The SVD is too expensive for high-resolution factorizations and it always computes a full approximation, which is often not necessary, as a few terms usually suffice for a good approximation. The Normalized Decomposition (ND) algorithm can be used instead in many situations.

Consider first a single-term approximation

$$f_P(\mathbf{x}, \mathbf{y}) \approx \tilde{f}_{P1}(\mathbf{x}, \mathbf{y}) = g_1(\mathbf{x}) h_1(\mathbf{y}).$$

If $\mathbf{x}$ is fixed, $g_1(\mathbf{x})$ is a constant, scaling a profile given by $h_1(\mathbf{y})$. To find a single-term separable approximation, find the average normalized profile along $\mathbf{y}$ and store it in $h_1(\mathbf{y})$, then store the normalization factors in $g_1(\mathbf{x})$.

Although the ND method does not guarantee optimality, tests show that single-term approximations using the SVD are in most cases visually similar to single-term approximations found using the ND.

A wide class of approximations can be computed using the p-norm:

$$g_1(\mathbf{x}) = \left(\int_Y |f_P|^p (\mathbf{x}, \mathbf{y}) \, d\mathbf{y} \right)^{\frac{1}{p}},$$

$$h_1(\mathbf{y}) = \frac{1}{|X|} \int_X \frac{f_P(\mathbf{x}, \mathbf{y})}{g_1(\mathbf{x})} \, d\mathbf{x}.$$

To implement the ND algorithm these integrals must be computed numerically.

Normalized decomposition (ND), besides being considerably faster than an SVD, takes much less memory. We can sample the BRDF and compute the average profile and norms incrementally, rather than having to store and operate on a large matrix. The only memory needed is that for the two output functions $g_1(\mathbf{x})$ and $h_1(\mathbf{y})$. The averaging process used to compute the output functions also reduces noise, so the technique can be used with good results on noisy measured data.

A single-term ND expansion contains only positive factors, since the BRDF f must be positive everywhere. For multi-term expansions, approximation of sequential residuals can be used. However, since the residuals will contain negative values, the additional terms will contain factors with negative values.

5 Parameterization

The parameterization of the BRDF can significantly affect separability. Figure 1 visualizes the effect of reparameterization. Two images are decomposed and reconstructed by the ND algorithm. The original image is not reconstructed very well. The reparameterized image, which is rotated in order to align the object with the boundaries, is much better approximated.

As we focus on hardware rendering the parameterization of the functions of the resulting separable form must also be compatible with the linear interpolation of texture map coordinates performed in hardware. If this technique is used with per-pixel evaluation of texture coordinates any bijective parametrization of BRDFs can be used.

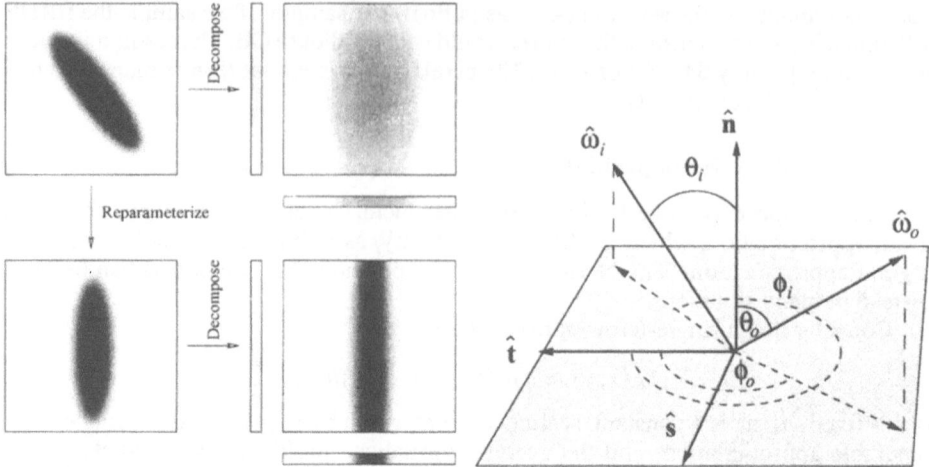

Fig. 1. *Reparameterization can improve the performance of decomposition. In this case the SVD would result in a perfect single-term reconstruction. The ND algorithm used in this figure results in a blurrier reconstruction.*

Fig. 2. *Surface coordinate system used to parameterize a BRDF. The surface normal is $\hat{n}$, the primary surface tangent is $\hat{t}$, and $\hat{s}$ is the secondary surface tangent perpendicular to $\hat{n}$ and $\hat{t}$.*

We have not found a single parameterization that works well for all BRDFs, although we have found parameterizations that work well for broad categories of BRDFs. This is to be expected due to the different surface phenomena that contribute to variation in reflectance, as shown in Figure 3. Each of these phenomenon aligns the features the BRDF along different axes. We will show examples of these tradeoffs in Figure 5.

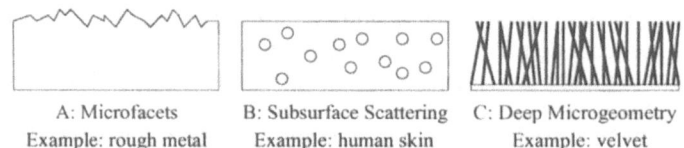

A: Microfacets | B: Subsurface Scattering | C: Deep Microgeometry
Example: rough metal | Example: human skin | Example: velvet

Fig. 3. *Surface phenomena that contribute to BRDFs.*

5.1 BRDF Parameterization

The standard parameterization of a BRDF is with respect to the incident direction $\hat{\omega}_i$ and viewing direction $\hat{\omega}_o$ relative to a local surface frame at $\underline{x}$. A unit length vector $\hat{a}$ can be expressed in spherical coordinates $(\theta(\hat{a}), \phi(\hat{a}))$ relative to the local surface frame $\{\hat{n}, \hat{t}, \hat{s}\}$ (see Figure 2) as follows:

$$\cos\theta(\hat{a}) = \hat{n} \cdot \hat{a},$$
$$\tan\phi(\hat{a}) = (\hat{s} \cdot \hat{a})/(\hat{t} \cdot \hat{a}).$$

Let $\theta_i = \theta(\hat{\omega}_i)$, $\phi_i = \phi(\hat{\omega}_i)$, $\theta_o = \theta(\hat{\omega}_o)$ and $\phi_o = \phi(\hat{\omega}_o)$.

Many BRDFs are not especially separable with respect to the standard incident/view, or $(\theta_i, \phi_i) \times (\theta_o, \phi_o)$ parameterization.

Very good results can usually be obtained using an elevation/azimuth, or $(\theta_i, \theta_o) \times (\phi_i, \phi_o)$ parameterization, which is unfortunately not directly compatible with hardware texture mapping; see Section 5.3.

Rusinkiewicz [22] has parameterized the BRDF in terms of the halfway vector $\hat{\mathbf{h}}$ (the vector halfway between the incident and outgoing ray) and a "difference vector" $\hat{\mathbf{d}}$:

$$\hat{\mathbf{h}} = \text{norm}(\hat{\omega}_i + \hat{\omega}_o),$$
$$\hat{\mathbf{d}} = (\text{Rot}\{\hat{\mathbf{s}}, -\theta(\hat{\mathbf{h}})\} \circ \text{Rot}\{\hat{\mathbf{n}}, -\phi(\hat{\mathbf{h}})\})\, \hat{\omega}_i.$$

The two rotations are chosen to rotate $\hat{\mathbf{h}}$ to the pole of a new coordinate system, which is visualized in Figure 4; $\hat{\mathbf{d}}$ is in fact $\hat{\omega}_i$, but parameterized with respect to this transformed frame. The Rusinkiewicz reparameterization can be interpreted as a change of basis with the new basis found by a Gram-Schmidt orthonormalization of $\{\hat{\mathbf{h}}, -\hat{\mathbf{n}}, \hat{\mathbf{n}} \times \hat{\mathbf{h}}\}$:

$$\hat{\mathbf{h}} = \text{norm}(\hat{\omega}_i + \hat{\omega}_o), \qquad \hat{\mathbf{u}} = -\text{norm}(\hat{\mathbf{n}} - (\hat{\mathbf{n}} \cdot \hat{\mathbf{h}})\hat{\mathbf{h}}),$$
$$\hat{\mathbf{v}} = \hat{\mathbf{h}} \times \hat{\mathbf{u}}, \qquad \hat{\mathbf{d}} = [\hat{\omega}_i \cdot \hat{\mathbf{h}}, \hat{\omega}_i \cdot \hat{\mathbf{u}}, \hat{\omega}_i \cdot \hat{\mathbf{v}}]^T.$$

Although the Rusinkiewicz parameterization makes many BRDFs much more separable, it is numerically unstable if $\hat{\mathbf{h}} \approx \hat{\mathbf{n}}$. This makes it unsuitable for hardware interpolation; see Section 5.3.

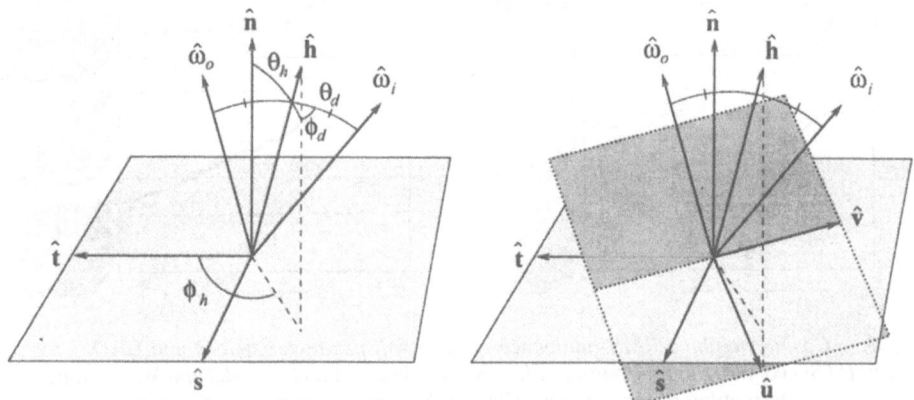

Fig. 4. *Two different views of the Rusinkiewicz parameterization. View 1 (left): The angles (θ_d, ϕ_d) of the "difference" vector $\hat{\mathbf{d}}$ are relative to $\hat{\mathbf{h}}$ and the plane containing $\hat{\mathbf{h}}$ and $\hat{\mathbf{n}}$. View 2 (right): The Rusinkiewicz parameterization generates a new orthonormal frame consisting of $\hat{\mathbf{h}}$, a vector $\hat{\mathbf{u}}$ perpendicular to $\hat{\mathbf{h}}$ and in the same plane as both $\hat{\mathbf{h}}$ and $\hat{\mathbf{n}}$, and a third vector $\hat{\mathbf{v}}$ perpendicular to both $\hat{\mathbf{h}}$ and $\hat{\mathbf{u}}$. The vector $\hat{\omega}_i$ is analyzed against this new frame to obtain the difference vector coordinates.*

To avoid the numerical instability, we can instead apply Gram-Schmidt orthonormalization to $\{\hat{\mathbf{h}}, \hat{\mathbf{t}}, \hat{\mathbf{s}}\}$:

$$\hat{\mathbf{h}} = \text{norm}(\hat{\omega}_i + \hat{\omega}_o), \qquad \hat{\mathbf{t}}' = \text{norm}(\hat{\mathbf{t}} - (\hat{\mathbf{t}} \cdot \hat{\mathbf{h}})\hat{\mathbf{h}}), \qquad (4)$$
$$\hat{\mathbf{s}}' = \hat{\mathbf{h}} \times \hat{\mathbf{t}}', \qquad \hat{\mathbf{d}} = [\hat{\omega}_i \cdot \hat{\mathbf{h}}, \hat{\omega}_i \cdot \hat{\mathbf{s}}', \hat{\omega}_i \cdot \hat{\mathbf{t}}']^T.$$

254

Note that $\hat{h}$ cannot equal $\hat{t}$ for any true surface frame. For vertex frames that are not exactly aligned with the surface, as used in computer graphics, it is theoretically possible for $\hat{h}$ to be close to $\hat{t}$ but only for glancing retroreflection (for which the majority of BRDFs are 0), and even then for only one view direction.

This parameterization may not align anisotropic features of the BRDF and does not have the same symmetries as the Rusinkiewicz parameterization, but in practical applications it is numerically stable and it is compatible with hardware interpolation.

5.2 Error Analysis

To compare these parameterizations, we tested a number of analytic and measured BRDFs [10]. Each BRDF was sampled 32 times along each dimension and a separable decomposition was computed using the SVD. To obtain a consistent parameterization-independent comparison the RMS error of the outgoing radiance was estimated using 8000 Monte Carlo samples evenly distributed over both the incident and view hemispheres. Each sample was computed by multiplying the value of the approximated BRDF with the cosine of the incident elevation angle (i.e. θ_i). This choice was made because outgoing radiance corresponds to what is actually perceived by the eye.

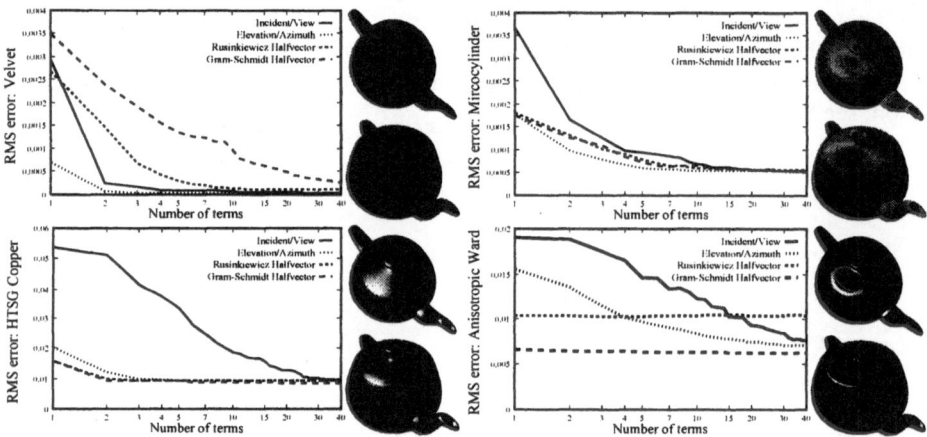

Fig. 5. *Cosine weighted RMS luminance error for all parameterizations and BRDFs for the velvet, HTSG copper, Poulin-Fournier microcylinder brushed metal model and Ward's model, as a function of the number of terms in an SVD. The non-zero asymptotic error is due to sampling and the bilinear interpolation used to reconstruct a continuous version of each factor.*

Results are shown in Figure 5. The non-zero asymptotic error is due to the bilinear interpolation used to reconstruct a continuous version of each factor. The asymptotic errors shown in Figure 5 are also highly dependent on the size of the texture maps used and the average value of each BRDF. Figure 6 shows the dependency between texture map size and RMS error. Note that the asymptotic error may not decrease monotonically, depending on how the BRDF interacts with the sampling grid, and how antialiasing is performed during BRDF sampling.

RMS error is not a totally appropriate error metric, as it tends to overweight the peaks while underweighting the diffuse colour. Future research should consider appropriate error metrics for BRDF approximations, perhaps by analyzing shape-from-

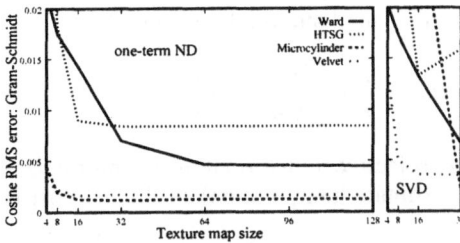

Fig. 6. *Cosine weighted RMS error with respect to the original BRDF for single-term ND and single-term SVD approximations with Gram-Schmidt parameterization using varying texture map sizes.*

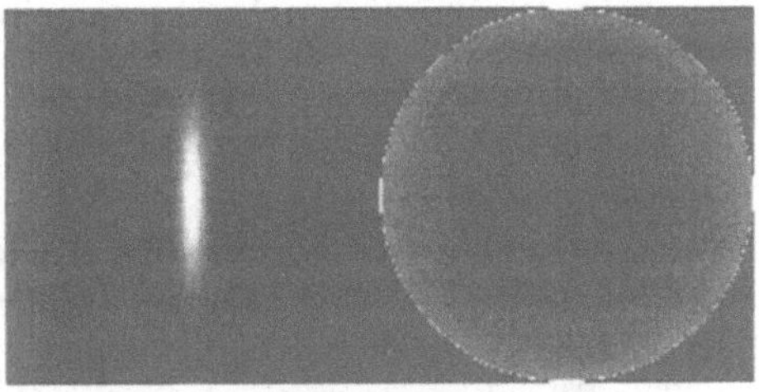

Fig. 7. *The resulting texture maps (as XY hemisphere maps) after decomposing Ward's model in the Gram-Schmidt parameterization with the ND algorithm. See Figure 10 for an image rendered with these texture maps.*

shading algorithms in the context of the nonlinear intensity sensitivity of the human visual system.

With respect to RMS error, we found that no single parameterization was the best for all the BRDFs we tested. BRDFs that are dominated by specular or near-specular reflection off randomly oriented microfacets (Figure 3A), such as HTSG models of rough metal or Ward's model, were usually best approximated by halfvector parameterizations. Matte materials in which "thick" microgeometry and self-shadowing were present and that had colour shifts at normal viewing angles, such as matte translucent paints or velvet (Figure 3B&C), had BRDFs that usually were most separable using the standard incident/view parameterization. Certain BRDFs, such as glossy iridescent paints, may be best approximated using a sum of two terms with different parameterizations. The elevation/azimuth parameterization was surprisingly effective in most cases.

5.3 Factor Parameterization

Now we have to find a suitable representation of the functions in a separable expansion that allows for a good interpolation of the parameters. Several possible representations [9, 14, 17] permit bilinear interpolation in the (u, v)-space of texture maps to approximate spherical interpolation of unit vectors.

Mapping a spherical coordinate (θ, ϕ) representation directly onto the coordinates of a texture map does not give the desired result, since interpolation does not correctly wrap around in ϕ using the shortest path over the hemisphere.

Hemisphere maps are a better solution to angular interpolation. The XY hemisphere map just projects a given unit vector $\hat{\mathbf{a}}$ onto the tangent vectors:

$$a_x = \hat{\mathbf{a}} \cdot \hat{\mathbf{t}}, \qquad a_y = \hat{\mathbf{a}} \cdot \hat{\mathbf{s}}.$$

Now we have to map a_x and a_y into the usual range of texture coordinates:

$$a_u = \frac{1}{2}(a_x + 1), \qquad a_v = \frac{1}{2}(a_y + 1). \tag{5}$$

If problems with backfacing vertex frames are encountered it is better to use parabolic maps [9], which automatically take care of negative $a_z = \hat{\mathbf{a}} \cdot \hat{\mathbf{n}}$ and scale the other coordinates so they lie outside the unit circle and extend out to infinity smoothly:

$$a_u = \frac{1}{2}\left(\frac{a_x}{1+a_z}+1\right), \qquad a_v = \frac{1}{2}\left(\frac{a_y}{1+a_z}+1\right).$$

This computation can be accomplished with a projective transformation and normalization (required anyways for correct texture coordinate interpolation) so the net cost is just another dot product to compute a_z.

The Rusinkiewicz parameterization does not work well with hemisphere map representations. Our approach calculates texture coordinates only at vertices; linear interpolation of texture coordinates is used within polygons. The difference vectors at the vertices of polygons covered by a highlight tend to be parameterized with wildly different values (i.e., vary heavily in ϕ_d) in the Rusinkiewicz parameterization. Bilinear interpolation then calculates incorrect texture coordinates, which introduces very visible errors.

The elevation/azimuth $(\theta_i, \theta_o) \times (\phi_i, \phi_o)$ parameterization is also not compatible with hemisphere maps. When interpolating azimuth angles the shortest direction of interpolation needs to be chosen, taking into account the periodicity of both ϕ_i and ϕ_o. Neither hemisphere maps nor periodic textures satisfy this requirement.

The incident/view $(\theta_i, \phi_i) \times (\theta_o, \phi_o)$ parameterization works with hemisphere maps, and certain "deep microgeometry" BRDFs (such as velvet) are more separable with respect to this parameterization.

The new Gram-Schmidt halfvector parameterization combined with an XY hemisphere map representation of the functions g_k and h_k has proven to be a good combination for many near-specular BRDFs and is given in full by the following:

$$
\begin{aligned}
\hat{\mathbf{h}} &= \mathrm{norm}(\hat{\omega}_i + \hat{\omega}_o), & \hat{\mathbf{t}}' &= \mathrm{norm}(\hat{\mathbf{t}} - (\hat{\mathbf{h}}\cdot\hat{\mathbf{t}})\hat{\mathbf{h}}), \\
& & \hat{\mathbf{s}}' &= \hat{\mathbf{h}}\times\hat{\mathbf{t}}', \\
\mathfrak{h}_u &= (\hat{\mathbf{h}}\cdot\hat{\mathbf{t}}'+1)/2, & \mathfrak{d}_u &= (\hat{\omega}_i\cdot\hat{\mathbf{t}}'+1)/2, & (6)\\
\mathfrak{h}_v &= (\hat{\mathbf{h}}\cdot\hat{\mathbf{s}}'+1)/2, & \mathfrak{d}_v &= (\hat{\omega}_i\cdot\hat{\mathbf{s}}'+1)/2,
\end{aligned}
$$

The bottom left image of Figure 10 shows Newell's teapot rendered with a single-term decomposition of Ward's model using the ND algorithm and the above parameterization. Figure 7 shows the corresponding texture maps that were used to render the single-term approximation.

6 Rendering

Compositing and texturing operations, which are already available in current graphics hardware through OpenGL or Direct3D, can be used for interactive reconstruction of a separably decomposed BRDF. Frame buffer and texture map arithmetic is used to reconstruct the outgoing radiance (eq. 1) in parallel for each pixel.

For each term, first render the scene with one diffusely illuminated texture map factor. Without clearing the colour or depth buffers, render the scene again with constant illumination and the second texture map. Texture coordinates have to be recalculated at each vertex whenever the view or relative light source position changes. For the second pass, set the depth test to "equality" and set the compositing operation to "multiply". The accumulation buffer can then be used to sum multiple terms. With multitexturing,

1. Calculate texture coordinates $\mathfrak{h}$ and $\mathfrak{d}$ for each vertex (see Equation 6).

2. Clear the colour and depth buffers.

3. Set up a simple Lambertian lighting model.

4. Render the scene using $g_k(\mathfrak{h})$ as a texture map on the diffuse reflectance. The result in the colour buffer is $g_k(\mathfrak{h})I\cos_+\theta_i/r^2$.

5. Set the z-test to ``equality''.

6. Set the compositing operator to *multiply* colours.

7. Turn off hardware shading.

8. Render the scene using $h_k(\mathfrak{d})$ as a texture map. The result in the colour buffer is $g_k(\mathfrak{h})h_k(\mathfrak{d})I\cos_+\theta_i/r^2$.

Fig. 8. *Pseudocode for rendering using contemporary graphics hardware.*

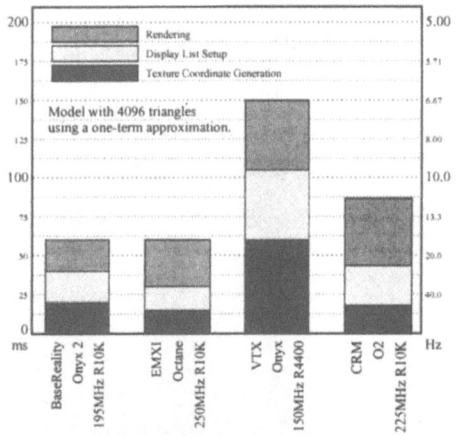

Fig. 9. *Rendering times and rates on different platforms using a one-term, two-factor approximation. A breakdown into stages is shown; the lower two stages (texture coordinate generation and display list regeneration) must currently be done by the host CPU.*

the product of two texture maps and the diffuse lighting can be formed in a single pass. See Figure 8 for pseudo code for this algorithm.

For a single-term, two-factor decomposition and a model with 2048 quads, we achieved rates of 6.7-17Hz; see Figure 9. Performance was strongly dependent on bus and CPU performance, as it was necessary to perform tangent vector transformation and texture coordinate generation on the host.

Texture mapping a diffuse term can reintroduce a dependence on $\underline{x}$ that can add visual complexity; see Figure 13. As well, MIP-mapping can be used to avoid highlight aliasing, by generating a pyramid of factorizations at different resolution levels and prefiltering the BRDF for each level. Alternatively, at some loss in accuracy, the factors of a single high-resolution decomposition can be filtered and downsampled independently.

6.1 Hardware Rendering Issues

Our implementation needed to address the limitations of current graphics hardware, specifically lack of dynamic range and precision, limited texture coordinate generation capabilities, and lack of negative numbers and signed arithmetic. In this section we only sketch how to overcome these limitations; for more detail see [10]. Some of these limitations had a moderate impact on performance, but it would be relatively easy to address them in new hardware designs.

Cosine Term: We use hardware lighting to multiply the term $g_k h_k$ by $\cos_+\theta_i$. It could be built into the reflectance function, but this might affect the separability.

Signed Arithmetic: Multiterm approximations will have negative values in the expansion, which are incompatible with contemporary graphics hardware. We can use biasing to convert the expansion to a form that uses only multiplication of positive values. Three additional rendering passes are then required to correct for

Fig. 10. *Comparison of rendering modes using Ward's anisotropic BRDF model [25], using $k_d = (1.0, 0.0, 0.0)$, $(\alpha_x, \alpha_y) = (0.21, 0.048)$, and $k_s = 0.3$. Top left: Gouraud interpolation of the BRDF evaluated at the vertices. Top right: the BRDF evaluated in a raytracer at every pixel, with interpolation of the frame vectors from the vertices. Bottom left: ND with one term (128 × 128 pixels), rendered with hardware acceleration. Bottom right: SVD with five terms (32 × 32 pixels), rendered with hardware acceleration.*

the bias [10]. Note that all passes use the same set of texture coordinates. See Figure 11 for an example of a multi-term rendering.

Precision: Frame buffers often only have 8 bits of precision. While this is sufficient for some BRDFs, deeper frame buffers increase quality. If multitexturing is used, only the multitexturing unit needs to have high precision.

Dynamic Range: Frame buffers usually clamp intermediate colour components to the range $[0, 1]$; texture maps can likewise only store values in the range $[0, 1]$. Unfortunately, BRDFs are defined over the range $[0, \infty)$. To avoid clamping we multiply the textures by scale factors chosen to ensure that no possible pointwise product will exceed the limits of the frame buffer, while maximizing the available precision. In a final rendering step, the result must be scaled by a product of the reciprocals of these scale factors. To avoid precision issues in the frame buffer, we limit the range of the original BRDFs to $[0, 5]$.

Texture Map Resolution: A texture map resolution of 128 × 128 has proven to be adequate for all the BRDFs we tested. Usually 64 × 64 and sometimes even less is enough; see Figure 6.

While the algorithm runs now at interactive rates on current hardware (Figure 9), some relatively simple extensions to the graphics hardware (and/or the graphics API and drivers), most importantly some new texture coordinate generation modes, would permit much better performance and ease of use [16].

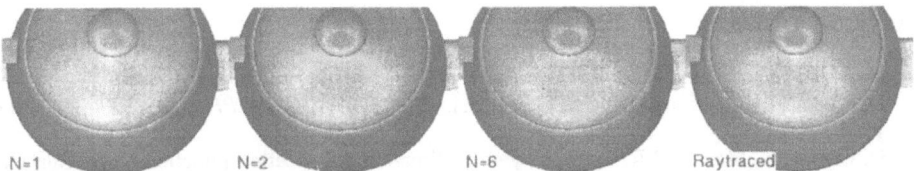

Fig. 11. *The microcylinder model rendered with different numbers of terms using OpenGL. The incorrect extra highlight that appears using one term disappears with two or more terms.*

6.2 Software Rendering

So far we have presented what has to be done to use a separable representation in hardware accelerated rendering. A separable representation can easily be used in software rendering: We do not have to even limit ourselves to parameterizations that are compatible with linear texture coordinate interpolation if texture coordinates are evaluated at each pixel.

To evaluate a BRDF at a certain position, one has to compute a sum of products at that position (eq. 3). As we have seen, a few terms are often sufficient to visually approximate a given BRDF. Thus the evaluation boils down to a few texture lookups, multiplications and additions. Implementation in a renderer or in a shading language is straightforward.

7 Conclusions

We have investigated different parameterizations and decomposition algorithms to improve the visual convergence of the separable approximation to BRDFs, and have shown how reconstruction from this compressed representation can be accomplished at interactive rates using current graphics hardware.

A modification of the Rusinkiewicz half-vector/difference vector parameterization [22] combined with a hemisphere map parameterization of the factors stored in texture maps gave excellent results for "microfacet" BRDFs.

The proposed representation of BRDFs can also be used for software renderers. Separable decompositions are a good choice for a compact general-purpose data format to store compressed BRDFs, as they allow for fast and accurate evaluation of BRDFs, including those reconstructed from measured data.

Acknowledgements

Holly Rushmeier and Greg Ward Larson were extremely helpful in retrieving data from Ward's imaging gonioreflectometer, used here for the vinyl BRDF. The velvet and feather BRDFs were reconstructed from data provided by the group at Columbia-Utretch. The HTSG analytic model was implemented by Glenn Evans. The implementation of the Poulin-Fournier model was provided by Szymon Rusinkiewicz. Some additional BRDF data was provided by Heinz Mayer of the Graz University of Technology.

This research was funded by a grant from the National Sciences and Engineering Research Council of Canada.

References

1. H. Andrews and Hunt. *Digital Image Restoration*. Prentice-Hall, 1977.
2. D. Banks. Illumination in Diverse Codimensions. In *Proc. SIGGRAPH*, pages 327–334, July 1994.
3. B. Cabral, N. Max, and R. Springmeyer. Bidirectional Reflection Functions from Surface Bump Maps. In *Proc. SIGGRAPH*, pages 273–281, July 1987.
4. J. DeYoung and A. Fournier. Properties of Tabulated Bidirectional Reflectance Distribution Functions. In *Proc. Graphics Interface*, pages 47–55, May 1997.
5. A. Fournier. Separating Reflection Functions for Linear Radiosity. In *Eurographics Rendering Workshop*, pages 383–392, June 1995.
6. J. Gondek, G. Meyer, and J. Newman. Wavelength Dependent Reflectance Functions. In *Proc. SIGGRAPH*, pages 213–220, July 1994.
7. X. He, K. Torrance, F. Sillion, and D. Greenberg. A Comprehensive Physical Model for Light Reflection. In *Proc. SIGGRAPH*, pages 175–186, July 1991.
8. W. Heidrich and H.-P. Seidel. Efficient Rendering of Anisotropic Surfaces Using Computer Graphics Hardware. In *Image and Multi-dimensional DSP Workshop (IMDSP)*, 1998.
9. W. Heidrich and H.-P. Seidel. Realistic, Hardware-accelerated Shading and Lighting. In *Proc. SIGGRAPH*, August 1999.
10. J. Kautz. Hardware Rendering with Bidirectional Reflectances. Technical Report CS-99-02, University of Waterloo, 1999.
11. A. Keller. Instant Radiosity. In *Proc. SIGGRAPH*, pages 49–56, August 1997.
12. J. Koenderink, A. van Doorn, and M. Stavridi. Bidirectional Reflection Distribution Function Expressed in Terms of Surface Scattering Modes. In *European Conference on Computer Vision*, pages 28–39, 1996.
13. E. Lafortune, S.-C. Foo, K. Torrance, and D. Greenberg. Non-linear Approximation of Reflectance Functions. In *Proc. SIGGRAPH*, pages 117–126, August 1997.
14. E. Lafortune and Y. Willems. Using the Modified Phong Reflectance Model for Physically Based Rendering. Technical Report CW197, Dept. Comp. Sci., K.U. Leuven, 1994.
15. R. Lewis. Making Shaders More Physically Plausible. In *Eurographics Workshop on Rendering*, pages 47–62, June 1993.
16. M. McCool and W. Heidrich. Texture Shaders. In *SIGGRAPH/Eurographics Workshop on Graphics Hardware*, August 1999. See also Technical Report CS-99-11, University of Waterloo.
17. L. Neumann and A. Neumann. Photosimulation: Interreflection with Arbitrary Reflectance Models and Illuminations. *Computer Graphics Forum*, 8(1):21–34, March 1989.
18. M. Olano and A. Lastra. A Shading Language on Graphics Hardware: The PixelFlow Shading System. In *Proc. SIGGRAPH*, pages 159–168, July 1998.
19. B.-T. Phong. Illumination for Computer Generated Pictures. *Comm. ACM*, 18(6):311–317, June 1975.
20. P. Poulin and A. Fournier. A Model for Anisotropic Reflection. In *Proc. SIGGRAPH*, pages 273–282, August 1990.
21. W. Press, S. Teukolsky, W. Vetterling, and B. Flannery. *Numerical Recipes in C: The Art of Scientific Computing (2nd ed.)*. Cambridge University Press, 1992.
22. S. Rusinkiewicz. A New Change of Variables for Efficient BRDF Representation. In *Eurographics Workshop on Rendering*, pages 11–23, June 1998.
23. P. Schröder and W. Sweldens. Spherical Wavelets: Efficiently Representing Functions on the Sphere. In *Proc. SIGGRAPH*, pages 161–172, August 1995.
24. B. Walter, G. Alppay, E. Lafortune, S. Fernandez, and D. Greenberg. Fitting Virtual Lights for Non-Diffuse Walkthroughs. In *Proc. SIGGRAPH*, pages 45–48, August 1997.
25. G. Ward. Measuring and Modeling Anisotropic Reflection. In *Proc. SIGGRAPH*, pages 265–272, July 1992.
26. S. Westin, J. Arvo, and K. Torrance. Predicting Reflectance Functions from Complex Surfaces. In *Proc. SIGGRAPH*, pages 255–264, July 1992.

Editors' Note: see Appendix, p. 374 for colored figures of this paper

An Illumination Model for a System of Isotropic Substrate- Isotropic Thin Film with Identical Rough Boundaries

Isabelle Icart, Didier Arquès

(icart@univ-mlv.fr, arques@univ-mlv.fr)
Université de Marne-La-Vallée
5, boulevard Descartes, Champs-sur-Marne, F-77454 Marne-La-Vallée CEDEX 2

Abstract. A new physically-based illumination model describing the interaction of light with a system composed of an isotropic substrate coated by an isotropic film with geometrically identical statistical rough boundaries (ITF) is presented. This model divides the intensity reflected from the system into three components: specular, directional-diffuse and uniform diffuse intensity. The formulas for the intensity reflected coherently (specular) and incoherently (directional-diffuse) from the system are derived within the framework of the scalar diffraction theory. Assuming that the slopes on the boundaries of the film are small, a first-order expansion of the reflection coefficient is used in the evaluation of the Helmholtz-Kirchhoff integral which allows to calculate the previous intensities. The consistency of the model is evaluated numerically and appraised visually by comparison with classic approximations.

1 Introduction

In the real world all materials are not polished nor perfectly smooth (soap films are an example of surfaces that can be considered as perfectly smooth [10]): the surfaces are assumed to be a collection of irregularities which scatters light into various directions, though certain directions are privileged. A smooth surface will reflect light only in the specular direction whereas a rough surface (roughness is a non intrinsic property which depends on wavelength and incidence angle - see e.g. the Rayleigh criterion [2] p.10) will show a diffuse-like behaviour due to diffraction by these irregularities. The results of Beckmann and Spizzichino [1] in physical optics, which gave rise to the illumination model of Cook and Torrance [5] and later to the more complete model of He, Torrance, Sillion and Greenberg [8] in computer graphics deal with calculating the coherent (specular) and incoherent (directional-diffuse) components of light diffracted by a single rough surface with uniform reflection coefficient. The problem of rendering systems consisting of rough thin films or rough multilayers is more complex because the reflection coefficient of such systems depends on the geometry (and then on the roughness) of each boundary and cannot be considered as uniform. People already achieved realistic pictures of rough thin films or multilayers by means of spectral BRDFs [7] or intuitive approaches (see e.g. [15] and [6]) coupled with classic illumination models. In 1994, Callet [3] obtained pictures of thin film coatings and metallic paints by means of the geometric optics model of Cook and Torrance [5] used together with some approximations. These approximations consist in calculating the bidirectional reflectance function for each boundary and using the interference formula valid for smooth films (see formula (1)) to deduce the total BRDF of the system (see [4] p. 203-205). Within the framework of the scalar diffraction theories, it is nevertheless possible to determine precisely (or at least with a given accuracy) the components of light reflected towards an observer from a system substrate-thin film under certain assumptions. In this paper, we first evaluate the coherent and incoherent intensities reflected from a system substrate-identical thin film towards an observer situated in the Fraunhofer diffraction zone ([2] p. 343), in a given direction. Then, we deduce the local illumination model as a sum of three intensities : specular, directional-diffuse and uniform diffuse. These results will be compared with those obtained by neglecting the spatial dependence of the reflection coefficient (which amounts to considering the system as an equivalent surface with a Fresnel coefficient equal to the amplitude reflection coefficient of the corresponding smooth plate formed by the mean planes of the boundaries). The assumptions entering into this model are specified in detail as follows:

1. The system consists of an homogeneous and isotropic thin film with complex refractive index and an isotropic substrate. Both ambient-film and film-substrate boundaries are geometrically identical (identical thin film denoted I.T.F afterwards) and generated by a stationary isotropic stochastic process.
2. The height-deviation ζ of the surfaces from their mean planes is characterised by a Gaussian probability density function involving two parameters : the surface RMS height σ, and the correlation length τ.
3. Boundaries are locally smooth (LSRS-type film : see [14] p.254)
4. The incident wave is plane and monochromatic.
5. The dimensions of the irradiated surface (2X, 2Y) are much greater than the wavelength λ of incident light and the surface correlation length τ.
6. The point of observation is in the Fraunhofer diffraction zone.

The paper is arranged as follows:

- Section 2 derives the general and simplified expressions of the amplitude reflection coefficient for a system substrate-identical thin film.
- In Section 3 we evaluate the coherent and incoherent intensities reflected from the system.
- Section 4 specifies the local illumination model.
- Section 5 provides a numerical and a visual estimation of the error committed on the directional-diffuse component by assuming a uniform reflection coefficient in the Helmholtz-Kirchhoff integral.
- Finally, the last section of this contribution presents the conclusions.

2 Amplitude reflection coefficient for a system substrate-identical thin film

The illumination model described by He, Torrance, Sillion and Greenberg in 1991 [8] was obtained by applying the scalar form of the Kirchhoff theory to the case of a single rough surface with uniform reflection coefficient. As it will be shown hereafter, the amplitude reflection coefficient of a system substrate-I.T.F. depends on space coordinates by means of ζ and thus, using the results of He, Torrance, Sillion and Greenberg for this kind of system is inappropriate. The model has to be extended to account for a non uniform reflection coefficient, the expression of which will be derived below.

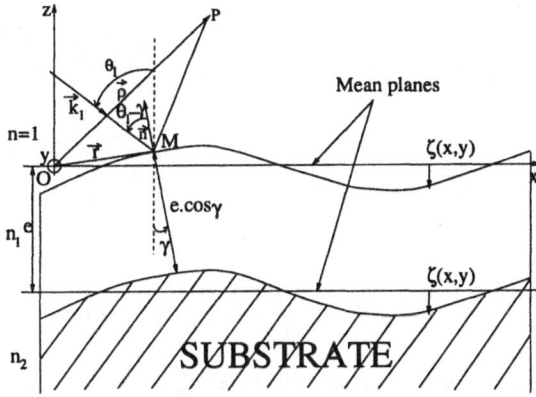

Fig. 1. Identical thin film

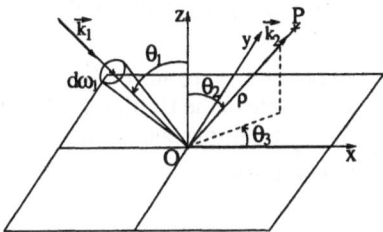

Fig. 2. Incident and scattered waves

2.1 General expression of the reflection coefficient of a system substrate-I.T.F

Consider a plane progressive monochromatic unpolarised wave incident under the angle θ_1 on the upper mean plane of the film (see Fig. 1). This wave shall be resolved into two linearly polarised components, with polarisation planes respectively parallel ($//$) and perpendicular ($\perp$) to the plane of incidence. The film is assumed to be the LSRS type, which allows us to make the tangent plane approximation. The I.T.F. is then represented locally by a plane parallel plate inclined under the angle γ to the (Ox) axis (see Fig. 1). Assuming that the transverse dimensions of this plate are much greater than wavelength, the amplitude of the local electric field can be obtained by summing the amplitudes of the multiple reflected waves, to infinity, for both components of the incident wave. The field reflected by the plate, E_{lsc} is then expressed by means of the following classic equations (see e.g. [9]):

$$E_{lsc} = R_l E_{lincident} \quad R_l = \frac{R_{01l} + R_{12l}e^{j\phi}}{1 + R_{01l}R_{12l}e^{j\phi}} \tag{1}$$

where $j^2 = -1$ and subscript l denotes either the parallel or perpendicular ($l = //$ or $\perp$) component with:

$$R_{01\perp} = \frac{\cos i - \sqrt{n_1^2 - \sin i^2}}{\cos i + \sqrt{n_1^2 - \sin i^2}} \qquad R_{12\perp} = \frac{\sqrt{n_1^2 - \sin i^2} - \sqrt{n_2^2 - \sin i^2}}{\sqrt{n_1^2 - \sin i^2} + \sqrt{n_2^2 - \sin i^2}} \qquad (2)$$

$$R_{01//} = \frac{n_1^2 \cos i - \sqrt{n_1^2 - \sin i^2}}{n_1^2 \cos i + \sqrt{n_1^2 - \sin i^2}} \qquad R_{12//} = \frac{n_2^2\sqrt{n_1^2 - \sin i^2} - n_1^2\sqrt{n_2^2 - \sin i^2}}{n_2^2\sqrt{n_1^2 - \sin i^2} + n_1^2\sqrt{n_2^2 - \sin i^2}}$$

where:

$$i = \theta_1 - \gamma \qquad \phi = \frac{4\pi e}{\lambda}\cos\gamma\sqrt{n_1^2 - \sin i^2}$$

As γ expresses by means of the partial derivatives $\zeta_x' = \partial\zeta/\partial x$ and $\zeta_y' = \partial\zeta/\partial y$ of the random height variable $\zeta(x, y)$ in the form:

$$\cos\gamma = 1/\sqrt{1 + \zeta_x'^2 + \zeta_y'^2}$$

it follows that R_l can also be expressed by means of ζ_x' and ζ_y'. However, as the gèneral expression of R_l is difficult to integrate in the Helmholtz-Kirchhoff integral (see Section 3), we will use the small-slope assumption, which allows to limit ourselves to a first order expansion of R_l in ζ_x' and ζ_y' [13].

2.2 First order expansion of the reflection coefficient

As locally smooth rough surfaces are characterised by small partial derivatives ζ_x' and ζ_y', $R_{//}$ and $R_\perp$ (see equations (1) and (2)) can be expanded to the first order in ζ_x' and ζ_y' as follows:

$$R_\perp = \alpha_\perp + \beta_\perp\zeta_x' + o(\zeta_x') + o(\zeta_y') \qquad R_{//} = \alpha_{//} + \beta_{//}\zeta_x' + o(\zeta_x') + o(\zeta_y')$$

with:

$$\alpha_\perp = \frac{(K - J_1)(J_1 + J_2) + (K + J_1)(J_1 - J_2)e^{j\phi_0}}{(K + J_1)(J_1 + J_2) + (K - J_1)(J_1 - J_2)e^{j\phi_0}}$$

$$\alpha_{//} = \frac{(n_1^2 K - J_1)(n_2^2 J_1 + n_1^2 J_2) + (n_1^2 K + J_1)(n_2^2 J_1 - n_1^2 J_2)e^{j\phi_0}}{(n_1^2 K + J_1)(n_2^2 J_1 + n_1^2 J_2) + (n_1^2 K - J_1)(n_2^2 J_1 - n_1^2 J_2)e^{j\phi_0}} \qquad (3)$$

$$\beta_\perp = \frac{2I\left[(J_1^2 - K^2)(J_1 + J_2)^2 + (K^2 - J_1^2)(J_1 - J_2)^2 e^{2j\phi_0}\right]}{J_1\left[(K + J_1)(J_1 + J_2) + (K - J_1)(J_1 - J_2)e^{j\phi_0}\right]^2}$$

$$+ \frac{8IK^2(J_1^2 - J_2^2)(2j\pi e J_2/\lambda - 1)e^{j\phi_0}}{J_2\left[(K + J_1)(J_1 + J_2) + (K - J_1)(J_1 - J_2)e^{j\phi_0}\right]^2}$$

$$\beta_{//} = \frac{2n_1^2 I\left[(J_1^2 - K^2)(n_2^2 J_1 + n_1^2 J_2)^2 + (K^2 - J_1^2)(n_2^2 J_1 - n_1^2 J_2)^2 e^{2j\phi_0}\right]}{J_1\left[(n_1^2 K + J_1)(n_2^2 J_1 + n_1^2 J_2) + (n_1^2 K - J_1)(n_2^2 J_1 - n_1^2 J_2)e^{j\phi_0}\right]^2}$$

$$+\frac{8n_1^2 I K^2[n_1^2 n_2^2(J_2^2 - J_1^2) + (2j\pi e J_2/\lambda)(n_2^4 J_1^2 - n_1^4 J_2^2)]e^{j\phi_0}}{J_2\left[(n_1^2 K + J_1)(n_2^2 J_1 + n_1^2 J_2) + (n_1^2 K - J_1)(n_2^2 J_1 - n_1^2 J_2)e^{j\phi_0}\right]^2}$$

$$\phi_0 = \frac{4\pi e J_1}{\lambda} \quad K = \cos\theta_1 \quad I = \sin\theta_1 \quad J_i = \sqrt{n_i^2 - \sin\theta_1{}^2}, i=1,2$$

These simplified expressions of $R_\perp$ and $R_{//}$ will be used instead of the full expressions of the reflection coefficient in the Helmholtz-Kirchhoff integral (see next section).

3 Evaluation of the coherent and incoherent intensities

In this section, we derive the expressions of the intensities reflected coherently and incoherently from the system, which are at the basis of our illumination model.

3.1 Field reflected from an ITF in the Fraunhofer diffraction zone

The scalar form of the Helmholtz-Kirchhoff integral [13] applied to both components of the incident wave provides an expression of the electric field diffracted at a point P in the far zone (see Fig. 2), in a direction defined by angles θ_2 and θ_3, as a function of the reflected electric field E_{lsc} and its normal derivative with respect to the normal on the surface S:

$$E_l(P) = \frac{1}{4\pi}\iint\limits_{S}\left[E_{lsc}\frac{\partial\psi}{\partial n} - \psi\frac{\partial E_{lsc}}{\partial n}\right]dS \quad \psi = \frac{e^{jk\rho - \vec{k_2}.\vec{r}}}{\rho} \quad k = \frac{2\pi}{\lambda}$$

Subscript l denotes either the parallel or perpendicular ($l = //$ or $\perp$) component, $\vec{k_2}$ the wave vector of the scattered wave, ψ the Green function, ρ the distance between the origin of the reference frame and point P, and $\vec{r}$ the vector from the origin to a point M on the upper boundary (see Fig. 1 and Fig. 2). The incident plane wave is represented by the scalar electric field $E_{linc} = E_{l0}e^{j(\vec{k_1}.\vec{r} - \omega t)}$ where E_{l0} is the amplitude of the wave, ω is its angular frequency and $\vec{k_1}$ is the incident wave vector. The time-factor $e^{-j\omega t}$ will be omitted subsequently. The reflected electric field E_{lsc} and its derivative along the normal $\vec{n}$ at point M then express as:

$$E_{lsc} = R_l E_{l0}e^{j\vec{k_1}.\vec{r}} \quad \frac{\partial E_{lsc}}{\partial n} = \left[jR_l\vec{k_1}.\vec{n} + \nabla R_l.\vec{n}\right]E_{linc}$$

For a surface with small partial derivatives ($|\zeta_x'(x,y)| << 1$ and $|\zeta_y'(x,y)| << 1$), it can be proved that the term $\nabla R_l.\vec{n}$ is negligible with respect to $R_l\vec{k_1}.\vec{n}$. It holds then that:

$$E_{lsc}\frac{\partial\psi}{\partial n} - \psi\frac{\partial E_{lsc}}{\partial n} = jR_l(\vec{v}.\vec{n})E_{linc}\psi \tag{4}$$

with:

$$\vec{v} = \vec{k_1} - \vec{k_2}\begin{pmatrix} v_x = (2\pi/\lambda)(\sin\theta_1 - \sin\theta_2\cos\theta_3) \\ v_y = -(2\pi/\lambda)\sin\theta_2\sin\theta_3 \\ v_z = (-2\pi/\lambda)(\cos\theta_1 + \cos\theta_2) \end{pmatrix} \quad \vec{n} = \frac{1}{\sqrt{1+\zeta_x'^2+\zeta_y'^2}}\begin{pmatrix} -\zeta_x' \\ -\zeta_y' \\ 1 \end{pmatrix}$$

After expanding equation (4) to the first order in ζ'_x and ζ'_y and replacing into the Helmholtz-Kirchhoff integral, we obtain:

$$E_l(P) = \frac{-je^{jk\rho}}{2\lambda\rho} E_{l0} \iint_S \left[(\alpha_l v_x - \beta_l v_z)\,\zeta'_x + \alpha_l v_y \zeta'_y - \alpha_l v_z \right] e^{j\vec{v}\cdot\vec{r}}\, dS$$

By analogy with the calculations of Beckmann and Spizzichino, and using the same assumptions, we find:

$$E_l(P) = K \left[F_l \iint_S e^{j\vec{v}\cdot\vec{r}}\, dS + \epsilon_l(X,Y) \right] \tag{5}$$

$$\text{with:} \quad K = \frac{-je^{jk\rho}}{2\lambda\rho} E_{l0} \quad F_l = \frac{\lambda}{2\pi}\left(\beta_l v_x - \alpha_l \frac{\vec{v}\cdot\vec{v}}{v_z} \right) \tag{6}$$

$$\epsilon_l(X,Y) = \frac{j\lambda}{2\pi v_z}\left[(\alpha_l v_x - \beta_l v_z)\int_{-Y}^{Y} [e^{j\vec{v}\cdot\vec{r}}]_{-X}^{X}\, dy + \alpha_l v_y \int_{-X}^{X}[e^{j\vec{v}\cdot\vec{r}}]_{-Y}^{Y}\, dx \right]$$

where S is the illuminated part of the surface. Beckmann and Spizzichino label the term $\epsilon_l(X,Y)$ "edge effects", as it involves values of $\vec{v}\cdot\vec{r}$ at the surface edges and neglect it in the calculation of the coherent component of the electric field, given that the dimensions of the surface are much greater than wavelength. It can nevertheless be shown that despite this assumption, the edge effects are negligible only close to the specular direction. However, making one further assumption ([12] p.86), it is possible to evaluate the average of the edge terms. It should be pointed out that if we take $\beta = 0$, equations (5)-(6) amount to the results found by Beckmann et Spizzichino in the case of a single rough surface ([1] p.28).

3.2 Coherent intensity

From equation (5), we draw the expression of the average intensity I_{lc} of the field coherently reflected from the whole surface at point P. If we label $\bar{E}_l(P)$ the conjugate of the electric field $E_l(P)$ and $\langle E_l(P)\rangle$ the average of $E_l(P)$ with respect to the statistical variable, we obtain:

$$I_{lc} = \frac{\rho^2}{A\cos\theta_2}\langle E_l(P)\rangle\langle \bar{E}_l(P)\rangle$$

with:

$$\langle E_l(P)\rangle = K\left[F_l \left\langle \int_{-X}^{X}\int_{-Y}^{Y} e^{j\vec{v}\cdot\vec{r}}\, dx dy \right\rangle + \langle \epsilon_l(X,Y)\rangle \right]$$

$$\left\langle \int_{-X}^{X}\int_{-Y}^{Y} e^{j\vec{v}\cdot\vec{r}}\, dx dy \right\rangle = A\,\mathrm{sinc}(v_x X)\,\mathrm{sinc}(v_y Y)\chi_1(v_z)$$

$$\langle \epsilon_l(X,Y)\rangle = \frac{\lambda A}{2\pi}\left(\alpha_l \frac{v_x^2 + v_y^2}{v_z} - \beta_l v_x \right)\mathrm{sinc}(v_x X)\,\mathrm{sinc}(v_y Y)\chi_1(v_z)$$

where χ_1 is the one-dimensional characteristic function of the rough surface and:

$$\text{sin}_c(x) = \frac{\sin(x)}{x}, x \in \Re.$$

This implies, after some simplifications:

$$\langle E_l(P) \rangle = \frac{je^{jk\rho}}{4\pi\rho}\alpha_l A v_z \, \text{sin}_c(v_x X)sin_c(v_y Y)\chi_1(v_z)E_{l0}$$

For a surface with a Gaussian height distribution, characterised by the probability density function $p(\zeta) = \frac{1}{\sigma\sqrt{2\pi}}e^{-\zeta^2/2\sigma^2}$, we have:

$$\chi_1(v_z) = \frac{1}{\sigma\sqrt{2\pi}}\int_{-\infty}^{\infty} e^{-\zeta^2/2\sigma^2}e^{jv_z\zeta}d\zeta = e^{-g/2}$$

with $g = (\sigma v_z)^2$. The coherent intensity then becomes:

$$I_{lc}(\theta_1, \theta_2, \theta_3) = \frac{A|\alpha_l|^2}{4\lambda^2\cos\theta_2}[\text{sin}_c(v_x X)\,\text{sin}_c(v_y Y)]^2(\cos\theta_1 + \cos\theta_2)^2 e^{-g}I_{linc}d\omega_1$$

where I_{linc} represents the incident intensity for the parallel or perpendicular component and $d\omega_1$ the incident solid angle. It should be noted that in the case when $X \gg \lambda$ and $Y \gg \lambda$, the coherent intensity is zero in all directions, excepted in the specular direction. In this case the coherent intensity will be identified with the specular intensity of our illumination model (see Section 4). For unidirectional incidence with solid angle $d\omega_1$, the specular intensity becomes (see [8] p. 186):

$$I_{lsp}(\theta_1, \theta_2) = |\alpha_l|^2 e^{-g}\Delta I_{linc} \tag{7}$$

Δ is a function which is unity in the specular cone of reflection and zero otherwise. We have to notice that formula (7) does not involve β_l: the specular intensity reflected by the system substrate-I.T.F. is equal to the specular intensity reflected by an equivalent surface with a Fresnel factor equal to the reflection coefficient of the corresponding smooth film (the parallel plate formed by the mean planes of the boundaries).

3.3 Incoherent intensity

The incoherent (or directional-diffuse I_{ldd}) intensity is given by the formula:

$$I_{ldd} = \frac{\rho^2}{A\cos\theta_2}\left(\langle E_l(P)\bar{E}_l(P)\rangle - \langle E_l(P)\rangle\langle\bar{E}_l(P)\rangle\right)$$

This expression can be developed using the one-dimensional (χ_1) and two-dimensional (χ_2) characteristic functions of the surface (see [12] p. 17). Assuming that the edge effects are non stochastic (so that they give no contribution to the incoherent intensity) we obtain:

$$I_{ldd} = \frac{\rho^2|KF_l|^2}{A\cos\theta_2}\left(\int_{-X}^{X}\int_{-Y}^{Y}\int_{-X}^{X}\int_{-Y}^{Y}e^{j(v_x(x-x')+v_y(y-y'))}\chi_2(v_z, -v_z, \rho)dxdydx'dy'\right)$$

$$-\int_{-X}^{X}\int_{-Y}^{Y}\int_{-X}^{X}\int_{-Y}^{Y}e^{j(v_x(x-x')+v_y(y-y'))}\chi_1(v_z)\chi_1(-v_z)dxdydx'dy'\Big)$$

For a Gaussian height distribution, the final formula for the directional-diffuse intensity is:

$$I_{l\,dd}=\frac{\pi\tau^2}{4\lambda^2\cos\theta_2}\left|\beta_l\hat{v}_x-\alpha_l\frac{\vec{\hat{v}}.\vec{\hat{v}}}{\hat{v}_z}\right|^2 e^{-g}\sum_{m=1}^{\infty}\frac{g^m}{mm!}e^{-\frac{\pi^2\tau^2(\hat{v}_x^2+\hat{v}_y^2)}{m\lambda^2}}I_{l\,inc}d\omega_1 \qquad (8)$$

where τ is the correlation length of the surface and $\vec{\hat{v}}=\vec{v}/\|v\|$.

It should be noted that taking $\beta_l=0$ in equation (8) leads to the formula of the directional-diffuse intensity given by He, Torrance, Sillion and Greenberg ([8] p.186) excepted that the Fresnel factor is replaced by the reflectivity $|\alpha_l|^2$ of the plane parallel plate formed by the mean planes of the surfaces.

4 Local illumination model

Like the model of He, Torrance, Sillion and Greenberg, our illumination model is presented as a sum of three terms : specular intensity, directional-diffuse intensity and uniform-diffuse intensity:

$$I_r(\theta_1,\theta_2,\theta_3)=I_{ud}(\theta_1)+I_{sp}(\theta_1,\theta_2)+I_{dd}(\theta_1,\theta_2,\theta_3) \qquad (9)$$

$I_{sp}(\theta_1,\theta_2)$ is the specular intensity given by formula (7), $I_{dd}(\theta_1,\theta_2,\theta_3)$ is the directional diffuse (see formula (8)) intensity, and $I_{ud}(\theta_1)$ is the uniform diffuse intensity which results from the multiple surface and subsurface reflections and can be approximated by the Lambert formula: $I_{ud}(\theta_1)=|\alpha_l|^2\cos\theta_1 d\omega_1$, where α_l is the zero-order term of the expansion of the reflection coefficient for the parallel or perpendicular component (see formula (3)). The local illumination model for N finite solid angle sources, accounting for both polarisation components is given by:

$$I_r(\lambda)\quad=\quad\sum_{k=1}^{N}\left(|\alpha_k|^2\cos\theta_{1k}d\omega_k+|\alpha_k|^2 e^{-g_k}S\Delta\right)I_{inck}$$

$$+\quad\frac{\pi\tau^2 S}{4\lambda^2\cos\theta_2}\sum_{k=1}^{N}|\beta_k|^2 e^{-g_k}\sum_{m=1}^{\infty}\frac{g_k^m}{mm!}e^{-\frac{\pi^2\tau^2(v_x^2+v_y^2)_k}{m\lambda^2}}I_{inck}d\omega_k$$

where subscript k denotes the kth light source, S is the shadowing function (see [8] equations (23)-(25)) and I_{inck} is the total (parallel + perpendicular) incident intensity for light source k. The terms inside the brackets respectively correspond to the three terms in equation (9) and:

$$|\alpha_k|^2=\frac{|\alpha_{//k}|^2+|\alpha_{\perp k}|^2}{2}$$

$$|\beta_k|^2=\frac{|\beta_{//}\hat{v}_x-\alpha_{//}(\vec{\hat{v}}.\vec{\hat{v}}/\hat{v}_z)|_k^2+|\beta_{\perp}\hat{v}_x-\alpha_{\perp}(\vec{\hat{v}}\vec{\hat{v}}/\hat{v}_z)|_k^2}{2}$$

5 Estimation of the error committed on the directional-diffuse component by assuming a uniform reflection coefficient

We have just seen that the first order term in the expansion of the reflection coefficient, β_l, only appeared in the directional-diffuse (incoherent) part of the reflected light. Neglecting this term (which amounts to considering the film as an equivalent surface with a reflection coefficient equal to the amplitude reflection coefficient of the plane parallel plate formed by the mean planes of the I.T.F.) will thus result in an error only on the directional-diffuse term. The next section aims at evaluating this error both numerically and visually according to the angular (θ_1, θ_2 and θ_3) and film (RMS height σ, correlation length τ, thickness e) parameters.

5.1 Directional-diffuse intensity obtained by considering the reflection coefficient to be uniform

A first approximation consists in using the formula given by He, Torrance, Sillion and Greenberg for a rough surface to compute the directional-diffuse intensity reflected in the direction (θ_2, θ_3) (see [8] p.186) by replacing the Fresnel coefficient $|F|^2$ by the reflectivity $|\alpha|^2$ of the plane parallel plate formed by the mean planes of the I.T.F. (which amounts to taking $\beta = 0$ in equation (8)). The directional-diffuse intensity (without shadowing) is then (see Fig. 1 and Fig. 2 for the notations):

$$I_{dd1} = \frac{\pi \tau^2 e^{-g}}{4\lambda^2 \cos\theta_2} \frac{|\alpha_{//}|^2 + |\alpha_\perp|^2}{2} \left(\frac{\vec{v}\,\vec{v}}{\hat{v}_z}\right)^2 \sum_{m=1}^{\infty} \frac{g^m}{mm!} e^{-\frac{\pi^2 r^2 (\hat{v}_x^2 + \hat{v}_y^2)}{m\lambda^2}} I_{inc} d\omega_1 \quad (10)$$

5.2 Directional-diffuse intensity obtained by means of a first order expansion of the reflection coefficient.

Using a first order expansion of the reflection coefficient, the total directional-diffuse intensity was obtained in the form (see equation (8)):

$$I_{dd2} = \frac{\pi \tau^2 e^{-g}}{4\lambda^2 \cos\theta_2} \frac{|\beta_{//}\hat{v}_x - \alpha_{//}(\vec{v}\,\vec{v}/\hat{v}_z)|^2 + |\beta_\perp \hat{v}_x - \alpha_\perp(\vec{v}\,\vec{v}/\hat{v}_z)|^2}{2} \cdot$$
$$\sum_{m=1}^{\infty} \frac{g^m}{mm!} e^{-\frac{\pi^2 r^2 (\hat{v}_x^2 + \hat{v}_y^2)}{m\lambda^2}} I_{inc} d\omega_1 \quad (11)$$

5.3 Numerical estimation of the error

The relative error committed by using I_{dd1} instead of I_{dd2} for the directional-diffuse intensity is evaluated by the function D which depends on wavelength, incidence angle θ_1 and viewing angles θ_2 and θ_3:

$$D(\lambda, \theta_1, \theta_2, \theta_3) = \frac{I_{dd2} - I_{dd1}}{I_{dd2}}$$

$$D = \frac{\left|\beta_{//}\hat{v}_x - \alpha_{//}\frac{\vec{v}.\vec{v}}{\hat{v}_z}\right|^2 + \left|\beta_\perp \hat{v}_x - \alpha_\perp \frac{\vec{v}.\vec{v}}{\hat{v}_z}\right|^2 - \left|\alpha_{//}\frac{\vec{v}.\vec{v}}{\hat{v}_z}\right| - \left|\alpha_\perp \frac{\vec{v}.\vec{v}}{\hat{v}_z}\right|}{\left|\beta_{//}\hat{v}_x - \alpha_{//}\frac{\vec{v}.\vec{v}}{\hat{v}_z}\right|^2 + \left|\beta_\perp \hat{v}_x - \alpha_\perp \frac{\vec{v}.\vec{v}}{\hat{v}_z}\right|^2}$$

270

It shall be noticed that D is independent of the surface parameters σ and τ. In order to

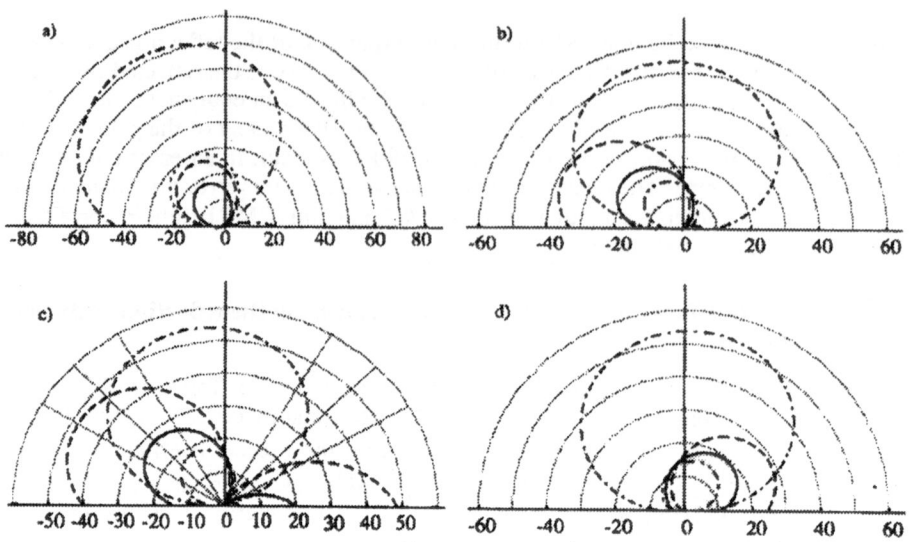

Fig. 3. a) Relative error for $\theta_1 = 60°$, $\theta_3 = 0°$ and for the four Meyer wavelengths:
—— 631.4 nm ····· 557.7 nm – – – 490.9 nm –·–·· 456.4 nm
b) c) d) Relative error for: b)$\theta_3 = 50°$ c)$\theta_3 = 0°$ d)$\theta_3 = 110°$
The four polar curves correspond to different values of the angle of incidence:
– – – $\theta_1=30°$ —— $\theta_1=45°$ –···–$\theta_1=60°$ –·–·· $\theta_1=80°$

estimate this error, we made a series of numerical simulations. The error was estimated for an I.T.F. of copper oxide (thickness $e = 800nm$) on a copper substrate. Figure 3a-d are polar representations of the relative error D as a function of the viewing angle θ_2 (the polar radius is D and the polar angle θ_2). Figure 3a displays the variations of D for an angle of incidence $\theta_1 = 60°$, in the plane of incidence ($\theta_3 = 0°$), for the four Meyer wavelengths [11]. It can be noticed that the error on the component with $\lambda = 631.4nm$ is quite small ($D = 18$ percent) whereas it is very important for the component with $\lambda = 456.4nm$ (about 73 percent). Similarly, the polar plots on Figures 3b,c,d represent the variations of the relative error in different viewing planes (characterised by angle θ_3) for several values of the angle of incidence θ_1 and for the red ($\lambda = 631.4nm$) component. It can be seen that the maximum value of the error strongly depends on the value of the incidence angle. For instance, in the plane of incidence (see Fig. 3b) the maximum of the error is 18 percent for $\theta_1 = 60°$ and 55 percent for $\theta_1 = 80°$. Note that the error is equal to zero for some values of the angle θ_2, which correspond to $v_x = 0$. As a conclusion, we can state that for given incidence and viewing angles, the relative error may be quite important, depending on the wavelength of light, and for a given wavelength and given viewing angles, the error can become very significant according to the angle of incidence of light.

5.4 Visualisation of the error

We have just seen that the relative error on the diffuse component was independent of the surface parameters (RMS height σ and correlation length τ) and could be great for some values of the angular parameters. The aim of this section is to appraise visually the difference between pictures rendered by both models according to the surface parameters.

The following pictures (see Appendix), generated by a spectral ray-tracing algorithm working on the four Meyer [11] wavelengths, display the evolution of the directional-diffuse component of light reflected by a system substrate-identical thin film according to the film parameters (correlation length τ, RMS height σ, film thickness). The spheres are made of a thin identical copper oxide film on a copper substrate (excepted for pictures 5c and 5f where the substrate is silver). The materials are characterised by their complex refractive indices, derived from experimental data for each one of the four Meyer wavelengths. The film spreading on the spheres was simulated by means of a sinusoidal variation of thickness from e_{max} at the top of the sphere to e_{min} at the bottom. Pictures 4-6 a, b, c were obtained by the use of formula (10) for the directional-diffuse intensity, whereas pictures 4-6 d, e, f were rendered by means of formula (11). The lighting consists of a single spherical light source situated behind the observer. It can be noticed that the visual differences between pictures rendered by the two models can be significant or negligible depending on the value of the film parameters. For instance there is a clear difference between pictures 4a and 4d: Fig. 4d displays a wider diffuse spot and a green fringe of interference which does not appear on figure 4a. As the correlation length increases with σ fixed at $100nm$ (see Fig. 4b and 4d), the surface becomes smoother with respect to the incident light, and the differences between the two pictures vanish (it can be noticed that the diffuse patch is smaller than on figures 4a and 4d: the surface becomes less diffuse as σ/τ decreases). Similarly, as the RMS height σ increases from $100nm$ to $130nm$ with τ fixed at $1.6\mu m$ (see figures 4c and 4f) the diffuse term spreads out slightly, but the visual differences between the two pictures remain small. Pictures 5a-f show the directional-diffuse term with σ and τ fixed at $100nm$ and $1\mu m$ respectively, for different values of the oxide film thickness, on a copper (5a,5b,5d,5e) or silver (5c,5f) substrate. It can be noted that whatever the thickness of the oxide film, pictures rendered by both models are quite different for such values of σ and τ. If now the ratio σ/τ is held constant at 0.1 (see figures 6a-f), increasing σ tends to attenuate the differences between pictures rendered by both models. As a conclusion, we can state that the influence of the surface parameters on the visual difference between the two models is clear: for given illumination and viewing angles, a visual difference which is not important can become significant for some values of the surface parameters.

Pictures 7a-d and 8 display scenes rendered by a full semi-global illumination model obtained by completing the local illumination model (see Section 4) by global reflection and transmission terms. Pictures 7a, 7b, 7c, 7d represent a piece of oxidised copper (Fig. 7a and 7b) or iron (Fig. 7c and 7d) piping illuminated by two spherical light sources. The thickness of the oxide film was taken to be a function of the space variables varying between 500 and $1000nm$. Pictures 7a and 7c were obtained by using formula (11) for the directional diffuse intensity whereas for pictures 7b and 7d, formula (10) was used. It can be noticed that on Fig. 7a, the yellow fringe is wider than on Fig. 7b, which exhibits a bigger green fringe of interference. The difference between Fig. 7c and Fig. 7d is less obvious, but the fringes seem brighter on Fig. 7c and the green interference fringe wider on Fig. 7d. The global reflection of the walls can be clearly observed on the iron piping.

Figure 8 depicts a set of saucepans made of an iron substrate coated with an iron oxide I.T.F.. The thickness of the oxide film on the discs forming the bottom of each saucepan is bounded by the values e_{min} and e_{max} (different for each saucepan) and increases irregularly from e_{min} at the centre of the disc to e_{max} at its edge. The reflection of the yellow table can be seen in the bottom of the saucepans. Computation times are similar to those obtained by any classic ray-tracing algorithm and quite identical for the two models. For instance rendering picture 7.b takes about half an hour for a resolution of 900x600, on a Pentium II 333 Mhz, whereas rendering Fig. 7a only takes 11 per cent more computation time.

6   Conclusions and future directions

We have presented a new illumination model for substrate-identical thin film-type systems. Based on scalar diffraction theories, it allows to evaluate with given accuracy the components of light reflected from a system substrate-identical thin film. We have shown both numerically and visually the consistency of this model by comparison with a simple classic approach. Future work consists in expanding this illumination model to account for systems of the kind substrate-general thin film (film with mutually independent rough boundaries) and to rough multilayer systems.

References

1. Beckmann, P., Spizzichino, A., "The Scattering of Electromagnetic Waves from Rough Surfaces", Pergamon Press, 1963.
2. Born, M. and Wolf, E, 1964, Principles of Optics (Pergamon Press, Oxford).
3. Callet, P., "Interférences, couches minces et peintures métallisées", International Journal of CADCAM and Computer Graphics, vol. 9, pp 251-264, Paris, 1994, Hermes.
4. Callet, P., "Couleur-lumière Couleur-matière", Diderot Editeur, Arts et Sciences, 1998.
5. Cook, R. L. and Torrance, K. E., "A Reflectance Model for Computer Graphics", ACM transactions on Graphics, 1, 1982, pp. 7-24.
6. Godlewski, J., Kalinowski, S., Davoli, I. and Bernardini, R., 1987, Thin Solid Films vol. 146, 115.
7. Gondek, J. S., Meyer, G. W, Newman, J.G., "Wavelength Dependent Reflectance Functions". Proceedings of Siggraph'94. In Computer Graphics.
8. He, X. D, Torrance, K. E., Sillion, F. X., Greenberg, D. P., "A Comprehensive Physical Model for Light Reflection", Computer Graphics, Vol. 25, N. 4, 1991.
9. Hecht, E., 1987, Optics, 2nd Edition, Adison-Wesley Publishing Co.
10. Icart, I. and Arquès, D., "An Approach to geometrical and Optical Simulation of Soap Froth", Computers & Graphics vol 23:3, Elsevier Science, 1999.
11. Meyer, G. W., "Wavelength Selection for Synthetic Image Generation", Computer Vision, Graphics and Image Processing, vol. 41, 57-59, 1988.
12. Ogilvy, J. A., "Theory of Wave Scattering from Random Rough Surfaces", Institute of Physics Publishing, Bristol and Philadelphia.
13. Ohlidal, I. and Lukes, F., "Ellipsometric parameters of rough surfaces and of a system substrate-thin films with rough boundaries", Opt. Commun. 5, 1972.
14. Ohlidal, I., Navratil, K., "Scattering of light from multilayer systems with rough boundaries", Progress in Optics, Vol. 34, Elsevier Science B.V, 1995.
15. Szczyrbowski, J., Dietrich, A. and Hoffmann H., 1982, Phys. Status Solidi a 69, 217.

Editors' Note: see Appendix, p. 375 for colored figures of this paper

Rendering of Wet Materials

Henrik Wann Jensen   Justin Legakis   Julie Dorsey

Laboratory for Computer Science
Massachusetts Institute of Technology

Abstract. The appearance of many natural materials is largely influenced by the environment in which they are situated. Capturing the effects of such environmental factors is essential for producing realistic synthetic images. In this work, we model the changes of appearance due to one such environmental factor, the presence of water or other liquids. Wet materials can look darker, brighter, or more specular depending on the type of material and the viewing conditions. These differences in appearance are caused by a combination of the presence of liquid on the surface and inside the material. To simulate both of these conditions we have developed an approach that combines a reflection model for surface water with subsurface scattering. We demonstrate our approach with a variety of example scenes, showcasing many characteristic appearances of wet materials.

Keywords: appearance, subsurface scattering, participating media, global illumination, Monte Carlo, rendering, ray tracing.

1 Introduction

It is well known that the appearance of materials is noticeably influenced by environmental factors. One common factor is the presence of water and other liquids, either on or within a material, leading to a "wet" appearance. For example, most rough or powdered materials, such as sand, asphalt, and clay, become darker when wet. Other materials, such as paper and cloth, become more transparent. Wet paper appears darker than dry paper under direct lighting conditions, but brighter than dry paper when illuminated from behind.

In these examples, the appearance is affected by water that has been absorbed into the material. A different situation can be observed when water is present on the surface of a material, such as water puddles on a road. The appearance of the road is changed so that it not only becomes darker but it also becomes more specular due to the smooth air-water interface.

The presence of water puddles on a road has been simulated in computer graphics by Nakamae et al. [12] for the purpose of driving simulations. They modeled water puddles using a two-layer reflection model with one layer of water above the asphalt. To account for the darkening of the road due to the presence of water, they use an empirical approach, introducing mud particles in the water and manually adjusting the diffuse and specular coefficients of the road. To simulate the transition from a dry road to a wet road with water puddles, they linearly interpolate the reflection coefficients and normal vectors of the smooth water surface and the bump-mapped asphalt. This approach made it possible to render some very convincing images. Dorsey et al. [4]

also applied an empirical approach to rendering surface water due to flow simulations, modulating the diffuse reflection depending on the wetness.

In the optics literature, there are two dominating theories regarding the appearance of wet materials, one considering a layer of water on the surface [10], and a second considering water inside the material [17]. In this paper we present a model that incorporates both of these theories, implemented in a general Monte Carlo subsurface scattering ray tracer. We find that these theories can be integrated effectively, and our results demonstrate that our model can be used to accurately simulate the appearance of wet materials.

1.1 Overview

The rest of this paper is organized as follows. In Section 2, we describe the two theories that explain why some materials change appearance when wet. We present our methods for rendering both surface and subsurface water effects in Section 3. In Section 4 we show our results of applying these methods to four test scenes. We discuss our results in Section 5, and in Section 6 we draw conclusions.

2 The Appearance of Wet Materials

There are two main reasons why materials look different when they are wet: a layer of water on the surface and a concentration of water beneath the surface. Both of these components influence the appearance of the material.

2.1 Water on the Surface

The presence of water on a surface (for example a puddle of water on a road) causes the surface to become specular due to the smooth air-water interface. The behavior of this interface is described by Fresnel's equations for dielectric media [3].

A thin water film on a Lambertian surface can also cause the surface to become darker [10]. The main cause for this darkening is the possibility of total internal reflection at the water-air boundary. Some of the light reflected from the Lambertian surface will be reflected back to the surface by the water-air interface. This light is then subject to another round of absorption by the surface (see Figure 1) before it is reflected again. This can lead to a sequence of multiple absorptions, resulting in a darkening of the surface.

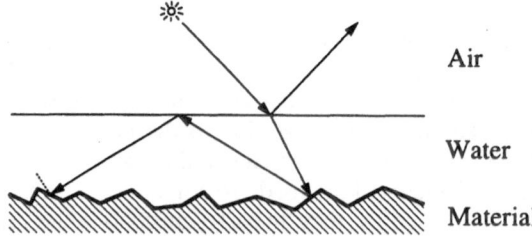

Fig. 1. A layer of water above the surface reflects less light due to the internal reflection at the water-air interface.

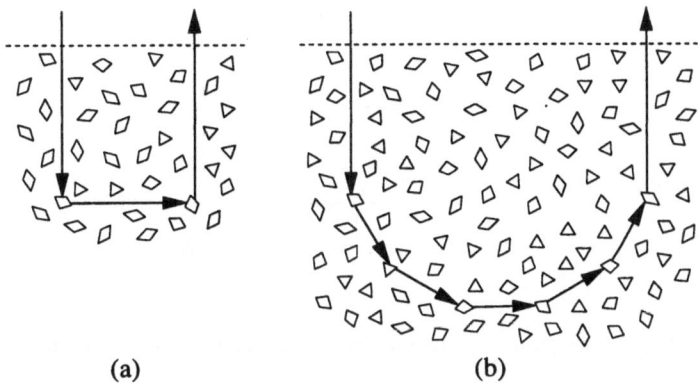

Fig. 2. After many scattering events, the shortest path a photon can take to leave the surface (a) with 90 degree average scattering angle and (b) with 30 degree average scattering angle. (Redrawn from [2].)

2.2 Water Beneath the Surface

The presence of water beneath the surface is another important factor influencing the appearance of a material. For rough or powdered materials, such as sand or clay, the water can usually enter regions previously filled with air. This changes the scattering properties of the material and makes the scattering more directional in the forward direction [17]. The main reason for this is that the index of refraction of water is higher than that of air and most often closer to that of the material. This again means that a ray of light entering the material will be refracted less due to the lower relative index of refraction. On a larger scale, this can be seen as a change in the scattering properties of the material, where the average scattering angle is reduced such that the scattered light diverges less from the previous ray. As illustrated in Figure 2, the influence of this reduced scattering angle on a ray of light is that it on average it undertakes a larger number of scattering events before leaving the surface. This increases the total amount of light that is absorbed, and the overall effect is a reduction in the reflectivity of the material.

3 Rendering Wet Materials

We use a combined surface and subsurface model to capture the appearance of wetness in and on a material. The surface model is used to simulate the interaction of light with a thin film of water or other liquid on the surface. The subsurface model is used to simulate the scattering properties of the material, and how they are changed by the presence of absorbed wetness.

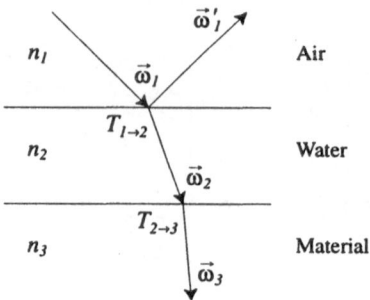

Fig. 3. Computing the light transmitted through a thin liquid film.

3.1 A Two-Layer Surface Reflection Model

To simulate the presence of a thin film of liquid on a surface, we use a two-layer reflection model. This model takes into account the interaction of light with both the air-liquid interface and the liquid-material interface (see Figure 3). By using Freṣnel's equation [3] we can compute the amount of light transmitted through each layer:

$$T_{1\to 2} = \left(\frac{n_1}{n_2}\right)^2 (1 - F_{1-2}(\vec{\omega}_1, n_1, n_2)) \qquad (1)$$

and

$$T_{2\to 3} = \left(\frac{n_2}{n_3}\right)^2 (1 - F^k_{2-3}(\vec{\omega}_2, n_2, n_3)), \qquad (2)$$

where n_1, n_2, and n_3 are the indices of refraction of air, the liquid, and the material respectively. $\vec{\omega}_2$ is the refracted direction into the liquid as given by Snell's law. F_{1-2} and F_{2-3} are the amount of reflected light at the air-liquid and the liquid-material interface respectively. The Fresnel term for the liquid-material interface is raised to a constant k. We use k as a simple technique for simulating surface roughness. A value of k larger than 1 increases the amount of light transmitted into the material — in particular for light entering the material at non-grazing angles.

The radiance leaving a surface, L_o, is computed as the sum of the reflected radiance, L_r and the transmitted radiance, L_t:

$$L_o(x, \vec{\omega}_1) = L_r(x, \vec{\omega}'_1) + L_t(x, \vec{\omega}_2), \qquad (3)$$

where $\vec{\omega}'_1$ is the direction of the reflected ray. Using Equations 1 and 2, we compute the transmitted radiance:

$$L_t(x, \vec{\omega}_2) = \left(\frac{n_1}{n_3}\right)^2 (1 - F_{1-2}(\vec{\omega}_1, n_1, n_2))(1 - F^k_{2-3}(\vec{\omega}_2, n_2, n_3))L_s(x, \vec{\omega}_3), \quad (4)$$

where L_s is the radiance due to subsurface scattering, and $\vec{\omega}_3$ is the refracted direction of the light as it enters the material. When light intersects the surface from the inside, we apply Equation 4 in reverse. Note that in this case there is the possibility of total internal reflection. For the shadow rays in the subsurface scattering simulation, we use Equation 4 to compute the amount of light entering the material at the point where the shadow ray intersects the medium. This assumes that the light source is distant compared to the optical thickness of the material.

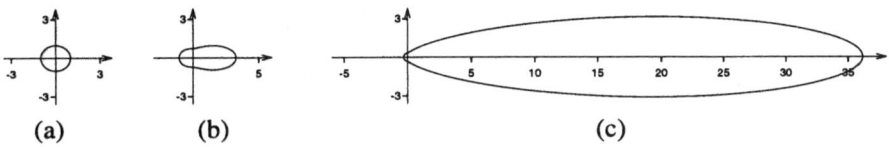

Fig. 4. Polar plots of the Henyey-Greenstein phase function. (a) $g_1 = g_2 = w = 0$, (b) $g_1 = 0.5$, $g_2 = 0.2$, $w = 0.5$, (c) $g_1 = 0.8$, $g_2 = 0.1$, $w = 0.8$.

3.2 Representing the Materials

Materials rendered with subsurface scattering are considered as participating media. The parameters controlling the appearance of participating media are the scattering coefficients, the absorption coefficients and the phase function. In a non-homogeneous medium these parameters can have different values depending on the position within the medium.

A number of different phase functions are available for different types of media. For the materials we consider here, the phase function is not known. One can assume that the sources of scattering (grains, cracks, air-bubbles, etc.) are larger than the wavelength of light [1] and thus the individual scattering events can be described reasonably well with Mie scattering [11]. Instead of simulating each scattering event, we use the empirical Henyey-Greenstein phase function [8] to approximate the accumulated effect of Mie scattering. To have control of both back scattering and forward scattering, we use the two-term Henyey-Greenstein phase function:

$$f(cos\theta, g_1, g_2, w) = w\frac{1 - g_1^2}{(1 - 2g_1 \cos\theta - g_1^2)^{1.5}} + (1-w)\frac{1 - g_2^2}{(1 - 2g_2 \cos\theta + g_2^2)^{1.5}}, \quad (5)$$

where θ is the angle between the current direction and the scattered direction. $g_1 \in [0, 1]$ controls forward scattering, $g_2 \in [-1, 0]$ controls backward scattering, and w is the weight of the forward scattering lobe relative to the backward scattering lobe. Figure 4 illustrates three configurations of the Henyey-Greenstein phase function.

4 Results

We have implemented the wetness model in a global illumination renderer. For the simulation of subsurface scattering we have implemented two techniques: Monte Carlo path tracing [15] and the volume photon map [9, 5]. For our results we have used the path tracing approach where practical. Even though this is slower than the photon map approach it has the advantage that the error from the subsurface scattering is visible only as noise.

All our results were rendered using a dual processor (Pentium II 400 MHz) PC running Linux, at a resolution of 1024x768. We supplied wetness functions and material parameters to all objects in our test scenes using a combination of hand-painted textures and procedural 3D functions [14].

Fig. 5. Wet Paper: (a) light source in front of the paper, (b) light source behind the paper.

4.1 Wet paper

Our first test scene demonstrates a wet spot on a piece of paper. The paper is modeled using an extruded Bezier patch with a thickness of 0.8 mm.

The wet spot is created by modulating the phase function from the dry value $g_1 = 0.05$, $g_2 = -0.05$ and $w = 0.2$ to the wet value $g_1 = 0.8$, $g_2 = -0.1$ and $w = 0.1$. This change makes the forward scattering much stronger, and this is the reason for the different appearance of the wet spot.

We rendered two versions of the paper scene: Figure 5(a) has the light source at the same side of the paper as the observer. As a result, the wet spot looks darker than the dry surrounding area. This is due to the fact that light striking the wet spot is scattered in the forward direction (away from the observer), while more light hitting the dry paper is scattered back toward the eye. Another observation is the increased translucency of the wet spot that can be observed by the fact that the pencil behind the paper is visible through the wet spot but not through the dry part of the paper. This, again, is due to increased forward scattering in the wet region. In Figure 5(b) we moved the light source behind the paper. This changes the appearance of the paper significantly. Due to the stronger forward scattering, the wet spot is brighter than the surrounding dry area.

For both paper scenes we used Monte Carlo path tracing using up to 1600 subsurface samples. Rendering the images took 110 and 190 minutes respectively. The high albedo of the paper (≈ 0.85) makes multiple scattering important, and it is the main reason why we used this relatively high number of sample rays.

4.2 Beach Scene

Our second test scene is a rock on a sandy beach. The model consists of 730,000 triangles, and we use subsurface scattering to render both the rock and the beach. We used procedural textures to control the scattering and absorption parameters of the rock and the sand. The wetness in this scene was modeled using a sum of turbulence functions simulating the water left from the four previous waves. Based on the wetness we changed the forward scattering from 0.1 to 0.8 for the rock and from 0.2 to 0.7 for the sand.

We rendered four different images of the beach scene. Figure 6(a) shows a completely dry version of the scene. Both the rock and the sand look light and diffuse.

In Figure 6(b) we have rendered the beach scene after applying the wetness function. Notice how the sand and the lower part of the rock look much darker.

To investigate the relative contribution of the surface model and the subsurface model, we rendered the beach scene from Figure 6(b) again but with water covering all of the rock. The result is shown in Figure 6(c). Note that the top of the rock does not look significantly darker. The main difference is at grazing angles, where the rock is more specular due to the smoother air-water interface. The main result of the presence of water on the rock is that it has a glazed appearance. Our final rendering of the beach scene is shown in Figure 6(d). Both the sand and the rock are completely wet and, as a result, much darker.

We rendered these images using Monte Carlo path tracing with approximately 500 subsurface samples. The rendering time was from 180 minutes for the dry scene to 300 minutes for the completely wet scene. The increase in rendering time for the wet material is mainly caused by the increased number of subsurface samples (as shown in Figure 2). The rendering time for this scene was largely due to the procedural 3D textures used for the stone material and the wetness function.

4.3 Spilled Cognac

Our last test scene shows a glass of cognac spilled on a wood table. The cognac glass is modeled as a surface of revolution clipped to form three separate dielectric interfaces: air-glass, air-cognac and cognac-glass. The wood table is rendered with subsurface scattering. A 2D texture map was used to control the absorption and scattering coefficients for the wood. This is similar to the way a 2D texture would be used to control the color of a surface-based wood material. By using a 2D texture for subsurface scattering, we assume that the scattering and absorption coefficients are constant in the direction orthogonal to the table. This is a reasonable approximation considering that most of the scattering happens close to the surface.

The wet area is another 2D texture map projected into the table and used for the subsurface samples. Since cognac is a colored liquid, we used the wetness function to modulate not only the phase function parameters but also the scattering and absorption coefficients. Note that we did not change the scattering and absorption coefficients to make the material look darker; the darkening is caused only by the change to the phase function. We used a bump map based on the wetness map to modify the normals at the edge of the spilled cognac. This mainly affects the highlights on the spilled cognac, but nonetheless adds to the impression that a liquid is present *on* the surface.

For the cognac scene we used the photon map approach [9] since Monte Carlo path tracing is too inefficient for sampling the caustic below the cognac glass. Note that this caustic as well as the rest of the indirect illumination of the table is due to photons stored in the volume photon map. Since the photons are stored in the wood medium and not just on the wood surface, we have to use more photons than for a surface-based approach. We used two million photons for this scene. The image was rendered with 4 samples per pixel in 28 minutes. The background is blurry due to a lens simulation.

5   Discussion and Future Work

A legitimate criticism of our approach is that we did not directly compare the predictions of our model with experiment. The predictions of our model and the influence of measured material parameters should be checked carefully.

Our results indicate that subsurface scattering is the most significant reason why materials are darker when wet. Water present on the surface of a material simply adds a "glazed" appearance. This observation is based on our assumption of how the phase function changes when water is applied to the material. We have been adjusting the phase function parameters to make the images look convincing. It would be very interesting if real measurements of phase function parameters were available for dry and wet materials in order to verify the results.

Real measurements would also be helpful for the absorption and scattering coefficients. For these parameters we also selected values to make the images look convincing.

Measuring the parameters for subsurface scattering is difficult, especially for non-homogeneous materials. An alternative to using measured data would be the use of a virtual gonio-reflectometer [18]. The main difficulty with this approach would be in modeling of the volumetric structure of the material.

A virtual gonio-reflectometer could also be used to compute a BRDF approximation for the subsurface scattering, similar to the approach of Hanrahan and Krueger [7]. We have not used this approach since we wanted to test the validity of the theories for wet materials without being limited by the BRDF. Moreover, the use of only a BRDF precludes the simulation of non-homogeneous materials with three-dimensional wetness functions.

One open issue that still needs to be addressed is the rendering of wet materials that are not dielectric. In our implementation, we use Fresnel's formula for dielectric surfaces. In contrast, the problem with conducting materials, such as metals, is that they are opaque. Consequently, subsurface scattering is less likely to occur. For conducting materials with a structure where subsurface scattering does occur, it will be primarily due to reflection rather than refraction. Therefore, a change in the index of refraction of the surrounding medium will have little effect.

It would also be interesting to combine the rendering of wet materials with actual simulations of the patterns due to the flow of water over surfaces [4].

We use a simple non-adaptive ray marching technique for integration inside a non-homogeneous medium. Making this ray marcher adaptive could reduce the number of evaluations of the functions controlling the behavior of the medium. This could have a large impact on the rendering times in particular when we use the costly turbulence function [14] to control the material structure.

6 Conclusion

We have presented a model that incorporates two theories for rendering wet materials: two-layer surface reflection and subsurface scattering. We have shown that not only do each of these theories produce convincing results, but they can be used in conjunction effectively. Our experiments have found the consideration of water inside the material to have the most dramatic effect. Using a full subsurface scattering simulation allowed us to render objects with translucency. Not only were we able to achieve the characteristic darkening of thick wet materials, but we were also able to render the increased translucency of thin materials caused by the absorption of water.

Acknowledgments

Thanks to Craig F. Bohren and to the reviewers for their helpful comments. This work was supported by an Alfred P. Sloan Research Fellowship (BR-3659), an NSF CAREER award (CCR-9624172), an NSF Postdoctoral Research Associates award (EIA-9806139), and an NSF CISE Research Infrastructure award (EIA-9802220).

References

1. Michael Bass (editor), *Handbook of Optics*, McGraw-Hill, Inc., 1995.
2. C.F. Bohren, *Clouds in a Glass of Beer*, Wiley, New York, 1987.
3. Max Born and Emil Wolf, *Principles of Optics*, Cambridge University Press, Cambridge, 1997.
4. Julie Dorsey, Hans K. Pedersen and Pat Hanrahan, "Flow and changes in appearance", *Proceedings of ACM SIGGRAPH 96*, pages 411–420, 1996.
5. Julie Dorsey, Alan Edelman, Henrik Wann Jensen, Justin Legakis and Hans K. Pedersen, "Modeling and Rendering of Weathered Stone", *Proceedings of ACM SIGGRAPH 99*.
6. Roy Hall, *Illumination and Color in Computer Generated Imagery*, Springer-Verlag, 1988.
7. Pat Hanrahan and Wolfgang Krueger, "Reflection from Layered Surfaces due to Subsurface Scattering", *In Proceedings of ACM SIGGRAPH 93*, pages 165–174, 1993.
8. L. G. Henyey and J. L. Greenstein, "Diffuse Radiation in the Galaxy", *Astrophysics Journal*, vol. 93, pages 70–83, 1941.
9. Henrik Wann Jensen and Per H. Christensen, "Efficient Simulation of Light Transport in Scenes with Participating Media using Photon Maps", *Proceedings of ACM SIGGRAPH 98*, pages 311-320, 1998.
10. John Lekner and Michael C. Dorf, "Why Some things are darker when wet", *Applied Optics*, vol. 27, no. 7, pages 1278–1280, 1988.
11. Gustav Mie, "Beiträge zur Optik trübcr Medien, speziell Kolloidaler Metallösungen", *Annalen der Physik*, vol. 25(3), pages 377–445, 1908.
12. Eihachiro Nakamae, Kazufumi Kaneda, Takashi Okamoto and Tomoyuki Nishita, "A Lighting Model Aiming at Drive Simulators", *In Proceedings of ACM SIGGRAPH 90*, pages 395–404, 1990.
13. F. E. Nicodemus, J. C. Richmond, J. J. Hsia. I. W. Ginsberg and T. Limperis, *Geometric Considerations and Nomenclature for Reflectance*, *National Bureau of Standards*, 1977.
14. Ken Perlin, "An image synthesizer", *Proceedings of ACM SIGGRAPH 85*, pages 287–296, 1985.
15. Holly Rushmeier, *Realistic Image Synthesis for Scenes with Radiatively Participating Media*, Ph.d. thesis, Cornell University, 1988.
16. Robert Siegel and John R. Howell, *"Thermal Radiation Heat Transfer"*, Hemisphere Publishing Corporation, 1992.
17. Sean A. Twomey, Craig F. Bohren and John L. Mergenthaler, "Reflectance and albedo differences between wet and dry surfaces", *Applied Optics*, vol. 25, no. 3, pages 431–435, 1986.
18. Stephen H. Westin, James R. Arvo and Kenneth E. Torrance, "Predicting Reflectance Functions from Complex Surfaces", *Proceedings of ACM SIGGRAPH 92*, pages 255–264, 1992.

Editors' Note: see Appendix, p. 376 for colored figures of this paper

Rendering Inhomogeneous Surfaces with Radiosity

L. Mostefaoui, J.M. Dischler and D. Ghazanfarpour

Laboratoire MSI
E.N.S.I.L. – Université de Limoges
TECHNOPOLE 87068 Limoges Cedex- France

Abstract. Natural surfaces are often complex: they nearly always exhibit small scale imperfections such as dirt, dust, cracks, etc., as well as large scale structural elements, as for wickerwork, brick walls, textiles, pebbles, etc., that are generally too complex to be modeled explicitly. In this paper, we propose a new multi-scale periodic texture model adapted to the efficient simulation of the previously mentioned features. This new model combines notions of virtual ray tracing (that we have recently introduced) with bi-directional texture function, while it also considers self-shadowing and inter-reflections at texture scale. In a second step, the texture model is integrated into hierarchical radiosity with clustering. Therefore, an extension of radiosity techniques, currently limited to texture maps, bump maps and general (homogeneous) reflectance functions, is proposed. The final rendering consists of applying a second ray tracing pass, based on a gathering methodology adapted to the model. The method provides images at a significant lower computation and memory consumption cost than with "explicit" models in the case of periodic features (wickerwork, grids, pavements, etc.) for a similar visual quality.

1 Introduction

Most natural surfaces such as streets, textiles, walls, floors, etc., are not uniform, neither concerning the local geometry (wrinkles, cracks, etc.), nor concerning the reflectance behavior: color variation, and more generally non constant bi-directional reflectance distribution function (BRDF). Various texturing techniques such as texture mapping, "Bump mapping" Blinn [1], solid texturing [2, 3], displacement mapping [4], hypertexturing [5], texel mapping [6], etc. have been developed in computer graphics to simulate such complex effects. All of these techniques help to enrich the visual quality of the scenes, without increasing the geometric complexity, e.g. the number of patches.

In spite of their importance, only a low number of radiosity approaches have addressed the problem of integrating textures, or more generally "inhomogeneous" surfaces. In [7], a first method was proposed for texture maps by considering an average color on the patches. [8] proposed an efficient hierarchical technique, based on a Galerkin radiosity. The problem of including bump maps into radiosity simulations was addressed in [9]. Also general reflectance behaviors (general BRDFs) were considered in [10]. However, this model does not consider inhomogeneous cases, that is, a BRDF variation over the patches. Likewise, we recently developed a method allowing for procedural features (displacement maps, hypertextures, fractals, etc.) to be integrated into radiosity simulations without using intermediate "high precision" meshes [14]. But, the formulation is not hierarchical. In addition "micro-scale" inter-reflection phenomena are not considered (inter-reflections at texture scale). Currently, complex features are integrated into radiosity simulations using a high rate subdivision into small triangles. The resulting geometric complexity is often enormous and overloads the memory and computation capacity (in spite of clustering strategies [11, 12]). In fact, finite elements techniques still suffer from being limited to scenes of rather poor visual complexity, compared to ray tracing (or more generally path tracing) rendered scenes that already reach impressive performances [13].

The aim of this paper is to propose a texture model adapted to the efficient realistic rendering of the previously mentioned complex surface structures, and to integrate this model into hierarchical radiosity simulations with clustering. Our texture model is adapted to the rendering of periodic features (as for texel maps) such as for example wickerwork. It is based on the notion of bi-directional texture function (BTF), that was introduced in [15], and combines it with our virtual ray tracing technique [19] (see next section).

Once defined, the texture model is integrated into hierarchical radiosity simulations with clustering by generalizing the approaches of [20, 21] to the consideration of non-constant BRDFs over patches. We assume that the entire energy received by a piece of patch (covering a piece of the texture) is scattered towards all directions according to an average BRDF corresponding to that piece of texture. As opposed to radiosity for general reflectance functions [10], we consider different BRDFs at different levels of the patch hierarchy. In practice, we also used a discrete decomposition of the hemisphere into bins, as opposed to spherical harmonics.

Final pictures are computed using a gathering step based on ray tracing, which is necessary because of the inhomogeneous nature of the patches. Since the final gathering step is usually time consuming, we adapted the methodology to the use of bilinear interpolations, which is similar to techniques developed in [22, 23]. However, we also estimate the variance to avoid excessively smoothing shadows and discontinuities.

In the next section, we first present our multi-scale texture model. In section 3, this model is integrated into radiosity simulations. Then, we show how texture-scale light scattering effects can be pre-computed on samples, in particular inter-reflections at texture scale. In section 5, we explain the final rendering technique, based on ray tracing. Finally, in the last section, we show some graphical results, as well as a performance study.

2 Modeling inhomogeneous surfaces

The texture principle presented [15], consists of using a map (like a usual texture map), that, instead of containing a color information on each pixel, contains a "full" BRDF. Such a map is called a bi-directional texture function. Because of the very important storage requirements of BRDF MIP-maps [16] (a thin 128^2 MIP-map for example requires storing 21845 BRDFs), we proposed in [19] a BTF model limited to the consideration of some finite sets of materials only. The formulation is reduced to a view dependent multi-resolution map of normals, colors, transparencies, etc.

Generally, there are two problems common to nearly all approaches based on discrete multi-resolution samples [17, 18, 19]: memory consumption and the fact that the sampling may become visible in some cases (for example the pixels of a low resolution texture map). For this reason, it becomes interesting in some cases to keep a continuous description of the considered domain. A continuous description avoids the problem of visible sampling and excessive memory consumption, while aliasing can be partly prevented using oversampling.

In this paper, we follow the suggestion of [17] by preserving both levels of the texture description: a continuous one (rendered directly using the virtual ray tracing technique developed in [19]), and a sampled one (a BRDF MIP-map) for efficient antialiasing in extreme cases. The height of the MIP-map pyramid determines the memory consumption / computational efficiency ratio, while the continuous description allows us to avoid the "pixel" effects. Figure 1 illustrates the principle of combining BRDF MIP- maps with virtual ray tracing. A periodic texture is first modeled by the user using a usual geometric modeler, such that the continuity, when repeating the sample, is preserved (as for the wickerwork model in figure 1). This geometry can be mapped directly onto a 3D surface S using a kind of "secondary" ray tracing technique that we called "virtual ray tracing" [19].

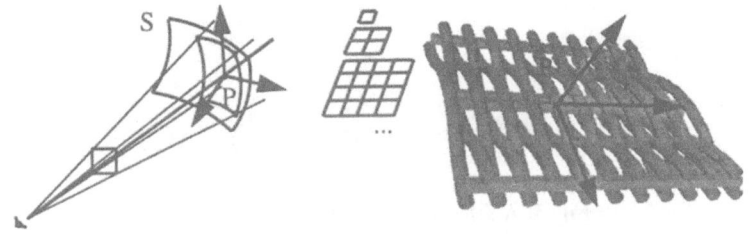

Fig. 1. Combining virtual ray tracing with BRDF MIP-maps (BTFs).

A computer simulation (as it has been done in [25], for example) can be used to compute a BRDF corresponding to the previously modeled texture. In our case, we directly use the radiosity technique developed in the next section. The left part of figure 2 illustrates the BRDF that we obtained for the wickerwork of figure 1. In the same way, it is also possible to compute BRDFs corresponding to sub-parts of the texture, and thus to build a complete BRDF MIP-map pyramid $\Gamma(l, u, v, \lambda)$. l represents the level in the hierarchy, $1 \leq u, v \leq 2^{l-1}$, and λ the wavelength. Figure 1 shows a pyramid of height three. Furthermore, transmittance can be considered (as shown in the middle part of figure 2), by constructing a BTDF (bi-directional transmittance distribution function) MIP-map. We also consider an "opacity" coefficient, which accounts for "holes" in the texture (as for a grid). Therefore, we compute a "transparency" coefficient representing the portion of energy that goes through the texture without any changes (as opposed to the BTDF). The right part of figure 2 shows the transparency (the ratio of holes) for the wickerwork. This coefficient is only view dependent as opposed to the bi-directional nature of the BRDF and BTDF. Though it is possible to include the transparency directly as a part of the transmittance (BTDF), we separated both. The reason is that both can be handled differently during the radiosity simulation, as will be explained in the next section.

We now dispose of two texture descriptions: a continuous geometric model, and a discrete pyramid. Both can be combined during rendering as follows. Oversampling is first applied. Therefore, each pixel is sampled into a certain number of sub-pixels. For each of these sub-pixels, we determine a compression rate to find out the "appropriate" level into the MIP-map (recent investigations have been made on determining that level [24] efficiently). If the level does not exist (below the bottom of the pyramid), we use for the shading computation the virtual ray tracing technique, which avoids "pixel" effects. For all of our examples (see results), we used at most pyramids of height two or three (as shown in figure 1).

Unfortunately, the previously described combination of virtual ray tracing with

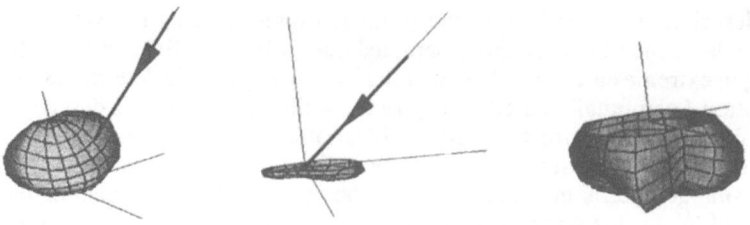

Fig. 2. BRDF, BTDF and view dependent "transparency" obtained for the wickerwork sample.

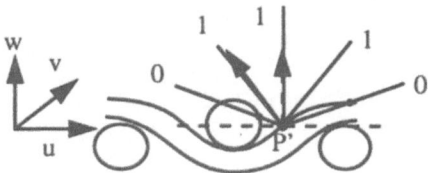

Fig. 3. A self-shadowing directional map.

BRDF MIP-maps might introduce a certain discontinuity at those regions of the textured surface S that are precisely at mid-way between the virtual ray tracing level and the bottom level of the BRDF pyramid. The reason is that the BRDF accounts for all "internal" light reflection phenomena, as opposed to the virtual ray tracing technique. These phenomena are mainly: inter- reflections at texture scale and self-shadowing. Some parts of the texture may emit energy directly towards neighboring parts, or on the contrary may cast some shadows. The problem of inter-reflections at texture scale will be discussed in section 4. The problem of self-shadowing can be resolved as for bump mapping [29] within the virtual ray tracing computation, by shooting secondary rays in different directions. In fact, it is possible to build a directional shadow map on the texture point P' (see figure 3) to obtain a hemisphere of Boolean values (or a sphere in the case of transparent textures), that can be used as indicator during the shading computation. Results concerning self-shadowing are given in section 4, in parallel with examples concerning inter-reflections.

3 Hierarchical radiosity with clustering

Once the texture has been modeled, it needs to be integrated into realistic rendering and lighting simulation techniques. Radiosity allows us to determine the global lighting of the scene using as subdivision into finite elements. We will integrate our textures into hierarchical radiosity simulations with clustering, including general reflectance functions [20, 21]. However, we do not consider "mirror-like" specular to diffuse transfers, but only directional diffuse transfers, mainly because of simplicity.

We will consider four kinds of energy transfers: (1) direct transfers, (2) reflected indirect transfers, (3) transmitted indirect transfers, and finally (4) direct transfers going through patches that have holes (in fact, (1) and (4) represent the same type of transfer; the only difference is the way that the visibility is processed). Note that in the case of transmittance, it becomes necessary to consider double-sided patches, which also doubles the radiance information to be stored. Often, the transmittance can be neglected (for example for a grid), the predominance being mainly "transparency" (the proportion of holes).

The different energy exchanges taking place in a scene can be described as an integral equation, generally called in computer graphics the "rendering equation" [26]. In the case of scenes, composed of patches, we obtain:

$$L_{out}^r = L_e + \sum_{i=1}^{Np} \int_{A_i} L_{in} \rho_r(\vec{d_{in}}, \vec{d_{out}}, u, v) \frac{\cos(\theta)\cos(\theta')}{r^2} V dA_i$$

where L_{out}^r represents the outgoing radiance, Np the number of patches, ρ_r the BRDF and V the visibility. The same applies for the transmittance with ρ_t, the BTDF. Note that for including the textures, we need to consider an "inhomogeneous" structure on the patches. Therefore, the BRDF ρ_r, as well as the BTDF ρ_t, were both made (u, v) dependent in our equations. Various radiosity techniques have been developed to resolve the radiance equation presented above. We will combine the method of [10], developed for general reflectance functions, with the clustering strategy of Smits et al. [12]. It turns out that the transcription is straightforward.

Recall that in the previous section, we have computed a BRDF MIP-map $\Gamma(l, u, v, \lambda)$ (respectively a BTDF map) corresponding to the texture world. These BRDFs (respectively BTDFs) describe the mean reflectance (respectively transmittance) properties of the texture at different scales. As for [10], we need to store a directional energy emission information (an energy hemisphere, or two in the case of transmittance) on each patch (and sub-patch if introduced during the hierarchical radiosity). For practical reasons, we used a discrete decomposition of the hemisphere into bins, as opposed to spherical harmonics. We shall assume that one initial patch matches the size of the modeled texture sample (figure 4.a); that is, the mapping makes the vertices of the patch match the four corners of the texture sample. Thus, the global mean reflectance property of the patch is entirely captured by the corresponding top level of the texture BRDF pyramid, provided that the distortion introduced by the mapping is not too important. Also, the reflectance behavior of eventually introduced sub-patches, is captured by the corresponding lower levels in the pyramid. We note that for triangular patches, that generally cover triangular parts of the texture map, it is also possible to build BRDF pyramids matching these triangular parts. In the remainder of this paper, we mainly consider quadrilateral patches. Now, the energy transfer from one source patch P_i to another receiver patch P_j (figure 4.b), is given by:

$$L_{P_j} = L_{e,P_j} + \int_{P_i} L_{P_i} \Gamma_{P_j} \frac{\cos(\theta)\cos(\theta')}{r^2} V dP_i$$

where L_{P_j} represents the outgoing radiance. As for [10], we may use a disk approximation by sampling the emitter into N sub-elements. Normally, due to the inhomogeneous nature of the patches, each element emits the energy in a different way, which has been discussed in [27] in the case of general light sources. Storing on each patch multiple elements, where each of these elements contains its own energy hemisphere is unfortunately extremely memory consuming. Therefore, we actually stored on the emitter patch (and all of its sub-patches) only the global mean (directional) outgoing energy, plus for patches that have no sub-patches at most four elements (four hemispheres) to get more precise results. Since, sub-patches contain their own energy emission hemispheres, it is not necessary to store additional explicit elements. For example, the emitter P_i of figure 4.b contains four sub-patches, and one of these sub-patches contains again four. If we approximate the energy transfer from P_i to P_j using four disks,

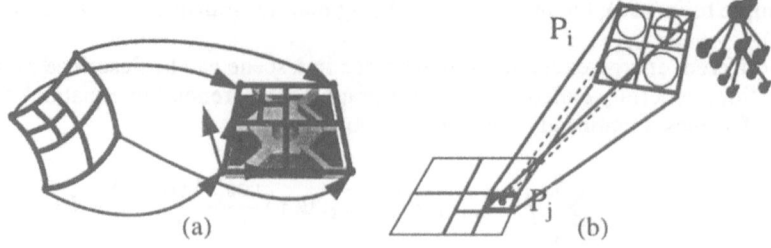

Fig. 4. (a) The vertices of the patch must match the corners of the texture map. (b) extended energy transfer, considering different BRDFs for inhomogeneous surfaces.

then we will consider the energy hemispheres of the four sub-patches, instead of that of P_i. Note also that it is important to use the appropriate BRDF level of the pyramid on the receiver P_j according to its depth in the hierarchy, since the BRDF is not constant across P_j (in the formula we called $\Gamma_{P_j} = \Gamma_{l,u,v,\lambda}$, where l, u, v are chosen according to the position of P_j in the hierarchy). We finally obtain following approximate transfer formula:

$$L_{P_j} = L_{e,P_j} + \sum_{k=1}^{N} L_{P_i}^k \Gamma_{P_j} \frac{\cos(\theta_k)\cos(\theta_k')\pi\delta P_i^k}{\delta P_i^k + \pi r^2} V_k$$

Once the transfer is completed, the energy is pushed / pulled inside the patch hierarchy by simple addition of the energy hemispheres (downwards, the energy is split according to the respective areas of the sub-patches). Apart from the transfer between two patches, there is no real difference with usual hierarchical radiosity. The same error bounds and "oracles" can be used to decide whether to subdivide or not. Also clustering can be processed identically. We used a technique based on α-links (as described in [12]) using a BFA criterion (radiosity, form factor and area). Before shooting the energy from one cluster towards an other cluster or towards a certain patch, the energies of all included patches (the leafs of the cluster) are summed up according to an internal visibility, that is computed using a software Z-buffer technique. Inversely, all energy received by a certain cluster is directly distributed among the enclosed patches. This process allows us to avoid storing a certain spherical energy information on each clusters. For the internal visibility, it is just important to consider the eventual low opacity of some patches. We used a software Z-buffer technique, that first projects all of the opaque patches, and then the transparent ones (with similarity to alpha maps). If transmittance is considered, patches are double-sided (they contain two hemispheres), thus, it is important to take into account the particular orientation of a certain patch.

4   Inter-reflections at texture scale

As we have mentioned in section 2, some parts of the geometric features of the texture might emit some energy directly towards neighboring features. For rather "flat" textures, this term can be completely neglected, as opposed to rough textures. Computing an inter-reflection term for textures, actually has some similarity with the estimation of irradiance values within complex geometric structures. Often statistical approaches are used. In our case, the textures are periodic, and repeated over the surfaces. This opens

Fig. 5. An example of inter-reflection at texture scale.

the way to a simpler deterministic approach. In fact, we shall simplify the model by considering only the secondary indirect illumination (obtained after one bounce only). Let A be the radiance leaving a point P' of a patch i of the texture world, due to the secondary reflections occurring in the texture, when the latter is illuminated by a certain radiance L. A can be linearly expressed as $A = LF_i(\alpha, \beta)$, where F is a function depending only on the incoming directions (α, β) of the incident radiance L. F is also assumed to be view "independent", which excludes high specularity, and relates it to the irradiance.

The function $F_i(\alpha, \beta)$ (one for each patch of the texture) can be directly computed "on the fly" during the BRDF pyramid construction technique that we have presented in section 2, since we basically apply a radiosity simulation, that can be used to compute also the secondary reflections.

Figure 5 illustrates an example of texture. From left to right, the figures illustrate: first, the initial energy, due to the direct illumination only, second, the result after considering secondary reflections , and last (on the right) the difference between the two previous results, e.g. the total secondary indirect illumination. We obtained this result for an illumination due to a normalized incoming radiance (as shown by the arrow). Since L has been normalized, the result of the right figure can be used directly as value for the function F_i for this direction. Applying the same technique for all directions, we obtain for each patch i of the texture world, the corresponding function $F_i(\alpha, \beta)$.

We note that it is important to duplicate the texture for the computation of F_i, otherwise there would be visual artifacts, especially on the patches at the "frontiers" of the texture (they don't have neighbors if the texture is not repeated).

The left part of figure 6 illustrates some tori, rendered using the virtual ray tracing technique (inter-reflections are already implicitly considered when the BRDF pyramid is used, as opposed to virtual ray tracing). The left picture shows the result using no inter-reflection and no self-shadowing. The middle picture integrated self-shadowing, and the last one all effects. Note that there is no real difference between the two pictures on the right, except on the shadow regions in the texture that are completely black for the middle part, as opposed to the right one.

5 Rendering using ray tracing

The radiosity simulation provides a global solution of the rendering equation. Unfortunately, only mean values are given on the patches. These mean values cannot be turned into individual radiance values (at least without introducing serious errors) in the case of important variances (for example of the local BRDF). Final gathering [28] is a technique that helps to improve the quality of the final rendering. It has been used in the context of radiosity with clustering, as for example in [21], or in the context of Monte Carlo techniques, as for example in [23]. This technique is best suited for inhomogeneous surfaces, since it consists in a complete re-computation of the integral equation. In addition, it provides high quality results.

Basically, the global solution computed by the radiosity simulation can be "re-used" to compute the outgoing radiance on each point P of a surface S, by summing up over the hemisphere of P (a sphere in the case of transmittance). Rays can be "re-traced" towards all clusters (or patches) to determine more precisely shadows. Unfortunately, using a complete integration on all points of the scene induces excessive computational requirements, making such an "extremely accurate" approach nearly unusable in practice. To avoid such an excessive computation, we use interpolations in regions of low variance by constructing a data structure similar to the 5D tree of [22], except that we use a 4D tree (two dimensions for the surface u and v parameters and two for the directions). In [14], we also used a similar approach. Nonetheless, to avoid excessively smoothing sharp shadows, we also keep track of those clusters and patches that produce important variations. Therefore, we also add a "gathering" list l_i to the data structure.

Let be P_i the patch containing the point P, where the shading must be computed. If P_i is "visited" for the first time, a certain data structure is initialized (the data structure consists of a hemisphere of energy on each vertex, plus the gathering list l_i). For each cluster Cl_j (or eventually each patch P_j at the lowest level) – starting from the global scene cluster, and refining according to an error bound criterion, with similarity to radiosity – the amount of incoming radiance is computed on the vertices of P_i (as well as on some randomly chosen points to get a better estimation of the variance). If the variance of energy is below a given error threshold ϵ, then the radiance coming from Cl_j (or respectively P_j) is stored in the 4D structure (in the hemisphere defined on each vertex, which has been previously initialized to zero). Otherwise Cl_j (or respectively P_j) is added to the gathering list l_i. Now, the shading on P can be computed by using both the hemispheres on the vertices (using a bilinear interpolation, as done in [22] in a 3D case) and the list l_i. For the latter, stochastic rays are traced, since these clusters (respectively patches) produce important variances (shadow frontiers for example). The data structure on P_i needs only be computed once. For low variances the list l_i will be nearly empty, thus only a very low number of rays will be traced, which considerably accelerates the rendering (compared to usual gathering). On the other hand, some discontinuities may appear in the case of high error bounds around the patches, since for two neighboring patches, the gathering lists may be different.

6 Results

Figure 7 illustrates a comparison between using textures and using "explicit" models. The two upper pictures correspond to the texturing approach. In this case, the scene contains only 1165 patches. The radiosity simulation required 13 seconds on an PC Pentium II 350MHz with 128Mb RAM for 3 iterations and with a low error bound of 1.0 (this corresponds to 0.4 percent of the initial light source value). 2870 links were created and the memory required for storing the scene and during the radiosity was about 3.1Mb. The left part shows the final result obtained with the previously described ray tracing approach without considering self-shadows. We used a medium error bound $\epsilon = 0.1$ to decide whether or not to add the emitter to the gathering list. The rendering took 33.2 minutes for a resolution of 500x400 pixels, with 9 rays per pixel. An average of 2 gathering rays per patch point was traced. The right part shows the result with self-shadows (the difference is mainly visible on the walls). In this case, the ray tracing took about 85 minutes.

The bottom part of figure 7 illustrates an approach based on "explicit" patches. In this case, the scene contains 65477 patches. The radiosity simulation required 16.22 minutes for 4 iterations and with an error bound criterion of 2.0 (this corresponds to 1.0 percent of the initial light source value). 12407 links were created and the memory required was about 31.2Mb. The obvious difference concerning the computation time and memory requirement of the radiosity compared to the texturing approach is mainly due to the fact that there are nearly 53 times more patches. The ray tracing required 24.5 minutes. Unfortunately, we could not run the previously described gathering methodology because of memory limitations (storing lists and hemispheres on more than 100000 vertices was not possible). We also tried to apply a gathering step without "optimization" using interpolations, but in this case the computation time became excessive (we stopped the computation after several hours). The rendering shows only an interpolation on the patches, in particular the shadows are of poor quality. Nonetheless, it allows a visual comparison with the texturing approach. For example, we used a self-shadow map of low resolution (8x4 directions), which may explain the difference on the bottom of the walls. Also the mapping has "stretched" the spheres.

We note that it would be interesting to develop a fast technique to directly visualize the radiosity solution in the case of textures, without using a final ray tracing approach.

Figure 8 illustrates an additional example. All of the surfaces except the ceiling are textured (even the floor). We show results for two different lighting conditions. The radiosity solution for both figures required approximately 3 minutes, and the final ray tracing 40 minutes (left) and 130 minutes (right). The difference is due to the number of light sources.

7 Conclusion

In this paper, a solution for integrating general inhomogeneous surfaces (surfaces with complex non-constant reflectance behaviors and complex macro-geometry) into radiosity simulations was proposed. Therefore, some light scattering behaviors were precomputed at different scales using simulations similar to BRDF computation techniques. Nearly all inter-reflection phenomena, including inter-reflections at texture scale and self-shadowing, were considered. Aliasing was also addressed using a transition between virtual ray tracing and BRDF MIP-maps (BTFs). The final gathering step provides high precision results, while the hierarchical formulation and the error bounds allow one to control the ratio between quality and computational efficiency. The method can also be extended (with minor changes only) to more advanced texturing techniques such as texel maps for example.

However, several topics need to be further investigated. For example, in this paper, we do not consider specular to diffuse transfers, but only directional diffuse transfers. Therefore, caustics (due to metal links [19] for example) cannot be rendered. An other important problem is the fact that we always repeat "the same" texture sample (periodicity), as for texel mapping. For some random textures (street pavement for example), the repetition effect might become unpleasant.

References

1. Blinn J.F., "Simulation of wrinkled surfaces", Computer Graphics 12, 1978, pp. 286–292.
2. K. Perlin, "An Image Synthesizer", Computer Graphics 19(3), 1985, pp. 287–296.
3. Peachey D., "Solid Texturing on complex Surfaces", Computer Graphics 19(3), 1985, pp. 279–286.

292

4. R.L. Cook, "Shade Trees", Computer Graphics 18 (Siggraph'84), pp. 223–231, 1984.
5. K. Perlin and E.M. Hoffert, "Hypertexture", Computer Graphics 23(3), pp. 253–262, 1989.
6. J.T. Kajiya, and T.L. Kay, "Rendering fur with Three Dimensional Textures", Computer Graphics 23(3) (Siggraph'89), pp. 271–280, 1989.
7. M.F. Cohen, S.E. Chen, D.S. Immel and P.J. Brock, "An Efficient Radiosity Approach for Realistic Image Synthesis", IEEE CGA 6(3), pp. 26–35, 1986.
8. R. Gershbein, P. Schroeder and P. Hanrahan, "Texture and Radiosity: Controlling Emission and Reflection with Texture Maps", Computer Graphics (Siggraph'94), pp. 51–58, 1994.
9. H. Chen, and E-H. Wu, "An Efficient Radiosity Solution for Bump Texture Generation", Computer Graphics 24(4)(Siggraph'90), pp. 125–134, 1990.
10. F.X. Sillion, J.R. Arvo, S.H. Westin and D.P. Greenberg,"A Global Illumination Solution for General Reflectance Distributions", Computer Graphics 25(4), pp. 187–196, 1991.
11. F.X. Sillion, "Clustering and Volume Scattering for Hierarchical Radiosity Calculation", Fifth EGWR, June 1994.
12. B. Smits, J. Arvo and D.P. Greenberg, "A Clustering Algorithm for Radiosity in Complex Environments", Computer Graphics (Siggraph'94), pp. 435–442, 1994.
13. M. Pharr, C. Kolb, R. Gershbein and P. Hanrahan, "Rendering Complex Scenes with Memory-Coherent Ray Tracing", Computer Graphics (Siggraph'97), 1997.
14. J.M. Dischler, L. Mostefaoui and D. Ghazanfarpour, "Radiosity Including Complex Surfaces and Geometric Textures Using Solid Irradiance and Virtual Surfaces", Computers and Graphics 23(4), 1999 (to appear).
15. Dana K.J., Nayar S.K, van Ginneken B. and Koenderink J.J., "Reflectance and Texture of Real-World Surfaces", IEEE Conf. on Comp. Vision and Pattern Recognition, 1997.
16. L. Williams, "Pyramidal parametrics", Computer Graphics 17(3), pp. 1–11, 1983.
17. T. Noma, "Bridging between surface rendering and volume rendering for multi-resolution display", Proc. EGWR, pp. 31–40, 1995.
18. F. Neyret, "A general and multiscale method for volumetric textures", Proc. Graphics Interface'95, pp. 83–91, 1995.
19. J.M. Dischler, "Efficiently Rendering Macro-geometric Surface Structure with Bi-directional Texture Functions", Proc. EGWR, pp. 169–180, 1998.
20. F.X. Sillion, G. Drettakis and C. Soler, "A Clustering Algorithm for Radiance Calculation in General Environments", Proc. EGWR, pp. 196–205, 1995.
21. P.H. Christensen, D. Lischinski, E.J. Stollnitz and D.H. Salesin, "Clustering for Glossy Global Illumination", ACM TOG 16(1), pp. 3–83, January 1997.
22. E. P. Lafortune and Y. D. Willems, "A 5D Tree to Reduce the Variance of Monte Carlo Ray Tracing", Proc. of 6th EGWR, 1995.
23. H. W. Jensen and N. J. Christensen, "Photon Maps in Bi-directional Monte Carlo Ray Tracing of Complex Objects", Computers and Graphics 19(2), pp. 215–224, 1995.
24. J.P. Ewins, M.D. Waller, M. White and P.F. Lister, "MIP-map Level Selection for Texture Mapping", IEEE TVCG 4(4), pp. 317–329, 1998.
25. Westin S. H., Arvo J. R. and Torrance K. E., "Predicting Reflectance Functions from Complex Surfaces", Computer Graphics 26(2), pp. 255–263, 1992.
26. Kajiya J., "The Rendering Equation", Computer Graphics 20(4), pp. 143–150, 1986.
27. P.M. Deville and J.C. Paul, "Modeling the spatial Energy Distribution of Complex Light Sources for Lighting Engineering", Proc. of EGWR, pp. 147–159, 1995.
28. M.C. Reichert, "A Two-pass Radiosity Method Driven by Lights and Viewer Position", Master's thesis, Program of Computer Graphics, Cornell University, 1992.
29. Max N., "Horizon mapping: shadows for bump-mapped surfaces", The Visual Computer 4, 1988, pp. 109-117.

Editors' Note: see Appendix, p. 377 for colored figures of this paper

Face Cluster Radiosity

Andrew J. Willmott, Paul S. Heckbert and Michael Garland[1]

Computer Science Department
Carnegie Mellon University
Pittsburgh, PA 15213, USA

Abstract. An algorithm for simulating diffuse interreflection in complex three dimensional scenes is described. It combines techniques from hierarchical radiosity and multiresolution modelling. A new face clustering technique for automatically partitioning polygonal models is used. The face clusters produced group adjacent triangles with similar normal vectors. They are used during radiosity solution to represent the light reflected by a complex object at multiple levels of detail. Also, the radiosity method is reformulated in terms of vector irradiance and power. Together, face clustering and the vector formulation of radiosity permit large savings. Excessively fine levels of detail are not accessed by the algorithm during the bulk of the solution phase, greatly reducing its memory requirements relative to previous methods. Consequently, the costliest steps in the simulation can be made sub-linear in scene complexity. Using this algorithm, radiosity simulations on scenes of one million input polygons can be computed on a standard workstation.

1   Introduction

The hierarchical radiosity algorithm in its various forms is probably the most promising radiosity method in existence. The best hierarchical radiosity methods, using clustering, permit scenes of moderate complexity (several hundred thousand input polygons) to be simulated in a few hours. Unfortunately, current radiosity techniques, even with clustering, use excessive memory and their speeds are not competitive with other, less realistic rendering methods. We would like to be able to apply radiosity methods to the complex scenes common in special effects. Such scenes routinely use objects each employing 100,000 polygons or more. We therefore seek an enhancement to the hierarchical radiosity algorithm that will permit very complex scenes — scenes with millions of input polygons — to be economically simulated on a standard computer.

One of the greatest difficulties with existing radiosity methods is that their memory use is at least linear in the number of input polygons. This is not a problem if the scene is small, but if the input polygons cannot fit in physical memory, the algorithm will thrash and performance will degrade dramatically. To deal with very complex scenes, we need methods which in practice have memory and time cost that is sub-linear in the number of input polygons.

In this paper we describe the face cluster radiosity algorithm, a technique that achieves this goal. Its three main phases are preprocessing, solution, and postprocessing. Preprocessing converts the scene description into a multiresolution, hierarchical model. The time cost of this is super-linear in the number of input polygons, but preprocessing can be done on an off-line, object-by-object basis, so its memory costs are

---

1. {ajw|ph|garland}@cs.cmu.edu

modest and its time costs can be amortized over multiple solutions. Next, one or more radiosity solutions are found. This is the costliest step, in practice. The solution phase is sub-linear in cost because it accesses only the coarsest levels of detail from the hierarchy that are necessary. Consequently, often large portions of the hierarchy need never be paged in during this phase, with huge physical memory savings. After solution, postprocessing evaluates the radiosity of the finest details of the scene. This requires linear time. The overall cost, being dominated by solution, is thus sub-linear in practice.

A preview of the technique is shown visually in Figure 7. If one of the best existing radiosity algorithms (hierarchical radiosity with volume clustering) is used on a detailed model, a solution takes over ten minutes (Figure 7a). If, on the other hand, the input geometry is simplified by cutting the number of triangles by a factor of 100, and the same algorithm is applied to the simplified model, a solution can be calculated much more quickly (Figure 7b, 7 seconds). This is fast, but the accuracy and visual quality are poor. Our face cluster radiosity technique allows a solution not much more expensive than this to be calculated and propagated to the fully detailed model, yielding Figure 7d. This is much faster than the full solution and almost as accurate.

2   Hierarchical Radiosity

We review previous work, and describe at a high level how our new method differs. Hierarchical radiosity [3, 9] has a cost linear in the number of elements, n. Unfortunately, because the initial light transport 'link' from each polygon to every other polygon must be computed, the cost is also quadratic in the number of input polygons, k. The cost is thus $O(k^2 + n)$. Classical hierarchical radiosity algorithms work well on scenes with a small number of large polygons, but they become impractical in time and memory consumption for scenes of several hundred polygons.

Hierarchical Radiosity with Volume Clustering. To combat this problem, clustering methods for hierarchical radiosity were developed [2, 7, 14, 15, 16]. These methods group the input polygons into *volume clusters*, building a hierarchy above the input polygons that culminates in a root cluster for the entire scene. The lower nodes in this hierarchy are elements in quadtrees (small surface patches, with normal and reflectance), as before, but the upper nodes are different. They are octree or k-d tree boxes containing a set of disconnected polygons with potentially varying normal vectors and reflectances. The use of clusters reduces the number of links needed from quadratic to linear.

Several methods for handling the light incident on a cluster have been explored. The simplest is to sum the incoming light. This approach, called beta links by Smits, turns out to be fast, $O(k + n)$, but inaccurate. A more successful alternative is to push the light down to the leaves of the tree (Smits' alpha links) [15, 16, 17]. This raises the cost of the algorithm to $O(k \log k + n)$. A third alternative, proposed by Sillion and Christensen [2, 14], is to represent a cluster as a point that emits and reflects light according to a directional distribution. Both latter methods require light to be pushed down the tree, as with alpha links. Christensen's algorithm appears to be asymptotically the fastest, achieving good quality results in $O(k + n)$ time. Although any of these clustering methods is significantly faster than classical hierarchical radiosity, the need to touch all of the input polygons on each solver iteration causes their working set to be excessively large for complex scenes.

Figure 1 is a schematic comparison of variants of hierarchical radiosity on a scene with two large polygons A & B in close proximity, and eight small polygons C-J, more distant. Simple hierarchical radiosity (a) yields a forest of quadtrees. Polygons A and B are subdivided and some of their children are linked. The large number of links between the small input polygons C-J makes the algorithm inefficient. Figure 1b shows hierarchical radiosity with volume clustering. If cluster Q is sufficiently small and distant from cluster P then a single link between them suffices. Since a cluster can illuminate itself, a self link on Q is necessary as well. The algorithm is still slow because it is necessary to push light down to polygons C-J.

Face Cluster Radiosity. We propose that volume clusters be replaced by multiresolution models for all groups of input polygons that represent a sur-

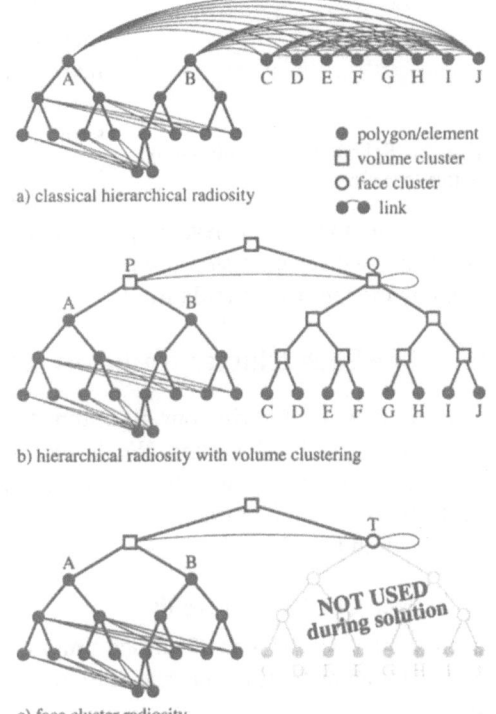

Fig. 1. Three approaches to hierarchical radiosity.

face. The use of such models allows pushing of light to the leaves to be avoided, and they often provide a better fit to the original surfaces than volume clusters. The particular multiresolution representation that we use, face clustering, groups adjacent faces that have similar normals, and thus can approximate largely planar surfaces well.

With this scheme, the data structures for elements coarser than and finer than the input polygons are more similar, since both face clustering and quadtree refinement yield a contiguous piece of surface with a normal. Hierarchical radiosity is now free to subdivide below the level of the input polygons and to "unsubdivide" above this level. This reduces the hitherto inordinate role of the input polygons, permitting hierarchical radiosity to represent light transport at more natural levels of detail, and to operate more efficiently in complex scenes.

The use of multiresolution models improves the accuracy of our representations and permits our algorithm to avoid touching the lowest portions of the hierarchy during iterations. In Figure 1c we see how a tree of simplified models is built above the input polygons. The tree nodes below T and above C-J are now face clusters, not volume clusters, while the highest levels of the tree, above connected objects, are volume clusters. Note that the subtree below T can be paged out during simulation, saving time and memory. The hierarchy is seen schematically in Figure 2.

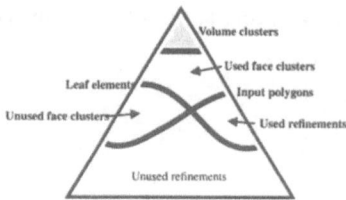

Fig. 2. Schematic of a hierarchy using face clusters.

The use of simplified models in radiosity has previously been proposed. Rushmeier et al. demonstrated the feasibility of the concept, but their method employed manually-constructed simplified models, making it impractical for complex scenes [13]. Greger et al. showed how a radiosity simulation of a simple scene could be applied to a more detailed version of that same scene by using an *irradiance volume* [8]. Both these methods require the user to judge the level of pre-simulation simplification; simplification and simulation are two separate steps, whereas in our algorithm, the level of simplification is driven by the radiosity simulation.

3 The Face Cluster Radiosity Algorithm

In this section we describe our algorithm for simulating radiosity on multiresolution models that use face clustering. We discuss our approach to building the necessary hierarchies, and then show how the standard radiosity equations can be modified to better suit the use of these hierarchies, starting with the standard formulas governing diffuse interreflection [3].

3.1 Face Cluster Hierarchies

Recent work from the area of surface simplification provided a starting point for our research into radiosity using multiresolution models. Iterative edge contraction, one of the currently popular simplification techniques, can be used to construct a hierarchy of progressively larger vertex neighbourhoods on the surface. Each edge contraction collapses the two vertices at either end of the edge to a single, new vertex. The hierarchy is created by treating the endpoints as the children of this new vertex. These vertex hierarchies have been used primarily for view-dependent refinement of models for real-time rendering [10].

In our original algorithm we used vertex hierarchies directly, but they sometimes proved problematic, because vertex nodes don't have a well defined area and normal. These properties are easier to establish for face hierarchies than for vertex hierarchies.

To address this problem, we developed an algorithm for generating *face cluster hierarchies* [4] that is a dual form of the quadric-based simplification algorithm of Garland and Heckbert [5]. Rather than iteratively merging pairs of vertices to directly simplify the mesh, we iteratively merge groups of topologically connected faces, which we refer to as face clusters, thereby partitioning the original mesh (see Figure 8). This process does not change the original geometry of the surface in any way; it merely groups surface polygons into progressively larger clusters. These merge operations can be used to create a simplification hierarchy in the same manner as edge collapses; an example is shown in Figure 3.

In [5] quadric functions of position, $\mathbf{v}^T\mathbf{A}\mathbf{v} + 2\mathbf{b}^T\mathbf{v} + c$, are used to represent the set of planes associated with a vertex node, and can be used to find the best-fit point to those planes. When we are working in the dual space, we instead use quadric functions of the face normal, $\mathbf{n}^T\mathbf{A}\mathbf{n} + 2\mathbf{b}^T\mathbf{n} + c$, to represent the set of vertices in a cluster node, and to find the best-fit plane to those points. Because of this, it can be shown that by applying the quadric error approach to the dual problem, face clusters can be made to preserve planarity where possible, in the same way that vertex simplification tries to preserve shape. We can also add an additional error term to ensure the clusters are well-shaped, in the sense of being as close to circular as possible. More detail can be found in [4].

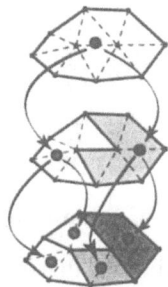

Fig. 3. A Face Cluster Hierarchy

For each node i in the face cluster hierarchy, we calculate an oriented bounding box for the faces it contains using principal component analysis [11]. We also store the sum of the area-weighted normals of those faces

$$\mathbf{S}_i = \sum_j A_j \hat{\mathbf{n}}_j \tag{1}$$

where face $j \in$ cluster i. As we will show later, this is a useful approximation of the reflective qualities of the faces within the node.

3.2 Notation

Each element i has a known reflectance ρ_i, emittance e_i, area A_i, normal $\hat{\mathbf{n}}_i$, and unknown radiosity b_i, where bold symbols denote vectors. The distance between elements i and j is r_{ij}, and the unit vector from i to j is $\hat{\mathbf{r}}_{ij}$. The average visibility between two points on these elements is $\bar{v}_{ij}$: 1 for no occlusion, and 0 for total occlusion.

The *irradiance* E_i is the incident power per unit area. Calculating it exactly is typically intractable, so we approximate it using the point-to-point approximation of the form factor [3],

$$E_i = \sum_j \frac{(\hat{\mathbf{n}}_i^T \hat{\mathbf{r}}_{ij})(\hat{\mathbf{r}}_{ji}^T \hat{\mathbf{n}}_j)}{\pi r_{ij}^2} \bar{v}_{ij} A_j b_j. \tag{2}$$

We have written the traditional dot products in matrix notation because we will shortly be exploiting the associativity of matrix multiplication to rewrite this formula.

3.3 Vector-based Radiosity

The classical radiosity method assumes piecewise constant (Haar) basis functions and planar surfaces. In a hierarchy, the children are coplanar with the parent. For the purposes of projecting radiosities up and down the tree, radiosities are scalar quantities. If this method is applied to a multiresolution model, it causes curved or bumpy portions of the model to be shaded a flat colour, leading to a faceted appearance that hides the geometric detail (Figure 7c). This is similar to the step-function effect in constant-basis radiosity, but applying a post-process smoothing step at the leaves is no longer sufficient to cover up these discontinuities.

298

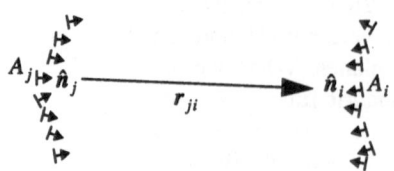

Fig. 4. Radiosity transfer between clusters of faces.

We now adapt the radiosity method to multiresolution models that use face clustering. Consider the light transfer from one cluster to another (Figure 4). We let j be an element in the source cluster and i be an element in the receiver cluster. If we assume that all (i,j) pairs are intervisible and that the sources are close together and far from the receiver, then $\hat{r}_{ij}$, $\hat{r}_{ji}$, r_{ij}, and $\bar{v}_{ij}$ are independent of j, and we can approximate the irradiance from a single cluster as:

$$E_i \approx \hat{n}_i^T \left[\frac{-\hat{r}\hat{r}^T}{\pi r^2} \sum_j \hat{n}_j A_j b_j \right] \bar{v}_i \tag{3}$$

This allows us to rewrite the transfer in terms of two vector quantities, so that:

$$E_i = \hat{n}_i^T \mathbf{E}_i \tag{4}$$

where

$$\mathbf{E}_i = \bar{v} \left[\frac{-\hat{r}\hat{r}^T}{\pi r^2} \right] \mathbf{P} \tag{5}$$

and

$$\mathbf{P} = \sum_j \hat{n}_j A_j b_j = \sum_j \mathbf{S}_j b_j \tag{6}$$

We refer to $\mathbf{E}$ as the irradiance vector [1], and $\mathbf{P}$ as the power vector.

The irradiance vector $\mathbf{E}_i$ is a 3-vector whose components are the irradiances on planes normal to the x, y, and z axes, respectively, positioned at the receiver. Recording this information, rather than a scalar irradiance to the average plane of the receiver, allows coarse variations in the irradiance as a function of orientation to be modelled. This eliminates most of the faceting effects of Figure 7c, as seen in Figure 7d.

Fig. 5. The power vector. The radiosity emitted by the surfaces on the left is approximated by the elemental surface on the right, whose direction is the power-weighted sum normal.

Standard hierarchical radiosity effectively assumes that outgoing power is diffuse (isotropic) over the hemisphere above a planar surface. But the outgoing power from a cluster can be anisotropic due to occlusion. To permit nonplanar clusters to approximate their outgoing power compactly and quickly, we employ a 3-dimensional power vector. The magnitude of the vector approximates the total power leaving the cluster, and the direction of the vector indicates the hemisphere toward which most of the energy is directed (Figure 5).

These formulas are generalizations of the standard radiosity equations; in the case of co-planar clusters, they reduce to the familiar hierarchical radiosity push-pull formulas.

We can substitute these vector quantities directly for the irradiance and radiosity in a standard hierarchical radiosity algorithm, although as $\mathbf{P}$ is already area-weighted, when pulling radiosity up the hierarchy we sum the power vectors of a node's children, instead of averaging them. Instead of a single transfer coefficient, we store the *transfer vector*, $\mathbf{m} = \mathbf{r}/\sqrt{\pi r^2}$, which allows us to apply Equation 5 more simply as

$$\mathbf{E} = -\bar{v}\mathbf{mm}^T\mathbf{P}. \tag{7}$$

At the leaves of the hierarchy, where we must transform the accumulated irradiance vectors into the power vector we apply the equation

$$\mathbf{P}_j = \mathbf{S}_j(\rho_j\hat{\mathbf{S}}_j^T\mathbf{E}_j + e_j). \tag{8}$$

As with standard radiosity, whenever these equations are applied, dot products must be clipped to zero to account for occlusion by the tangent plane to the surface.

The above treatment of vector-based transfer assumes a monochromatic world. It can easily be extended to the familiar RGB colour model; we simply store $\mathbf{P}_R$, $\mathbf{P}_G$, $\mathbf{P}_B$, $\mathbf{E}_R$, $\mathbf{E}_G$, $\mathbf{E}_B$, and operate on each pair of irradiance and power vectors independently. Note that the transport vector, $\mathbf{m}$, is still wavelength independent.

3.4 Algorithm Description

There are three types of nodes in the hierarchy used by our algorithm. At the top, volume clusters contain all unconnected parts of the scene. In the middle, face clusters contain connected surface meshes. At the bottom, there are polygonal elements, and refinements of those elements. In our implementation, all of these nodes use a common object-oriented interface to communicate with each other. Usually much of each face cluster hierarchy remains unused; only those face clusters at the top of the tree are paged in during the solution phase.

Radiosity using vector-based transfer proceeds in much the same manner as the irradiance/radiosity method first popularised by [6], and outlined in Figure 6. In Gershbein's method, irradiance is gathered to each node in the hierarchy, and then pushed down to the leaves, whereupon it is converted to radiosity by the application of reflectance and emittance operators, and pulled back up the hierarchy. In our algorithm, the irradiance vector, rather than scalar, is pushed to the leaves, and the

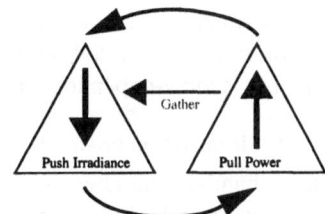

Fig. 6. Schematic of the Face Cluster Radiosity Cycle.

power vector, not scalar radiosity, is pulled back up the hierarchy. Below is an outline of the algorithm.

Preprocessing. Face cluster hierarchies are generated for the input models. These hierarchies are dependent only on the geometry of the models, and can be reused over multiple instantiations of each model. This process is done off-line, and typically only once, whenever a new model is acquired.

Initialisation. The scene description and its constituent models are read in. Hierarchical radiosity elements are then created for the small number of root face clusters in the scene, and these are volume clustered to complete the initial element hierarchy.

```
solve()
   while (not converged)
      gather(root)
      pushpull(root, 0)
      refine(root, ε )

gather(element i)
```

$$\Delta \mathbf{E}_i = - \sum_{\text{links } j \text{->} i} \bar{v}_{ij} \mathbf{m}_{ij} \mathbf{m}_{ij}^{\mathrm{T}} \mathbf{P}_j$$

```
   for (all children c of i)
      gather(c)

pushpull(element i, vector E )
   // E is irradiance on i from parent
```

$$\mathbf{E} = \mathbf{E} + \Delta \mathbf{E}_i$$

```
   if (i is a leaf)
      // convert irradiance to power
```

$$\mathbf{P}_i = \mathbf{S}_i(\text{Max}(\hat{\mathbf{S}}_i^{\mathrm{T}} \mathbf{E}_i, 0)\rho_i + e_i)$$

```
   else
```

$$\mathbf{P}_i = 0$$

```
      for (all children c of i)
         pushpull(c, E )      // push irradiance
```

$$\mathbf{P}_i = \mathbf{P}_i + \mathbf{P}_c \qquad \text{// pull power}$$

Solution. The solver proceeds according to the pseudocode at left.

The **refine** procedure follows that outlined in [3]. When a face cluster element needs to be subdivided, its two child elements are created using position and average normal information retrieved from the cluster file on disk. Storage for power vectors and other such element information is only required for those face cluster nodes actually being used by the solver.

Post Processing. After the algorithm has terminated, the radiosity solution is propagated to the leaves of the model by applying the irradiance vectors at the leaves of the transport tree to all their descendents (e.g., node T of Figure 1c). This final process is again $O(k)$, but is typically insignificant compared to the solution time. The radiosities of the vertices of the models in the scene are then written out to disk. An alternative that we don't use is to perform a final gather on the hierarchy generated by the solution. This can generate extremely good quality results, but is view-dependent and is quite slow.

3.5 Estimating Transfer Coefficients and Error

We must handle a number of different types of transfer; radiosity exchange between face clusters, standard planar elements, and volume clusters. This can lead to problems in choosing an error metric that is consistent for all transfers. To handle these in a common framework we use sampling across the receiver to estimate the error in the transfer at the same time as we estimate the transfer itself. We use the L_1 norm to measure error, i.e., the *BFA*-weighted refinement discussed in [16]. A fixed number of sample points are generated across the cluster or face, and used both for estimating fractional visibility and determining bounds on the transfer [7, 12]. For links that are partly occluded, the refinement epsilon is reduced to encourage subdivision at shadow boundaries. (The refinement epsilon controls link subdivision; links with transport error greater than this are split.)

We estimate the transport vector as

$$\bar{\mathbf{m}} = \frac{1}{n} \sum_{i=1}^{n} \mathbf{m}_i = \frac{1}{n} \sum_{i=1}^{n} \frac{\mathbf{r}_i}{\sqrt{\pi} r_i^2} \qquad (9)$$

where $\mathbf{r}_i$ is the vector from sample point i of n on the source s to sample point i on the destination d. The L_1 norm can then be estimated by using the samples $\mathbf{m}_i$ to evaluate

$$\Delta BFA = (\lceil \mathbf{S}_i^{sT}\mathbf{m}_i\mathbf{m}_i^T\mathbf{S}_i^d \rceil - \lfloor \mathbf{S}_i^{sT}\mathbf{m}_i\mathbf{m}_i^T\mathbf{S}_i^d \rfloor)\frac{\|\mathbf{P}^s\|}{\|\mathbf{S}^s\|}, \tag{10}$$

where $\lceil \ \rceil$ and $\lfloor \ \rfloor$ denote upper and lower bounds. This effectively measures the range of FA, weighted by the average emitted radiosity of the source. The problem of generating correlated area-weighted normal samples $\mathbf{S}_i$ and transport samples $\mathbf{m}_i$ can be addressed by using a constant number of children of each face cluster in question to generate the samples.

3.6 Implementation Details

To build volume clusters, we followed the methods described in [7, 15]. An octree that encloses the scene is created, and scene polygons are placed within that octree according to their size and position. Visibility is sampled using ray-tracing; the spatial data structure used for acceleration is a nested grid data structure.

Compared to the storage required for a face in standard hierarchical radiosity, we store 9 real numbers per hierarchical element instead of 3, and 3 reals per link instead of 1. Although the face cluster hierarchical elements are more expensive than standard Haar elements, they are in general more lightweight than volume cluster elements, which require 8 child pointers in our implementation, and much more lightweight than storing a general radiance distribution.

4 Results

We have compared face cluster radiosity to our own implementation of hierarchical radiosity with volume clustering, which follows those of Sillion and Gibson [7, 15].

4.1 The Museum Scene

We designed an indoor scene typical of those seen in the radiosity literature. This scene is lit by both sun and sky, and internally by three spotlights. Much of the light in the room is reflected from the overhead skylight by the detailed stone floor, providing a good test of complex interreflection.

The scene contains a number of high resolution scanned models, a polygonized implicit surface (the podium), and a displacement-mapped surface (the floor). These models range in complexity from 4,140 polygons to 1,000,000 polygons; it took from 1s to 600s to generate their associated face cluster hierarchies, for a total time of 1500s.

4.2 Empirical Complexity

Using the quadric-based surface simplification method [5] we applied progressive radiosity, hierarchical radiosity with volume clustering, and our face cluster radiosity algorithm to versions of the museum scene with varying polygon counts, to demonstrate the effect of using ever more detailed models on these algorithms. While previous experiments have investigated the effect of increasing the lighting or geometric complexity of a scene on radiosity algorithms [18], this experiment shows the effect of increasing model complexity in a scene with fixed geometric layout. The results were collected on

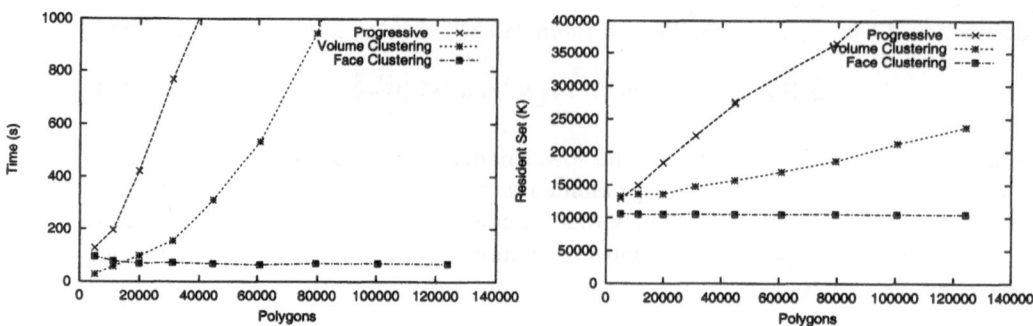

Fig. 7. Performance of hierarchical, progressive, and face cluster radiosity as model complexity increases. The graphs show (left) solution time and (right) maximum resident set size (memory usage).

an SGI Power Challenge with a 195MHz R10000 MIPS processor and 1Gb of main memory. While exact error comparisons between the solutions were not available due to the difficulty in generating a reference solution, we took care to use similar parameter settings for all three methods. When compared by eye, the solution meshes from the two hierarchical radiosity methods looked much the same. The progressive radiosity method did somewhat better on generating first order shadows, but very poorly on simulating second bounce illumination. At higher resolutions, almost no secondary illumination was detectable.

Figure 7 shows graphs of solution time and memory use for the methods tested. Notably, the time cost of the face cluster radiosity algorithm stays approximately constant, while previous methods have a cost that is super-linear in the number of input polygons. As suggested in Figure 1c, this is because fine levels of detail of the cluster hierarchy are never accessed, in spite of the increasing polygon count. In fact the solution time for face cluster radiosity is slightly greater for very low resolution versions of the test scene where face clustering provides little benefit and a significant number of leaf polygons must be refined.

The memory use of the face cluster radiosity algorithm also stayed constant at around 100MB maximum resident set size, and 120MB total memory use, significantly below that of the other methods. While the total memory use of the progressive radiosity method is typically better than that of hierarchical methods, it is apparent from this graph that its memory locality is much poorer. Also, because the highly tessellated floor accounts for much of the indirect illumination in the scene, the number of shooting steps is $\Theta(k)$, and the performance of progressive radiosity is the worst case $\Theta(k^2)$. The HRVC curve is approximately $\Theta(k \log k)$.

4.3 A Highly Complex Museum Scene

The use of face cluster radiosity enables an increase in quality and scene size over previous methods. We were able to run a radiosity simulation on the full museum scene, containing 2.7 million polygons, in under two minutes, including both solution and preprocessing time. (Neither of the two other radiosity methods could handle this complex a scene on our test machine.) The result is shown in Figure 9. Initialisation and solution for the illumination in the scene, i.e., running the core face cluster radiosity algorithm, took 56 seconds. A further 53 seconds was devoted to postprocessing, which included both the final push-to-leaves phase, and refining the mesh locally for better visibility results when viewing the output mesh.

Preprocessing time for the models in this scene took a total of 1500s. We think that preprocessing time could be sped up significantly; our current algorithm is $O(k^2)$, which could be reduced to $O(k \log k)$ by using a convex hull algorithm to help calculate bounding boxes. As pointed out previously, this cost can be heavily amortized; the same models can be reused over multiple scenes and radiosity simulations. Indeed, this is the reason we have not yet optimized our face cluster hierarchy code.

4.4 Discussion

Our algorithm gives the greatest benefit for finely tessellated objects. For more intricate, space-filling objects such as trees, we rely on volume clustering to provide a good simulation. This is because of the limitation in our algorithm that each topologically connected surface has its own face cluster tree. For instance, a pile of pebbles might need a separate tree for each pebble, if those pebbles were modelled separately. While we currently aggregate disconnected components by using volume clustering, better methods for tightly packed components such as the pebble pile are an avenue for future research.

Many of the input polygons in Figure 9 are invisibly small. Arguably a similar picture could be generated using a much simpler scene. However, this ignores the possibility of using the output mesh for a walk-through, where we might wish to pass much closer to some of the models in the scene. Also, it is tedious to manually preprocess a scene in a view-dependent manner to optimise radiosity simulations. Ultimately, we wish the radiosity simulation to be as independent of the model resolution chosen for viewing as possible.

5 Conclusions

We have designed and implemented a new hierarchical radiosity algorithm based on face clustering and a vector formulation of radiosity. The algorithm yields sub-linear performance in the number of input polygons, an improvement over the linear performance of the previous fastest volume clustering algorithms. The principal reason for this speed-up is that the face cluster radiosity algorithm greatly reduces memory use. Unlike previous clustering methods for hierarchical radiosity, it does not require that information be pushed down to the leaves of the hierarchy during the solution phase.

This is possible because of the combination of face clustering and vector-based radiosity. Face clustering ensures that each cluster of faces has a (reasonably) small range of normal vectors, so it can more accurately be approximated by a single normal than could a volume cluster containing a set of faces with a wide range of normals. Vector-based radiosity provides an inexpensive representation for gross directional variation in irradiance and outgoing power. The vector representation is intermediate in complexity between the traditional representation of radiosity algorithms, a scalar quantity, and the more sophisticated directional techniques employed in radiance algorithms [2, 14].

Face cluster radiosity paves the way for the application of radiosity to high-complexity scenes, implicit surfaces, and displacement-mapped polygons. Together with the ability to handle textures, this makes the creation of animation using radiosity solutions more practical.

Several ideas for future work present themselves: A more complete error analysis of the approximations made in this algorithm should be done. This could help reduce the cluster artifacts that sometimes appear with this method. We are currently exploring the use of conservative bounds in vector radiosity transfer, and results look promising. By generalizing the method to work with directional distributions, not just vector irradiance, global illumination in non-diffuse scenes could be simulated.

Acknowledgements

Funding was provided by NSF grants CCR-9505472, CCR-9357763, and DMI-9813259, and the Schlumberger Foundation. Thanks to Joel Welling for machine access and Francois Sillion for discussions.

References

[1]   James Arvo. The irradiance Jacobian for partially occluded polyhedral sources. In *Proceedings of SIGGRAPH '94 (Orlando, Florida, July 24–29, 1994)*, Computer Graphics Proceedings, Annual Conference Series, pages 343–350. ACM SIGGRAPH, ACM Press, July 1994.

[2]   Per H. Christensen, Dani Lischinski, Eric J. Stollnitz, and David H. Salesin. Clustering for glossy global illumination. *ACM Transactions on Graphics*, 16(1):3–33, January 1997.

[3]   Michael F. Cohen and John R. Wallace. *Radiosity and Realistic Image Synthesis*. Academic Press Professional, Boston, MA, 1993.

[4]   Michael Garland. *Quadric-Based Polygonal Surface Simplification*. PhD thesis (Technical Report CMU-CS-99-105), Carnegie Mellon University, 1999. http://www.cs.cmu.edu/~garland/thesis.

[5]   Michael Garland and Paul S. Heckbert. Surface simplification using quadric error metrics. In *SIGGRAPH 97 Conference Proceedings*, Annual Conference Series, pages 209–216. ACM SIGGRAPH, Addison Wesley, August 1997.

[6]   Reid Gershbein, Peter Schröder, and Pat Hanrahan. Textures and radiosity: Controlling emission and reflection with texture maps. In *Computer Graphics (Proceedings of SIGGRAPH '94)*, pages 51–58, July 1994. http://www-graphics.stanford.edu/papers/texture.

[7]   S. Gibson and R. J. Hubbold. Efficient hierarchical refinement and clustering for radiosity in complex environments. *Computer Graphics Forum*, 15(5):297–310, 1996.

[8]   Gene Greger, Peter Shirley, Philip M. Hubbard, and Donald P. Greenberg. The irradiance volume. *IEEE Computer Graphics & Applications*, 18(2):32–43, March–April 1998.

[9]   Pat Hanrahan, David Salzman, and Larry Aupperle. A rapid hierarchical radiosity algorithm. *Computer Graphics (SIGGRAPH '91 Proceedings)*, July 1991.

[10] Hugues Hoppe. View-dependent refinement of progressive meshes. In *SIGGRAPH 97 Proc.*, pages 189–198, August 1997.

[11] I. T. Jolliffe. *Principal Component Analysis*. Springer-Verlag, New York, New York, 1986.

[12] Dani Lischinski, Brian Smits, and Donald P. Greenberg. Bounds and Error Estimates for Radiosity. In *Computer Graphics Proceedings, Annual Conference Series, 1994 (ACM SIGGRAPH '94 Proceedings)*, pages 67–74, 1994.

[13] Holly Rushmeier, Charles Patterson, and Aravindan Veerasamy. Geometric simplification for indirect illumination calculations. In *Proceedings of Graphics Interface '93*, pages 227–236, Toronto, Ontario, Canada, May 1993. Canadian Information Processing Society.

[14] François Sillion, G. Drettakis, and Cyril Soler. A clustering algorithm for radiance calculation in general environments. In *Eurographics Rendering Workshop 1995*. Eurographics, June 1995.

[15] François X. Sillion. A unified hierarchical algorithm for global illumination with scattering volumes and object clusters. *IEEE Transactions on Visualization and Computer Graphics*, 1(3):240–254, September 1995.

[16] Brian Smits, James Arvo, and Donald Greenberg. A clustering algorithm for radiosity in complex environments. In *Proceedings of SIGGRAPH '94 (Orlando, Florida, July 24–29, 1994)*, Computer Graphics Proceedings, Annual Conference Series, pages 435–442. ACM SIGGRAPH, ACM Press, July 1994.

[17] M. Stamminger, W. Nitsch, and Ph. Slusallek. Isotropic clustering for hierarchical radiosity – implementation and experiences. In *Proc. Fifth International Conference in Central Europe on Computer Graphics and Visualization '97*, 1997.

[18] Andrew J. Willmott and Paul S. Heckbert. An empirical comparison of radiosity algorithms. Technical Report CMU-CS-97-115, School of Computer Science, Carnegie Mellon University, April 1997. http://www.cs.cmu.edu/~radiosity/emprad-tr.html.

Editors' Note: see Appendix, p. 378 for colored figures of this paper

Effective Compression Techniques
for Precomputed Visibility

Michiel van de Panne
A. James Stewart
Department of Computer Science, University of Toronto
{van,jstewart}@dgp.utoronto.ca

Abstract. In rendering large models, it is important to identify the small subset of primitives that is visible from a given viewpoint. One approach is to partition the viewpoint space into viewpoint cells, and then precompute a visibility table which explicitly records for each viewpoint cell whether or not each primitive is potentially visible. We propose two algorithms for compressing such visibility tables in order to produce compact and natural descriptions of potentially–visible sets. Alternatively, the algorithms can be thought of as techniques for clustering cells and clustering primitives according to visibility criteria. The algorithms are tested on three types of scenes which have very different structures: a terrain model, a building model, and a world consisting of curved tunnels. The results show that the natural structure of each type of scene can automatically be exploited to achieve a compact representation of potentially visible sets.

1 Introduction

The visibility problem is to determine which scene elements are visible from a particular viewpoint. Algorithms that solve this problem are very expensive in time, in memory, or in complexity. For these reasons, real–time applications will often precompute visibility information, store it, and later use it to accelerate rendering.

Storage of the precomputed visibility information can require a very large amount of memory. This paper describes two effective techniques to compress precomputed visibility information. These techniques are very general and may be used in applications as varied as architectural walkthroughs, terrain flyovers, and tunnel roaming.

Techniques that precompute visibility typically divide space into regions and determine what parts of scene are visible from each region. This is a common strategy: Teller and Sequin [17] divide a building into rooms and, for each room, compute the other rooms visible from it. Yagel and Ray [19] subdivide space into a regular grid of cells and use a different method to compute cell–to–cell visibility. Games in maze–like environments often have room–to–room visibility explicitly stored in a table.

These techniques can be thought of as using a very coarse form of clustering to reduce memory requirements: By storing cell–to–cell visibility, rather than cell–to–polygon visibility, groups of polygons in the same cell are clustered and do not need to be exhaustively enumerated.

This coarse form of clustering has several drawbacks: polygon clusters are restricted to correspond one–to–one to viewpoint regions; viewpoint regions themselves are not clustered at all; a polygon cluster must be entirely rendered if even a tiny fraction of it is visible; and it is unclear how to create optimal clusters in less well-structured environments, such as terrains.

In this paper, the space of viewpoints is divided into small regions and a precomputation step determines which *polygons* are visible from each region. A boolean **visibility table** encodes this information: entry (i, j) of the table is TRUE if polygon j is potentially visible from some point in region i. Given the fine subdivision of space and the possibly large number of polygons, the visibility table is potentially huge.

This paper's principal contribution consists of two methods to compress the visibility table:

- The first is a **lossy compression method** which merges viewpoint regions and merges polygons. This method may conservatively deem a polygon to be visible when in fact it is not. Like all conservative visibility algorithms, this does not pose a problem as long as hidden surface elimination (e.g. Z–buffering) is performed during rendering.
- The second is a **lossless compression method** which contructs a graph of viewpoint and polygon clusters. Visible polygons can be enumerated by performing a very simple traversal of this graph. This lossless method never mistakenly deems a polygon to be visible when it is not.

These compression methods have several desirable features:

- A combination of the two compression techniques yields better compression than either alone.
- The level of compression may be chosen to optimize memory, occlusion information, or some ratio of the two.
- These techniques permit very efficient "random access" decompression: For any particular viewpoint region, all visible polygons can be quickly enumerated.
- The polygon and viewpoint clusters are automatically adapted in a natural way to the environment, making this a very general method. For example, in our experiments (presented in Section 6) we discovered:
  - in terrains, polygons are clustered in separate valleys and on peaks;
  - in tunnels, viewpoints are clustered in contiguous tunnel sections; and
  - in buildings, polygons are clustered around "open corridors" from which all of the polygons of the cluster are visible.

The beauty of using the visibility table is that viewpoint clusters and polygon clusters may be treated identically: one consists of a cluster of rows, while the other consists of a cluster of columns. This observation yields very simple algorithms which do not need to know anything about the underlying structure of the viewpoint regions or the scene polygons.

2 Related Work

In work of similar spirit to ours, Yagel and Ray [19] precompute visibility information for a two–dimensional scene using a regular subdivision of space. Their principal contribution is an elegant algorithm to compute cell–to–cell visibility, but they also suggest clustering cells of similar visibility using criteria like those of our lossy compression algorithm. Wang et al.[18] combine precomputed potentially-visible sets with detail simplification in regions where the sets become very large.

Most methods that precompute visibility divide the viewpoint space into cells and compute cell–to–cell visibility. This has the implicit effect of clustering polygons in each cell, which reduces the memory requirement at the cost of not taking advantage of detailed visibility information. Teller and Sequin [17] divide a building into rooms and compute room–to–room visibility. Coorg and Teller[6] exploit the presence of large occluders to perform occlusion culling for a viewpoint. Cohen-Or et al.[2] exploit large convex occluders to compute cell-to-object visibility. Plantinga[13] uses a small set of effective occluders and computes visual events among the occluders in order to partition the viewpoint space into 2D cells.

Coorg and Teller [5], Gigus and Malik [7], and Cohen-Or and Zadicari[4] all exploit features of aspect graphs to produce incremental updates of visibility. Yagel and Ray [19] also suggest recording only changes in visibility in order to compress their cell–to–cell visibility information.

Another class of visibility methods computes visibility during the rendering process. Some examples include the hierarchical Z–buffer of Meagher [12] and of Greene, Kass, and Miller [9], the hierarchical coverage masks of Greene [8], and the hierarchical occlusion maps of Zhang *et al* [20]. An advantage of these techniques is that they can cope with dynamic scenes. However, these techniques work best when a set of large occluders can rapidly be identified for the current viewpoint, which is not always possible. These techniques can potentially be used in conjunction with a compressed visibility table, using a table to achieve the same result as a large occluder.

There has also been a substantial amount of work in clustering for global illumination. Hierarchical radiosity [10], for example, imposes a hierarchical structure on the scene surfaces and computes energy transfer between different nodes in this hierarchy. An alternative "hierarchy of uniform grids" is described by Cazals, Drettakis, and Puech [1]. However, the principal expense in global illumination lies in determining whether one surface sees another, and clustering usually occurs *before* visibility is computed, which is opposite to what we do when compressing the visibility table.

3 The Visibility Table

Visibility is encoded in a boolean table, in which each row initially corresponds to one viewpoint cell and each column initially correponds to one polygon. The table ideally encodes the *partial visibility*: the entry in row i, column j is TRUE if and only if polygon j is at least partially visible from some point in cell i. However, our lossy compression can allow some occlusions to be lost, in which case the table will encode a conservative visibility set[2], which is a superset of the exact partial-visibility set.

Any division of viewpoint regions may be used; our experiments used a regular voxel subdivision of space. One could just as well use another subdivision, such as an oct–tree, a binary space partition, or a k–d tree. Similarly, any division of the scene may be used; our experiments used single polygons. One could also pre–cluster polygons manually, given some knowledge of the scene, or one could go in the opposite direction, subdividing very large polygons (e.g. imposters) if it is likely that only a part of the polygon will be visible at any time.

Given a visibility table, rendering is simple: Locate the row corresponding to the region containing the viewpoint and render each polygon whose corresponding column contains the value TRUE. In order that the rendering time be proportional to the number of visible polygons, each row of the table can be stored as a linked list of the TRUE entries, or alternatively, the FALSE entries must be run–length encoded. We choose the latter. A row is represented by a sequence of integers, where each integer is the number of FALSE entries before the next TRUE entry. For example, the sequence 5, 3, 0, 0, 1 indicates that TRUE entries occur in columns 5, 9, 10, 11, and 13:

0	1	2	3	4	5	6	7	8	9	10	11	12	13	14	15	16	17	
0	0	0	0	0	1	0	0	0	1	1	1	0	1	0	0	0	0	...

The run-length encoding scheme described above can be used as a simple low-cost method for storing the visibility table in an easy-to-decode fashion, comparable to conventional sparse-matrix storage techniques. The job of our compression algorithms is to do much better than this, and thus our compression algorithms make use of this run-length encoding only as a last step. It is worth remarking that, unlike conventional sparse-matrix storage, it would also be possible to run-length encode the non-zero (TRUE) elements, given that there is only one assignable non-zero value. Thus, the sequence 5, 1, 3, 3, 1, 1, 5, 1 could indicate that there are 5 FALSE entries, followed by one TRUE entry, 3 FALSE entries, etc. In many situations, however, this will be less compact than simply run-length encoding the FALSE entries, given the expected sparsity of TRUE entries in densely occluded environments. As well, our compression techniques will first produce visibility tables which are even sparser (but encode the same information), and then use a run-length encoding step as a final compression step.

Experiments have shown a preponderance of short runs of FALSE entries. In order to encode these runs with little memory, each run is represented with either one byte or three bytes: A run of 0 to 254 FALSE entries is encoded with a single byte containing the run length, while a run of 255 to 65535 FALSE entries is encoded with a single byte of 255 followed by two bytes containing the run length.

Given a set of viewpoint regions and a set of polygons, the initial visibility table may be constructed in any one of many ways. Since the initial table construction is not a contribution of this paper, we use a fairly naive approach that *samples* visibility using an item buffer: From several points within each viewpoint region and from six directions around each such point, the scene is rendered into an item buffer in which each polygon is assigned a unique colour. A quick traversal of the item buffer determines which polygons are visible. One problem with the item buffer method is, of course, that it is not conservative: Polygons can be missed due to the limited resolution of the item buffer and the discrete viewpoint sampling done within the viewpoint region. However, artifacts caused by such missing polygons will, by definition, likely be small. Another problem is that it is time consuming, since the scene must be rendered many times from many different viewpoints. For the experiments described in Section 6, the visibility tables took several hours to compute using software rendering on 166 Mhz PC. Other methods may be used to construct the initial visibility table using general methods[19, 15, 6], or methods for specific environments[16, 2].

4 Lossy Compression Algorithm

The lossy compression algorithm compresses the visibility table by merging rows and by merging columns.

- Two rows are merged if they have a similar set of TRUE entries. The merge deletes the two old rows and inserts a new row that is the logical OR of the original two rows. This corresponds to merging two viewpoint regions that have similar sets of visible polygons. The merge creates a new meta–region from which is visible the union of the polygons visible from the two original regions. The logical OR maintains conservative visibility: If a polygon was visible from one of the original regions, it is visible from the merged region.
- Two columns are merged if they have a similar set of TRUE entries. The merge

deletes the two old columns and inserts a new column that is the logical OR or the original two columns. This corresponds to merging two polygons that have identical visibility status in most viewpoint regions. That is, for most viewpoint regions either both polygons are visible or neither is visible. The merge creates a new meta–polygon which is visible from all regions from which either one of the original polygons was visible. Again, the logical OR maintains conservative visibility.

To determine which 'similar' sets of columns or rows should be merged, the lossy algorithm must determine the benefit and the cost of a potential merge.

The **benefit** of a merge is equal to the reduction in table size. Since the table is run–length encoded, its size is proportional to the number of TRUE entries and the benefit of a merge is equal to the number of TRUE entries that are eliminated.

The **cost** of a merge is equal to the number of occlusions that are "lost." An occlusion is represented by a FALSE entry, which indicates that some polygon is occluded from viewpoints in some region. An occlusion is "lost" whenever the logical OR is applied to two entries of *different* boolean values, TRUE and FALSE: The result of the OR is TRUE, and the original FALSE value, representing an occlusion, is lost. Note that no information is lost when two entries of equal value are ORed.

If a row or column is the result of n prior merges, each FALSE entry in that row or column represents n occlusions. If such a FALSE entry is lost in a merge, the cost is n lost occlusions, rather than one. Thus, in order that costs be correctly calculated, each row and column must record the number merges of which it is the result.

Our **slow greedy algorithm** evaluates all pairs of rows and all pairs of columns, and merges the pair with the largest ratio of benefit–to–cost. This is repeated until some user–determined criterion is satisfied. This algorithm is slow because each iteration takes time quadratic in the number of rows and in the number of columns. For large scenes with more than a few thousand initial viewpoint regions or initial polygons, the slow algorithm is unusable. However, the good feature of the slow algorithm is that it performs progressive compression, thereby allowing control over the compromise between lost occlusions and table size. A user might express their desired compromise in terms of a target table size or a limit on the percentage of lost occlusions. We use the latter in our experiments, stopping the lossy compression when 5% of occlusions have been lost.

An alternative **fast greedy algorithm** is used in practice, as follows: A fixed fraction of the rows are chosen as "seed rows." Each remaining "non–seed row" is tested against each seed row and is merged with the seed row of maximum benefit–to–cost ratio. A similar procedure is then performed with the resulting columns. In practice, we choose the seed rows using a regular sampling pattern. If the list of scene primitives has some structure, as we might expect, then this helps to distribute the seed rows in an equitable fashion around the scene. The fast greedy algorithm produces excellent compression and was used in all the lossy compression experiments reported in Section 6.

5   Lossless Compression Algorithm

An alternative compression algorithm can take advantage of locally-similar but globally-dissimilar visibility relationships. For example, viewpoints located in the hallway of a building all share the visibility of a room at the end of the hallway, but they may not share the visibility of rooms located along the hallway. Similar scenarios also occur in non-architectural scenes, as will be illustrated by the experimental results. In terms of the visibility table, these situations correspond to rows or columns that share a large number of TRUE values, but that are not merged by the lossy algorithm because they also differ in a large number of other entries (i.e. their merge cost is too high). The lossless compression algorithm, identifies these situations and merges *only part* of the row or column.

The **lossless compression algorithm** operates as follows (refer to Figure 1):

1. Find a set, V, of viewpoints regions that have a set, P, of visible polygons in common. Pick the set to maximize the product of the cardinalities: $|V| \times |P|$.
2. Create a single polygon cluster consisting of the polygons of P and allocate for it a *new column* in the visibility table. Since the polygon cluster is visible from each of the viewpoint regions in V, the new column has a TRUE value in each row corresponding to a region in V.
3. Symmetrically, create a single region cluster consisting of the viewpoint regions of V and allocate for it a *new row* in the visibility table. Since the region cluster sees all of the polygons in P, the new row has a TRUE value in each column corresponding to a polygon in P.
4. Set to FALSE all entries in the intersection of the rows and columns of V and P. (These entries are made redundant with the addition of the new row and column.)
5. Repeat with new V and P until no clusters remain above some user-defined size.

There is no cost to this operation, since no occlusions are lost. The benefit is that the visibility table becomes sparser. For a given cluster, the benefit can be computed as the number of TRUE entries which become FALSE, minus the number of TRUE entries created in the new row and new column. If $|V|$ and $|P|$ are the cardinalities of V and P, respectively, then the benefit is $|V| \times |P| - |V| - |P|$. By including the new region and polygon clusters as a new row and new column of the table, these clusters can participate in subsequent merges, as shown in Figures 1(b) and 1(c).

To determine which polygons are visible from a particular viewpoint region, the corresponding row of the visibility table is traversed, just as it is done with the lossy-compressed table. However, if (on that row) a TRUE entry is encountered in some column, j, and if column j corresponds to a polygon cluster rather than to a single polygon, then a recursive traversal of row j is performed. (It is easy to distinguish the cluster columns, since they all appear to the right of the rightmost polygon column.)

It is interesting to note that the same traversal may be performed with the roles of the rows and columns reversed (i.e. traverse each column). In this case, we enumerate all viewpoint regions that see a particular polygon. This symmetry is evident in Figure 1. For example, polygon c is visible from regions 0, 1, and 3.

6 Experimental Results

Our experiments applied both types of compression, as well as their combination, to three types of scenes. These scenes were chosen for their dissimilar structures in order to illustrate the generality of our method and to show that the compression techniques automatically exploit the natural structure of each scene in order to yield compact visibility descriptions. We first motivate the choice of each dataset or scene and then provide a summary of the key properties of each scene.

The terrain dataset is shown in Figure 2 and was procedurally generated using an iterative subdivide-and-displace approximation of a fractal terrain. The existence of occlusion-culling techniques specific to terrains [14] motivated the choice of this example, as well as the large number of simulation and gaming applications that involve

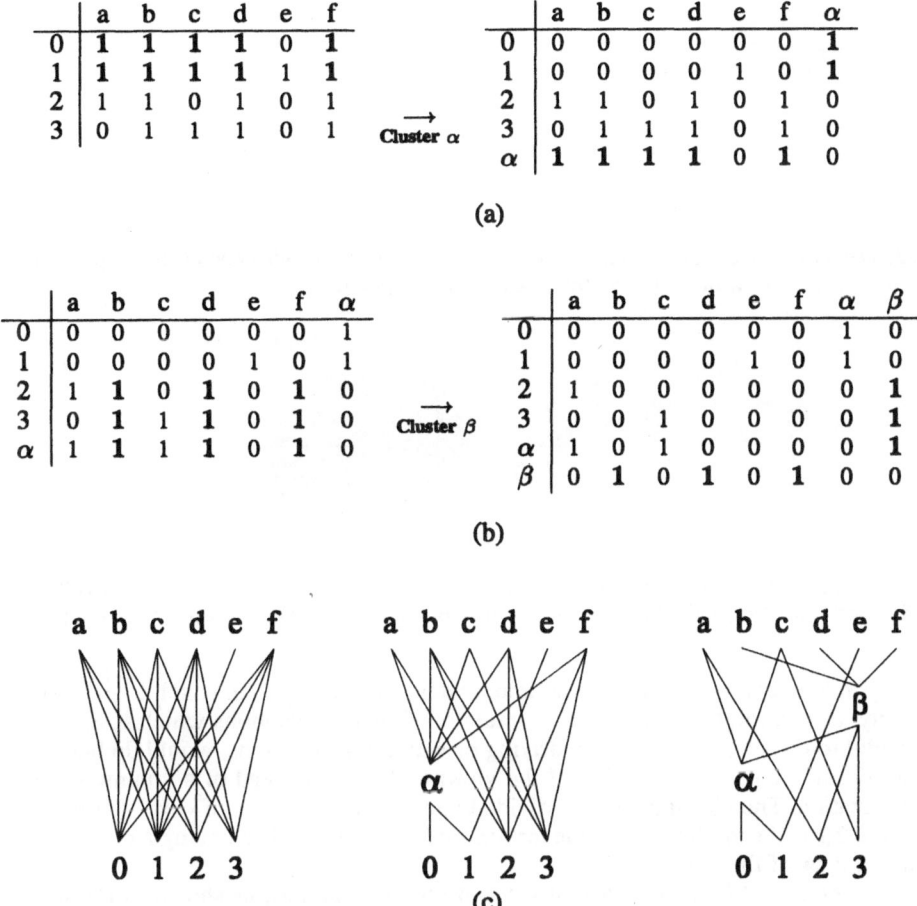

(a)

(b)

(c)

Fig. 1. An example of the lossless clustering algorithm, where letters denote polygons and digits denote viewpoint regions. (a) The visibility table is modified when a cluster, α, is created, consisting of $\{0, 1\} \times \{a, b, c, d, f\}$. (b) A second cluster, β, is created, consisting of $\{2, 3, \alpha\} \times \{b, d, f\}$. Included in β are the viewpoint regions of cluster α, but not the polygons of cluster α. (c) An alternative representation of the visibility table, where a line directed *upward* from i to j corresponds to TRUE entry in row i, column j of the visibility table. To enumerate the polygons visible in a region, i, *all upward paths* from i are followed. For clustered tables, these paths traverse intermediate clusters, such as α and β in the rightmost graph. For example, the polygons visible from viewpoint region 3 are b, c, d, and f. All polygons are visible from region 1.

312

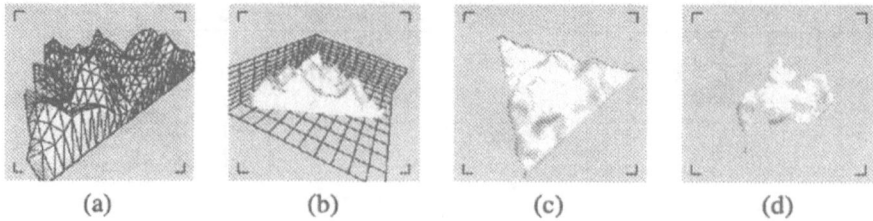

Fig. 2. The terrain dataset. (a) primitives (b) voxel grid defining the viewpoint cells (c) plan view of terrain (d) plan view of visible set for a particular viewpoint.

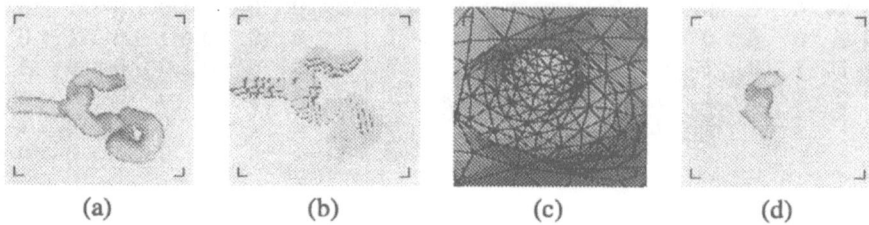

Fig. 3. The tunnels dataset. (a) exterior view (b) voxelization used for the viewpoint cells (c) interior view with diffuse lighting (d) exterior view of visible set for the viewpoint used in (c).

moving on or over terrains. In our example we deal specifically with voxel–to–primitive visibility, as one might use in a flight simulator. Other applications which restrict the viewpoint to the surface, such as in driving or walking simulations, would do better to use a 2D surface parameterization of the viewpoint space instead of a volumetric parameterization. The viewing space is divided into a $10 \times 10 \times 8$ set of voxels, as shown in Figure 2(b). Viewpoints below the terrain surface are treated as having a completely occluded view of the world.

Our second test scene consists of a set of winding tunnels, as shown in Figure 3. This dataset was motivated by applications such as colonoscopy [11]. The voxelization is constructed procedurally from the boundary representation of the tunnels. The viewpoint cell which contains a given viewpoint can be quickly located by computing a unique voxel ID based on the quantized xyz coordinates of the viewpoint, and then using a hash table indexed by this ID. This avoids allocating voxel storage for the large volume of space outside of the tunnel system, under the assumption that the viewpoint should always remain within the tunnels. Viewpoints that are outside the tunnel walls — even if they are inside cells that straddle the walls — are considered to see nothing, so treatment of straddling cells requires some care.

Lastly, we choose a building floorplan as a dataset, as shown in Figure 4. The floorplan exists on a 10×17 unit grid. All wall segments are broken into primitives, each no longer than 1 unit in length. The viewpoint cells consist of 1×1 unit squares on the grid. These are schematically illustrated in Figure 4(b). The scene is constructed as a 3D model, although the 2D floorplan effectively contains all the information about the structure of the scene. Each wall is double–sided.

The key properties that characterize each of the three example scenes are given in Table 1. Some details of this table bear further explanation. The maximum occlusion in the terrain and tunnel scenes is 100%, as some viewpoint cells are located below the terrain surface or outside the tunnel wall. The dataset size assumes an uncompressed

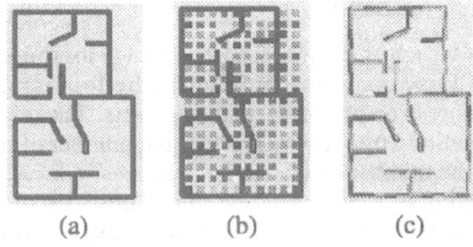

(a)   (b)   (c)

Fig. 4. The rooms dataset. (a) plan view (b) plan view showing voxels (c) plan view showing primitives

scene properties	terrain	tunnels	rooms
# viewpoint cells	800	1275	170
# primitives	1217	4166	242
mean occlusion	84%	82%	90%
min, max occlusion	48%, 100%	70%, 100%	80%, 94%
data set size	15 kB	50 kB	10 kB
uncompressed table size	122 kB	664 kB	5.3 kB
table size, gzip	26 kB	64 kB	1.2 kB
lossy compression			
reduction applied	2p, 2v	10p, 5v	200g
table size (compression)	22.1 kB (5.5×)	23 kB (29×)	0.2 kB (27×)
lossless compression			
# clusters	2000	2000	100
table size (compression)	28.5 kB (4.3×)	95 kB (7.0×)	1.3 kB (4.1×)
lossless compression			
table size (compression)	6.1 kB (20×)	4.4 kB (151×)	0.1 kB (53×)
% of original table size (gzip)	5% (21%)	0.7% (10%)	2% (23%)
% of dataset size (gzip)	41% (173%)	9% (128%)	1% (12%)

Table 1. Experimental Data and Results

representation of an indexed–vertex representation of the geometry. An xyz vertex triple is assumed to be represented in 12 bytes, while an index is assumed to be stored as a 4–byte integer. The raw table size assumes a binary representation of the visibility table. The run–length encoded versions of the raw table are comparable in size to the binary–encoded raw tables for our examples.

We use `gzip` to provide a simple point of comparison for our compression techniques. In practice, the requirement for random access to the rows in order to answer visibility queries means that individual rows should be compressed instead of the entire table. We use `gzip` as applied to the entire table as an upper bound on the performance of a row–based compression algorithm. It should also be noted that a further advantage of our compression schemes is that they produce enumerated lists of visible primitives, unlike binary compression algorithms which only reproduce the original rows of the visibility table. Lastly, we note that gzip is only a 'fair' comparison for the lossless compression algorithm.

6.1 Lossy Compression Results

The compression tests we apply to the test scenes are (1) lossy compression, (2) lossless compression, and (3) lossy compression followed by lossless compression. We first look at how lossy compression performs on the datasets. The results are summarized in Table 1, where the notation 10p, 5v means that the number of primitives was reduced by a factor of 10 and the number of viewpoint cells was reduced by a factor of 5. In all cases, the lossy clustering procedure was continued until 5% of the occlusions present in the original visibility table were lost. The fast greedy algorithm was applied in the case of the terrain and tunnels datasets because of their size. The slow greedy algorithm could be applied to the room scene (for 200 iterations) because of its small size. In all cases, the lossy compression took less than 20 minutes to complete as computed on a 166 MHz PC.

The results show that the lossy compression scheme can reduce the size of the pre-computed visibility table by a factor of 29 for the well–structured tunnel scene. It also does very well on the rooms scene (27× compression), although not as well for the less–structured terrain scene (5.5×). Figure 5(a) (see color plates) shows the clusters which are formed for the terrain scene, resulting from reducing the number of primitives by a factor of 30, showing a plan view on the left, and an interior view on the right. Clusters typically consist of connected polygons, although this adjacency information is not explicitly present in the raw visibility table. As well, clusters tend to be based on mountain faces and valleys. The clusters produced for the tunnel scene, shown in Figure 5(b) show similar behaviors, creating a patchwork coverage of the tunnel walls. We do not show the viewpoint clusters for the terrain and tunnel scenes, as they are difficult to depict, given their 3D nature.

The viewpoint clusters formed for the room scene, shown in Figure 5(c) are mainly based on individual rooms, as one might intuitively expect. The primitive clusters are similarly organized. The two figures on the right illustrate examples of the lost occlusions that arise during the lossy compression. The viewpoint is indicated as a blue dot, while the blue wall segments indicate the original minimal–size PVS. The red wall segments indicate the additions made to the PVS in the interest of obtaining good compression.

6.2 Lossless Compression Results

The results for lossless compression are shown in Table 1 and Figure 6. Lossless clustering by itself produces compression factors of between 4 and 7. These results are comparable to gzip, keeping in mind that gzip is not amenable to the random–access and fast enumeration requirements of visibility applications.

The clusters formed by the lossless compression algorithm have a different structure than those of the lossy compression, as shown in Figure 6 (see color plates). Clusters formed early on appear high in the cluster hierarchy and result in the largest storage reductions. We illustrate some of these clusters in Figure 6 for the three test scenes. In Figure 6(a), the same cluster is shown twice; first in a plan view and then in a side view. Although the cluster looks to be an unlikely agglomeration of primitives in the plan view, the side view reveals that it is really a group of primitives facing a particular direction, and hence consistently visible as a group from a particular (large) set of viewpoints. The important clusters for the tunnel scene, shown in Figure 6(b), tend to be coherent cylindrical regions of the tunnels, although the clusters do not provide completely continuous coverage, as evident from the "holes." The appearance of these holes is unintuitive to us. The rooms dataset provides results having an intuitive interpretation, as shown in Figure 6(c). The figure on the left shows a cluster which groups together the primitives in a room. The remaining two clusters illustrate distributed clusters which effectively capture particular 'visibility corridors' within the scene.

6.3 Combining Lossy and Lossless Compression

An interesting characteristic of the lossy and lossless compression techniques is that they appear to operate in orthogonal fashions. The results of following lossy compression with lossless compression are given in Table 1. The occlusions which are 'lost' when using the combination of techniques are the same as those which are lost using the lossy technique alone. The compression ratios achieved for the terrain and tunnels scenes are approximately the product of the compression ratios achievable by each technique alone. For all three datasets, the combined compression performs 4 to 10 times better than gzip. More interestingly, the final compressed visibility table, only amounts to a small percentage of the storage space required for the uncompressed dataset geometry.

There are several caveats to be stated about Table 1. The rooms example has 3D geometry but a 2D visibility problem, and therefore the storage cost for the precomputed visibility is small when compared to the storage cost for the dataset geometry. The tunnels dataset is perhaps the most convincing result, storing 95% of the occlusion relationships with a memory cost of 9% of the uncompressed dataset geometry. However, this kind of results is probably restricted to scenes which have well structured visibility coherence. A last caveat is that any implementation that must decode the table must also build associated indexing data structures such as the hash table required for the tunnel scene in order to efficiently locate the viewpoint cell, given a particular viewpoint. These additional data structures could potentially double or triple the storage costs given in Table 1, although we have not yet evaluated their average costs. Nevertheless, the results show that remarkably little storage space is needed to encode precomputed visibility information.

7   Summary and Discussion

Precomputed visibility information can be used to answer the question "What is visible from this viewpoint?" The algorithms presented in this paper address a new problem (to the best of our knowledge): How can precomputed visibility information be efficiently compressed? Experimental results show that the proposed algorithms are effective for three very different types of datasets: a terrain, a series of winding tunnels, and a building interior. The result is a near–optimal method of occlusion culling which has low storage cost and which permits fast, random–access enumeration of visible primitives.

We propose a variety of future work which would extend these techniques to new application domains as well as addressing some caveats in their use.

- Scalability is an important issue. Large scenes likely need to be tackled with a top–down divide–and–conquer approach, in addition to the bottom–up approach proposed thus far.
- The compromise between storage cost and lost occlusions needs to be explored in terms of a trade-off between rendering time and storage cost.
- The viewpoint space could be expanded to include the viewing direction. The technique could also be applied to efficiently store voxel–to–voxel visibility.
- Models of the rendering cost could be incorporated into the clustering criteria.

References

1. Frédéric Cazals, George Drettakis, and Claude Puech. Filtering, clustering and hierarchy construction: a new solution for ray-tracing complex scenes. *Computer Graphics Forum*, 14(3):371–382, August 1995. Proceedings of Eurographics '95. ISSN 1067-7055.

2. D. Cohen-Or, G. Fibich, D. Halperin, and E. Zadicario. Conservative visibility and strong occlusion for viewspace partitioning of densely occluded scenes. 1998.

3. D. Cohen-Or and A. Shaked. Visibility and dead-zones in digital terrain maps. *Computer Graphics Forum*, 14(3):C/171–C/180, September 1995.

4. D. Cohen-Or and E. Zadicario. Visibility streaming for network-based walkthroughs. In *Proceedings of Graphics Interface '98*, 1998.

5. Satyan Coorg and Seth Teller. Temporally coherent conservative visibility. In *Proceedings of the Twelfth Annual Symposium On Computational Geometry (ISG '96)*, pages 78–87, New York, May 1996. ACM Press.

6. Satyan Coorg and Seth Teller. Real-time occlusion culling for models with large occluders. In *Proceedings of the 1997 Symposium on 3D Interactive Graphics*, 1997.

7. Z. Gigus and J. Malik. Computing the aspect graph for the line drawings of polyhedral objects. *IEEE Trans. Pattern Analysis and Machine Intelligence*, 12(2), February 1990.

8. N. Greene. Hierarchical polygon tiling with coverage masks. *Computer Graphics*, 30(Annual Conference Series):65–74, 1996.

9. N. Greene, M. Kass, and G. Miller. Hierarchical Z-buffer visibility. In *Computer Graphics (SIGGRAPH '93 Proceedings)*, 1993.

10. Pat Hanrahan, David Salzman, and Larry Aupperle. A rapid hierarchical radiosity algorithm. *Computer Graphics (SIGGRAPH '91 Proceedings)*, 25(4):197–206, July 1991.

11. Lichan Hong, Shigeru Muraki, Arie Kaufman, Dirk Bartz, and Taosong He. Virtual voyage: Interactive navigation in the human colon. In Turner Whitted, editor, *SIGGRAPH 97 Conference Proceedings*, Annual Conference Series, pages 27–34. ACM SIGGRAPH, Addison Wesley, August 1997.

12. Donald J. Meagher. Efficient synthetic image generation of arbitrary 3–D objects. In *Proceedings of the IEEE Conference on Pattern Recognition and Image Processing*, pages 473–478, June 1982.

13. H. Plantinga. Conservative visibility preprocessing for efficient walkthroughs of 3d scenes. In *Proceedings of Graphics Interface '93*, pages 166–173, 1993.

14. A. James Stewart. Fast horizon computation at all points of a terrain with visibility and shading applications. *IEEE Transactions on Visualization and Computer Graphics*, 4(1):82–93, March 1998.

15. Seth Teller and Pat Hanrahan. Global visibility algorithms for illumination computations. In *Computer Graphics Proceedings, Annual Conference Series, 1993*, pages 239–246, 1993.

16. Seth J. Teller. Computing the antipenumbra of an area light source. In *Computer Graphics (SIGGRAPH '92 Proceedings)*, volume 26, pages 139–148, July 1992.

17. Seth J. Teller and Carlo H. Séquin. Visibility preprocessing for interactive walkthroughs. In Thomas W. Sederberg, editor, *Computer Graphics (SIGGRAPH '91 Proceedings)*, volume 25, pages 61–69, July 1991.

18. Y. Wang, H. Bao, and Q. Peng. Accelerated walkthroughs of virtual environments based on visibility preprocessing and simplification. *Computer Graphics Forum (Eurographics 98 issue)*, 17(3):187–194, 1998.

19. R. Yagel and W. Ray. Visibility computation for efficient walkthrough of complex environments. *Presence*, 5(1):45–60, 1995.

20. H. Zhang, D. Manocha, T. Hudson, and Kenneth E. Hoff III. Visibility culling using hierarchical occlusion maps. In *SIGGRAPH 97 Conference Proceedings*.

Lighting Design: A Goal Based Approach Using Optimisation

António Cardoso Costa[I] [II]
acc@dei.isep.ipp.pt

António Augusto Sousa[III] [II]
augusto.sousa@inescn.pt

Fernando Nunes Ferreira[III]
fnf@fe.up.pt

Abstract

There is a need for reliable lighting design applications because available tools are limited and inappropriate for interactive or creative use. Architects and lighting designers need those applications to define, predict, test and validate lighting solutions for their problems. We present a new approach to the lighting design problem based on a methodology that includes the geometry of the scene, the properties of materials and the design goals. It is possible to obtain luminaire characteristics or other kind of results that maximise the attainment of the design goals, which may include different types of constraints or objectives (lighting, geometrical or others). The main goal, in our approach, is to improve the lighting design cycle. In this work we discuss the use of optimisation in lighting design, describe the implementation of the methodology, present real-world based examples and analyse in detail some of the complex technical problems associated and speculate on how to overcome them.

Key words: lighting design, inverse design, optimisation, global illumination, light transport.

1. Introduction

In a 3D space for which we know the geometry and materials within, where should we place luminaires and what characteristics should they have to satisfy the lighting design goals?

This question hides very complex and challenging problems. The people that need answers to this question — architects, engineers and designers — would benefit very much if tools were available to define, predict, test and validate their lighting design solutions; instead, existing tools are limited in scope and inappropriate to interactive or creative use. Computer tools are capable of providing more detailed analyses than real or small-scale models. Designers are increasingly computerised and seek prediction and analysis tools for their problems. In this paper we describe and analyse a new approach that solves the problem of finding lighting solutions from the geometry, the materials and the design goals (an inverse approach). The calculation engine is a global illumination simulation program that uses the geometry, the materials and the light sources (as in a direct approach). The inverse approach is more complex because there can be many incompatibilities between the input information. These incompatibilities have a physical meaning and can be dealt with by changing some of the input data (geometry, material properties or design goals). This inverse approach also allows the exploration of lighting design solutions in virtual or real spaces. Fig. 1 shows our approach, where the designer includes design goals in the input data. A

[I] Departamento de Engenharia Informática do ISEP-IPP, Rua S. Tomé, 4200 Porto, Portugal.
[II] INESC Porto, Praça da República 93 R/C, Apartado 4433, 4007 Porto CODEX, Portugal.
[III] Faculdade de Eng. da Univ. do Porto, Rua dos Bragas, 4099 Porto CODEX, Portugal.

318

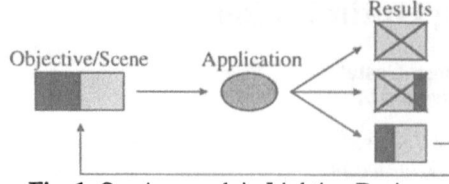

Fig. 1. Our Approach in Lighting Design

user-driven computational search iterates until some preset termination criteria is achieved. The best solutions are shown and a decision can then be made. The three types of solutions in the right part of Fig. 1 show that it is possible to generate impossible, unwanted or adequate solutions. The designer can choose to refine the design goals and restart the process or, alternatively, to apply his own judgement and choose the most suited solution available. The abstract description in Fig. 1. hides many difficult and resource consuming problems, for which available solutions are yet very unsatisfactory. The main goal of this work is to qualitatively improve the lighting design cycle. Improvement is achieved by letting the user include the design goals in the search for solutions and explore the different solution paths. If this is accompanied by technical improvements, then we would also attain another important goal: shortening the design cycle. The "Related Work" section describes other research work, while the "Overview" section explains our approach and methodology. The "Implementation" section describes the algorithm implemented and methods/techniques used. The "Results" section presents examples, problems found, technical solutions developed and some performance analyses. In the "Open Questions" section we discuss questions related to lighting design and our approach. Finally, conclusions are presented in the last section.

2. Related Work

In [Costa99], within the context of the proposed approach, the authors describe the methodology, the algorithm and an initial implementation, but without going into details. Schoeneman *et al.* [Schoe93] and Kawai *et al.* [Kawai93] tried to address the inverse lighting design problem, but solved it only partially for mostly diffuse environments and seem to have ignored many types of design constraints. Both used a radiosity-based algorithm [Cohen93]. Poulin *et al.* [Pouli97] described an approach that allows the interactive positioning of simplified luminaires from sketches of shadows, umbra, penumbra or highlights (as design constraints), but their approach does not seem capable of handling indirectly lit spaces. The Design Gallery approach of Marks *et al.* [Marks97] is also interesting, because it presents a new methodology for the exploration of solutions in large multidimensional problems, different from conventional methodologies like interactive evolution or inverse design. Results may be questionable because it seems they used a local illumination algorithm. Also, their dispersion phase (solution generation and filtering) can become prohibitively expensive in computation time if many solutions have to be generated for the following reduction (browse and select) phase.

3. Overview

In [Costa99] an overview of our approach was presented which explained the concept of an "ideal" lighting design approach – the inputs are:
- the geometry of the scene
- the properties of the materials
- a set of statements about lighting design goals.

The outputs are:
- a set of solutions (possibly empty)
- suggestions to overcome the limitations found.

Due to the complexity of the problem and the insufficiency of current technological resources, alternative "practical" approaches must be found that allow the implementation of computerised solutions with reasonable resource consumption – storage, time, etc. This work describes one "practical" approach and the algorithm, methods and techniques that we have found appropriate for its implementation. Lighting is a very complex mix of physical phenomena [Feynm85], but for most real world environments, some of those phenomena are very rare and simplifications can be made that allow simpler theories and models to be derived. Some of the simplifications that were made for developing a feasible implementation are:
- geometric optics – assumed (particle theory of light)
- media – non participating media
- *BSDF*[1] – symmetrical (no change if incoming and outgoing rays are switched)

Although the *BRDF* (reflected components of the *BSDF*) of real surfaces is symmetric, the *BTDF* (transmitted components) seldom is and that may invalidate the reversibility of lighting calculations. One way to circumvent this is to use the *basic radiance* concept of [Veach97]. To provide lighting data for our implementation it is important to use a lighting calculation tool with at least the following requisites:
- physically valid symmetric *BSDF* model (*BRDF* only if no transmission exists)
- reversibility of lighting calculations
- no restrictions for the properties of surfaces
- light sources with arbitrary radiance distributions
- radiance calculation anywhere in space.

Lighting design goals are mostly modelled by fictitious luminaires that are artificially introduced in the scene to provide means for computing solutions (this is the reason why reversibility of lighting calculations is so important). These luminaires may be:
- PL – previous luminaire; a luminaire in the scene, ie, a design condition
- IL – inverse luminaire; a fictitious luminaire used as a design goal
- DL – desired luminaire; a lighting design result.

3.1 Methodology
In some cases, lighting design problems are based on scenes that have some initial radiance distribution: predefined luminaires, daylighting, etc – this initial illumination is represented by PLs. After the designer quantifies the lighting design goals using ILs, an initial step is performed to account for the effect of the initial radiance distribution in the scene. This lighting simulation computes the effect of the PLs in the ILs. If those effects do not lead to contradictory situations, then the ILs are decomposed into a new set of ILs that account for the initial scene illumination. Using the ILs as radiance emitters, we must find a way of computing the incoming radiance in selected points and directions in the scene's volume and correlate that with a particular design solution. With an optimisation algorithm it is possible to calculate automatically solutions that maximise some function of that incoming radiance, if we are able to define

---

[1] Bi-directional Scattering Distribution Function.

such a function – this will be a cost function $F(x)$ of the optimisation phase, whose main goal is to find the global maximum. In most lighting design problems, a solution may be represented by different sets of parameters: luminaire position, luminaire spacing or almost anything relevant to the scene. Usually, the n parameters can be converted from real to suitable integer values, which makes the configuration parameter space a large set of n-dimensional points. Exhaustive searches seldom are an efficient way to find the solutions. We must then resort to local search strategies [Pirlo96], which basically move from one solution to another one in its neighbourhood according to some well defined rules. In lighting design, straightforward strategies are not adequate to solve the problem because the solution may be very difficult to find if the cost function is complex. Simulated Annealing (SA) [Kirkp84] is a suitable strategy for difficult optimisation problems and is able to process cost functions with quite arbitrary degrees of non-linearities, discontinuities and stochasticity, arbitrary boundary conditions and constraints imposed on the cost function and is statistically guaranteed to find the optimal solution [Ingbe93]. The non-linearities or discontinuities of the cost function may invalidate the use of optimisation methods based on gradient calculations, but with a continuous and "smooth" cost function, a two step technique joining SA and a gradient-based search method might prove beneficial.

4. Implementation

Fig. 2 shows an outline of the our algorithm. The input data is the geometry of the scene, the properties of materials and the lighting design goals. The geometry and properties are usually described in a quantitative way using conventional data formats. PLs and ILs describe initial scene's luminaires and lighting goals. The double arrow in Fig. 2 represents the communication channel between the optimisation and the lighting calculation tools. We have chosen the *Radiance* computer program for lighting calculations because it has been photometrically and photorealistically validated [Ward94]. The lighting calculations performed inside the optimisation loop of Fig. 2 are the main responsible for the large computation times in our implementation. Each calculation is a light transport computation in a set of directions around a point. Radiance behaviour around a point is calculated by collecting radiance samples around that point (SRD – spherical radiance distribution). Due to the complexity of lighting, many samples are necessary. In our test cases, we have found that 2048 "well distributed" samples on the direction sphere are a good compromise between accuracy and performance, although in many cases 1024

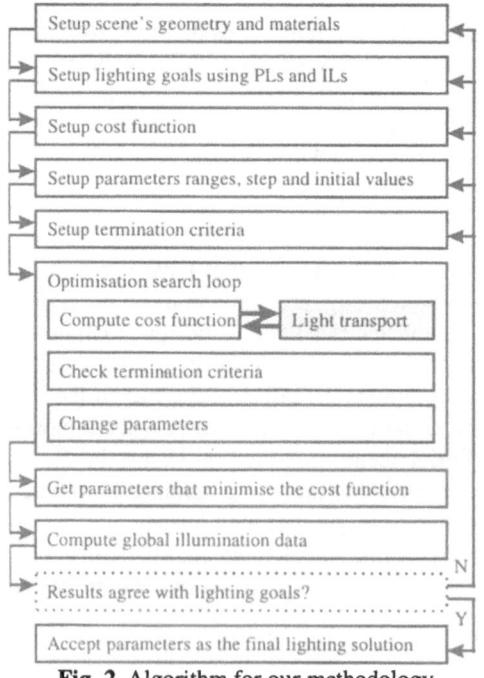

Fig. 2. Algorithm for our methodology

samples also work fine. We have also chosen the *ASA* [Ingbe1998] optimisation software (a SA algorithm). In all tested cases, it has produced good and reproducible results in less than 5000 iterations.

4.1 Design Goals and Cost Functions

The double arrow in Fig. 2 links the optimisation and the lighting calculation tools. The optimisation tool is basically a loop that tests different sets of configuration parameters while trying to maximise a cost function dependent on those parameters. To compute a cost function value, the parameters are passed to a user-defined script that manipulates them and calls the lighting calculation tool as necessary. This script (a representation of the cost function) is user definable and may include relationships, constraints, etc, between parameters and lighting data. Typically, the cost function script $F_{script}(x)$ will measure radiance arriving at particular points and produce a scalar value that is dependent on all the design goals included in this function. We have developed a script language for $F_{script}(x)$: the optimisation parameters are input parameters (x_1, x_2, etc) and it returns as result the calculation of the cost function value. This script language is like a programming language with operators (geometrical, logical, etc), flow instructions (choice, loop, etc) and is implemented with standard tools like GNU *flex* and *bison*. To compute radiance values arriving at a point within a solid angle, there is a special function **Importance**() that actually calls the lighting calculation tool to do it. If luminaire candlepower data is available and essential to the lighting design, then it can be used when computing the radiance values by scaling them with the appropriate candlepower factor (the candlepower distribution must be tabulated or defined analytically). The input parameters represent any design variable relevant to the lighting design problem that must be optimised. As such, they may represent spatial co-ordinates, angles, distances, etc. If a designer says "*I would like to enhance the lighting of this room by adding a projector type luminaire hanging from the ceiling so that illumination on the top of this table improves, but without glare effects or excessive lighting in the user face*", this lighting design problem can be defined by the use of 2 ILs, one for the table top (positive) and another for the user face (negative). The cost function script must verify if the geometrical and directional constraints are respected and compute the fictitious radiance (emitted by ILs) arriving at points dependent on the input parameters to produce its final cost value. In this example, the input parameters represent the luminaire position and direction (5 parameters). The cost script in Code 1. represents those lighting design goals:

```
1.  # (x₁,x₂,x₃):position (x ₄,x₅):direction
2.  # other variables have user defined values
3.  V= Vector (Face Center,(x₁,x₂,x₃))
4.  if Angle (Face Perp,V)<V threshold and
5.      Angl e(Face Perp,Dir (-x₄,-x₅))<A threshold return FAILURE
6.  W L1CL1 = Importance (Scene L1,x₁,x₂,x₃,x₄,x₅)
7.  W L2CL1 = Importance (Scene L2,x₁,x₂,x₃,x₄,x₅)
8.  return -(K ₁*W L1CL1 -K₂*W L2CL1 )
```

Code 1. Cost function

- *line 4* - avoids the luminaire inside the user view
- *line 5* - avoids direct lighting on the user face
- *line 6* - measures the importance of table top IL_1
- *line 7* - measures the importance of user face IL_2
- *line 8* - computes the weighted effect of both ILs.

The contributions of the two ILs have opposite signs in *line 8* because IL_1 represents an objective to maximise while the IL_2 represents an objective to minimise.

5. Results

Radiance has a useful and reliable cache technique that accelerates the calculation of diffuse inter-reflections. In the initial light transport calculations, *Radiance* has to compute a lot of information to build the diffuse inter-reflection cache; after that, it is able to produce light transport data much more quickly, because most of the required information is cached. When working with complex geometries, it is also advantageous to use *Radiance* in persistent mode (it reads the input data and then executes ray-tracing commands when requested without being restarted in each design iteration). This way *Radiance* saves a lot of time setting up its internal data structures again and again. All the simulations were performed on PC's running *Linux* with recent versions of *Radiance* (3R1) and *ASA* (17.19) software. Each simulation was repeated at least 5 times and the best result was taken as the final result. All positional parameters were converted to integer 5cm units and all directional parameters were converted to integer 2° units to reduce the parameter search space to a reasonable size (but still too big to do exhaustive searches).

5.1 Test Case #1

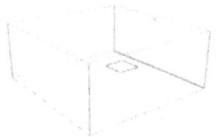

Fig. 3. Geometry of simple scene

Fig. 4. SRD - PL

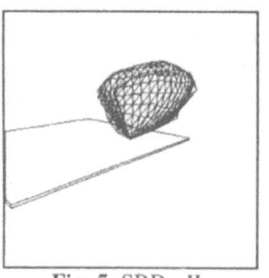

Fig. 5. SRD - IL

The scene is a simple room (6x6x2.5m) with an initial luminaire (PL), located in the right wall near the ceiling, as shown in Fig. 3. The table top is at height 0.8m above the floor and it is not centred in the room. The materials are slightly specular. The lighting design goal is to add another projector type luminaire near the ceiling (above 2.4m) so that the lighting on the table top becomes homogeneous. This lighting goal is modelled with a positive IL on the table top. To account for the PL lighting effects on the table top, it is necessary to calculate the initial lighting distribution over that table top and decide whether or not to subdivide the initial IL into smaller ILs. Fig. 4 shows the radiance distribution due to the PL in a point on the table top. This SRD shows how radiance arrives at the specified point (the larger lobes represent greater incoming radiance in the corresponding direction). If the designer wants a uniform radiance distribution around the point, then there will be some directions where the incoming radiance may already be greater than the desired threshold. For those directions there is no need to shoot fictitious radiance into the scene. For other directions where the desired radiance is not yet achieved, the missing radiance is emitted into the scene as fictitious radiance and it will be used to search for the best luminaire characteristics. The radiance distribution in Fig. 5 is a SRD representing a set of directions where the desired incoming radiance is not yet achieved. In this example, we subdivided the initial IL into four ILs to accurately account for the initial lighting on the table top. To add one projector type luminaire (DL) to the scene, the cost function can be the sum of incoming fictitious radiance emitted by the four ILs. We can anticipate that the solution should be symmetric

Fig. 6. Solution evolution

to the PL, near the ceiling in the opposite wall. The cost function script will call the lighting calculation tool four times (one for each IL) to compute a weighted sum of incoming radiances for each candidate point and solid angle. The image in Fig. 6 shows the evolution of solutions during the optimisation (arrows represent successive intermediate solutions and the final solution is shown with a small sphere). It can be noticed that initial solutions are near the table top, but the directional ILs make the intermediate and final solutions settle in a high region near the left wall. For this design study, because the geometry is very simple, each simulation produces good results in less than 2000 iterations. One simulation with 2000 iterations runs in less than 1 hour.

5.2 Test Case #2

Fig. 7. Geometry of NRC office scene

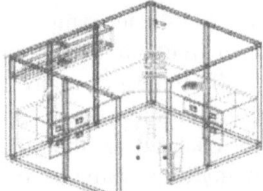

Fig. 8. Working cell in NRC office

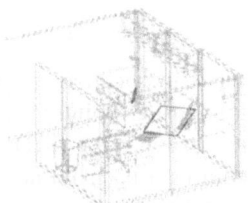

Fig. 9. ILs inside NRC working cell

The previous test case had a very simple geometry, but to show the advantages of this methodology a more complex and realistic scene is used. The next test case uses a scene that is based in a real office (Fig. 7). This scene has 10550 geometric objects (mainly polygons) and some of the materials are specular. The office is composed of 6 working cells and corridors. Each working cell is surrounded by vertical panels and has a L-shaped desk top, a computer screen, some drawers (below and above the desk top) and other small objects over the desk top (Fig. 8). An empirical lighting design solution is shown in Fig. 11 (see Appendix), where the solution is composed of 10 (2x5 grid) rectangular flat panel luminaires in the ceiling (ambient lighting) and 12 projector luminaires on the desk tops (task lighting). This design solution does not take into consideration some important design factors:

- best placement of luminaires for lighting
- glare in user faces for standard sitting positions
- shadow boundaries on the panels and desk tops
- redundancy in the amount of luminaires.

It would be desirable to have a lighting design solution where those factors could be accounted for during the design study, not in the end. The first step to achieve this is to define appropriate lighting design goals:

- lighting on the desk tops – positive IL
- avoid glare in user faces – negative IL
- luminaires in volumes – constraint
- luminaires in row – constraint.

The IL for each desk top has been defined as a rectangle in front of the computer screen and the IL for each user face is a small rectangle corresponding to a human face in standard sitting position – these ILs are represented by the black rectangles in Fig. 9. Let us suppose that the designer wanted to try several types of luminaires and arrangements.

5.2.1 Luminaire Type #1

```
1.  # (x1,x2,x3,x4,x5,x6),(x7,x8,x9,x10,x11,x12),(x13,x14,x15,x16,x17,x18)
2.  # position and direction of each luminaire
3.  # IL1: all the desk tops; IL2: all the user faces
4.  angle=60
5.  WL1DL1 =importance   (Scene L1,x1,x2,x3,x4,x5,x6,angle)
6.  WL1DL2 =importance   (Scene L1,x7,x8,x9,x10,x11,x12,angle)
7.  WL1DL3 =importance   (Scene L1,x13,x14,x15,x16,x17,x18,angle)
8.  WL2DL1 =importance   (Scene L2,x1,x2,x3,x4,x5,x6,angle)
9.  WL2DL2 =importance   (Scene L2,x7,x8,x9,x10,x11,x12,angle)
10. WL2DL3 =importance   (Scene L2,x13,x14,x15,x16,x17,x18,angle)
11. diff y12=Abs (x2-x8); diff y23 =Abs (x8-x14)
12. K0=1/(1+diff fy12+diff y23)
13. K1=1; K 2=100
14. return -K 0*(K 1*(WL1DL1 + WL1DL2 + WL1DL3 )-
           K 2*(WL2DL1 + WL2DL2 + WL2DL3 ))
```
Code 2. Cost function

This design study was made with conical projector luminaires with 120° aperture to analyse the effect of few small sized luminaires located asymmetrically in the room: 3 of those luminaires (DLs) were optimised in one side of central vertical panel, although all desk tops and user faces were considered as ILs. The luminaires were also restricted to point downwards, to be above working cells and preferentially aligned in a row. The cost function script is in Code 2. To favour aligned luminaire arrangements; a weighting factor dependent of the Y differences (smaller horizontal dimension) was also included (*lines 11* and *12*). Each set of luminaire parameters was defined with suitable ranges: near the ceiling over each working cell and directed downwards. To effectively prevent glare, the user face IL was scaled to be 100 times bigger than the desk top IL (*line 13*). Fig. 12 (see Appendix) shows the design solution for this setup (geometry of scene, properties of materials, cost function and parameter ranges). Because this study has a complex geometry and many degrees of freedom, each simulation takes 6 hours to complete (2000 iterations). After 200/300 iterations many candidate solutions tend to concentrate in some part of the configuration search space that corresponds to a small set of positions and directions for each DL. Although *Radiance* has an acceleration technique that is very effective, many times radiance distributions are being calculated in points near previously used points (whose radiance distributions can be saved for later reuse). This led us to the development of a new acceleration technique.

5.2.2 Acceleration Technique for SRD Calculation

Whenever a radiance distribution (SRD) has to be calculated in a certain point, it would be useful to reuse available radiance data from neighbouring points, because that could mean a significant reduction in computation time. In Fig. 10 a SRD must be calculated for point A. This technique (see Code 3.) requires a user defined distance threshold (T_{dist}) to decide if a radiance sample from a neighbouring point is used or not – if the perpendicular distance between parallel radiance directions is smaller than T_{dist}, the radiance value is used and no ray-tracing operation is performed. Previously calculated SRDs from points inside the sphere of radius T_{dist} around A are completely used (point B). If necessary, a sorted list of near points is computed and those points are subjected to the T_{dist} check to reuse the available radiance information (for point C in Fig. 10, radiance values from solid angles α_1 and α_2 would be reused in point A). In the end, if there are missing radiance samples, they are computed with ray-tracing operations. To avoid the propagation of radiance val-

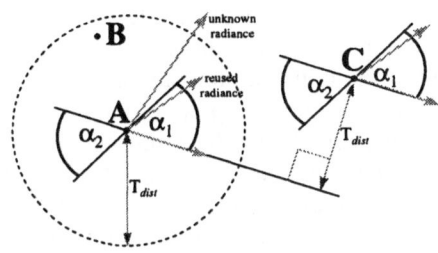

Fig. 10. Acceleration technique

```
1.   calculate_sum_radiances(   Px,Py,Pz,Dx,Dy,Dz,Ap,Tdist )
2.   if SRD( Px,Py,Pz,Dx,Dy,Dz,Ap) already exists
3.      return weighted sum of radiance values
4.   initialise this_SRD
5.   set list_near_SRDS with the nearest SRD's in cache of SRD's
6.   for each near_SRD in list_near_SRDS
7.      if radiance values from near_SRD are valid and not reused
8.         add those radiance values from near_SRD to this_SRD
9.      if this_SRD is fully computed
10.        return weighted sum of radiance values
11.     else
12.        mark radiance values as reused
13.        compute missing radiance values usin    g Radiance
14.        mark those radiance values as new
15.        add those radiance values to this_SRD
16.        save this_SRD in the cache of SRD's
17.        return weighted sum of radiance values
```

Code 3. Acceleration technique

ues from SRD to SRD, which could introduce large radiance errors, each radiance sample carries a flag to indicate if it has already been reused – if so, it is ignored. It is also important to test only a small amount of neighbouring points (less than 30) or else the computation time of this technique becomes greater than the ray-tracing operation. The previous design study was also performed using this acceleration technique with T_{dist} as 5cm and 20 neighbouring points. Design results obtained were very similar (radiance maximum relative error less than 5%). Reduction in computation time was very significant (more than 50%). In a simulation with approximately 6500 iterations, the total amount of radiance calculations was reduced from 18795564 to 5173812 (27.53%). Although this technique requires a considerable amount of bookkeeping, it is not difficult to implement. It produces good results with a significant reduction in computation time even in spaces where desired luminaires are small, very directional and its number is insufficient.

5.2.3 Luminaire Type #2

To overcome the undesirable shadow boundaries generated by spotlight type luminaires, this design study uses 6 omni-directional spherical luminaires with the same design conditions. The lighting design solution is shown in Fig. 13 (see Appendix). The suggested luminaire placement is similar to previous design studies. Although the small size of the spherical luminaires is responsible for some shadow boundaries, ambient lighting is better than in the previous case.

5.2.4 Luminaire Type #3

In this design study an alternative lighting solution was tried to reduce the existence of shadow or penumbra boundaries (mainly due to the small luminaire size). This study uses the original luminaires shown in Fig. 11 (see Appendix), but tries to find an alternative arrangement that optimises the aforementioned lighting design goals. To accomplish this, it was predefined that 5 luminaires would be in a row along the major room dimension, but allowing different spacing distances between them. The design parameters were:

- x, y – reference corner of the leftmost luminaire: over leftmost working cell
- d_1, d_2, d_3, d_4 – spacing between successive luminaires: between 1.5m and 2.5m.

The luminaire height and orientation were also predefined. This originates an optimisation problem with 6 degrees of freedom, but because the luminaires have a large area, each one must be reasonably sampled. We have chosen to sample each luminaire in 4 interior points, which leads to 40 SRD computations per iteration (5 luminaires x 4 points x 2 ILs). Using the reference point of the leftmost luminaire and the 4 spacing distances, the cost function script computes the reference point of the remaining 4 luminaires and samples each at 4 interior points, calculating the contributions of both ILs. Those contributions are finally weighted and combined to produce the cost function value. Fig. 14 (see Appendix) shows an image of the corresponding lighting design solution. It seems to be a good lighting solution because desk top lighting is homogeneous and there are no sharp shadow boundaries visible near the sitting position or any undesirable glare effects. In this study, because the number of SRD calculations per iteration is very big, our acceleration technique produces a significant decrease in computation time. The total amount of radiance calculations for 2300 iterations was reduced from 45258295 to 5147580 (11.37%) and the computation time decreased to less than 30%.

6. Open Questions

Our approach to lighting problems using inverse design seems promising, but there are still many open questions. It is very difficult to convince end users to work with an application based on our methodology and algorithm in its current state. Some of the open questions are discussed next.

6.1 Define lighting design goals

This is a very important question because without a good answer there is no way of solving the design problem. Although it is a difficult question, our experience has shown that most designers are usually trying to solve similar problems, in which the physical component of lighting is the most important and other components (aesthetics, etc) are secondary. Using the IL concept, we think most of the basic lighting design goals can be well described. Lighting design goals related to perceptual aspects, aesthetics, etc, are more difficult to define because they cannot be described by a simple concept (like the IL). Our examples have shown that these goals are more easily defined with some sort of programmable tool like the cost function script we presented. Unfortunately, programming is not a common skill of designers. Some sort of abstraction must be developed to hide this complexity and allow people to clearly and easily state their real lighting design goals.

6.2 What is input data

To solve a lighting design problem, a very basic geometry and little knowledge about the properties of materials is insufficient. Because lighting is closely related to geometry and properties of materials, any design study in which detailed knowledge about those elements is missing will not be able to provide real useful answers. There is even the danger of producing incorrect ones that may completely fail to attain the lighting design goals. This also rises the question of knowing what detail is needed for the geometry and the properties of materials to get correct design solutions in the fastest time possible. Empirically, we can think that small sized objects with mostly diffuse properties could be removed from the geometry, but this must be done carefully and can even lead to serious errors, so it is not generally applicable.

6.3 Find the optimal solution

In our algorithm we are currently using the *ASA* software. Being a simulated annealing algorithm means that it may run for large periods of time until the search is exhausted or something stops its execution. The statistical guarantee of finding the optimal solution is not very useful, because that means that *ASA* finds the optimal solution when it exhausts the search space or with an infinite number of iterations. Our experience with optimisation has shown that veritable solutions are usually found after several thousand iterations (less than 5000), but we cannot ensure that the solution found is optimal or measure its distance from optimality. When the lighting problem context was simple and empirical evidence helped, all solutions found by our algorithm were in agreement with that evidence. But for difficult lighting design problems with complex geometries or complex design goals, empirical evidence is of little help or may even have a negative influence in the solution search. One way to answer this question is by avoiding it. In this case the search would be completely user driven and/or helped by some sort of "intelligent" agents, model based knowledge, genetic algorithms, etc. To accomplish this, the designer should use an interactive graphical interface to test candidate solutions in real time and make decisions on the fly. Unfortunately, this does not seem to be feasible with the existing technology.

6.4 Solve the real problem

Even if it is possible to ensure that quasi-optimal or optimal solutions are generated, there is always the possibility that the solution is not the appropriate one. Errors or uncertainties in the input data (geometry, etc), incorrect specification of goals or other factors may lead to solutions for a problem which is not the designer actual problem. This has to do with the sensitivities between the elements of the problem and the way solutions are generated. For instance, if a highly specular material is described as being only slightly specular, generated solutions may be very different from what they should have been if that specification was correctly made. It seems difficult to measure these sensitivities, but this is an important question because it may affect the designer's confidence in the generated solution.

6.5 Change input data

Up to now, all our lighting experiments have been made with static geometries of the scene and properties of materials. It would very interesting to solve lighting design problems in which the designer could change small elements in the input data (some small subset of the geometry or some property of a certain material) without having to restart the whole process and discard all previously produced data. This seems to be a very big challenge, but the benefits would be huge and the possibilities fascinating. Probably this will require the development of new lighting algorithms which are able to separate and classify meticulously all the lighting exchanges so that partial recalculations become possible without loosing accuracy.

6.6 Future work

In the future we will try to address and give answers to some of the simplest questions raised. The large computation times are a consequence of the simplicity of our algorithm and methods/techniques chosen, so further research has to be made to replace them with more efficient alternatives. The optimisation part of our algorithm also needs to be improved so that quasi-optimal solutions are produced as soon as possible and the amount of iterations performed to produce them decreases significantly. If improved, these two factors will have a great influence in reducing the computation times. The main goal of a project named CASSILDE (*Computer ASSIsted Lighting DEsign*), funded by portuguese ministry of Science and Technology, is the development of an easy to use and intuitive prototype application for designers based on this research work.

7. Conclusions

The main objective of our work is to develop new approaches that can solve the lighting design problem while trying to improve and shorten the design cycle. This paper explains in detail some developments in that approach. It has originated a methodology and an algorithm that semi-automatically tries to solve the lighting design problem. Our algorithm uses well-known tools from Global Illumination and Optimisation fields and links them in a new innovative way. We also present a new acceleration technique for radiance calculations within our algorithm. It allows a faster calculation of radiance distributions and seems to be very effective in reducing the computation times (50-75% reductions in all tested cases). The examples presented in this paper are complex and show the possibilities of this new approach. The solutions found for the several examples seem consistent with empirical evidence, feasible and veritable. In this paper we also present some important open questions related to lighting design and discuss some ideas and possible answers.

References

[Cohen93] Cohen, M.F.; Wallace, J.R.; *Radiosity and Realistic Image Synthesis*; Academic Press 1993.

[Costa99] Costa, A.; Sousa, A.; Ferreira, F.; *Optimisation and Lighting Design - WSCG'99 Proceedings*, Short Papers, pages 29-36; WSCG 1999.

[Feynm85] Feynman, R.; *QED: The Strange Theory of Light and Matter*, Princeton University Press 1985.

[Inbge93] Ingber, L.; *Simulated Annealing: Practice versus Theory - Journal of Mathematical Computer Modelling*, V. 18, N. 11, pages 29-57; 1993.

[Ingbe98] Ingber, L.; *Adaptive Simulated Annealing*; ftp://ftp.ingber.com/pub; Lester Ingber Research; 1993-1998.

[Kawai93] Kawai, J.K.; Painter, J.S.; Cohen, M.F.; *Radioptimization - Goal Based Rendering - COMPUTER GRAPHICS Proceedings*, pages 147-154; SIGGRAPH 1993.

[Kirkp84] Kirkpatrick, S; *Journal of Statistical Physics*, V. 34, pages 975-986; 1984.

[Marks97] Marks, J; Andalman, B.; Beardlsey, P.A.; Freeman, W.; Gibson, S.; Hodgins, J.; Kang, T.; *Design Galleries: A General Approach to Setting Parameters for Computer Graphics and Animation - COMPUTER GRAPHICS Proceedings*, pages 389-400; SIGGRAPH 1997.

[Pirlo96] Pirlot, M.; *General Local Search Methods - European Journal of Operational Research*, N. 92, pages 493-511; Elsevier Science B.V. 1996.

[Pouli97] Poulin, P.; Ratib, K.; Jacques, M.; *Sketching Shadows and Highlights to Position Lights - Proceedings of Computer Graphics International 97*, pages 56-63, 1997.

[Schoe93] Schoeneman, C.; Dorsey, J.; Smits, B.; Arvo, J.; Greenberg, D.; *Painting with Light - COMPUTER GRAPHICS Proceedings*, pages 143-146; SIGGRAPH 1993.

[Veach97] Veach, E.; *Robust Monte Carlo Methods for Light Transport Simulation*, PhD Thesis, Chapter 7, pages 201-218, Stanford University, 1997.

[Ward94] Ward, G.J.; *The Radiance Lighting Simulation and Rendering System - COMPUTER GRAPHICS Proceedings*, pages 459-472; SIGGRAPH 1994.

Editors' Note: see Appendix, p. 379 for colored figures of this paper

Interactive Virtual Relighting and Remodeling
of Real Scenes

Céline Loscos†, Marie-Claude Frasson††, George Drettakis†,
Bruce Walter†, Xavier Granier†, Pierre Poulin‡

†iMAGIS[1]-GRAVIR/IMAG-INRIA
B.P. 53, F-38041 Grenoble, Cedex 9, France
‡Département d'informatique et de recherche opérationnelle, Université de Montréal

Abstract. Lighting design is often tedious due to the required physical manipulation of real light sources and objects. As an alternative, we present an interactive system to *virtually* modify the lighting and geometry of scenes with both real and synthetic objects, including mixed real/virtual lighting and shadows.

In our method, real scene geometry is first approximately reconstructed from photographs. Additional images are taken from a single viewpoint with a real light in different positions to estimate reflectance. A filtering process is used to compensate for inaccuracies, and per image reflectances are averaged to generate an approximate reflectance image for the given viewpoint, removing shadows in the process. This estimate is used to initialise a global illumination hierarchical radiosity system, representing real-world secondary illumination; the system is optimized for interactive updates. Direct illumination from lights is calculated separately using ray-casting and a table for efficient reuse of data where appropriate.

Our system allows interactive modification of light emission and object positions, all with mixed real/virtual illumination effects. Real objects can also be virtually removed using texture-filling algorithms for reflectance estimation.

1 Introduction

Designing the illumination of real environments has always been a difficult task. Lighting design for home interiors for example, is a complex undertaking, requiring much time and effort with the manipulation of physical light sources, shades, reflectors, etc. to create the right ambiance. In addition other physical objects may need to be moved or otherwise changed. The problem is even more complex on movie sets or exterior lighting design. The fundamental trial-and-error nature of the relighting process makes it painful and often frustrating; more importantly, the requirements of constructing and moving real objects and light sources make testing many different potential designs often impossible.

Ideally, we would like to perform such processes entirely synthetically. The lighting designer would simply photograph the environment to be relit and/or remodeled, and then create the different conditions by computer simulation so that they can be evaluated appropriately.

Evidently, such a goal is very hard to accomplish. In this paper we provide first solutions to a subset of this goal, inspired by techniques developed for computer augmented reality, and common illumination between the real and the synthetic scenes [2, 10].

Our method starts with a preprocess, in which real geometry is reconstructed from a series of photos [20], taken from several different viewpoints. A second set of im-

---

[1]iMAGIS is joint project of CNRS, INPG, INRIA and Université Joseph Fourier.

ages (which we call *radiance images*) are taken from a *fixed* viewpoint with a real light source in different positions. The geometry and radiance images are used to extract an approximate reflectance at each pixel for the given point of view. Because reflectance is harder to estimate in shadowed regions, we try to have each visible surface point unshadowed in at least one image. We compensate for geometric and photometric imprecision by filtering and combining results from the individual radiance images. The result of this new approach is an acceptable estimate of reflectance, called a *reflectance image*; in the process, shadows are removed in a satisfactory manner.

Our main goal is to provide *interactive* manipulation of mixed real and virtual environments with common illumination. To achieve this we have separated the calculation of direct and indirect illumination. The reflectance image is used to initialise a hierarchical radiosity system with clustering [23], optimized for dynamic updates [6]. This structure is used for rapid updates of *indirect* light, while *direct* light is computed on a pixel-by-pixel basis. For direct light many components can be pre-computed and cached in a table for rapid use, and in other cases the changes are limited to small regions of screen space, permitting interactive updates. Working on a pixel-by-pixel basis results in high quality direct shadows and also facilitates the removal of real objects, since we can simply manipulate the reflectance image using texture generation methods.

It is important to note outright that we do not attempt to extract *accurate* reflectance values. The goal is to achieve *convincing* relighting at interactive rates. To this end we can ignore inaccuracies and small artifacts, if the overall effect is believable.

2 Previous work

A large body of literature exists in computer vision on reconstructing 3D scenes from photos [8]. However the quality of the extracted 3D models has only recently become satisfactory for computer graphics applications with the presentation of interactive systems such as *Photomodeler* [19], *REALISE* [9, 15], *Façade* [4], and others [20]. While they all include some form of texture extraction and mapping, none treat the extraction of surface properties and re-illumination. Sato *et al.*[21] present a system to extract 3D geometry, texture, and surface reflectance, but it is limited to controlled environments.

With the development of an ever increasing number of computer augmented reality applications, it becomes important to handle the common illumination between real and synthetic scenes. While some previous papers [10, 5] present preliminary solutions, they all require significant user intervention and are limited in different ways in the lighting or geometric conditions they can treat. Recent developments to *Façade* [2] include surfaces property extraction, but rendering times of the *Radiance* [24] system used for image generation are far from interactive.

Nakamae *et al.*[18] developed a solution for merging virtual objects into background photographs, and estimated the sun location to simulate common illumination effects in outdoor environments. More recently Yu and Malik [27] proposed a solution to virtually modify the illumination with different virtual positions of the sun in outdoor scenes.

Loscos and Drettakis [16, 17] have developed an approach to remove shadows, thus enabling synthetic relighting. This technique attempts to remove shadows by computing the best possible approximation using a single image. Despite successful results for certain cases, certain visual artifacts remain in the shadow regions.

In our method, as mentioned in the introduction, we separate direct lighting, which can be easily computed for each pixel, from indirect, or global lighting. Since we will be interactively modifying the scene, we need to be able to update the global illumina-

Fig. 1. The 7 radiance images used for the example presented in this paper.

tion rapidly. To do this, we have used some of the ideas developed by Shaw [22] and Drettakis and Sillion [6].

Removal of real objects from a reconstructed scene requires some form of hole-filling in the real images/textures containing the real objects being removed. Heeger and Bergen [13] have developed a method to synthesize texture images given a texture sample. They use a series of linear filters to analyse the sample and create a texture that matches the sample appearance. Their method is successful on "stochastic" textures (e.g., stucco) but fails on "deterministic" textures (e.g., bricks). El-Maraghi [7] has provided a public domain implementation of their algorithm.

Igehy and Pereira [14] integrate a composition step into the Heeger and Bergen algorithm in order to "erase" flaws (e.g., stains or undesired features) from images. They manually create a mask which indicates which part of the image is to be covered by the synthesized texture and which part keeps its original texture.

3 Overview of the Method

Our goal is to allow interactive synthetic relighting and remodeling of real environments including both removing real lights or objects, and adding virtual ones. To accomplish this, we need to build approximate geometric and reflectance models of the environment and quickly estimate the illumination in modified configurations. We also want our method to be tolerant of measurement and modeling errors in order to work on a broad class of environments. Our process consists of several preprocessing steps followed by an interactive relighting session.

We begin by taking two sets of photographs of the target environment. The first is taken from multiple viewpoints under normal lighting conditions and is used to build an approximate geometric model provided by our photomodeling system [20]. The second set is taken from the fixed viewpoint that will be used during the interactive editing session. These photos use controlled lighting that consists of a single known light source that is moved between photos. We typically use between 5 and 7 such photos (e.g., Fig. 1). This second set, which we will refer to as the *radiance images*, is used to estimate the reflectance on all the visible surfaces.

To recreate sharp shadows, the direct lighting is estimated on a per pixel basis from the fixed viewpoint using ray casting. For each pixel we store its corresponding 3D point and surface, its estimated local reflectance, and its visibility and form-factors to each light. This structure is illustrated in Fig. 2.

Each radiance image is used to estimate the reflectances at each pixel, but may be unreliable in some regions such as shadows. We generate a more robust reflectance

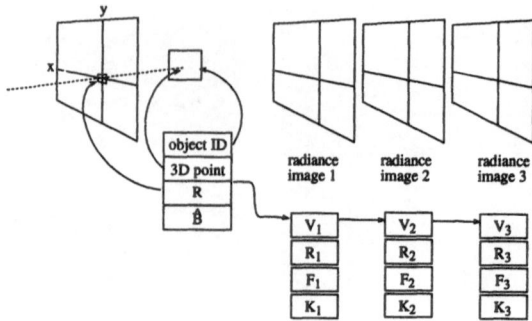

Fig. 2. A per pixel data structure is stored for the interactive view as well as for each radiance image. The visibility to each light V_i, the form-factor to each light F_i, the estimated reflectance at this pixel R_i, and the confidence level K_i of the pixel are stored for each radiance image i. The interactive view stores the merged reflectance R, the ambient term $\hat{B}$, the object's surface ID and the 3D point corresponding to each pixel.

estimator by assigning a confidence for each estimate and combining them from the multiple images accordingly. If we remove real objects, we also estimate the reflectance in regions of the image that become visible. This is accomplished by adapting a texture-filling algorithm.

Once the geometric and reflectance models are extracted, they are used to initialise an hierarchical radiosity system that enables dynamic simulation of the indirect lighting in the environment.

After completing these preprocessing steps, we are ready to interactively model and relight our scene. When we modify the lighting or the geometry of the scene (either real, virtual or both), we efficiently update direct and indirect light. The regions of the image for which direct illumination must be recomputed are efficiently identified in screen space using polygon ID maps and the shaft data structures used for dynamic global illumination. These same structures also allow efficient recomputation of indirect light.

4   Preprocessing

The main goal of the preprocessing steps is to initialise the data structures that will be used during the interactive session. First surface reflectance at each pixel is estimated, and a pixel-based data structure for precomputed direct lighting quantities is initialised. Finally the hierarchical radiosity system is set up for rapid indirect lighting updates.

The process begins by building a geometric model of the environment using our photomodeling system [20]. The user specifies a set of corresponding points in the set of photographs taken from multiple viewpoints. The system uses these to solve for the camera parameters and 3D positions of the points. The user connects these points together into polygons to form a geometric model of the scene and can specify additional constraints to improve the model. All further processing uses the radiance images, with the light source positions measured by the user.

4.1   Pixel Data Structure

The radiance images are all taken from the fixed viewpoint that we will use in our interactive remodeling session. The physical light source we used is a simple garden light covered by white semi-transparent paper to achieve a more diffuse effect. Using a fixed viewpoint simplifies the capture of the real scene (since we need a small number of images); in addition working in image space allows more efficient data structures to be used for display, and generally simplifies the algorithms developed.

Much of the computation is done on a per pixel basis for this viewpoint using an augmented pixel data structure. At each pixel we store (see Fig. 2):

- The 3D point P which projects to the center of this pixel
- The polygon ID of the visible surface containing this point
- The form-factor F_i to each light source from this point
- The visibility V_i to each light source from this point
- The estimated surface reflectance R at this point

We create one such data structure for each radiance image plus an additional one for interactive use which also stores the indirect radiance $\hat{B}$ estimated by the radiosity system for this point. The radiance images additionally store a confidence K_i (≤ 1) at each pixel which indicates how reliable we think its reflectance estimate is.

The polygon ID and 3D point P are obtained by using an item buffer [25] and z-buffer depth values. The form-factor F_i is computed using a standard point-to-polygon technique [1]. The visibility V_i is the fraction of the light source which is visible from point P and is estimated by ray casting from the point to the light source. The number of rays is varied adaptively from 4 to 64, with the higher number being used in regions of penumbra. Initially, confidence K_i is set equal to V_i, since we have less confidence in regions in shadow.

4.2 Reflectance Recovery Algorithm

If we assume that our surfaces are diffuse then there is a simple relation between the radiance L seen by a pixel in the camera, the reflectance R at point P, and the incident light on point P given by:

$$L = R\left(\sum_i F_i V_i E_i + \hat{B}\right) \qquad (1)$$

where E_i is the emittance of light i, $F_i V_i E_i$ is the direct illumination due to light i and $\hat{B}$ accounts for all indirect light. The emittance value is currently set arbitrarily, and an appropriate scaling factor applied to compensate during display.

If all the quantities in question were available and exact, we could solve exactly for the reflectance at each pixel using a radiance image i with its single light source via:

$$R_i = \frac{T^{-1}(C_i)}{F_i V_i E_i + \hat{B}} \qquad (2)$$

where C_i is the pixel color recorded by the camera and $T()$ is the response function of the camera. This function was unavailable for our camera[2] so we have used a simple scaling factor, though it could be accurately estimated using the method of Debevec and Malik [3].

As a first approximation to indirect lighting $\hat{B}$, we have used an ambient term equal to the average image color times a user specified average reflectance [10]. The resulting reflectance gives satisfactory results for our test cases, although more involved indirect

---

[2] A Kodak DC260 digital camera.

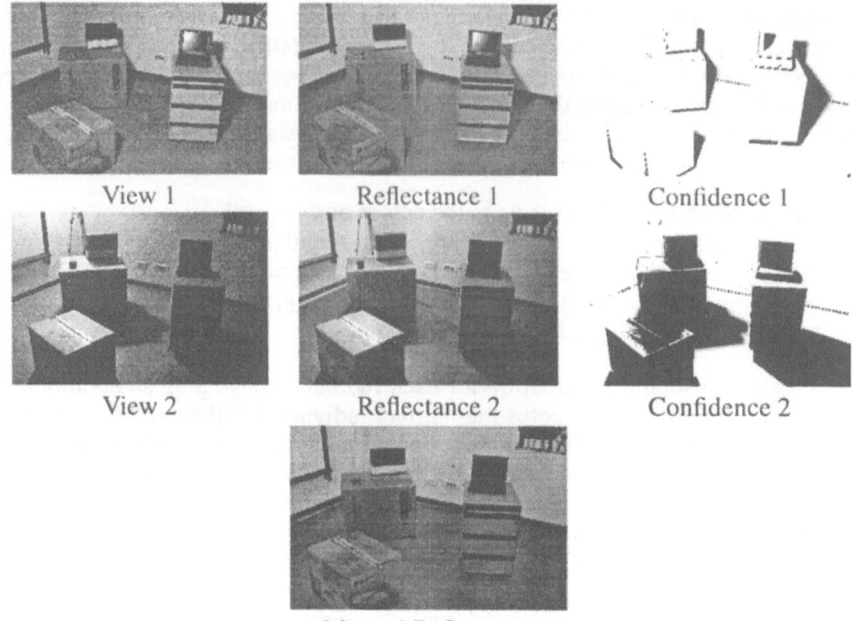

View 1 Reflectance 1 Confidence 1

View 2 Reflectance 2 Confidence 2

Merged Reflectance

Fig. 3. Two of the seven radiance image views (left), the confidence images (right), and the resulting reflectance (center), extracted using Eq.(2). Dark values are for lower confidences. The merged reflectance is shown at the bottom.

lighting calculations may be necessary in other contexts when more accurate reflectance is needed. Some experiments were performed with an iterative approach to reflectance estimation using our radiosity solution, without much improvement in the reflectance estimate. Nonetheless, this is clearly a topic of future work.

Because of the many approximations in our system including the geometry, indirect light, and diffuse assumption, we know that our reflectance estimates will sometimes be quite inaccurate (e.g., in shadow regions where the indirect term dominates). We compensate for this by combining the reflectance estimates from multiple radiance images to form a much more robust reflectance estimator.

For each radiance image i, we also estimate our confidence K_i for each pixel reflectance estimate. The computation of K_i values is explained in next section. The merged pixel reflectance is formed by a weighted average of individual reflectance estimates:

$$R = \frac{\sum_{i=0}^{n} K_i \times R_i}{\sum K_i} \qquad (3)$$

4.3 Filtering Confidence Values

As mentioned above, we initially set the confidence equal to the visibility V with respect to the light source, to reflect the fact that our reflectances are often inaccurate in shadow regions where indirect light dominates. However there are also other conditions that can cause inaccurate reflectance estimates including geometric error, specular highlights, saturation in the camera, and even the movable light source being visible in some images. We use a series of filters to try to identify and reduce the confidence in such problem regions.

Near shadow boundaries visibility V depends heavily on the exact geometry configuration and thus may be unreliable due to inaccuracies in our reconstructed model. To reflect this, we first expand low confidence regions using a 5×5 minimum filter where the pixels confidence is replaced by the minimum confidence in its neighborhood. Abrupt changes in the confidence can also cause objectionable artifacts in the combined results, therefore we next apply a 5×5 smoothing filter.

Lastly, to detect other problem regions, we apply an outlier filter. For each pixel, we compute the median of its high confidence reflectance estimates (e.g., those with $K_i > 0.75$) from the individual radiance images. Estimates which differ by more than a user supplied threshold from this median are assumed to be outliers and have their confidence set to zero. This allows to automatically detect and discount problem regions such as specular highlights and the light source tripod which is visible in some radiance images. Afterwards another smoothing filter (3×3) is applied. Examples of resulting confidence images are shown in Fig. 3 for two views.

Once the confidences have been computed, we combine the reflectance estimates using Eq. (3). The result is more robust and contains fewer artifacts than any of the individual reflectance estimates from the radiance images as shown in Fig. 3.

4.4 Texture Filling for Real Object Removal

Removing a real object from the scene leaves a gap, or previously invisible region, for which we need reflectance estimates. We fill in this missing information using texture synthesis in a technique similar to Igehy and Pereira [14]. We use El-Maraghi's [7] implementation of Heeger and Bergen's [13] texture synthesis in our system.

To synthesize the textures needed, we extract a texture sample from the *reflectance image* from every polygon that now covers the region to fill. The extraction of the sample is currently done manually, but we are experimenting with automatic extraction procedures. This sample is fed to the synthesis algorithm which generates a texture of the same size as the region to fill. The generated texture is applied to the reflectance using a masking process, described in Section 5.3. The generated textures are stored for objects marked as "removable" accelerating the interactive remodeling operations.

It should be noted that texture generation is performed on the reflectance image and is thus not hindered by shadows or lighting variations during the object removal. The reprojection of the shadows with the new scene will generate a correct image of the scene without the real object.

4.5 Initialising the Hierarchical Radiosity System

To bootstrap the hierarchical radiosity system, the reflectance values recovered by Eq. (3) are reprojected onto the corresponding polygons, initialising the reflectance values. For the polygons invisible in the image used for the interactive session, we take a sample of the texture during the photomodeling session and get an average value using Eq. (2). For parts of polygons invisible from the fixed viewpoint, we use an average reflectance value computed from the visible parts.

With this approximation, a first radiosity solution is computed by our system, using an implementation of hierarchical radiosity with clustering [23]. The subdivision is set to a relatively coarse level since such a level is sufficient for computing indirect light, which varies slowly. An example mesh is shown in Fig. 4(b).

Recall that direct effects, including direct shadows, are treated separately for display. Direct light is however computed by the radiosity system, but simply ignored for display. The subdivision is fixed at the beginning of the process to a minimum area

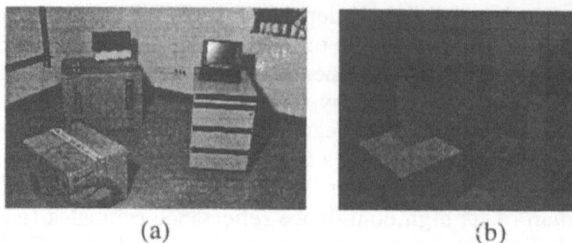

(a)   (b)

Fig. 4. (a) The original view of the scene and (b) the corresponding radiosity mesh used to simulate indirect light and dynamic updates; note the coarse subdivision.

threshold. Nonetheless, we maintain the hierarchical nature of the radiosity algorithm, since links are established at different levels of the hierarchy, using a "standard" BF refiner [12]. Thus we will only need to update links and the radiosity values when performing interactive modifications.

5 Interactive Modification of Scene Properties

Once the reflectance has been computed for each pixel and the radiosity system set up, we can perform interactive modification of scene properties. The modifications that our system permits are related to lighting and geometry. The former includes changing a real light or adding virtual lights; the latter includes adding and moving virtual objects and removing real objects.

The web page *http://www-imagis.imag.fr/Membres/Celine.Loscos/relight.html*, contains high-resolution images and online movie sequences of interactive sessions. All timing results reported below have been taken on a SGI R10000 195Mhz processor.

5.1 Modifying Illumination

When we modify a light source emittance, two operations need to be performed:

- For indirect illumination, we need to compute a new radiosity solution. Given that the subdivision and the link structure are fixed after the initial solution, updating indirect illumination simply requires a few successive sweeps of the hierarchy to "gather" and "push-pull" [12] radiosity and is very fast (less than .05 seconds in our test scenes, since their polygon count is low).
- For display, the direct lighting component is recomputed at each pixel. Indirect illumination is displayed using hardware smooth-shading of the elements of the hierarchical radiosity subdivision, which are then blended into the final image. This results in the addition of the indirect irradiance $\hat{B}$ at each pixel.

In the pixel structure, we have stored the visibility and form-factor with respect to each light source. Thus the computation of the direct component is very rapid.

When displaying an image, we compute the following color at each pixel:

$$C = R\left(\sum_{s=0..n_s} F_s V_s E_s + \hat{B}\right) \qquad (4)$$

for the n_s (real or virtual) light sources in the scene. Before inserting any virtual light source, the scene is lit only with its original light ($n_s = 0$). Shadows are *reprojected* due to the visibility term V_s, since they have been removed from the reflectance.

An example is shown in Fig. 5. The original photo is shown in (a), reprojected initial lighting conditions in (b), and we show the addition of a virtual light source in (c). The entire update for adding the virtual light takes 3.1 seconds broken down as follows: visibility 2.5 sec., shaft/radiosity operations 0.4 sec., indirect light blending and other 0.2 sec. Recall that in the case of the light source insertion, we are required to update *all* the pixels of the image. During dynamic updates, we cast a small number of rays to the light sources, resulting in aliased shadows. An additional "shadow clean-up" could be performed when the user stops modifying the scene, with a higher shadow sampling rate.

5.2 Modifying Scene Geometry

To allow interactivity when adding, removing or moving objects and lights, we maintain a shaft data structure [11], inspired from the work of Drettakis and Sillion [6]. Updating the entire table requires in the order of a few minutes for visibility values, especially when using many rays per light source; using the method described below reduces this time to fractions of a second.

A hierarchical shaft [11] data structure is constructed from the first radiosity solution, and corresponds to each light transfer link. When we add an object it is first attached to the root cluster of the scene; links are established to the light sources as appropriate, based on the refinement criterion, and visibility information is computed.

The hierarchy of shafts is used for two purposes: (a) to identify the pixels for which *direct* illumination has changed (i.e., the shadow regions of the new object); and (b) to identify the links for which visibility needs to be updated (i.e., all links whose shaft is cut by the new object), for both direct and indirect light transfers.

To achieve the above, we descend the hierarchy of shafts, finding those intersected by the new object. The hierarchical elements attached to the end of a shaft originating at a light source are marked as "changed". While descending, the visibility of the modified links is updated. With all necessary links updated, we recompute a radiosity solution with only gather and push-pull steps.

The pixel data structure is then updated and displayed. The bounding box of the initial and final position of the moving object are first projected onto the image-plane, limiting the region of the screen directly affected by the motion. For this region a new item buffer is performed, and the pixels under the previous object position are found as well as those under the new position, since the polygon IDs will have changed. For these pixels, reflectances are kept to the original values for the "uncovered" pixels and updated to that of the virtual object for the newly covered pixels. New form-factors and visibility values are then computed for all the pixels changed in the modified region.

For the pixels associated with patches tagged as "changed", visibility with respect to the sources is recomputed. These are not as localized as the directly affected pixels, but their number is often small.

The entire pixel table is then traversed to update the indirect illumination value at each pixel, based on the new global illumination calculation; again, this is performed with hardware rendering of the hierarchical radiosity patches.

When inserting a new light source, the form-factor and visibility with respect to the source need to be computed for every pixel.

When removing an object, we perform a similar process. We delete every link and all corresponding shaft structures of the removed object.

When moving an object, the process is equivalent, but we do not have to delete the links. We just have to update the information (form-factors and visibilities). Shafts due to the moving object are deleted and reconstructed with its new position.

In Fig. 5(d) we show the insertion of a virtual object in a scene lit with the original light and an added virtual light source. The insertion requires 1 sec., of which visibility accounts for .5 sec., shafts .1 sec. and the rest .4 sec. When moving the virtual object, we achieve update rates of about 1 sec. per frame, with a similar breakdown to that of the object insertion (Fig. 5(e)).

5.3 Removing Real Objects

When the user chooses to remove an object, she indicates the object to the system. Similarly to virtual objects, we know *exactly* which region of the screen will have to be filled, since the correspondences between polygons and pixels are known through the polygon IDs stored in the pixel data structures. We automatically create two masks corresponding to this region: a weight mask and a texture mask [14]. At first, each contains "1" over the region to fill and "0" elsewhere. We extend the weight mask a few pixels to compensate for inaccuracies in the removed object geometry (to avoid leaving any color from the removed object in the image).

The object is then removed from the scene and a new item buffer is performed to update the polygon IDs. The polygon IDs present in the region to be filled indicate from which polygons we have to extract textures. The texture mask is filled with these new IDs and the weight mask is blurred around its "0/1" borders. This allows the composition of the synthesized texture with the texture from the image: when the mask is 0, the color of the pixel will be the color in the reflectance image, when the mask is 1 the color will be taken from the synthesized texture and a fractional weight will allow a smooth transition from the synthesized texture to the original image (e.g., the original colors present in the image).

The reflectance is then updated for the pixels affected, as well as the visibility and form-factors, as in the case of virtual object motion/removal. Results of object removal are shown in Fig. 6.

A second example of real object removal is shown in Fig. 7. In the context of an interior redesign, we may want to remove doors for example, which is hard to do in the real world. This is shown Fig. 7(b). Note that due to approximate reflectance estimation, the texture generation results in slightly visible discontinuities. A virtual object has been added in (c) and a different lighting configuration created in (d).

6 Conclusion

We have presented a new approach to synthetic relighting and remodeling of real environments. Our approach is based on a preprocessing step to recover approximate reflectance properties from a sequence of radiance images. Radiance images are taken from a fixed viewpoint with varying illumination (i.e., different positions of the same light source), using a simplified reconstructed model of the scene. Using the information in the images and the 3D reconstructed model, we create reflectance images for each light position by estimating direct illumination and light source visibility as well as indirect light. The reflectance images are merged by a weighted average based on the confidence level we have in the reflectance at each pixel in each radiance image. In our case, this is based on visibility (points in shadow have low confidence); a filtering step is applied to compensate for errors in geometric reconstruction and illumination computation.

After the reconstruction has been performed we can interactively modify scene properties. This is achieved by efficiently identifying regions of the screen which need updating, and performing a pixel-by-pixel update for direct light. Indirect lighting is treated separately with an efficient hierarchical radiosity structure, optimized for dynamic updates.

In our implementation we can virtually modify real light intensity, insert and move virtual objects, and even remove real objects *interactively*. Despite inevitable artifacts, the quality of the images is sufficient for the purposes of interactive lighting design and limited remodeling.

Independently to our work, Yu *et al.*[26] have recently developed more robust techniques for reflectance estimation, including specular effects in particular. These are based on capturing images of the entire scene, and computing radiosity to estimate the reflectance using clever iterative methods and high-dynamic range images. We believe that our approach can benefit from such improved reflectance estimation (for example to remove the artifacts in texture generation in Fig. 7) as well as for the reflectance of objects which are not visible in the radiance image. On the other hand, we believe that both our interactive approach, especially for global illumination, as well as our confidence maps could be useful for such approaches.

In future work, using the high dynamic range radiance images of Debevec and Malik [3] will allow us to achieve more accurate reflectance extraction. Once we have more confidence in the original radiance most of the errors in the reflectance estimation will be due to indirect light. The hierarchical radiosity framework has the added advantage that it can be used to bound indirect illumination errors and thus should allow us to achieve better results.

We also need to investigate ways to allow motion of the viewpoint, which is currently an important limitation of our approach. Also, the texture generation approaches we have used are limited to stochastic textures. With some user intervention, it may be possible to achieve satisfactory results with deterministic textures also.

From a more practical point of view, we can add the synthetic motion of real objects simply into our system. A view-independent texture of the real object is required, which can be provided by our photomodeling system, as well as a modified rendering routine. As was discussed in the results, the largest expense in the updates is the calculation of visibility for direct lighting. These calculations can be easily parallelized, and we hope to achieve good speedups in a parallel version, enhancing interactivity.

References

1. D. R. Baum, H. E. Rushmeier, and J. M. Winget. Improving radiosity solutions through the use of analytically determined form-factors. In *Computer Graphics (SIGGRAPH '89 Proceedings)*, volume 23, pages 325–334, July 1989.
2. P.E. Debevec. Rendering synthetic objects into real scenes: Bridging traditional and image-based graphics with global illumination and high dynamic range photography. In *SIGGRAPH '98 Conference Proceedings*, Annual Conference Series, pages 189–198, July 1998.
3. P.E. Debevec and J. Malik. Recovering high dynamic range radiance maps from photographs. In *SIGGRAPH '97 Conference Proceedings*, Annual Conference Series, pages 369–378, August 1997.
4. P.E. Debevec, C.J. Taylor, and J. Malik. Modeling and rendering architecture from photographs: A hybrid geometry- and image-based approach. In *SIGGRAPH '96 Conference Proceedings*, Annual Conference Series, pages 11–20, july 1996.
5. G. Drettakis, L. Robert, and S. Bougnoux. Interactive common illumination for computer augmented reality. In *Rendering Techniques '97 (8th Eurographics Workshop on Rendering)*, pages 45–56. Springer-Verlag, June 1997.

6. G. Drettakis and F. Sillion. Interactive update of global illumination using a line-space hierarchy. In *SIGGRAPH '97 Conference Proceedings*, Annual Conference Series, pages 57–64, August 1997.

7. T. El-Maraghi. An implementation of Heeger and Bergen's texture analysis/synthesis algorithm with source code. http://www.cs.toronto.edu/~tem/2522/texture.html.

8. O. Faugeras. *Three-Dimensional Computer Vision — A Geometric Viewpoint*. MIT Press, 1993.

9. O. Faugeras, S. Laveau, L. Robert, G. Csurka, and C. Zeller. 3D reconstruction of urban scenes from sequences of images. Tech. report 2572, INRIA Sophia-Antipolis, May 1995.

10. A. Fournier, A.S. Gunawan, and C. Romanzin. Common illumination between real and computer generated scenes. In *Proc. of Graphics Interface '93*, pages 254–262, May 1993.

11. E. A. Haines and J. R. Wallace. Shaft Culling for Efficient Ray-Traced Radiosity. In *Photorealistic Rendering in Computer Graphics (Proceedings of the 2nd Eurographics Workshop on Rendering)*, New York, NY, 1994. Springer-Verlag.

12. P. Hanrahan, D. Salzman, and L. Aupperle. A rapid hierarchical radiosity algorithm. In *Computer Graphics (SIGGRAPH '91 Proceedings)*, volume 25, pages 197–206, July 1991.

13. D.J. Heeger and J.R. Bergen. Pyramid-Based texture analysis/synthesis. In *SIGGRAPH '95 Conference Proceedings*, Annual Conference Series, pages 229–238, August 1995.

14. H. Igehy and L. Pereira. Image replacement through texture synthesis. In *Proceedings of the 1997 IEEE International Conference on Image Processing*, 1997.

15. F. Leymarie, A. de la Fortelle, J. Koenderink, A. Kappers, M. Stavridi, B. van Ginneken, S. Muller, S. Krake, O. Faugeras, L. Robert, C. Gauclin, S. Laveau, and C. Zeller. Realise: Reconstruction of reality from image sequences. In *International Conference on Image Processing*, volume 3, pages 651–654, Lausanne (Switzerland), 1996. IEEE Signal Proc. Soc.

16. C. Loscos and G. Drettakis. Interactive relighting of real scenes. Tech. report 0225, INRIA Rhône-Alpes, November 1998.

17. C. Loscos, G. Drettakis, and L. Robert. Interactive modification of real and virtual lights for augmented reality. In *SIGGRAPH '98 Technical Sketch (Visual Proceedings)*, July 1998.

18. E. Nakamae, K. Harada, T. Ishizaki, and T. Nishita. A montage method: The overlaying of the computer generated images onto a background photograph. In *Computer Graphics (SIGGRAPH '86 Proceedings)*, volume 20, pages 207–214, August 1986.

19. Photomodeler. http://www.photomodeler.com.

20. P. Poulin, M. Ouimet, and M.-C. Frasson. Interactively modeling with photogrammetry. In *Rendering Techniques '98 (9th Eurographics Workshop on Rendering)*, pages 93–104. Springer-Verlag, June 1998.

21. Y. Sato, M.D. Wheeler, and K. Ikeuchi. Object shape and reflectance modeling from observation. In *SIGGRAPH '97 Conference Proceedings*, Annual Conference Series, pages 379–387, August 1997.

22. E. Shaw. Hierarchical radiosity for dynamic environments. *Computer Graphics Forum*, 16(2):107–118, 1997.

23. F. X. Sillion. A unified hierarchical algorithm for global illumination with scattering volumes and object clusters. *IEEE Transactions on Visualization and Computer Graphics*, 1(3):240–254, September 1995.

24. G.J. Ward. The RADIANCE lighting simulation and rendering system. In *Proceedings of SIGGRAPH '94*, Annual Conference Series, pages 459–472, July 1994.

25. H. Weghorst, G. Hooper, and D. P. Greenberg. Improved computational methods for ray tracing. *ACM Transactions on Graphics*, 3(1):52–69, January 1984.

26. Y. Yu, P.E. Debevec, J. Malik, and T. Hawkins. Inverse global illumination: Recovering reflectance models of real scenes from photographs. In *SIGGRAPH '99 (to appear)*, 1999.

27. Y. Yu and J. Malik. Recovering photometric properties of architectural scenes from photographs. In *Computer Graphics (ACM SIGGRAPH '98 Proceedings)*, July 1998.

Editors' Note: see Appendix, p. 380 for colored figures of this paper

Beyond Photorealism

Stuart Green

LightWork Design Ltd., 78 Clarkehouse Road, Sheffield, S10 2LJ. UK
stuart.green@lightwork.com

Abstract. For around 30 years the computer graphics research community has pursued photorealism as though it were the ultimate form of visual expression. Yet, as an art form, photorealism is one of many abstractions that an artist might use to convey ideas, shape, structure, emotion and mood. In this paper we describe how techniques and wisdom learned from photorealistic computer graphics can be adapted and applied to a diverse range of alternative styles for visual expression.

1 Introduction

From the first moments of the pioneering work in computer graphics some 30 years ago, the quest for realism has been an enduring goal. The term *photorealism* has been coined to denote techniques and art forms in which proponents strive to create synthetic images that are so lifelike they might be mistaken for photographs of real world scenes and objects. While advocates of photorealism have, over the years, conceived a wide range of methods and algorithms for synthetic image generation, the purest and dominant form of these has been *physically-based* techniques. These are inspired and driven by observations of the physical world, in which the interaction of light with the surfaces and objects in an environment, and the projection of an image on the film within a camera, are the key processes to be emulated.

The techniques of ray tracing and radiosity have become established as powerful complementary tools in the photorealistic rendering toolbox. In both cases, the physical behavior of light is *simulated* within a virtual world to yield, in the best cases, fine examples of the hallmarks of photorealism.

Pursuit of photorealism through simulation is the most demanding of tasks. Our world is incredibly rich and diverse; the processes of nature are complex and often hard to predict precisely. Today, researchers can define synthetic environments that contain just the right kind of objects made from the right kind of materials, illuminated by the right kind of lights, and from these create a convincing image. But we are still not quite ready to respond to the challenge of the general case. Many researchers have focused on the diverse elements of the physical world, such as materials simulation, light interaction, performance of optical systems and of the chemical process that transforms a momentary exposure of light on the surface of photographic film into a permanent image. To solve the general photorealism problem there is still original research work left to do.

It is curious to note that often researchers set about a solution to these demanding physical simulations not because there is necessarily a clearly identified need for a solution, but because the technology can be applied to arrive at a solution. This is often the case of technologists with a solution in search of a problem. Certainly, there are plenty of viable applications of photorealism, including special effects in film and design visualization, however, the techniques applied are often empirical rather than physically-based – simulating reality is not so important as creating the *illusion* of reality in the mind of the observer.

2 Photorealism Defined

Before defining NPR, it is necessary to understand what is *really* meant by the term 'photorealistic rendering'. **Photo** comes from the Greek *phos*, meaning light, or produced by light. **Realistic** means depicting or emphasizing what is real and actual, rather than abstract or ideal.

Rendering, in this context, is traditionally regarded to mean a perspective drawing showing, for example, an architect's idea of a finished building. In the computer graphics community, rendering is taken to refer to the process by which the representation of a virtual scene is converted into an image for viewing.

The art of photorealistic rendering had many proponents long before the birth of computer graphics. The work of the artist Johannes Vermeer (1632-1675) exhibits properties that are photographic in their quality. The perspective within the subject matter is very closely observed, and brush

Figure 1: *The Music Lesson* by Vermeer.

strokes are short and subtle and cannot easily be discerned in the finished painting. It is widely believed that Vermeer used a *camera obscura* to compose his paintings – a lens system and a projection screen was placed in front of the subject (an indoor scene) and the projected image was copied precisely. Despite whatever mechanical aids Vermeer may have used, his work stands as a most impressive example of photorealistic rendering at its best. However, some critics of his day were less appreciative of the work, accusing it of being cold, inartistic and prone to displaying 'spiritual poverty'. Since the advent of photography, photorealism in art has become less fashionable, and has given way to more abstract and stylized forms of representation.

It is interesting that the criticisms of Vermeer's work in the 17th century are equally true of some modern practitioners of photorealistic computer graphics. Certainly, the early attempts at photorealistic computer graphics, while technically impressive, were regarded as sterile and cold, being too perfect and lacking feeling. The efforts of numerous researchers over the last 30 years have placed a rich set of tools in the hands of the artist. Yet it is important to recognize that photorealistic rendering is not nor ever will be the panacea of the artist; it is simply one of many art forms at the artist's disposal. An important skill of the artist is in choosing the right medium for each job, which will be guided by such considerations as aesthetic appeal and effectiveness of communicating the visual message.

Prior to the impressionist movement, the majority of fine art was intended to capture a view of nature – the talent of the artist was measured by how closely a painting resembled its subject. Impressionism introduced a popular art form in which the painting style was not necessarily an accurate reflection of reality. Impressionist artists were ridiculed by the critics of the time. A key differentiation of the art form was that the canvas itself was an active part of the picture – the shape of the brush strokes and the texture of the layers of paint were used to convey emotion and mood, with colors often being bold and exaggerated. Brush strokes can be used to direct the eye, and focus attention on the important elements of a composition. Long flowing strokes and short, sharp jabbing strokes convey stark contrasts of emotion, just as the choice of palette can evoke sensations of warmth or coldness.

3 Introducing NPR

A few years ago, a number of researchers began to pursue alternative forms of artistic expression in computer graphics. This research was often in marked contrast to that of the photorealistic rendering advocates, and became known as **nonphotorealistic rendering** (NPR). It is rather absurd to describe a field of research and development after that which it is not, yet the term has endured and has become adopted by the computer graphics community to denote forms of rendering that are not inherently photorealistic. The terms *expressive, artistic, painterly* and *interpretative* rendering are often preferred by researchers of the field since they convey much more definitively what is being sought.

The term NPR is used in this paper in deference to current popular terminology, but that term is itself a hindrance to the NPR movement. By analogy, it would be like categorizing the whole of fine art into 'Impressionist' and 'Non-Impressionist', and using the latter term to categorize all art forms by the fact that they are not in keeping with the Impressionist style. To do so has the effect of de-emphasizing and degrading other art forms. A richer vocabulary is needed to enable the art forms to develop through the written and spoken word as well as through the practice of the art itself.

So what is NPR? A definition along the lines of "a means of creating imagery that does not aspire to realism" is fundamentally flawed. For example, the images of Figure 2 fit this definition, but could they be regarded as examples of NPR? To strive for a definition of NPR is as pointless as defining "Non-Impressionist". The field is in its infancy, and it is hard to be specific about what it is (and therefore more convenient to state what it is not). The richness and diversity of computer-assisted art forms is at least as wide as those of traditional art. Photorealism is but one form of representation; in time the term NPR will be replaced by others that are more specific to the branches of computer assisted art forms.

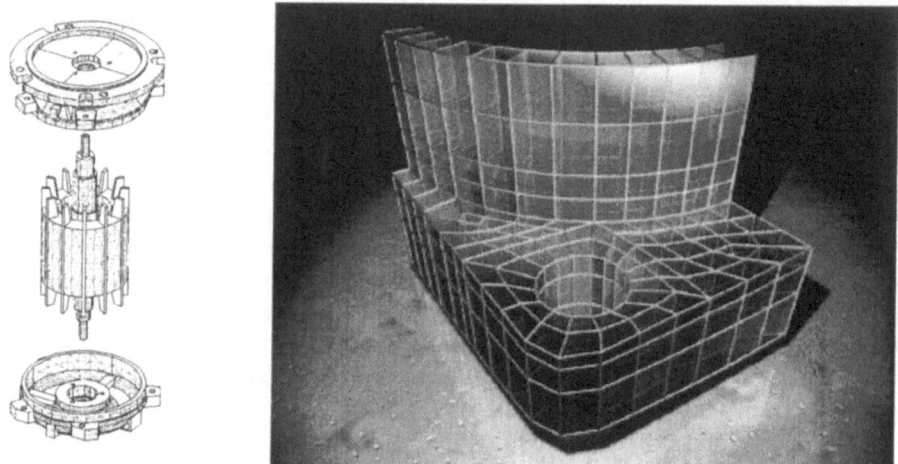

Figure 2: These images are not regarded as photorealistic. Are they NPR?

Not surprisingly, early proponents of NPR have focused their attention on *natural media emulation* – the reproduction of traditional art forms, such as styles based on the media of pen and ink, watercolor and oil on canvas. Natural media emulation can be regarded as one branch of NPR research. But NPR offers a much wider scope than this and the opportunity to experiment with new art forms that have not previously been popularized, either because they have not been 'discovered' or because those art forms would be impractical to create by hand.

In contrast to photorealism, in which the driving force is the modelling of physical processes and behavior of light, the processes of *human perception* can drive NPR techniques. This can be just as demanding as physical simulation but for different reasons – a technologist may find comfort in developing algorithms to reproduce a certain physical phenomenon that is objective and relatively predictable. The fact that the photorealistic rendering problem can be expressed as a single equation [Kajiya86] provides a comforting focal point of the quest – a notion that there is a single, correct solution. Developing techniques to replace, augment or even assist the subjective processes of an artist requires a shared understanding of the use to which these techniques will be put, and the creative processes the artist undergoes. The finest examples of NPR work will be produced when artists and technologists work together to identify a problem and develop solutions that are sympathetic to the creative processes. For NPR there is no single correct solution – no rendering equation to solve.

The inclination of the technologist is often to pursue techniques that require minimal intervention by the user, and a goal might be to devise schemes that generate images fully automatically. This is certainly a guiding principle of photorealism, where involvement of the user to provide 'hints' for the software is generally regarded as a bad thing. A number of NPR researchers have demonstrated that generation of certain styles can be automated quite successfully, most notably the pen and ink emulation of Winkenbach [Winkenbach94], and the impressionist effects of Litwinowicz [Litwinowicz97] and Hertzmann [Hertzmann98]. However, it is important to differentiate between expressive *style* (such as impressionism, expressionism, photorealism) and the artistic *medium* (watercolor, pastel, charcoal). For the latter, it seems valid to express algorithmically how charcoal might appear on heavily textured paper, or a wet wash might cause bleeding in watercolor. However, simulating artistic expression is another matter – we should recognize that computers are not creative or inventive, but should be treated as tools that allow users to express themselves. When the task of generating a complete, stylized picture is delegated to the computer, this can give rise to results that are amateurish and simplistic.

Apodaca describes some of the techniques that are used for computer generated imagery in film making which he calls *photosurrealism* [Apodaca98]. Although based in realism, there are techniques that are distorted and shaped under the guidance of the director to arrive at the false reality that is deemed necessary to tell the story. Story telling is about creating illusion – convincing the audience that the unreal is real. Digital cinematographers require the most extreme flexibility in the tools that they use to create the required end result, usually resorting to effects that are inherently non-physical.

4 Comparing and Contrasting Photorealism and NPR

Table 1 provides a comparison of the trends of photorealism and NPR.

	Photorealism	NPR
Approach	Simulation	Stylization
Characteristic	Objective	Subjective
Influences	Simulation of physical processes	Sympathies with artistic processes; perceptual-based
Accuracy	Precise	Approximate
Deceptiveness	Can be deceptive or regarded as 'dishonest'; viewers may be misled into believing that an image is 'real'	Honest – the observer sees an image as a *depiction* of a scene
Level of detail	Hard to avoid extraneous detail; too much information; constant level of detail	Can adapt level of detail across an image to focus the viewer's attention
Completeness	Complete	Incomplete
Good for representing	Rigid surfaces	Natural and organic phenomena

Table 1: Comparing and Contrasting Photorealism and NPR

5 An Overview of NPR Research

Here we provide a short overview of the trends in NPR research in recent years. This is not intended to be exhaustive, but simply to give an indication of approaches that have been popular.

Historically, NPR research can be regarded as having originated in early 2D interactive paint systems, such as Quantel Paintbox. These systems provided synthetic artist drawing objects, such as air brushes and pencil, and the user applied these to a canvas to create pixel-based effects. Researchers have developed these techniques further and two prominent areas emerged: 2D brush-oriented painting involving more sophisticated models for brush, canvas, strokes, etc., and 2D/2½D post-processing systems in which raw or augmented image data is used as the basis for image processing. A number of researchers have explored techniques that can be applied to photographic images to synthesize painterly renderings of those images.

One of the key approaches that separate branches of research in the field is the degree to which user intervention is required. Some researchers have favored automatic techniques that require no or very limited user input, while others use the computer to place strokes at the guidance of the artist. 2½D paint systems have been developed in which augmented image data is used to automate paint actions initiated by the artist on pre-rendered scenes.

A more recent trend of NPR research has been the adoption of 3D techniques. The classic 3D computer graphics rendering pipeline exposes a number of opportunities within which NPR techniques can be applied to manipulate data in both 3D and 2D forms. A number of researchers have focused on providing real time algorithms for NPR which afford stylized visualizations of 3D data that can be manipulated interactively. The view-independence of some of these approaches provides obvious benefits for the generation of animation sequences.

Taxonomy for NPR is provided by [Teece98b], in which different approaches are classified primarily according to whether they are 2D or 3D, and whether user intervention is required. This provides four principle categories of NPR research as summarized in Table 2.

	2D or 2½D	3D
No User Intervention	Saito90 – Rendering 3D Shapes Bakergem91 – Free-hand Plotting Buchanan96 – Effects with Half-Toning Litwinowicz97 – Video Processing Treavett97 – Automated NPR Images Hertzmann98 – Using brushes of multiple sizes	Sasada87 – Drawing Natural Scenery Winkenbach94 – CG Pen & Ink Illustr. Strothotte94 – Rendering Frames Elber95 – Line Art Rendering Meier96 – Painterly Rendering Lebaredian96 – Rendered Cel Look Claes97 – Networked Rendering Markosian97 – Real-time NPR Gooch98 – Technical Illustration Gooch99 – Interactive Technical Illustration
User Intervention	Strassman86 – Hairy Brushes Haeberli90 – Paint by Numbers Litwinowicz91 – Inkwell Cockshott92 – Modelling Paint Texture Hsu94 – Skeletal Strokes Salisbury94 – Pen & Ink Illustration Schofield96 – Piranesi Curtis97 – CG Watercolor	Teece98a/b – 3D Expressive Painter

Table 2: A taxonomy of NPR systems, adapted from [Teece98b]

6 Kazoo and Non-Photorealistic Rendering

LightWork Design has developed LightWorks®, a photorealistic rendering toolkit over the last ten years which is used primarily by 3D design products [LightWorks]. Over the past few years the company has observed a growing desire amongst users for forms of visualization other than photorealism. Photorealistic computer graphics has its place, but the visual messages conveyed can be too precise and sterile for certain applications. A designer often has the need to convey work in progress, which is incomplete and imprecise, or to express a design idea to inspire a client. Realistic rendering is not well suited to this.

To respond to this need, the company has developed the **Kazoo**™ family of software for providing NPR styles to application programs [Kazoo]. The Kazoo Toolkit offers a configurable rendering pipeline that provides a software infrastructure within which a wide range of existing and new NPR styles can be developed. Some example styles are illustrated in Figure 3.

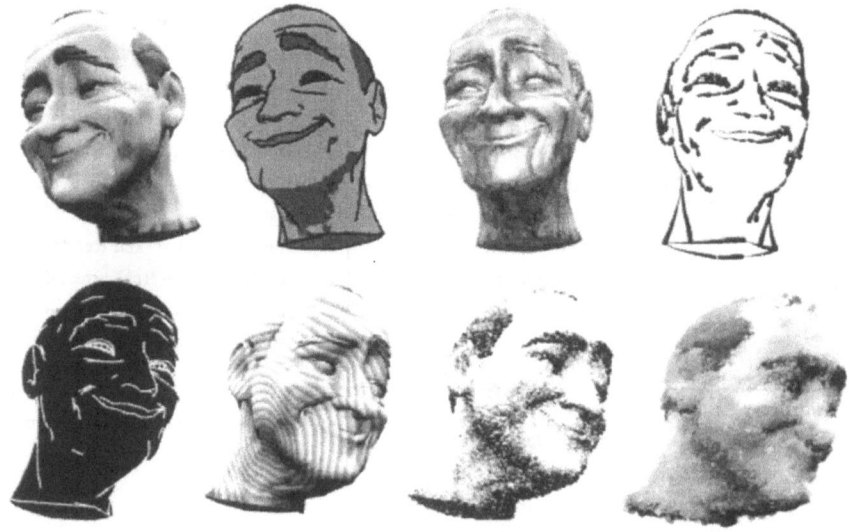

Figure 3. Example Kazoo Styles

The requirements of flexibility and configurability for NPR are much the same as those required in a photorealistic rendering system. Consequently, LightWorks served as an effective core technology on which to build Kazoo. Kazoo was designed to accommodate two configurable rendering pipelines. These are a *shading pipeline* and a *stroke pipeline*. The former accepts 3D surface geometry and yields raster image data. The latter also accepts 3D surface geometry and yields both 2½D resolution-independent stroke data (curves) or image data. A *Kazoo style* is implemented using one or both of these pipelines configured to deliver the required result. When both pipelines are used, this may be in parallel (when usually the stroke output is superimposed on the shading output) or sequentially (when usually the output of the stroke pipeline drives the input of the shading pipeline). There is no limit to the number of passes through the pipelines that can be performed for the generation of a single image.

The Kazoo shading pipeline is an enhanced photorealistic renderer, with each stage being configurable such that it may be substituted with purpose-written software by the style writer. Input to the pipeline is 3D data represented as polygons, implicit surfaces and parametrically defined surfaces. A style may begin by optionally performing some deformation to the geometry, for example, to give a false perspective. This distorted geometry is then passed to the visibility-processing step to yield a collection of surfaces for shading. These surfaces are divided into multiple sample points within the visible region beneath each pixel. The sample points are shaded by a series of steps that treat orthogonal characteristics of the surfaces, including their illumination and reflectivity. Finally a post-processing step provides a framework within which image-based effects can be implemented. This step, as indeed are most others, is multi-pass in that repeated occurrences of the step can be applied as required.

The Kazoo stroke pipeline also begins with 3D surface data that may be optionally deformed. But it differs from the shading pipeline in that the visibility processing is designed to determine visible edges (boundaries and silhouettes) that are classified against surfaces. A stroke generation stage then evaluates these edges to yield continuous 2½D strokes. Intuitively, a stroke is a single line that would be placed on the canvas by an artist. The stroke generation combines the geometric properties of the edges and applies a series of heuristics to arrive at a candidate stroke drawing sequence. Note that at this point the strokes can be regarded as 2½D because their appearance is view-dependent.

Having evaluated a collection of strokes, the next stage in the pipeline is to optionally deform the strokes, for example, to provide randomness or to distort them. After deformation, the strokes can be either rasterized then post-processed as in the shading pipeline, or alternatively they can be used directly as resolution-independent strokes. Although the strokes are at this point recorded as a 2½D data set, sufficient geometric interaction is maintained with them so that 3D surfaces can be reconstructed through a back-projection stage. The resulting 3D data can be passed through one of the pipelines again for further processing.

These pipelines can be combined and programmed to enable a wide range of styles to be designed and developed. Further examples of Kazoo styles are given in the color plates.

7 Conclusion

It is remarkable that photorealism has endured for so long as the goal of the work of so many researchers in computer graphics. For a community that is so culturally diverse and technologically advanced, the focus on so pure an art form to the exclusion of virtually all others is almost without precedent. But this begs the question: is computer graphics art or science? While the development of computer graphics systems is predominantly the domain of the scientist, it is artists who are responsible for the *application* of those systems. Computer-generated imagery is at its finest when technologists and users work together to define and solve common problems. Much of the work of researchers is done in environments that lack any art or user direction, or any strong sense of application or practical purpose. This can give rise to proliferation of solutions that lack tangible accompanying problems.

For the research community, NPR represents a gold mine of opportunity, with recent proponents having addressed a wide range of subject matter, including various artistic media such as pen and ink, watercolor and pencil sketch.

One of the refreshing aspects of NPR is that it brings closer together the disciplines of art and science; its value is far less on the technical brilliance of the techniques but on the aesthetics of the results, and the scope to convey shape, structure and artistic expression. It is an area that requires artists and engineers to work together to solve new and challenging problems in computer graphics.

References

[Apodaca98]   A.A. Apodaca. "Photosurrealism", in Rendering Techniques '98, Proceedings of the Eurographics Workshop in Vienna, Austria, pages 315-322, 1998.

[Bakergen91]   W. D. van Bakergen and G. Obata, "Free-hand plotting - is it Live or is it Digital", CAD Futures 91, Vieweg, Wiesbaden.

[Berman94]   D. F. Berman, J. T. Bartell and D. H. Salesin, "Multiresolution Painting and Compositing", Computer Graphics (Proc. Siggraph), ACM SIGGRAPH, ACM Press, July 1994.

[Buchanan96]   John W. Buchanan, "Special Effects with Half-Toning", Eurographics '96 proceedings, Volume 15, Number 3, Blackwells Publishers, 1996.

[Claes97]   Johan Claes, Patrick Monsieurs, Frank Van Reeth and Eddy Flerackers, "Rendering Pen-drawings of 3D scenes on networked processors", WSCG '97 proceedings, Volume 1, February 1997.

[Curtis97]   Cassidy Curtis, Sean E. Andersen, Joshua E. Seims, Kurt W. Fleischer and David H. Salesin, "Computer-Generated Watercolour", Computer Graphics (Proc. Siggraph), ACM SIGGRAPH, ACM Press, August 1997.

[Elber95]   Gershon Elber, "Line Art Rendering via a Coverage of Isoparametric Curves", IEEE Transactions on Visualization and Computer Graphics, Volume 1, Number 3, September 1995.

[Gooch98]   Amy Gooch, Bruce Gooch, Peter Shirley, and Elaine Cohen. "A Non-photorealistic Lighting Model for Automatic Technical Illustration." Computer Graphics (Proc. Siggraph), ACM SIGGRAPH, July 1998.

[Gooch99]   Bruce Gooch, Peter-Pike Sloan, Amy Gooch, Peter Shirley, and Richard Riesenfeld. "Interactive Technical Illustration". Interactive 3D Conference Proceedings, April 1999.

[Haeberli90]   Paul Haeberli, "Paint by Numbers: Abstract Image Representations", Computer Graphics (Proc. Siggraph), Vol. 24, No. 4, ACM SIGGRAPH, ACM Press, August 1990.

[Hertzmann98]   Aaron Hertzmann, "Painterly Rendering with Curved Brush Strokes of Multiple Sizes".Computer Graphics (Proc. Siggraph), pages 453–460. ACM SIGGRAPH, July 1998.

[Hsu94]   Siu Chi Hui and Irene H. H. Lee, "Drawing and Animation using Skeletal Strokes", Computer Graphics (Proc. Siggraph), ACM SIGGRAPH, ACM Press, August 1994.

[Kajiya86]   J.T. Kajiya. "The Rendering Equation" In Computer Graphics (SIGGRAPH '86 Proceedings) pages 143-150, 1986.

[Kazoo]   Kazoo™. LightWork Design Ltd. http://www.kazoo3d.com

[Lebaredian96]   Rev Lebaredian, "Traditional Cel Animation Look with 3D Renderers", Siggraph 96 Visual Proceedings, ACM SIGGRAPH, ACM Press, 1996.

[LightWorks]   LightWorks®. LightWork Design Ltd. http://www.lightwork.com

[Litwinowicz91]   Peter Litwinowicz, "Inkwell: A 2½-D Animation System", Computer Graphics (Proc. Siggraph), Vol. 25, No. 4, ACM SIGGRAPH, ACM Press, 1991.

[Litwinowicz97]   Peter Litwinowicz, "Processing Images and Video for An Impressionist Effect", Computer Graphics (Proc. Siggraph), ACM SIGGRAPH, ACM Press, 1997.

[Markosian97]   Lee Markosian, Michael A. Kowalski, Samuel J. Trychin, Lubomir D. Bourdev, Daniel Goldstein and John F. Hughes, "Real-Time Nonphotorealistic Rendering", Computer Graphics (Proc. Siggraph), ACM SIGGRAPH, ACM Press, 1997.

[Meier96]   Barbara Meier, "Painterly Rendering for Animation", Computer Graphics (Proc. Siggraph), 1996.

[Saito90]   Takafumi Saito and Tokiichiro Takahashi, "Comprehensible Rendering of 3D Shapes", Computer Graphics (Proc. Siggraph), Vol. 24, No. 4, ACM SIGGRAPH, ACM Press, August 1990.

[Salisbury94]   Michael P. Salisbury, Shaun E. Anderson, Ronen Barzel and David H. Salesin, "Interactive Pen-and-Ink Illustration", Computer Graphics (Proc. Siggraph), Vol. 28, No. 4, October 1994.

[Salisbury96]   Michael P. Salisbury, Corin Anderson, Dani Lischinski and David H. Salesin, "Scale-Dependent Reproduction of Pen-and-Ink Illustrations", Computer Graphics (Proc. Siggraph), ACM SIGGRAPH, ACM Press, 1996.

352

[Salisbury97]   Michael P. Salisbury, Michael T. Wong, John F. Hughes and David H. Salesin, "Orientable Textures for Image-Based Pen-and-Ink Illustration", Computer Graphics (Proc. Siggraph), ACM SIGGRAPH, ACM Press, August 1997.

[Sasada87]   Tsuyoshi T. Sasada, "Drawing Natural Scenery by Computer Graphics", Computer-Aided Design, Vol. 19, No. 4, May 1987.

[Schofield94]   Simon Schofield, "Nonphotorealistic Rendering", Doctoral Dissertation, Middlesex University, England, 1994.

[Schofield96]   Simon Schofield, "Piranesi: A 3-D Paint System", Eurographics UK 96 Conference Proceedings, 1996.

[Strassman86]   Steve Strassman, "Hairy Brushes", Computer Graphics (Proc. Siggraph), Vol. 20, No. 4, ACM SIGGRAPH, ACM Press, August 1986.

[Teece98a]   Daniel Teece, "3D Painting for Non-Photorealistic Rendering", SIGGRAPH '98 Conference Abstracts and Applications, ACM SIGGRAPH, ACM Press, July 1998.

[Teece98b]   Daniel Teece, "Three Dimensional Interactive Non-Photorealistic Rendering", PhD Thesis, University of Sheffield, England, 1998.

[Treavett97]   S.M.F. Treavett and M. Chen, "Statistical techniques for the automated synthesis of non-photorealistic images", Proc. 15th Eurographics UK Conference, March 1997.

[Winkenbach94]   Georges Winkenbach and David H. Salesin, "Computer-Generated Pen-and-Ink Illustration", Computer Graphics (Proc. Siggraph), Vol. 28, No. 4, ACM SIGGRAPH, ACM Press, 1994.

[Winkenbach96]   Georges Winkenbach and David H. Salesin, "Rendering Parametric Surfaces in Pen and Ink", Computer Graphics (Proc. Siggraph), ACM SIGGRAPH, ACM Press, 1996.

Editors' Note: see Appendix, p. 381–382 for colored figures of this paper

Appendix: Colour Images

Myszkowski et al. (pp. 5–18)

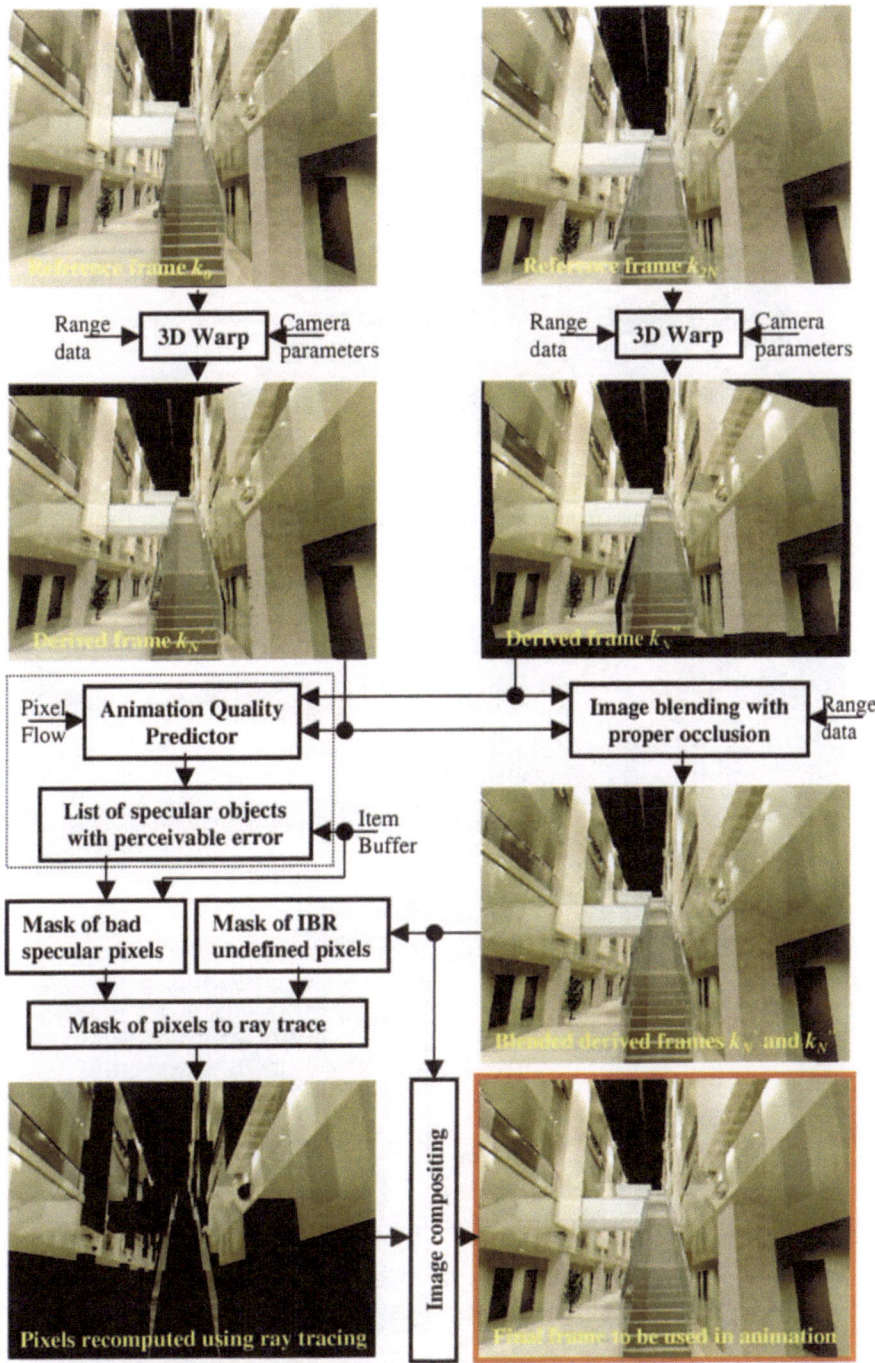

Fig. 1. The processing flow for inbetween frames

Walter et al. (pp. 19–30)

Fig. 2. Some frames from a render cache session. See main text for more detail

Fig. 8. Some example images captured from interactive sessions. Some approximation artifacts are visible but the overall image quality is good. All scenes are ray traced except the lower right which is path traced. In the upper right image we have just moved the ice cream glass and you can see its shadow in the process of being updated on the table top

Bala et al. (pp. 31–44)

Plate A: Tunnels and Interpolant Dependencies

 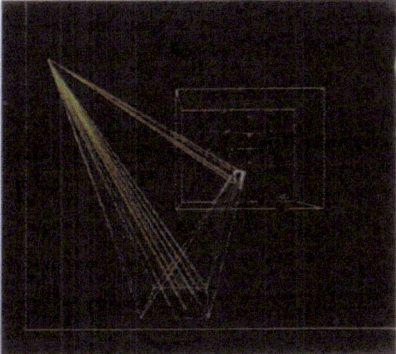

Fig. 1. 3 spheres. On the right, one interpolant for the red sphere is shown. The interpolant has: a reflection tunnel to the ground, and a direct tunnel to the light

 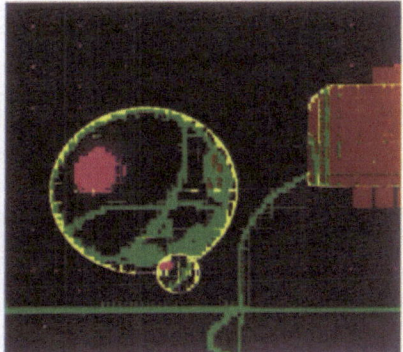

Fig. 2. Scene edit. The green sphere is replaced by the yellow cube. On the right, a color-coded image shows the impact of the edit. Blue-gray pixels are interpolated. Green, yellow and magenta pixels fail due to the error predicate. Interpolants are only invalidated and rebuilt for the dark red pixels

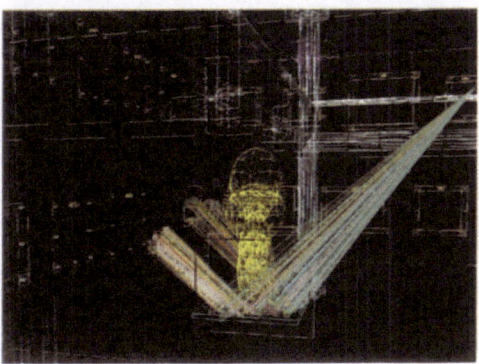

Fig. 3. Museum scene, interpolant dependencies. Interpolants that depend on the reflective mirror

Plate B: Scene Edits for Museum Scene

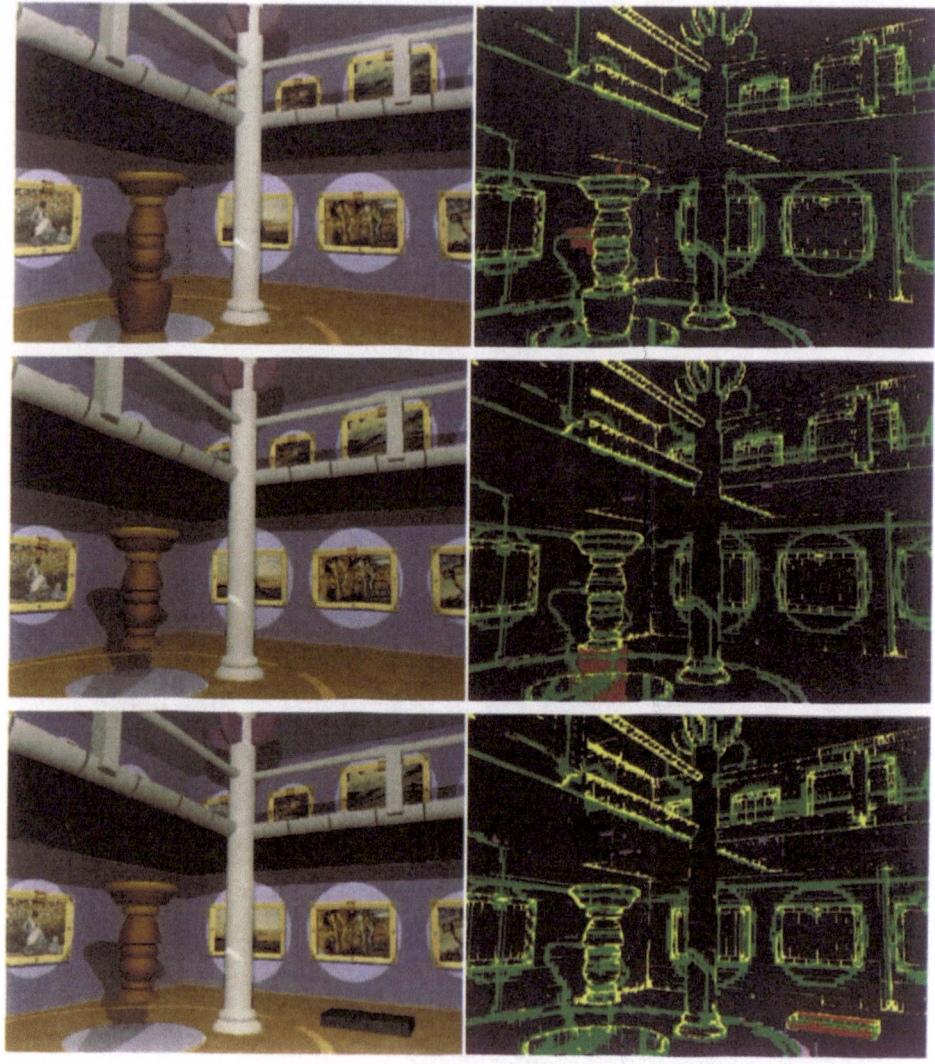

Museum scene

Top to bottom:
Edit-(a) – delete top of sculpture
Edit-(b) – delete bottom of sculpture
Edit-(c) – add green bench

Westermann et al. (pp. 45–56)

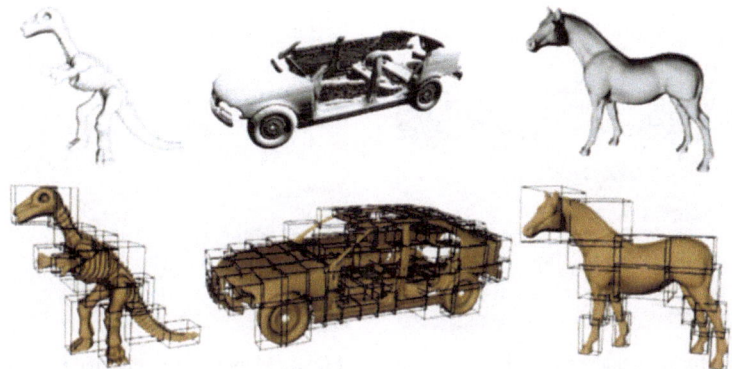

Fig. 6. Different polygonal models have been converted into sets of distance volumes (bottom row) and rendered via 3D textures (top row)

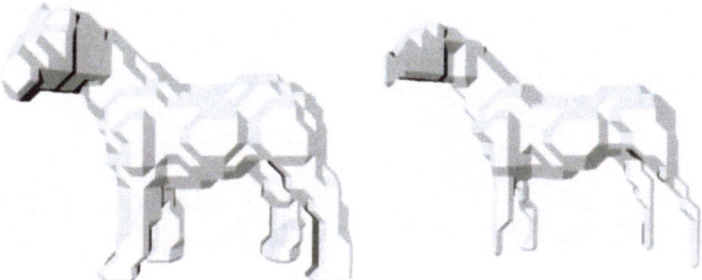

Fig. 7. The outer and the inner mesh used to render the thin boundary region around the surface of the voxelized horse data set

Fig. 8. The shading of voxelized models on a per-pixel basis using Phong's illumination model

Max et al. (pp. 57–62)

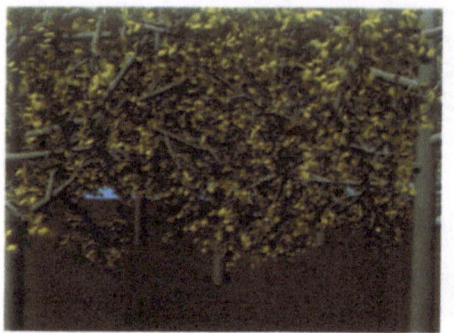

Fig. 1. Maple forest, rendered by IBR

Fig. 2. Maple forest, rendered with polygons

Fig. 3. Mixed oak and maple forest, by IBR

Fig. 4. Closer view of maple and oak forest

Fig. 5. A close-up, showing leaf texture

Fig. 6. A long view of the whole forest

Udeshi and Hansen (pp. 63–76)

a Direct lighting

b Gray-level shadow (25 light samples)

c Indirect lighting (brightened
for display. 32 virtual light
sources shown in green)

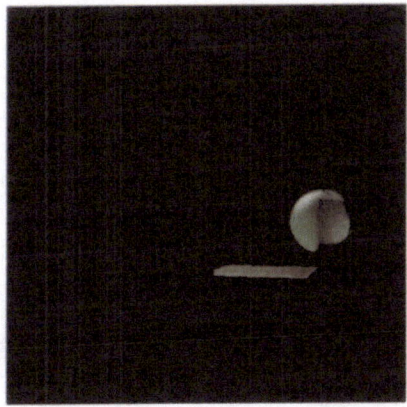

d Raytraced portions

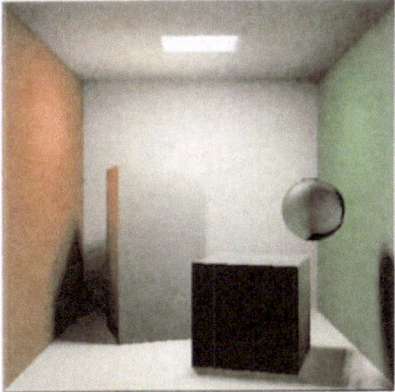

e Final blended image

Fig. 10. Images showing different stages of rendering. These images were generated using four pipes

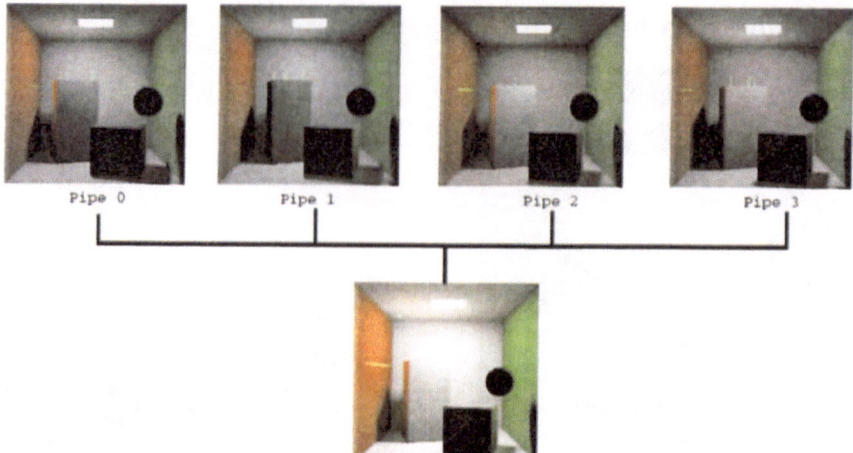

Fig. 11. Images rendered by different pipes. Each pipe contributes to both the shadow and indirect lighting generation

Fig. 12. Office scene rendered at over tour frames a second using 8 pipes and software compositing

Premože et al. (pp. 107–118)

Fig 2. A rendering of the same data as used to generate Fig. 1, after processing using the techniques from this paper

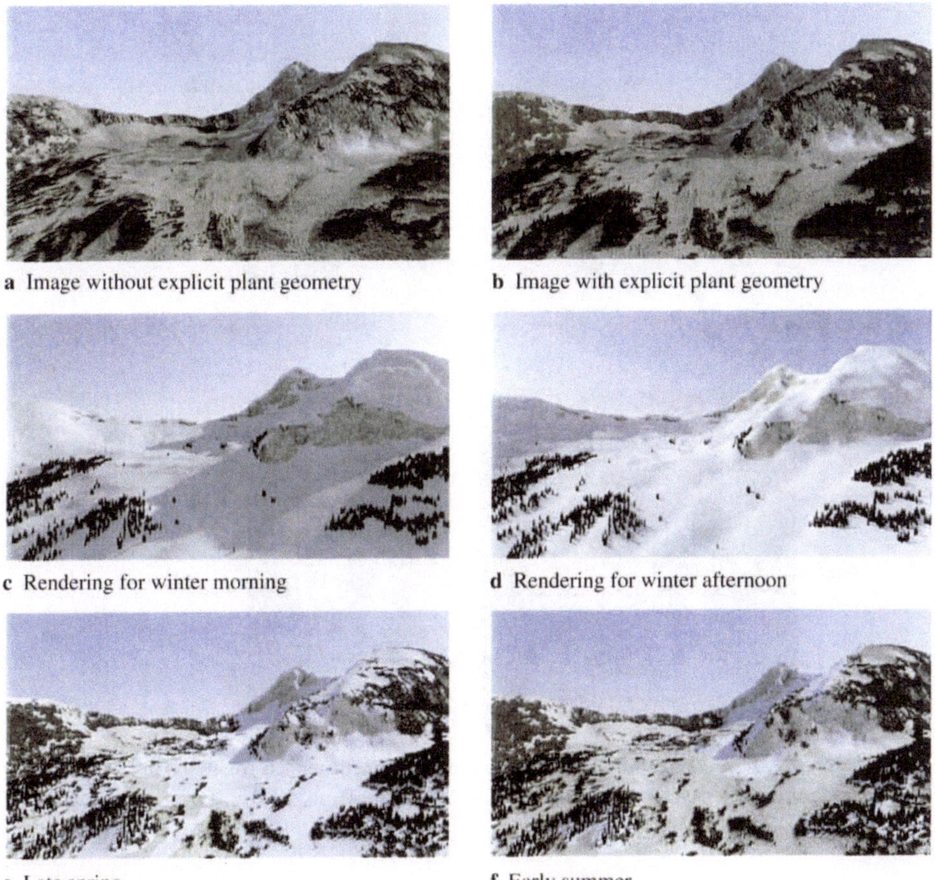

a Image without explicit plant geometry

b Image with explicit plant geometry

c Rendering for winter morning

d Rendering for winter afternoon

e Late spring

f Early summer

Fig 7. Renderings of a 2 km by 2 km region in the Wasatch Mountains at different time of day/year

Rocchini et al. (pp. 119–130)

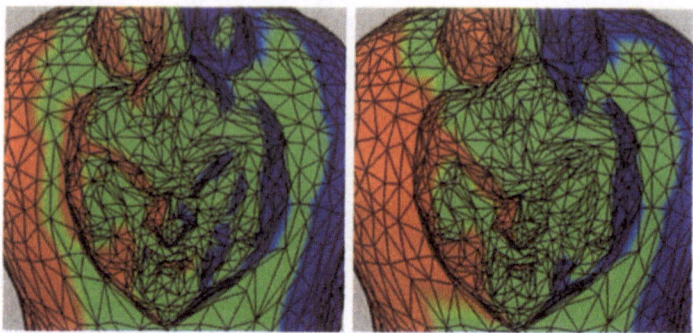

Fig. 1. An example of optimized frontier faces management: in the initial configuration on the left we have 1,137 frontier faces out of the total 10,600 faces; after optimization (on the right) we get only 790 frontier faces

Fig. 2. A comparison of the accuracy of the synthetic models (right) *wrt* the original object images (left)

Marschner et al. (pp. 131–144)

Plate 1. A rendered image showing a scene containing objects made of the measured materials

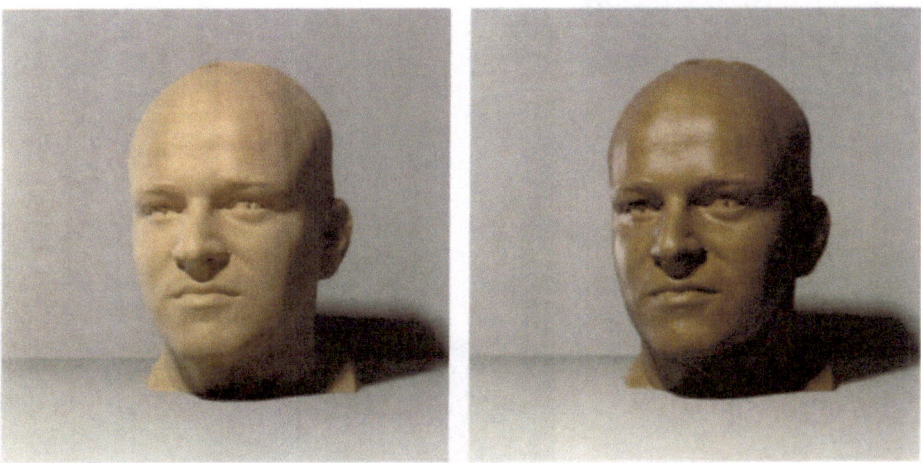

Plate 2. Rendered images showing BRDFs measured from two different subjects

McAllister et al. (pp. 145–160)

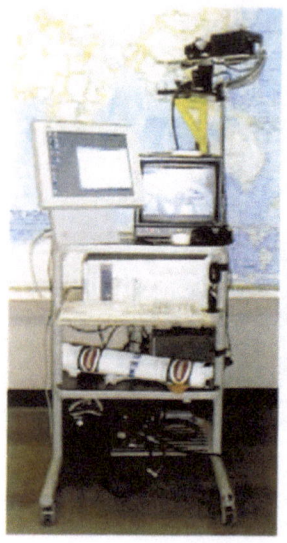

Left: The scanning rig used to acquire environments. **Middle:** A range scan registered with a color image. White lines are silhouette edges. **Right:** An item buffer resulting from warping a source image to the viewpoint of another source image with Z comparison (McAllister et al.)

Upper Left: An environment made from two scans – one with Henry, one without. **Lower Left:** A plant scanned from four positions, composited using quadratic splats. **Right:** Library with plants and leather chairs, composited from two scans (McAllister et al.)

Fu et al. (pp. 161–174)

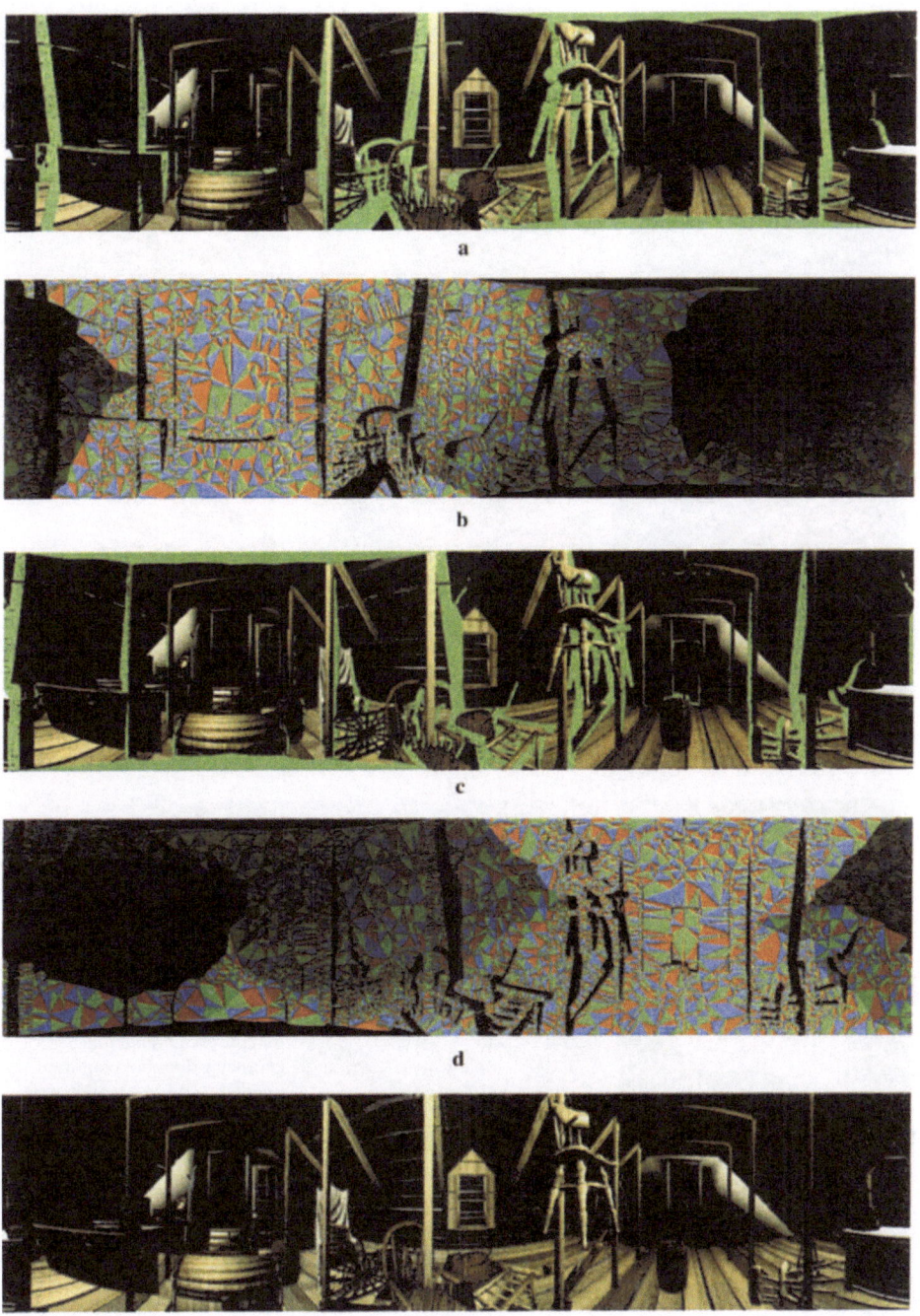

Fig. 13. Blending of two warped panoramas

Schaufler and Priglinger (pp. 175–186)

Fig. 12. The system for interactive frustum placement: The main window shows the object together with the frusta. One is highlighted for editing. In the lower left corner the view obtained using this frustum is given. **Left:** Displacement mapped globe. **Middle:** Scanned dragon head from the Stanford 3D Scanning Repository. **Right:** Polygons to be displaced into the dragon head (the image planes of the frusta)

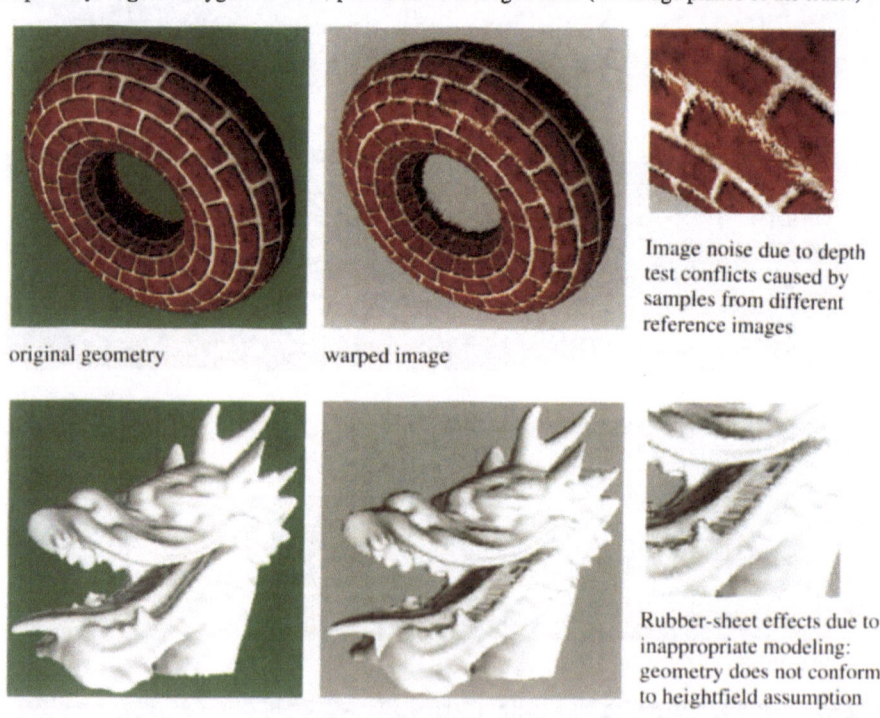

original geometry   warped image

Image noise due to depth test conflicts caused by samples from different reference images

Rubber-sheet effects due to inappropriate modeling: geometry does not conform to heightfield assumption

Fig. 13. Comparison of images obtained from original geometry and from warped reference images

Heidrich et al. (pp. 187–196)

Light field rendering with decoupled geometry and illumination, the latter being provided through an environment map. **Top:** color coded texture coordinates for the environment map, as extracted from the geometry light field. **Bottom:** final renderings. Compare Fig. 3

The glossy torus on the left is the result of a geometry rendering with a prefiltered environment map. The torus in the center represents the refraction part. Both parts have been weighted by the appropriate Fresnel term. The right image shows the combination of the two parts. Compare Fig. 4

Rendering of vector-quantized light fields. **Left:** uncompressed, **center:** reduced resolution on the (u, v)-plane, **right:** reduced resolution in all 4 dimensions

Keating and Max (pp. 197–212)

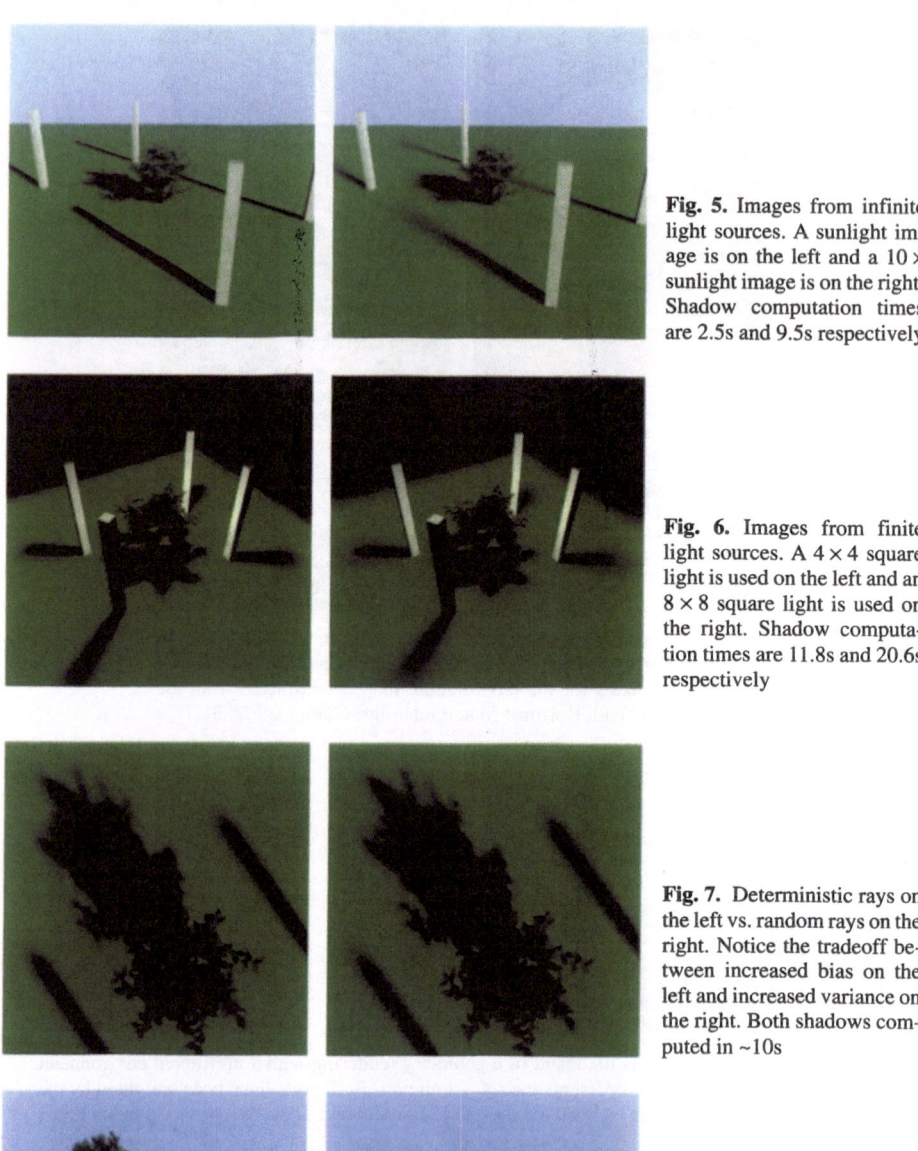

Fig. 5. Images from infinite light sources. A sunlight image is on the left and a $10 \times$ sunlight image is on the right. Shadow computation times are 2.5s and 9.5s respectively

Fig. 6. Images from finite light sources. A 4×4 square light is used on the left and an 8×8 square light is used on the right. Shadow computation times are 11.8s and 20.6s respectively

Fig. 7. Deterministic rays on the left vs. random rays on the right. Notice the tradeoff between increased bias on the left and increased variance on the right. Both shadows computed in ~10s

Fig. 8. Left: A demonstration of self-shadowing using a dense tree in sunlight, shadow computed in 18.6s

Fig. 9. Right: Using filter weights to simulate multiple light sources with one filter

Schöffel and Pomi (pp. 225–234)

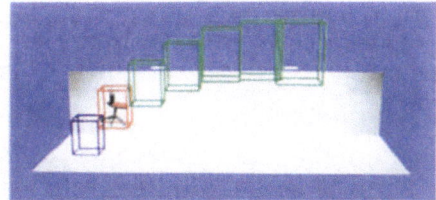

Fig. 4. Examples of predicted bounding volumes: The red wireframe box indicates the current position of the dynamic object, the blue box outlines the previous one. Predicted volumes are drawn in green. In the left example, two future positions have been calculated, while in the right image, five predicted positions are shown, taking into account object translation and rotation

Fig. 5. Dynamic shaft management: In the bottom row, links are displayed for those shafts that are stored (only links for the light sources are shown); the same scene without links is shown above. The chair is being moved from the right to the left. **Left:** Shafts at the old position of the chair. **Middle:** Shafts for the new position are added. **Right:** After line-space update, outdated shafts are removed by the garbage collector

Fig. 6. A more complex test environment. Only links from the light source to the floor that are affected by moving the seat are shown. Note that due to balancing, mesh resolution on the floor appears finer than link resolution

Damez and Sillion (pp. 235–246)

ACTOR   LIGHT

Fig. 4. Representative frames from example animations

Kautz and McCool (pp. 247–260)

Raytraced

OpenGL
single–term
ND + L2 norm

Fig. 12. HTSG copper, Poulin/Fournier's brushed metal, Lafortune/Willems' modified Phong, measured velvet, measured peacock feather, and measured grey vinyl

Fig. 13. Diffuse texture maps can be added to single-term separable decompositions for the specular highlight. **Left to right:** Ward's anisotropic BRDF; Ward's anisotropic BRDF (oriented orthogonally to the first example); (measured) varnished wood

Icart and Arquès (pp. 261–272)

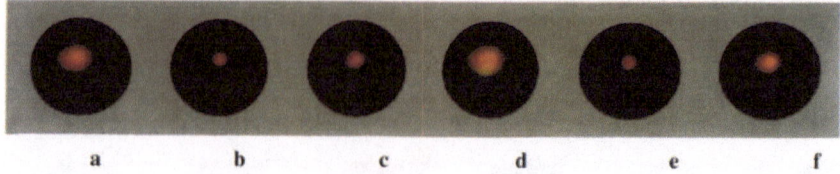

Fig. 4. Directional diffuse intensity for $e_{min} = 800$ nm, $e_{max} = 1000$ nm
a, d $\sigma = 100$ nm, $\tau = 800$ nm **b, e** $\sigma = 100$ nm, $\tau = 1600$ nm **c, f** $\sigma = 130$ nm, $\tau = 1600$ nm

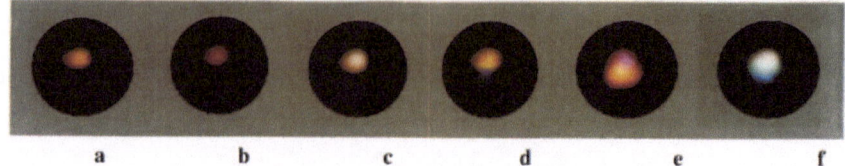

Fig. 5. Directional diffuse intensity for $\sigma = 100$ nm, $\tau = 1$ μm
a, d $e_{min} = 0.8$ μm, $e_{max} = 1.2$ μm **b, e** $e_{min} = 1.5$ μm, $e_{max} = 1.7$ μm **c, f** $e_{min} = 0.8$ μm, $e_{max} = 1$ μm

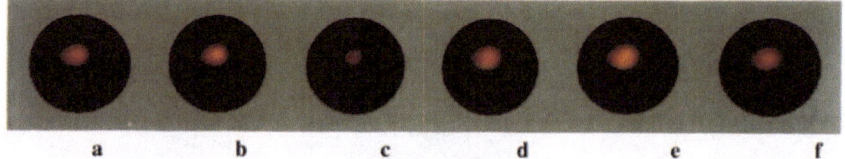

Fig. 6. Directional diffuse intensity for $e_{min} = 800$ nm $e_{max} = 1000$ nm
a, d $\sigma = 80$ nm, $\tau = 800$ nm **b, e** $\sigma = 120$ nm, $\tau = 1200$ nm **c, f** $\sigma = 150$ nm, $\tau = 1500$ nm

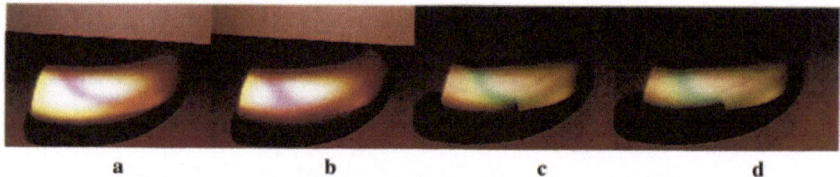

Fig. 7. a, b A piece of copper/copper oxide piping. **c, d** A piece of iron/iron oxide piping

Fig. 8. A set of iron saucepans coated with identical iron oxide thin films with different thicknesses: From left to right: $e_{min} = e_{max} = 0$ nm; $e_{min} = 250$ nm $e_{max} = 450$ nm; $e_{min} = 500$ nm $e_{max} = 650$ nm; $e_{min} = 650$ nm $e_{max} = 800$ nm

Jensen et al. (pp. 273–281)

Fig. 6. Rock on sandy beach with different wetness functions. **a** Dry, **b** mixed wet and dry, **c** water covering the rock, **d** completely wet

Fig. 7. Cognac spilled on wood table

Mostefaoui et al. (pp. 283–292)

Fig. 6. Three tori showing from left to right the difference between considering: no effect, self-shadowing and self-shadowing plus inter-reflections

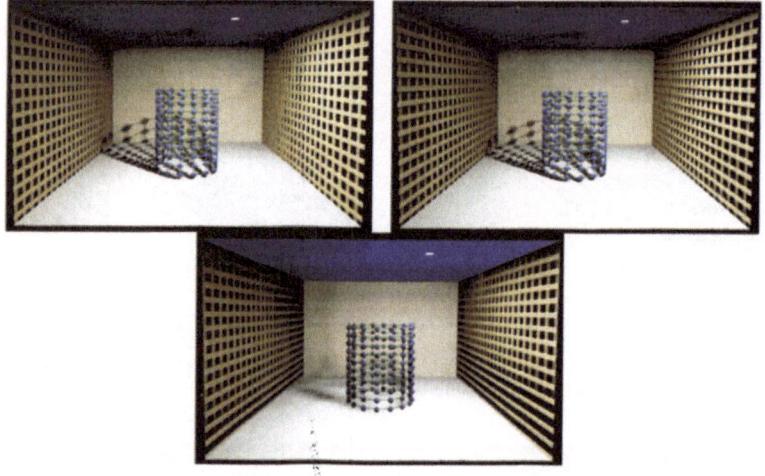

Fig. 7. A comparison between a texturing approach and an "explicit" approach

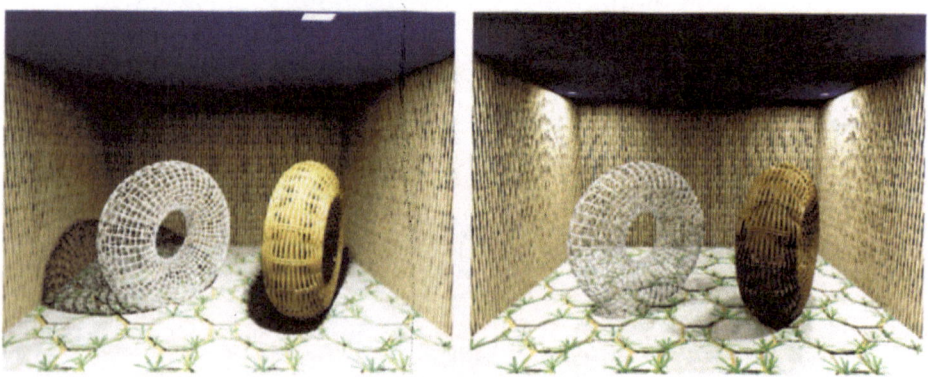

Fig. 8. A scene showing textures under different lighting conditions

Willmott et al. (pp. 293–304)

a HRVC, 108,000 triangles, 707s

b HRVC, 1000 triangles, 7s

c Scalar FCR, 108,000 triangles, 7s

d Vector FCR, 108,000 triangles, 8s

Fig. 7. Face cluster radiosity (FCR) and hierarchical radiosity with volume clustering (HRVC) algorithms applied to a detailed dragon model

Fig. 8. Face clusters on the Venus head model. A total of 8000 randomly coloured clusters are shown

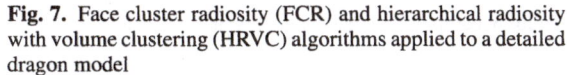

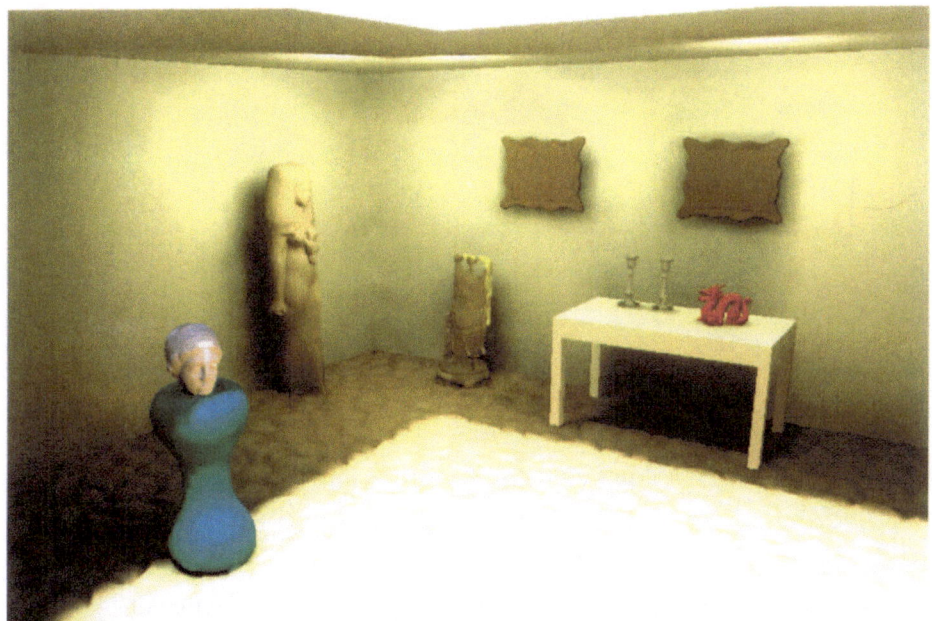

Fig. 9. The museum scene: diffuse interreflection simulated with face cluster radiosity. The input scene contained 2,700,000 polygons. Solution plus post-processing took two minutes and 120MB of memory to generate

van de Panne and Stewart (pp. 305–316)

Fig. 5. Clustering resulting from lossy compression. **a** Terrain dataset, **b** tunnels dataset, **c** rooms dataset

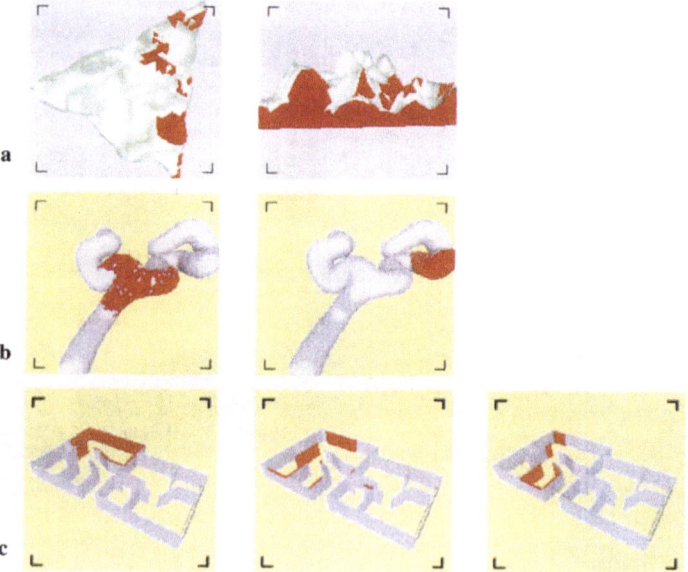

Fig. 6. Clustering resulting from lossless compression. **a** Terrain dataset, **b** tunnels dataset, **c** rooms dataset

Costa et al. (pp. 317–328)

Fig. 11. Empirical lighting design solution

Fig. 12. Lighting design solution for 120° DLs (3)

Fig. 13. Lighting design solution for 360° DLs (6)

Fig. 14. Lighting design solution for predefined DLs (5)

Loscos et al. (pp. 329–340)

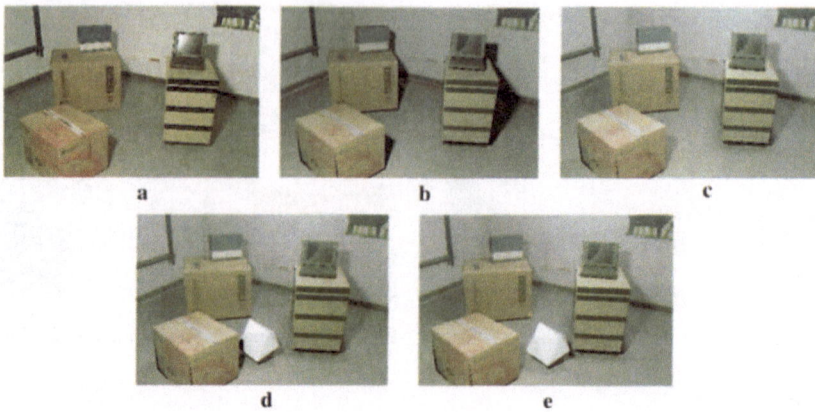

Fig. 5. a The original radiance image (photo). **b** Original reprojected lighting conditions, displayed using the recomputed direct and indirect components, **c** a virtual light has been inserted into the scene adding the light took 3.1 seconds (for 400 × 300 resolution). **d** A virtual object has been inserted into the scene with both lights on; adding the object required 1 sec. **e** Moving the virtual object requires 1.1 sec.

Fig. 6. Texture filling examples for real object removal. **a** Initial reflectance image. **b** The laptop is removed. The laptop was removed entirely *synthetically* since no additional image was captured. **c** The original relit image. **d** The relit image after removal. Removal of the laptop took 0.7 sec., since generated textures are pre-computed for "removable" objects

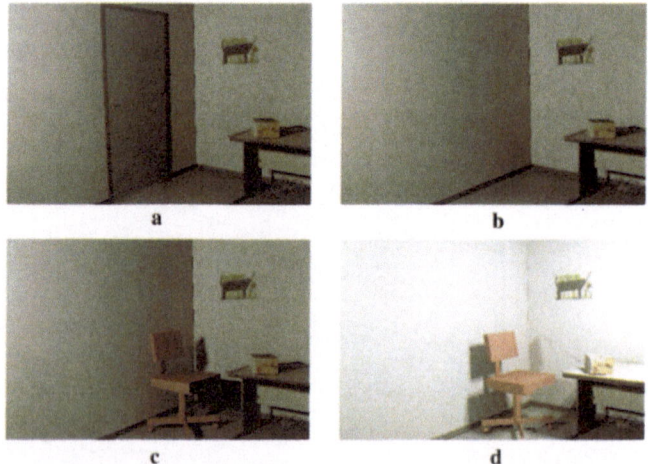

Fig. 7. A second real object removal example. **a** The original relit image, **b** the relit image after removal of the door, which took 2.9 sec., for a resolution of 512 × 341. **c** A virtual chair has been added to the scene, requiring 3.4 sec., and **d** a virtual light added (needing 6.6 sec.)

Green (pp. 341–352)

Single model rendered in a range of Kazoo Styles

Sample non-photorealistic image (courtesy of Scott Pritchard)

SpringerEurographics

Eduard Gröller,

Helwig Löffelmann,

William Ribarsky (eds.)

Data Visualization '99

Proceedings of the Joint EUROGRAPHICS
and IEEE TCVG Symposium on Visualization in Vienna, Austria, May 26–28, 1999

1999. XII, 340 pages. 230 partly coloured figures.
Softcover DM 118,–, öS 826,–, sFr 107,50
ISBN 3-211-83344-7. Eurographics

In the past decade visualization established
its importance both in scientific research and
in real-world applications.
In this book 21 research papers and 9 case
studies report on the latest results in volume
and flow visualization and information visualization. Thus it is a valuable source of information not only for researchers but also for
practitioners developing or using visualization applications.

Michael Gervautz,

Axel Hildebrand,

Dieter Schmalstieg (eds.)

Virtual Environments '99

Proceedings of the Eurographics
Workshop in Vienna, Austria,
May 31–June 1, 1999

1999. X, 191 pages. 78 figures.
Softcover DM 85,–, öS 595,–, sFr 77,50
ISBN 3-211-83347-1. Eurographics

The special focus of this volume lies on
augmented reality. Problems like real-time
rendering, tracking, registration and occlusion of real and virtual objects, shading and
lighting interaction and interaction techniques in augmented environments are
addressed. The papers collected in this book
also address levels of detail, distributed
environments, systems and applications and
interaction techniques.

All prices are recommended retail prices

 SpringerWienNewYork

Sachsenplatz 4–6, P.O.Box 89, A-1201 Wien, Fax +43-1-330 24 26, e-mail: books@springer.at, **Internet: http://www.springer.at**
New York, NY 10010, 175 Fifth Avenue • D-14197 Berlin, Heidelberger Platz 3 • Tokyo 113, 3–13, Hongo 3-chome, Bunkyo-ku

SpringerEurographics

Bruno Arnaldi,

Gérard Hégron (eds.)

Computer Animation and Simulation '98

Proceedings of the Eurographics
Workshop in Lisbon, Portugal,
August 31–September 1, 1998

1999. VII, 126 pages. 82 figures.
Softcover DM 85,–, öS 595,–, sFr 77,50
ISBN 3-211-83257-2. Eurographics

Contents:
- J.-D. Gascuel et al.: Simulating Landslides
  for Natural Disaster Prevention
- G. Besuievsky, X. Pueyo: A Dynamic
  Light Sources Algorithm for Radiosity
  Environments
- G. Moreau, S. Donikian: From
  Psychological and Real-Time Interaction
  Requirements to Behavioural Simulation
- N. Pazat, J.-L. Nougaret: Identification
  of Motion Models for Living Beings
- F. Faure: Interactive Solid Animation
  Using Linearized Displacement
  Constraints
- M. Kallmann, D. Thalmann: Modeling
  Objects for Interaction Tasks
- M. Teichmann, S. Teller: Assisted
  Articulation of Closed Polygonal Models
- S. Brandel, D. Bechmann, Y. Bertrand:
  STIGMA: a 4-dimensional Modeller
  for Animation

Jürgen Landauer, Ulrich Lang,

Matthias Wapler (eds.)

Virtual Environments '98

Proceedings of the Eurographics Workshop
in Stuttgart, Germany, June 16–18, 1998

1998. VIII, 335 pages. 206 partly coloured figures.
Softcover DM 128,–, öS 896,–, sFr. 116,50
ISBN 3-211-83233-5. Eurographics

Ten years after Virtual Environment research
started with NASA's VIEW project, these
techniques are now exploited in industry to
speed up product development cycles, to
ensure higher product quality, and to encourage early training on and for new products.
Especially the automotive industry, but also
the oil and gas industry are driving the use of
these techniques in their works.
The papers in this volume reflect all the different tracks of the workshop: reviewed technical papers as research contributions, sum-
maries on panels of VE applications in the
automotive, the medical, the telecommunica-
tion and the geoscience field, a panel dis-
cussing VEs as the future workspace, invited
papers from experts reporting from VEs for
entertainment industry, for media arts, for
supercomputing and productivity enhancement. Short industrial case studies, reporting
very briefly from ongoing industrial activities
complete this state of the art snapshot.

All prices are recommended retail prices

Martin Göbel,

 SpringerWienNewYork

Sachsenplatz 4–6, P.O.Box 89, A-1201 Wien, Fax +43-1-330 24 26, e-mail: books@springer.at, Internet: http://www.springer.at
New York, NY 10010, 175 Fifth Avenue • D-14197 Berlin, Heidelberger Platz 3 • Tokyo 113, 3–13, Hongo 3-chome, Bunkyo-ku